STUART
SYMINGTON

Missouri Biography Series
William E. Foley, Editor

STUART SYMINGTON

A Life

James C. Olson

UNIVERSITY OF MISSOURI PRESS
COLUMBIA AND LONDON

Copyright © 2003 by
The Curators of the University of Missouri
University of Missouri Press, Columbia, Missouri 65201
Printed and bound in the United States of America
All rights reserved
5 4 3 2 1   07 06 05 04 03

Library of Congress Cataloging-in-Publication Data

Olson, James C.
   Stuart Symington : a life / James C. Olson.
     p.   cm. — (Missouri biography series)
Includes bibliographical references (p.) and index.
   ISBN 0-8262-1503-3 (alk. paper)
   1. Symington, Stuart, 1901– 2. Legislators—United
States—Biography. 3. United States. Congress. Senate—
Biography. 4. United States—Foreign relations—1945–
1989. 5. United States—Politics and government—1945–
1989. 6. Missouri—Politics and government—1865–1950.
7. Missouri—Politics and government—1951– I. Title.
II. Series.

E748.S95 O47 2004
328.73'092—dc22

                                  2003017200

Text designer: Kristie Lee
Jacket designer: Jennifer Cropp
Typesetter: Crane Composition, Inc.
Printer and binder: Thomson-Shore, Inc.
Typefaces: Adobe Garamond, Bodoni, and Vladimir Script

The University of Missouri Press acknowledges the generous
contributions of the Sosland family and the Gaylord Foundation toward the publication of this book.

For Vera Farrington Olson

Contents

Preface

STUART SYMINGTON lived at or near the center of American power during most of his adult life. He moved easily in the upper echelons of government and politics, the military, business, entertainment, and "society." He counted among his friends presidents and royalty, labor leaders and prize fighters, movie stars, professors, and politicians of both major parties. He seemed to know everybody who counted.

Tall, handsome, and athletic, he was looked upon by some as a playboy, a characterization that was far from accurate. He built an impressive career as a successful businessman with a reputation for rescuing failing companies; a government official unanimously confirmed by the Senate for six top administrative posts in the Truman administration, including first secretary of the air force; and a four-term senator from Missouri. He was a candidate for the Democratic presidential nomination in 1960, and for a time appeared to be Kennedy's choice for vice president.

Known as "Harry Truman's Troubleshooter," he played major roles in reforming the Surplus Property Administration, the National Security Resources Board, and the Reconstruction Finance Corporation. As surplus property administrator, he successfully led an effort to break up the aluminum monopoly. As assistant secretary of war for air, he was a central figure in the negotiations leading to the National Security Act of 1947 that created the Department of Defense, the CIA, and a separate air force. As secretary of the air force he oversaw the Berlin airlift and the racial integration of the air force. He was involved in early discussions regarding use of the atomic bomb. He waged an incessant campaign for increased funding for the air force, and when he failed, resigned.

After a stunning victory in 1952, Symington represented Missouri in the U.S. Senate for twenty-four years. As U.S. senator, he was in the forefront of the fight against Joe McCarthy. As the only senator to serve simultaneously on the armed services, foreign relations, and space committees, he had a unique role in discussions of defense and diplomacy in the postwar period. He traveled widely, making numerous trips to Vietnam during the war. He changed from being one of the Senate's most ardent hawks to one of its most celebrated doves. His investigations of the CIA provided important evidence in the Watergate scandal.

Despite his preoccupation with national and international affairs, he was an effective advocate for Missouri and its people. Next to Harry Truman, he was *the* man from Missouri.

THIS BOOK had its origin—appropriately in view of the subject's love of athletics—at a University of Missouri football game. Vera and I were sitting with Stuart (Tim) and Janey Symington. In the course of the afternoon, I asked Tim what was going to be done with his father's papers, recently deposited in the Western Historical Manuscripts Collection, administered by the University and the State Historical Society of Missouri, but closed during the senator's lifetime except by his permission. If I were interested, Tim thought permission could be arranged, but suggested that I also talk to his brother Jim (James W. Symington, former four-term representative from Missouri's Second District, practicing law in Washington.) That conversation occurred at a delightful lunch, hosted by William H. Leedy, a mutual friend, at the Metropolitan Club. Jim's response was equally positive, although he wondered whether a full-length biography wasn't a little ambitious for a person of my age!

Shortly before he died Senator Symington granted me full access to his papers, and expressed the hope that I would use them. The senator's death before I was able to begin my research made the question of permission moot. Once I got at the project, I could not have asked for more generous cooperation than was given by the senator's two sons. They made available twelve large manuscript boxes of "personal papers," not included in the papers deposited in the Western Historical Manuscripts Collection. As the footnotes attest, these proved to be indispensable. They also allowed me to use family scrapbooks chronicling their mother's career as a singer in New York, and they made available numerous photographs. Most important, they gave freely of their time, answering innumerable questions and providing useful information. They read the manuscript and corrected a number of errors, particularly about family matters. They understood that I was working as an independent historian, and made no effort to influence my interpretations.

Aside from the personal papers, my most important sources were the Symington Papers in the Western Historical Manuscripts Collection. The staffs of that remarkable institution in both Columbia and Kansas City were most helpful. I especially thank David Boutrous and his staff in Kansas City for providing space in their cramped quarters for piles of manuscript boxes sent from Columbia for my use.

The Harry S. Truman Library in Independence contains many of Symington's papers from his years in the Truman administration, plus the papers of colleagues. The staff was most helpful. I worked particularly with Dennis Bilger, Elizabeth Saffly, and Pauline Testerman. The staffs of the Eisenhower, Johnson, and Kennedy libraries were equally welcoming and helpful, as were the staffs of the National Archives and Records Administration, the Manuscript Division of the Library of Congress, the Historical Office of the Department of Defense in Washington and the Air Force in Washington and at the Air University, Maxwell Air Force Base, Alabama, the State Historical Society of Missouri, the Minnesota Historical Society, the Oral History Research Office of Columbia University, the Seeley Mudd Manuscript Library at Princeton University, the Mercantile Library of St. Louis, the Miller Nichols Library, University of Missouri–Kansas City, the Manuscript Library, Washington University, the Harvard University law library, and the Sterling Library at Yale University. Providing assistance by telephone were the staffs of the William Fulbright Papers, University of Arkansas; the Frank Church Papers, University of Idaho; and the Richard Russell Papers, University of Georgia.

Many persons, other than those mentioned, provided help. Among them: Diane Blair, Clark Clifford, General Benjamin O. Davis, Jay Dillingham, John Dillingham, Lynn Genzler, Toby Godfrey, Alfred Goldberg, James Goodrich, Amelia Graves, Paul Nitze, General Bernard A. Schriever, Kathryn Nelson Smith, Elmer B. Staats, Cinde Sherman, Hugh Sprague, Robert Utley, George Weaver, Herman Wolk, John Zentay, and Eugene Zuckert. George Watson, Air Force Historian, read the entire manuscript and provided helpful comments, as did Robert Ferrell of Indiana University, whose detailed comments vastly improved the manuscript. My daughter, Sarah Olson, despite her heavy schedule as Superintendent of the Roosevelt-Vanderbilt National Historic Sites, read the entire manuscript and suggested numerous stylistic improvements. The University of Missouri provided financial assistance and supported the employment of an administrative assistant. Among those who served in that capacity I give thanks to Delores

Wilson, Teresa Koch, Patricia Stogsdill, and especially Mary Roberts, who secured permissions and put the final draft through the computer.

I would like to acknowledge, especially, a recently published book which makes a significant contribution to an understanding of Symington's career: Linda McFarland, *Cold War Strategist: Stuart Symington and the Search for National Security.* This excellent study, which originated as a doctoral dissertation in history at the University of Missouri–Columbia, treats certain aspects of Symington's career in greater detail than I do. I recommend it.

I also would like to acknowledge the staff of the University of Missouri Press who assisted with this book: Beverly Jarrett, editor in chief; Jane Lago, managing editor; John Brenner, manuscript editor; Karen Renner, marketing director; Kristie Lee and Jenny Cropp, book designers; and Dwight Browne and Nikki Waltz, production manager and assistant.

Vera Farrington Olson, my wife of more than sixty-two years to whom this book is dedicated, assisted in research, read several drafts with a critical eye, and most of all provided moral support throughout the effort.

I alone, of course, am responsible for any errors of fact or sins of omission or commission this work may exhibit.

STUART
SYMINGTON

1

Beginnings

ALTHOUGH Stuart Symington's thirty years of public life in Washington were as a man from Missouri—in his later years as *the* man from Missouri—his roots were in the East, deep in the soil of Maryland and Virginia.

According to family tradition, the original Symington in America, James, arrived from Scotland in 1785.[1] He landed in Philadelphia, where he worked as a stonecutter. Aboard ship he had met Margaret Ogilvie, a young Scotswoman traveling alone. Her marital status at the time remains unclear. Either she was the widow of a man named William Ogilvie, or she was running away from an unhappy marriage with him. Divorce was hard to come by in Scotland in the eighteenth century. Margaret had left behind two children, apparently with her mother, and was pregnant with a third. Pregnant or not, she completely captivated young James Symington, who was making his way to America from Ayrshire.

How Margaret paid for her passage to America is unknown. Numerous immigrants financed their passage by indenturing themselves to American employers for a period of years. At some point she became acquainted with another passenger, Robert Morris, the wealthy Philadelphia banker and signer of the Declaration of Independence who was famed as the "financier of the Revolution." Morris invited her to join his household as housekeeper or governess. Her child, a daughter initially named Deborah Morris, was born in the Morris home, and when in 1787 her shipboard acquaintance persuaded her to marry him, she was given away by Morris. About a year after their marriage, James and

Margaret Symington moved to a house on Brandywine Creek, near Wilmington, where James operated a mill for grinding flint. In 1800 they moved to Baltimore and James resumed the stonecutting trade. Apparently he did rather well. When he died in 1827, he left an estate of seventy-five thousand dollars, a substantial sum in the early nineteenth century.

James adopted Deborah, and he and Margaret eventually had two more daughters and three sons, one of whom was Thomas, born December 23, 1793, on Brandywine Creek. Thomas served as an apprentice to his father in the stonecutting trade, and then as a young man went to work for William Stuart, who had a stonecutting and marble business. Stuart, whose father had fought in the War of the Revolution, became lieutenant colonel of the U.S. Infantry defending Baltimore during the War of 1812, being credited, according to family legend, with "saving" Fort McHenry during the British naval bombardment the night of September 13, 1814, when he took over from the commandant, alleged to have been drunk. In addition to being a war hero, William Stuart was a successful businessman who was active in politics. He served several terms on the Baltimore city council and as a member of the Maryland House of Delegates. He had a short term as mayor of Baltimore, after which he became president of the Maryland Institute of Arts.[2] His daughter, Angeline, whom Thomas Symington married in 1825, was obviously quite a catch.

Nothing is known about the appearance of the earlier Symingtons, but there is a portrait of Thomas, dating from about 1860 when he was sixty-seven years of age. He was a handsome man, an appropriate forebear of a family that through the generations has produced unusually handsome men and beautiful women. With his penetrating eyes and strong jaw, he looks like a man in the prime of life. Apparently he was. At the age of seventy-one, after Angeline had died, he married Mary Wilson, thirty-seven, whom he had met at the Episcopal Church, where she was the church organist; she bore him two children before he died in 1875 at the age of eighty-two.

Thomas Symington did well financially, making substantial sums in real estate, marble quarries, and chemicals and fertilizer. He furnished much of the marble for the 1850 addition to the capitol building in Washington. He provided the cornerstone of the Washington Monument as a gift.[3] Unlike many others, including his son, he seems to have survived the Civil War financially intact. In 1862 he retired to a farm outside Baltimore, which he named "Indian Spring," managing his various business enterprises in addition to farming. When he died, he left an estate of one hundred thousand dollars in cash and what apparently was a substantial unrecorded balance that he divided among his children.

Thomas and Angeline had two daughters and four sons. The oldest of the sons, born January 5, 1839, they understandably named William Stuart, after Angeline's father.

This first W. Stuart Symington—as is true of all his descendants who have borne the name, he dropped "William"—enlisted in the Virginia Militia at the age of twenty-two to fight for the Confederacy in the Civil War. He became a second lieutenant at the outset and about a year later was appointed first lieutenant in the Confederate Army. Stuart became an aide to his first cousin by marriage, General George E. Pickett, and served in that capacity throughout the war. He fought with Pickett at Five Forks, Drewry's Bluff, Gettysburg, and Petersburg. Near the end of the Seven Days in June 1862, he disobeyed Pickett's orders to join him in Richmond and stayed behind to participate in the Battle of Frayzer's Farm. His horse was shot seven times and finally killed. He also had a horse shot out from under him during the futile, bloody assault on Cemetery Ridge in the waning hours of the Battle of Gettysburg. In command of Union troops at Cemetery Ridge was Brigadier General James S. Wadsworth, whose granddaughter Evelyn would become Mrs. W. Stuart Symington III.[4]

Lieutenant Symington remained with Pickett during all of the dreary months from Gettysburg to Appomattox and was among those cited by Pickett, in his final report to General Lee, "for gallantry and untiring zeal."[5] He surrendered his sword as a captain, but throughout the rest of his life he was referred to as "Major." Whatever his rank, his devotion to the Lost Cause remained undiminished. In its obituary of him, the *Baltimore Sun* wrote, "wild horses would not have dragged an admission from him that he believed that the South was in the wrong."[6] Rather than sign the Oath of Allegiance required of all former Confederate officers, he went to Germany, studying at the University of Heidelberg, until the frenzy calmed down. He was vice president of the Society of the Army and Navy of the Confederate States in Maryland, and in the last year of his life the society gave a testamentary dinner for him, the only person they had ever so honored up to that time. Three days before his sudden death on June 9, 1912— he collapsed after a game of golf on a hot Sunday afternoon—he had led a parade of Confederate veterans celebrating the Confederate Memorial Day.

After returning to Baltimore from Germany, Major Symington went into the fertilizer business. Apparently, he was not very good at it. The company went into bankruptcy, and its owner lost everything. The family had to sell their big house on Charles Street and move into a small, rented house on North Avenue, not a particularly fashionable part of the city. Later he recovered somewhat, serving as secretary of the Consolidated Gas Company in Baltimore. By the time of his death, he was looked upon as one of Baltimore's leading citizens and, even in the midst of the family's most serious financial vicissitudes, they moved in Baltimore's most fashionable society.

One reason for that could well have been the woman Major Symington had the good fortune to marry. While in Richmond during the war on a recruiting trip, he attended a debutante ball at which he met a beautiful young woman named Lelia Skipworth Powers, daughter of a prominent Episcopal clergyman. In addition to her beauty, she possessed an impeccable Virginia lineage. Through her mother she was a direct descendant of Benjamin Harrison, who was married to Anne Carter, daughter of Robert "King" Carter, whose descendants included the Lees. After returning from Germany, Major Symington went back to Richmond and persuaded Lelia to marry him. They made a handsome couple, and, before Lelia died at the age of forty-four, they had a daughter and seven sons. The sons were all strapping young men, inheriting physiques that reflected their father's strength and their mother's beauty. All of them, with one exception, went into business and became financially successful.[7]

The exception was W. Stuart Symington, Jr. He had no interest in business, but instead went to Johns Hopkins University, where he studied language and literature. He became fluent in three foreign languages and ultimately received a Ph.D. in French literature. An athlete as well as a student, he was captain of the football team at Hopkins and played lacrosse on a Baltimore club team that won a national championship. At the age of twenty-three he received an appointment as an associate professor of romance languages at Stanford; after a year he returned east to become a full professor at Amherst College. Two years later, on November 17, 1897, he married Emily Haxall Harrison, a young woman of rare beauty and, apparently, rather daunting determination. Like many southerners, the Harrisons had lost everything in the Civil War, and Emily brought little to the marriage except her beauty, her strong personality, deep religious convictions, and some fine antique furniture.[8]

Stuart and Emily Symington had six children: a daughter, Louise, and five sons, the oldest being W. Stuart Symington III, born June 26, 1901.

With a growing family, the young professor and his wife found it difficult to make ends meet on a salary that was never more than one hundred dollars per month. Moreover, teaching may have lost some of its allure, possibly because of the situation at Amherst. Family legend has it that from the beginning of his tenure, Professor Symington had difficulty with the college janitor. Then one day, so the story goes, he used some blackboards that were still wet. The janitor, observing this from the door, shouted, "He wrote on them boards." The students laughed, and young Symington, knowing that his control of the class was in jeopardy, collared the janitor and threw him out. Deciding that he had better report the incident to the president, he was met with the comment, "This man is the first janitor we have had here in many years who is able to keep Amherst warm in the winter; so, especially in that you are relatively new, if it came to which one of you would have to leave, I wouldn't give much for your chances with the Board of Trustees." After this episode, he is supposed to have gone home and told his wife, "Pack up. The janitor has more weight than I do."

In any event, in 1903 Professor Symington resigned his post at Amherst and moved his family to New York, where he enrolled in the law school at New York University. They had virtually no money, and Emily was too proud to take any help from their relatives, some of whom were quite well off. As a result, her husband eked out a living as a translator while attending school. Their son remembered the first years of his life "as years of real poverty."[9]

After his father finished law school at the University of Maryland, he took his family back to Baltimore, where he began the practice of law. He met with only sporadic success, and complicated his life by engaging in a number of unsuccessful business and real estate ventures. As a result, the family's fortunes waxed and waned. At times they were very poor, and even when they enjoyed a degree of prosperity, there never seemed to be enough money, at least not enough to support the way of life to which they aspired and which their ancestry would seem to predict. Moreover, they felt disadvantaged when they compared their situation to that of the other Symington brothers, all of whom were successful in business. Stuart envied his cousins, who always seemed to have plenty of money. The family had a pleasant home, built with help from Uncle Tom, in Roland Park, one of the pioneering upscale residential developments in the country,[10] but after a few years they had to give it up and move back to the city, living first in a small apartment and then a small house.

In the summer of 1914, however, Emily took all of the children—by then numbering six—on an extended tour of Europe. Stuart, age thirteen, kept a diary—a practice which, unfortunately, he did not continue. Emily settled the family in a small Swiss hotel in Vevey, a pleasant little town between Lausanne and Montreux on the shore of Lac Leman. She put the children in school, primarily to learn French; Stuart frequently recorded the number of French words he had learned during the day.

Apparently, she had no specific plans to return home. She rarely heard from her husband, but his infrequent letters were red-letter events for the entire family—Stuart wrote in his diary that his father "certainly writes wonderful letters." Father rarely sent money, and before long the family was desperately short of funds. (One wonders where Emily found money for the trip in the first place.) On August 17, Stuart wrote, "Mother's money is rapidly giving out and goodness only knows what we are going to do after that." On August 20 he noted, "We are now staying entirely on credit." Father sent twenty-five hundred francs on August 22, but that soon ran out, and Emily had to borrow three hundred francs from the relief fund maintained by the American consul.

Whatever Emily's plans, the outbreak of World War I cut them off. After some hesitation, she decided that she should return home. She took the family to London and with help from Uncle Powers, a captain in the navy, booked passage on the *Britannia,* arriving in New York on October 22.[11]

Then it was back to the little house in Baltimore. Indeed, the transition from summer in Switzerland to winter in Baltimore was symbolic of the roller-coaster kind of existence the family endured. Their finances, never equal to Emily's aspirations, created severe tensions between an easygoing father and a strong-willed, determined mother.

They were not a close-knit family, and Stuart Symington III did not look back on his childhood with much fondness. He was never particularly close to his father. Their personalities were too far apart, and young Stuart, who always played to win, found it increasingly difficult to relate to his low-key, quizzical father who believed, for example, that in games the result was less important than the pleasure of participation.[12] Moreover, the elder Symington frequently drank more than was good for him. This made a lasting impression on his son, who throughout his life enjoyed a cocktail—usually having one before dinner—but never drank to excess.

Just as Stuart was not particularly close to his father, he was not his father's favorite child. This was forcibly brought to his attention one day when he was home from Yale on vacation. He was visiting a ball-bearing plant that his father was trying to run—unsuccessfully, as was the case with virtually all of his business ventures. He overheard the plant superintendent say, "That son of yours is a fine boy," and his father reply, "Oh Stuart's all right, but wait till you see one of my other sons."[13]

He admired but was not particularly close to his mother. Emily, with her striking beauty, strong will, and religious fervor, dominated them all. A devout Episcopalian, she became prominent in the church and made sure that all of the children were brought up in the faith.[14] None of them, however, developed their mother's religious zeal. She also instilled in them a strong sense of honor, conscience, and love of country. An ardent suffragette, she once picketed the White House on behalf of votes for women.

Emily's other abiding passion was helping the downtrodden. She focused particularly on the problems of blacks in Baltimore, helping them to find food and jobs. She frequently preached in black churches, and she strove to instill in family and friends her ideas—advanced for the time—of racial equality. Years later, when her son was president of Emerson Electric Company, he was visited by a delegation of black leaders demanding more equality for their people in the plants of the city. As their demands became more strident, Symington reminded them that racial issues were rather sticky in St. Louis. "It is neither northern nor southern, rather a border town, comparable to, say, Baltimore," he said.

"What do you know about Baltimore?" their leader asked, adding, as an afterthought, "By any chance are you related to Mrs. Emily Symington?" When Symington replied that she was his mother, the man said, "Let's get out of here. This man's mother did as much as anybody to help our people in Baltimore."[15]

Despite her strong views, Emily Symington apparently provided little supervision of her children, and they tended to come and go pretty much as they pleased. Stuart recalled that when he was about six he hitched a ride on a grocery wagon; he was discovered, far from home, and was chased off the wagon. On the way back, investigating a house under construction, he fell into the basement, shattering his left elbow. He was never able to straighten his left arm completely, but that did not keep him from becoming a champion left-handed tennis player.

Stuart's tennis began at an early age on the grass courts of the Baltimore Country Club, just a few blocks from the family home in Roland Park. He hung around the courts a lot, and occasionally the greenskeeper, a former British professional named Latham, would hand him a racquet and say, "Let's play a few." Latham, Symington remembered, chewed tobacco constantly, and was proud of the fact that he spit only once a day, for lunch.[16]

As a boy, Stuart took every opportunity to earn money. He sold magazines, and for a time sold spring water that he hauled around the neighborhood in a wagon pulled by the family dog. Perhaps his most interesting sales experience occurred during the Democratic National Convention of 1912, held a few blocks from home. Along with Beverley Smith, later a well-known correspondent for the *Saturday Evening Post,* he hawked candy, peanuts, chewing gum, cigars, and cigarettes to delegates on the convention floor. The convention dragged on for days during the hot Baltimore summer as the delegates remained deadlocked over Woodrow Wilson and Speaker of the House Champ Clark of Missouri. Finally, William Jennings Bryan was able to break the deadlock and move the delegates toward Wilson. Smith later recalled, "About noon . . . my friends . . . and I went down to a candy store at Dolphin Street for some licorice sticks. As we sucked at these, we saw Stuart Symington streaking down the street, his blond hair flopping. 'Woodrow Wilson has been nominated,' he cried, 'unaminously.'(Stuart always had trouble with words. Thirty-odd years later, when he was Secretary of the Air Force, I remember he had trouble distinguishing 'fission' bombs from 'fusion' bombs.")[17]

Stuart's favorite part-time job was as a sports reporter for the *Baltimore Sun.* He covered all sports, but tennis was his favorite. "I would go to New York to play in the Nationals at Forest Hills, lose in an early round, then cover the entire tournament for $25.00 a week plus expenses; the life of Riley."[18]

Stuart was not a particularly popular child with either his sister and brothers or with his classmates. He was too competitive, too aggressive. He was a handsome child, as were all the Symington children, and he came off as something of a know-it-all. Moreover, he always seemed to win the prizes. Once, according to a family story, their mother offered a tennis racket to the child who by the end of the summer best memorized certain psalms. One of the younger brothers said, "Please, Mama, give it to Stuart now, so we can have it to play tennis all summer."[19]

Stuart and Emily Symington would have sent their children to private schools had it been possible, but unfortunately most of the time there was not enough money. Young Stuart started his formal education in the Roland Park Public School. During the summer months he and his sister, Louise, spent time at a camp started by Charlotte Noland in Middleburg, Virginia. Among the campers was Wallis Warfield, who as the Duchess of Windsor years later entertained Symington and General Hoyt Vandenberg during a respite from the Berlin Airlift.[20] After two years in public school, Stuart enrolled in the nationally known Gilman Country School, just north of Baltimore, on a scholarship obtained by his father. Stuart lost the scholarship when at the end of his third year he joined a number of others in flooding the basement in protest against the school's refusal to pipe hot water into the showers. So it was back to a public school, this time not in suburban Roland Park but in Baltimore, where he finished the eighth grade. It was at this point that Emily took the children to Europe, and when they returned Stuart was enrolled in Donaldson School, a small private school in Ilchester, Maryland. He hated the place, and after two years persuaded his parents to send him to Baltimore City College—actually a high school—where he graduated in the spring of 1918. At City College, he captained the tennis team, played lacrosse, and boxed, a sport that brought him a broken and slightly disfigured nose. He also got into a scrape that haunted him years later.

One spring evening in 1918 Stuart and a number of friends piled into a car that one of their group had taken from a neighbor's driveway. Rounding a curve at high speed, the car went off the road, fell into a ditch, caught on fire, and was demolished. All the passengers were hurt, some seriously. Stuart broke his right arm and was slightly burned. The boys were brought before a magistrate and fined twenty-five dollars each; their fathers sent the car's owner, a friend and neighbor, a check to cover the cost of his demolished vehicle, and everyone thought this would be the end of it. The prosecuting attorney of Baltimore County, however, decided to make some political capital by bringing the boys before a grand jury. Stuart's father was told that if the boys would tell who was driving, all but the driver would be released. He refused to ask the boys to do this, and none did, with the result that all were paroled to their parents. The senior Symington, irritated with his son but angry at this turn of events, appealed the case; the superior court ruled that since there had been no sentence, no further action was needed. It remained on the record, however, and years later Symington's political opponents dredged it up.[21]

When Stuart graduated from high school in the spring of 1918, he wanted to enlist in the regular army, but his father refused to let him unless he could get into officer's training. He was only sixteen, but he lied about his age and was admitted to the junior Plattsburg Training Camp in New York. In the fall he was accepted for the regular army and sent to the Officers Training School at Camp Zachary Taylor, near Louisville, Kentucky. Life at Zachary Taylor was hard and lonely, but fortunately it did not last long, and he was kept too busy to be homesick. He later recalled:

> The only time I remember being really homesick was Christmas Eve, 1918; could not get home, was in Louisville by myself, and went to the theater. Two people—I think their names were Van and Schenck—sang a song called Roses of Picardy. The melody was truly beautiful. In the balcony, by myself, I suddenly felt sad and lonely, homesick. To the best of my knowledge that was the last time. We were never a close family.[22]

When the war ended November 11, Officer Candidate Symington, along with most of his class, decided to stay on in the hope of obtaining a commission. That hope was realized January 18, 1919, when he was commissioned a second lieutenant in the field artillery and released from the service, the youngest second lieutenant in the army.[23] Later, he reminisced:

> To say that I was proud of those gold bars and my excessively polished cordovan boots would be an understatement.
> One day, however, those boots got me in trouble. My mother was in Baltimore and included me in a party at the Lyric, then the opera house in Baltimore. We were sitting in a box. My boots were too small. My legs began to itch terribly. I could not stop moving them. My mother whispered several times, "Keep still." I tried, but it was very difficult. Finally a young and exceptionally good looking Brigadier General leaned over and tapped me on the shoulder, saying, "Next time, Lieutenant, buy them a little bigger." That was the first time I saw General Douglas MacArthur.[24]

Meanwhile, the family had moved to Chicago, where their father, having given up his not-too-successful law practice in Baltimore, was running an ammunition plant for his brother Tom. Stuart joined the family, but soon decided that he wanted to return to Baltimore. His mother made this possible by arranging for him to live with her sister Anne, Mrs. George Jackson, whose husband was a successful Baltimore businessman.

After spending the summer playing tennis—he competed in the national singles championship at Forest Hills—and taking a course in chemistry at Johns Hopkins, Stuart enrolled in Yale. "There was no particular reason for me to go to Yale," he recalled. "Except for my older cousin, Tom Symington, whom I much looked up to, I had no friends there. But Tom was a big man on campus. He had returned to Yale after leaving naval aviation, and sold me on the idea."[25]

Stuart enjoyed life at Yale. He was still aggressive and competitive, but he had lost some of the arrogance he had exhibited as a child. From an attractive little boy he had grown into a handsome, albeit gangling, six-footer. He was gregarious and well liked. Using the entree provided by his cousin Tom, he became something of a big man on campus himself, serving as an assistant editor of the *Yale Daily News* (Henry Luce was the editor), press manager of the Yale Dramatic Association, and a member of Yale's championship tennis team. He made Delta Kappa Epsilon and the Elihu Society. His grades were only fair, because he really didn't work very hard in class. "I guess nobody ever showed me that knowledge could be useful," he once said. "Maybe that sounds dumb, but it's true." Although he would become the most prominent alumnus of his class, he ranked next to last in a vote of his classmates on who was "most likely to succeed."[26]

Shortly after Stuart enrolled in Yale, the family moved back to Baltimore, where his father resumed the practice of law. He had made some money in Chicago, and did better at the law than he had earlier. He was able to provide Stuart a generous allowance, but it was never enough, so Stuart spent his summers as a reporter for the *Baltimore Sun,* covering sports and politics. He particularly enjoyed covering tennis tournaments, and, as earlier, he combined reporting with playing. He was still good enough to play in the national championships, so, as before, he would enter a tournament, lose after a round or two, and cover the remaining matches for the *Sun.* His last National was in Philadelphia in 1922; the tournament had been transferred there while the Forest Hills Stadium was being built. Also in the summer of 1922, Stuart was assigned to cover the senatorial campaign of William Cabell Bruce, whose son David was dating Stuart's sister, Louise. They didn't get married, but David, whose brilliant career as a diplomat extended into the Reagan years, remained a close friend.

Before Stuart could return to Yale, his father suffered severe reverses in an ill-fated real estate speculation. He had invested heavily in an effort to develop Gibson Island, some twenty miles from Baltimore in Chesapeake Bay, into a tennis, golf, and yachting center. Ultimately Gibson Island became one of the most successful resorts on the East Coast, but W. S. Symington lost almost everything he possessed in the early stages of its development, which unfortunately was under way during the postwar depression of 1921–1922. His son later commented, "The thought that a single such mistake could put my brilliant but relatively unbusinesslike father in such financial straits, to the loyal and deep distress of my mother, made a permanent impression on me; to the point where I never again personally borrowed anything from anybody; millions for companies, but never a cent personally."[27]

Stuart desperately wanted to return to Yale for his senior year, but the Gibson Island fiasco made it impossible for his father to provide the money. He asked his uncle George Jackson, with whom he had stayed for a few months in 1919, for a loan. Uncle George agreed to lend him the money without interest, and he went back to Yale.

By now, however, the whole focus of his life had changed. He had fallen hopelessly, irretrievably in love.

Beginning with his sophomore year, he roomed with Henri de Sibour, a member of a socially prominent Washington family. Through him at a Washington charity ball during the Christmas holidays of 1920 he met Evelyn Wadsworth, a lovely ash blonde with twinkling blue eyes and a stunning smile. They danced a few times and he found that she was a good dancer and as witty and vivacious as she was beautiful. He discovered, too, that she had brains as well as beauty. At the end of the evening, he asked her for a date, and she accepted.

If there was an American aristocracy, Eve Wadsworth belonged to it. Her father's family had been in America since 1632, an ancestor had fought with Washington in the Revolution, and for generations the Wadsworths had played leading roles in the life of New York State. They lived in baronial houses set on vast tracts of land in the Genesee Valley. They fought in the nation's wars and engaged in meaningful public service. Brigadier General James S. Wadsworth served as military governor of Washington, D.C., during the Civil War and died a hero's death in the Battle of the Wilderness.[28] His son, James W. Wadsworth (Eve's grandfather) played a dominant role in New York's politics for a generation, serving in the New York General Assembly, as state comptroller, and for more than a decade as chairman of the House Committee on Agriculture in the U.S. Congress. Eve's father, Senator James W. Wadsworth, Jr., a man of great landed wealth based on gifts from his father, had just been reelected to a second term in the Senate and was a power in the Republican party both in New York and nationally.

On her mother's side, Eve's family was even richer and more prominent. Her maternal grandfather was John Hay, who as a young man had been Abraham Lincoln's private secretary, and who in his later years had served as the American ambassador to England and as secretary of state under both Presidents McKinley and Roosevelt. His wife, Clara, had inherited great wealth from her father, Cleveland industrialist Amasa Stone. Eve's Aunt Helen (her mother's only sister) had married the fabulously rich Payne Whitney, and Eve spent lots of time with her cousins, John Hay, "Jock," and Cornelius Vanderbilt "Sonny" Whitney.

When in Washington, the Wadsworths lived in the elegant mansion that H. H. Richardson had designed for John Hay just across Lafayette Square from the White House—he created a duplicate house next door for Hay's closest friend, Henry Adams.[29] Alice Wadsworth, Eve's mother, had inherited a third of the building from her father. She bought the other two-thirds from her brother and sister, and soon restored the great house to the central place in Washington society it had occupied when it served as the home of the secretary of state.

It was at the imposing recessed door of this Romanesque mansion that Stuart Symington presented himself for his first date with Evelyn Wadsworth. Dressed in a new, fourteen-dollar suit, he had come over from Baltimore on the train and then had taken a streetcar to 800 Sixteenth Street. The door was opened by an imposing man in a full dress suit. Stuart thrust out his hand and said, "How do you do, Senator. I'm Stuart Symington."

The man at the door, however, was not Senator Wadsworth, but Danny Spillane, the family butler. Symington's Baltimore background had prepared him only for Negro servants, and he had never seen a senator at close range. This unprepossessing beginning apparently did not damage his position with the family. Danny Spillane became one of his close friends and strong supporters. Senator Wadsworth took to his daughter's suitor almost from the beginning, despite the fact that the young man came from a long line of Southern Democrats and did not hesitate to express his opinions. He once wrote a friend: "Young Symington is the kind of man who looks you straight in the eye."[30]

Eve, apparently, was not so easily persuaded. She liked the handsome young man from Baltimore who was an engaging conversationalist and a divine dancer, but she saw no particular reason to settle down in marriage. She was one of the belles of Washington society; her beauty, brains, money, and prestige produced a long line of suitors. Stuart, for whom it had been love at first sight, wrote her frequently, came down from New Haven whenever he could afford it, and visited her at the Wadsworth home in Geneseo, New York. When school finished in 1923, he abandoned his plans to go to law school and enter practice with his father. He wanted to get into business and make some money—he had watched with envy the good life lived by his uncles who were successful in business, and at the Wadsworths' he had been introduced to money that was both big and old. He was so impatient that he left Yale without receiving his degree. He was short of credits in mathematics, and try as he might he could not sell the dean on the notion that he should graduate without making them up. (In 1945 Yale relented and awarded his degree retroactive to the Class of 1923.)

His father's oldest brother, Tom, operated a thriving plant in Rochester, New York, making heavy railroad equipment. The Wadsworth home in the Genesee Valley was only thirty miles away; Eve would be there in the summer, and it would be easy to get over to see her. Stuart asked his Uncle Tom for a job, and was taken on as an apprentice iron molder at a salary of $150 a month, not much by Wadsworth standards, but high for an apprentice iron molder. The work was hard and dirty and the hours were long, but Stuart kept at it, living in a cheap boardinghouse for ten dollars a week and getting up with the aid of an alarm clock so he could be at work at seven in the morning. In a few months he became a journeyman iron molder, but he had no intention of remaining an iron molder for long. Indeed, he had been hired with the understanding that he would go through the shops to learn the business.

He had a lot to learn. Ed Burrows, the vice president in charge of the Rochester plant, reminded him that he had been given the job only because he was a nephew of the owner, and that his liberal arts course at Yale "didn't do one damn thing to help you in this business." Stuart responded by asking Burrows for his advice, and was told that he should study engineering and mathematics. Burrows urged him to enroll for an engineering course in the International Correspondence School, volunteering to lend him some books Burrows had left over from an earlier course he had taken. Stuart followed Burrows's advice, spending several evenings a week working on his correspondence course lessons. The company also let him off early twice a week so he could take a course in mathematics at the Rochester School of Optometry.[31]

The most important part of Symington's education at Rochester came from his fellow workers, who introduced him to an entirely new way of life. Living in Baltimore, he hadn't known any blacks who worked in other than subordinate positions; in the plant at Rochester, the shipping foreman was black. "I got to knowing that man and respecting him and liking him for his ability and character, and it opened up a whole new world to me that I've never forgotten: that Negroes are the same as white people, some good, some bad, some with ability, some not, but people with people's feelings and problems and hopes and disappointments."[32]

He ran into cases of incredible sacrifice and hardship. He became well acquainted with a yard foreman "who got up every morning and made all the meals for his wife, who was so crippled that she couldn't get out of her chair; all of the food had to be put where she could get at it, because they didn't have any servants, of course. And then he'd come home and have to clean up everything. And that was *his* life. But he never complained. Never once." Another man he came to know well "got up at four in the morning, went to a diner for breakfast so he wouldn't disturb his family, rode the bus for an hour, worked until four, another hour on the bus, spent an hour with his family, ate and went to bed. And that was his life. . . . But he explained it to me: he was putting his two children through the Conservatory of Music."[33]

Throughout his public life, Stuart Symington expressed a genuine, credible concern for those who worked with their hands for a living, and his experience at Rochester helped shape that concern in a way that no amount of theoretical knowledge could ever have accomplished. His living situation also contributed to his knowledge of how poor working people got along. He lived in a cheap boardinghouse, where he shared one bathroom with two other boarders. Life was not altogether unpleasant, however; the food was good and he remembered his landlady, Mrs. Vernon Carr, as "one of the finest women I've ever known." Moreover, as often as possible he "washed up," got in the old Essex Four that he owned jointly with one of his fellow boarders, and drove the thirty miles to Geneseo to see Eve.

During the summer Stuart and Eve came to an "understanding." Their engagement was announced in the fall, and on March 1, 1924, they were married in St. John's Church, just across Sixteenth Street from the Wadsworths' Washington home. President and Mrs. Coolidge headed the guest list, which included cabinet members, ambassadors, senators, and congressmen. Governor and Mrs. Albert Ritchie came over from Annapolis in honor of the groom's father, who was serving as a judge in Baltimore. Both families were there in full force, including the Payne Whitneys, John Hay Whitney, and the Clarence Hays from Boston. Eve's cousin Joan Whitney served as maid of honor. The couple was preceded to the altar by the largest bridal party ever assembled in St. John's. The Episcopal Bishop of Maryland officiated at the service, along with the rector of St. John's. Following the ceremony, those at the church joined four hundred additional guests for a reception at the bride's home. Among the throng was a young army officer named George C. Marshall. (Twenty-two years later, Symington, as assistant secretary of war for air, visited General Marshall in China. As they were riding together in the general's car through the streets of Nanking, Marshall suddenly turned and said, "Symington, you make me feel old. I danced with your mother-in-law at your wedding reception when I was a captain.")[34]

After the reception and a sit-down dinner for the bridal party, Stuart and Eve drove to the Union Station in Eve's mother's car—no more riding around in an old Essex—to board a train for New Orleans as the first stop on their way to Havana. They arrived at the station only to find that there had been a schedule change and the train had departed. They spent their wedding night at the Willard Hotel and took the train the next day. After a few days in New Orleans they boarded a ship for Havana. On the return trip they stopped in Miami and New Orleans.

Then it was on to Rochester. Eve, whose life had alternated between the vast estate in the Genesee Valley and the imposing mansion in the heart of the nation's capital, found herself living in a tiny, two-room apartment, the wife of an iron molder. But she knew and he knew that it would not be for long. Stuart Symington was not an ordinary apprentice; both Eve's heritage and his dramatized that. Moreover, he was determined to achieve success, and he was going to do it fast.

2

A Rapid Rise in Business

THE LITTLE two-room apartment on South Union Street, not one of Rochester's more prestigious locations, seemed an unlikely springboard for Stuart Symington's drive to succeed in business, and the first few months there augured for a slow rise if there was to be one at all. Stuart continued as an iron molder, coming home at nights so covered with sand, grime, and sweat that, as Eve recalled later, "it took two baths to remove the smudge." Then, after dinner prepared by the twenty-one-year-old Eve—who was having her first experience at keeping house and preparing dinner for anyone—Stuart buried himself in his books. When not studying, he went to classes in mechanical engineering at the Mechanics Institute, and two evenings a week a math tutor from the Rochester Gas and Electric Company came to the apartment.[1]

In what spare time he had, he played tennis and squash. He lifted weights to improve his physique. Six feet, two inches tall, weighing about 185 pounds, with the erect stature and graceful stride of a superior athlete, he developed a commanding presence that never deserted him. His arresting blue eyes were blessed with acute vision.[2]

Stuart Symington wasn't an ordinary iron molder. He was the owner's nephew and was expected to learn the business. He stayed in the shops for about a year and then began to move from department to department, observing operations and fulfilling various staff assignments. He learned quickly and did not hesitate to give advice, some of it not particularly welcome. Moreover, he was becoming impatient with not having a regular assignment. He and Eve had bought a house on Canterbury Road—considerably more fashionable than Union

Street—with money that Eve had received as a wedding gift; he had joined the Masonic Order; and on June 12, 1925, a son, Stuart Symington, Jr. (Tim), was born. It was time for a regular job.

The young man went to Ed Burrows, vice president in charge of the plant, to ask for a line assignment. Burrows, who had been somewhat antagonistic but nevertheless helpful when Stuart arrived, listened patiently to his young employee's presentation. Stuart thought he had made his point and would get a regular position. A few days later, however, his Uncle Charlie, who had bought the Rochester plant from Uncle Tom Symington, called to ask him to spend the weekend at his home on Long Island. Charlie, a kindly man, tried to let his nephew down as easily as possible, but he delivered a devastating blow: Stuart was no longer wanted in Rochester.

Instead of going up, the young man in a hurry was on his way out. "Walking from my uncle's house to the Huntington Railroad Station on that soft summer evening had me as low in spirits as I have ever been, or ever would be. No money, no job, a family to support."

As might be expected, his family came to the rescue. Uncle Tom, who had given Stuart his first job in Rochester, was at work in Baltimore developing new products for the railroad industry and thought Stuart might be of some help in the business. So Stuart and Eve sold their house in Rochester, packed up Baby Tim, and moved into "a weird little apartment in Baltimore," part of the Garden Apartments on University Avenue, bordering on the exclusive Roland Park neighborhood where Stuart lived for a time while growing up.[3] "Eve was completely understanding and loyal, which bolstered me plenty," Symington later wrote.

The young couple did not remain long in Baltimore. Through the works manager at the Rochester plant, who was more of a friend than the vice president had been, Stuart got word of a company in Rochester that made sewer pipe and clay conduit for telephone lines which was about to go into receivership. The company owned a bed of clay in Pennsylvania that the works manager said would be excellent for producing the molding sand used in the manufacture of iron and steel castings. Stuart, who apparently had ready access through his uncles to large sums of money, persuaded Uncle Tom that the clay bed would be a good investment, and early in 1926 he went to Rochester with a certified check for three hundred thousand dollars to bid on the property. While in Rochester he met an oil man from Pennsylvania, Vernon Taylor, who also was interested in the property. Taylor suggested that they form a partnership and buy the land together. This was satisfactory with Tom, who joined in the establishment of the Eastern Clay Products Company, with Stuart as president. The company sold clay products to large foundries all over the country, and during the first year made a profit of 40 percent. Clearly, young Stuart knew how to run a company.

Uncle Charlie asked him to return to Rochester as his executive assistant. (His uncles for some years had assumed a familial responsibility for his well-being, and with the rather sudden death of his father on February 19, 1926, that sense of responsibility increased.[4] They were learning, however, that in young Stuart they had a man who could run a business and make money on his own. He would come to them for help from time to time, but he surely did not need to be taken care of.) Charlie's company had expanded rapidly, purchasing the Gould Coupler Company in Buffalo and its subsidiaries, the Gould Storage Battery Company and the Gould Car Lighting Corporation. The entire operation they renamed Symington-Gould.

So it was back to Rochester. Stuart kept his interests in the Eastern Clay Products Company, arranging with Taylor for someone else to serve as president. The young family moved into a house on fashionable East Avenue in the Brighton section of Rochester, "one of Rochester's proudest addresses."[5] While living there, a second son, James Wadsworth Symington, was born.

The family didn't stay long in Rochester. Stuart's uncles offered him the presidency of the battery company in Buffalo. After thinking about it for a while, he turned them down, saying that he knew nothing about selling batteries, but was confident he could manufacture them. He suggested that they make him operating vice president. They agreed, and the family moved to Buffalo, taking up residency in a new high-rise apartment on Park Circle.[6]

In a short time, however, Stuart found himself at odds with the newly appointed president of the company, a likable person who apparently found it difficult to make tough decisions. Stuart's efforts to clean up the operation ran afoul of some of the senior executives, who understandably took umbrage at having a twenty-six-year-old boy tell them how to run their business. Two of them threatened to quit unless Stuart resigned, and the president told Stuart that he had no choice but to support them. Stuart went down to Baltimore to talk to his Uncle Donald, president of the Baltimore Trust Company and a major investor in Symington-Gould. He suggested that the brothers get rid of the battery company's management and make him president, assuring his uncle that he had become convinced he could handle selling as well as manufacturing. Uncle Donald replied that they couldn't do that, but told Stuart he could have a position in a company in Baltimore in which the uncle had an interest. Stuart countered by suggesting that the uncles let him use a building in Rochester, which was being vacated because they were selling the car lighting business, to manufacture radio parts. They agreed, and set up a new company called Valley Appliances, Inc., with Stuart as president.[7]

Stuart had been successful as president of Eastern Clay Products, but he had not done well as an operating vice president—he was simply not cut out to be number two in anything. He would now have another chance to run his own show—and he would demonstrate once again that he knew how to run a business and make money. He would also use his family and other contacts more aggressively than ever before.

Radio was still in its infancy. It had advanced beyond the crystal set with earphones to a vacuum-tube receiver with a separate speaker, a large horn-shaped device which sat on top of or alongside the receiver. Valley Appliances concentrated on the manufacture of parts for the speakers and almost immediately began to show a profit. The Peerless Company in Rochester agreed to buy Valley parts for all of the loudspeakers they manufactured. This worked well for about a year, but early in 1929 Peerless merged with a company that manufactured receivers, loudspeakers, and all component parts. Valley lost its only customer and faced the prospect of closing down. Stuart responded by going to all of the companies to whom Peerless had been selling speakers made with Valley parts with an offer to provide complete speakers at prices below those of the competition. Once again, Valley Appliances had all of the business it could handle, working three shifts, seven days a week. Once again, however, the flurry of prosperity was short-lived. The autumn Crash of 1929 greatly reduced the demand for radios. At the same time, most manufacturers began to incorporate the speakers into self-contained cabinets. It was clear that the future in radio lay in manufacturing complete sets.

The manufacture of radios was tightly controlled by the Radio Corporation of America. Stuart applied for a license, but was turned down. Believing that RCA's practices might be in violation of the antitrust laws, he decided to go ahead without a license. He would manufacture all of the parts in the Valley plant, then ship them across town to an abandoned warehouse where a separate corporation would assemble them. This worked well for a while, and Stuart was selling all the radios he could put together. Then one day an attorney for RCA showed up at the plant with a warning that if they did not cease manufacturing radios without a license they would be sued. Stuart explained Valley's corporate structure and took his visitor over to the warehouse to show him what RCA would acquire if the suit was successful—a few tables and chairs.

Shortly thereafter, Senator Wadsworth received a letter from RCA's general counsel—a friend from college days—complaining about the unethical actions of his son-in-law. Stuart, called on the carpet, was able to convince the senator that the problem resided wholly in RCA's arbitrary and restrictive patent policy, and that, indeed, RCA, by pooling patents with General Electric, Westinghouse, AT&T, Western Electric, and United Fruit, had created a situation that was in violation of the antitrust laws. Senator Wadsworth replied to his friend at RCA that their patent policies were arbitrarily restrictive, and that he could envision the need for corrective legislation if they were not modified. Meanwhile, he urged his son-in-law to hire a good lawyer and arranged for him to obtain the services of his close friend, Colonel William J. "Wild Bill" Donovan, the World War I hero who was rapidly making a name for himself in New York's political and legal circles.[8]

Donovan soon had an impressive complaint drawn up against RCA and several others. At this juncture, Stuart turned to his Uncles Charlie and Donald for help. They owned 50 percent of the stock of a company known as the Locke Insulator Corporation; the other half was owned by General Electric. Stuart asked his uncles if they would make it possible for him to see Owen D. Young, chairman of GE's board, about getting to David Sarnoff, president of RCA. They suggested that he should first see George Baldwin, GE's senior vice president, and arranged for Stuart to visit Baldwin in his apartment in the old Savoy Plaza. Baldwin said that there was no use talking to Young, who didn't like Sarnoff. Stuart should call Sarnoff himself: "He knows about you and your family."

"Many thanks, but I have tried to see him before, and it takes weeks."

Baldwin thought that if Stuart told Sarnoff that he was going to sue on an antitrust basis he would get in. Stuart made the call from Baldwin's apartment, and at three o'clock that afternoon was in Sarnoff's office. There is no record of the conversation (Sarnoff later became a fairly close friend), but in due course Stuart got the license.

The license was particularly important, because now new vistas were opening up for the radio business, and twenty-eight-year-old Stuart Symington intended to make the most of them.

Opportunity came in the form of a suggestion from Dr. Fulton Cutting, owner of the Colonial Radio Company of Long Island City, that Valley and Colonial be merged. Cutting, a physicist, was an able scientist who had become fascinated by radio. His company, however, was undercapitalized, and he was having difficulty obtaining a license from RCA. Stuart had his license and saw that an association with Cutting could be highly beneficial. So, as he wrote later, "Somehow we raised the money and Valley and Colonial were consolidated." They retained the name Colonial, although Stuart became president; Cutting became chairman of the board and head of the engineering department. Both families moved to Buffalo, where the new company would operate in a plant formerly owned by the King Radio Company, a subsidiary of Sears, Roebuck and Company, which at that time was divesting itself of all of its manufacturing units.

The Sears connection was a prime example of Stuart Symington at his entrepreneurial best. While Valley Appliances was still concentrating on the manufacture of loudspeakers, they obtained an order from King to provide speakers for the Silvertone radios being manufactured for Sears. Shortly thereafter, the head of the furniture plant in North Carolina that provided the cabinets for the radios "confided" to Stuart that the plant manager at King Radio was demanding fifty cents a set on the side, suggesting that out of fairness Stuart should assume half the burden and pay him twenty-five cents a unit. Stuart immediately went to Buffalo and confronted the plant manager, who emphatically denied that he was involved in any such activity. A few days later, whether by coincidence or design, Arthur Barrows, head of the hardware department at Sears, dropped off the early morning train from Chicago for an unannounced visit. Stuart showed him through the plant and then took him to lunch. During lunch, Barrows burst out laughing and said that their North Carolina cabinetmaker had reported that Symington was asking for a personal cut on each speaker. When Stuart gave him the facts, he laughed and said that the King radio people had already told him the story.

In a few days, Barrows, who would become president of Sears and later would accept Symington's offer of appointment as undersecretary of the air force, called Stuart to say that General Robert E. Wood, president of Sears, would like to see him. At their meeting, Wood, emphasizing that Sears was a merchandiser and not a manufacturer, wondered if Stuart would be interested in buying King Radio. Stuart was definitely interested, but until he could complete his merger with Colonial, he was hardly in a position to move. Wood held the offer open, and with the merger completed, Stuart was ready to negotiate.

He did not negotiate from strength. Radios were still looked upon as something of a luxury, and the depression following the Crash of 1929 hit the radio business particularly hard—Colonial lost five hundred thousand dollars in May alone because of the need to write down inventory. Despite all this, the twenty-nine-year-old fledgling in the radio business worked out a very good deal with the hard-bitten head of the largest merchandising firm in the country. Colonial would take over the operation of the King Radio plant in Buffalo and assume responsibility for their contracts to purchase materials. In addition, Colonial would add five hundred thousand dollars to its working capital. In return, Sears agreed to give Colonial two million dollars a year in radio business, and four hundred thousand dollars in agricultural implements. Wood then said that in return for these contracts he wanted 29 percent of Colonial's stock. "No you don't," Symington replied, "you want 49." When Wood asked what all this was about, Symington said, "We want a partner, not just a customer."[9]

Symington later wrote: "That was about the smartest single proposal I ever made in my life."

It was indeed a good arrangement. As the depression deepened, the radio business all but collapsed. In the summer of 1932, Symington went to Wood ready to call the whole deal off: "No matter how well or how inexpensive we make these sets, you can't sell them. People just don't have money. So let's shake hands and call it a day, and we'll apply for receivership." The general responded by asking how much it would cost Colonial to operate until the end of the year if Sears gave them no business at all. Symington did not know but said he could find out in twenty-four hours. The next day, back in Wood's office, he said it would take $570,000. Wood called his financial vice president and told him "to give Symington a line of credit of $570,000 and let him draw on it as needed." Symington recalled that he literally choked up as he thanked the general. Wood replied, "You said you wanted a partner, not a customer, didn't you; and I have faith in the future of this country."

He obviously had faith in his young partner as well, and, as it turned out, his faith was more than justified. The depression started to lift a bit in 1933, and, as the New Deal pumped money into the economy, people began to have a little disposable income. Almost everyone wanted a radio—to listen to the news, the weather, and sports, to say nothing of Jack Benny and the Marx Brothers. Sears knew that they could profit from this demand if they could only find a product which people could afford. Colonial had developed a portable radio—the Silvertone Compact—and Sears wanted to retail it for less than ten dollars. Symington thought he could never deliver the sets at a figure that would make such a price possible, but at Wood's insistence he agreed to give it a try. As it turned out, Colonial made more profit on the compact set than on any other unit they manufactured.

Business was good, but despite the happy relationship with Sears, Stuart was uneasy with Colonial's dependence on one customer. Thanks to his brother Charlie, who had made a tremendous success of the car radio business in Detroit—the Symington boys were all much more successful in business than their father had been—Stuart was able to move Colonial into the manufacture of radios for automobiles, gadgets that rapidly caught on as Americans combined their passion for motor cars with their appetite for being entertained and kept up to date while they drove around. As far as home sets were concerned, Sears took all of their production, marketing them under the "Silvertone" name.

Once again Symington's supreme salesmanship came into play. He talked the Graybar Electric Company, a national distributor of home radio sets, into switching from giant General Electric to Colonial as their principal supplier, thus demonstrating, as he had in the patent scuffle with RCA, that he could take on a monster and win. The deal gave Colonial two national distributors of home sets, and, of course, the car radios that were being marketed through Charlie's company in Detroit.

Stuart, though, was restless, and in the fall of 1933 moved to New York, ostensibly to further develop Colonial's jobber-dealer relationships with Graybar. General Wood, who had taken a shine to the young man, thought he was making a mistake, that he would lose close contact with the plant and thus with the entire operation. In later years, Symington ruefully admitted that the general had been right, recalling Eve's grandfather Wadsworth's comment about farming: "the best fertilizer for any land is the foot of the owner."

Stuart's restlessness may have been caused by diminishing interest in the radio business. Colonial was doing well and making a nice profit, but the field was becoming increasingly competitive, and the prospect of trying to beat the giants such as RCA and Sylvania could have dimmed the attractiveness of the enterprise. In any event, shortly after moving to New York he began to have conversations with Charles Payson—who had married Eve's cousin, Joan Whitney—about becoming president of the Rustless Iron and Steel Company, a corporation manufacturing stainless steel under patents that made it possible to produce both rustproof and completely stainless steel at prices well below anything competitors could offer. The conversations continued through 1934; finally Payson made an offer that Stuart couldn't resist. He became president of Rustless on January 1, 1935.

By this time Symington had concluded that the way to riches in business was not through salary but through ownership. Income from his Colonial stock had made him financially independent. (He retained the stock, realizing a handsome profit when the company was sold to Sylvania several years later). His interest in Rustless centered around the acquisition of stock, and on becoming president he received an option on fifty thousand shares at $2.50 and twenty-five thousand shares at $7.50. At the time Rustless stock was selling for a dollar a share over the counter; in eighteen months it was quoted at $17.75. Just as Symington had developed Colonial Radio into a profitable enterprise, he made Rustless a thriving corporation. Payson sold Rustless to ARMCO in 1936 and they took over the management of the company.[10] Symington was out of a job, but Rustless and Colonial had made him a millionaire. At age thirty-five he could easily have retired.

Retirement, however, would have been impossible for Stuart Symington. He got involved with his friend Vernon Taylor, with whom he had founded Eastern Clay Products Company, in the manufacture and sale of a new device known as a parking meter. They formed a company called the Karpark Corporation, with Symington as president, and had their meter designed by Raymond Loewy, an internationally famous industrial designer.[11] With automobiles beginning to clog the streets and hard-pressed cities looking for additional sources of revenue as well as parking spaces, the new device seemed to have a bright future. Parking meters, however, were sold almost exclusively to local governments, and before a sale could be made a city council had to pass the necessary legislation. The process was entirely too cumbersome for the impatient Symington, and he soon lost interest in the parking meter business. He wrote later, "making something for $8 or $9, then selling it for around $60 was just not in my line."

He was "ready and anxious for a change." Meanwhile, he and Eve were enjoying to the full the good life in New York, and Stuart was developing—undeservedly, he always maintained—a reputation as a playboy.[12]

The Symingtons moved easily in the upper echelons of New York society. They had money, family background, and good looks. Charming and witty, they were an asset to any party—and they loved parties. Eve recalled, "Of course we had fun. We both love parties and we both love dancing and we danced a lot and we played bridge . . . We always had fun." Stuart told an interviewer, "We were young. We could be up all night someplace and go right on through and play tennis the next morning." (It would have been Stuart only for tennis. Eve suffered a spinal injury as a child and played little tennis and no golf, although she was a superb dancer and became an expert markswoman.)

They lived in a comfortable apartment at 1165 Park Avenue, "just past the very high rent district," close to the border between Harlem and Yorkville. Stuart Symington, Jr., recalled: "Jimmy and I used to get the hell beat out of us. We got it from both ends . . . gangs from Harlem on one side and Yorkville on the other." Michael and Peter Forrestal, sons of the future first secretary of defense, had similar problems as they made their way from the Forrestal home on Beekman Place to the school bus on Park Avenue. They wanted their father to provide a chauffeur to take them to school, but he refused, arranging instead for them to take boxing lessons. Occasionally, Peter was pitted against Jim Symington, who, unlike the Forrestal boys, loved boxing, and who, according to his father, developed into "the best amateur lightweight I ever saw." Jim recalled, "We stood toe to toe and exchanged fake, featherweight punches. Not a blow was struck in anger."[13]

Symington and Forrestal, whose careers would mesh and tragically fall apart in a celebrated controversy over air power, became close friends. They played tennis at the River Club and regular weekend golf at Piping Rock or the Creek Club in a foursome which included, among others, Robert Lovett, a future secretary of defense, and Di Gates, who was married to Alice Davison, daughter of Henry P. Davison, a Morgan partner who during World War I had been chairman of the governing board of the World League of Red Cross societies. (Symington still played a wicked game of tennis—Payne Whitney's pro once told one of the boys, "You should see your old man at this game"—but he was turning more and more to golf, which he learned to play well and which became almost a passion.)[14]

Summers were spent in a house at Greentree, the Payne Whitney estate, on the North Shore of Long Island, among the great estates of the super-rich and the imposing summer homes of many whose fortunes, though huge, were not quite as great. They saw a lot of Eve's cousins, Jock and Sonny Whitney, and through them mingled with not only the business rich but also the literati and celebrities from the theater, Hollywood, and the world of sport. When, for example, Liz Altemus married Jock Whitney in what society columnist Maury Paul, "Cholly Knickerbocker," described as "THE match of the season," with Robert Benchley serving as best man, "also in attendance at the splendid ceremony were many of Jock's other illustrious intimates, including Fred Astaire, author Donald Ogden Stewart, polo great Thomas Hitchcock, Jr., Charles Payson, Whitney's brother-in-law, and fellow Yalemen James J. Wadsworth and W. Stuart Symington, Wadsworth's brother-in-law."[15]

In common with New York business leaders of his day, Symington wore a bowler hat in winter and a stiff straw hat in summer. He and movie actor Adolphe Menjou shared the same tailor, Frank Gez. His suit coats were tailored to conceal his deformed left arm. He belonged to the Madison Square Garden Club. He and Eve frequently went to the fights; the world heavyweight champion Gene Tunney was a good friend. Most years they went out to Louisville for the Kentucky Derby, mingling with the horsey set from around the world— among their friends was the noted horseman and social lion, Serge Obolensky.[16] They regularly were guests at the most glamorous parties in town. It was a heady existence, and they both enjoyed it. Small wonder that Stuart began to be thought of as something of a playboy. That reputation was reinforced when Eve started making headlines as "Eve Symington, the Society Singer."

It all began one May evening in 1934 at a benefit for the Bellevue Children's Cardiac Clinic at the Place Pigalle, a swank midtown nightclub. Toward the end of the evening, which had featured a number of professional entertainers, some of Eve's friends, who had heard her sing at parties, urged her to perform. Finally she went to the microphone, and, looking exquisite under the spotlight, began to sing. "There she was, with this unbelievable voice, and she was standing with this lovely mass of blonde hair," her husband fondly remembered, and she brought down the house.[17]

A few weeks later, the management offered her a four-week contract at five hundred dollars per week. She wanted to accept. Stuart encouraged her, but suggested that she check with her father. He was in politics, and while singing in nightclubs was becoming a glamorous thing for rich young women to do— Cobina Wright, Jr., was at the Waldorf and Sally Clark, a Roosevelt relative, sang at the Plaza—he might have some difficulty with the idea. James Wadsworth, who after his defeat for reelection to the Senate in 1926 was in the first term of what would be two decades in the House of Representatives and was being mentioned as a possible Republican nominee for the presidency, asked his daughter only one question. "Is Place Pigalle east or west of Broadway?" When she told him it was two doors west, he replied, "Well, I guess that's all right."[18]

Opening night was a great success. The place was jammed with celebrities. The Whitneys were all there, as were the Wadsworths, who had come up from Washington for the event. Cholly Knickerbocker wrote, "Wotta party—wotta jam. The 'red plush' set was out in full force." The *New York News* carried a top-of-the-page row of pictures, headed "Social Set Goes Hi-de-ho . . . Screen Stars Go La-de-da . . . as Society Gal Goes Crooner." Among those pictured were tobacco heiress Doris Duke and screen stars Douglas Fairbanks, Sr., and Kay Francis. Introduced by Phil Harris, Eve stood under a bright spotlight, "a slim figure in a glistening gold satin," singing the torch songs that would become her trademark: "The Very Thought of You," "A Good Man Is Hard to Find," "Moonglow," "Two Loves," and "All I Do Is Dream of You." Cholly Knickerbocker reported, "Eve's debut as a singer received such an ovation as I have seldom heard. Her relatives and friends rallied 'round, whistled, roared, stamped, cheered and applauded until the synthetic lampposts in the room literally swayed on their foundations."[19]

She became the toast of Cafe Society. After two successful stints at Place Pigalle, she went to Le Mirage at 125 East Fifty-fourth Street, described by the *New Yorker* as "one of the most charmingly decorated spots in town." The magazine went on, "La Symington, statuesque and smiling, relies on her incredibly deep voice for all her effects, singing without chichi or dramatics. She gives the impression, by deliberate design, of being an amateur. Which helps the inty feeling of the whole place." When the Waldorf-Astoria opened the Sert Room, Eve headed the bill, and again, "everyone who counts" was there.[20]

Eve's success inspired others. The legitimate nightclub was just emerging after the repeal of Prohibition and managers were scrambling to find new ways to lure customers. The society singer with a built-in following of wealthy friends seemed like a sure bet. So pronounced was the trend that the American Federation of Actors filed a complaint. Eve fired right back. "I can't see why any girl hasn't a right to take a job and keep it on her own merits," she said. "Everybody's got responsibilities, and in society the family and children are just as important to you. I need the money, but that's got nothing to do with it."[21]

Eve, however, was in a class by herself. She brought in the crowds every night, not just on opening night when the place was filled with her friends. Inez Callaway commented, "And you might think that night club proprietors would have added two and two together by this time, given up the hunt for another Eve Symington and hired themselves some professional talent." Even with the so-called professional talent, Eve more than held her own. As Jack Gould wrote in the *New York Times,* Eve was "entitled to slap the wrists of the wags who once upon a time claimed her employment as a singer was merely a come-on for the customers who do not eat peas off their knives. To eardrums throbbing from the scratchy gigglings of many torch singers, her low and cultivated voice is melodic glycerine."[22]

When she took the job, Eve wasn't sure that she would do more than fulfill her four-week contract, but she liked the work and continued to perform for several weeks each spring and fall for the next four years, moving from the Place Pigalle to the Iridium Room in the St. Regis, the Persian Room at the Plaza, and, finally, the Sert Room of the Waldorf-Astoria, where she spent two years, earning about one thousand dollars a week, singing alternately with Xavier Cugat and Leo Reisman.[23] Her husband recalled with pride, "Cool, collected, beautiful, with total poise, she caught the heart of New York with her appealing voice."

She became a genuine celebrity, known for her beauty and her clothes as well as her voice. Her picture appeared regularly in the fashion magazines and roto-gravure sections of the newspapers, frequently in a smart bathing suit that showed her figure off to great advantage. In 1937, the Fashion Academy named her as one of the five best-dressed women in the public eye, along with Jessica Dragon-ette, Carole Lombard, Lily Pons, and Helen Gleason.[24]

Her performing horizon expanded beyond the nightclub circuit. She appeared on the Rudy Vallee show and with Major Bowes' Amateur Hour. Paramount Pictures asked her to take a screen test and offered her a contract. There was only one hitch. They wanted her to have her front teeth filed down and straightened.

"I can't begin to tell you how relieved I was," she told a reporter for the *New York Woman.* She really didn't want to go to Hollywood, and this took the decision out of her hands.[25]

Apparently, the Paramount offer got her to thinking about whether she really wanted to continue as an entertainer. In January 1938 she terminated her engagement at the Waldorf, "to give herself and her vocal chords a rest." She and Stu flew to Trinidad and then took a small freighter to Tobago, where they spent a month rusticating with Stuart's sister, Louise, and her husband, Lawrence Balliere of Baltimore.[26]

Shortly after returning from Tobago, Eve, apparently without consulting her husband, called her manager, David (Sonny) Wirthlin of the Music Corporation of America, and told him to cancel all her contracts. "What's come over

Eve?" a startled Wirthlin asked Stuart, who was equally surprised. She told her husband, "I had to decide whether I really wanted to be a singer, or a wife and mother."

In an interview with society columnist Dorothy Kilgallen she said, "I just want to see how it feels to go to bed nights for a change." When it was suggested that she was going to stay home to take care of her children, she smiled, "Heavens! If I said that people would say, 'High time!'"[27]

By all accounts she had done a remarkable job of balancing the demands of her career with those of motherhood. Her singing engagements were only for a few weeks each year, and when she was working she always managed to have dinner with the boys. It was a fast life, however, the kind that could put a strain on even the solidest of marriages, especially in a milieu where monogamy, if practiced, was serial at best. Danton Walker, gossip columnist for the *Daily News,* wrote that "Stuart and Eve Symington are straining at the marital leash." Apparently, there were other rumors, but there seems to have been no basis for any of them.[28] Stuart was proud of his wife and reveled in her success. He was in her audience almost every night, "the only stage door Johnny who could take her home."

Little wonder that he developed a reputation as something of a playboy.

He was at loose ends, and had he not found something more interesting to do than manufacture parking meters, he might have indulged his playboy proclivities even further. He was rich; his wife was rich and was earning a handsome salary. He and Taylor expanded the parking meter operation by forming a second company, Vehicular Parking, Ltd., to gain further market share, but he was becoming increasingly disenchanted, and in the summer of 1938 sold his stock at five cents on the dollar. He later described his connection with the parking meter business as "an unfortunate undertaking," saying that the industry, "having started wrong, would not be straightened out."[29]

Meanwhile, he was involved in negotiations that would culminate in a development second in importance only to his marriage to Evelyn Wadsworth.

3

Turnaround in St. Louis

IN THE SPRING of 1938, David Van Alstyne, head of the New York investment banking firm of Van Alstyne and Noel and chairman of the board committee charged with finding a new president for a failing motor and fan manufacturing company in St. Louis, called on James Forrestal, president of Dillon, Read and Co., to ask whether he knew anyone who could take over the company and turn it around. Forrestal suggested his good friend Stuart Symington as just the man Emerson needed.[1]

Van Alstyne followed up on Forrestal's suggestion, and soon agreed that Symington was ideally suited to lead the Emerson Electric Manufacturing Company back to profitability. Symington had wide experience in the electrical manufacturing business, he was a super-salesman, and, as he had demonstrated at both Colonial Radio and Rustless Iron and Steel, he knew how to build a profitable business. For his part, Symington, having extricated himself from the unfortunate parking meter venture, was looking for a new challenge.

Emerson surely offered one. Founded in 1890 by a small group of men excited by the possibilities of the new electrical industry, the company soon found its niche in the manufacture of small motors and electric fans. Growing with St. Louis, which at the time of the Trans-Mississippi Exposition in 1904 had become the fourth-largest city in the United States, Emerson supplied forty-two wholesalers in twenty states by the end of World War I. At this juncture, the principal owners decided to expand capacity by moving into a new eight-story building on Washington Avenue in downtown St. Louis. They helped pay for the move by issuing one million dollars' worth of preferred stock.

As Emerson's official history puts it, "The company's decision to expand immediately after World War I could not have come at a worse time." The postwar recession stifled sales, and, in addition, Emerson faced increasing competition from manufacturers who installed their own motors in appliances. Moreover, Emerson's new factory, a dusty, multistoried building, was ill-suited to the manufacture of the newer motors, especially the hermetically sealed refrigerator motors, which required clean assembly conditions. The company enjoyed a brief, fragile profitability in the mid-1920s, but the Great Depression nearly wiped it out. Sales declined by more than two-thirds between 1929 and 1932, making it impossible for the company to meet its dividend commitments and producing a bitter stockholders' fight.

The preferred stockholders won and brought in a new manager, Joseph Newman, a thirty-five-year-old executive who had been chief financial officer of the St. Louis–based Lesser Goldman Cotton Company. Newman increased sales, but profits remained elusive, thus forcing the company to skip dividend after dividend and further exacerbating the tension between the preferred and common stockholders. In an effort to cut costs, Newman laid off 240 employees (about a tenth of the workforce), producing in the spring of 1937 a bitter fifty-three-day sit-down strike—the longest, to that date, in American history. At the same time, in an attempt to obtain new capital, Newman persuaded the board of directors to take the company public, with the issuance of forty thousand shares of common stock. By the end of the year, only twenty-eight shares had been sold. Clearly, the company was in serious trouble. David Van Alstyne, whose firm was handling the unfortunate stock offering, persuaded a majority of the board that new leadership was needed—leadership which he hoped Stuart Symington would provide.

In July 1938 Symington went to St. Louis with Van Alstyne to meet with Emerson's directors. The meeting did not go well. Symington had assumed that the directors were interested in his manufacturing and merchandising abilities. Some of them, it seemed, were more interested in his money, and when it became clear that he would be expected to invest a considerable sum of his own in the company, he declined the offer. That night, sitting in the club car of the Pennsylvania Railroad's "Spirit of St. Louis" en route to New York, Van Alstyne tried to persuade Symington to reconsider. He had put his own company at risk by guaranteeing the stock offering. "If Emerson goes broke," he said, "then Van Alstyne, Noel and Company goes broke, too."

The talk continued. Symington had developed considerable respect for Van Alstyne, and the challenge at Emerson intrigued him. Finally he said, "Dave, if you'll go back and get me the exact deal I asked for, then I'll reconsider."

That "deal" consisted of twenty-four thousand dollars a year in salary and an option on 15 percent—seventy-five thousand shares—of the company's common stock. Van Alstyne persuaded the directors to agree, and Symington went back to St. Louis for another, more satisfactory meeting, during which the details of his employment were worked out. His appointment as president and general manager, effective October 1, 1938, was announced on September 6.[2]

Symington took Eve to Bermuda for a couple weeks' vacation before heading out to St. Louis. The family had no plans to move, at least for a while. Eve no longer was singing at the Waldorf, but the boys were in school, and Stuart was not at all sure that things would work out at Emerson. He took a room at the Jefferson Hotel, from where he could walk to his office, and then, after becoming a member of the St. Louis Racquet Club, he lived there for several months. While living at the Racquet Club he became acquainted with Clark Clifford, beginning a friendship that was to become increasingly close and would last a lifetime.[3]

The new president found the problems even greater and more complex than he had assumed. Sales were down; the warehouses were loaded with outmoded and overpriced inventory; the company's finances were shaky; the workforce was sullen and unproductive; top management was loaded with deadwood. As Emerson's official history put it, "What Symington didn't know was that . . . his hard-won stock option was practically worthless."

With characteristic dash and energy, he attacked all his problems at virtually the same time. By 8:30 on his first morning at work he had fired the purchasing agent, and within a few months he had replaced most of the company's senior executives. Two whom he retained—Oscar Schmitt in sales and John Driy in production—became trusted lieutenants who worked hard and enthusiastically with their new boss. Symington recalled, "many was the evening, after a long day, that Schmitt, Driy, and I worked late at night upstairs in my room at the [Racquet] club." Symington reciprocated their loyalty with promotions and seats on the board of directors. He also persuaded the board to transfer to the two men twenty-five thousand of the seventy-five thousand shares on which he had options. Although the company was losing about a thousand dollars a month, he convinced the directors to put up $22,800 to hire the Trundle Engineering Company of Cleveland, whom he had used at Colonial and Rustless, to do an industrial engineering study of the company's organization and operating methods. In a few months he had completely revamped both.

On the afternoon of his first day at work he called a meeting of all the foremen, the union heads, the works manager, and the plant superintendent. He had been well briefed on the history of Emerson's labor troubles. Before going to St. Louis he had lunch with Jim Carey, president of the United Electrical Workers Union and an old friend. Carey knew that Symington, unlike most industrialists, believed in strong unions—Symington had cooperated fully when he organized the workers at Colonial Radio. When Symington asked him about the union's plans for Emerson, he responded, "To put them out of business at the earliest opportunity." He pointed out that Emerson's facilities and methods were so outmoded that the only way they could stay competitive was to skimp on wages, and when Symington told him that he had just become president of Emerson, Carey advised his friend to "get out as fast as you can and keep your losses to a minimum." Symington, however, wanted to know what they could do together. Before lunch was over the two men had agreed on a union shop, and Carey said the union would be patient as Symington tried to improve wages. When Symington asked about William Sentner, an avowed Communist who headed the union's local, Carey breezily replied, "He's not so tough. He's only been arrested twenty-nine times. I've been arrested fifty-seven."

The new president faced a hostile audience. The union had bitter memories of the company's intransigence during the prolonged strike of the year before, the average take-home pay was only sixteen dollars a week, and management seemed to be dragging its feet on implementing even the small concessions wrung from them as the result of the strike. Symington later wrote:

> At this first meeting I pleaded for understanding, emphasized Ben Franklin's comment, "If we don't all hang together, surely we'll hang separately," said we wanted to establish true profit-sharing, with seniority in years as important as position; in other words, we would all win together or we would lose together.
>
> While talking at this first meeting with the plant people, a man previously introduced to me as the union "in-plant" representative, would laugh, in jeering fashion, at most of my observations; so I finally turned on him, "Why don't you shut up? You are supposed to be the representative of these people, are being paid by the union heads from out of town while these men and women are nearly starving and the company is going broke. As their representative, you are a disgrace." This man yelled something back and started towards me. A new voice then said, "Sit down, Bob"; and for the first time I had a look at William Sentner, the International Vice President of the United Electrical Workers. Sentner then asked, "Do you really mean what you are saying?"
>
> "Yes, or I wouldn't be saying it."
>
> "Well, we'll give it a try."

Symington thanked him, and the meeting broke up.

William E. Sentner, president of District 8 of the United Electrical, Radio and Machine Workers of America (UE), one of six children of a Russian Jewish immigrant, had helped to organize St. Louis's first International Ladies Garment

Workers local in 1909. He grew up in a milieu of labor activism. He recalled, "When I was a kid I used to break windows in strikes for two-bits a piece." In 1924 at the age of sixteen he enrolled in Washington University's School of Architecture. Becoming alienated from campus life, he took up with a radical intellectual and began to read Karl Marx. When his money ran out, he hit the road, winding up with the Merchant Marine. He traveled the world as a laborer and fireman, studying Marx and American labor history. He returned to St. Louis in 1933 to work as a draftsman, and in 1933 he joined the local John Reed Club. Before the year was out, he had become a member of the St. Louis branch of the Communist party, and soon was devoting himself full-time to radicalizing the labor movement. Sentner, though openly avowing his party membership, was no ordinary, doctrinaire Communist. Rather, he thought of himself as an intellectual and a proponent of "civic unionism," which sought to make a connection between the union and the community, and he was perfectly willing to cooperate with management if he thought it would benefit the union.[4]

There could hardly have been a greater contrast between two men than that between Symington and Sentner: Symington, the scion of an old-line Maryland family; Sentner, the son of a Russian immigrant; Symington, who by and large had led a life of privilege, part of the country's social and financial upper crust; Sentner, who had led a life of poverty, part of the country's underclass, hounded by bill collectors and the police. Despite their differences—and their views were as divergent as their backgrounds—they developed a grudging respect for each other, exchanging books and pamphlets and arguing economic and social questions. They both joined a discussion group, "The Serious Thinkers," organized by William Scarlett, Protestant Episcopal Bishop of St. Louis, one of the most liberal men in the church (who, over the years, would become one of Symington's closest friends) and made up of some of the city's leading business and professional men. Sentner was an occasional visitor in the Symington home. Stuart Symington, Jr., remembers seeing his father and Sentner standing by the fireplace in their living room and hearing his father describe Sentner's career in the Merchant Marine and his rise in the labor movement. "I remember how embarrassed Sentner was as Dad praised him to the skies."[5]

Symington moved quickly to take advantage of Sentner's apparent willingness to cooperate. Following up on his earlier conversation with Carey, he offered Sentner a check-off system through which the company would collect the union's dues in return for deferring wage demands—the company was losing money and simply couldn't afford to increase wages. When Sentner seemed skeptical, Symington showed him the books. Convinced that the company actually was losing money and amazed that Symington's salary was only about half of what he had thought it was, Sentner agreed. In sharp contrast to its traditional policy of confrontation, Emerson seemed to be moving toward a new policy of cooperative labor relations. Sentner, despite his visceral suspicion of management, was developing an entirely new style of union leadership. Some charged that he had succumbed to Symington's "soft soap," but most realized that he was simply facing up to the facts of life, that if workers were to have good jobs, their companies must be profitable.

It was not all smooth sailing. The bargain with UE placed two union stewards in the time-study department, which determined wage rates. The union felt that this provided labor with an opportunity to participate in the establishment of wage rates, but Symington soon let the union know that wage rates would be fixed by management. He threatened to withdraw the check off, but later compromised by agreeing to the establishment of a joint union-management committee to deal with future rate changes.

Despite occasional difficulties, union and management continued to cooperate for the benefit of the company. Dramatic evidence of this came in the fall of 1939 when Emerson received an offer from Evansville, Indiana, to relocate there. The offer was tempting. Emerson's production facilities were scattered among five buildings in downtown St. Louis, none of them on a railroad siding, and none of them equipped to support the production Symington knew he would have to achieve to make Emerson profitable. He suggested to Sentner that unless there was some way for the company to find the money to rebuild its facilities in St. Louis, he might have to accept the Evansville offer.

Sentner responded with an almost unheard of effort for a labor leader, particularly one from the far left. He launched a "civic campaign" to solicit money from business and real estate groups to keep the company in town. This failed. The Chamber of Commerce thought it would set a dangerous precedent—actually, some of their leaders would not have been unhappy to see Symington go, although they liked him personally. Sentner, rebuffed by the Chamber of Commerce, persuaded Local 1102, the company's union, to guarantee a $140,000 loan, with funds to be derived from payroll deductions, and to be reimbursed through a profit-sharing plan that Symington was promoting.

As it turned out, Emerson didn't need the union's money. Using personal contacts, Symington was able to persuade the Bankers Trust Company in New York, which had considered calling its loan, to stick with Emerson, and to convince the Marine Midland Trust Company to extend a new line of credit. He was also successful in persuading important St. Louis bankers, notably Walter Smith of First National and Hord Hardin and Sidney Maestre of the Mississippi Valley Trust Company, to support his efforts—someone suggested that the bankers came through because they "shuddered at the thought of unions going into the banking business."

Although the money wasn't needed, the offer dramatized how far Emerson had come. In a year and a half, Stuart Symington had redefined the relationship between the company and its workforce, transforming it from confrontation to cooperation, and making Emerson stand out like a beacon—or a sore thumb, depending on your point of view—in essentially conservative St. Louis. A union pamphlet, reciting the history of the effort to keep Emerson in St. Louis, described the suspicion and lack of trust that had characterized labor-management relations at Emerson and then went on to praise Symington as instituting the "First real attempt on the part of the company to arrive at a common and workable understanding with the Union," an understanding based on "mutual respect and good will."[6]

Emerson became known as a good place to work, and Symington after a few short months had become recognized as one of the most progressive employers in town. This didn't endear him to many of his fellow businessmen, who found their own labor relations complicated by his open cooperation with the union— although he probably was never in danger of being kicked out of the Racquet Club or run out of town, as he sometimes jokingly asserted.[7] He did, however, build a solid record with organized labor, which in later years gave him consistent and unstinting political support.

Emerson also took the lead in the racial integration of its workforce. Neither completely northern nor completely southern, St. Louis was a border city, not unlike the Baltimore in which Stuart Symington had grown up. In the late 1930s, aside from public transportation, St. Louis was completely Jim Crow, and many of its business leaders were content to let it stay that way. Symington had inherited "advanced" views on racial questions from his mother, and he had worked side by side with blacks in his uncles' plants in Rochester. At Emerson, with Sentner's cooperation, he moved quickly to break the bonds of segregation at the plant. He desegregated the cafeteria and the "smoking islands" where workers took their breaks to avoid smoking near flammable material. He provided opportunities for blacks to move into skilled and semiskilled jobs. As a result, although Emerson did not employ as many blacks as such industries as steel and meatpacking, it was looked upon in the black community as the best place in town to work—and again, Stuart Symington's record at Emerson provided part of the basis for the consistent support he later received from Missouri's black voters.

All of this, however, would have come to naught had Symington not been able to make Emerson profitable. It did not prove to be easy.

Heavy dependence on electric fans made the company vulnerable to a host of competitors and, more ominously, to the looming specter of air-conditioning. Emerson needed new products and new customers, and it needed them fast. The company's fledgling president sought both simultaneously, using, as he had in his search for financing, what *Fortune* called his "vast catalog of those mysterious things known as 'contacts.'"[8]

His most important contact was that with his old friend at Sears, Roebuck and Company, General Robert E. Wood, who had put him on the road to success in the radio business. He went up to Chicago to see the general and found him receptive. Wood handed Symington a copy of the Sears catalog and told him to look through it to see if there was anything in it that Emerson could manufacture. It wasn't going to be quite that simple, however. Sears had become a large and complex corporate bureaucracy. Wood referred Symington to Arthur Barrows, head of the hardware department—and future president—whom Symington also knew from his days at Colonial Radio. Barrows, in turn, asked him to see Tom Dunlop, who handled purchasing for the hardware department. Dunlop proved to be rather difficult. "Don't think that just because you once sold us radios," he said brusquely, "and just because you're a friend of the General's, that you can come in here and automatically get business. If you want any, you'll have to start from scratch. In fact, you'll come in here on your knees, barking like a dog."

Symington stalked out, his temper understandably rising—but then his instincts as a salesman took over. He got down on his knees and went back into the office, barking like a dog, grinning, and saying, "If competitive, some business please." Dunlop's office was a partially open, cagelike affair, and all of this took place in full view and hearing of the office workers on the floor. They burst into applause, and Symington, having demonstrated that he would do almost anything to make a sale, was on his way to working out a very lucrative arrangement as a Sears supplier.

Most of Emerson's production for Sears consisted of small motors, which could be manufactured with very little retooling. Late in 1939, Emerson took over the manufacture of electric arc welders, which Sears marketed under its well-known Craftsman label. This all came about through one of Symington's characteristic snap decisions. As he and Emerson's official historian tell it, Symington had gone to Chicago to see Dunlop about a number of business matters and was kept waiting for several hours. Symington and Dunlop had become good friends, and when Symington chided Dunlop about his treatment, Dunlop told him that he (Dunlop) was in deep trouble. The company from which Sears bought its electric welders had just gone broke and he needed to find a new owner right away to protect his catalog. Symington replied that if Dunlop would talk to him about what he had come to discuss, Emerson would buy the company.

"But you don't even know where the company is."

"That's right, but if you have the welders in your catalog, they must be pretty good, so I'll take a chance."

Dunlop jumped up, and said, "Let's go right down and see the General." On the way down, Symington asked, "By the way, where is the company?"

"Cincinnati," was the answer, and by evening Symington and Dunlop were on the train for Cincinnati. General Wood, who approved of the deal, said, "Don't buy the stock, Stuart, just the assets."

Within twenty-four hours Emerson owned the Commonwealth Manufacturing Company of Cincinnati. Symington sold all parts of the business (including the manufacture of artificial flowers) except the production of welders, and soon the welder-manufacturing equipment was shipped to St. Louis and put into production.

The manufacture of welders added to Emerson's product mix, and with Sears taking the entire output the venture created a profit from the beginning. Making welders, however, would never be a core business for Emerson. The company had built its reputation on the manufacture of small motors, particularly those which powered the famous Emerson fans. Management had long realized, though, that the demand for electric fans was declining. For a time, the company made money by producing motors for refrigerators, but in the mid-1930s refrigerator manufacturers began putting their compressor motors inside hermetically sealed cooling units. Joe Newman had tried to make hermetically sealed motors, but with no success. Emerson's dusty old multistoried buildings simply were not suited for the manufacture of hermetics.

To Symington it made no sense whatever to give up such a large and lucrative market. Refrigerators were replacing iceboxes in homes all across America. Most of the motor market was controlled by the giants such as General Electric and Westinghouse, which also produced complete refrigerators. The smaller, independent refrigerator manufacturers would jump at the chance to secure a quality motor from an independent supplier. Convinced by his engineers that Emerson could build hermetically sealed motors if they had adequate facilities, Symington started looking; it was at this juncture that the offer from Evansville, Indiana, came in, and the union rallied to his support. As has been indicated, he did not need union support, but was able to get bank financing to remain in St. Louis. On March 12, 1940, Emerson announced that it was purchasing twenty-two acres at West Florissant Road and the Wabash Railroad tracks in the then relatively rural St. Louis County suburb of Ferguson to build a hermetic motor production facility. The company also announced that it was taking an option on 140 adjoining acres for possible expansion.

By the fall of 1940, the Florissant Road plant was up and going. Most important of all, in 1940 the company began to show a small profit, and Symington was able to inaugurate the profit-sharing plan he had talked about during his first meeting with union leaders—a plan he felt was the key to improved labor relations and increased production. In the beginning no one seemed to be particularly enthusiastic. Sentner and the other union leaders were only moderately interested. Most business leaders considered profit-sharing a radical idea that upset the balance between management and labor and that couldn't possibly work. Symington, nevertheless, went ahead.

The plan provided that 22 percent of the earnings applicable to common stock were to go to the employees, with two-thirds based on salary and one-third on longevity. There weren't many profits to share that first year. The total available for distribution amounted to only $21,420.[9] William Drohan, one of Emerson's labor representatives, recalled that his first check was for twelve dollars, "but when you were making only eighteen bucks a week, that twelve looked great." Profits grew steadily, and Symington increased the amount available for distribution to 30 percent. In 1944, employees shared in a total of $1,256,100, and the checks ranged upwards from five hundred dollars. An important reason for the profitability, Symington asserted, was "primarily because the organization, from top to bottom, was working together as a team":

> As illustration, one Sunday afternoon my wife and I were motoring to a Cardinal doubleheader, when a large but very old Cadillac, loaded with some who clearly already had had a few beers, cut us off sharply. One of them looked back in derision. We heard him suddenly yell, "My God, that's Mr. Symington." Their driver got out, volunteered, "Sorry about that." Then, pointing to the old Cadillac with obvious pride, "Look what I bought with my profit-sharing check."[10]

Symington told the stockholders, "correlated with the desire to share profits with all the people responsible for creating them is the aim to have this company known as a desirable place to work. We are sure that such a reputation is to the interest of every stockholder."

Emerson indeed was becoming known as a most desirable place to work. Union leaders looked upon Symington as the most progressive employer in St. Louis. Cooperation had replaced confrontation in labor-management relations, and during Symington's presidency, Emerson never had a union-voted strike. Black workers, still living in what was essentially a Jim Crow city, found expanded opportunity and genuine integration. In their minds Emerson was the best employer in St. Louis.

Even among business leaders who had looked askance at the brash young newcomer's liberal ideas, Symington began to gain acceptance. This proved to be more difficult than winning over labor, in part because many of the more conservative St. Louis businessmen thought that he had sold out to the unions—a charge Symington hotly denied. Symington got off to a bad start with some St.

Louis leaders when, shortly after he arrived, he was in a meeting at which it was suggested that he adopt a spy system at Emerson—apparently in line with practices in certain other St. Louis plants—in which selected workers would be hired to eavesdrop on their fellows and write up reports for management. Symington responded that they ought to be ashamed of themselves for suggesting such a thing. Further complicating Symington's relations with his fellow business leaders was the whispering campaign against the new president conducted by some former Emerson executives and their allies on the board. Sid Maestre, Hord Hardin, and Walter Smith, in addition to their continuing financial support, did much to help Symington gain acceptance in the St. Louis business community.

But most important was Symington himself, his outgoing, athletic personality, his ability to sell himself to virtually everyone he encountered. A senior Emerson executive observed, "Symington was one of the outstanding salesmen of all time—fantastic at the art of putting himself across to others. He could sell himself so well, and he could therefore sell whatever he decided to sell."

Even before these evidences of success had occurred, Symington had decided that he could make it at Emerson and had arranged for Eve and the boys to move to St. Louis. The family moved in the fall of 1939, in time for the boys to begin school. They bought a house at 6 Lenox Place in the Central West End. A syndicated gossip columnist wrote, "The famous . . . Eve Symington, the first society torch singer, is moving to St. Louis with her husband. . . . St. Louis is all agog over the famous folk moving in on them."[11]

This was something of an exaggeration, to be sure, but the new couple almost immediately moved into the top echelons of St. Louis society. Although some of the high-society men might look askance at Stuart's unorthodox views and his dalliance with labor leaders, their wives could hardly ignore Eve with her background, her glamour, and her connections, or Stu with his elegant good looks and his irresistible charm—as Clark Clifford's wife, Marny, once said, "Stuart is the kind of man who makes any woman, however unglamorous, feel lovely."[12] But, as had been the case in New York, Stuart and Evelyn Symington were sought out for themselves. They were great party people. Soon they joined the St. Louis Country Club, the cachet of acceptance in St. Louis society.

Sid Maestre put Stuart on the board of the Mississippi Valley Trust Company, and the Chamber of Commerce elected him to its board and asked him to serve on its very important and active airport committee—signs that he was gaining acceptance. Shortly he would be recognized as one of St. Louis's leading businessmen, and his performance at Emerson gained recognition beyond the city.

In April 1940, he delivered a talk on "Getting the Production Job Done" at the spring conference of the Society for the Advancement of Management in

Cleveland. It was the first time he had addressed a national audience, and he began with a modest disclaimer, saying that for him to address this group on production was "like a college player explaining to the Yankee infield how to play ground balls; perhaps more analogous, comparable to an interne [*sic*] instructing the staff on the details of an intricate operation." He talked for a while about ways to achieve management efficiency—fairly routine, textbook stuff— but then he must have startled his audience by launching into a spirited defense of the Wagner Act, the establishment of the National Labor Relations Board, and other New Deal legislation covering wages and hours and unemployment compensation. He noted that the pamphlet sent out in advance of the meeting called these "handicaps." He argued that properly administered, they could well promote industrial efficiency. Buoyed by his experience at Emerson, he expounded at length on the importance of collective bargaining and strong, well-led unions. "We hear a lot of talk about dishonest people getting hold of unions. It is possible. They apparently even get hold of nations. They have been known to get hold of banks, and of great industrials." He also talked at length about one of his favorite subjects, profit sharing. If profits are not shared, he warned, "the capitalistic system will fall."[13]

Symington's optimistic views of the New Deal's labor laws made him stand out among American industrialists, just as they had among his peers in St. Louis. But the overriding story in St. Louis was the dramatic turnaround he had achieved at Emerson. He would soon face other and greater challenges as he and Emerson sought to find their role in the war that was sweeping over much of the world.

4

Five E's for Excellence

FOR A TIME Emerson seemed quite uninterested in participating in the massive industrial effort President Franklin Roosevelt had called for in response to the Nazi juggernaut's sweep across western Europe. At a June 1940 dinner honoring Emerson's longtime employees, Symington reported that the company had "avoided seeking any business connected with the war now in progress." For Emerson, "concentration on our own products . . . [was] the wise course to follow."[1]

In the summer of 1940, Emerson turned down a contract from the St. Louis branch of the Army Ordnance Department to make boosters for artillery shells.[2] The company was moving into the new Florissant plant, and everyone wanted to get on with the business of producing hermetics without losing momentum. Symington soon concluded, however, that with Free World prospects deteriorating almost by the day, a company with Emerson's capabilities could not and should not remain aloof from defense work. Moreover, it was becoming clear that if Emerson were to continue to prosper it would have to get into some kind of defense production. In the fall, the company undertook a production study for the Ordnance Department, and by year's end had accepted a small contract to produce boosters for artillery shells—the same contract they had turned down a few months earlier. Soon, the new Florissant plant had been completely retooled for booster production. By July 1942 Emerson had produced two million boosters, and by war's end the total exceeded ten million.

Symington took a leadership role in the production of boosters. His good friend August Busch, Jr., head of the vast Anheuser-Busch Brewing Company based in St. Louis, had gone to work for the commandant of the Ordnance Department as a colonel, and Busch persuaded Symington to become national chairman of the civilian army ordnance booster committee. The two of them toured the country checking on booster production. Despite this, and the fact that Emerson won its first "E" for boosters, Symington was interested in moving the company into something that would make use of all its talents—Emerson's highly talented engineering department, for example, had little involvement with booster production, which was a relatively simple build-to-print operation with designs supplied by others.[3]

As Symington searched for additional war contracts, he got a suggestion from David Van Alstyne, the investment banker who had been responsible for his move to Emerson. A man named Preston Tucker, who had built racing cars in Detroit before the war, had developed a design for a power gun turret, something in which the British, based on their experience against the Luftwaffe, were most interested. Tucker, the flamboyant entrepreneur who after the war would develop the much ballyhooed but short-lived "Tucker Torpedo" automobile, lacked the facilities to put his plans into production. Emerson, with its experience in manufacturing small motors, might be able to retool for the job. Symington visited Detroit, and Tucker came to St. Louis; they both went to Washington to talk to Air Corps officers. Ultimately the negotiations broke off—Tucker wanted to be put on Emerson's payroll at a relatively high salary, and Symington's engineers questioned certain aspects of the Tucker design—but Symington did make contact with a number of people in the Tucker organization who impressed him favorably and who later went to work for Emerson.[4]

The whole turret matter seemed dead, but in mid-April it came up again, quite by accident. Symington, who was vacationing in Florida, called an Air Corps acquaintance on another matter and was asked, "by the way," whether he would be interested in having Emerson manufacture turrets, based on British designs, for use in both British and American planes. Indeed, he would be, and before the day ended he was in Washington to begin discussions. That was on Tuesday, April 14. The next eight days were pure Symington, as he conducted whirlwind negotiations in Washington and St. Louis with side trips to New York, Cleveland, and Detroit, using his contacts from prior years and demonstrating for all observers the validity of his reputation as a super-salesman. "I wish you could have seen Stuart at work," R. H. McRoberts, Emerson's legal counsel, told an interviewer. "In one day he could cut through so much red tape that the progress he made should have taken weeks, even months under the law. We consulted with [Assistant] Secretary [of War for Air] Lovett [an old friend] and we saw this general and that admiral, and with the force of Stuart's drive and intelligence, and the confidence people quickly felt for him, he produced decisions and got commitments without waiting."[5]

On Wednesday, his second day in Washington, Symington's first stop, after brief conversations with army and navy officials, was to see William S. Knudsen, former head of General Motors, whom Roosevelt had persuaded to take over the Office of Production Management. Knudsen knew nothing about Emerson, and wondered if Symington could recommend a mutual friend whom he might call. Symington suggested Charles Wilson of General Electric, and waited while Knudsen called. In a few minutes he was told, "Charlie says you'll do whatever you say you'll do. OK. And good luck."

That same day, Symington and a group of OPM officials flew to St. Louis, "for a frenetic conference with [Emerson] executives [and] a horse-trader's inspection of Emerson-owned land adjoining the hermetic-motors plant." The next day they all went back to Washington to draw up a rough contract. Friday, Symington flew to New York and Buffalo, "to grab up some engineers who knew something about turrets from Bell, Curtiss-Wright, and others." On Saturday he went out to Cleveland to visit with another group of engineers, some of whom had come in from Detroit, including Arthur R. Lardin, whom Symington had met during his negotiations with Tucker and who would become his principal adviser. Then it was back to St. Louis, where Symington led a group of architects over the land on which the government would build a fifteen-million-dollar turret plant.

All of this occurred so rapidly that Symington had little opportunity to inform his board of directors, let alone to secure their approval. On Monday morning, April 21, Emerson's directors met to listen to their president lay before them what essentially amounted to a fait accompli: OPM had selected Emerson to build standardized Army-Navy-British (ANB) .50-caliber gun turrets at the rate of one thousand units per month; the government, in addition to buying most or all of the newly completed Florissant plant, would build a huge new facility on the adjoining land; and finally, Symington and a group of engineers would be going to England immediately to learn as much as they could about the British-designed turret Emerson was soon to build. The directors sat in stunned silence as Symington outlined the plans—at the end of the presentation, one director is supposed to have said, "Stuart, what the hell is a turret?"[6]

Nevertheless, in what for many of them must have been an act of almost blind faith, the board ratified their president's plans—and began a process which turned Emerson from a small regional electric manufacturer into one of the country's industrial giants.

On Tuesday Symington and Lardin returned to Washington to be sworn in as special consultants to OPM so they could qualify for diplomatic passports. The next day—Wednesday, April 23—formalities completed, they flew to New York to board a Pan-American Clipper for Lisbon. Taking off at eight in the morning accompanied by Air Corps Major John T. Murtha, they put down in Bermuda for lunch, flew all night to the Azores, and arrived in Lisbon the next evening. Here they cooled their heels while they waited for space to open up on a flight to London.

Finally, the party obtained seats on a Dutch DC-3, which the British had acquired when the Germans overran Holland. They went not to London, but to Bath, and as they droned through the skies they were mindful of the fact that they could easily be attacked by Focke Wulfs returning from a strike on Allied shipping—a plane carrying the noted actor Leslie Howard was shot down on the same route a few minutes later. From Bath, Symington flew to London at one thousand feet in a small two-seater that dropped a colored flare every two or three minutes for identification——the Germans were using small British planes that they had captured in France for daytime attacks on specific targets.

The great city of London lay almost in ruins. Few cities in the history of the world had ever taken such continuous battering. Between September 7 and November 3, 1940, an average of two hundred German planes attacked every night, with the night raids being accompanied by almost continuous daylight attacks by small groups and sometimes single planes. As Winston Churchill, who was there through it all, rallying his countrymen to the defense of their beleaguered island, wrote in his magisterial *History:* "Our outlook at this time was that London, except for its strongest buildings, would be gradually and soon reduced to a rubble-heap. I was deeply anxious about the life of the people of London, the greater part of whom stayed, slept, and took a chance where they were."[7]

Symington and his party were among those who "stayed, slept, and took a chance where they were." Many years after the war, Symington wrote Air Vice Marshal H. D. Spreckley, in response to a Christmas card, ". . . what memories it brought back—those long dreary nights during the blitz and all the pleasures we had far below ground—the sirens and ack ack and the pleasure of knowing you during those days. . . . I was thinking the other night how we would put out all the lights and go out at your country place to listen to the German bombers on their way to Liverpool, hoping we would see a streak of fire and [hear] the high whine which showed that one of the Bowfighters had made its kill."[8]

Symington, along with most Americans in England, was amazed by the way Britons could take their nightly pounding, remain reasonably cheerful, and still keep working. He sensed, as did many others, that even though most of the rest of the world had written off the British, they believed they would survive, that the gallant airmen who went up night after night in their tiny Spitfires were beginning to have an effect. He recalled that when he arrived at his office the morning after the great raid of May 10—when more than five hundred bombers attacked London, and in which his British secretary was badly injured and one of his American engineers was crippled for life—everyone seemed quite cheerful, even though the fires were still burning.[9]

All of this had a profound effect on the young American businessman who really hadn't thought much about the war, except perhaps in connection with the opportunities it might provide for making money. Returning to England during the blitz changed all that. He observed, "the courage . . . the tremendous courage. Life went on, bombs or no bombs." Coming home late one night, he once recalled, "I asked the cabbie if there had been an alert, and a big one landed close enough to shake the cab, but the cabbie just kept on going and said, 'Ordered that one special for you, Gov'ner.'"[10]

In "Memories," Symington wrote, "It was about this time all isolationist thinking left me. I realized, months before Pearl Harbor, that together we must stop Hitler." He may have been influenced some by *Collier's* war correspondent Quentin Reynolds, with whom he spent considerable time—and who later would write very favorably about his work in Washington.[11]

It was one thing to admire the British for their courage; it was quite another to try to work with them. As General Raymond E. Lee, military attaché and head of U.S. Intelligence in London during 1940–1941—and an astute, sophisticated and sensitive observer—wrote in his *Journal*, "One hardly knows how to deal with the British in their worst moments."[12]

And these were their worst moments, those anxious days in the spring of 1941, with around-the-clock bombings and the specter of invasion looming on the horizon. When Averell Harriman arrived in March as President Roosevelt's special envoy to oversee Lend-Lease, Britain was close to starvation. Even so, when the first shipments of food arrived under the Lend-Lease program, the Britons, while grateful, were less than enthusiastic about what they were receiving. They much preferred their own cheeses, for example, and they found little to commend in the canned luncheon meats that came to be known generically as Spam. Kathleen Harriman, who was with her father, wrote her sister Mary: "The great difficulty is reeducating the people. They prefer to go without, rather than change their feeding habits."[13]

So it seemed in the matter of gun turrets. Almost every day Symington and his party went out from London to visit one of two plants working around the clock to produce the newly developed gun: the Boulton Paul plant in Wolverhampton or the Frazier-Nash Company in Bath. Both were producing turrets for .30-caliber guns, which the British thought were adequate for their bombers flying at night. The United States wanted .50-caliber guns to provide protection for daylight as well as night bombing. The British had no faith in daylight bombing, and their early experience with Lend-Lease B-17s confirmed their views. Trial runs on July 8, before the planes were properly modified and the crews adequately trained, were a complete failure: of the three B-17s sent to bomb the naval barracks at Wilhelmshaven from thirty thousand feet, none hit the target. Other early daylight missions were equally unsuccessful—in thirty-nine sorties none hit their targets and eight aircraft were lost. This produced a great deal of controversy, and discussions of strategy, tactics, and equipment, Symington recalled, "invariably ended in disagreement."[14]

But obviously some kind of agreement was essential. Harriman was particularly helpful, with contacts and with arrangements. According to Symington, "he really did a superb job for the Allies, not only in facilitating supplies, but also in holding down the increasing irritation of the British over our not entering the war."[15] The key, however—as it had been in numerous other negotiations—was Stuart Symington himself. General Lee, in writing about the difficulties in getting things done, said:

> A very good instance is the matter of turrets. For weeks and months we had cables galore and negotiations back and forth about manufacturing turrets for airplanes in the United States. We simply could not get anywhere. Finally a man named Symington (and he is one of the most admirable Americans I think I have ever seen) came over with an Air Corps officer, and in two weeks they have straightened the whole thing out, made final arrangements, got the plans and are leaving for the States again."[16]

Symington and Murtha left for home in late May, going first to Bournemouth on England's south coast.[17] From Bournemouth they went by car at 4 A.M. to the port of Pool, where they boarded a Sunderland flying boat, presumably for Lisbon. After they were airborne, however, the captain announced that because of the naval battle raging off the coast of France—the British were engaged with the *Bismarck*—they would detour to Foynes on the west coast of Ireland. Putting down at what would become the great tourist entrepot of Shannon, they were taken to the Dunraven Arms in the lovely little town of Adair to spend the night. The trip had not been particularly pleasant. As they were boarding the plane at Pool, an elderly British artillery captain, complete with swagger stick, stood at the door. As the passengers stepped off the launch, he asked, "What is your nationality?" All but Americans were given comfortable seats to the rear; the Americans were assigned small, newly installed iron seats at the front of the cabin. After they had landed at Foynes, Symington announced in the presence of some of the crew that he knew Lord Adair, "hoping this might improve our seats on the way down to Lisbon." He called Adair from the inn, and while he and Major Murtha enjoyed a pleasant dinner in the Adair castle (now the top hostelry in Adair), knowledge of the friendship did nothing to improve their seats on the flight to Lisbon.

They were given the same little iron seats, and were provided no service. They had brought an ample supply of spirits aboard, and soon were serenading the whole cabin with song and complaints about their treatment, all to no avail.

Before the plane reached Lisbon, a young brigadier came forward to ask what the problem was. He seemed sympathetic, and apparently reported the situation. In any event, when the group landed in Bermuda, en route from Lisbon on the Pan American Clipper, the British authorities went out of their way to be accommodating.

Symington tended not to forget incidents such as this—and it did illustrate the difficulties the British and Americans sometimes had in working together. Stopping in Washington, he reported it all "to the very pleasant British Air Marshal with whom we worked," commenting that if he could get that elderly captain relieved of his job, he would see that the other American passengers were informed, and "it would help our mutual effort." A few days later, back in St. Louis, he received a wire from the air marshal, "Mission Accomplished."

Anyhow, the trip from Lisbon to New York passed more pleasantly than the long hours in the Sunderland flying boat. The Pan American Clipper carried thirty-two passengers—a record for the westward crossing. Among them was CBS correspondent Elmer Davis, who told the *New York Times* that though the British expected an invasion they seemed rather confident of their ability to defend themselves.[18] Symington reported that he found "business as usual and normal." Returning to St. Louis, he amplified his account considerably for the local press, expressing great confidence in the Britons' ability to defend themselves. He also began to position himself on the side of those who felt the United States should enter the war, commenting that the British considered St. Louis's Charles Lindbergh—then a leading spokesman for the America Firsters— as "England's worst American enemy."[19]

Back in St. Louis, the monstrous new government-owned building was going up next to Emerson's new hermetics plant. On September 17, Symington's good friend Robert Lovett came out to dedicate the new structure to the memory of Captain Colin P. Kelly, who had been killed at Clark Field during the December 10 attack on the Philippines.[20] In October—four months after the first contracts were let—the first unit, totaling 140,000 square feet, went into production. When completed in 1942, the 700,000-foot structure would be the largest turret-producing facility in existence. Meanwhile, Emerson engineers, using rented facilities downtown, tried to develop workable production blueprints from the plans Symington brought back from England—no easy task as they attempted to adapt the English turrets, designed to accommodate .30-caliber guns, to the requirements of the .50-caliber weapons that the Army Air Force needed to protect its daylight bombers.

Equally urgent was the need to expand the labor force. Emerson's twenty-five hundred employees were fully occupied in the company's regular production, including the boosters for artillery shells. When the first unit of the new plant opened in October the company would need at least thirty-five hundred more workers, most of them skilled or semiskilled. Complicating all this, the contract with the United Electrical Workers would expire on August 1, and negotiations with the War Department were such that the company would not be able to begin formal discussions with the union until mid-July. Symington persuaded the union to continue working under the existing contract, in part by providing $250,000 to be divided among union members by the leadership, the equivalent of a five-and-a-half cent an hour raise. He also began informal discussions with Sentner, in which he agreed to the establishment of a union shop in exchange for a no-strike pledge and a good-faith effort to help the company recruit and train new employees. By August 4 a new two-year contract had been signed, establishing a union shop at Emerson.[21]

Emerson managed its mushrooming payroll—by 1945 the workforce totaled more than twelve thousand—with notable success, despite enormous problems of recruitment and training. The company had already established itself, among both blacks and whites, as a good place to work, and that reputation stood it in good stead as it competed in the dwindling labor market of World War II. Morale, which had improved steadily after Symington's arrival, remained high, and through skillful educational programs the company kept the importance of their mission constantly before its employees. Emerson workers enthusiastically supported the war effort. They regularly led St. Louis, for example, in war-bond subscription drives. Partly as a result of all this, Emerson enjoyed remarkably good labor relations during the war, experiencing only one short-lived strike—based on a grievance over an employee who had been demoted after breaking a critically needed tool, and called off after Sentner reminded the strikers of the CIO's no-strike pledge and of the no-strike clause in their contract.[22]

Although Symington gave much of the credit for Emerson's smooth labor relations to John Driy, "as able a shopman as there was,"[23] his own leadership was critical. The image of their vigorous young president, working literally around the clock—he had a cot and shower installed in his office—made an impression on the shop floor, as did the fact that he frequently was there to see for himself the problems faced by those on the line. His relations with William Sentner also helped. Their relationship gained national attention when Eliot Janeway, in a major *Fortune* article entitled "A Yaleman and a Communist," proclaimed, "In St. Louis they met: despite their divergent views, they worked together for the benefit of Emerson—and the war."[24]

But the story of Emerson's contribution to the war effort was by no means a saga of uninterrupted success. There were problems almost from the beginning, and at times it appeared that the venture would end in ignominious failure.

In the first place, Emerson's engineers found it impossible to produce a satisfactory turret from the plans Symington had brought back from England. The navy promptly rejected a prototype completed in the summer of 1942, and for the remainder of 1942 Emerson produced turrets designed by other companies, particularly Sperry and Grumman. Even before the rejected prototype was completed, Emerson's engineers were asked to design a tail turret for the B-24 bomber. This they accomplished with complete success, and in January 1943 the first "homegrown" turret was installed in a B-24—Emerson employees contributed a dollar each to "buy" the turret and donate it to the Army Air Force in ceremonies at the plant. The Army Air Force also asked Emerson to modify the tail turret for installation in the nose of the B-24, and this they also accomplished with success. Symington, and, it is safe to say, most Emerson employees, swelled with pride as they read accounts of the B-24 attacks on the Nazi war machine, knowing that many of those planes returned safely to their bases in England and elsewhere because they were equipped with Emerson turrets.[25]

Second, Emerson's accounting system proved totally inadequate to meet the needs of doing business with the government. Emerson's contracts, in common with those of most other defense contractors, were written on a cost-plus-fixed-fee basis, which meant that the company had to justify all of its costs to receive payment. Because of what Emerson's historian described as "the company's haphazard approach to its bookkeeping,"[26] by the spring of 1942 it was facing more than twenty million dollars in unreimbursed costs and possible termination of all its contracts. William Snead, Emerson's treasurer and one of Symington's most trusted lieutenants, found an accountant in Chicago, Ralph Petering, who seemed to possess the qualifications to help the company work out of its mess. Petering came to St. Louis for an interview, and Symington hired him on the spot—another quick decision and another good one. Petering solved the reimbursement problem—at one time he had four hundred Emerson employees and one hundred government auditors working together—and devised an accounting system that met the needs of the war contracts. (Petering spent the rest of his career with Emerson, becoming vice president and treasurer.)

Finally, there were incredible difficulties with the government in addition to accounting problems, exacerbated by Symington's quick temper and his freely expressed contempt for bumbling bureaucrats. Many of the AAF officers assigned to work with defense contractors were poorly equipped for their responsibilities, and, in addition, as Symington later recalled, "the degree of vacillation and delay characteristic of the growing bureaucracy in Washington had to be seen to be believed."[27]

An early problem surfaced in connection with negotiations over the cost-plus-fixed-fee contract. After representatives of Emerson and the contract officers at Wright Field had agreed on the terms, the War Department changed its policies on maximum allowable fees. When Symington asked to see a copy of the directive, he was told by the chief of the contract division that it was contrary to policy to release such administrative memoranda.[28]

More serious problems came from Wichita, Kansas, headquarters of the Army Air Forces' inspection division, which included St. Louis, and "where a dedicated but elderly colonel in charge knew little about manufacturing." Symington recalled:

> One morning a tall and somewhat assured Air Corps captain came to Emerson and announced he had orders to inspect the turret plant. He did so, returned to Wichita, and apparently made a critical report; then came back to "investigate" us further. While he was in the shop on this second visit, our Operating Vice President, John Driy, as able a shop man as there was, came in with a white face to announce that he was quitting because the captain in question was out on the assembly line telling his foremen how to do their job. Obviously this had to be handled, and quickly, so I went out to the line, found said captain, told him the only person he should talk to in the future was me; that if he couldn't handle his visits on that basis he was no longer acceptable. (Heavy talk on my part, primarily to raise the morale of our own supervision.) The captain replied, "You'll be hearing from me," and walked out. That was the last time we ever saw him.[29]

But that was by no means the end of it. Somehow Emerson came to the attention of Congressman Andrew Jackson May of Kentucky, chairman of the House Armed Services Committee, and in due course, committee investigators presented themselves at the plant. Symington opened the company's books and gave them access to every bit of information they requested, with the understanding that if any questions were raised the company would have an opportunity to respond. After an investigation of "many weeks," Chairman May, without any consultation whatever, charged on the floor of the House of Representatives on July 20 that Emerson received a fee of two million dollars in connection with their contract to build the plant; that the company did not have the expertise to produce turrets and brought in outsiders at great cost; and that the principal executives built lavish offices for themselves and were given salary increases averaging 66 percent, and that Symington's salary was increased from fifteen thousand to twenty-five thousand dollars a year.[30]

When Symington heard about the attack, he immediately called May's office, but was told that the congressman was on his way to Kentucky by car and could not be reached. Unable to contact May, he took the first available plane for Washington to talk to his father-in-law, Congressman James Wadsworth. Wadsworth called Walter G. Andrews of New York, the ranking Republican on the committee, who, when he failed to persuade May to return, got the rest of the committee to agree to meet on July 28 to hear Symington.[31]

Meanwhile John Cochran, veteran Democrat from Missouri's Thirteenth District, which included Florissant, took the floor of the House on July 20 to refute May's charges one by one. Calling Symington "one of the youngest presidents of a very large corporation in this country" and "a great success," he said that "the statements made by the gentleman from Kentucky can by no stretch of the imagination be supported by the facts." He went on to say that May "must have confused the Emerson Electric Co. with testimony in the file concerning some other corporation."[32]

After Cochran's defense on the House floor, Symington's appearance before the military affairs committee on July 28 was a little anticlimactic. At the conclusion of the testimony, Congressman Andrews told the subcommittee that he had discussed the case with Undersecretary of War Robert Patterson, who reported that Emerson had cooperated more completely in the war effort than any other industrial company in the country. In any event, nothing further was heard from Congressman May, who was having troubles of his own—he would soon be indicted, convicted, and jailed for accepting bribes from armament manufacturers.[33]

The air force inspectors from Wichita, however, were still around, and daily becoming more of a nuisance. The shop heads reported that some of the civilian inspectors were suggesting money on the side. Symington reminded them that under no circumstances were there to be any payoffs and asked each of them to keep a daily log of inspector contacts. In a few days, "a pleasant reserve colonel from Wichita" appeared at the plant to say that he was sorry but that reports from his inspectors were so bad that he was going to Washington to tell his superiors that Emerson was not capable of running the turret side of the business. Symington handed him the daily logs and suggested that he had better read them before filing his report—also reminding him that his chief civilian inspector had been arrested for the attempted rape of a fourteen-year-old girl. In a few days, Robert Lovett suggested that Symington come to Washington to talk about the inspection problems. Lovett turned him over to Major General Lucius Clay, who after reading some of the reports told Lovett that he would handle it—and apparently he did, because there was no more trouble from Wichita.[34]

But Emerson's troubles with the government were not over. The Senate Committee on the National Defense Program, headed by Harry Truman, the junior senator from Missouri, decided that it would investigate Emerson. At the committee's first meeting, held in Detroit in May 1942, a man by the name of John A. Weber, president of the Weber Machine Tool Company, described how he had created a series of paper engineering firms to defraud the government, how through contacts at Emerson—he had been fired the previous June—he had won a six-hundred-thousand-dollar subcontract, and how he had run this contract through several of his paper companies, each time making a handsome profit. In addition, the committee had received a number of negative reports from inside the plant. As a result, they decided to conduct a formal investigation.[35]

When Symington received notice of the investigation, he blew up. Emerson was making good money with its regular lines, and the thought of going through yet another investigation was more than he could bear. He called in his personal lawyer, Sam Fordyce, and told him to draw up the necessary papers to get Emerson out of the turret business, "and get me a brass key with lots of vaseline on it. I'm going to Washington to tell those people what they can do with this turret plant."[36] Fordyce told his friend to slow down, that he was moving too fast. When Symington threatened to find another lawyer, Fordyce agreed to prepare the papers.

Fordyce, however, was not going to let his impetuous young friend make a fool of himself. A few days later he took him to lunch at the Noonday Club in downtown St. Louis. They were joined by John Snyder and Senator Truman. Snyder was one of Symington's bankers and a good friend; Truman, Symington had barely met.

Toward the end, Sam Fordyce said, "Harry, Stuart says he is going to quit the gun turret business because of all the red tape in Washington, and especially now that your committee has decided to investigate the operation." Truman looked at Symington for a time, then asked, "So you are going to quit, are you?" Symington replied, "Yes sir. Your planned investigation is the last straw. The morale of our people just can't take any more. We are already loaded up in our regular lines, the surtaxes make any real profit off of turrets doubtful, our shop people have worked their hearts out to no avail, so let the government take it over and to hell with it." Truman responded, "The boys on the Anzio beachhead aren't quitting." Symington replied, "The boys on the Anzio beachhead have a different enemy. They don't have to fight their way through all this red tape and interference which makes it impossible to operate properly."

Senator Truman said, "If I give you my word nothing will be done that is not right and proper, and tell you now that my door will be open to you personally anytime you want to see me, will you reconsider?"

Symington, who must have been somewhat embarrassed by the look of his friends, Sam Fordyce and John Snyder, remembered what the future president had said about Anzio, and replied, "Under those circumstances we will go ahead and do our best."[37]

Harry Truman kept his word. The harassment stopped, and when the Truman Committee issued its final report, Emerson and its president were completely exonerated.[38]

One is tempted to ask, in view of this outcome, why the investigations occurred in the first place, and, in particular, why they produced such serious charges. Symington attributed the whole thing to incompetence, venality, and worse—and he was partly right. The incredibly rapid buildup during the months before and after Pearl Harbor brought many men to positions of authority for which they were poorly equipped by education, experience, and, in some cases, character. Both the Congress and the Executive felt obliged to assure themselves and the public that the vast sums of newly appropriated money were being spent wisely, creating a climate that produced many overzealous functionaries. But there was more to it than that. Emerson did have serious problems as it tried to superimpose turret production onto its already overloaded plant, and the company's official history forthrightly deals with those difficulties.[39] Moreover, despite generally good—one can easily say excellent—labor relations, there were bound to be grievances and disgruntled employees in the rapidly expanding labor force anxious to pour their complaints into willing ears from the outside. It was easily possible for an uninformed outsider to get the impression that Emerson's management was incompetent or worse.

But the record proved exactly the opposite. Symington put together a management team and a labor force that worked wonders. A relatively obscure company before the war, best known for producing small motors and electric fans, Emerson by war's end was the largest turret manufacturer in the country. On October 21, 1942, Defense Production Chief William Knudsen, who as recently as April 1941 had never met Stuart Symington, came out to St. Louis for the opening of the Florissant plant, and presented Emerson with an army-navy "E" pennant for outstanding war production. By war's end, the company had garnered five "E's" for excellence, and Stuart Symington, then forty-four years old, was rapidly assuming a place as one of America's brightest and most promising young business executives.

5

From Business to Government

As the war wound down, Emerson's management realized that the good times would hardly last beyond the day of victory. Symington reported in January 1944 that "an extraordinarily large amount of peacetime business" had been booked, but he knew that once the war was over and the demand for turrets declined or ceased altogether Emerson would face some painful readjustments. "We all know that Emerson is a 'war baby,'" he told a company dinner in February 1943. "The question is, What will we do after the war?"[1]

Publicly, he expressed considerable optimism. There would be a tremendous demand for labor-saving devices such as Emerson knew how to produce, and there would still be some demand for armaments, "because we all agree that never again are we going to live in this country without large, multimotored bombers watching what other people are doing." Privately, however, he worried about the effects of rapid demobilization and Emerson's return to dependence upon just a few products, particularly the highly cyclical electric fan business. To help meet postwar challenges, he established a consulting relationship with the Radiation Laboratory at the Massachusetts Institute of Technology, not only to get their expertise in gyroscopes and radar—crucial for the war effort—but to tap MIT's general technological sophistication. He thought of new products, such as a typewriter and a shotgun, never developed, and reopened contacts with Sears. His most revolutionary idea, however, was a merger with International Telephone and Telegraph in an arrangement that would make Emerson the manufacturing arm of ITT as Western Electric was for AT&T.[2]

Sothenes Behn, founder and chairman of ITT, approached Symington in the spring of 1944 to talk about a merger, asking him to lunch on the top floor of the ITT building in New York—"the only business lunch I ever attended where, in addition to two kinds of wine, there was a footman behind each chair." Symington had known Behn in New York—he was one of the socialites who showed up at Eve's openings—and rather liked him, but he did not think the scheme as outlined by Behn would work, so the discussions broke off. About a year later, however, Behn called again, this time proposing a merger along lines Symington originally had suggested, with Symington becoming executive vice president and ultimately taking over the management of the company. Symington definitely was interested, but before presenting the matter to his board he wanted to go to Washington to check the antitrust implications with the attorney general. He had met Tom Clark, but asked his good friend John Snyder, who had just been appointed director of the Office of War Mobilization, to arrange an appointment. Snyder readily agreed, but added, "The president told me this morning he wanted to see you. Call and make an appointment."[3]

That afternoon in the Oval Office with Harry Truman, Symington recalled, the new president said, "Stu, I want to dump a load of coal on you. After World War I there was a lot of scandal incident to the disposal of surplus property. This war is now over in Europe. I hope and expect it to be over shortly with Japan; and would like you to take the chairmanship of the Surplus Property Board. I just do not want any scandal."[4]

Stuart Symington had never held a political job and had expressed little interest in politics. He came from an old-line Democratic family, and his father had been active in Maryland politics. Eve's father, however, was the quintessential conservative Republican, and, indeed, one of the most powerful figures in the Republican party. Most of their friends were Republicans, many of them ardent Roosevelt-haters. As Frederick Lewis Allen wrote, "This hatred of Roosevelt . . . was strongest and most nearly unanimous among the very rich and in those favored suburbs and resorts where people of means were best insulated against uncomfortable facts and unorthodox opinions." Suburban Creve Coeur and the St. Louis Country Club provided just such insulation. Symington himself, though quite out of sympathy with many of his friends' attitudes—their anti-labor, anti-black prejudices, for example—had become quite disenchanted with FDR. He voted for Wendell Willkie in 1940, and as late as October 1941, William Sentner reported that Symington "hates Roosevelt as much as ever and believes him responsible for all goody-good red tape."[5]

Symington and Truman got to know each other during the Truman committee's investigation of war production at Emerson, and apparently got along well from the beginning, with their relationship being fostered by John Snyder, a close friend of both. Despite his lack of enthusiasm for Roosevelt, Symington supported Truman's campaign for the vice presidency, and at least on one occasion made Emerson's Twin Beech craft available to him. Shortly after the election Symington and Snyder flew over to French Lick Springs, Indiana, where the newly elected vice president was recuperating from the stress of the campaign. They had dinner and spent the night. The next morning, Truman and Snyder invited their friend "to join us in an old artillery habit," and, Symington recalled, "Thereupon each of us had a stiff bourbon." Sometime later, Snyder asked Symington to join a group he was taking to Lamar, Missouri, Truman's birthplace, to participate in the ceremonies officially notifying Truman of his election as vice president. Then, on Inaugural Day, Symington and Snyder gave a reception at the Carlton Hotel in honor of the new vice president and Mrs. Truman. For Symington it was "a rewarding occasion, the first time I met many who later became friends and associates in the government." Later in the day, he attended a reception given by his good friend Secretary of the Navy James Forrestal, where he met a young congressman from Texas who was on the House Naval Affairs Committee, Lyndon B. Johnson.[6]

When Harry Truman was thrust into the presidency on April 12, 1945, he instinctively turned to his old friends from Missouri. Bob Hannegan, chairman of the Democratic National Committee, was in town and was among those who gathered in the cabinet room to witness the oath of office. Truman called Snyder, vacationing in Mexico, to come to Washington immediately. Snyder asked Symington to join him to help with the president's first speech to Congress, to be delivered on April 16. "My thoughts were asked for," Symington later wrote, "but I contributed little because I knew very little about what should be said under such circumstances."[7]

Back in St. Louis, he wrote the president:

> My dear Friend:
>   From here on it is Mr. President, but perhaps this once I can be privileged to so address you.
>   The loss of Mr. Roosevelt was a shock to the world, but those of us who know you have no apprehension about the future of our country.
>   The shadows of Robert E. Lee and Bedford Forrest, and Lincoln, too, are all around you; and I see all the little people of this our country, miners, shop workers, farmers, looking to you with faith and confidence.
>   If at any time you ever felt I could be of service in any way, you know what a very great privilege it would be.
>   My wife joins me in asking that God bless you and your family, and that His wisdom will guide you in the days to come.[8]

The president responded with a form letter, but his fellow Missourians, especially Snyder and Hannegan, were hard at work trying to recruit their young friend for a place in the new administration. Snyder asked him to come to Washington for the ceremony on April 30 at which he was sworn in as federal loan administrator. On the same day, Symington watched his good friend Ed McKim of Omaha sworn in as the president's chief administrative assistant; the Associated Press photograph of the ceremony shows Symington between the president and McKim. On May 25, Snyder and Secretary of the Navy Forrestal flew out to St. Louis to attend a dinner Symington gave for a group of industrialists, thus providing evidence to the St. Louis community that Symington had considerable influence with the new administration.[9]

Symington recalled that he asked the president for twenty-four hours to consider whether he would accept the "load of coal." He discussed the offer with a number of friends and was advised "not to touch that job. In World War I most of those handling surplus sales went to jail."[10] That evening he dined alone with his father-in-law in the Wadsworths' Georgetown home

> and told him of the offer and how negative my friends had been; added that I had decided to turn it down. I felt confident he would agree. (Senator Wadsworth was extremely conservative, long convinced both President Truman and President Roosevelt were far too liberal.) To my surprise, my father-in-law turned and said with some heat, "You've been lucky under our system. If the President of the United States has asked you to help him in the difficult job he now faces, you should be honored to accept." I was startled. The Senator, the Boss as we called him, had never talked to me quite that way before. After thinking it over, the next day I called Mr. Behn to say that I could not be considered for what he had in mind, then went to the White House and accepted Mr. Truman's offer.[11]

Symington's memory of the sequence of events was hazy at best. By early June the press began to speculate that he was being considered for the chairmanship of the Surplus Property Board. Charles Ross, Truman's boyhood friend from Independence and now his new press secretary, would say only that the question was under consideration. Symington, when contacted by the *St. Louis Post-Dispatch*, "said he had not had any official notice that his name was being considered."[12]

It is fairly clear, however, that Symington by this time had accepted the appointment. On May 22, 1945, he wrote the president, accepting the job and promising that "it will be done as you would want it, in a goldfish bowl." Truman responded on May 25, 1945, signing his letter simply "Harry."[13]

Truman had discussed the matter with Snyder on May 19 and made this note on his appointment sheet: "Saw John Snyder and discussed Surplus Property situation, which is bad—we have been trying to find a solution in order to get Surplus Property in circulation and also get the government a square deal on it. It has all the elements of a Teapot Dome in it and also the Forbes." On June 5 the president had Snyder, Charles Ross, and Samuel Rosenman for lunch in the family dining room of the White House, during which they "discussed sale of war plants, surplus property board chairman and F.E.P.C. All loaded with political dynamite."[14]

Two days later he announced Symington's appointment as chairman of the Surplus Property Board. The appointment, one of several announced by Truman on June 7, was seen as a move by the president to bring "stronger, more liberal administrators" into his administration, and generally it was well received. The press made much of Symington's "gift for repairing broken-down businesses," his ability to work with labor, and his leadership in improving race relations. At the same time, they noted he had voted for Willkie in 1940 and was the son-in-law of James W. Wadsworth. In some quarters Eve created more interest than did her husband. George Dixon wrote: "A presidential announcement which failed to create much stir was that W. Stuart Symington, an industrialist from a place out west called St. Louis, Missouri, had been appointed . . . chairman of the Surplus War Property Board. Washington society, however, will be more than academically interested because Mr. Symington's wife, Evie, is quite a girl." Evelyn Peyton Gordon, society columnist for the *Washington Daily News,* commented, "The appointment of . . . Stu Symington as head of the Surplus Property Board should bring back to Washington one of its most glamorous girls."[15]

Clearly the new chairman of the Surplus Property Board was not one of those ordinary Democratic political functionaries Truman seemed to have a penchant for placing in high office—but for a time it appeared that Symington might not be confirmed. Drew Pearson wrote in his widely syndicated column, "Washington Merry-Go-Round," that despite Truman's "extraordinarily good luck" in getting his appointments through the Senate, he would have difficulty with Symington—"some senators are afraid he picked a lemon." The problem, according to Pearson, was that Symington, who would be responsible for guarding the interests of small business in the disposal of surplus property, "has been cited by the U.S. courts as a flagrant monopolist."[16]

The "citation" derived from a civil suit filed by the Justice Department against Symington's unfortunate business enterprise, Vehicular Parking, Ltd., long after he had severed all connections with the company. On June 15, Joseph C. O'Mahoney, Democrat from Wyoming and chairman of the subcommittee of the Senate Military Affairs Committee, grilled him intensely on his past business connections, particularly those with Vehicular Parking and Rustless Iron and Steel, which had been sued for patent infringements. Symington successfully dissociated himself from both, making an impassioned defense of his record against monopolies. "I am sensitive to charges of favoring monopoly," he said, "because I have always fought big combinations." Although Symington felt good about the proceedings and observers predicted favorable committee action, O'Mahoney adjourned the hearing without setting a date for a vote.[17]

Meanwhile, Pearson published additional columns rehashing the monopolist charges, and others joined the fray, including Thomas L. Stokes, who charged that the Symington appointment provided a good example of what could happen when appointments were turned over to a political operative such as Bob Hannegan. With all of this and with no movement by O'Mahoney—Senator Scott Lucas of Illinois criticized the committee for its unnecessary delay—Symington, never one to suffer uncertainty gracefully, began to lose patience. He told the president that in view of the trouble in the Senate, Truman should feel free to withdraw his name. Truman replied, "I'm not behind you 100 percent. I'm behind you 200 percent. Now don't you take any nonsense from that O'Mahoney."[18]

Despite O'Mahoney's seeming lack of enthusiasm, on Thursday, July 12, Warren Austin, ranking Republican member of the Senate Military Affairs Committee, asked for unanimous consent that the nomination be confirmed, and the request was granted. Stuart and Eve flew in from St. Louis on Sunday, July 15. The next morning, July 16, 1945, in a ceremony attended by numerous dignitaries, forty-four-year-old Stuart Symington moved from business to government.[19]

6

The World's Largest Merchandiser

ALTHOUGH he thought the chairmanship of the Surplus Property Board would be temporary—perhaps lasting only a few months—Symington severed all connections with Emerson, resigning the presidency and selling his stock. The boys were both in the service, so Eve joined him in Washington, where they took a small apartment in the Shoreham Hotel. They would live in the Shoreham for five years, thinking of themselves as "temporaries," and though Stuart liked to characterize himself as a businessman temporarily working for the government, he would spend the rest of his active career in government and politics. His friendship with Harry Truman, already well established, would grow warm and close, albeit there were times, particularly during the air force years, when he sorely tried his good friend's patience. He became a regular participant in Truman's legendary poker weekends on the presidential yacht *Williamsburg,* and while his background and bearing were noticeably patrician, he happily referred to himself as one of "the Missouri gang." For the moment, however, he had to try to work himself out from under "the load of coal" the president had dumped on him.[1]

Although everybody recognized the importance of developing a workable scheme for the disposition of the billions of dollars of surplus property that would become available after the war—everything from paper clips to mammoth manufacturing plants—neither President Roosevelt nor the Congress, for obvious reasons, wanted to call too much attention to the problem until after victory had been achieved. It remained a secondary responsibility of the Bureau of the Budget.

The disposal of surplus property, of course, was but one of the issues surrounding reconversion to a peacetime economy. Its solution, however, would have a profound effect on the nature of that economy. President Roosevelt asked Bernard Baruch, the famed financier and park-bench philosopher, to study the whole question of reconversion and to recommend policies for the disposal of surplus property. Baruch and John M. Hancock, a prominent industrial banker who had been a member of the War Resources Board, produced a report designed to get the government out of business as soon as possible. Responsibility should be concentrated in one agency headed by an administrator "of proven executive capacity, business sagacity, unquestioned integrity, and great courage." The report's conservative tone alarmed old New Dealers and other liberals—Harold Ickes wrote that it looked like "a build-up for big business"—and when Roosevelt, at Baruch's insistence, appointed Texas cotton tycoon Will Clayton to head the Surplus War Property Administration (which he had created by executive order), the liberal press charged the president with a complete abandonment of New Deal principles.[2]

Clayton, described as "one of the half-dozen most capable businessmen of his generation," confirmed neither the hopes of his supporters nor the fears of his detractors. He established an organization and promulgated rules, but he realized from the beginning that a new entity being created by Congress would supersede his agency. Congress, convinced that surplus property disposal should not be left to a department created by executive order and presided over by a single administrator who could be too easily influenced by big business, established a surplus property board whose three members required senatorial confirmation.[3]

Roosevelt's appointees were not a particularly impressive lot. Robert A. Hurley, former governor of Connecticut, and Lieutenant Colonel Edward Heller, a San Francisco banker, barely gained confirmation. Guy M. Gillette, recently defeated for reelection as senator from Iowa, easily won confirmation as a former member of the Senate, but he possessed no particular qualifications for the position. Harry Truman, who shortly after Gillette's appointment inherited the "mess" in surplus property, complained to his diary, "Guy can't make up his mind on anything. If God told him to take charge of heaven, he'd be dead sure that Hell would be an easier place to run. I have known him to change his mind three times in as many conferences on one issue. He's very religious, very good looking and is so anxious to do what is right. But he can never make up his mind on what God wants. If he had the power of decision he'd be a great man. Too bad he hasn't."[4]

Whatever his powers of decision, Gillette from the beginning faced an impossible situation. Hurley and Heller had largely abandoned their decision-making responsibilities to the board's administrator, William E. Howse, a dynamic Wichita businessman serving as a colonel in the army reserve. Howse did not get along with Gillette, but, supported by Hurley and Heller, ran things pretty much as he saw fit—when Gillette resigned after only four months in office, he complained that he had been reduced to the status of a minority member.[5]

The common wisdom around Washington held that the new chairman would be able to do little to alter the situation at SPB—Howse, with the support of Heller and Hurley, would continue to run things as he saw fit.[6] The common wisdom, however, failed to reckon with Stuart Symington and his ability to make changes.

On Symington's second day in office, Howse walked in with a stack of books and deposited them on his desk, saying, "After you have read these you'll know something about what you are supposed to do." Symington, sensing a confrontation, swept the books off his desk and said to Howse, "What do you do around here?" Howse turned and walked out. The next day a most unflattering picture of the new chairman appeared in the press. When he tried to discover where they got it, the man in charge of public relations, an army captain, was so evasive that Symington concluded that Howse was behind it all. There were other incidents, and in a few days Symington told Howse he had better leave. Howse refused, saying the other members of the board would back him. Symington immediately called a meeting and laid out the whole matter. Howse, seeing his support slip away—Hurley and Heller would back him against the indecisive Gillette, but not against the very decisive Symington—resigned on the spot.[7]

With Howse out of the way, Symington moved quickly to establish his own team at Surplus Property. First, he recruited Eugene Zuckert to be his executive assistant. Eliot Janeway had introduced Zuckert to him in New York in 1943. Over a drink at "21" he formed such a favorable impression of Zuckert, then teaching at the Harvard Business School, that he offered him a job on the spot. Zuckert wanted to get into the navy, not move to St. Louis and work for Emerson. Symington, thinking of Zuckert as a possible future employee, worked with Forrestal to help him obtain a commission. Now he intervened with Forrestal again to get Zuckert transferred to the Surplus Property staff.[8] Zuckert would follow Symington to the Pentagon, become assistant secretary of the air force, and ultimately secretary.

Symington next turned to his brother-in-law, James J. (Jerry) Wadsworth, appointing him director of the Public Benefits Division. Wadsworth was working for Curtiss-Wright in Buffalo; he had experience in New York state politics and was someone Symington liked and trusted—the close family relationship did not seem to bother anyone. Wadsworth, a Republican, worked in government off and on during most of his life, serving for a time as Eisenhower's ambassador to the United Nations.[9]

As general counsel Symington appointed Hugh Cox, then serving as an assistant attorney general. Tom Clark had recommended Cox, but told Symington he wouldn't be able to get him because he wanted to return to private practice in New York. Symington called on Cox in his office in the Justice Department and in half an hour had him signed up to work for the Surplus Property Board.[10]

Rounding out the senior team was Joseph F. Carroll, whom Symington got on a loan from J. Edgar Hoover, head of the Federal Bureau of Investigation. Early on he had decided that the opportunities for graft and corruption in the disposal of billions of dollars of surplus property were so great—he had been offered a bribe himself—that the organization needed an efficient compliance division. He did not know Hoover, but Clark introduced him. They got on well from the beginning—they soon became fairly close friends—and Hoover lent him "one of my best."[11] Carroll remained "on loan" to Symington after he went to the Pentagon and ultimately became a major general in the air force.

Symington ran an easy, relaxed, informal office, but, as at Emerson, there was never any question as to who was boss. Staff members soon learned that they could expect to get a buzz on the squawk box shortly after eight-thirty to see if there were going to be any particular problems during the day, and they had better be ready. Symington told the staff at an early meeting, "Gentlemen, let's get this straight. In this office we arrive at eight-thirty because that is official regulations. And we stay late when necessary because we love our work." As Zuckert put it, "With Stuart it wasn't the hours. In a sense, he worked twenty-four hours a day. You could get a call at home anytime."[12] Zuckert also remembered Symington's ability to determine what was important: ". . . as somebody once said, he had an instinct for the jugular."

Immediately after the Senate confirmed Symington's appointment as chairman of the Surplus Property Board, Senator Tom Stewart of Tennessee, a persistent critic of the disposal program, introduced legislation to replace the board with a single administrator. Five days later, the president, long known to be impatient with the government's progress in disposing of the war surplus, called upon Congress to replace the surplus property board with a single administrator who would be responsible for selling the property as well as for making policy. At Symington's first press conference—held in the police "show-up" room of the old Washington Municipal Building, because there was no room in the SPB offices in the same building—he expressed surprise at the president's recommendation, and "then he spent 40 minutes evading questions which sought to lead him into an expression of his own views on a one-man board." Demonstrating what came to be recognized as an easy ability to handle the press, he said, "If I disagree I'm disagreeing with the President and if I agree I'm talking about something that I know little about." He did assure his questioners, however, that, contrary to a story in the *New York Times,* he had not stipulated to the president that he would take the job only if it became a one-man operation— "no one stipulates to the President."[13]

Congress, after being prodded again by Truman in his annual message on September 6, acted on September 12 with a simple bill, which replaced the surplus property board with a single administrator. Truman promptly appointed Symington as the administrator and the Senate again unanimously confirmed the appointment, on September 26, with little discussion.[14]

Symington thus became personally responsible for the disposal of more than ninety billion dollars' worth of federal surplus property. He became the world's largest merchandiser. As one observer put it, he was "the first person in history to run a one-hundred-billion-dollar secondhand store."[15]

Symington, despite the coyness with which he initially approached the question of a board versus a single administrator, had, along with the other members of the board, testified in favor of a single administrator, and found the new arrangement much more to his liking. Despite this improvement, the other difficulties inherent in surplus property disposal remained. One of them became painfully apparent during the transition from a board to a single administrator.

Truman dispatched Symington and Snyder, now director of the Office of War Mobilization and Reconversion, to Western Europe to survey stockpiles of surplus material and try to determine what to do with them.[16] They found that no one really knew what was on hand or what to do with it. Symington estimated that the army surplus in the European theater was "somewhere between 3,000,000 and 6,000,000 tons at an estimated cost of many billions of dollars." Transportation costs ruled out bringing the material home; it would have to be sold or given away in Europe, and to foreign governments rather than individuals— aside from questions of U.S. policy, some foreign governments were refusing to let their citizens buy directly from the United States. Above all, the process needed to be streamlined. Symington recommended that a new agency be created within the State Department for foreign surplus, with the army and navy acting as custodians. He urged quick action: "According to the Army, if present disposal regulations are followed in the European theater alone it will take at least 100,000 men, at a cost of some $30,000,000 to $40,000,000 monthly to handle the surplus remaining just in that theater."[17]

Despite all this, the military seemed unable to move rapidly. Symington sent the president an article by Joseph Hanlon, a Washington correspondent of the *Post-Dispatch,* which he said "clearly illustrates the problem."[18] Hanlon cited a number of horror stories about army policy such as the fact that the army had a reserve supply of fifty-three million blankets, which were in short supply on the civilian market. "That would be more than five blankets for every soldier we had in the Army at the peak," he wrote, "but these 53,000,000 are only the reserve supply. They were acquired on the theory that a blanket in storage could be kept for 20 years and that over a period of 20 years the Army might need 20,000,000 blankets."[19]

The nub of the problem both abroad and at home was that too many agencies were involved. The surplus property administrator could set policy, but he had control over neither inventory nor sales. The military decided what goods would be declared surplus, and supply officers were not known for the rapidity with which they disposed of material that they might possibly need at some future date—the blankets, for example. On the other side of the ledger, actual disposal was handled by the Department of Commerce (for consumer goods) and the Reconstruction Finance Corporation (for industrial materials, including plants).

Symington had policy control over both organizations respecting surplus property, but found it difficult to get them to move as quickly or efficiently as he desired. Henry Wallace, secretary of commerce, had little interest in surplus property disposal, so Symington persuaded the president to give the RFC responsibility for all surplus sales.[20]

Regardless of the organization, the problems were so vast and complicated that no one could hope to solve them to everyone's satisfaction. By all standards, the task was big. "It is the largest merchandising operation ever undertaken by any business or governmental organization," Symington told the Congress. He presented a few comparisons to illuminate the size and character of the disposal job. The surpluses were more than half the value of the 1940 gross national product; surplus machine tools were equivalent to the total value of machine tools produced in the fifteen years preceding 1940; surplus agricultural land and buildings were the equivalent of all agricultural holdings in the state of Texas.

The job was as complex as it was big. As Symington pointed out, sales had to be completed quickly and there were restrictions on what could be sold to whom; the inventory was out of the control of the merchandiser; many of the products were designed for war rather than for commercial use; the inventory was widely scattered in many inconvenient locations.[21]

Symington remarked to George Hall of the *Post-Dispatch* that being the world's largest merchandiser was "a real bone-crusher, but it's damned interesting." He expected to get brickbats rather than bouquets, but, he said, "I can take it."[22]

He made an easy target, but in most instances his unerring sense of salesmanship and public relations enabled him, if not to turn the brickbats into roses, at least to deflect them. A case in point involved Fiorello La Guardia, mayor of New York City, who in testifying October 11 before the Senate Subcommittee on Surplus Property, headed by New York Democrat James M. Mead, declared that Symington was "not competent or suited to administer the law" and urged that he and his whole staff be replaced.[23]

It turned out that La Guardia had written Symington September 26 wishing him luck "in the tough job you have assumed," and calling attention to some practices which he considered "nothing short of disgraceful," and which, he had been assured, had been stopped. Symington learned when he got to the office October 12 that the letter had been filed pending the preparation of a reply. He called La Guardia immediately, offering to come to New York to apologize. Once again the Symington charm worked. He smoothed the mayor's ruffled feathers, and the two agreed on a procedure for addressing New York's problems with surplus property disposal. The two men became good friends. A year later, when Symington was on an around-the-world tour as assistant secretary of war and La Guardia was working for the United Nations Relief Administration, the two met, by prearrangement, in Cairo, where they had a grand time touring the pyramids—"La Guardia could put away a tremendous amount of scotch whiskey without [sic] it hardly showing."[24]

When Senator William Langer of North Dakota complained that buyers in his state were being subjected to long lines and inefficient service, Symington got hold of a converted B-25 bomber and took Langer to Bismarck to listen to the complaints; while they were in the West they went on to Cheyenne to meet with disaffected citizens there. Nothing specific came from the trip, "but it was an investment of purest gold in congressional relations."[25]

Symington knew that time was of the essence in developing an effective disposal program. "The old story that time is money was never more true than it is in this situation," he told the *Post-Dispatch*. "Whatever you're going to get for what we have to sell, you'll get less tomorrow than you will today." He kept framed on his office wall a letter from Bernard Baruch that advised, "When in doubt, sell."[26]

And Symington from the beginning tried to speed disposal. Immediately after being sworn in as surplus property administrator, he announced a reorganization of the agency to decentralize decision making and to attack four broad problems: making it simple for veterans to buy surplus, expediting the clearance of government property from plants, moving surplus goods more rapidly to state and local governments, hospitals, and educational institutions, and speedily disposing of war plants and their tools for peacetime uses.[27]

In all of this, his first concern was the creation of jobs and providing aid to small business. Assuaging the fears of those who had felt that he was a monopolist, he said, "If we do not promote local, independent business, we will end up with a few companies. That would be most unfortunate for the economy."

Veterans posed particularly difficult problems. The Mead committee called on Symington to explain the shabby treatment veterans had received at surplus sales in Massachusetts and Maryland, where hundreds waited in the rain for hours and then were sent away because nothing was available except a few broken-down jeeps. He demonstrated once again that he was learning well the art of dealing with Congress. Instead of being defensive, he opened his testimony by saying, "Gentlemen, I have had this disgraceful affair investigated thoroughly by Mr. Joseph Carroll, who, as you know, is one of the investigators of the FBI. Here is Mr. Carroll's report."[28]

He then went on to detail what had happened in a way that calmed most of his congressional critics, pointing out that the problem resulted from a complete breakdown of communication between the Smaller War Plants Corporation and the Department of Commerce, and outlining specific steps he proposed to take to prevent it from happening again.

But he did more than finesse congressional critics. He responded to the criticism by instituting substantial changes that, in his words, "would give the veteran every break possible in the disposition of these surplus war assets." He greatly increased the outlets available to veterans and made it possible for them to buy surplus property for business purposes on terms similar to those enjoyed by large dealers.[29]

The veterans' problem was but one of a thicket of complications facing the Surplus Property Administration, but it was illustrative of the whole range of difficulties confronting Symington. Shortly before he left office, he reminded a Senate committee investigating the disposal of surplus property that "goods are not distributed by statements of principle or by statutes no matter in what detail or with what precision they are drawn." The problem of distribution was a problem of administration and operation. "In our private economy," he added, "goods are distributed through an elaborate and intricate series of relationships. . . . The system . . . is not so arranged that it can easily give a priority to one group of ultimate buyers as against another." Yet this, in effect, is what he was being forced to do.[30] It was not surprising that he had not been wholly successful. He was admitting the difficulties so that the public, and particularly the veterans, would not believe "that the task is easy or that our failures have been intentional."

This uncharacteristically gloomy disclaimer was hardly necessary. Symington had numerous critics, but, in the words of a historian of disposal, he had "brought ability, energy and dedication to his work."[31] As the president observed when accepting Symington's resignation, he had accomplished the task he had been given; his last weeks as surplus property administrator were dominated by news of his successful assault on the aluminum monopoly—an effort reminiscent of his earlier attack on David Sarnoff and the Radio Corporation of America.

Prior to World War II, the Aluminum Company of America (Alcoa) had dominated the aluminum industry. Indeed, it had been under almost continuous indictment since shortly after passage of the Sherman Act in 1890 for its monopolistic control of light metals production. On March 12, 1945, Judge Learned Hand had issued an interim decision in a suit that the government had brought in 1937. Judge Hand found Alcoa guilty of monopoly, but delayed implementing his decision until the results of the disposal of government-owned aluminum facilities could be evaluated.[32] Outgoing Attorney General Francis Biddle held, before he left office, that in view of Hand's decision, none of the surplus aluminum plants could be sold to Alcoa.

The problem first hit Symington at a board meeting on July 24—eight days after he took office—and he found himself confronted by two diametrically opposed recommendations. The board had hired two experts to advise it on the aluminum question: Samuel Moment, a career bureaucrat who was chief of market analysis for the Bonneville Power Administration; and Gordon W. Reed, an official of the aluminum division of the War Production Board who had an interest in the Apex Smelting Company, a large secondary aluminum smelter with close ties to Alcoa. Moment wanted a disposal plan that would encourage the development of competition in the aluminum industry; Reed argued that no disposal plan could succeed if it did not recognize Alcoa's continuing monopoly.

Symington was much more comfortable with Reed, the straight-talking businessman, than he was with Moment, whom he found to be quite theoretical, but if he adopted Reed's approach he could be accused of going back on his pledge to discourage monopoly in the disposal process. Moreover, Hugh Cox, the board's new general counsel, whom Symington had hired on Attorney General Clark's recommendation, found legal difficulties in both plans. Symington asked the lawyers to come up with a plan that in cooperation with business would move the plants quickly at a good return to the government and at the same time would achieve competition in the aluminum industry.

Although Symington vacillated for a while as he sought to sort out the far-from-perfect options that seemed to be available—Harold Stein described him as remaining "poised in uncertainty"—he soon took control of the process, working closely with his good friend John Snyder and Attorney General Clark, with whom he was developing a very cordial relationship.[33]

By early August most people in the administration had adopted the view that any acceptable solution to the aluminum problem must foster competition, but no one knew quite how to proceed. Alcoa's leases ran until 1948. They contained a complicated cancellation clause, but with the war still on, invoking it would create a political firestorm fueled by unemployment resulting from closure of the plants. Sam Husbands, director of the Reconstruction Finance Corporation, suggested short-term leases with the government guaranteeing the operators against loss. Further complicating matters, Alcoa held the key patents, and even with government guarantees, there would be no way for a new operator to succeed.

The collapse of Japan on August 14 intensified the need to move on disposal and at the same time removed one impediment to canceling the leases—interfering with war production. Snyder called an interagency meeting in his office on August 17. Symington was there, along with Hugh Cox and the other members of the Surplus Property Board, together with representatives of Justice, Interior, and the RFC. The meeting accomplished very little. Wendell Berge, assistant attorney general in charge of antitrust litigation, announced that sale of the plants to Alcoa was unacceptable to the Justice Department. Symington and Snyder wanted everything possible done to keep the plants running and the employees at work. They did not want the government to contribute to the growing unemployment that loomed on the postwar horizon. Finally, those present agreed that if the lawyers could find a legally acceptable means of canceling the leases, Alcoa should be given the opportunity to continue operations on a sixty-day cancellation basis. This would keep the plants operating while the government searched for a buyer, and at the same time would make them available for transfer to a new operator. If Alcoa refused, responsibility for the resulting unemployment would be theirs rather than the government's.

Symington, becoming impatient with the lawyers, decided to try his powers of personal persuasion on Arthur V. Davis, chairman of Alcoa's board. The powers didn't work. Accompanied by Cox, Symington called on Davis August 27 in his room at the Carlton Hotel. The aged Davis—he was nearing eighty—apparently offended that this young upstart would try to persuade him to change a publicly announced policy, categorically refused and told Symington that he would hear from his lawyers before the end of the month.

Symington, angry at the treatment he had received and convinced that cooperation with Alcoa was impossible, now moved aggressively and publicly to force Alcoa to cooperate. He recommended the cancellation of Alcoa's long-term leases, replacing them with sixty-day operational permits. Alcoa refused to accept this arrangement, and Symington's efforts to find another operator were unsuccessful—the only companies with enough capacity to replace Alcoa were Reynolds and Kaiser, and they were not interested unless they could secure government subsidies and access to Alcoa's patents.

The country faced the specter of no aluminum production, and Alcoa found plenty of defenders. Newspapers, chambers of commerce in the affected cities, and some congressmen joined in a chorus of criticism of the RFC and the Surplus Property Board for shutting down the plants and causing widespread unemployment.[34]

Inevitably, Congress got involved. Three committees of the Senate held joint hearings October 15–19: the Subcommittee on Surplus Property of the Committee on Military Affairs, the Special Committee to Study and Survey Problems of Small Business Enterprises, and the Industrial Reorganization Subcommittee of the Special Committee on Postwar Economic Policy and Planning. The transcript fills 336 tightly packed pages.[35]

As far as the administration was concerned, the hearings were quite unsatisfactory, and Symington did not get the subsidy recommendation he sought. Most of the Democrats on the committee represented states affected by the Alcoa closings. The Republicans opposed subsidies as a matter of principle. Senator Kenneth Wherry of Nebraska inserted in the record an editorial from the *New York Times* highly critical of Symington for suggesting that the way to attack monopoly was through governmental subsidization of competitors. This view got strong support from an unexpected source when, on the last day of the hearings, President Truman, in response to a question at a press conference, expressed the opinion that the aluminum plants could be disposed of without subsidies.[36]

Symington seemed to be back at square one, but he moved out quickly on two lines of attack. On the one hand, he negotiated quietly with Reynolds to see if he could get agreement on an arrangement that did not include governmental guarantees; Reynolds, understandably reluctant about trying to compete with Alcoa without governmental guarantees, finally agreed to lease the Hurricane Creek and Jones Mills plants in Arkansas if Alcoa would grant royalty-free licenses on certain of its patented processes. Alcoa categorically refused—"why give trade secrets to competitors?" To try to break the impasse, Symington decided, despite his earlier experience, to go directly to Davis—he still had great confidence in his powers of persuasion. Davis agreed to see him in his suite at the Carlton Hotel. "But," as a historian of Alcoa put it, "the smooth Missouri politician, who had great confidence in his reputation for charm, was entirely unprepared for the distinctly uncharmed response he got from the gritty little Alcoa chairman. After being regaled at length with all the wonderful public service benefits of coming to terms with the needs of competitors, Davis reportedly replied in words much like the following: 'My father was a Congregational minister, and we were taught that if we felt we're doing right that we don't have to take the shirt off our back and give it to somebody else.'"

Symington left in a rage. Irving Lipkowitz, an attorney with the Anti-Trust Division of the Justice Department, recalled, "It took much careful soothing from his staff to keep the SPB administrator negotiating."[37]

Despite his anger, Symington kept negotiating, but he also made it clear that he was perfectly willing to take on one of the country's most powerful conglomerates. He repeatedly assailed Alcoa and its president for being recalcitrant and uncooperative, capping it all on January 6 with what *Fortune* called "the shot heard round the aluminum world," a statement that "The time has come to say frankly to Congress that it may well be that no disposal of any of the plants to competitors will be possible unless Alcoa changes its attitude, or unless the courts, acting under the Sherman Act, reorganize Alcoa so that its monopolistic power is broken."[38]

Alcoa's attorneys now moved quickly to try to get the matter resolved. Apparently, they were feeling the heat from Symington's attacks, and they concluded that Symington meant what he said. In a rather sudden about-face they agreed to grant the royalty-free licenses, provided that Reynolds and/or other operators would share any improvements on a royalty-free basis. Symington was ecstatic. He told Wilson they would have a joint press conference the next day, that he would get a letter from the attorney general and from Senator O'Mahoney. Symington did have to get approval from the Justice Department, and though there was a little quibbling by some of the lawyers, by the next morning he had not only Clark's approval but also his congratulations.

The press conference went well. Symington read a letter he had written to Davis complimenting him on his "constructive" action. Davis was a little grudging, but in his letter to Symington he said, "Except for the public considerations which you have presented to us so effectively, we could not consider a royalty-free license under such a valuable asset."

Fortune, commenting on the love feast that seemed such a quick departure from the hostilities of a few days earlier, wrote, "The only question was whose tongue was in whose cheek."[39] The press all over the country commented favorably on the action, which was universally interpreted as breaking the monopoly in the aluminum industry, a result that the Department of Justice had been trying to achieve for years. As George Smith put it in his careful history of Alcoa: "Thus, it happened that a temporary agency of the Federal Government established competition in an industry where free-market forces and the federal courts had failed to do so. It was a stunning event in the history of American business-government relations . . ."[40]

Many people played important roles in the negotiations—Wendell Berge particularly, and also Sam Moment and Hugh Cox of Symington's staff—but Stuart Symington, in government less than six months, deservedly received most of the credit. I. F. Stone, the ultra-liberal journalist, wrote in *The Nation,* under the heading, "Salute to Symington," that though "the liberal crowd in Washington had been dismayed at his appointment," Symington had "won a resounding victory over one of the toughest troglodytes of American industry." He concluded, "In this rather unhappy Truman Administration," Symington "deserves a salute."[41]

While Symington's assaults on Alcoa captured most of the headlines during his last months as surplus property administrator, he was quietly working behind the scenes to disengage himself from the job. On January 11, 1946, he wrote President Truman, submitting his resignation, "to take effect at your convenience, but I hope not later than February 1." The surplus property administration was limited to policy making; the actual selling was done by the Reconstruction Finance Corporation. Symington suggested that both policy making and selling be concentrated in the newly created War Assets Administration.[42]

The president and others in the administration (particularly Secretary of the Treasury Snyder) agreed that a surplus property administrator as such was no longer necessary, and that, indeed, it would be better to concentrate the disposal of surplus property in one agency—the War Assets Administration, created for the purpose. Although Symington was asked if he had any interest in heading the new agency (he did not), he seems not to have been much involved in the discussions that led to its establishment—he favored giving full responsibility for surplus sales to the Reconstruction Finance Corporation, with which he had enjoyed fairly cordial relationships. Snyder, now secretary of the treasury, and others wanted to relieve the RFC of all of its sales responsibilities rather than add to them, arguing that the people at RFC were bankers, not salesmen. Symington responded that you didn't need to be a salesman if you took the best honest offer—"That's all that's needed so long as there's nothing crooked." He said many years later, "But I couldn't sell that, . . . so I resigned."[43]

In accepting Symington's resignation, the president praised him for establishing "sound and comprehensive policies" for the disposal of surplus property. He accepted the resignation "with less reluctance since I have today sent your nomination to the Senate of the United States as Assistant Secretary of War for Air."[44]

7

Assistant Secretary of War for Air

SYMINGTON had assumed when he was appointed chairman of the Surplus Property Board that once he finished the job he would return to St. Louis to resume the presidency of the Emerson Electric Company.

President Truman, however, wanted him to stay on. It is easy to understand why. The administration's relations with Congress were becoming increasingly strained, and its reputation had been repeatedly tarnished by reports of incompetence and corruption. Symington got along famously with members of Congress, both Republicans and Democrats, and he enjoyed a generally favorable press. He was receiving high marks for his performance as surplus property administrator and his reputation for integrity was unblemished. Truman could ill afford to lose him.

Snyder and Hannegan, acting as emissaries for the president, offered Symington his choice of three positions: assistant secretary of state for commercial air problems, assistant secretary of the navy for air, or assistant secretary of war for air, a post that had just opened up because of the resignation of Robert Lovett, whom Symington knew well. He did not take long to make up his mind. As president of Emerson, he had been involved with both the army and navy. The navy he found to be experienced and efficient; the air force, however, "was sort of a bastard child of the Army, much like the Marines with the Navy." He was sure his business experience would be of greater use to the Army Air Forces than to the air arm of the navy.[1] Moreover, if the president's plans for reorganizing the defense establishment were ever realized, the Army Air Forces could well become a separate service on an equal footing with the army and navy.

The president felt that he needed to check the appointment with the secretary of war, Robert P. Patterson, who was on a trip around the world. He had spoken about it before with Judge Patterson, but had received no definite response. He called Kenneth Royall, undersecretary, asking for Judge Patterson. When told that the secretary was on a trip around the world, he said, "Oh, I thought he was going to let me know about Symington, appointing Symington." Truman then asked Royall to come to the White House and talk about the matter. At the president's request, Royall contacted Patterson and obtained his rather grudging approval. "Well, if the president really wants him, tell him it is all right."[2]

The president really wanted him, and with Patterson's approval, no matter how grudging, he went ahead with the appointment, announcing it on January 18, 1946.[3] The Senate, faced with the task of confirming Symington for the third time in six months, quickly gave unanimous approval, and the new assistant secretary of war for air was sworn in at the Pentagon on February 1 before what his father-in-law described as "quite an impressive gathering."[4]

When Symington moved into his spacious suite in the Pentagon's E-ring—a far cry from his former office in the old Municipal Building on Vermont Avenue (Zuckert located it at "the intersection of Rape and Homicide")—he found himself part of a sprawling bureaucracy both encrusted with tradition, and, in the case of the air arm, seething with demands for reform. Patterson had been in office only since September 21 when he had succeeded the venerable, war-weary Henry L. Stimson, who had resigned at the age of seventy-eight. He had been in the War Department since 1941, however, first as assistant secretary, then as undersecretary. "The Judge," as he was called by virtue of his ten years on the federal bench—Hoover had appointed him to the U.S. district court and Roosevelt had elevated him to the circuit court—was a lifelong Republican. Truman did not hesitate to ask him to succeed Stimson. Despite Patterson's apparent lack of enthusiasm for Symington's appointment, the two men worked well together. Patterson gave Symington responsibility for heading the War Department's efforts in the struggle for unification of the armed forces; Symington for his part described Patterson as "wonderful."[5]

Royall was a North Carolinian with a law degree from Harvard. He saw service in France during World War I, and between the wars built a successful law practice in North Carolina, where he was active in Democratic politics. During World War II he was chief of the legal section and then deputy fiscal director of the Army Service Forces. He served for a time as Stimson's special assistant. In October 1945, Truman named him undersecretary. Royall and Symington got along fairly well, but were never particularly close. Royall found Symington "a very pleasant fellow . . . but he always seemed to have some axe to grind." The "axe" probably was unification. Royall, alone among senior officials of the War

Department, had little enthusiasm for the president's unification plans. For his part, Symington once said, "Ken was a little nervous about me because I came from Missouri and he was Under Secretary of War. But we got along fine and had no problems of any kind."[6]

Howard Petersen, the other assistant secretary, had succeeded John McCloy, who had left at about the time Lovett departed.

General Eisenhower, who had become chief of staff when George Marshall retired, was Symington's close friend and golfing companion. The Symingtons and the Eisenhowers frequently played bridge together—Stuart once complained that Ike took all his spending money—and though a deep rift later developed between them, their relationship at this time was warm and cordial. Stuart and Eve were guests of the Eisenhowers at the Augusta Golf Club (Ike proposed Symington for membership). At Ike's urging they attended the general's inauguration as president of Columbia University, and they occasionally went up to New York for an evening with Ike and Mamie. Eisenhower was a source of great strength during the unification struggle.[7]

The military man with whom Symington would work most closely was General Carl Spaatz, who had succeeded General Henry H. Arnold as commanding general, Army Air Forces. Symington first met Spaatz at Lovett's Florida home during a short vacation between the surplus property and War Department assignments. From both Eisenhower and Lovett, he had heard nothing but the highest praise for the salty general who had led the Army Air Forces to victory in both Europe and the Pacific—Eisenhower once described him as "probably the ablest of all active airmen." Symington wrote, "From that day in Florida on, Tooey Spaatz and I, as well as our wives, became fast friends. Spaatz had it all—ability, integrity, the courage to stand up for what he thought was right; and a priceless asset in that all who served under him became completely devoted to him."[8]

Symington made it clear from the beginning that he expected Spaatz and his staff to make the military decisions, that his efforts would be directed toward improving the logistics and management of the AAF, its relations with the War Department and with Congress—and, as he wrote later, "It worked. Spaatz and I never had a major disagreement."[9]

Between the time Lovett resigned and Symington took over, Colonel Thetus C. Odom, executive officer, managed the Office of the Assistant Secretary of War for Air. Odom, who was much interested in administrative arrangements, developed an organization chart—something that Lovett apparently had neglected—established office policies, including the hours of work expected of each staff member, and wrote a number of memos for the benefit of the new assistant secretary of war for air.[10]

Symington generally followed Odom's suggestions, but within weeks of his appointment he persuaded Zuckert, his right arm at Surplus Property, to join him as a special assistant. During the war Zuckert had taught statistical control for the AAF so he knew something about the way the Army Air Forces operated. Zuckert recalled, "I gradually picked up little chores, and Symington and I worked together very well." Symington soon established his own personal imprint on the office, and as Zuckert once said, created a place that was "alive. . . . [and] fun."[11]

Symington, never noted for patience, found much to be impatient about in the War Department with its cumbersome procedures. He soon learned that the War Department was not Emerson, or even Surplus Property, and he found that he could not always do things his way. Early in his tenure, for example, he discovered that a secretary in his office had to stay on the line until a long-distance call was completed. He complained to the War Department's director of communications that the two women in his office spent a great deal of their time waiting for calls to go through. He would "like to know the reasons for the ruling and what, if anything, can be done to have it rescinded." He received a lengthy reply, setting forth numerous reasons for the policy and stating that it could not be rescinded.[12]

Of much greater importance, Symington apparently had difficulty in getting access to the files of the Joint Chiefs of Staff. In a memo that really put civilian authority in its place, Colonel B. L. Boatner, executive to Lieutenant General Ira Eaker, deputy commander of the Army Air Forces, responded to a request from Symington's office for access:

> The matter has been discussed with General Eaker who states that headquarters AAF is not in a position to duplicate or furnish copies of JCS classified publications to other than designated JCS repositories without clearance from JCS.
>
> General Eaker suggests that, if Mr. Symington . . . desires to see JCS papers . . . in General Spaatz' possession, he is sure General Spaatz will be pleased to show them to him.[13]

The problem of access was symptomatic of a larger problem of cooperation between the air secretary's staff and the air staff, who might well have resented the rather considerable number of civilian assistants Symington assembled in his office. In August, Spaatz sent a memo to the air staff reminding them that he expected full cooperation with the air secretary's staff.[14]

Efficiency improved, but not always fast enough to satisfy the impatient Symington. He complained to Zuckert, "Gene, will you tell me why every time I want a figure about the Air Force I have to send out a search party."[15]

He was constantly after facts. He was conscious that he had been appointed because of his business expertise, and, leaving military operations in the hands of the airmen, he devoted his restless energy to the business side of the AAF.

Through the fortunes of war and the remarkable leadership of Lovett and Arnold, the Army Air Forces had become operationally almost coequal with the army and navy. When Symington took over, the drive for unification was well under way and AAF leaders looked forward with confidence to achieving separate status within the defense establishment. Symington recognized that one of his responsibilities was to prepare the AAF for independence.

There was much to do, and the task was complicated by the nation's headlong rush to break up its war machine and return to the pleasures of peace. As Surplus Property administrator, Symington had pushed the military to dispose of its excess war materials as rapidly as possible; as assistant secretary of war for air, he pressed the War Assets Administration and the War Department as well as the AAF to expedite disposal. Within the AAF he insisted on aggressive action, simplified paperwork, and complete records. He wanted to demonstrate to Congress "that the Air Forces were doing an excellent job."[16]

More troubling than the disposal of surplus property was the manpower shortage resulting from rapid demobilization—a shortage that threatened to invalidate the 70-Group Program, the centerpiece of the AAF's postwar plans. Those plans, developed in the closing months of the war by enthusiasts who saw air power as the key to national survival, were based on the assumption that seventy combat groups were necessary to protect U.S. interests at home and around the world.[17] Symington uncritically accepted the 70-Group concept—his job, he was fond of saying, was not to develop strategy but to sell it.

The 70-Group Program created controversy from the beginning, and would be a key element in Symington's difficulties as secretary of the air force. As assistant secretary of war for air he fought an unsuccessful rearguard action against personnel reductions that, he asserted, would "cut to pieces the planned program of the Air Force." He complained to Patterson that "any further semblance of a 70-Group Program cannot be maintained without kidding the War Department, the administration, the Congress, and the people."[18]

Given budgetary constraints and, even more important, the need to demonstrate that the AAF could be trusted to manage its own affairs, he stressed the necessity of rigid cost controls in all aspects of AAF operations. Lovett had foreseen the need and had moved to establish a comptroller's office. Symington, faced with greater urgency and driven by his experience in business, moved aggressively to achieve meaningful controls. Cost control did not come naturally to the military mind, but with the enthusiastic support of General Spaatz, Symington managed to get the senior officers thinking about it, at least, thus laying the groundwork for what became a successful program of management control through cost control.[19]

Some in the War Department held that most AAF officers were too inexperienced to manage a successful program. Symington recognized that. He reminded Patterson that the Air Materiel Command had had sixteen commanding officers since 1942, adding, "This command was far larger than General Electric. Can you imagine the latter having 16 Presidents in four years?" While recognizing a lack of experience on the part of many AAF officers, Symington argued that War Department criticism of the AAF as an inefficient organization because its officers were young and inexperienced was "bunk." They were not burdened by habits learned in the bureaucracy, they could "change easier than some of the old and only experienced in bureaucratic methods men who throng other branches. You can't teach old dogs new tricks." To help promising AAF officers, he arranged for courses in business management.[20]

From the beginning Symington recognized that the AAF could not achieve completely successful business methods so long as it was dependent upon a system that gave other services responsibility for the procurement of much of its matériel, and that gave those services—such as the Army Quartermaster Corps—de facto control over substantial parts of the AAF budget. He complained to Patterson, "it is apparent that a major factor operating against efficient management in the Air Force is the present policy of not allowing the Air Force to control its own funds. . . . As things now stand, it is a fact that top Air Force management does not know how much money in all categories it has available. This prevents accurate planning; and without accurate planning, you cannot have efficient management."[21]

"From the standpoint of either good management or military doctrine," he argued, "if the Commanding General of the Air Forces is supposed to be the Commander of the Air Forces, how can one justify any logistic authority having veto power over the Command responsibility?"[22]

As air force historian George Watson observed, "Symington envisioned an air arm with the same authority as the Army and Navy, with a civilian head equal in power and status to the Secretaries of the Navy and War, and with full responsibility for its own research, development, and procurement." Indeed, he saw this as the heart of what independence was all about, and as the struggle for unification went on he pushed as hard as possible for procedures that would make it work.[23]

Symington fretted a great deal over the AAF's public relations, which he considered abysmal, particularly when compared with the navy's publicity successes—he once sent some navy clippings to General Eaker with the observation that they represented "the kind of publicity we might continue to get if we had a live publicity department."[24]

The AAF managed to get its own public relations department, but the initial budgetary allocations were so small as to make it almost impossible for the department to function. Symington complained to Patterson that the AAF received far too little for entertainment, noting that he personally had paid for two dinners, "for some of our columnist and press friends carefully gotten together to help the cause, this after the War Department Budget office had turned them down." He asked, "Shouldn't we get this matter ironed out once and for all? Otherwise, if we get no money to do the right job, passing over Public Relations to the Air Forces has killed good relations." A short time later he asked the secretary for authority to establish a private lunch room: "many times people ask to come over here for lunch, want to talk privately. Mr. [John L.] Sullivan, Assistant Secretary of the Navy for Air, has a lunch set-up which is good, next to his office. He tells me he has only been out of it four times since July."[25] In the same vein, he complained to Patterson about a proposed order prohibiting transportation of government employees and members of Congress in War Department planes: "Why should the Army endeavor to give up the one 'sales-plus' it can offer, to wit, rapid transportation under proper circumstances to those people who decide its destinies?"

> In this connection, and inasmuch as it has much to do with the scope of my work—Air—may I respectfully present that in my opinion we are going too far in taking away the planes of the Secretary of War and the Chief of Staff?
> General Eisenhower is a national figure. The country is grateful to him and you. This plane helps you both in your work.
> In my opinion, taking away your personal plane lowers the prestige of both the office of the Secretary of War and the Chief of Staff.
> The Secretary of the Navy has a yacht, uses it nearly every day to advance the interests of the Navy. I understand so have and does the Chief of Naval Operations.[26]

The AAF took a long step toward improved public relations when Symington persuaded Stephen F. Leo to head the department. Symington first met Leo, a Maine newspaperman with close ties to Governor Sumner Sewall, during the Truman committee's investigation of Emerson—Leo was a member of the committee's staff—and immediately formed a favorable opinion. When Symington became assistant secretary of war for air, he asked Leo to conduct a study of the AAF's public relations. Shortly after the study, he asked him to take over the operation—actually to serve as an assistant to Major General Emmett (Rosie) O'Donnell, who, in the tradition that all major staff functions had to be headed by a uniformed officer, served as director. Leo was interested, but he had promised

Governor Sewall to accompany him to Germany as part of General Lucius Clay's military government staff. Symington and Spaatz finally persuaded Clay to release him, and in September Leo was back in Washington, where, despite his unimpressive title, he became a key player on the air force team.[27]

Regardless of who served as head of public relations, Symington paid attention and was, indeed, the AAF's most effective communicator. He entertained journalists, congressmen, and other important people—he got his private dining room; he and Eve gave dinners, usually at the 1925 F Street Club—they still were living at the Shoreham. He even struck up a cordial relationship with his nemesis Drew Pearson.[28] On one occasion he took a group of men to New York to have dinner at "21" with his friend Toots Shor and afterwards to watch the fights at Madison Square Garden. The party included Congressman Lyndon Johnson; Matt Connelly, the president's secretary; Leslie Biffle, secretary of the Senate; Joseph Nunan, commissioner of Internal Revenue; Postmaster General Hannegan; Assistant Postmaster General Gael Sullivan; Quentin Reynolds, editor of *Collier's;* James Conzselman, coach of the Chicago Cardinals professional football team; Supreme Court Justice William O. Douglas; and Attorney General Clark.[29]

Symington did not confine his public relations activities to Washington. In March he accepted an invitation from the Democratic National Committee to speak at a Jackson Day dinner in Salt Lake City, and apparently was a great success. In April he responded to a request from Congressman Johnson, with whom he had developed a close friendship, to visit Texas for an inspection of air bases, with luncheon and dinner talks in San Antonio and Austin, which Johnson hosted, and in the process enhanced his political standing both in his district and throughout the state.[30]

Unlike any other assistant secretary, Symington had direct and easy access to the president: poker sessions, meetings in the Oval Office, and frequent correspondence. He took interest in the preparation of Truman's new presidential plane—the DC-6 "Independence"—assuring him that it would be "the finest 'air yacht' in the land." On at least one occasion he wrote directly to the president to complain about the disparity between the AAF and the navy in appropriations for the purchase of airplanes, asserting that if this were not corrected, the navy would "take over the whole show." Truman expressed appreciation for the letter, saying, cryptically, "These matters will work out, as they should, if we ever get to the point where we can actually get a practical result."[31]

Symington occasionally asked for a favor, as in the case of a nephew of Joseph Pulitzer of the *Post-Dispatch* who wanted to get a job with the United Nations so he could be in New York with his invalid mother, who had lost her two other sons in the war. Truman responded, "I have spoken to Ed Stettinius about young Moore, although his kinship with Joe Pulitzer doesn't help him much with me."

The assistant secretary of war for air evidently felt close enough to the president, so that in thanking him he could lecture him a little: "Relative to Joe Pulitzer, anybody can go around cussing those people who don't agree you are doing a magnificent job, but I believe I can serve you better by moving in on them and attempting to show them where and why they are wrong."[32]

In any event, he was soon proving to be one of the president's most effective spokesmen. *Collier's* published a glowing article, "Mr. Charm, of Washington," describing Symington as "The One Man Lobby" and declaring that in the short time since his appointment, "The headlines coming out of Washington . . . indicate that the downward trend of Army prestige has been checked." His ability to sell Congress was an important reason "why Symington has come as far as he has in the government in so short a time. With the present rift between Congress and the administration, a man who can get along with senators and representatives is valuable. And Symington certainly can do that."

> As one senator put it, "That feller is Mr. Charm himself." He breezes into a committee meeting, well dressed and smiling. He is respectful, helpful, always candid and co-operative. He sits cross-legged in the witness chair, illustrates every point with an anecdote, and never attempts to gloss over unpleasantness. . . .
>
> Some people in Washington do not care for Symington and do not consider that he is big enough for the job. But the attitude of much of Washington is that of a newspaperman at an interview with Symington recently. They were discussing the Army-Navy merger. "I'll tell you," said Symington finally. "Give me a pencil and paper and I'll sell you on certain advantages of this merger plan in thirty seconds." "Mr. Symington," said the reporter. "In thirty seconds, I'm quite sure you could sell me anything."[33]

Symington got an unusual opportunity for travel, education, and prominence when the president appointed him one of three representatives of the executive branch to serve on the commission representing the United States at the Philippine independence ceremonies in Manila on July 4. This would be part of a round-the-world trip that would enable the assistant secretary for air to gain "personal knowledge of the problems of the Army Air Forces overseas and the problems of AAF personnel stationed on our overseas bases." An unstated purpose was to observe the projected nuclear bomb tests near Bikini Atoll in the Central Pacific. (Forrestal also observed the Bikini tests as part of a round-the-world tour of his own, which did not include the Manila ceremonies. He and Symington traveled independently, although they visited many of the same places at different times.)[34]

Symington left Washington's National Airport on June 26 in one of the Air Transport Command's specially equipped C-54 "Skymasters." With him were the other representatives of the president: Postmaster General Hannegan and J. Weldon Jones of the Bureau of the Budget. Also along was Senator Millard E. Tydings of Maryland, coauthor of the Tydings-McDuffie Philippine Independence Act and one of Symington's close friends—Eve and Eleanor Tydings had been debutantes together in Washington. Rounding out the passenger list were Assistant Postmaster General Sullivan (future chairman of the Democratic National Committee), and Lieutenant General John K. (Joe) Cannon, wartime commandant of the Twelfth Air Force, who had become director of the army's air training program.

They spent the night at a California air base and then went on to Honolulu, where Symington addressed a meeting of the Chamber of Commerce. He gave what was coming to be his standard air-power talk, with local assurances that Hawaiian forces would be increased, but—possibly presaging his late-in-life stand on disarmament—he mentioned that he agreed with the views of his friend Bernard Baruch that all existing atomic bombs should be destroyed and their manufacture stopped. He used the occasion to mention the B-36, the giant, six-engine bomber being developed in Fort Worth, declaring it could "fly 10,000 miles with an atomic bomb."[35]

The group then went on to Kwajalein, headquarters for the Bikini operation. Symington stayed with Brigadier General Roger Ramey, who was in charge of the tests. He found Ramey desperately trying to adjudicate conflicts over the assignment of space on the observation planes. He had assigned the congressmen and scientists who had come out to see the tests to the same plane; the scientists, it seemed, wanted their own plane. Symington solved the problem by suggesting that the congressmen go with him. They were fortunate: Symington's plane was closest to the explosion. Symington wrote,

> The test itself was awesome. A group of old Navy ships had been placed as targets in a lagoon. The sky was clear. We were the closest plane, some 17 miles off; were given dark glasses to protect our eyes, and warned not to be concerned at the shock wave which would hit our plane a few seconds after the explosion.
>
> There was the flash of light, then the mushroom cloud, and shortly thereafter our plane was rocked by the shock wave. I noticed a large ship turn over in the lagoon as a child would turn over a toy boat in a bathtub.[36]

Symington's plane returned to Kwajalein and immediately took off for Guam. Listening to the radio in his room at the Guam naval base, he was disturbed at the way in which various commentators, encouraged by the navy, were downplaying the results of the test and the importance of nuclear power in warfare.[37] He made a quick decision to skip the Manila ceremonies and go back to Kwajalein to view the results of the test. The next morning he persuaded General Kenney to take the C-54 and its passengers to Manila and loan him his B-17 to go back to Kwajalein. Kenney had not been scheduled to go to Manila and jumped at the chance—he had commanded MacArthur's air force during the war, and was pleased to be able to attend the Independence ceremonies.

So Kenney's crew took Symington back to Kwajalein, where he picked up a navy PBY for Bikini. Accompanied by Major General William E. Kepner and Vice Admiral William Blandy, he inspected the target ships. They donned rubber shoes and rubber coats. Then, led by a man with a Geiger counter, they started off in two small boats to view the damage. They boarded the *Nevada,* the *Arkansas,* and the heavy cruiser *Pensacola.* Symington wrote later, "The force shown us was unbelievable. On one ship a steel door was blown off and in, and then blown around and out of another entrance. Clearly, this was a great new force with which the world would have to contend."[38]

Back at Kwajalein, Symington boarded General Kenney's B-17 for the long flight to Tokyo, stopping en route at Iwo Jima and Okinawa. At Okinawa he took a helicopter out to the Island of Ie to dedicate a monument over the grave of the war correspondent Ernie Pyle, who had been killed the year before by a Japanese sniper. In Tokyo Symington stayed with Lieutenant General Ennis Whitehead, commander of the Far Eastern Air Forces. Tydings and Hannegan had rejoined him, and the three were treated to a series of parties and high-level briefings. On Sunday, Tydings and Symington were guests of the MacArthurs for lunch in the palatial house they had requisitioned as a residence—"one of the two most beautiful I had seen outside of this country. (The other, also in silver and blue, was that of the Duke and Duchess of Windsor on the coast of Southern France.)" Symington had first met General MacArthur back in Baltimore;[39] lunch "was all pleasant, but pretty formal." Both Symington and the senator were nonplussed when shortly after lunch, Mrs. MacArthur announced that the general had excused himself to take a nap. The next day, Symington met alone with MacArthur. He had assumed that the general might be interested in his views regarding recent developments in Washington, "but the conversation was one long monologue." After about an hour, Symington said that he must go—he had a dinner date with the T. V. Soongs (he was Madame Chiang Kai-shek's brother) in Shanghai. MacArthur insisted that he stay—"I haven't heard what you think." The monologue continued, but after another half hour Symington finally was able to leave.

The Soongs' driver met them at the airport, and they dashed through the crowded streets of Shanghai at breakneck speed—Symington was sure they hit at least one pedestrian—to the heavy iron gates of the Soong residence, where they "entered a different world; a beautiful park, nightingales singing in the trees; then on to a truly exquisite house." Laura Soong had spent much time in Washington. Symington had met her, and both she and her husband were well aware of their guests' close association with the American president. The Soongs gave the Symingtons embarrassingly extravagant attention. When Symington went to Nanking to see General George Marshall, then nearing the end of his frustrating mission to China, the Soongs provided him with a palace in which to spend the night and came from Shanghai for breakfast. The sojourn with Marshall, who reminded him that he had danced with Eve's mother at their wedding reception, "was a sad visit" despite the cordiality with which he was greeted. Mrs. Marshall was ill, and the heat was stifling. Marshall himself "appeared tired," and he was apprehensive about the future of the Chiang Kai-shek government, which fell a short time later. Symington's impression "was of a great American somewhat out of his field as a diplomat, but carrying out the orders of the Commander-in-Chief to the best of his ability under truly trying circumstances."[40]

Most of the rest of the trip consisted of high-level, privileged tourism, although Symington visited air bases and Hannegan inspected postal facilities along the way. In Cairo, Symington by prearrangement met Fiorello LaGuardia to bring him up to date on the work of UNRRA in China. In Berlin, he had a number of visits with General Lucius Clay. Although Clay's warning about Russian intentions would touch off the "war scare" of 1948, at this time—virtually alone among U.S. policy makers—he felt some optimism about the future of U.S.-Soviet relations.[41] As Symington reported to the president after his return, Clay provided "the first counter thinking to the heavy anti-Russian sentiment characteristic of previous opinions on our trip around the world." Clay felt that a part of the problem with the Russians derived from their mannerisms. Even when they were trying to please, they were "very clumsy." Clay agreed with General Bedell Smith, who had visited Berlin a day in advance of Symington. Smith was sure the Soviets would not fight until they had the atomic bomb.

When Symington asked Clay how he correlated his thinking with John Foster Dulles's statement that the Russians felt they could not live in a world that contained capitalistic countries, the general replied, "But we are planning now for what might happen in 15 or 20 years, for our children. If things go on this way, a scrap with Russia is inevitable. I am one who believes we can get to know them, and they can get to know us. I believe we can, over a period, work out the prevention of that war which so many people think inevitable."[42]

After he returned home, Symington reported much the same thing at a party given by Hannegan for the president, a number of cabinet officers, Democratic senators, and others. Secretary of Commerce Wallace noted in his diary, "Symington said that in talking with Bedell Smith and Clay he reached the conclusion that Russia definitely did not want war; that she couldn't possibly be ready for war in less than ten years, and it would probably take fifteen; that she certainly could not be pressed into war until she had the atomic bomb. Symington said, however, that one thing the Russians should realize was that we can be pushed so far and no farther." Wallace, who in less than a month would break with the administration over its "get tough" policy toward the Soviets, added, "What Symington told me indicated that we shall go on being tough and building up armaments and making sure that the next war and the next depression will be bigger and worse than the last one."[43]

From Berlin the travelers went to London, where they were guests of Ambassador Harriman. Symington knew Harriman from his years in New York, but Hannegan was meeting him for the first time. Symington remembered Hannegan saying, "This man has class. President Truman needs people like him in Washington. Let's see he gets there." Apparently they did—on September 22, two days after he took Wallace's resignation, the president called Harriman, asking him to return to become secretary of commerce.[44]

For Symington, the London stopover provided an opportunity to renew acquaintances from the time he had spent in England prior to America's entry into the war. He went out to Bracknell in Berkshire to play golf with Lord Anthony Rosslyn, with whom he had worked on matters relating to turret production. At the embassy he joined, among others, the venerable Lord Hugh Montague Trenchard, the "father" of British military aviation, and Lord Charles Portal, air chief marshal during World War II, to observe a flyover of Royal Air Force veterans to commemorate the Battle of Britain. He was distressed to note the small number of planes, "a practical demonstration of Churchill's remark that never in history had so many owed so much to so few."[45]

It was a good visit. The day after returning home, Symington wrote Spaatz, "We had a great day in London. . . . Ambassador Harriman was pleased with it all. We have good friends in that group of English officers abroad, no reservations." Major General Clayton Bissell, military and air attaché in the embassy, wrote: "The Ambassador and the Royal Air Force personnel with whom you came in contact have all been very complimentary in their remarks about your visit. I am sure that it has done inestimable good for the Air Force group here and will be helpful to us in our relations with the Royal Air Force."[46]

Back home, Symington turned again to the public relations problem and relationships with the navy. From St. Louis, where he had gone to vote in the

Missouri primary, he wrote Spaatz: "On my trip around the world, I became convinced that the Navy is attempting to give a 'front' that they are our first line of defense all over the world, not only from a diplomatic standpoint but also from a military standpoint." Citing front-page headlines in the Paris editions of the *New York Herald Tribune* on the navy's maneuvers in the Mediterranean in response to the growing crisis in Yugoslavia, he wondered what had happened to the plan to have a B-29 or two fly over the area.[47] Whatever the fate of the original idea, Symington thought the notion should be pursued. "What is the difference," he asked Spaatz, "between putting carriers, cruisers, etc. into the Mediterranean and putting B-29s over there to fly on our side of the line?"

"The only difference I see," he continued, "is that the B-29s could defend themselves adequately and knocking off ships would be like shooting fish in a barrel. Therefore if we are going to create an incident, why don't we create one through a strong representation instead of a relatively weak one."[48]

The State Department, agreeable to a show of force but trying to avoid an incident, was cool to the idea. Symington went ahead on his own, announcing in October that the Army Air Forces would send a flight of B-29s around the world, "if the State Department approves." Although there was some favorable comment—the *San Antonio* [Texas] *Express,* for example, said that the proposed flight was simply recognition of the fact "that airpower has become more important than seapower to national strength"—the idea found little support. *Time* commented that though the stated purpose of the trip was to work out technical problems associated with long-distance missions, "the real reason was the Air Forces' concept of its own manifest destiny—either enforcing the peace under the United Nations or keeping the U.S. secure." The editorial warned, "Far from strengthening U.S. diplomacy, the Air Forces' trigger-happiness was likely to embarrass it. State would have to be doubly careful now in approving the flight."[49]

The flight was approved, but only in a scaled-down version—so reduced that, as Symington later wrote, "it could not express what we originally wanted," and the project was abandoned. In November the Strategic Air Command sent a flight of six B-29s from Davis-Monthan Field in Arizona nonstop to the American base at Rhein-Main in Germany, but the diplomatic aspects of the mission were minimized.[50]

All of this jockeying for position, of course, was but part of the larger struggle over the unification of the armed forces, in which Symington, as the War Department's point man, found himself in almost constant conflict with representatives of the navy.

8

Unification

SHORTLY AFTER he became assistant secretary of war for air, Symington received a memorandum from Secretary Patterson stating that though he had failed to mention it when they were discussing unification at a meeting of the War Council, he assumed that everyone present knew that Symington had been delegated responsibility for handling unification. But just in case they did not, he was sending a copy to everyone who was present. He wanted "no doubt" as to who was responsible.[1]

Symington responded with a note—copied only to Generals Spaatz, Eaker, and Norstad—thanking the secretary for the honor, but suggesting, "there are reasons why I think this may be a net grave mistake." He asked for the privilege of setting them forth over the weekend when he would be in New York. The "reasons," as he laid them out in an uncharacteristically rambling memorandum, were primarily that he had more than enough to do to improve the business operations of the AAF, and that designating him to head the effort would strengthen the opinion that "the real fight is between the Navy and the Air Forces."[2]

There is no record that Patterson responded to this request, and though the War Department never issued a statement to that effect, there was no doubt that Symington was spearheading unification. Nor did anyone doubt that the real fight was between the navy and the air forces.

The fight had been brewing for months, even years, as the military establishment sought to reckon with the impact of air power on warfare. Although World War II was neither fought nor won solely in the air, air power was a key element in Allied victories in both Europe and the Pacific. In Europe the air war had been carried to the enemy almost solely by the Army Air Forces, but in the Pacific both the navy and the AAF had been responsible for air attacks on Japan. Both contributed to victory, and the partisans of each tended to overemphasize their own contributions.

The Army Air Forces wanted independence. Indeed, since the end of World War I most airmen had championed the cause of a separate air force, coequal with the army and navy. They achieved a high degree of independence during World War II, but they were still part of the army, and at a disadvantage in exploiting the force of modern air power. At war's end, General Arnold wrote General Spaatz, then commanding the U.S. Army Strategic Air Forces in the Pacific:

> While I am naturally feeling good about peace with Japan, as far as the Army Air Forces are concerned, it is, I shall say, unfortunate that we were never able to launch the full power of our bombing attack with the B-29s. The power of those attacks would certainly have convinced any doubting Thomases as to the capabilities of a modern Air Force. I am afraid that from now on there are certain people who will forget the part we have played. As a matter of fact, I see evidence of it right now in the writings of the columnists—probably inspired by interested parties.[3]

On October 1, 1945, Arnold informed his subordinate commanders that he favored a Department of the Air Force as part of an overall unified command, and in his last annual report he called for "one integrated, balanced United States military organization."[4]

Arnold's thinking was very much in tune with that of the army leadership in general. Although there was regular grumbling about the AAF's push for independence, army planning assumed almost from the beginning the establishment of a separate air force—indeed, there is a considerable body of opinion that the principal reason why AAF leaders were so enthusiastically in support of the War Department's plans for reorganization is that they believed those plans offered their best hope for independence. Thus when Lieutenant General Joseph T. McNarney, deputy chief of staff, testifying for the War Department before the House Select Committee on Post-War Military Policy in the spring of 1944, presented a chart showing a separate Department of the Air Force as part of a single Department of Defense, he had the full support of AAF leaders. Representatives of the navy, caught off guard by McNarney's proposals, argued that the case for consolidation had not been made and urged further consideration. The committee took no action, but recommended that the Joint Chiefs of Staff study the matter. Meanwhile, Senator David I. Walsh of Massachusetts, chairman of the Committee on Naval Affairs, urged Forrestal to come up with a navy plan for reorganization to counter the War Department's proposal that seemed to him to be gathering momentum in Congress.[5]

Forrestal turned to his longtime friend and former lawyer, Ferdinand Eberstadt, whose brilliant legal career had been followed by a not particularly successful government experience as chairman of the Army and Navy Munitions Board and vice chairman of the War Production Board, from which post he had been relieved by Donald Nelson, WPB chief, in 1943.[6] Eberstadt, although reluctant to return to government service, finally came to the aid of his friend. Assembling a staff that consisted primarily of active-duty naval reserve officers, he worked through the summer of 1945 to produce a 251-page report that countered virtually every one of the War Department's recommendations—except that which called for a separate air force. Forrestal was generally pleased with the report, which essentially recommended continuation of the status quo, with coordination provided by the Joint Chiefs of Staff. He had concerns with Eberstadt's proposal for a separate air force. Along with most ranking naval officers, he resented the repeated assertions by AAF spokesmen that air power had replaced sea power as the nation's first line of defense, and he was fearful that a separate air force would gobble up naval aviation.

Meanwhile, President Truman, whose experience in the Senate had convinced him that there was a lot of wasteful duplication in the army and navy and who during his campaign for the vice presidency had urged unification of the armed forces, decided to get into the discussion. The JCS study called for by the House Select Committee on Postwar Military Policy had failed to produce agreement; hearings during the fall by the Senate Committee on Military Affairs on a bill proposing a single military department treated the country to the unseemly spectacle of its highest officers engaged in juvenile arguments about how to organize the nation's defense. The committee established a subcommittee to prepare a new bill that would take into account the testimony presented. On December 19—two days after the Senate hearings ended—Truman sent a special message to Congress proposing a bill of his own.

Acknowledging that "the American people have all been enlightened and gratified by the free discussion which has taken place within the Services and before the committees of the Senate and House of Representatives," he declared, "there is enough evidence now at hand to demonstrate beyond question the need for a unified department." He proposed a single Department of National Defense, headed by a civilian secretary who would be a member of the cabinet and who would have jurisdiction over three coordinate branches, one for the land forces, one for the naval forces, and one for the air forces. He did say that the navy should retain its own carrier, ship, and water-based aviation and the Marine Corps should be continued as part of the navy. He provided for a single chief of staff who with "the commanders of the three coordinate branches of the Department should together constitute an advisory body to the Secretary of National Defense and to the President."[7]

The army and the AAF were ecstatic. They had achieved virtually everything they wanted. The navy was close to mutiny. Eberstadt, chagrined that the president had adopted so little of his plan, wrote Forrestal that Truman was a fool and urged that everything possible be done to prevent his plans from becoming reality. Forrestal, though disappointed, was not prepared to lead a mutiny—at least not overtly. On the day of the president's message, he sent a communiqué to "all hands" urging them to refrain from opposing the president in their public utterances, with the understanding, of course, that they were free to state their opinions if called upon by congressional committees and always to defend the importance of the navy to the nation's defense. Truman endorsed this position, although he soon had more than enough of naval opposition to his proposals for military reorganization.[8]

Symington quickly became embroiled in the controversy. Shortly after his confirmation he wrote Forrestal, reporting that he had heard "from a naval officer of rank" that an organization was being formed with the support of naval people to fight unification. He thought it a "sad commentary" that high-ranking officers were publicly flaunting their opposition to the commander in chief.[9]

On the surface, Forrestal and Symington maintained their friendship throughout the unification controversy. They played golf at the Chevy Chase Club, they exchanged friendly notes, and they never criticized each other directly in public. Yet it was evident that the controversy severely strained their longtime friendship. Clark Clifford, who as counsel to the president had responsibility for developing the administration's tactics in the unification struggle, wrote that he was close to both men. His original principles has been "strongly pro-navy," but while he retained his friendship for Forrestal, "he gradually began to feel he was showing excessive rigidity."[10]

Symington criticized Forrestal in private, but never lost his ability to negotiate with him. This was not true of Eberstadt. In a long, "eyes only" memorandum to Patterson, Symington urged the secretary not to negotiate with Eberstadt, "the kind of man who will take a job and then cut the throat of his boss behind his boss' back," because it put Patterson in a bad light with the president and the public. "Forrestal brings in Eberstadt and the next thing you know it is Patterson vs. Eberstadt, with Forrestal on the sidelines ready to agree or disagree. . . . Of course this well known trick in negotiating much improves Forrestal's position with the President, in that he Forrestal appears as a mediator, you as an aggressor."[11]

Earlier, Major General Norstad, the young AAF officer who was serving as chief of the War Department's plans division and who became a key player in the struggle for unification, had urged Patterson to turn discussions with Eberstadt over to Symington, who could counter Eberstadt's presumed organizational expertise with his "great amount of practical business experience, particularly in the field of organization," and because of "the political angle." Norstad's comments reflect the attitude of AAF officers regarding Symington's participation in unification. They welcomed it. He had clout with the president and with the Congress; he had accepted AAF doctrine without reservation; he had a reputation as a super salesman; he was about their age and shared many of their interests; he was comfortable with them and they with him. Many of them agreed with Colonel Barton Leach, who on his return to the faculty of the Harvard Law School after a four-year stint in AAF headquarters wrote Spaatz: "The Air Force . . . must insist upon young, aggressive civilian leadership. Mr. Symington has the basic requirements for civilian leadership of the Air Force and Judge Patterson does not."[12]

Despite his demurral to Patterson, Symington from the time of his appointment was involved in the unification struggle as well as the controversy with the navy. On the evening of May 7 he invited Clifford and Norstad to his Shoreham apartment to discuss progress. He and Norstad were concerned about the impact of Forrestal's testimony before the Senate Naval Affairs Committee on S. 2044, which had been introduced by Senator Elbert Thomas of Utah in basic support of the president's proposals. Forrestal had said that while the navy was "solidly behind" what it believed to be the basic objective of the president's proposals, he did not believe that S. 2044 would work. He did not like the single chief of staff and was worried about the future of navy and marine aviation; moreover, the structure envisioned was too complicated and cumbersome.[13]

Symington began the conversation by expressing the hope that they could have "a free and frank discussion" of the more controversial aspects of S. 2044. Norstad said he thought Forrestal was misinterpreting the role of the proposed chief of staff. Clifford responded by saying that he had worked with Forrestal in the preparation of his testimony and that while he did not feel there was any danger of "a man on horseback," he shared Forrestal's concerns. Symington and Norstad agreed that the single chief of staff was not the crux of the matter and they would not insist on it at the cost of delaying the legislation. Symington wanted to move onto a discussion of what could be done to expedite action. Clifford was quite sure that S. 2044 could not be passed in its present form. Symington was not so sure, but he acknowledged that there was no use trying to push the bill as it was then written. Clifford reported that he would recommend to "the Boss" that he call the two secretaries in and direct them to report on their specific areas of agreement and disagreement, with the understanding that he would decide on the points of disagreement. Symington and Norstad said that this seemed to be an acceptable course of action. As the meeting broke up they agreed that their conversations had been exploratory only, that no commitments had been made, and that for the time being they would keep the substance of their talk to themselves.[14]

The president followed Clifford's advice, and in the letter which Patterson and Forrestal wrote in response to Truman's request that they try to work out their differences, the War Department dropped its insistence upon a single chief of staff. There remained disagreement on the need for a single department of defense, a separate air force, the control of military aviation, and the role of the Marine Corps. Essentially, the president adopted the War Department's position on all disputed points, except he did agree that the navy should have jurisdiction over "ship, carrier and water-based aircraft essential to Naval operations, and aircraft of the United States Marine Corps," and over land-based aircraft essential to administration, transport, and training. He also agreed to guarantees of the Marine Corps' integrity as part of the navy.[15]

Although Symington participated in development of policy and in negotiations—during discussions of the president's request, for example, he had urged Patterson to make every effort to cut the areas of disagreement to "simplify the problem for the President"[16]—and would be more heavily involved in negotiations later in the struggle, his principal role at this juncture was that of a salesman. By midsummer he had emerged as the War Department's most visible proponent of unification and, especially, of a separate air force. As Bill Davidson wrote in *Collier's,* "The main reason that Symington is now a key man in government is that he is a super salesman." Davidson credited him with restoring the army's image with the public and slowing down the navy's tidal wave of anti-unification publicity.

Publicity, Symington believed, was one of the most important weapons in the arsenal, and for that reason he fretted over what he felt to be the War Department's wretched public relations. He applauded Spaatz's plans to send senior air officers around the country to talk up air power and unification, but when he saw the list of speakers he cautioned: "Some of your speakers are not very expert at public speaking, General LeMay for example. He is a fine officer but a poor speaker. . . . Believe the subject of unification calls for our best. Let's discuss."[17]

He talked about the importance of air power in his speeches in Texas and Utah, but he gave his first major speech on unification at a luncheon given by the Detroit Economic Club on June 17. He could not have asked for a better occasion. A thousand people, including some of the leading industrialists of the country, crowded into the ballroom of the Book Cadillac Hotel, and Symington was flanked by a dazzling array of AAF brass. Using these men as a backdrop, he delivered a hard-hitting speech on the importance of air power in the nation's defenses, the need for unification of the armed forces with separate status for the air force, and, especially, the need for adequate financial support. Here he entered into direct comparisons with the navy, charging that the navy was receiving more money for the procurement of airplanes than was the AAF. "Is there one American in 50,000," he asked, "who knows that in this, the first postwar year, the navy is getting millions of dollars more than the Air Force to buy hundreds more planes than is being allowed the Air Force?"[18]

Citing a speech made in Chicago by Vice Admiral Arthur Radford, he charged that the navy was trying to build a second strategic air force. "If there are two separate and complete air developments, where does the taxpayer get off? Should we have the development of strategic air by both services, at the expense of the billions involved, or should it be under the people who developed it and who, under General Hap Arnold, fought successfully against the entire world to prove its merit?" Then, with obvious relish, he introduced the officers who were with him—Spaatz, Eaker, Kenney, George, LeMay, Vandenberg, plus Doolittle, by then a civilian—citing with pride their accomplishments: "the men who did the job, the men to whom now is entrusted much of the defense of our country."

He concluded by repeating his call for unity, and "for a full and equal place for air, especially as the major new weapons coming up are primarily weapons of the air . . . we want the young eagles of America strong and high over our land; and that is why we are out here today to ask you to help us carry out our mission—the provision of adequate air defense for our country."[19]

He sat down to a standing ovation. Spaatz handled a question-and-answer period. At the end of the meeting, a show of hands indicated almost unanimous approval of unification with full status for the air force. That plus favorable press comment should have been encouraging. Symington worried in a telephone conversation with Norstad the next morning, from Dayton, where he had spent the night, about Patterson's reaction and that of the president. Norstad assured him that Patterson was pleased, as was General Eisenhower, and he saw no reason why the president should not be. Over at the navy, however, "there was a little boiling over it. They didn't know what the hell to do about it."[20]

Symington interrupted his speech-making for the trip around the world. Although his purpose was to view the Bikini bomb tests and to inspect AAF installations, he talked unification and a separate air force whenever it seemed remotely appropriate. He gave MacArthur a copy of his Detroit speech. The general told him that he agreed with every word of it. He also delivered a long anti-navy lecture, and wondered why the president put up with the navy's efforts to sabotage his policies. He said if the president would "discharge one high-ranking official" the sabotage would stop. General Marshall, visited two days later in Nanking, expressed himself as in favor of unification but felt that the navy would resist it to the end. He warned Symington that "ill-timed and incorrect statements of certain Air Force officers" contributed to the navy's intransigence.[21]

Back home, Symington resumed the campaign for unification and a separate air force, speaking on the subject to the Wings Club in New York and at the first postwar meeting of the Air Reserve Association in Memphis. He sounded similar themes in each: the savings that would result from unification, the need for economy, the importance of air power, and the strategic need for a separate air force. He toned down his attacks on the navy, which the *New York Times* reported "have been credited with having induced Congress to postpone action on President Truman's program at the last session." Symington's attacks and those of various AAF officers may have had something of a backlash effect, but it is difficult to make a case for the charge that they were a major cause of congressional delay. The navy wanted delay and navy partisans in Congress were strong enough to effect it; the columnist Doris Fleeson reported that "in a secret session called . . . by Commanding Gen. Spaatz to discuss budget problems, the top brass of the Army Air Forces somberly agreed that the Navy had licked the projected Army-Navy merger."[22]

AAF leaders may have been pessimistic, but Symington remained confident that he could sell unification and a separate air force. He called on his friends for help: Eve's cousin, J. H. "Jock" Whitney, a power in the financial and entertainment worlds; Mary Pillsbury [Mrs. Oswald] Lord, prominent New Yorker identified with many war-related causes; Tex McCreary, the entertainment mogul; and others. General Doolittle, now working for the Shell Union Oil Corporation, as head of the Air Force Association, spent almost full time on the problem.

Perhaps no one was more enthusiastic or effective than the famed aviatrix Jacqueline Cochran. Jackie Cochran, high school dropout and former beauty parlor operator, had learned to fly during the war and gained fame as a ferry pilot, when the few women who ventured into the male world of aviation became wartime celebrities. Married to Floyd Odlum, millionaire owner of the Atlas Corporation and Convair, she developed a line of cosmetics and became rich in her own right. She had an almost uncontrollable passion for the Army Air Forces and became convinced that the future of the country depended upon getting the AAF out from under the dead hand of the army. She persuaded Arnold to take her on as an unpaid assistant to promote the idea. Arnold assigned a young colonel, Jake Smart (later a major general), to work with her, and she spent a year barnstorming the country. Shortly after Symington became assistant secretary, she came to see him. "I had anticipated a tomboy," he recalled, "so when she walked in, I was surprised. Attractive and very well dressed, she was obviously proud of her physique. She could be a seducer." Years later she said, "Senator, that first time we met, you were looking at my legs."[23]

They became friends. Symington frequently visited the Odlum ranch, a luxurious spread in the hills of Southern California not far from Los Angeles, where Floyd in time became almost confined because of his arthritis. It would be easy to draw inferences, but as was the case with many other women whom Symington charmed and was charmed by, there is no evidence that there was anything between them but close friendship and mild flirtation. "For us in the Air Force," he wrote, "she was a great thing—a kind of ambassadress because she had Floyd to support her—and because of her own brass. Her passion was to get attention and she wouldn't hesitate a minute if she were certain she was right about something. . . . Around the Air Force, she was sort of a goddess."[24]

In pursuit of his campaign, Symington became increasingly involved in negotiations with the navy. Forrestal, under pressure because his ambivalent attitude toward some of the specifics in the president's proposals had made him appear at odds with the commander-in-chief, was trying to seek an accommodation between navy interests and what the president wanted.

On November 7, Forrestal invited Symington and Norstad to have lunch with him at his Georgetown house. They all recognized that continued disagreement between the services on unification would jeopardize national security, and that every effort must be made to reach agreement before the new Congress convened.

After lunch they were joined by Admirals Sherman and Radford. The meeting turned out to be productive. They recognized that two issues still separated them: the role and authority of the "top secretary," and the roles and missions of each of the services. Forrestal, influenced by Eberstadt, still clung to the notion that the head of the new department should have only coordinating authority,[25] although he seemed to agree that the head should have ultimate authority but not the ability to interfere with the operation of the component services. With regard to the marines and land-based aircraft, two matters that the navy insisted must be resolved before they could support any unification plan, Symington and Norstad argued at length against trying to legislate roles and missions. With regard to the marines, they said they would not go beyond the president's position as expressed in his letter of June 15—the wording of which, they pointed out, had been proposed by the navy. As for land-based air, they would agree "that for a period of 3 years, without prejudice to the ultimate allocation by competent authority of the roles and missions involved, the navy would be authorized to maintain their 160 land-based aircraft plus 100% reserve for anti-submarine patrol and shipping reconnaissance." As this seemed to provide a satisfactory basis for further discussion, Symington and Forrestal asked Norstad and Sherman to work out a statement on which they all could agree.[26]

Symington went off for a week in Texas and Mexico while Sherman and Norstad tried to reach an agreement. It was not easy. The normally reasonable Sherman, taking his cue from Forrestal and the navy brass, would agree to a position only to then back away. This was particularly true in the matter of roles and missions. When the navy insisted that roles and missions would have to be determined by the president rather than the department head, the War Department agreed, only to have the navy decide that a presidential directive was not enough, that roles and missions would have to be determined by Congress. A frustrated Norstad wrote, in a memorandum for the record, his favorite device for recording his thoughts and opinions, "it was apparent . . . that my personal participation in any further negotiations would serve no useful purpose and that I proposed to withdraw. (I propose to convey the idea that the reason I no longer feel I can be a party to further discussions on the question of Unification is that I no longer have confidence in the good faith of the Navy on this particular subject.)"[27]

Norstad continued to participate in the discussions. On November 20 he and Symington met with Forrestal, handing him a paper that set forth their views on organization, roles, and missions. Forrestal indicated that he had no problems with the War Department's position on roles and missions, but he did note that "there was considerable feeling on this subject in the Navy." Norstad replied that there was equal feeling in the Army Air Forces on the other side of the question, which Forrestal recognized as the case.[28]

The Symingtons spent Thanksgiving at the Wadsworth farm in Geneseo, and the occasion gave Symington an opportunity to unburden himself to his father-in-law, who in the new, Republican-controlled Eightieth Congress would be even more influential than in the past. Symington returned to Washington with the feeling that unification might be easier to get through the new Congress than it had been in the old. He mentioned that to Forrestal when they met alone on Sunday, December 1. Forrestal was not so sure, except that he did think that the War Department's position would be stronger. He seemed to be quite on the defensive, complaining that the War Department's approach from the beginning had been "unilateral and nonconsultative," and that the navy, in trying to improve the original proposal, had been "accused of stodginess, lack of cooperation, and almost disloyalty." Although, as has been indicated, Symington had refrained from criticizing Forrestal publicly, he had not spared the navy as an institution, and he criticized Forrestal privately—for example, he wrote his father-in-law, "I think you are right in that Forrestal's letter [to the President] was a hedge. He is not playing the game." There is no record of Symington's response to Forrestal's complaints, but he did suggest as they were breaking up that it might be possible to get the AAF to agree to some statutory assignment of land-based aircraft to the navy for anti-submarine and reconnaissance. This was nothing new; Norstad had advanced the same idea in his talks with Sherman. The two men agreed to get together again the next Wednesday.[29]

At lunch on Wednesday, the two civilian leaders were joined by Norstad together with Sherman and Radford. Why Forrestal invited Radford to join the group is a mystery—at least if he had any hope that the luncheon would be productive. Radford had become increasingly strident in his opposition to a separate air force, and, indeed, to the whole idea of unification.[30] He ran true to form at lunch, launching into a tirade against the Army Air Forces and questioning the basis for a belief that there would be a place for a strategic air force in future wars. Forrestal noted in his diary, "The meeting broke up with a feeling on my part that we were farther away than ever from reaching an agreement."[31] It could hardly have been otherwise.

For several weeks after the luncheon, there seems to have been little interservice discussion of unification. Norstad left for a couple of weeks, and on his return reported to Symington that he had just talked to Sherman on the telephone, wondering if anything had been done. Nothing had. Norstad reminded Sherman that when he left he had a paper ready that he thought would be satisfactory, and that in any event the time was approaching when they must get together or admit that agreement was impossible. He thought Sherman's reluctance reflected Forrestal's position.[32]

Despite Sherman's reluctance, he and Norstad continued to meet—almost on a daily basis—to try to agree. Symington, in addition to orchestrating public support, monitored the conversations. He and Norstad got along so well and were in such agreement that "monitoring" was hardly required. Their concern was a separate air force and avoidance of legislated roles and missions. They were willing to compromise on virtually everything else. Not so with Eisenhower and Patterson, who had not taken a particularly active role in the discussions— Patterson admitted to Forrestal that he "had not paid much attention to the conversations that Symington had with Norstad and Sherman"[33]—but they gave no indication that they were willing to abandon the army's original preference for a straight line of command through a single chief of staff.

Clifford, who was handling the matter for the president and who was bombarded from both sides by his two good friends, Symington and Forrestal, records in his memoirs that "as the battle lines hardened, I spent as much time as possible with General Eisenhower, trying to gauge his willingness to compromise."[34] A breakthrough seems to have occurred late in the year when the

Symingtons invited the Eisenhowers and Cliffords to their apartment for Sunday evening dinner. After dinner, the three men went into the bedroom and talked until well after midnight. Eisenhower, as both Clifford and Symington knew, was strongly for unification—he said "it would be unconscionable to fight another war organized the way we had been in World War II"—and he felt that the War Department's position was the better one. To get the process started, he would be willing to compromise.

Clifford remembered this as "a very important meeting." In any event, the process moved rapidly after the first of the year. After the cabinet meeting on January 3, Patterson rode with Forrestal to the Navy Department. He told Forrestal that he was not "rigidly or stubbornly" committed to any plan, that he was willing to be quite flexible. Forrestal, Symington, Norstad, and Sherman met frequently over the next several days, and on January 16 they agreed on the draft of a letter to the president to be signed by the two secretaries—Symington during these negotiations seems to have been representing the War Department totally, with Norstad's assistance; Patterson does not seem to have participated. Forrestal called Clifford, who wanted to release the news immediately. Forrestal persuaded him to wait until six o'clock to give him time to inform the navy's friends in the House and Senate.[35]

The letter revealed how much the War Department had given up for the sake of a separate air force and the avoidance of congressionally mandated roles. On all of the other points on which there had been disagreement in the letter of May 31, the navy's position prevailed: the Secretary of National Defense would have only coordinating powers, and the command structure would be headed by the Joint Chiefs of Staff. Even in the matter of roles and missions, the two secretaries attached a suggested draft of an executive order that gave the navy control over its land-based patrol and reconnaissance aircraft and assured the marines of their primary role in amphibious operations.[36]

The bill went through eight drafts before it was ready for submission to Congress. No one in the White House was particularly happy with it. Clifford's assistant, George Elsey, who did most of the drafting, commented angrily in a handwritten note to his boss, "President's intention was merger. We are not getting merger. . . . I think Pres. Truman's orig[inal] aims have been subverted. . . . What we have is a Navy and Air Force betrayal of Army's merger idea—they have ganged up to get 3 depts with only the most nominal nod at merger."[37]

Elsey may have overstated it, but the only two services that got anything at all out of unification were the air force and the navy. Symington and Norstad, representing the War Department, were willing to compromise on virtually everything to obtain a separate air force. Clifford, representing the president, wanted a unification bill even if it had imperfections. So did Eisenhower, and his willingness to drop insistence on a single chief of staff, according to Clifford, was critical to making an agreement possible. The winner was Forrestal. He skirted dangerously close to administrative disloyalty, but managed to keep pressing, wearing everyone else down. In a telephone conversation with Symington, he said, "If it had been anyone else but Mr. Truman I think I would have been fired long ago."[38]

Symington expected to help the bill through Congress. From his earliest days in Washington he had cultivated senators and representatives on both sides of the aisle, and he got along well with almost all. Both Symington and his friends in the AAF anticipated the use of his well-known powers of persuasion to convince the doubting and bolster the faith of the converted. With the shift to Republican control, his father-in-law, a staunch supporter of unification, assumed a more influential position.[39]

Before the president's bill was ready for submission, Symington had to withdraw from the struggle. For years he had suffered from headaches, at times so severe as to require hospitalization. Shortly after becoming assistant secretary of war for air, a bout drove him to a hospital, this time in New York. The doctors found dangerously high blood pressure; they put him on a diet and told him to take it easy. There was no way, of course, that he could or would follow such instructions, and in the spring of 1947 his blood pressure was out of control and the headaches almost unbearable. There were other symptoms of difficulty. Zuckert remembered that at times, especially in the late afternoon, Symington's eyes turned a deep blue. He finally was persuaded to get out of town; he and Eve went to Cat Cay in the Bahamas for a few days' rest in the sun—interrupted only by a visit to Key West for a "purely social" lunch with the president and Samuel Rosenman—and then home to St. Louis. Clifford brightened his spirits by writing, "Your efforts in obtaining ultimate agreement to a plan of unification were of such primary importance that I thought you would be interested in reading the end result to which you contributed so greatly. I enclose herewith a copy of the bill which we have sent up to the Congress for their consideration. . . . I told the President what a valuable contribution you made to this result and he is more than grateful."[40]

Prior to leaving for Cat Cay, Symington had gone to Boston to consult with Dr. Reginald Smithwick of the Massachusetts Memorial Hospitals, who had developed a procedure for severing the sympathetic nerves near the spine as a means of treating severe cases of high blood pressure.[41] The procedure, since supplanted by drugs, was long and complicated, and it was successful only about a third of the time. Symington reacted so well to the tests, however, that both Dr. Smithwick and his physicians in St. Louis thought the operation was worth trying.

He contemplated stopping in Washington en route to Boston to testify on the unification bill working its way through Congress. No one believed this was a good idea. Members of his staff, Clifford, and others sought to dissuade him. Eisenhower wrote a two-page, single-spaced letter on the subject. He was "shocked and astounded to learn from Tooey [General Spaatz]" that Symington was planning to come to Washington to testify. "You owe it to yourself and your family and—from my viewpoint—you owe it to the whole service to get yourself well now and to give yourself the maximum opportunity to do so." He reminded Symington, somewhat in jest, that he was commander-in-chief of the army and could order the pilot, on pain of court-martial, not to land in Washington: "Wouldn't that be something?"[42]

Symington's friends prevailed, and he went directly to Boston, where Dr. Smithwick performed the operation in the Evans Memorial Hospital. It was a complete success. As Symington said later, "Since the day I had the operation, I've done anything I wanted to, eaten everything I wanted, drunk anything I wished, no low-salt diet, nothing." He remained in the hospital, however, for about a month. Eve, staying at the Ritz-Carlton, served as a conduit for a steady stream of messages from Washington, as the air staff and others kept the ASWA apprised of the progress on unification. General Eaker wrote, "the battle has not gone so well since you left as it did while you were here energizing the creaky old machine." He thought "the critical stage has not been reached and probably will not be for some weeks."[43]

Forrestal wrote, "I have had the feeling in the last two weeks that unification was rather bogged down. Norstad, Sherman, Clifford and I had lunch last Friday to consider ways and means of speeding it up. I do not believe there will be real trouble in the Senate but the House doesn't look so good, the danger not being opposition but rather apathy."[44]

Eisenhower was more optimistic. He wrote Eve to tell Stuart, "provided he shows any interest in the matter, that the proceedings on the Hill are developing pretty much as I predicted."[45]

Clifford also exuded optimism. "The hearing is going well on the Unification Bill," he wrote. "Patterson and Forrestal both did splendidly and Eisenhower gave them the full treatment. I have read Admiral Sherman's statement and I believe it is exceptionally good. All in all I believe I can report real progress."[46]

By mid-April Symington was able to go home to Creve Coeur. The operation had gone well, and his friends in St. Louis, he wrote Clifford, were "really wonderful. . . . They got me a new radio and Wes McAfee and [David] Calhoun had Union Electric put television in the house . . . and I feel like a thoroughly spoiled one." The president asked his personal physician, Dr. Wallace Graham, taking an air medicine course in San Antonio, to fly to St. Louis and look in on him. Dr. Howard Rusk, who had been the Symington family's physician prior to the war, called to examine his record. Both found the patient improving steadily. The president expressed pleasure with the results, but admonished Symington in the avuncular tone he was coming to adopt when writing to his assistant secretary to follow the doctors' orders.[47]

Symington was bored, and anxious to get back to work. As he wrote his good friend Justice Douglas, "I don't know just what I am going to do, but the big Doc in Boston says I shouldn't kick away what looks like a fantastically good recovery by coming back to work too soon."[48]

Even though he did not return to Washington, he did, for all practical purposes, go back to work. He kept in close touch with the air staff in Washington, with Clifford in the White House, and with Zuckert and Leo of his own office. He exchanged long, chatty letters with Forrestal and Eisenhower—Forrestal remained gloomy, but Eisenhower retained his optimism. Symington, too, remained optimistic, although taking nothing for granted. He warned General Kenney not to irritate possible congressional opponents of unification by over-emphasizing strategic bombing. The AAF was in the final round of a fight that "if we don't win . . . the Air Force reverts to its previous impossible position as a minor addendum to the War Department."[49]

On June 24 he wrote Dr. Smithwick a progress report. He was encouraged. He had gone out to dinner several times, but always had been home by midnight, and "except for a period of nervousness that comes on me periodically, I feel pretty good even then." The same day he wrote Matthew Connelley, the president's secretary, asking for an appointment for July 8 or 9 to pay his respects—"I really could stay down there and work now but the Doc advises periodic visits instead of a steady routine, this for a few more weeks. In any case I am rounding into proper shape for '48."[50]

By the time Symington called on the president on July 8, the struggle for unification was virtually over. The Senate approved its bill on July 9. The House passed a similar bill on July 19. A conference committee took very little time to iron out the differences, and by July 25 the bill was ready for the president's signature. He signed it in the cabin of *The Sacred Cow* just before taking off for Grandview, Missouri, to visit his dying mother. Clifford, who had brought the bill to the president, recalled, "As I began to leave with the papers, President Truman turned and handed me one of the pens with which he had signed the bill—the first such gesture he made toward me—and asked me to give the other pens to Patterson, Forrestal, Royall, and Symington."[51] In carrying out his responsibility, Clifford wrote:

> The President asks that I inform you of his deep appreciation for the splendid contribution that you made in the attainment of the unification of this country's armed services. . . .

The President expressed the opinion that this pen would be of particular significance to you because it was the instrument used in the final step in which, for the first time in our history, a separate Air Force was created.[52]

For Symington and others in the AAF who for the past eighteen months had devoted most of their energies to achieving unification—Symington gave most of the credit to Norstad[53]—the creation of a separate air force was by far the most important part of the new legislation, bringing to fulfillment the dreams of almost every airman since the days of Billy Mitchell. The legislation also created the Department of Defense, the Central Intelligence Agency, and the National Security Council.

But it was not a good bill; as Symington later said, "it wasn't the bill we wanted at all." The navy, led by Secretary Forrestal and abetted by powerful friends in Congress, managed to curb the powers of the Secretary of Defense so that he had little more than coordinating authority.[54] Much of the trauma associated with the birth of the U.S. Air Force had its roots in the ambiguous command structure in which it occurred.

Judge Stuart Symington.
Symington family
photograph.

Emily Harrison Symington and baby Stuart. Symington family photograph.

Second Lieutenant Stuart Symington. Symington family photograph.

Eve Symington, Red Cross driver in St. Louis. Courtesy of Stuart Symington, Jr.

Lord Halifax (right) inspects a turret, with unidentified man and Symington. Courtesy of the Stuart Symington Papers, Western Historical Manuscript Collection, Columbia, Missouri.

Refuting Congressman May, Symington talks with Congressman Charles I. Faddis, chairman of the House Military Affairs Subcommittee. Stuart Symington Papers, Western Historical Manuscript Collection, Columbia.

Poker on the *Williamsburg,* July 1949. Clockwise: President Truman, Clark Clifford, Symington, Oscar Ewing, Tom Clark, unidentified man, George Allen, Mon Wallgren. Courtesy of the Harry S. Truman Library, Independence, Missouri.

Relaxing at Key West: President Truman, flanked by Eric Johnston and Symington, out for a stroll. Harry S. Truman Library.

Chief Justice Fred Vinson swears in Symington as secretary of the air force. Looking on are Kenneth Royall, secretary of the army; James Forrestal, secretary of defense; and John Sullivan, secretary of the navy. U.S. Air Force photo, courtesy of the Harry S. Truman Library.

Justice Stanley Reed swears in Arthur S. Barrow as undersecretary of the air force. Looking on are General Carl Spaatz and Assistant Secretaries Eugene M. Zuckert and Cornelius Vanderbilt Whitney. U.S. Air Force photo, courtesy of the Harry S. Truman Library.

Symington and General Carl Spaatz. Harry S. Truman Library.

Symington and General Hoyt Vandenberg. Stuart Symington Papers, Western Historical Manuscript Collection, Columbia.

Symington emerging from a B-36, Carswell Air Force Base. Acme Telephoto, courtesy of the Stuart Symington Papers, Western Historical Manuscript Collection, Columbia.

President Truman signs the proclamation establishing Air Force Day. Looking on are General James Doolittle (ret.), General Hoyt Vandenberg, General Lauris Norstad, and Symington. Harry S. Truman Library.

Symington and Bob Hope visit the troops in Alaska. Stuart Symington Papers, Western Historical Manuscript Collection, Columbia.

Stuart Symington leaves the Pentagon as he retires as secretary of the air force. Left to right: Secretary of Defense Louis Johnson, Symington, General Hoyt Vandenberg. At far right, saluting, is General Omar Bradley. Official U.S. Air Force photo.

Symington, chairman National Security Resources Board, with William Green, president, American Federation of Labor. Acme Photo, courtesy of the Stuart Symington Papers, Western Historical Manuscript Collection, Columbia.

Symington with President Truman at the president's birthplace, Lamar, Missouri, April 19, 1959. Courtesy of the Harry S. Truman Library.

Symington and Lyndon Johnson. Honorary degree from Baylor University. Stuart
Symington Papers, Western Historical Manuscript Collection, Columbia.

President Truman presents Symington with the Distinguished Service Medal as Eve looks on. Used by permission of Wide World Photos.

9

First Secretary of the Air Force

ALTHOUGH Forrestal, the new secretary of defense, observed to the president that "one's friends were frequently more difficult as partners than strangers," President Truman, as had been expected, appointed Symington secretary of the air force. At the same time he announced the appointment of Sullivan as secretary of the navy and Royall as secretary of the army. All three had served in roles that could be considered stepping stones to their new positions; all had served in World War I; all had built successful civilian careers between the wars (Royall and Sullivan as lawyers); all were highly regarded in Congress. The appointments elicited a favorable response from all parts of the country.[1]

Jackie Cochran sent Symington a clipping of a *New York Times* story that had Sullivan's name in larger type than Symington's with this comment:

> The Government's Secretary for Air
> Should be sore at the "Times" like a bear
> They used small typesetting
> Thus completely forgetting
> The coequal status that's there.[2]

Cochran's limerick was more than a little prescient. The newly minted air force, despite the overconfident braggadocio with which some friends of air power advanced its claims, did have to struggle, in large ways and small, to achieve recognition of "the coequal status that's there." Senior AAF officers welcomed

Symington's appointment as the best possible choice to lead the development of the new air force. General Arnold, who had created the Army Air Forces during World War II, spoke for many of them when he wrote from his retirement office at Hamilton Field in California, "It's a tremendous satisfaction to know you are going to be where you so surely belong. . . . The Air Force and the country as a whole, should feel mighty fine about having in this new position, a man whose stature matches the bigness of the task ahead of him."[3]

The air force had many reasons to be pleased. Aside from his proven administrative ability and compatibility with air force aims, Symington was closer to the man in the White House than anyone in the Department of Defense—surely much closer than the new secretary of defense. Indeed, the secretary of the air force occupied a unique position in the Truman administration. He provided a link between the eastern, Ivy League establishment—men such as Acheson, Forrestal, Harriman, Lovett, McCloy—and the "Missouri gang." His antecedents aligned him more closely with the former, but he was equally at home with the president's cronies from Missouri—indeed, two of his closest friends were Snyder and Hannegan. Adding further to Symington's support in the administration was the presence of Clifford in the White House.

Although Truman had announced Forrestal's appointment the day after he signed the unification bill, he delayed appointment of the service secretaries for a month. He had assumed that he would preside over their swearing-in ceremonies after he returned from a trip to Rio de Janeiro to sign a Western Hemisphere collective security pact. Forrestal persuaded Clifford that in view of the tense international situation—American intelligence had reported that Yugoslavia might seize the Italian border city of Trieste still occupied by American and British forces—he and his associates should be sworn in without waiting for the president, who was on the USS *Missouri*, four days away from Washington. The president agreed, and in a hurriedly organized ceremony in the Navy Department, Chief Justice Fred M. Vinson administered the oath of office to the new secretary of defense.

The next day, in Secretary Royall's office in the Pentagon, the chief justice administered similar oaths to Symington and Sullivan—Royall, it was decided, did not need to take a new oath inasmuch as he was already serving as secretary of war, having been appointed upon Patterson's resignation some weeks earlier. The ceremony was held on such short notice that Symington did not even have an opportunity to invite his two sons, who were studying at Yale. Eve, coming in on a train from New York, barely made it. Even so, about two hundred spectators crowded into Royall's office for the ceremony, including the top leaders of the army, navy, and air force, cabinet officers, and friends of the two men. There had been concern about whether Symington had fully recovered from his operation, but Raymond P. Brandt, chief Washington correspondent for the *Post-Dispatch,* reported that "wearing a brown suit, white shirt and brown tie, [he] spoke the oath clearly and without nervousness . . . [and] appeared in excellent health."[4]

Following the ceremony, Symington and Royall signed an agreement transferring many administrative functions from the army to the air force. The agreement, which had been worked out by a group headed by Major General William P. Hall, AAF officer in Eisenhower's office, was far from perfect from the air force point of view in that it left the chaplain corps, medical service, and much of engineering with the army. Indeed, there was a feeling among some members of the air staff that the agreement had been forced upon the air force while it was still a part of the army.[5]

Be that as it may, Symington moved quickly to establish the air force and to assert his authority over it.[6] He brought with him key people from his office who simply carried on their former duties with new titles: Eugene Zuckert became an assistant secretary; Stephen F. Leo, director of public relations; Brackley Shaw, general counsel. For the position of undersecretary, Symington turned to Arthur Barrows, who had recently retired as president of Sears, Roebuck and Company. Symington had known Barrows since the early thirties when he was a purchasing agent for Sears. As a second assistant secretary, Symington chose Eve's cousin, polo-playing "Sonny" Whitney, who despite his playboy image had impressive business credentials and had been a pilot in both World War I and World War II, serving for a time on Eisenhower's staff. He was a Democrat. Whitney tired of government service after a few months and was replaced by Harold C. Stuart, a lawyer who had served in the AAF during the war as a reserve colonel and had performed a number of special tasks for Symington.[7]

The new secretary continued the administrative style he had developed at Emerson and in earlier governmental posts—free and easy with minimal bureaucratic rigidities, lots of give and take, but with everyone knowing who was boss. He was a hard, demanding man to work for. He frequently lost his temper. One day Colonel John B. Montgomery, who served for a year as the department's executive officer, placed a batch of papers in the secretary's in basket at about 7 P.M. Symington, irritated that he had received them so late, picked them up and scattered them all over the floor. He frequently acted on impulse. Zuckert once commented, "[w]e used to say don't tell him something if you are not willing to have him pick up the phone and do something about it."[8]

He arrived at the office between eight and eight-thirty, and seldom left before seven. Once home, he would get on the phone. Norstad, with whom Symington had developed a close relationship during unification, recalled that many a night Symington telephoned him between ten and eleven, and frequently would call at seven the next morning. Leo was another frequent recipient of the secretary's late-night phone calls. When Symington complained about Leo's absence from staff meetings, he is reported to have said, "Well, Stuart, I'll make a deal with you; if you don't call me at 11 o'clock in the evening or after, I'll make staff meetings." Zuckert, who recalled the conversation, went on the say, "That was typical of the whole atmosphere, how alive it was, it was fun."[9]

Although Symington had a capacity for absorbing details, he never got immersed in them. He delegated freely and expected subordinates to assume the responsibility that went with authority. He told them, "If I have to make your decisions, then I don't need you."[10]

As a businessman he had said that to be successful one needed a good lawyer, a good accountant, and a good publicity man. He felt the same about government, but an administrator's strategy had to be defensive. He was always being shot at by somebody: Congress, the General Accounting Office, the press, and the public. Symington developed defensive administration into an art.[11]

He gained a reputation, as *Time* stated in a cover story, "for energy and forcefulness. He is a formidable looking figure, sprawling in his red leather chair, a spectacular executive when transacting business over the telephone."[12]

Although he dominated the civilian side of the air force, he left military matters to the chief of staff, General Spaatz. During his months as assistant secretary, Symington had developed reverential respect for the dour, wise, and patient man who led the AAF.[13] Spaatz, however, was tired—at fifty-six, he was old for an active-duty airman—and shortly after the Department of the Air Force was created he told Symington he wanted out; he had tried to retire in 1945 but was persuaded to stay on until autonomy had been achieved. He wanted no elaborate ceremonies, but Symington insisted that he permit himself to be honored at a black-tie, stag dinner at the 1925 F Street Club. Held May 21, it brought together the top group of the air force (civilian and military), cabinet members, congressmen, and newspaper people.

Spaatz recommended as his successor Hoyt Vandenberg, the tall, handsome, youthful—at forty-eight he was the youngest man in the armed services to wear four stars—vice chief of the air staff. Spaatz had made him vice chief over a number of officers senior in rank, and had been grooming him to head the air force. As Clifford remarked, "In a city . . . filled with war heroes, Vandenberg was clearly marked as a star of the next generation."[14]

If Spaatz had been something of a father figure, Vandenberg was more like a fraternity brother. As leaders of the air force, the two men—Symington and Vandenberg—could have come straight from central casting. They not only looked the part, they acted in almost perfect harmony. As a Vandenberg biographer put it, "The two comprised a rare team. . . . and it was no coincidence that the United States Air Force made some of its greatest strides under this great team."[15]

One of Symington's goals was to improve business operations. If the air force was to receive anything like the money it required from an economy-minded president and Congress, it would have to demonstrate that it could give Americans full value for their tax dollars. As assistant secretary he had instituted cost control to bring expenditures into line, and as secretary he elaborated it into what he called "Management Control through Cost Control," designed to reward efficiency and at the same time deal with inefficiency. He gave Zuckert responsibility for administering the program. Zuckert, who had similar responsibility before unification, once said that "God alone" knew what the phrase "Management Control through Cost Control" actually meant, but "it was a great rallying cry and it enabled us to inject Ed Rawlings [Lieutenant General Edwin W. Rawlings, the Air Comptroller] into situations where . . . [his] good business judgment could be used." Rawlings, who had an MBA from Harvard—and who later became chief executive at General Mills—instilled sound business practices. No one may have known what the phrase meant, but Symington could talk with confidence about "Management Control through Cost Control." The air force developed a reputation for lean, hard administration and for spending the public's money wisely.[16]

He assigned Barrows responsibility for streamlining air force purchasing. No one could completely streamline government purchasing, but like Zuckert on the management side, Barrows injected a heavy dose of business procedure into the air force procurement system. He ruffled a few feathers along the way, as he insisted on strict new rules for contractors in honoring their agreements. When some of them complained that they were being unfairly criticized, he was reported to have replied, "We haven't said anything bad about you, we've just let it be known that we think you're a bunch of cheap, chiseling thieves."[17]

Not all the "cheap, chiseling thieves" were contractors. Shortly after he became secretary, Symington had to deal with a scandal involving Major General Bennett E. Meyers, who during the war had been deputy chief of logistics on the air staff. The case was messy. Meyers had created a company through which he funneled AAF contracts at great profit to himself. In 1945 he retired on what later was proved to be a nonexistent disability. A Senate committee headed by Homer Ferguson, a Republican from Michigan, came upon the Meyers case while investigating wartime contracts. It began to ask some embarrassing questions. Why had the AAF ignored an anonymous letter accusing Meyers of wrongdoing? Were others in the high command involved? Was Meyers's retirement a means of easing him out of the service?

Symington had become acquainted with Meyers during the war and rather liked him. He was "brilliant and effective," with "a logistic business concept not many of the Air Force people had."[18] Symington knew that the investigation, if not properly handled, could do harm to the air force. He took an interest in the case, directing Colonel Desmond O'Keefe, the air judge advocate general, to furnish him with weekly reports. He learned that Meyers had told the committee's counsel, a young lawyer named William P. Rogers (who would later be secretary of state in the Nixon administration) that he had stayed in Symington's house and that Symington had approved all of his actions. Symington went to Rogers, told him that Meyers had been his house guest in St. Louis on one occasion before the war, but that far from approving Meyers's actions he knew nothing about them. He said, "Please don't hurt this brand new Air Force." Rogers replied, "Let me tell you something—if after this investigation the Air Force is hurt, I will feel worse than you do." Symington assured the committee that the AAF had been neither dilatory nor collusive, but once the investigation turned up evidence of Meyers's guilt, he moved quickly to turn the matter over to the Justice Department. Symington also assured Forrestal that the air force was "properly covered."[19]

Meyers wanted a court-martial rather than a civil trial. Symington advised the Justice Department that he would authorize a court-martial only if the department directed him to do so. When, however, Meyers, meeting with Symington and Spaatz, threatened to implicate others in the air force, including General Arnold and him, if he were not given a court-martial, Symington told him, "Any chance you ever had of a court-martial just went out the window."[20]

Meyers was tried in federal court and ultimately spent almost three years in prison. Symington denounced Meyers as a "crook" and saw to it that he was stripped of his decorations and his pension. After Meyers had been convicted, Symington wrote to Senator Ferguson: ". . . in the name of the Air Force, I want to thank you and your Committee and also Mr. Rogers for the way you localized this investigation on the man in question with minimum criticism of the Air Force as a whole."[21]

Symington was determined to prevent a Meyers-type case from happening again, and it was this determination that prompted Barrows's assignment to take charge of all air force procurement. He also decided that the air force needed its own investigative unit. He turned to FBI director J. Edgar Hoover, again requesting the services of Joseph R. Carroll, the agent who had set up the investigative service at the Surplus Property Administration. Hoover assented, and Carroll transferred to the air force, becoming director of a new Office of Special Investigations. He was a colonel in the reserve when he came in. Symington made him a brigadier general immediately. He ultimately became a lieutenant general and inspector general of the air force—another example of Symington's ability to recognize talent.[22]

Symington's insistence on developing sound business practices was rooted in the belief that they were a necessary ingredient for achieving recognition of the air force's newly acquired independence. The desire for this recognition motivated virtually all of his actions as secretary.

At the third meeting of the National Security Council, he insisted that the air force should have primary responsibility for air intelligence. Predictably, Secretary Sullivan objected, arguing that the navy would lose naval air intelligence. Forrestal asked that the matter be delayed until he had time to reconcile the opposing views of the two services. A month later he announced the kind of compromise that would characterize much of his administration of the Department of Defense: "the Air Force has the dominant interest in air intelligence, but . . . the Navy should not be denied what it needs in this field."[23]

Then there was the matter of a uniform for the new air force. Symington took a special interest in this, believing that it was important for morale. The airmen liked the blue cloth and clean lines of the new design, and they also appreciated the fact that aside from insignia, the design was the same for both enlisted men and officers. The air force took considerable ribbing from the other services and the press—even the president joined in. He approved the uniform, but after he had done so he sent Symington a suggestion he had received with this note: "I'm sorry I didn't know about the suggestion when you were here. It looks to me like something to think about, particularly the 'Flight Pay Pocket.'"[24]

Symington worried about manpower for the new air force. Low pay, poor housing, and frequently unpleasant working conditions made it difficult for the air force to compete with private industry for the technicians needed to maintain and operate its increasingly complicated equipment. Particularly troubling was the shortage of officers. The air force had no source of supply, having to depend on West Point, Annapolis, college ROTC programs, officer candidate schools, and aviation cadet training programs. Moreover, the percentage of college-trained officers in the air force was considerably below that in the army or navy. The army and navy agreed that up to 25 percent of the graduates from West Point and Annapolis could accept commissions in the air force, but this was not a satisfactory permanent solution. Symington was convinced that the air force needed its own academy. In November 1949 he appointed a board headed by General Spaatz to find a suitable location. The next month President Truman endorsed the idea, and Lieutenant General Hubert R. Harmon, who would become the first superintendent, was put in charge of planning for the new academy.[25]

Once the word got out that the air force was planning an academy, the secretary's office was deluged with proposals from communities in all parts of the country. Civic leaders in Alton, Illinois, and Sedalia, Missouri, thought that, with the head of the air force from St. Louis, their chances were particularly good. Privately, Symington favored Alton, but he made no effort to influence the site selection board. He generally turned the importuning delegations over to Zuckert.[26] Symington was in the Senate before the location was decided upon and the academy was finally authorized. In recognition, however, of his pioneering support of an air force academy, a handsome bust sits on a pedestal in the foyer of the library.

The Air Force Academy was the most visible of a substantial array of training and educational institutions created by the air force as it sought to develop its training programs after it achieved separate status. The Air University, established in 1946 at Maxwell AFB, Alabama, while Symington was assistant secretary of war for air, developed rapidly under the leadership of Major General Muir S. Fairchild. As the need for additional air crews became increasingly acute, the Air Training Command was expanded despite serious shortages of civilian personnel—the air force could not compete with private industry.[27]

From his first association with the air force, Symington pushed for research. He didn't have to push very hard within the air force. General Arnold had laid a strong foundation for research during the war, and at war's end had persuaded the Douglas Aircraft Company to establish the RAND corporation. Spaatz was equally committed.[28]

Budgetary and organizational problems were not so easy to solve. The National Security Act provided for a Research and Development Board at the Department of Defense level, but Symington wanted the air force to have greater control over its research than this implied. He was particularly fearful of a proposed interdepartmental committee on scientific research and development that would include the army, navy, and air force along with nonmilitary agencies. Arguing that the problems faced by the military and nonmilitary agencies were "so unrelated that combining the two under a single committee structure would be most difficult," he urged that DOD not participate. Neither the army nor the navy shared air force fears. Symington again appealed to Forrestal. Noting that the other agencies proposed for membership on the committee were agreed that it should not concern itself with military research, he argued that there was no need for DOD participation. He concluded that despite "unjustifiable" criticism that the military took over activities that should be under civilian control, the Department of Defense should not voluntarily turn essential research activities over to civilian control.[29]

Symington didn't prevail, but he continued to push for more air force control over its research and development. He was more successful with the Air Force

Engineering Development Center, although he had to use his political skills to the fullest to persuade Congress that it was needed and to beat down competing parochial interests to get approval for its location at Camp Forrest, Tennessee, as recommended by Sverdrup and Parcel, the St. Louis firm chosen to select the site. The Arnold Engineering Center, as it came to be known, included a sophisticated wind tunnel and other tools needed to "bridge the gap," as Symington put it, "between our present limited capabilities and our requirements for coping with the problems incident to supersonic speeds." He also insisted that the air force needed to "maintain technical superiority and . . . assume a place of predominant importance in our peacetime military planning."[30] That insistence was a key element in his unrelenting struggle on behalf of the air force and air power.

Politics permeated all of Symington's efforts to establish the new air force. His wide circle of friends in high places, his charm, and his impressive talents as a salesman became weapons in the air force's political arsenal.

First and foremost among his friends in high places was the president himself. Truman became irritated with Symington occasionally during the budget battles of 1948–1949, and there was some press speculation that he would replace him after the election of 1948, but there was no foundation for that speculation and no basis for the occasional rumor that the president was considering dismissal of his air secretary. On the contrary, their relationship remained warm. Symington continued to be a regular at the president's poker sessions on the *Williamsburg* and elsewhere—one night they played poker until four o'clock at the home of Attorney General Howard McGrath. Symington was one of the few who made purely social visits to the presidential vacation retreat at Key West. Mrs. Truman came to St. Louis for Tim's wedding.[31]

On another level, Symington was active in furthering the president's political agenda. He was in Philadelphia for most of the 1948 Democratic National Convention, staying with his cousin, Clare McLean, whose husband owned the *Philadelphia Evening Bulletin*. He had calls from both Hannegan and Clifford saying that the president had decided upon Justice Douglas as his running mate and they wanted him to approach Douglas, a friend, but Symington felt that he was not the person to contact him. He suggested Paul Porter, member of the Washington law firm Arnold, Fortas and Porter and an active Democrat, also staying at the McLeans'. Porter wanted to pass the task to Fortas, former Interior Department counsel and a Douglas protégé. They found Fortas fishing in southwestern Virginia. He agreed to make the call, but wanted Symington and Porter to come up to Washington to help him. Late in the afternoon they all met at Fortas's Georgetown home and placed a call to Douglas, who was out in Oregon. As Symington later wrote: "For over an hour, Fortas, Porter and I took turns working on him to accept the President's offer. Douglas was adamantly against acceptance. At a point towards the end of our conversations I began to believe he was certain in his own mind that Mr. Truman would lose, probably did not want to risk his lifetime appointment to the highest court."[32]

The next day, at a luncheon given by Martin Clement, head of the Pennsylvania Railroad, at Philadelphia's Merion Cricket Club, Symington was upbraided by Leslie Biffle, secretary of the Senate and close friend of Alben Barkley, for trying to promote Douglas. He denied that he was trying to promote anybody, he was just following instructions from the White House. That evening Symington, Hannegan, and Ed Flynn, New York Democratic boss, watched Barkley's electrifying keynote address on a television set in the suite of Frank Walker, former chairman of the Democratic National Committee. As the four of them listened to Barkley and watched him bring the convention to its feet, they became convinced that he was the obvious choice. Flynn was not particularly enthusiastic—he thought Barkley at seventy-three was too old and being from Kentucky would not bring much strength to a ticket headed by a Missourian. Finally, however, the three others brought him around to reluctant approval.

The next day Symington participated in a tragicomic effort to find a campaign treasurer. At the suggestion of Snyder and Clark he accompanied them to Howard McGrath's penthouse hotel suite. McGrath had just become chairman of the Democratic National Committee and had a direct telephone line to the White House. He was preoccupied with finding someone to serve as treasurer of the party to raise money for the fall campaign. They tried Robert Woodruff, head of Coca-Cola, but he couldn't do it. Bernard Baruch also turned them down, for which Truman never forgave him.[33] Truman himself suggested Bill Pawley, in McGrath's suite. Pawley had gained fame during the war as a Flying Tiger and amassed a fortune selling airplanes to the Chinese. He was a friend of both the president and Hannegan. He replied that he would be glad to do the work, if they could find a well-known figure to take the treasurer's job.

Symington suggested Eve's cousin, Cornelius Whitney, then assistant secretary of the air force. He had lots of money, and he was well known in financial circles. Truman knew him as a good Democrat who had run unsuccessfully for Congress from Long Island. When Truman wondered whether Whitney would take it, Symington assured him that he would if the president personally asked. Truman did, Whitney accepted, and the meeting broke up with the problem solved.

A couple of days later Joseph and Stewart Alsop published a revealing account of the disarray in Democratic fund raising. They charged that the Democratic strategists expected to run up a big tab, and then leave Whitney to pick it up.[34]

The next day, McGrath called Symington, furious. Whitney had reneged on his promise. Distressed, Symington called Whitney in utter disgust. Whitney replied, "I had had a few beers when the President called. The next morning I realized I was not capable of doing the job." Symington reminded him that he wouldn't have had too much to do, that Pawley would have done most of the actual work. "Oh, I forgot to tell you," Whitney answered. "I called Pawley's office and they said he had left for Europe and would not be back until after the election."[35]

As Truman's biographers have pointed out, the last days of August and the early part of September were desperate for the beleaguered president. Virtually no one thought he could win. Symington was among the doubters—he said later that the only two of his friends who believed strongly that the president would win were Clifford and Hannegan—but unlike his boss, the secretary of defense, who remained aloof from the campaign, he did everything he could to help the election effort.[36]

Early in September, he was among a small group that met with the president at the White House. In what Symington described as "probably the finest talk of his life" the president discussed his and the party's financial problems. He told his friends that recently he had to call a friend in Kansas City for the money to get his campaign train back to Washington from Oklahoma. A majority of the group reassembled at Democratic headquarters in the Ring Building. They faced the prospect of the president of the United States not having enough money to present his views on the issues. They all doubled their previous contributions, and finally they hit upon a man for treasurer who not only was willing to take the job but also would raise enough money to enable the president to conduct his famous whistle-stop campaign: Louis Johnson, a West Virginia politician who was close to Harry Vaughan, the president's military aide, and who—to Symington's later distress—would become secretary of defense.[37]

The Berlin Airlift kept Symington in Europe during much of the fall, but he campaigned for Truman whenever he could, particularly in Missouri, and, despite his doubts, remained steadfast in his public expressions of confidence in the president's ultimate victory. He began to have some hope that the president might win when he and Lyndon Johnson participated with Dewey on a *New York Herald Tribune* Forum. They were talking about the farm problem. Johnson had given a hard-hitting talk about farm issues. Dewey observed that he was interested in farmers. "I have a farm in Pawling, with a tiny brook running right through it," he said. Johnson turned to Symington and whispered, "Hell, that just won't go over with our farmers in Texas."[38]

Riding the presidential train from St. Joseph to Kansas City, Symington found "the confidence of this quiet man . . . hard to believe." On the Saturday night before the election, the Symingtons and the Hannegans were at the Kiel Auditorium in St. Louis for the president's last campaign speech. They had been at a dinner where all the other guests were toasting a Republican victory. They had a great time at Kiel, listening to the crowd repeatedly roar, "Give 'em hell, Harry." They left the meeting with a surge of hope. Leaving by a side door, they found the president quietly sitting in his car, beside a Secret Service man, waiting to go to the station to take the night train to Kansas City. Symington commented, "Boss, you were never so convincing as you were tonight." Truman replied, "Well, anyway it's over."

The common wisdom, repeated by many of Truman's biographers, is that he was extremely confident of victory.[39] His comment in St. Louis, and the fact that he chose to spend election night alone at the Elms Hotel in Excelsior Springs, convinced Symington that the president "was not as sure of victory as his basic courage made him appear." He contrasted that night with election night, 1944, when he ran the radio in the president's suite at the Hotel Muehlebach in Kansas City—"the contrast could only make one think."

After voting in St. Louis, the Symingtons returned to Washington. Symington stayed up all night in their Shoreham apartment, listening to the returns. Next morning he went to his office in the Pentagon, where he wrote the president a short note in longhand: "All congratulations. There will be people who say they knew it all the time, but I believe you are as surprised as I am." Truman did not answer the letter, but a few weeks later as they were playing poker at the home of Ambassador Joseph P. Davies, the ambassador observed, "You know, Mr. President, I too want you to know I knew it all the time." Truman was dealing. Symington recalled that he "stopped dealing; looked at me hard for a few seconds, then continued."[40]

Although the president was Symington's most important friend, another friend was Lyndon Johnson, who, if not then in a particularly high place, was beginning the ascent—and Symington assisted in the climb. From their first meeting in Forrestal's office the afternoon of Roosevelt's fourth inauguration, Symington and Johnson had got on. Symington took a liking to the brash young congressman from the Texas hill country, and the congressman could not have helped being impressed with Symington's connections. Johnson became one of Symington's allies in the House, and Symington used every opportunity to remind the people of Texas that it was important for the nation's defenses to keep Johnson in Washington. He campaigned for Johnson's reelection to Congress in 1946 and went to Texas in 1948 to help in the hard-fought battle against Coke Stevenson for the Democratic senatorial nomination. In San Antonio he helped bring the normally antagonistic Paul Kilday and Maury Maverick factions together behind Johnson, turning a twelve-thousand-vote defeat in the first primary to a ninety-nine-vote victory in the runoff.[41] In Dallas, he may have made it possible for Johnson to continue his campaign. In town for a meeting of the Air Force Association, he found Johnson almost incapacitated with a violent attack of kidney stones. The local doctors seemed unable to do much for him. He wanted to go to the Mayo Clinic in Minnesota, but didn't know how to get there without causing press speculation. Jackie Cochran had flown in from California in her Lodestar to hear Symington speak. Symington was sure she would be willing to fly Johnson to Rochester. She was, and she got him there in complete secrecy. The Mayo doctors successfully removed the kidney stones, and seven days later he was back on the campaign trail without a word about his mysterious absence.[42]

Johnson remained in close communication. Once, after returning from Berlin, Symington met Eve at the Sea View Inn at Biddeford Pool, Maine, where he had gone as a child. He was exhausted and gave instructions that he was not to be disturbed. The next morning, about eight o'clock, the phone rang. "I told you not to call me," he reminded the clerk. "There's a Mr. Johnson calling you from Texas," she replied. "He says he's not interested in any of your instructions and wants to talk to you."[43]

Although Symington remained attuned to the demands of the campaign and helped wherever he could, his principal tasks in 1948 were integrating the air force and supervising its efforts in carrying out the president's program in Berlin.

Both require separate treatment.

10

Integrating the Air Force

ON JULY 26, 1948, ten days after the Democratic party had seen its southern wing depart in protest against the platform and the candidate's stand on civil rights, Harry Truman issued Executive Order No. 9981, which provided "that there shall be equality of treatment and opportunity for all persons in the armed services without regard to race, color, religion, or national origin." The policy was to go into effect "as rapidly as possible, having due regard to the time required to effectuate any necessary changes without impairing efficiency or morale."[1]

His fellow Missourian, the secretary of the air force, asked the president if he really meant it. "I not only mean it," the president snapped, "I'm counting on you to see it is done."[2]

And, one might add, as a history of the effort, "It was done." Assistant Secretary Zuckert, who had responsibility for monitoring the process, said later, "He did it in a way that was typical Symington. If it had not been Symington, it probably couldn't have happened, but it happened, and it was surprisingly easy."[3]

The operative phrase here is "surprisingly easy." Although the effort went smoothly, it was not easy to change habits and practices that were ingrained in military custom and civilian attitudes. The AAF, as part of the army, had adopted War Department policies regarding segregation of the races. During the war, at President Roosevelt's insistence, they had created two black flying units composed of graduates of the Tuskegee Army Airfield. The 332d Fighter Group compiled an enviable record as part of the Ninth Air Force, flying hundreds of escort missions and never losing a friendly bomber to enemy fighters while shooting down more than a hundred enemy aircraft in air-to-air combat. The 477th Medium Bombardment Group got into a mutiny against a bigoted commander and lost any chance to get into action.[4]

After the war, despite pressures for racial reform, it appeared that there would be little change in the army and the air force, that the patterns of racial segregation would continue, perhaps with minor modification. In the fall of 1945 the War Department established a three-man board headed by Lieutenant General Alvan C. Gillem to study the problem of Negro troops. The Gillem Board found ample evidence that small units, such as platoons in white companies, were "eminently successful when ably led." It recommended the continuation of such units, also finding opportunities for individual Negro soldiers in clerical, supervisory, and maintenance work without regard to race. The Gillem Board said the ultimate object should be the use of all army manpower "without regard to antecedents or race," but it avoided specific proposals.[5] The army could salve its conscience by adopting laudatory goals, but it would be under no pressure to realize them.

Most ranking officers of the army and the AAF were comfortable with the Gillem Board's recommendations. General Omar N. Bradley, the Missourian who succeeded Eisenhower as chief of staff, opined that the army could not move ahead of society as a whole in the matter of integration. As late as April 1948, Secretary of the Army Royall expressed the view that the army policy of segregation did not represent discrimination. This view found strong support in the air force. General Kenney argued that integration would be unfair to blacks because it would force them to compete with whites.[6] Lieutenant General Elwood "Pete" Quesada, who had led the IX Tactical Command during the war and was one of the country's most celebrated fighter pilots, was more emphatic. He declared that "anyone who says the Negro is up to the white man is just not telling the truth." Even General Vandenberg, preoccupied with the problems of building a nuclear striking force, was not disposed to place racial integration high on his agenda.

There was no way, however, that Symington would preside over a segregated organization. He had learned to respect the rights of blacks at his mother's knee. He had worked alongside blacks in his uncle's plant at Rochester and when he got into management took pride in promoting blacks to positions of responsibility. Against substantial opposition in the border city of St. Louis, he had integrated Emerson to the extent that blacks came to look upon it as the most desirable place in the city to work.

Symington believed that segregation was inefficient, but as Eugene Zuckert once said, "With Symington, it was principle first, efficiency second." He traced the origin of his opposition to segregation to "a quotation from Bernard Shaw in

Myrdal's book, *American Dilemma,* which went something like this—'First the American white man makes the Negro clean his shoes, then criticizes him for being a bootblack.' All Americans should have their chance. And both my grandfathers were in the Confederate Army."[7]

He was always impressed by the dramatic situation, and as he talked about integration in the air force, he liked to reflect on an incident that occurred during the war. Because of his record at Emerson, he had been appointed to the mayor's committee on race relations. On December 12, 1944, the city organized "Captain Wendell O. Pruitt Day" in honor of the first Negro fighter pilot from St. Louis to return from overseas. Pruitt had compiled an impressive record, including the sinking of a German destroyer. The mayor brought him out to Emerson to see Symington, who was immediately impressed. Near the end of their conversation, he asked the young man if there was anything he could do for him. Pruitt quietly responded, "Give my people a chance." Symington never forgot the incident nor the answer—nor the fact that Pruitt was killed on his first combat mission after returning to duty.[8]

Shortly after becoming secretary of the air force Symington made clear that he intended to move toward complete integration. He directed Major General Idwal Edwards, a senior staff personnel officer, to develop a plan. Edwards needed no prodding. He had been involved in racial matters during and after the war. He understood the frustrations that led to such disturbances as the mutiny of the 477th, the race riots at MacDill Army Airfield in 1946, and racial troubles at the Fort Worth Army Air Field in 1947. He participated in the work of a War Department Advisory Committee on Special Troop Policies, headed by Assistant Secretary McCloy. This gave him a broad view of the impact of segregation in the army and the AAF. He became convinced that segregation was a wholly inadequate personnel practice—segregated units could not rise above the low performance of their members, thus forcing the air force to underemploy many skilled and well-educated blacks. When the air force became independent, he directed Lieutenant Colonel Jack Marr, a member of his staff, to conduct a study to determine whether it would be wise to abandon segregation. Marr confirmed Edwards's own view that segregation was inefficient. He used it to reinforce Spaatz's inclination and to help convince Vandenberg, who was not opposed to integration but was more concerned with building the 70-Group air force. Air force thinking made it relatively easy for Symington to move ahead with desegregation before the president's executive order, and to respond with confidence when it was issued. Indeed, by then the air force had developed a plan that eventually became the basis for integration.[9]

Symington had support from the top. As secretary of the navy, Forrestal had moved that service toward policies that provided greater opportunities for blacks than existed in either the army or the Army Air Forces. As secretary of defense, he issued no sweeping directives—that was left to his successor—but he was clear in his opposition to continued segregation. He appointed a black civilian assistant, James C. Evans, son of a Baptist minister. Symington told Evans that he believed blacks in the air force should have whatever they could get on merit. Zuckert handled personnel matters, but if Evans needed to see Symington, his door was open. Symington recalled that he would meet Evans in the hall and ask, "Why don't you come to see me?" Evans would reply, "I don't have anything to see you about—you're doing all right."[10]

At the time he issued his Executive Order, Truman established a Committee on Equality of Treatment and Opportunity in the Armed Forces. Headed by Charles H. Fahy, former solicitor general, it was a distinguished biracial group that served both to prod and monitor the services. The Fahy Committee, consisting solely of civilians, took the discussion out of military channels. For the first time the services had to defend their personnel policies before a group of well-known civilians that enjoyed a presidential appointment.[11]

The air force welcomed the Fahy Committee as a forum that would enable it to bring its program to the attention of the president and the public—and it was apparent from the first meeting that the president needed to be informed. He attended that meeting—held January 12, 1949, in the Cabinet Room of the White House—and during his rambling remarks said, "The Navy's made some progress; Army, of course, has made great progress. I don't know about the Air Force."

Forrestal came to the defense of the air force: "The Air Force has come along—what they have in mind, Mr. President, is a very progressive—" Truman interrupted to say that he hoped that the entire government would move toward providing equal opportunity, and that if anyone had any suggestions he would be glad to listen to them. Just before the meeting ended, Symington, obviously unhappy with the president's lack of knowledge about the air force, reminded him that the air force had a plan to "completely eliminate segregation." The president responded with, "That's all right," and the meeting adjourned.[12]

The Fahy Committee met again the next day, and the air force was ready. Neither Symington nor Zuckert was present, but Major General R. E. Nugent, acting deputy chief of staff for personnel, and Colonel Marr presented in detail the plans that Zuckert, Edwards, Marr, and others had spent months developing. The plans would be modified in the months ahead, partly in response to suggestions from the Fahy Committee, but essentially they replaced segregation with integration.[13]

In line with Symington's oft-repeated assertion that the air force must operate as efficiently as possible, the plan found its rationale in efficiency. Segregation made it impossible for the air force to use its manpower efficiently. As Zuckert pointed out in a memo for Symington, the Marr study on which the plan was based demonstrated that the distribution of skills in the Negro civilian population did not correspond to the air force's requirements and "resulted in never-ending problems for which there appear to be no solution under the 'Negro unit' concept." At the other end of the spectrum, there was "a definite loss to the Air Force of the capability of highly-skilled Negroes in fields for which no 'Negro vacancies' exist." Moreover, "Where Negroes and whites have been integrated in the Air Force on the basis of individual qualifications rather than separated on the basis of color, the 'Negro problem' has disappeared."[14]

The only solution, in the minds of air force planners, was to abandon the policies of the past and adopt a policy of integration and consideration of individual merit and ability rather than color. This had Symington's enthusiastic approval. Indeed, he pushed for greater and faster progress. When Zuckert relayed a report from Evans that on a visit to Randolph Field he was gratified to find nine Negroes in unsegregated aviation cadet training, he got back a terse memo, "Gene: Why not more?"[15]

Consideration of each airman and officer because of individual merit did not necessarily mean the immediate elimination of all Negro units. Segregated service units would continue, although individuals would be considered for transfer and educational opportunities based on merit. It did mean that segregated combat units would be eliminated, specifically the all-Negro 332d Fighter Wing stationed at Lockbourne Air Base in Ohio. This action, besides being an important part of the air force's integration effort, was also part of the new 48-group program—Symington had lost his battle for the 70-Group air force. On February 17, Symington urged Forrestal to give early approval to the air force's desegregation plan.[16]

The ailing Forrestal—who in little more than a month would plunge to his death—was in no condition to make any important decisions, let alone on an issue that had become highly controversial within the Defense Department. The controversy arose because the army—which President Truman thought had made such great progress—did not want to change. Neither Royall nor Bradley felt that Negroes were suited for combat. Royall argued that because segregation was the normal condition in civilian life, forced integration would damage morale, since most of the army's volunteers came from the South. He felt that segregation provided Negroes with opportunities they would not have if forced to compete with whites in integrated units. He accused the air force of grandstanding and urged that, in the spirit of unification, the secretary delay a decision until all could agree on plans.[17]

So the matter dragged on. Testimony before the Fahy Committee on March 28 dramatized the nature and extent of confusion among the services on the issue. During a morning session Royall described the army's plan for meeting the terms of the president's executive order—a plan that in effect sought to provide equal opportunity without integration. Neither Symington nor Sullivan had been present at the morning session, and during the afternoon professed to know little about it. They were uncertain about why they were there. Fahy thought the secretaries had requested the meeting. They were under the impression he had asked to see them. They had only an hour before they needed to go to a meeting called by the new secretary of defense. While neither of them would want to adopt the army's plan, they recognized that the army's problem was different from those of the navy or the air force—Symington said at one point, "I think the Army has probably more of a problem. They have a lower grade of people from the standpoint of education, both white and colored." He was perfectly willing to go along with different approaches by each service, but he wanted action. The air force directive had been signed. It just awaited a date.[18]

On April 6, Secretary Johnson issued an order that, when carried out, would abolish segregation in the armed forces. He requested each of the service secretaries to conduct a study to determine what current practices conformed to the executive order and to prepare a plan to bring those practices into compliance. The army and navy both replied that they were in compliance—an assertion that Johnson summarily rejected. Symington resubmitted the department's earlier study and the draft of his order detailing changes designed to bring the air force into compliance.[19] Johnson approved the plan on May 6, and on May 11 General Vandenberg, "by order of the Secretary of the Air Force," issued Air Force Letter No. 35-3, detailing the new air force personnel policy. The policy was specific and direct; it represented a dramatic break with the past. From now on, the air force would provide "equality of treatment and opportunity for all persons . . . without regard to race, color, religion, or national origin." The order charged commanding officers with direct responsibility for implementing the policy, and "Commanders of all echelons of the Air Force will insure that all personnel in their command are indoctrinated thoroughly with the necessity for the unreserved acceptance of the provisions of this policy."

Earlier, General Edwards—by now wearing a third star—had addressed an air force commanders' conference at Maxwell Field on the subject. He recognized that there would be friction and incidents, but was sure they would be reduced "if commanders give the implementation of this policy their personal attention and exercise positive command control."

In general, that is what happened. It soon became widely understood that the new policy was not a collection of pious statements to be ignored at will, but that everyone in the top echelons, from Secretary Symington on down, wanted integration to succeed. As Lieutenant General Daniel (Chappie) James, Jr., the first black to become a four-star general in any of the services, recalled, those who thought to frustrate the process risked serious trouble. All echelons understood what was meant by command responsibility. Illustrative of the specificity with which the order was transmitted as it went down the chain of command, Major General Lawrence Kuter wrote subordinates in the Military Air Transport Command, "Commanders who cannot cope with the integration of Negroes into formerly white units or activities will have no place in the Air Force structure."[20]

The most serious problem was that posed by the all-black 332d Fighter Wing at Lockbourne. Symington had wanted to deactivate it as part of the belt-tightening forced on the air force by the 48-group budget and as a step in desegregation. The challenge was to accomplish deactivation without sacrificing—or giving the appearance of sacrificing—many black airmen and officers. Many were over age in grade and not trained in anything more advanced than the World War II P-51. The long delay in obtaining approval of desegregation had fueled suspicions at Lockbourne that retrenchment would win. The *Washington Post* reported that they were the logical victims of any reduction in force.[21]

As it turned out, however, the process went smoothly, and to the satisfaction of most of the officers and airmen concerned. The screening was accomplished quickly; reassignment was drawn out because of uncertainty regarding the fate of Lockbourne itself. The base continued to be operational, but the 332d was deactivated on July 1. By the end of the year all of its officers and airmen had been reassigned throughout the air force. The same situation prevailed elsewhere. Despite the initial announcement that some black units would continue to exist, by the end of the first year, practically all units were integrated. General Nugent, who had charge of carrying out integration, reported to Zuckert that integration had progressed "rapidly, smoothly and virtually without incident." On his recommendation, the air force canceled its monthly check on the program.[22]

"To some extent," as one historian remarked, "the Air Force's integration program ran away with itself." There were incidents, to be sure, but they generally were dealt with on the basis of Symington's dictum that "trouble-makers will get into trouble," and life on the air bases provided as low a degree of racial discrimination as could be found anywhere in the America of 1950s. Off base, of course, it was another matter. Here local mores prevailed, and there was little the air force could do to change them. Symington, visiting the Great Falls Air Base in Montana, learned in questioning Negro airmen that while everything was fine on the base, in town nothing was available to them. He got in touch with the mayor and told him that unless this changed, he would declare the whole town off-limits.[23] He was bluffing. He knew, and everyone in the air force knew, that off-base segregation was a matter for civilian rather than military decision.

Yet where the military had the power of decision, integration became almost complete, and the air force got extensive national publicity on the success of its program. In its final report, the Fahy Committee lauded the success of air force efforts. Both the national press and the black press gave the air force fulsome praise. The *Minneapolis Spokesman* called the air force program "the swiftest and most amazing upset of racial policy in the history of the U.S. military." The *Pittsburgh Courier* said that integration in the air force had been "better than most dared hope."[24] And as Zuckert, who with Edwards had developed the program and managed its progress, said, "It was surprisingly easy." The personnel of the air force—highly skilled and relatively well educated—made it easy. The airmen were much more receptive to the idea of integration than many officers had assumed, and, with few exceptions, the officer corps was ready to make it work. Zuckert and Edwards deserve much credit—Zuckert for his management of the program, and Edwards for his determination to bring it about. There were others: Vandenberg, once he gave the matter his attention; Nugent, for his careful monitoring of the program's progress; Marr, for his work on the plans.

In the end, however, the person principally responsible was Symington. He was not a crusader, but he felt as deeply on this question as on any he confronted during his entire career. Unlike Royall of the army, he recognized that problems existed and was willing to take a chance on solving them. He left the details to others, but he set the tone and gave the directions. Twenty years later he wrote to military historian Morris J. MacGregor, "I turned the actual operations of the job over to my Assistant Secretary Eugene Zuckert. . . . It all worked out routinely." MacGregor, an authority on the desegregation of the armed services, had this comment: "To call 'routine' the fundamental change that took place in Air Force manpower practices stretches the definition of the word."[25]

Zuckert summed it up this way: "If it had not been Symington, it probably couldn't have happened."

Symington recalled that during the war when Captain Wendell Pruitt said, "Give my people a chance," he might have replied, "we already had, but I didn't think it was fitting."[26]

Perhaps in 1950 he might have thought differently.

11

The Berlin Airlift

NOTHING illustrates the way Symington operated as effectively as the Berlin Airlift, the largest operation during his tenure. From the beginning, he had left strategy and operations to the experts, and he did so in Berlin. He confined himself to securing public and congressional support, and to looking after the needs of the airmen involved.[1]

The initial commitment to the airlift was made in Europe, not in Washington, by those two strong-willed men who ran the country's European operations: General Lucius D. Clay, U.S. military governor in Germany, and General Curtis E. LeMay, commander of U.S. Air Forces in Europe.[2]

Although the danger of imminent war, implicit in General Clay's telegram of March 5, 1948, had subsided, conditions remained tense in Berlin. The four-power occupation of the city, deep in the Soviet zone, was not working. The Russians, using their control of the area surrounding Berlin, imposed one restriction after another on the movement of Allied goods and personnel into the city. On March 30 they announced that effective April 1, all Allied personnel and goods traveling through the Soviet zone by train would be subject to inspection. This Clay would not tolerate. He told his superiors in Washington that he was going to instruct his guards to open fire if Soviet inspectors attempted to enter U.S. trains. Army Chief of Staff Omar N. Bradley, speaking for Forrestal, urged caution: "Our guards should not fire unless fired upon." Clay replied that he would follow the instructions to the letter, but added, "I do not agree that this is a fair instruction to a man whose life may be in danger."

The American trains were denied access to Berlin when their commanders refused to permit searches, and Clay decided to try to supply his forces by air. His British counterpart in Berlin, General Sir Brian Robertson, had agreed to follow the U.S. lead, and on April 1 Clay and Robertson inaugurated a small combined military airlift to bring supplies into Berlin from West Germany. After a few days the Soviets relaxed their restrictions on rail traffic and the airlift tapered off. Tensions continued, however, with the Soviets imposing one annoying condition after another. Finally, on June 24, ostensibly in response to the Allied decision to introduce West German marks into Berlin, the Soviets cut off all surface traffic into the city from the west.

If the Allies were going to stay in Berlin, they would have to respond. Washington, however, had yet to develop a clear strategy. Some were not sure that staying in Berlin was worth the inevitable cost, and even the president might have been vacillating.[3] Neither Spaatz nor Vandenberg, who succeeded him as chief of staff on July 1, had much enthusiasm for supplying Berlin by air. Flying supplies into Berlin was a transportation job, and it would divert aircraft and crews from being held in readiness for the air force's principal mission—strategic bombing. Symington adopted their position. He recalled, "There was a meeting in the Pentagon after we got Clay's telegram as to whether we should put in a train or go airlift. I think the vote was twenty something to three. Spaatz and I were two of the people who voted to put in a train because we figured that Stalin would never shoot American soldiers off of any train. I don't know who the third one was, but remember it was three."[4]

General Clay had no doubt about how to proceed. Having been satisfied by Ernst Reuter, mayor of West Berlin, that the Berliners would remain loyal to the Allies, he arranged with General LeMay to begin airlifting supplies into the beleaguered city.[5] LeMay went into action immediately. On Sunday, June 26, using C-47s, the only transports available, and commandeering a few "desk pilots," he flew eighty tons of flour, milk, and medicine into Berlin's Tempelhof Airport. The British began airlift operations the same day. U.S. and British forces operated in close coordination from the beginning and ultimately established a combined force to conduct the operations.

LeMay immediately called for additional aircraft, and soon reinforcements were coming in from air bases in Texas, Alaska, and Hawaii. By July 20, LeMay had 54 C-54s and 105 C-47s, with a maximum daily capacity of 1,500 tons. The British, with their Yorks and Dakotas, could carry 750 tons a day. More aircraft were needed if the airlift was going to be able to meet Berlin's daily requirement of 3,000 tons.[6]

Clay, called back to Washington for consultations, told the National Security Council on July 22 that if the United States was going to remain in Berlin it would have to expand the airlift or use armed convoys. He did not think the

Soviets were prepared to go to war, but the risks were such that the armed convoy option should be reserved for later use. He recommended expanding the airlift. General Vandenberg argued that the airlift was impeding the air force's ability to conduct strategic air warfare and to expand it would further erode that capability. Moreover, he warned, should war break out the air force would have most of its transport aircraft tied up in Europe, and could lose many of them to enemy fire. At this juncture, President Truman, making one of his rare appearances at an NSC meeting, said that in his judgment, the airlift was the best way, short of war, to remain in Berlin. He directed the air force to provide maximum support.[7]

The next day Vandenberg directed the Military Air Transport Service (MATS) to send 72 additional C-54s to Germany with enough personnel to establish a task force headquarters. The effort required about 2,500 men—including three crews per aircraft—the construction of an additional airfield in Berlin, and the expansion of bases in West Germany. Ultimately, 319 of the 400 C-54s the air force had in active service were assigned to the airlift. The airlift was not only a combined operation with the British but also a joint operation involving the army and navy. The services proved that though they might jockey for position in Washington, they could work together in the field.

While expanding the airlift, the air force, in a highly publicized maneuver, deployed two groups of B-29s to England. Symington and Vandenberg accompanied the planes to inspect the bases, but more importantly to shore up British resolve regarding the airlift and to firm up arrangements for combined operations. Symington told a press conference that the transfer of the B-29s was a "prestige movement. . . . We just want to show them that our B-29s can get around if necessary." As one reporter noted, "He did not elaborate on the reference to 'them.'" LeMay was more explicit. He told the press that the B-29s would simulate bombing attacks in Germany, and engage in joint training maneuvers with sixteen jet fighters being flown to England from the United States. Always aggressive, air force leaders made it clear that they intended "to press home to the Russians and others on the continent the tremendous threat of globe-ranging aircraft that can carry atomic bombs."[8]

To further drive home the lesson of American air power, the air force on July 23 sent three B-29s on a flight around the world. Symington had proposed a much larger flight more than a year earlier, but the State Department had turned it down for fear that it would irritate the Russians.[9]

While in Britain, Symington emphasized to Ernest Bevin, British foreign secretary, that maintenance of a substantial supply of food and fuel was the best way to maintain an Allied position in Berlin. He assured Bevin that the United States was prepared to do whatever was necessary to meet the basic needs of

Berlin's population. Before going to Frankfurt to confer with Clay and LeMay, Symington and Vandenberg had lunch with Lord Tedder, chief of the British Air Staff, with whom Vandenberg had served during World War II. They also spent an afternoon with Major General Leon Johnson, who had just assumed command of the Third Air Division, administrative unit for the B-29 groups.[10]

In Frankfurt, they found things in critical condition. Berlin's reserves of food and fuel were exhausted, and the airlift was unable to make up the shortfall. Symington, however, exuded optimism. He told reporters in London that the purpose of their trip was "to congratulate Lieut. Gen. Curtis E. LeMay and his people on what they have already done and to make sure there is nothing else we can do to cooperate with them." He announced in Frankfurt that "many more" C-54s would soon arrive; he reassured the people of Berlin that they would maintain the airlift and that there would be no reduction in deliveries. Symington and Vandenberg also went to Berlin. Countering Russian claims that while warehouses in the Soviet zone were bulging with enough food to feed the entire city for forty days, the airlift had failed to achieve its goal, Symington reported that the Western sectors had a twenty-seven-day supply on hand and that the airlift "could be kept up as much as desired through the winter."[11]

Symington was encouraged by what he saw. At Tempelhof he "felt a lump rise in his throat as he watched little girls with pigtails, wearing white puff-sleeved blouses and velvet bodices, pressing nosegays of flowers on the pilots as they piled from their planes."

The little girls accurately reflected the mood of the city. Despite continuing shortages and sacrifices reminiscent of the last days of the war, the round-the-clock deliveries of food and fuel were beginning to inspire confidence that the Allies had the will and the ability to keep the city sufficiently supplied to hold out against Communist domination. "Berlin," Mayor Reuter pledged, "will be the German 'Stalingrad' that will turn back the tide of Communist pressure."

Conditions hardly justified the optimism. Reserves of food and fuel were almost depleted, and during the early weeks of the airlift the Allies barely were able to meet daily requirements, let alone build up reserves. With winter coming on the prospect of shortages—particularly of coal—loomed ominously. "The shortage of fuel can be tolerated now," wrote the Communist daily *Vorwaerts*, "but how will it be in the autumn and winter?"[12]

Although Symington exuded optimism in his public statements, that question plagued everyone. Yet even as Symington and Vandenberg arrived in Europe, things were looking up. The additional C-54s were coming in almost daily, and a new commander, Major General William H. Tunner, deputy commander of MATS and a veteran of the World War II hump airlift to China, took over the operation. As LeMay later wrote, ". . . when it looked like we were going into a long-term aspect . . . we yelled for Bill Tunner to come over and take the chore. He was the transportation expert to end transportation experts. . . . it was rather like appointing John Ringling to get the circus on the road."[13]

Tunner, with increasing support from Washington, developed an organization that made it possible for the United States to keep its promises to the people of Berlin. Symington called him "the great hero" of the airlift. While Symington was still in Berlin, things began to turn around. On August 10 the air force moved 2,450 tons into Berlin. These, combined with approximately 1,600 tons moved by the British, amounted to 4,000 tons, or 1,000 tons more than the city's daily requirements.[14]

From Germany, Symington and Vandenberg planned to go to Athens to confer with leaders of the U.S. military mission in Greece. They were not allowed to fly over Yugoslavia, and would have to detour over the Mediterranean. Vandenberg, who had been working nearly around the clock for several days, wondered if they could not find some place where they might rest and get in a couple of days of golf. Again, Symington's extensive contacts provided the answer. He remembered that the Duke of Windsor was living in the south of France, near Antibes. He knew the Duchess of Windsor well from their Baltimore days. He called, and was immediately invited. The two men were royally entertained for the weekend, playing golf and spending time on the beach, where, Symington recorded, he saw his first bikini.

After lunch on Sunday they took off for Greece. They had dinner Sunday evening with General James Van Fleet, commanding U.S. forces in Greece. Athens was going full blast. When Symington commented on the well-dressed people on the streets, Van Fleet observed that they represented much American aid. Even so, Symington was impressed with the job Van Fleet—"an outstanding officer"—and the Greeks were doing in holding back communism. The presence of the two highest-ranking people in the air force touched off a spate of rumors in the Athens press, including the suggestion that a number of Thunderbolt fighters would be transferred from Turkey to Greece.[15]

In Turkey to inspect American air units, they spent an hour with President Inonu, reviewing the situation in Germany and in Europe generally. The visit was largely a courtesy call. When Inonu stated that, in view of the continued threat from the Russians, he must seek assurance that American aid to revitalize the Turkish armed forces would continue, Symington replied that this was a State Department problem, although he assured the president "that the Turkish people were held in high regard by all Americans; and that Mr. Lovett had given hearty approval to our visit as an expression of mutual friendliness and respect." The defense minister gave them "a sumptuous dinner" in a house that, they were told, had been a favorite of Kemal Ataturk, the founder of modern Turkey.[16]

Before returning home, Symington and Vandenberg stopped off in Paris for a visit with Ambassador Harriman. They found him encouraged by changes in attitudes in Western Europe, particularly in France, which exhibited "a will to win" not present before. He insisted that the United States should be firm and work "in practical fashion to effect practical military aid . . . if the occasion demanded."[17]

Back home, Symington involved himself some in the president's reelection campaign, and in seeking support for the airlift. He told the *New York Herald Tribune*'s annual Forum that the airlift could carry on during the winter months despite the weather. He made a point of praising the contributions of the army and navy, calling the airlift "a striking example of the new military unification of the armed forces."[18] Speaking to the second annual convention of the Air Force Association in New York on September 25, he said that if the Berlin airlift was faltering, as some critics had charged, the fault was with Congress, which had not provided sufficient money to buy all the aircraft needed. The air force had opted for combat planes over transports. "You can't transport anything through the air unless your fighter planes control it," he asserted.

The convention was celebrating the air force's first year of operation as a separate entity. Symington used the occasion to review progress and to make a dramatic announcement: an air force plane had flown "hundreds of miles faster than the speed of sound." He gave few details, except to identify the plane as an experimental, rocket-powered XS-1 and the pilot as Captain Charles E. "Chuck" Yeager. He followed this by reporting that a new Boeing B-47 bomber had outrun its jet escorts, the new Lockheed F-80 Shooting Stars. Symington combined his reports of spectacular technological progress with assurances—which he could hardly have believed—that unification was going well. Blunting an effort in the association to call for placing all air power under air force command, he assured his audience that relations with the army and navy were in good shape. "I can report to you in all sincerity," he declared, "that the situation is improving steadily because of the tactful and tireless efforts of the Secretary of Defense. The Air Force holds the Navy and all Naval airmen in the most complete respect. It has been fine to see how this relationship, at all levels, has improved in recent months."[19]

Back to the airlift—they were now calling it "Operation Vittles," and results were improving steadily. Traffic soon exceeded the capacity of the two big American bases, Rhein-Main and Wiesbaden. General Tunner expanded his operations, first to Fassberg and then to Celle in the British zone. Besides providing relief for Rhein-Main and Wiesbaden, these two bases were nearer to both the sources of supply and Berlin. Berlin's Tempelhof became overcrowded, even with the addition of new runways. German workers toiling around the clock built a new field at Tegel in the French sector. Ironically, much of the material came from the rubble left by the American bombardment of Berlin during the war.

At the height of the airlift, the transportation corps loaded seventy C-54s every six hours. They landed in Berlin at the rate of one every three minutes, day and night, in all kinds of weather. Average turnaround time at the loading base was one hour and twenty-five minutes, at the unloading bases, forty-nine minutes. While the planes were being unloaded, the crews grabbed a bite at mobile snack bars.

As summer gave way to autumn and autumn became winter, the foul weather and heavy traffic put a severe burden on the air crews; the long hours with little sleep told heavily on the ground crews. Although Symington left strategy and tactics to the military, he took a deep personal interest in the welfare of the men who flew the planes and did the work. As the holiday season approached, he decided that he would spend Christmas with the men of the airlift, and would bring with him some of the biggest names in the entertainment world.

Fortunately, he had the connections to make it possible. Through Jock Whitney he had come to know Tex McCreary, the popular radio entertainer who was now an executive with the National Broadcasting Company. McCreary put together a star-studded show, including such luminaries as Jinx Falkenberg, Irving Berlin, and Bob Hope. The "Christmas Caravan," as they called it, performed at Wiesbaden, Rhein-Main, and some smaller bases. Symington went with them, as did Vice President-Elect Alben Barkley, who had flown to Europe in Symington's plane. On Christmas Night hundreds of officers and men crowded into the main hangar at Tempelhof to watch the show. The pilots reveled in Hope's crack about the fog, "Soup I can take—but this stuff has noodles in it," but the hit of the show was the airlift anthem composed by Irving Berlin.[20]

Symington spent Christmas Day inspecting Rhein-Main with General Tunner and Lieutenant General John K. Cannon, who had succeeded LeMay as USAFE commander. They covered the entire working section of the base. Symington introduced himself and quickly put the men at ease. In the easy give-and-take that followed, he learned of the difficult working conditions and unpleasant living situations. Tunner described an encounter with a mechanic:

> In the maintenance section we stopped behind a grimy mechanic working on an engine. He looked around to see this obviously important civilian standing over him, flanked by a lieutenant general and a major general, and tried to come to attention.
>
> "Relax," Symington said for the hundredth time that day. "I'm Stu Symington. Just wanted to see how you're getting along with that engine."
>
> "Oh, I'm going to get it fixed all right, sir," the mechanic said, "but I could do it better if I had better tools."

"What's the matter with your tools?" Symington asked.

The mechanic held up a screw driver, a wrench, and a pair of pliers. "See these?" he asked. "Well, I bought 'em myself right here in Germany and they're all I got, and I can't get any more, and they ain't worth a good god-damn."

The mechanic's story was typical. At the completion of the tour, Symington told the generals he wanted information immediately so that he could inaugurate remedial action. Tunner wrote, "None of us could have asked for a more wonderful Christmas present than this opportunity to present the facts where they would receive action."

Supplies began flowing in. Tunner was "amazed at both the amount and the immediacy." He decided that "Symington must have gone straight to his office from the airport and started pushing buttons right away."

Tunner also talked to Symington about the need for larger transports. The C-54, he argued, was obsolete. Had he been given the new C-74 transports, he could have lifted the 4,500 tons required each day with 68 planes rather than the 178 C-54s required to do the job. Symington could not supply the C-74s, but, impressed by Tunner's arguments, he accelerated development of the large transport, resulting in the C-124 Globemaster that could carry 50,000 pounds and became the backbone of air force transport. Characteristically, he gave Tunner credit for being the father of the big plane.[21]

Hearing that things were particularly bad at Burtonwood, the English base that the air force had established to provide two-hundred-hour inspections for the C-54s, Symington asked the "Christmas Caravan" to visit the base with him and put on a show before heading back to the United States. He wanted to give the troops a boost, but he also wanted to examine conditions for himself. He was appalled at what he found:

> . . . twenty men in one hut with mud over the floor, only two dim lights in the barracks, a stove which was red hot on all sides—an old coal stove— they could not put anything on it; terrible lockers, bedding which they said was full of bedbugs (one of the boys volunteered they had tried to get some DDT but had not been able to). . . . They showed us the showers, which were bad, they said there was little warm water—dirt and mud on the floors and the latrines unspeakably filthy—worse than any I have ever seen on any base housing American soldiers and even worse than any of my experience in World War I.[22]

That night, during the Bob Hope show, he took the microphone and told the troops, "I am over here to get this depot straightened out, and if it isn't straightened out in two months there are going to be some heads fall." Major General Leon Johnson, whose command included Burtonwood, thought Symington was "playing to a gallery and a pretty cheap thing, because he knew we were going to get it straightened out if it was humanly possible. He had an audience, and that's what they wanted to hear, and so he said it."[23]

Symington saw it differently. He told Vandenberg, "I think I had Johnson and the boys almost crazy by the time I left," but he was confident that he would get action. Despite what Johnson thought of his motives, he was certain that his promises boosted morale at Burtonwood. Moreover, he backed up his words with action, committing four hundred thousand dollars for immediate improvements to the barracks and mess halls. Symington did not have the four hundred thousand dollars available, but in a hard bargaining session with the comptroller general he succeeded in getting use of ECA counterpart funds to make good on his commitments.[24]

Before returning to Washington, Symington went to London for another lunch with Lord Teddar. He described the conditions at Burtonwood and told Teddar frankly that he did not think the British were doing all they could to help maintain the depot. Teddar agreed and promised to give the matter immediate attention—which he did.[25]

Finally, on December 29, Symington took off for home. Accompanying him were Bob Hope and the rest of the "Christmas Caravan." They stopped in the Azores for refueling, and, although it was 2:30 in the morning, the cast put on a show for troops stationed there, "and probably had the best audience of the trip." As for the trip itself, Symington thought it "could not have been better from every angle."[26] As for his own performance, it, too, could hardly have been better. He was doing the things he did best, serving as salesman, cheerleader, negotiator, and troubleshooter. Regarding the airlift, he told Lyndon Johnson, in response to a statement of approval the senator had read into the *Congressional Record*, "It has been a difficult job, but it has been handled by typical American boys in a typical American fashion."[27]

By January the airlift was clearly succeeding; it could continue indefinitely. Symington worried about the cost and its impact on the air force budget. He asked Forrestal to request that the president "determine in principle" that the air force receive supplemental funds as needed. Forrestal replied that they had already established the principle and the action was unnecessary. As it turned out, they paid the total cost—approximately $252 million—"out of regular air force appropriations, using money freed up by a slowdown in aircraft procurement."[28]

On May 12 the Soviets lifted the blockade, although at the request of the State Department, involved in complex four-power negotiations on the future of Germany, the airlift continued. By July the buildup of supplies in Berlin seemed sufficient to begin phasing down operations; the president announced publicly that the airlift would be terminated on October 31. Actually, operations ceased on September 30.

The airlift had been an outstanding success. It delivered a total of 2,325 million tons of fuel, food, and supplies to Berlin.[29] It showed the effectiveness of large-scale air transport. It dramatized the truth of the claim by air power proponents that the air force could provide vital support for the nation's diplomacy. It provided convincing evidence that despite the noisy, unseemly quarrels in Washington, army, navy, and air force could work together for the common good when the occasion demanded. Symington took pride in the accomplishments of the men who operated the airlift and never let pass an opportunity to praise their efforts. In his first annual report, he called the airlift "a timely and impressive showing of . . . United States airpower, and . . . an example of great significance in showing what it means to any nation to be able to use the air space at will in pursuit of national and diplomatic aims."

He warned, however, against overconfidence. The summer months permitted a gradual buildup that made it possible to meet the demand even though the air force was in only an intermediate stage of readiness. "We cannot count on future crises being so ineptly timed by those who would put pressure on us," he wrote. "The instant readiness to be accomplished under the Four-Year program is essential if we are to have air power capable of crisis use."[30]

The airlift was a transport operation, and neither Symington nor Vandenberg thought of it as the central mission of the air force. That mission was strategic bombardment, and throughout the airlift both men continued their preoccupation with preparing the air force to fulfill its mission—and Symington, as his priority effort, with seeking the funds and the authorizations to make it possible.

12

The Fight for Air Power (I)

BY THE TIME Symington became assistant secretary of war for air, AAF leaders had committed to an air force of seventy groups as the minimum required for security in the postwar world. Symington accepted the 70-Group Program without question. General Spaatz was for it, and that was good enough for him. His job, as he was fond of saying, was not to develop strategy but to sell it—and from the moment he took office, he devoted himself to selling a 70-Group air force.

It was a hard sell. The country was tired of war. Most Americans had little interest in spending money on the military. They wanted to get on with living, to enjoy the fruits of victory: a new house, a new car, new kitchen appliances, new everything. President Truman, sensing the mood of the country, placed severe limits on military spending. In 1946 he decreed that it could not exceed one-third of the government's total income. His early budgets provided for only a fraction of what the services thought they needed. Encouraged by James Webb, his conservative budget director, he firmly believed that excessive military spending was inflationary. Moreover, the effort to create political stability in Europe through such devices as the Truman Doctrine and the Marshall Plan required vast sums that were to be found in part by reducing military expenditures.[1]

Although Truman was able to hold defense spending somewhat in check, there was no way that he could actually reduce military expenditures from their record peacetime levels. By the winter of 1946-1947 it was apparent that hoped-for cooperation with the Soviet Union would not materialize. Few knowledgeable people believed that war with the Soviets was imminent, but few informed observers completely discounted the danger posed by Soviet meddling in such trouble spots as Iran, Greece, and Turkey. As Barton Leach, professor of law at Harvard—and a wartime reserve colonel who remained close to Spaatz and Vandenberg, and who developed a close relationship with Symington—wrote in February 1947, "If we have war it is going to be with Russia. If we have no war with Russia, we shall have no war at all for at least two decades." General Spaatz began to speak openly of a war "with a continental empire" and the "problem of winning against great masses of people with great internal resources."[2]

Moreover, the armed forces faced steadily increasing costs. Part of the increase resulted from inflation, part came from the high cost of new, sophisticated weapons. For example, a B-17 bomber in World War II cost $218,000, but a B-36 in 1949 cost more than $3.6 million; the cost of fighter planes increased from $54,000 for a P-51 to $855,000 for an F-89.[3]

Symington never achieved the 70-Group air force he and the generals hoped for, but by capitalizing on the perceived dangers from abroad, he was able to sell both the president and the Congress on steadily increasing appropriations. He made enemies in the process, and even irritated the president, but he kept the needs of the air force effectively before the country.

Prior to unification, and to some degree even after, the air force submitted its budget through the War Department. The FY 1948 budget was in place before the Department of Defense came into being, and the FY 1949 budget process was so far along that Forrestal thought it best to let the process proceed as begun and concentrate on the development of a separate DOD budget for FY 1950. As assistant secretary, Symington expressed alarm over the cutbacks in defense funds. He warned that they threatened to wreck the AAF's planned program. For 1948, the War Department approved funds only for fifty-five groups, fifteen short of the minimum Symington and Spaatz felt to be essential. Spaatz went ahead and activated seventy groups, but left fifteen of them at skeleton strength.[4]

Symington intensified his efforts to get funding for the full seventy groups. He found willing and powerful allies in the American aircraft industry. He knew many of the leaders socially, and others from business. Moreover, his wartime experience at Emerson had given him an understanding of the industry's problems and the mentality of its leaders.

Initially some in the industry thought they might make the transition from war to peace by building a domestic market and increasing exports. Neither proved realistic. Commercial and private air traffic greatly expanded, but the higher speeds and greater capacity of the new transport planes reduced the number required to fill the demand. Further exacerbating the industry's problems, the British made steady inroads on the export market.[5] The only hope for a viable American aircraft industry lay in continued sales to the military services. At the same time, military leaders—especially Robert Lovett, Symington's predecessor as assistant secretary of war for air—clearly understood that an adequate air defense depended upon a healthy aircraft industry. Lovett worked to develop a federal aviation policy that would assure the country's continued superiority in the air. This meant, in his view, that the aircraft manufacturers needed to be encouraged to maintain their research and development facilities and pushed to pursue continued improvements. Largely because of his leadership, an interdepartmental Air Coordinating Committee was established in March 1945.[6]

Symington, too, understood the relationship between a healthy aircraft industry and an adequate defense, but at first he wanted the industry to pay its way without large government subsidies for research and development. This may have resulted, in part, from his preoccupation with cost control in the AAF, but he developed rather prickly relationships with some industry leaders, particularly Eugene E. Wilson, president of United Aircraft and, as president of the Aircraft Industries Association, principal spokesman for the industry. Wilson wanted a National Air Policy Board. The navy liked the idea, but representatives of the AAF vigorously opposed it on the grounds that it would delay unification. Wilson's criticisms of the AAF clearly damaged the cause of unification, and, in Symington's view, reduced the effectiveness of what should have been a major source of support. He and Spaatz made no secret of their unhappiness with Wilson, or of their pleasure when at the end of 1946 Major General (ret.) Oliver P. Echols became head of the AIA. Echols, as assistant chief of air staff, had directed air procurement during the war and was as familiar with the aircraft industry as anyone in the AAF. He was an aggressive and effective spokesman for the needs of the industry, and could be depended upon to maintain the AAF position on unification.[7]

Symington was encouraged to modify his opposition to subsidies for the aircraft industry by Brigadier General Turner Sims, who became executive officer when Colonel Odom retired. During the war, Sims had been with the Air Materiel Command at Wright Field; he understood, as well as anyone in AAF headquarters, the technological requirements of modern warfare. During the spring and summer of 1947, while Symington was at his home in St. Louis recuperating from his operation, Sims ran the office of assistant secretary. In memos to Symington, he forcefully stated the case for subsidizing the industry if necessary to keep it healthy, citing the delays that had occurred at the beginning of the war as something which must be avoided at all costs if the air force were to function as the nation's first line of defense. He urged that the AAF seek to stabilize the industry at some agreed-upon level of production and research.[8]

Although Symington continued to feel that the industry should assume some responsibility for its future, he did not need to be convinced of its importance to the country's defense. In February 1947 he observed to Spaatz that the air force would have to "face the problem of what is going to happen to the aviation industry." Later, he wrote to Echols: "It looks as if our airplane industry is in trouble and it would seem to be the obligation of our little shop to do the best we can to help where such assistance is right and proper. . . . I am sure General Spaatz feels the same way about it."[9]

There is no question about General Spaatz's attitude. Indeed, everyone in the defense establishment, including Forrestal, making the transition from being secretary of the navy to becoming secretary of defense, understood the importance of a healthy aircraft industry.[10]

Because of his absence in St. Louis, Symington did not participate in the discussions of the Air Coordinating Committee in the spring and summer of 1947. Undersecretary Royall represented the War Department. Although Royall was ambivalent about the merits of unification, he did not question the need for a larger air force and the importance of the aircraft industry. Under his leadership, the ACC, after a good deal of discussion, voted to recommend to the president that he appoint a commission to study the needs of the aircraft industry and to recommend an air policy. Brackley Shaw, Symington's legal aide—and later air force general counsel—headed the committee that drafted the letter.[11]

Truman did not act on the letter until July 17, when he announced the appointment of a President's Air Policy Commission. We do not know just why Truman decided to appoint the commission. Frank Kofsky, in his generally hostile treatment of Truman, says that he did it simply to prevent the Republicans from preempting the air power issue. There may be some truth to that, particularly in the matter of timing. The Republican Eightieth Congress was busy on legislation to create a permanent Air Board; as it turned out, a few days after Truman announced his decision Congress created the Congressional Aviation Policy Board, headed by Republican Senator Owen Brewster of Maine and Republican Congressman Carl Hinshaw of California. Aside from politics, both Truman and the Republican leadership in Congress were aware of the growing concern about the adequacy of the nation's defenses, and both understood that a healthy aircraft industry was a key ingredient in a strong defense. The president's commission and the congressional board cooperated fully, with the latter depending to a great extent on testimony provided by the former.[12]

Although Symington did not participate in the discussions leading up to the appointment of the commission and apparently had no voice in the selection of its members, he had every reason to be pleased. He knew most of them; some were close friends, especially the appointed chairman, Thomas K. Finletter, a prominent Philadelphia lawyer who had been active in the State Department. Other friends on the commission were Henry Ford II and Palmer Hoyt, publisher of the *Denver Post*. Ford resigned after a few weeks and was replaced by John A. McCone, prominent California industrialist, who was a friend of both Symington and Forrestal.[13]

The Finletter Commission and the Brewster Board offered the AAF golden opportunities to get its message out. Symington, now back in Washington and completely recovered from his operation, intended to take full advantage of them. He had the commissioners for lunch in the secretary of war's dining room on September 16, at which time senior air force officers briefed them on the air force and world situations. He left nothing to chance, directing that the briefing officers engage in not one but two dry runs before meeting the commissioners. Convinced that the commission's hearings would provide a wonderful forum for discussing air force needs, he urged that prominent military and civilian leaders be invited to testify as much as possible on the record. Spaatz suggested that Finletter discuss the question with Arthur Sulzberger, publisher of the *New York Times*. Finletter did so, and Sulzberger did not disappoint the air force. He urged that there be broad, on-the-record participation, and that the witnesses go "all out" in "advising the people as completely as possible the current and future dangers to which this country is exposed in just as specific terms as possible without jeopardizing sources of our intelligence."[14]

The air force team followed its careful preparation with hard-hitting, aggressive testimony that made headlines all over the country. General Spaatz led off. He warned the commission of the "folly" of lowering defenses in the face of the Soviet threat. He reiterated his call for a permanent peacetime air force of seventy groups, asserting that heavy, long-range bombers, escorted by fighters, were the only weapon that could penetrate enemy territory at vast distances. Carrier-based aircraft simply could not do it.[15]

Symington, testifying on September 27, supported Spaatz. In a second appearance on November 26, he reiterated the need for seventy groups, declaring them to be the "bedrock minimum." He urged the commission to weigh the costs against the possible consequences of not meeting defense requirements. "The Air Force," he argued, "must be prepared to carry out the air defense of the United States. . . . it must be prepared to undertake immediate and powerful retaliation, a capacity which is itself the only real deterrent to aggression in the world today." With General Vandenburg at his side, he candidly described the present condition of the air force and set forth in precise detail the composition of the seventy groups he was requesting. A reporter for *Aviation Week* who covered the hearings described the testimony as "exceeding anything previously put out on the subject. . . . one of the most amazing statements in recent Washington memory." He suggested that it "appeared to be a security violation of a very generous nature. If we had asked for that dope, we would have been given a severe lecture on security." The reporter surmised correctly. The information, still classified, was being readied for presentation in connection with the next budget. Symington advanced the time of public release. His action had a stunning effect. Newspapers and magazines all over the country published the figures—and generally endorsed Symington's position.[16]

Fleet Admiral Chester Nimitz, testifying for the navy, took vigorous exception to the air force's claims. Reliance on land-based bombers would be neither sound nor workable. "Unless we retain our ability to control the sea," he told the commission, ". . . we may eventually find ourselves exchanging long-range air attacks which will be indecisive alike against ourselves and our enemies, but at the same time damaging to our own cities and vital installations."[17]

It was clear that the old animosities had not died with unification. Forrestal, by now secretary of defense, tried to calm the controversy by refusing to endorse either position. He asserted that no one could be sure how future wars would be fought. He agreed with the president that defense expenditures should not be higher than the economy could support. Forrestal's feeble effort did nothing to stifle the controversy. Instead, it gave rise to an uneasy suspicion that the new secretary of defense might not be up to his job. On his prepared testimony, *Fortune* commented: "Seldom has a mimeograph machine worked so hard in the conveyance of so little information." The magazine continued: "Even some tart cross-examination by Chairman Finletter did little except arouse a possible suspicion that Mr. Forrestal was really as blank as he sounded."[18]

The commission ignored both Forrestal and the navy, and came out strongly for a defense strategy that relied heavily on air superiority. It called for substantial increases in air force appropriations. It supported the 70-Group Program, recommending that appropriations be increased sufficiently to enable the air force to reach full seventy-group strength, with modernized reserves, by the end of 1952. It recommended smaller increases for the navy, with most of the money going for aviation. As for the aircraft industry, the commission suggested that if its recommendations relative to the air force and the navy were followed, "the necessary base for expansion . . . will exist."[19]

This was all Symington and Spaatz could have asked for, but it was clear that the report was not going to solve their budget problems. The commission published its report on January 1. The president submitted his FY '49 budget estimates on January 13. Although the 70-Group Program would have required $5.2 billion for fiscal 1949, the air force, cognizant of the need to keep budgets as low as possible, had submitted an estimate for $4.21 billion, barely enough to maintain fifty-five groups. The Bureau of the Budget, however, cut this to $2.904

billion. Symington's reaction was quick and pointed. As soon as he saw the figures, he fired off a long letter to Budget Director Webb, with copies to Forrestal and Clifford. The recommendations had "grave implications which should be thoroughly understood before the estimate is submitted to Congress." They would make it impossible to maintain even a scaled-down version of the fifty-five-group program. Research and development would be so adversely affected that "in the event of an emergency in the next five years we will be fighting with obsolete weapons and materials." He added, "remember that not one airplane whose development started after Pearl Harbor was ever used in combat."[20]

Copying Forrestal, with an urgent plea for help, he wrote, ". . . we are more shocked at this decision of the Bureau than at anything that has happened since we came into Government." He said the same thing to Clifford.[21]

Despite Symington's warning, the budget went in as originally proposed. Truman was determined to hold the line on defense spending, his determination strengthened when the Eightieth Congress passed a tax cut by veto-proof margins. He was not going to let the Republicans force him into deficit spending, regardless of what the services felt they might need.[22] Then, events combined to turn things around. The Congressional Air Policy Board, reporting early in March, echoed the Finletter Commission in calling for a 70-Group air force. Both the Finletter Commission and the Brewster Board had based their recommendations on a deteriorating international situation, and particularly on increasing tensions with the Soviet Union. The Czech coup early in February, which resulted in a pro-Communist government backed by the Red Army, sent shudders down many a Washington spine. Then, on March 5, Lieutenant General Stephen J. Chamberlain, army chief of intelligence, received an "eyes only" telegram from General Clay reporting "a subtle change in Soviet attitude which I cannot define but which now gives me a feeling that . . . [war] may come with dramatic suddenness." Subsequent studies have revealed that there was little basis for believing that war with the Soviets was imminent, but Clay's observation provided further evidence that tensions were mounting.[23] The Soviets had replaced the Nazis as the primary threat to peace in Europe, and no one knew where Soviet expansion would end.

Symington took the Soviet threat more seriously than did most high-ranking officials in Washington, and he was concerned that Americans generally did not appreciate the country's lack of preparedness. For example, David Lilienthal, chairman of the Atomic Energy Commission, reported that at a dinner in the Pentagon on March 6 with Forrestal and the three service secretaries, "Symington said the American public was completely misinformed about how quickly we could go into action and what we could do." Air force intelligence consistently overstated Soviet air strength and generally was more pessimistic about the U.S. position vis-à-vis that of the Soviets than their counterparts in the other services.[24]

President Truman, though not subscribing to the immediate war scare, went before Congress on March 17 to warn the country of the growing Soviet menace. He did not call for an increase in defense appropriations, but confined himself to three requests: approval of the Marshall Plan, universal military training, and a temporary extension of selective service.[25]

Truman's push for universal military training posed a dilemma for Symington. Spaatz and most senior air force officers had no interest in universal military training. It would do little to provide the bright, trainable personnel the air force required, and it would absorb money that could be used to support increasing air strength. The Air Board, Spaatz's principal advisory group, argued that UMT was secondary in importance to the development of an air force in being—in other words, the 70-Group Program—and should be opposed on that ground.[26] Symington shared the generals' views even though they ran counter to those of the president. At the same time, he repeatedly insisted that both he and Spaatz supported the president on UMT. On March 29, for example, in response to a comment from Truman that "the opposition of the Air contingent to universal training is an exceedingly short-sighted approach because even the aviators ought to have the fundamentals of discipline if we are going to have an effective Force," he wrote, "I want to assure you that the Air Force, including General Spaatz and myself, has not only been backing, but has been working for your policies on Universal Military Training and Selective Service." He went on, "In the past ten days, General Spaatz and I have both voluntarily supported whole-heartedly UMT and Selective Service before the Senate Armed Services Committee and the House Appropriations Committee. I would like to face in front of you the person or persons who told you the Air Force was not supporting UMT. I think in short order you would find out who was telling the truth."[27]

As far as the record shows, Truman never called for the confrontation. He seems to have been completely satisfied with Symington's protestations. "Dear Stuart," he wrote on April 1, "I appreciated your letter of March 29th very much and I am most happy that the three branches of the Service are cooperating fully for Universal Military Training."[28]

They were not, of course, even though Forrestal and all three service secretaries, meeting privately with the Senate Armed Services Committee, joined in urging the adoption of UMT, declaring that in light of recent world conditions, it had become "not only necessary but mandatory." Actually, the air force and the navy had never favored UMT; only the army thought it would be of help. Symington always insisted that he supported UMT "in principle," but he was quick to add, "not at the expense of an adequate air force." He rationalized his position by falling back on the report of the President's Advisory Committee on Universal Military Training, headed by Karl Compton, president of the Massachusetts Institute of Technology. The report came out strongly for universal military training, but added, "If the introduction of universal training should have . . . an indirect effect of weakening rather than strengthening, the other elements of our national security, then our Commission is of the firm opinion that the adoption of universal training would be a mistake, and would diminish, rather than increase, our national security."[29]

The core of the matter was the budget. Symington subordinated everything—including UMT—to achieving budgetary support for an air force in being of seventy groups.

On April 7, testifying before the Senate Armed Services Committee, he stated that as between a 70-Group Program and UMT, he would take the seventy groups. A week later he followed this widely quoted statement with an even more pointed remark. During Symington's testimony before the House Armed Services Committee, his good friend Lyndon Johnson asked what can only be construed as a leading question: "Mr. Secretary, if you had to make a choice of methods of insuring the security of this Nation, do you think we are more likely to insure the security of this Nation with a strong effective 70-group Air Force or with UMT?" Symington responded, "Well, if my two boys had to go back again into the Army and the Marines, I would rather see them have a minimum Air Force than I would a group of younger boys trained for 6 months or a year."[30]

Symington's testimony has been credited with applying the coup de grâce to UMT. The stories about his role in killing UMT irritated him no end. Talk about his insubordination, and particularly his criticism of the president, "incensed" him. In an "eyes only" memo to Forrestal, who had mentioned the stories in conversation, he heatedly denied ever having criticized Truman. He "keenly regretted" the way the air force program was presented to Congress, "in conjunction with U.M.T., Selective Service, and a larger Army and Navy." He complained that the decision to do so was a sure way to kill UMT. He was upset that neither he nor Spaatz had been consulted: ". . . this was especially unfortunate to us, in that nobody who ever served a day in the Air Force was either a member of your permanent top staff or was one of those you called in temporarily to work on this matter."[31]

Actually, UMT never had a chance. Few voices supported it in the country; the Republicans who controlled the Eightieth Congress opposed it on both ideological and fiscal grounds; and within the administration itself, no one except the president and Secretary of State Marshall expressed much enthusiasm for it.

As UMT went under, it left in its wake disturbing evidence of the almost complete disarray in the Defense Department. During hearings on Selective Service, Symington declared that American security would be better served by taking the money the president had requested for UMT and spending it on the air force. The next day, General Bradley asserted that what was needed was not a 70-Group air force, "or even a 1000-group Air Force," but eight hundred thousand more men in the army. Commenting on the proceedings, Hanson W. Baldwin, pro-navy military columnist for the *New York Times* and one of Symington's most persistent critics, charged, "'Unification' becomes a joke when the Secretary of the Air Force goes over the head of the Secretary of Defense and of the President himself."[32]

Within the Defense Department, Symington pursued a steadily more independent course. When Forrestal was able to persuade Truman to increase his 1949 supplemental appropriations request from $3 billion to $3.375 billion, Symington complained about both the package and the process by which it was developed—a process in which there was virtually no air force participation. He protested to Forrestal that no one on the secretary of defense's staff had any air force service and that the cost figures being used by the Defense Department were wholly inaccurate. From the beginning, Forrestal had paid lip service to the idea of air force expansion, but he always insisted that it be carried out as part of a "balanced forces" program. To enable the air force to achieve seventy groups would require a total defense appropriation of $18 billion, $3 billion more than the $15 billion the president had established as an absolute ceiling for defense spending. In a sharply worded "eyes only" memo to Forrestal commenting on a draft of a letter to be sent to Chan Gurney, Republican from South Dakota and chairman of the Senate Armed Services Committee, Symington charged that the $18 billion figure, "which was given to you, and which you, thereupon, in good faith, gave to the Senate Armed Services Committee as the cost of the increase from 55 groups to 70 groups cannot be justified on any basis whatever, unless the post-D-day mobilization figures for the two other services are correlated with an air force mobilization requirement for the same period."

If Forrestal persisted in using the $18 billion figure, he would put himself, and the armed services generally, in "a difficult, if not impossible, position with the Congressional committees who may conclude: 1. That you are sacrificing air power and a force in being to get UMT and Selective Service, or 2. That Congress is not being treated with complete candor." He closed by reminding Forrestal that "The press, the Congress, and the people are all sold on this Air Force program." If the Congress had to choose between the air force and a balanced program, they would choose the air force.[33]

The letter to Senator Gurney created quite a tempest in the Defense

Department. Symington felt that no letter should be sent. Robert Cutler, president of the Old Colony Trust Company in Boston, whom Forrestal had asked to help with the budget, charged that the air force was not particularly cooperative in developing it.[34] When air force representatives at a drafting conference reported to their boss that Cutler had wondered whether Symington had ever read the drafts and had told them to tell him that he expected to have Symington's written comments by noon the next day, Symington lost his temper. Reaching for the "squawk box," he told Cutler just what he thought of the letter and of him—Cutler said Symington called him "an offensive name." Cutler switched off the intercom and went into Symington's office, where, according to his story, "I went up to Symington's desk. 'Stuart,' I said calmly but certainly, 'you can't talk to me like that. I came down here as a volunteer, at the request of Jim and General Marshall, to help them. I'm trying to do the best I can.' I held out my hand. 'Here, let's shake hands and forget what happened and go back to work.' After a moment, Symington stood up and we shook hands."

Although Cutler wrote Symington that the letter "was a better one because of the discussions I had with you, General Spaatz, Gene Zuchert [sic], and General Norstadt [sic]," the letter that Forrestal finally sent was little changed from the draft to which Symington had objected. Forrestal sent Symington a curt note, "Don't send any letter to Senator Gurney without first checking with me." Whether he checked with Forrestal or not—if he did, it must have been verbally, and the record does not even show a copy to the secretary of defense—Symington wrote directly to Senator Gurney, responding to questions Gurney had asked during the hearing.[35]

Whatever the situation—Symington to all appearances was deliberately disobeying his boss—Forrestal was becoming somewhat irrelevant as far as air force appropriations were concerned. Symington, emboldened by a favorable press and signs of strong congressional support, assumed an increasingly independent course outside the department as well as within it. At one point Forrestal told him that if he couldn't support the budget, he should quit. "I won't support it," Symington replied, "and I won't quit."[36] Forrestal clearly had lost control of his secretary of the air force. If he were to be brought into line, the president himself would have to do it.

Shortly before the Senate Armed Services Committee began hearings on the budget, Truman summoned the Pentagon leaders to the Oval Office to make sure they were all going to support his recommendation. Looking straight at Symington, he said, "I want everybody to back this budget. If you have anything to say against it, say it now." Symington responded, "Mr. President, are you asking me, in effect, to perjure myself if I am asked a question as to whether the Air Force can carry out its mission with this amount of money?" No,

Truman wouldn't ask anyone to perjure himself, but, looking hard at Symington, he asked, "Will you give me your word that you won't originate the question?" Symington gave his word.[37]

Symington didn't need to originate the question. The Senate Armed Services Committee, meeting behind closed doors on April 7, was much interested in hearing Symington's views on the president's budget, and he did not hesitate in giving them. The air force needed seventy groups in being, and the president's budget barely provided for fifty-five groups. As for Universal Military Training, in a colloquy with Senator Wayne Morse, Symington said that he had "always been for Universal Military Training. My father-in-law had worked at it for 25 years in the House and Senate." But, he added, "If it comes to the question of what we think is best for the country, we think it is better to have a 70 group peace time program than it is to have a Universal Military Training program and I think if I feel that way you would want me to tell you."[38]

Symington dominated the hearings, with Forrestal being reduced to trying to modify some of his rebellious associate's more extreme statements, particularly with respect to his estimates regarding Soviet air strength. Symington had made a number of speeches around the country comparing U.S. and Soviet air power, and had published an inflammatory article in the February issue of *American Magazine,* "We've Scuttled our Air Force."

"If we had kept strong," he wrote, "there might not even had been a threat of World War III today. If we hurry and catch up, the threat may recede. But the very nature of our preparedness demands that we waste not another single day."[39]

He was even more apocalyptic at the hearings. "We have only asked this year what we asked the year before," he reminded the senators. "We have not taken advantage of any tenseness in the world. We said three years ago that your Air Force was going to pieces, we said that two years ago, and we say this year it is going to pieces. We say this year, no matter how you try to fix it, you are not going to have it by the time the Russians have the bomb. It is too late."[40]

The immediate question, though, was the amount of money required to build a 70-Group air force. Symington and Spaatz assured the committee that $3.5 billion was needed. When Forrestal was asked for his views, he went back to the $18 billion figure, the amount required to maintain a balance of forces if the air force were to go to seventy groups.

The hearings and the extensive press coverage Symington's testimony received posed a dilemma for both Forrestal and the White House. Forrestal had assured the committee that Symington was free to express his own views, but, as the *New York Times* suggested, "In going directly to Congress to plead for a program larger than that recommended by Defense Secretary Forrestal, the Air Force leaders are exercising a prerogative under unification that hardly was expected to be exercised so soon." Forrestal issued a noncommittal statement and advised the White House to do the same.[41]

To the discomfiture of both Forrestal and the White House, Symington's efforts were beginning to produce results. Led by Georgia Democrat Carl Vinson, the ranking minority member on the House Armed Services Committee, the House Appropriations Committee on April 7 voted to add $822 million to the Defense Department's budget to enable the air force to begin a five-year buildup to seventy groups. A week later, in what was widely interpreted as a victory for Symington at the expense of the president and Forrestal, the full House approved the committee's recommendation by the overwhelming vote of 343 to 3. The president was asked if he intended to "spank" his secretary of the air force for continuing to advocate the 70-Group program. As in the past, he ducked the question, saying he would answer it at a later date.[42]

Publicly, Forrestal continued to defend Symington's right to speak his mind, but privately he fumed at his air secretary's "disloyalty," wondering darkly if Symington was out to get his job.[43] His paranoia surfaced in a semi-public setting at a meeting of the service secretaries to consider the Defense Department's response to the House vote on air force appropriations. The record is not inspiring. Forrestal charged that information had come to him that Symington was "in a conspiracy with someone in the White House to try to get me out." Symington responded, "That's one hundred percent adulterated nonsense." When Symington said that they should get hold of the people who were passing the rumor, Forrestal replied that he already had. This exchange was part of an hour-and-a-half meeting, with most of the attention being focused on which service was being treated unfairly in the budget process. The record reveals further evidence that Forrestal was unable to control the three strong-willed men who were supposed to serve under him.[44]

The next day Forrestal went before the Senate Armed Services Committee to testify on the supplemental bill. Earlier he had secured approval from the Joint Chiefs of Staff for a plan to allocate a total supplemental appropriation of $3.481 billion—about $500 million more than originally had been discussed. This plan would enable the air force to expand from fifty-five to sixty-six groups by the end of Fiscal Year 1949 and to reach seventy groups by the beginning of FY 51.[45]

Although the president and Senator Gurney both endorsed Forrestal's proposal, air power advocates in the House of Representatives expressed strong reservations. Lyndon Johnson stated that Forrestal's plan would give the nation "66 T-model groups, not jet model groups." Others joined in. Vinson declared the "fight for the 70 group Air Force had just begun." John Taber, New York

Republican and chairman of the House Appropriations Committee, said that he was still disposed to back up the House action despite Mr. Forrestal's proposed compromise. House Speaker Joseph W. Martin, Jr., agreed, stating that air supremacy was the country's best guarantee of peace and for that reason it must have a seventy-group air force. Powerful Republicans in the Senate also came out in support of the 70-Group program. Robert A. Taft, de facto majority leader, inserted in the *Congressional Record* a speech he had made in Fremont, Nebraska, in which he had stated, "Surely the Air Force must be our first line of defense and our first concern when it comes to spending money." Styles Bridges, New Hampshire Republican and chairman of the Senate Appropriations Committee, whom Symington had converted from a critic to a supporter, said after Forrestal's presentation that he was still for seventy groups.[46]

Armed with such support, Symington and Spaatz urged the Senate Appropriations Committee to support the House action over the Forrestal compromise. The committee agreed, and the Senate, with only two dissenting votes, adopted the House bill. Air power enthusiasts were ecstatic. General Eaker, now retired and working for the Hughes Tool Company in Houston, wrote: "I have talked to a number of old Air Force people lately and all have been enthusiastic about the victory you have won for the 70-group Air Force. You succeeded beyond my most optimistic expectations."[47]

But the air power victory was more apparent than real. The legislation provided that the $822 million addition to the supplemental appropriation could not be spent without a finding by the president that the "contracts let are necessary in the national defense," and that the procurement would result in the "maximum utilization of improvements in aircraft and equipment consistent with the defense needs of the U.S." As he signed the bill, Truman indicated that he was asking the secretary of defense and the director of the budget to assist him in making the necessary determinations.[48]

This was the kiss of death for the $822 million. Forrestal had not supported it, because without additional appropriations for the army and especially the navy it would "unbalance" the forces. Jim Webb thought that even the $3.481 billion submitted by Forrestal was too high.

Clearly, the fight for air power was far from over.

13

The Fight for Air Power (II)

THE PRESIDENT'S refusal to spend the $822 million appropriated by Congress and his budget for FY 1949, limiting total defense expenditures to $15 billion, shattered any hope that the air force would achieve the 70-Group strength which Symington had long insisted was the absolute minimum required for the nation's defense. Symington, in his annual report issued in July 1948, pointedly wrote of the importance of moving ahead on what he was now calling "the Four-Year Program. . . . often referred to as the 70-Group Plan." The schedule, he reminded his readers, called for fifty-five groups in January 1948, sixty-six groups in June 1949, and seventy groups in September 1949.[1] The president's budget, however, mandated a reduction from fifty-five groups, authorized earlier, to forty-eight. This had a profound impact on air force thinking generally and procurement decisions specifically.

By the summer of 1948 the air force had won reluctant recognition of its primary responsibility for strategic bombing, believed by many air force planners to be the key to victory in modern warfare. This recognition did not come easily and it was never unqualified. Throughout the struggle over unification the navy had insisted that it, too, had a role in strategic bombing, that, indeed, its carrier aircraft, launched from mobile platforms within easy range of enemy targets, were more effective than long-range bombers flying from distant airfields. Unification did nothing to dampen the navy's enthusiasm for strategic bombing as part of its primary mission.

In an effort to resolve differences over roles and missions, Forrestal had assembled the Joint Chiefs at the Key West Naval base on March 11. Significantly, he did not include the service secretaries, thus, by inference at least, asserting his primary role in the development of strategy. (Spaatz, it should be noted, kept in close touch with Symington throughout the conference.) After three days of intense discussion, the best the Joint Chiefs could do was to arrive at a compromise. Perhaps, under Forrestal's leadership, they could not have been expected to do more. The air force recognized the "right" of the navy to develop atomic capability, but the navy was not to create "a separate strategic air force." This was reserved exclusively to the air force. The Joint Chiefs also agreed that the marines should not develop a separate land army. They had no problems in agreeing that the president should be asked to seek a supplemental appropriation "to bring our total strength up to the point where it more nearly met the realities of the world situation."[2]

Although Forrestal expressed confidence that there was "now general accord on practically all matters which were previously unresolved," such was not the case. Each service continued to build its budgets without reference to the roles and missions of the other branches and with no regard for the president's announced budgetary ceilings. Moreover, interservice sniping accelerated rather than declined, with the navy being particularly aggressive. In May the navy had leaked to Drew Pearson an internal memorandum which argued that the air force was incapable of carrying out effective strategic bombing. That should be left to the navy's carrier aircraft, while the air force confined itself to continental defense.[3] The memorandum ignited a firestorm. Symington complained to Secretary of the Navy John L. Sullivan; Forrestal, who above all wanted to dampen the controversy, joined in expressing alarm at the navy's intemperate tactics.

The controversial memorandum was but one of a series of charges and countercharges that filled the air during the summer of 1948. The air force was not reticent in pressing its claims, with both Symington and General Vandenberg, who had succeeded Spaatz as chief of staff, being much in the news. In the face of the Berlin blockade, the crisis in Czechoslovakia, and mounting problems in the Far East, it seemed that the Department of Defense was in danger of flying apart.

In desperation, the beleaguered Forrestal turned to the recently retired Spaatz and retired Admiral John H. Towers to study the applications of air power and the efficacy of the Key West agreements. The two highly respected battle veterans agreed that the Key West decisions were essentially sound but "needed interpretation." They spoke of the need for unity, and Spaatz even agreed that the navy should be permitted to continue to develop its atomic capability—which meant continuing to develop the earlier-authorized but still highly controversial super carrier. They could not agree, however, on control of the nation's stockpile of atomic bombs. Towers held that operational control should not be vested in any one service; Spaatz insisted that control should be in the hands of the air force chief of staff, acting as an agent for the Joint Chiefs.[4]

While Spaatz and Towers were working on their memo, Forrestal decided to convene the Joint Chiefs in another out-of-Washington session to see if they could come to greater agreement on the meaning of the Key West decisions. They assembled at the Naval War College in Newport on Friday evening, August 20, and met through lunch on Sunday, August 22. A Defense Department press release stated that the three service secretaries participated in the meeting,[5] but no other record indicates that they were present. Vandenberg and Norstad spoke for the air force.

Newport did help to "clarify" the Key West agreements, but the equivocation that had characterized Forrestal's position from the beginning on roles and missions remained to dilute the hoped-for clarification. Speaking of the agreement before a gathering of about three hundred senior military officers at the Pentagon, Forrestal said he was convinced "that at the top command levels, there is a clear understanding of the exclusive role of the Air Force in the field of strategic air warfare and conversely the intent of the Air Force not merely to permit but to seek all the help it can get from Naval Air in the use of air power, either strategically or tactically." The decisions reflected his views, "and, if followed through with sincerity and tenacity, will mean a victory for the country."[6]

In short, the agreements would depend on mutual goodwill, something that was in limited supply. It could hardly have been otherwise. The president's ceiling of $15 billion on total defense expenditures could in no way accommodate what the services considered to be their legitimate needs.[7] As the service chiefs fought for what they considered to be their fair share of the pie, the goodwill that might have been present during preluncheon cocktails on that last day at Newport rapidly disappeared.

Symington left the details of the budget struggle to Vandenberg, who slugged it out on a regular basis in meetings of the Joint Chiefs of Staff. Frequently Bradley joined Vandenberg in making common cause against what they felt were the navy's excessive demands. In every instance, the navy refused to compromise, becoming steadily more stiff-necked. On October 4, at a meeting of the JCS attended by Forrestal, the service secretaries, and Admiral William Leahy, the president's chief of staff, Admiral Louis Denfield, read a long statement in which he declared, "The Navy has honest and sincere misgivings as to the ability of the Air Force successfully to deliver the [atomic] weapon by means of unescorted missions flown by present-day bombers, deep into enemy territory in the face of strong Soviet air defenses, and to drop it on targets whose locations are not accurately known." Navy carriers, however, could do the job.[8] This was a reprise of the anonymous memo leaked to Pearson in May, and must have made it clear to Forrestal that the goodwill he had hoped for at Newport had completely evaporated.

So had Forrestal's effectiveness with the president. He repeatedly tried to persuade Truman to lift his $15 billion ceiling, but to no avail. Ironically, by this time he had come to have more confidence in the efficacy of strategic bombing and would have assigned most of any additional money to the air force to develop its strategic bombing capacity[9]—and by 1948 strategic bombing was centered on use of the atomic bomb.

Air force planners had begun to place the bomb at the center of their thinking almost as soon as the clouds over Hiroshima and Nagasaki had drifted away. Symington, it will be recalled, had been impressed at Bikini by "the great new force with which the world would have to contend." Truman's decision in 1948 to limit the air force to forty-eight groups propelled the atomic bomb to the center of air force strategy. Rather than weakening everything equally, Symington and Vandenberg adopted the recommendation of a board of officers headed by Major General Muir S. Fairchild that the air force maintain its capability to strike at least one paralyzing blow in any war that should develop.[10] That paralyzing blow, everyone assumed, would be delivered by an atomic bomb.

As in other matters of strategy, Symington accepted without question the military view that the atomic bomb, powerful as it was, should be thought of as any other weapon to be deployed in accordance with the best judgment of the commanders in charge. Indeed, his attitude toward the use of the atomic bomb exhibited him at his most hawkish—he warned in a meeting of the National Security Council, at which the president's request for the development of a non-nuclear war plan was being considered, that "if we gave up the use of the bomb we might as well give up our Air Force." Later, when the Chinese entered the Korean War, he proposed that the United States immediately employ atomic bombs against China and threaten Russia with their use. David Stowe, a longtime Truman aide, recalled, "Stu Symington in those days was really one of the biggest hawks we had, and I can recall on at least two occasions the President asked Admiral Souers [executive secretary of the National Security Council, 1947–1950] and myself to visit with him and as he said, 'tie a can to this rocket.' "[11]

Symington's insistence that the air force not be prevented from using the bomb was accompanied by a strongly held view that the air force—or at least the Department of Defense—be given custody of the nation's supply. The Atomic Energy Commission, created in 1946, had been given responsibility for the manufacture and storage of all atomic weapons. The commission was obliged to consult with the legislatively established Military Liaison Committee, representing the Department of Defense, on all matters relating to the military applications of atomic energy. Despite these guarantees, the armed services remained fearful that they would not have access to atomic weapons when they needed them, nor would they be able to participate satisfactorily in the development of policies regarding their manufacture and use. As Steven Rearden put it in his excellent discussion of the custody and use issues, "In the search for answers to these critical questions, these years [1947-1950] would prove as formative, and sometimes as stormy, a period for the atomic energy program as for service unification."[12]

Symington may have been the most hawkish of the president's advisers in his position on use of the bomb, but he was joined by Forrestal, Royall, and Sullivan, as well as the JCS, in his view that the military should have custody. Truman, however, would have none of this. "As long as I am in the White House," he told Clifford, who relayed the message to David Lilienthal, chairman of the Atomic Energy Commission, "I will be opposed to taking atomic weapons away from the hands they are now in, and they will only be delivered to the military by particular order of the President issued at a time when they are needed."[13]

At Forrestal's urging, however, Truman agreed to a meeting with the service secretaries and Lilienthal to discuss the custody issue. Also present was Donald F. Carpenter, a Remington Arms Company executive who was chairman of the Military Liaison Committee of the Department of Defense. It was not a particularly happy meeting, and Symington appears to have contributed considerably to its unfortunate outcome. The session got off to a bad start when Carpenter, presenting the case for military custody, read a long memorandum setting forth the reasons why the bomb should be under the control of the Joint Chiefs of Staff. The president, obviously impatient, cut him off with a curt "I can read." Symington, apparently not sensing the president's mood, launched into an account of a recent visit to Los Alamos where "our fellas" told him that they should have the bomb. "They feel they might get them when they need them, and they might not work."

"Have they ever failed to work?" the president asked.

"No," Symington replied, "but our fellas need to get used to handling it."

Forrestal and Royall tried to reinforce Symington's point that those responsible for delivering the bomb needed to have familiarity with it, but the president was not impressed. They needed to understand, he told the group, that he had other considerations to weigh. "This is no time to be juggling an atom bomb around," he said as he abruptly adjourned the meeting.

Lilienthal, who had made the point for continued presidential control, wrote in his diary that night: "If what worried the President, in part, was whether he could trust these terrible forces in the hands of the military establishment, the performance these men gave certainly could not have been reassuring."[14]

Two days later, at the close of a cabinet meeting, Truman told Forrestal that the bomb would remain in civilian custody. Despite this, the air force continued to push its case. Many shared the view of various congressional leaders that there was "a pacific and unrealistic trend" in the Atomic Energy Commission. Regardless, custody of the bomb was central to the air force's ability to fulfill its mission. As Major General Hugh Knerr, the inspector general, argued, despite the fact that the air force had the mission of conducting strategic bombardment and that its principal weapon was the atom bomb, the air force had little control over the type of weapons the AEC produced for it, creating a situation "so confused and unstable as to practically guarantee a blow-up." Truman nevertheless remained adamant. As he told Forrestal, when advising him that he would keep the decision as to use of the bomb in his own hands, he "did not propose to have some dashing lieutenant colonel decide when would be the proper time to drop one."[15]

Truman was worried about more than the lieutenant colonels. As David McCullough suggests in his biography of the thirty-third president, Truman was beginning to have serious doubts about Forrestal's ability to lead.[16]

Forrestal and Symington seemed to be working in tandem during the custody controversy. Both were hawkish; both were preoccupied with the Soviet threat; both believed that responsibility for the development and control of nuclear weapons should be in military rather than civilian hands. As they worked together on this issue, however, their personal relationships, frayed by the months of jockeying over unification and by constant conflict over the budget, came close to collapsing.

The two men had a semi-public confrontation on April 20 in front of Sullivan and Royall when Forrestal alluded to but did not pursue charges that Symington was in a conspiracy against him. Forrestal had reacted with bitterness to the congressional appropriation for the support of a seventy-group air force, blaming Symington and declaring darkly that he "can't get away with a vote like that." Jack Anderson, Drew Pearson's assistant, told his boss: "It looks as if Forrestal still has blood in his eye, and is out to purge Symington. This has been dropped at cocktail parties where Forrestal has drank [*sic*] and talked too much, and the warnings have drifted back to Symington's office." Anderson added in his June 5 memo, "Leo [Stephen F. Leo, Symington's director of public relations] and Symington exchanged notes last night, agreed that the storm was about to break."[17]

The storm broke over a speech Symington gave to the Institute of Aeronautical Engineers in Los Angeles on July 17. Like many storms in the West, it produced much thunder and little rain. Gladwin Hill, writing in the *New York Times,* reported that Symington, "in a gloves-off talk before 500 aviation engineers roundly criticized the administration of the country's armed forces. . . . Assailing 'axe-grinders dedicated to obsolete methods' of warfare who contended that large air appropriations might 'unbalance' the three services, Mr. Symington declared air power should be put in balance not with the Army or the Navy, but with the power of potential enemies, and that 'the American people have put their money on air power.'" Hill also reported that when Symington arrived in Los Angeles he was handed a prepared speech, "presumably as approved by higher quarters in the Department of Defense," but, "considering it as too inconsequential to deliver . . . he summarily rejected it, and spoke 'off the cuff,' with frequent undisguised tinges of acerbity."[18]

Hill's story appeared in the Sunday *Times.* Forrestal wrote in his Diary for that date:

> I sent this message today to Mr. Symington:
> "If the account of your speech in Los Angeles on Friday evening, as reported by Gladwin Hill in today's *New York Times,* is accurate, it was an act of official disobedience and personal disloyalty.
> "I shall await your explanation.'

He also noted that he had called on the president during the afternoon "and told him I would have to ask for Mr. Symington's resignation unless he could provide a satisfactory explanation of his conduct in Los Angeles. I said I did this with reluctance but I had come to the conclusion that it was the only possible course. The President agreed and asked me to report to him on the conversation."[19]

The next evening the three service secretaries joined Forrestal at his home for dinner. Symington arrived early to explain what had happened in Los Angeles. The speech as originally drafted was unsatisfactory both to him and to the DOD public relations people. He asked that a revised version be sent to him by wire. It arrived in such bad shape as to be almost unusable, and was still unsatisfactory, particularly in its treatment of unification and of Forrestal. He was staying with John A. McCone, a prominent California industrialist who was also a friend of Forrestal, and the two of them worked over the speech to remove the objectionable material. Indeed, they put the finishing touches on the speech while Mrs. McCone drove them to the meeting. There wasn't time to make copies available to the press, some of whose representatives had received the earlier version released in error by air force public relations. Symington didn't speak "off the cuff," as Hill had charged, but—as he told Turner

Catledge, publisher of the *Times*—he read the speech "out of a large black book in front of everybody."[20]

Forrestal excused himself for a few minutes. When he returned, he said that he had called McCone, who had confirmed Symington's story. Symington said much later that he was furious with Forrestal for not believing him, but the matter seemed to be settled. An investigation by Harold Hinton, Forrestal's newly appointed director of public relations, further substantiated Symington's account. On July 20, R. W. Berry, Forrestal's assistant, wrote John O'Donnell of the *New York Daily News* in response to a story which O'Donnell had published that morning that Forrestal had "No idea of taking any action whatever." A review of the text showed that "instead of applying criticism," Symington had praised Forrestal's efforts to eliminate duplication.[21]

Three days later, after a cabinet meeting, Forrestal, in Symington's presence, told the president that "Mr. Symington had related extenuating circumstances" and that he wanted to be sure that the president was "fully informed on the subsequent developments."[22]

This seemed to settle the matter, but Symington remained concerned. He wrote Eisenhower, then serving as president of Columbia University, that his Los Angeles speech had been badly misreported. "It makes little difference to me what most people think," he wrote, "but it does make a difference what you think." He enclosed his letter to Catledge and Berry's to O'Donnell. He assured the general that there was "no basic difference" between the army and the air force, but warned that there was a "fundamental difference" between the air force and the navy, "and if it isn't decided soon, it will, in my opinion, become more and more dangerous from the standpoint of the security of the country."[23]

Symington also asked Arthur Krock, chief of the Washington Bureau of the *New York Times,* to join him for lunch at the Pentagon, during which, according to Krock, Symington supplied him "with chapter and verse to demonstrate that he had never merited Forrestal's doubts of his loyalty that were constantly being engendered by the troublemakers who abound in political Washington." Krock told Symington that he would publish the material if Forrestal agreed that it was accurate. He went to Forrestal's office, discussed what he proposed to write and asked if Forrestal had any objection to having it published. Forrestal replied that he would be pleased. Shortly thereafter the *Times* carried Krock's column, "The 'Insubordination' of Mr. Symington." The column related the history of policy differences between the two, concluding, "So far as this correspondent can determine, insubordination by Mr. Symington has never entered the equation and Mr. Forrestal does not think it has."[24]

The whole incident remains clouded in controversy and uncertainty. Symington discovered while he was giving the speech that a naval officer was hidden behind a curtain with a tape recorder, recalling that the man had wired a microphone near the podium so poorly that it could have electrocuted him—at one point during his speech he was heard to say, "This thing is hot!" The tape was sent to Sullivan's office in Washington. Symington asked Sullivan whether he could have a transcript and it was readily furnished. Shortly thereafter the transcript disappeared from air force files. There is no record of who read it or what it said, although Vice Admiral Fitzhugh Lee reported that Symington had said, when confronted with the tapes, that it was his understanding that his talk would be "off the record."[25]

In *Driven Patriot,* Townsend Hoopes and Douglas Brinkley paint a totally unfavorable picture of Symington's actions and his motives. They suggest that his conduct "was due in part to the fact that he suffered from extremely high blood pressure, a condition which was corrected in 1950." Actually, the condition was corrected in 1947. Hoopes and Brinkley intimate that Forrestal was afraid to fire Symington because of his powerful friends in the White House, industry, and the Congress: to have done so "would have exacerbated the explosive air force–navy dispute and could have embarrassed the President, thus further reducing his already fading prospects for election in the fall."[26]

Forrestal may have been worried about the president's "fading prospects" for reelection, but he took no part in the campaign and appears to have been negotiating with Dewey to stay on as secretary of defense. More important, he was showing increasing signs of fatigue, nervousness, and an alarming degree of paranoia. Krock later wrote that at the time of the Los Angeles speech, "I felt for the first time that there was some basis for being concerned about my old and beloved friend."[27]

Many others were equally concerned, as the secretary's increasing fatigue and nervousness became steadily more apparent, falling at times into paranoia, directed most regularly against Symington. Forrestal accused Symington of feeding information to Pearson and Winchell, who seemed to be trying to outdo each other in their attacks on the secretary of defense. Symington, declaring that "neither directly nor indirectly have I ever been party in any way or any kind whatever in any campaign against you," flatly denied the charge: "I have seen Drew Pearson twice in the last year, once at a party; your name did not come up. The last time I saw Walter Winchell was as a guest in your home at dinner. He has never spoken unfavorably to me of you."[28]

Forrestal apparently had also mentioned David Niles, administrative assistant to the president, as someone whom Symington had talked to about him. Symington wrote, "I have never discussed you with Dave Niles." Be that as it may, Symington apparently was fairly free in discussing his difficulties with Forrestal with his friends in the White House. Clifford understood them clearly. Eben Ayers, the president's assistant press secretary, wrote as follows of a conversation in the

Oval Office at which Clifford, Charles G. Ross, the president's press secretary, and General Vaughan were present, in addition to the president: "Vaughan said he had met Symington between the White House and the executive office, and that Symington's comments on Forrestal were pretty strong. Clifford and the rest of us said that the two were acting like a couple of small boys. The president said something about he might have to fire them both . . ."[29]

There was never any serious possibility that the president would fire his good friend from Missouri, irritated with him though he might have been at times. By January of 1949, however, Forrestal definitely was on the way out. Truman was not a forgiving man, and he never forgot Forrestal's perceived effort to court Dewey during the campaign in the hope that he might remain as secretary of defense. Moreover, he had become increasingly disenchanted with Forrestal's inability to make decisions and his failure to get control of the defense department. On January 11 he let Forrestal know that he intended to replace him with Louis Johnson after a transition period of several months during which Johnson's appointment would be kept a secret. Johnson's insistence plus Forrestal's obvious deterioration caused Truman to shorten the transition period. Johnson's appointment was announced March 4, and farewell ceremonies for Forrestal were scheduled for March 28.

During Forrestal's last weeks in office, the budget remained under active discussion, but most attention was being focused on efforts to reorganize the Defense Department to give the secretary greater authority, a change which both Symington and Forrestal favored. Correspondence between the two men slackened somewhat, but Forrestal continued to meet regularly with the three secretaries. On Saturday, February 5, Symington and Forrestal lunched alone, and on the ninth the Symingtons, along with the Clarks, the Snyders, and "others," were Forrestal's guests at dinner. On February 23, Forrestal and Symington spent forty-five minutes together on air force matters, and on March 4 Forrestal and the three service secretaries held an "off the record" meeting with the president about the armed forces budget.[30]

Symington had ample opportunity to observe Forrestal's condition, and noted with concern his steady deterioration. Early in 1949—and this surely contradicts many of the stories about the enmity between the two—Forrestal called and asked him to get him a good lawyer, " 'because,' he said, 'you are one of two people left I can trust and I want to change my will.' I asked if he was sure. The reply, 'Yes.' So I got him a top lawyer, Paul Porter, who was very experienced in Washington politics. After they met, Porter called to say, 'He's not in his right mind.' "[31]

Symington was present at Forrestal's farewell and Johnson's swearing-in on March 28. Forrestal apparently spent an hour with the three service secretaries in the afternoon. The next day, after a ceremony in the capitol honoring the departing secretary of defense, Symington rode back to the Pentagon with Forrestal and Louis Johnson. In an untitled memorandum, most of which dealt with the appointment of the next chairman of the Joint Chiefs of Staff, Symington wrote that he mentioned the importance of the cancellation of the B-54 program, and that Forrestal "volunteered to Mr. Johnson and myself that he was writing a memorandum to the effect he believed it was wise."[32]

This was probably the last time Symington saw Forrestal alive. In the early morning hours of May 22, Forrestal plunged to his death from the sixteenth floor of the U.S. Naval Hospital in Bethesda. Symington joined virtually all of official Washington in expressing shock and grief at the tragedy, telling the *New York Times,* "After years of personal and official association with Mr. Forrestal, his death comes as a great shock. On my behalf and that of the Air Force, I extend deepest sympathy to members of Mr. Forrestal's family and to his many close associates and friends."[33] He undoubtedly attended the funeral, but he was not among the twenty persons (including Sullivan and Royall) listed as honorary pallbearers. No one from the air force was included.

Years later Symington was asked about Forrestal's breakdown. He mentioned personal problems, problems at home, his wife's drinking, "But the main reason was the unification controversy. This destroyed Forrestal."[34]

The "unification controversy" permeated Forrestal's entire tenure as secretary of defense. Largely at his insistence, the Congress had created an organization that even a strong, resolute leader would have been unable to manage, and Forrestal was neither strong nor resolute. Moreover, Truman's fiscal policies, severely limiting the amount of money available for the armed services, set up a situation that made conflict inevitable. To this was added genuine differences between the air force and the navy regarding strategy.

Symington accepted without question air force doctrine on strategic bombing, and as civilian head of the air force he devoted his great energy and very considerable talents to selling that doctrine. He was frustrated at every turn by Forrestal's insistence upon the maintenance of "balanced forces," which in Symington's view was simply a means to justify the politically easy equal distribution of funds among the army, navy, and air force without reference to their roles in the nation's defense in the atomic age. Moreover, he looked upon the navy's efforts to develop strategic air capability as unnecessarily and dangerously duplicative. Many in the air force remained suspicious of what they considered to be Forrestal's pro-navy bias and attributed his lukewarm support of the air force to this prejudice.

The press, with its penchant for personalizing issues, made much of the conflict between Forrestal and Symington. They talked of Symington's "insubordination" and of his "victories" over the secretary of defense. Symington repeatedly insisted that his differences with his longtime tennis and golfing partner were based solely on principle, but he seems to have been fairly free in talking about Forrestal with his friends in the White House. Symington had numerous friends there; Forrestal had relatively few. Forrestal, as his paranoia increased, became convinced that Symington was disloyal and was out to do him in—yet his request to Symington to "get him a good lawyer" was at least a break in the paranoia.

Forrestal's biographers have generally accepted the journalistic view, and in one instance even intimated that Symington contributed to Forrestal's breakdown. Symington, unfortunately, did little to correct the record. Throughout his life, he maintained the policy of "Never speak ill of the dead." For example, in response to a series of statements regarding his relationship with Forrestal submitted by a person who was writing a biography, he wrote: "With respect to the assertions given you and to which you refer, some are false in implication, some are just not true; therefore, I believe it is best not to comment on them. Jim Forrestal was an American Patriot who did his best." At one time he was asked to compare Louis Johnson with Forrestal. He replied, "He was not in the same league."[35]

But it was Louis Johnson with whom Symington would be dealing as he carried on the fight for air power and faced the greatest crisis of his years as secretary of the air force—the controversy over the B-36 and the Revolt of the Admirals.

14

Showdown with the Navy

THE NAVY'S uniformed leaders never accepted the decision made at Key West and reaffirmed at Newport to grant the air force primacy in strategic bombing, including use of the atomic bomb. The result was an unseemly public brawl over strategy and organization that shook the newly created Department of Defense to its foundations and spread great confusion in the public at large.[1]

At first naval spokesmen questioned the wisdom of relying on strategic bombardment; later they directed their criticism against the long-range heavy bomber as the principal delivery vehicle, asserting that carrier-based planes were much more efficient. To launch and land aircraft capable of carrying an atomic bomb, the navy would need a larger carrier than anything then in the fleet. To meet the need, Fleet Admiral Chester V. Nimitz, who had led the navy to victory in the Pacific and was now serving as chief of naval operations, began in January 1948 to seek authorization and funding for a sixty-five-thousand-ton super carrier costing $120 million. With Truman's $15 billion cap on defense expenditures, both the air force and the army saw this as a serious threat to their own appropriations. In addition the air force saw the super carrier as an unwarranted expansion of the navy's mission.

In making their case before Congress, naval spokesmen repeatedly emphasized that the super carrier had been approved by the Joint Chiefs of Staff. The big carrier never went before the Joint Chiefs for approval. Forrestal simply told them at Key West that the president had approved it. Spaatz, still serving as air force chief of staff, replied that the decision of his commander-in-chief was acceptable to him as a subordinate. When Admiral Louis Denfield told the House Armed Services Committee that the JCS had approved the carrier, Vandenberg, who had succeeded Spaatz as chief of staff, protested to Forrestal that such an interpretation was wholly unwarranted. "I have not felt nor do I now feel," he wrote, "that I can give my approval to the 65,000 ton carrier project."[2]

Forrestal did not correct the navy's version of events, and Congress authorized construction. Johnson, who succeeded Forrestal, was determined to reduce expenditures and put down interservice rivalry, hinting that he might have to "knock some heads together." He was an ardent believer in air power and had little use for the navy. Symington, in a long letter to his father-in-law complaining about the navy's tactics in getting approval for the super carrier, wrote, "I am confident Secretary Johnson will put a stop to all this queer business."[3]

On June 23, five days after its keel had been laid with great fanfare, Johnson canceled all work on the *United States,* apparently after very little consultation. Sullivan, who learned of the decision after the fact while visiting naval installations in Corpus Christi, Texas, hurried back to Washington and penned an indignant letter of resignation. Although no one defended Johnson's heavy-handed tactics, the decision itself attracted general support. The chairmen of both the House and Senate Armed Services Committees supported it. Carl Vinson, erstwhile "father of the modern navy," commented, "The Navy with this big carrier would have been trespassing into the field of strategic bombing which belongs to the Air Force."[4]

With its penchant for designating "winners" and "losers," the press trumpeted or lamented the air force's "victory." In a perceptive article, the *U.S. News and World Report* observed that the cancellation of the super carrier "formally signaled" the "basic change" taking place in defense policy. "The Air Force . . . has been moving up to replace the Navy as the first line of defense and as the favored service. This change in roles is now fixed by the decision to deny the Navy the offensive air weapon it had shaped as a bid to retain its position."[5]

The navy and its partisans had no intention of giving up. They maintained a steady drumbeat of criticism of the whole idea of intercontinental strategic bombing, and particularly of the B-36, the mammoth six-engine plane with which the air force proposed to carry out its mission. David Lawrence, who despite his friendship with Symington tended to follow the navy line, wrote that Truman and Johnson, in relying solely on the air force and its long-range strategic bombers, were "willing to risk the loss of American cities." The *New York Times*'s Hanson W. Baldwin, no friend of Symington or the air force, declared that cancellation of the super carrier and the subsequent resignation of Secretary Sullivan "may provide the powder train that will lead to explosive events in the National Military Establishment."[6]

The "explosive events" were not long in coming.

On May 26, Pennsylvania Republican James E. Van Zandt, a naval reserve captain, rose in the House, in the midst of a discussion on aid to Greece and Turkey, to say that "ugly, disturbing reports" were beginning to circulate through Washington about the B-36 and the air force's procurement practices. He charged that even after having found the B-36 to be unsatisfactory as a bomber, the air force canceled contracts for other planes in order to purchase additional B-36s. All of this, he asserted, was done to benefit Floyd Odlum, who had acquired control of Consolidated Vultee, manufacturer of the B-36. Odlum, he said, had helped Louis Johnson raise money for the president's reelection campaign and was a good friend of Symington's. "It is reported," he hinted ominously, "that Mr. Symington is a frequent week-end visitor at the Palm Springs, Calif., ranch home of Mr. Odlum and his wife, the former Jacqueline Cochrane; that the logbooks of the 'Dew Drop' plane, which Mr. Symington uses as his personal aircraft, will record many visits to Palm Springs." He also reported that he had heard that Odlum was in the process of setting up "a huge aircraft combine" and that "there is a plan under way for Mr. Symington to resign as Secretary of Air as soon as the 1950 budget containing more funds for the B-36 is approved and head this huge aircraft combine." He admitted that he could not prove any of his statements, "though I do emphatically assert that they are so prevalent and so persistent as to require a congressional investigation without further delay."[7]

Symington fired off an angry letter to Vinson, who had indicated that the House Military Affairs Committee would look into the matter, hand-carrying it to Vinson's office. He categorically denied all of Van Zandt's charges, calling them "damaging to the good name of the armed services, to the morale of the patriotic men who serve in them, and to the national interest." He concurred in Vinson's decision to investigate the whole matter and expressed the hope that it would prove possible to trace the anonymous charges to their source.[8]

Symington asked Barton Leach to come down from Harvard to help in preparing testimony for Vinson's committee. Leach thought it was important that the whole history of the B-36 be reviewed in preparation for the hearings. More important than the personal attacks was the process by which the decision was reached to concentrate air force efforts on the B-36. It was an open secret that the big plane had been controversial from the beginning. Even if one could successfully counter the charges of personal malfeasance, there was always the question of judgment.[9]

The origins of the B-36 can be traced to 1941, before the United States entered the war. AAF planners, faced with the prospect of a defeated Britain, became convinced that they needed a bomber capable of reaching European targets from bases in the United States. Consolidated Vultee, Boeing, Douglas, Martin, and Northrup were asked to prepare design studies.[10] Because the demands of the war required planes in being rather than on the drawing board, the project languished during the early months of the conflict. The War Department gave Convair a production order for one hundred B-36s in the spring of 1944, but without a priority rating. There had been some thought earlier that the B-36 might be useful in the Pacific war, but this action made it clear that the United States planned to win the war without it.

In postwar plans, however, the B-36 came to the fore as the key to fulfilling the AAF's primary mission—strategic bombing. The AAF Materiel Command at Wright Field proclaimed the B-36 as "more than 200 percent efficient as the B-29," calling it "our only completely new design toward the further development and advancement of the conventional heavy bomber to which so much of the success of AAF operations may be attributed."[11]

Unhappily, neither Convair nor the B-36 lived up to expectations. Delays and cost overruns soured many in the AAF, and the maiden flight on August 8, 1946, despite AAF and Convair public relations hype, did little to sweeten their attitudes. Design flaws and performance that fell short of expectations made it clear that much work needed to be done before the B-36 could become a viable addition to the nation's air arsenal.

Symington, as assistant secretary of war for air, joined the public relations parade. It will be recalled that a few weeks before the plane's first flight, he told a Chamber of Commerce gathering in Honolulu, "The B-36 . . . can fly 10,000 miles with an atomic bomb." At his home in St. Louis, where he had gone to rest after his around-the-world trip, he told reporters, "Our new 10,000-mile bombers can fly easily across the North Pole and the Arctic Region. From bases in the continental U.S. or from our outlying bases, they can reach any of the capitals or industrial centers of Europe. They can reach the heart of all those countries that have in the past engaged in world wide war."[12]

Symington was a salesman, not an engineer, and a little hyperbole perhaps could be excused. Moreover, his exaggerations were not as extreme as those of some of the officers on whom he depended for his information—Spaatz, for example—or the air force public relations people whose enthusiasm, he soon concluded, was getting out of hand. He cautioned Rosy O'Donnell, chief of AAF public relations, "From here on out, I would play it down, down, down."[13]

There was ample reason to play it down. The first flight, despite all the hoopla, had been disappointing. George Kenney, commander of the newly formed Strategic Air Command, whose men would have to fly the plane, was openly hostile. The B-36, he charged, was too slow, it was poorly designed, and its effective range had been grossly overstated. He was "seriously concerned about the practicability of continuing production on the scale now planned." He believed they should scrap it and start over. On the other hand, Lieutenant General Nathan F. Twining, commanding general of the Air Materiel Command, argued that the plane's potential should not be judged solely by the early experimental models, pointing out that the B-17, which performed so effectively over Germany in World War II, was a far cry from the early experimental model. Besides, he argued, "With the recent severe slash of research and development funds, it becomes imperative that the Army Air Forces maintain its potency to the highest possible degree." This argued for staying with the B-36 and trying to improve it. Most of the high command, including Spaatz, sided with Twining. They had become convinced that strategic bombing with atomic weapons would be the primary mission of the air force in any future war, and they placed a much higher priority on forces in being than those which could be developed over a period of time. Spaatz, however, recognized some of Kenney's concerns by authorizing the replacement of the original engines with new variable discharge turbines plus certain design changes, including the installation of self-sealing gasoline tanks.[14] The additional cost would be absorbed by reducing the number of planes on order from 100 to 92 or 93.

Even so, costs zoomed out of sight. Shortly after he became secretary, Symington, understandably worried, asked Arthur Barrows, his newly appointed undersecretary, "When you get around to it, please look into quietly the B-36 contract with Consolidated Vultee—this from the standpoint of price, delivery, value, nature of contract, allowable costs, GAO auditing (I understand it is cost-plus-fixed-fee), etc."[15]

Symington had heard disquieting rumors, but he tended to attribute them to people around Forrestal who were hostile to the air force. An investigation by the inspector general, however, revealed that there were many aspects of the air force's negotiations with Convair that were less than straightforward. Colonel B. C. Kelsey, chief of the Air Materiel Command's control group, wrote Lieutenant General Howard Craig, deputy chief of staff, materiel: "Through a combination of errors and apparent mismanagement, the B-36C situation has been permitted to reach a situation where it may be difficult if not impossible to salvage the program with any degree of satisfaction." He was highly critical of both Convair and air force supervision of the project, which he called "extremely casual, if not negligent." The VDT engine, in particular, had proven to be a costly mistake, and various other design features had not borne up under rigorous inspection. Norstad, concurring in the decision to abandon the VDT, recommended that the entire B-36 project be cut back.[16]

A meeting in Symington's office on April 21 found senior air force officials badly split. McNarney, Vandenberg, and Wolfe favored cancellation. Arguing for continuation, Fairchild spoke convincingly about the B-36 as a deterrent to potential enemies. Barrows opposed cancellation on the basis of cost. Symington, who had tended to favor cancellation, came down on the side of continuation. The other three agreed to go along.[17]

Faced with divided counsel and mounting uncertainties, Symington flew to Fort Worth to look over the Convair plant and talk to his good friend, Amon Carter, publisher of the *Fort Worth Star-Telegram*.[18] Carter strongly supported the B-36—as might be expected—and urged Symington to watch it perform. He did that, studied performance data, and talked to Convair officials and Major General Roger Ramey, commanding the Eighth Air Force. All of this convinced him that they should go ahead, and before he left Fort Worth he used a Consolidated Vultee letterhead to send a "secret eyes only" memorandum to General Montgomery for delivery to Forrestal, charging that most of the criticism "was just a lot of nonsense."[19]

Symington's Fort Worth trip was something of a turning point for the B-36 program. Within the air force criticism of the plane virtually dried up. Even Kenney became converted. "This is the airplane for the strategic destruction of any conceivable enemy, anywhere, in any war within the next five years," he told a press conference in Fort Worth.[20] LeMay, who succeeded Kenney at the Strategic Air Command, strongly supported the B-36 as the best heavy bomber available, and the only one which would enable the air force to carry out its strategic bombing responsibilities, pending the delivery of jet bombers (the B-47 and B-52) then on the drawing boards. Moreover, the president's refusal to increase the defense budget beyond $15 billion (and the air force beyond forty-eight groups) made it imperative that the air force concentrate its purchases on as few aircraft as possible.

Acting on the recommendation of a small board of senior officers headed by General McNarney, Symington announced on January 11, 1949, the cancellation of a number of orders to free about $300 million for buying "a substantial additional number of B-36's and extensive modernization and improvement of other B-36's and B-50's [an extensively modified B-29], which are now on contract."[21]

The announcement created great consternation in the aircraft industry, and the aggressive manner in which Convair's public relations people trumpeted the decision added fuel to the flames. Their press release not only contained exaggerated claims for the B-36 but also included unfavorable remarks about other planes, particularly the Northrup B-49 "Flying Wing," which had been passed over.

Sources in the aviation industry hinted darkly that the Flying Wing had lost out because Northrup had failed to follow a suggestion from Symington that they merge with Convair, which had been bought by the Atlas Corporation, headed by Floyd Odlum.[22] These circumstances were the stuff of which good, long-lasting rumors are made, but the facts do not support this one. It is true that the air force had considerable interest in the Flying Wing as a possible alternative to the B-36. It was generally believed, however, that Northrup's facilities in Hawthorne, California, were inadequate for production. General Mc-Narney, who was favorably impressed with the B-49, suggested that Northrup and Convair arrange to produce it jointly in Convair's plant at Fort Worth. Several meetings were held to try to work it out, but no agreement could be reached. At this juncture Symington arrived in Los Angeles for his celebrated speech to the Institute of Aeronautical Science. John McCone suggested to Odlum and Northrup that they meet at his home with Symington to see if something could be worked out. Odlum suggested that Northrup merge with Convair. This seemed like a good idea to Symington, but Northrup objected. He wanted an interim solution of subcontracting the production work to Convair, and this was agreed on.

Meanwhile, as the B-36 improved, opinion in the air force solidified behind it, with General LeMay its leading proponent. With the limited funds available, the air force could not afford to develop two long-range bombers at the same time. The B-36 looked like the better bet.

Northrup was not the only aircraft manufacturer disgruntled by the B-36 decision. Boeing in Seattle lamented the cancellation of the B-54, although their sense of injury was ameliorated by work on the B-47 going forward in their Wichita plant. But not so the press in Seattle. Unimpressed by jobs in Wichita, Seattle newspapers complained that the decision to cancel the B-54 had never been satisfactorily explained, hinting darkly that politics might have been involved. Their unhappiness was assuaged somewhat by the decision to go forward with the new jet-powered B-52 in Seattle.[23]

Glenn L. Martin's complaints were not so easily disposed of. He lost the B-48 medium bomber, then in the research stage. The Air Materiel Command recommended, and Symington agreed, that no more than one medium bomber should be developed, and Boeing's B-47 had much greater potential. Unable to sell his product on its merits, Martin went the political route, asking Senator Millard Tydings to intercede. Tydings and Symington were good friends, and their wives were particularly close. Moreover, the Maryland senator was chairman of the Senate Armed Services Committee. Tydings's influence probably got Martin more extended consideration than he otherwise would have received, but in the end Symington refused to budge from the recommendations of the Air Materiel Command, supported by Vandenberg, that they not go forward with the B-48. In addition, the air force decided not to order Martin's medium transport plane, the 2-0-2. Martin felt badly mistreated.[24]

It was in this atmosphere that Van Zandt hurled his charges on the floor of the House. Symington had categorically denied them all in his letter to Vinson, but he was anxious to refute them in detail before the committee. Senior air force officers also were anxious to set the record straight. As George W. Watson put it, "At stake was much more than an investigation into the merits of the plane. Air Force missions and strategic doctrines were under fire, as well as Air Force leaders."[25]

In the weeks leading up to the hearings the air over Washington grew thick with charges, most of them centering on Symington and, to an increasing degree, Louis Johnson, who during the war had worked for Convair. The charges played heavily on Symington's friendship with Odlum, with assertions made that the two men were planning to form a huge aircraft manufacturing combine after Symington left office. Symington denied these and other charges, challenging Van Zandt to repeat them under oath. The congressman artfully replied that there was no need for that since he had conceded that he was in no position to prove anything, "and would be quite happy if the investigation establishes that all of the ugly rumors are false."[26]

Van Zandt continued his campaign throughout June and July, suggesting that if the charges against Johnson and Symington held up, "the '5 percenters' were playing a penny ante game by comparison." Van Zandt's credibility began to erode, however, even before the hearings began. Drew Pearson published a column pointing out that Van Zandt's charges followed almost word for word the language of an anonymous document, "first circulated by a well-known manufacturer of Navy planes."[27] That "well known manufacturer" turned out to be Glenn L. Martin, apparently seeking revenge for what he believed to be his shabby treatment at the hands of Symington and the air force.

The long-awaited hearings before the House Armed Services Committee began August 9. As far as Symington and the air force were concerned, they could not have gone better. As Murray Green analyzed their problem, they had to deal with three issues: whether the concept of strategic bombing was valid, whether the B-36 could carry out this concept, and whether any irregularities or improprieties had governed the decisions made since mid-1948 to retain and then to augment the program.[28] They scored direct hits on all three.

From the beginning, it was clear that Van Zandt had relatively little support. Indeed, several members of the House suggested that there really was no need for an investigation. Georgia Democrat Edward Cox told the Rules Committee that he thought the whole thing could be settled if Van Zandt would withdraw his statement and issue a public apology: "No man in Congress or in Washington or any where else that knows Stuart Symington would give any credit whatever to this statement." Howard Smith of Virginia commented, "I am convinced of one thing: When it is all over you will find Stu Symington is clean."[29]

Robert Lovett, who had been assistant secretary of war for air when planning for the B-36 was begun, led off. He denied that there had been any outside influences in the decision, and he talked convincingly about the need for an intercontinental bomber. Speaking about the Berlin blockade, he said, "The only thing . . . [that] restrained them [Russia] from aggression was the atomic bomb and a method of delivering them in some quantity."[30]

Lovett was followed by an impressive array of air force generals who testified to the importance of strategic bombing capability and the quality of the B-36. LeMay, who as commander of SAC had operational control of the heavy bombers, assumed direct responsibility for the decision leading to their purchase. When asked by Joseph B. Keenan, committee counsel, if he would assume responsibility as the chief advocate of the B-36, he said, "Yes, I certainly would . . . If I am called upon to fight, I will order my crews out in those airplanes, and I expect to be in the first one myself."[31]

General Vandenberg, who preceded Symington on August 12, defended both strategic bombing and the B-36. "We are convinced," he said, "that for the next few years the B-36 provides the spearhead of the ready-for-combat force in being which this country must constantly have at hand. Like any other aircraft it will in due time be superseded by a better one. Its successor is now in the design stage." He added a ringing defense of his boss: "That Mr. Symington could have entertained the idea of jeopardizing the security of this country by favoring inferior airplanes for the monetary advantage of a political party or because of the personal influence of an individual manufacturer is utterly unthinkable."[32]

When Symington took the stand, he assured the committee that the B-36 was a true intercontinental bomber, that nothing available would equal it, and that no consideration other than national security had influenced the decision to purchase it. He discussed in detail the process by which approvals for the B-36 had been secured, categorically denying all of Van Zandt's allegations. When he concluded, Vinson complimented him "on the frank, candid manner in which you answered each and every one of the allegations that has been made against you personally and against the Air Force." There followed some rather tedious questioning by Joseph Keenan, covering Symington's entire career in government, the operations of the air force, and the secretary's political views. Symington was not particularly happy with Keenan's handling of the investigation, and it is clear from reading the transcript that he was having some difficulty maintaining his patience. Louisiana Democrat Overton Brooks, possibly sensing Symington's irritation, said, "These are very serious charges against you personally and against the Air Force. I do not suppose this has given you any personal enjoyment in having these charges brought against you or the Air Force." Symington responded: "I mentioned in my comment, sir, that I do not see how you are going to get businessmen in Government—the only thing they get out of it is honor—and with such false charges you reward them, when they come in, by accusing them of dishonor."[33]

Committee members were interested in trying to track down the author of the famous "anonymous document" that seemed to be the basis of many of Van Zandt's charges. Symington said he knew who the author or authors were—as, indeed, he did—but Vinson did not want to discuss this at that time. The proceedings almost got out of hand. Van Zandt, trying to give some credibility to his sources, repaired to newspaper accounts. When he started reading from an article by Danton Walker in the *Washington Times-Herald* which suggested that Symington would soon be fired because Louis Johnson was "riding herd on the Missouri gang," Symington broke in, "Mr. Chairman, am I to understand that I have to sit here and listen to the Congressman read a lot of stuff from Danton Walker?"[34] Vinson decided that he didn't, that Van Zandt should turn his newspaper clippings over to the committee's counsel.

Symington was not through. He lashed out at Van Zandt for impugning the motives of the air force's high command and for "a rather disgraceful way of utilizing congressional immunity." Van Zandt once again tried to defend himself. He declared that he had only done his duty as a member of Congress, that he had made no accusations, that he had "simply repeated rumors, and they were ugly rumors . . . that were certainly detrimental to the morale of the armed forces." He hoped that the investigation would clear the air, "and those in charge of our armed forces will no longer have to work under a cloud of suspicion."

Vinson was not impressed. He said, "Mr. Van Zandt, you have given voice to rumors." He did not accuse his colleague of being the author of the anonymous document that seemed to be the source of most of the rumors, but he commented on "the funny coincidence" that Van Zandt's words were the same as those of the anonymous document. He recessed the hearings so that a subcommittee could go out to Los Angeles to take testimony from various aircraft manufacturers.[35]

Symington clearly had carried the day. Newspapers in all parts of the country commented on his challenge to Van Zandt to come out from under his cloak of congressional immunity, using such headlines as, "AIR BOSS DARES B-36 CRITIC: SAY IT AGAIN," "AIR BOSS DARES ACCUSER TO DROP LEGAL IMMUNITY."

The testimony in Los Angeles revealed no hint of impropriety on the part of Symington or others in the air force, nothing to substantiate Van Zandt's charges. Northrup's testimony was particularly interesting in view of the controversy surrounding the cancellation of the B-49 and stories about pressure on Northrup to merge with Convair. He denied that there had been any pressure whatever or any impropriety in connection with the decision to cancel the B-49. At the conclusion of the Los Angeles hearings, Illinois Democrat Melvin Price, subcommittee chairman, stated publicly that the charges against Symington and Odlum "have been completely exploded."[36]

Indeed they had. By the time the hearings resumed in Washington on August 22, everybody's attention was focused on the authorship of the notorious anonymous document upon which so many of Van Zandt's allegations were based. On August 21 Van Zandt heightened the suspense by releasing still another anonymous document. This one described the shabby treatment that Glenn L. Martin was supposed to have received at the hands of the air force and reiterated charges of favoritism in awarding the B-36 contract.[37]

Symington had suggested in his earlier testimony that he was quite sure he could identify the person or persons responsible for the original document. As soon as Van Zandt leveled his charges, Symington had asked Brigadier General Joseph Carroll, head of the air force office of special investigations, to see if he could track down the author.[38] Using his connections in the FBI, Carroll was able to trace authorship to Cedric R. Worth, a former lieutenant commander who was serving as an aide to Undersecretary of the Navy Dan Kimball. Symington had passed this information to Vinson, but the chairman, anxious to maintain "orderly proceedings," wanted to withhold discussion of the document until the scheduled witnesses had testified. Vinson, however, had a rebellion on his hands. Van Zandt, apparently trying to salvage some measure of credibility, angrily demanded that the anonymous writer be subpoenaed, "so we can bring these charges and the man who made them out in the open instead of blundering along in the dark." Several other members of the committee also insisted on finding out who the author was. Keenan joined the rebellion. "Mr. Chairman," he snapped, "in view of the turn taken by this hearing, I am not willing to proceed with any other witnesses until we hear from Mr. Deane [North Carolina Democratic Congressman Charles B. Deane, who had a copy of the document and who apparently knew who had written it] and Mr. Symington."

Vinson gave in and called Symington to come to the hearing. As Symington rushed over from his office in the Pentagon, the committee heard General Bradley. His important testimony, which assured the committee that the Joint Chiefs of Staff decision to approve the B-36 was based solely on merit, was lost on the committee and the growing crowd, anxious for the secretary of the air force to appear. As soon as Symington arrived he took the witness chair, but before he could begin Vinson asked him to stand aside. "Is Mr. Worth in the room?" he asked. "Yes, sir," came the reply, from a tall, graying man in the doorway. Called to the witness chair, Worth readily admitted authorship. He insisted that he was the sole author, although he admitted that he had assistance from Commander Thomas Davies, an aide to Admiral Radford, and Glenn Martin.[39]

Worth's confession completely discredited Van Zandt's charges, and for all practical purposes brought the procurement phase of the hearings to an end. Before recessing—the committee would still take up the whole question of strategic bombing—committee members of both parties unanimously approved a statement by Vinson declaring,

> There has not been, in the judgment of the committee, one iota, not one scintilla of evidence offered thus far in these hearings that would support charges that collusion, fraud, corruption, influence, or favoritism played any part whatsoever in the procurement of the B-36 bomber.
>
> There has been very substantial and compelling evidence that the Air Force selected this bomber, procured this bomber solely on the ground that this is the best aircraft for its purpose available to the Nation today.
>
> At this time I feel that the Nation should know that the Secretary of the Air, Mr. Symington, and the leaders of the Air Force, the Secretary of Defense, have come through this inquiry without the slightest blemish and that these men continue to merit the complete confidence of the American people in their past action and in the future.[40]

Symington's star had never shone brighter, but even before the congratulatory comments started to come in, he offered an olive branch to the navy. He wrote and made public a memorandum to Secretary Johnson expressing "complete confidence in the character and integrity of not only Secretary Matthews, but also Undersecretary Kimball, Admiral Denfield, the Chief of Naval Operations, and all those other fine officers of the Navy who have done and who are doing so much to protect the security of the United States."[41]

The memo was a bit too magnanimous and even self-serving. Stephen Early, who had been sent over from the White House to serve as Johnson's undersecretary, wrote, "There is a touch of U. S. Grant in your memo to Sec. Johnson re Kimball, etc.—they keep their horses. And this from a rebel." Paul Porter, who was serving on the United Nations Conciliation Commission for Palestine, wrote from Lausanne, Switzerland, "There is an old Arab proverb which says: 'When you make 'em eat it, don't put any perfume on it.'"[42] Whether self-serving or not, the memo was vintage Symington. He almost always leaned over backwards to be gracious. He was not a very good loser—perhaps that's why he seldom lost—but he was always a gracious winner.

The navy's top leadership reacted vigorously to the Worth fiasco. Matthews suspended Worth and ordered a court of inquiry. It failed to produce much. They tried to get a copy of the OSI report that had identified Worth, but Symington refused to give them one on the grounds that it was in the hands of the House Armed Services Committee and could be released only by them. As Murray Green wrote, "that plus the welter of contradictions among the witnesses and their seeming reluctance to cross-examine each other to develop some semblance of a coherent story as to what actually happened combined to augur a speedy end to the court. The net impact upon observers was one of utter confusion."[43]

Members of the court wanted Symington to appear as a witness, but he declined on the ground that the information he possessed was based on a report which had been turned over to the House Armed Services Committee, and that for him to testify "would in effect be doing indirectly what the Chairman has instructed that I not do directly." In addition, he felt that it would be inappropriate for him, "as Secretary of the Air Force . . . [to testify] on matters concerning the internal affairs of the Navy Department."[44]

The admirals on the court were irritated with Symington's refusal to appear voluntarily and threatened to subpoena him, but Matthews intervened to prevent it.[45] Meanwhile, a volunteer witness was making headlines.

Captain John G. Crommelin wanted very much to testify, and when the court's first recess prevented that, he issued a statement associating himself with Worth's charges, asserting that the navy's offensive power was being "nibbled to death" in the Pentagon.[46] Despite the drama associated with a young war hero putting his career on the line, Crommelin's charges might not have had much effect had they not been supported by others, notably retired Fleet Admiral William A. "Bull" Halsey and Rear Admiral Austin Doyle, commanding the navy's air training program. At the same time, the country was being flooded with another anonymous document, "The Strategic Bombing Myth," circulated by James G. Stahlman, a naval reserve officer who was publisher of the *Nashville Banner*. Relying heavily on reports of the United States Strategic Bombing Survey, the document purported to demonstrate that strategic bombing was the same as area bombing—therefore illegal as well as immoral—and that it had been a failure in World War II.[47]

Symington stated that he thought the new document was worse than the one Worth had written, but he expressed the belief that the navy was not responsible.[48] Despite his conciliatory public statements, there is little doubt that Symington was convinced certain high-ranking naval officers were determined to discredit the air force, and, if possible, derail unification. He had expressed these concerns publicly and privately on numerous occasions. There soon appeared dramatic evidence that his concerns were justified.

On October 4, the day before the House Armed Services Committee was to resume hearings, the *New York Times* published a letter from Vice Admiral Gerald Bogan, Commander, First Task Fleet, stating that the morale of the navy was "lower today than at any time since I entered the commissioned ranks in 1916." He attributed it to "a genuine fear in the Navy for the security of the country," a result of "policies followed by the Department of Defense since our National Security Act became law." Admiral Arthur Radford, commanding the Pacific Fleet, forwarded the letter with the comment, "rightly or wrongly, the majority of officers in the Pacific Fleet concur with Captain Crommelin and with the ideas expressed by Vice Admiral Bogan." Admiral Louis Denfield, chief of naval operations, forwarded the correspondence to Secretary Matthews, concurring in the sentiments expressed.[49]

The letters, which had been "handed to reporters by a naval source in a shadowy corridor of a downtown [Washington] office building," made it clear that the naval high command was prepared to go all out once it got before the committee. On October 7, the second day of the hearings, Radford laid out the navy's case. Calling the B-36 a "billion dollar blunder," the navy's number-one airman lashed out at a strategy that promised the American people "a cheap and easy victory should war come." Even if the strategy were sound, the B-36 was incapable of carrying it out. Relying on "technical witnesses" (primarily navy commanders and lieutenant commanders), Radford asserted that existing or soon-to-be-introduced fighter aircraft could easily track and destroy the B-36, and even if it got through to the target it would be unable to hit its target from high altitudes. The result would be area bombing that would produce the extermination of civilians and widespread destruction of the basis for achieving a stable postwar economy. He charged that Secretary Johnson "stifled" the navy and characterized his decision to cancel the *United States* as "a grave mistake." Radford was followed by other witnesses, notably Rear Admiral Ralph J. Ofstie, a member of the Military Liaison Committee to the Atomic Energy Commission, who argued that strategic bombing was not related to national policy, and Admiral Denfield. The CNO faced an awkward situation. As a member of the Joint Chiefs of Staff he had approved the joint emergency war plans that provided for air operations employing the atomic bomb, to be carried out by the Strategic Air Command, as the only major offensive action in the early stage of a war. He had also approved purchase of B-36s.[50] Nevertheless, he endorsed the views expressed by the earlier witnesses. He did not join Radford in criticizing Secretary Johnson.

The navy's testimony created quite a stir in the country and in the committee. It seemed for a time that Vinson might be wavering in his support of the air force and returning to his earlier pro-navy position.[51] The air force knew that it faced a daunting task.

Early in planning for the hearings, Leach, who was organizing the process, had urged that the air force attack the super carrier and the navy's ability to carry out its mission.[52] Symington, in line with his policy of never initiating criticism of a sister service, ruled this out. Instead, they would concentrate on defense of the B-36 and strategic bombing, and would devote their testimony to refuting the navy's charges.

Symington led off. In day-long testimony he lashed out at the navy's witnesses, particularly Radford,[53] questioning their motives and denying every one of their allegations. He charged the admirals with "spreading untruths" and endangering national security. He expressed contempt for the navy's "expert witnesses," comparing "these young officers" with Generals LeMay, Kenney, Norstad, and Vandenberg. "You decide, as you, of course, have the right to do . . . whose opinion you thought was right." He asked the committee how they would feel if junior air force officers would have attacked the experienced views of top navy officers on the efficacy of the aircraft carrier.[54]

As for the charge that strategic bombing was immoral, he said, "If this country's safety is at stake, for the life of me I can't see the difference in trying to stop the man on the lathe building a bomber to attack the United States and trying to stop a soldier. If civilians are going to be killed, I'd rather have them their civilians than our civilians."[55]

He denied that the air force was "putting all of its eggs in one basket." B-36 purchases amounted to only 16.3 percent of the total expenditures on air force planes. Only four of the authorized forty-eight groups were to be equipped with B-36 bombers, and even if the air force were able to go to fifty-eight or seventy groups it would still have only four groups of B-36 bombers. He pointed out that the cost of all additional B-36s purchased since the original contract for one hundred was let amounted to less than $1\frac{1}{4}$ percent of the budget of the Military Establishment for the fiscal years 1949, 1950, and 1951. He added: "That figure cannot but be impressive, not only because it so completely destroys the 'all eggs in one basket' fallacy, but also because it illustrates so well the relatively very little amount of money that has been, and is being, spent on the surest way to deliver the atomic bomb or any other type bomb against any aggressor and from our own shores."[56]

He also denied that the air force had gone around Secretary Forrestal, placing him in the awkward position of having to go along with air force plans or repudiating them after they had been announced. The record would show, Symington said, that Forrestal had concurred in all the basic decisions regarding the B-36. Seizing the opportunity to clinch his argument by coming to the defense of Forrestal, he added: "he [Forrestal] would not have hesitated to repudiate plans which he believed opposed to the national interest. To imply otherwise is to misjudge the character of a great American."[57]

Vandenberg followed. He reviewed the JCS decisions with respect to strategic bombing, emphasizing the air force at no time had intimated that it would be the only element in victory. He also defended the B-36 as the best strategic bomber available at the time. "I think the country should know," he said, "that the officers who are in charge of the strategic bombing program . . . have heard [the navy assertions] . . . and have concluded that the assertions are unfounded. The men who have arrived at that conclusion are the most experienced men in the world in conducting long-range operations."[58]

Vandenberg was assisted by Bradley. Indeed, Bradley made one of the major headlines to come out of the hearings when he referred to the admirals as " 'fancy dans' who won't hit the line on every play with all they have unless they can call the signals." In some respects, Bradley, aroused by what he believed to be the navy's efforts to subvert unification, was the most persuasive witness to appear before the committee. Laying out the strategic situation facing the United States, he brought up the question of the atomic bomb. Navy witnesses, in addition to criticizing the B-36, had repeatedly referred to the folly of "relying on an atomic blitz" to win a future war. He stated flatly that the combination of the atomic bomb and the Strategic Air Force was "one of our greatest deterrents to aggression both here and in Europe."[59]

The committee's final report reiterated the earlier vindication of the air force and its leaders in connection with the B-36. With respect to the airplane itself, the report concluded that was a matter for the military. As for organization and strategy, the committee affirmed its support for unification, the importance of strategic bombing, and the air force's primacy in carrying it out. The committee found fault with all of the services and urged greater cooperation. The "Revolt of the Admirals," however, had been quelled.[60]

Symington should have been elated. His reputation had survived the hearings unsullied. Across the country the air force had attained overwhelming popularity—a Gallup poll published near the conclusion of the B-36 hearings showed that three-fourths of the population thought that the air force would play the most important role in winning another war.[61]

Despite all this, within a month after the Vinson Committee issued its final report, Stuart Symington would have resigned as secretary of the air force.

15

Reorganization and Resignation

SYMINGTON always maintained that the root cause of Forrestal's breakdown and ultimate suicide lay in the failure of the defense structure which he had persuaded the president and Congress to adopt. From the beginning in 1947, virtually no one outside the navy and its coterie of partisans in Congress and the press thought the National Military Establishment, headed by a secretary of defense with virtually no powers beyond persuasion, would work. The presence of three strong service secretaries, each with direct access to the president as members of the cabinet, assured a minimal role for their nominal boss. Symington, by virtue of his forceful personality and powerful contacts, exploited his organizational independence with great effectiveness, but he also was one of the most persistent advocates of change. "There was no organizational sense," he commented late in life, "in my, for example, reporting to Forrestal in the Pentagon, and walking over and being equal to him at cabinet meetings in the White House. It made no sense."[1]

Forrestal gradually came to see that the system he had created was not working. He had no control over the service secretaries, and the Joint Chiefs of Staff continually frustrated him by their inability to reach decisions. In an effort to work his way out of the quagmire, Forrestal turned to his old friend, Ferdinand Eberstadt. He persuaded Herbert Hoover to appoint Eberstadt chairman of a task force to study the National Military Establishment as part of a study the former president, at Truman's behest, was conducting of the organization of the executive branch of the government.

Symington and his senior officers were aghast. They blamed Eberstadt's report of 1945, and his influence on Forrestal, for many of unification's failures.

To have him now in charge of making recommendations to improve the structure seemed like supreme irony. As Leach commented from Harvard, "you usually do not ask Damon for an objective appraisal of Pythias." Symington went so far as to suggest to Eberstadt that he not serve. Eberstadt had no intention of quitting. He called on Symington in the Pentagon to go over the whole matter again. By this time, Symington had changed his mind. In an "eyes only" memorandum to Forrestal, he reported that he had discussed the matter with Eberstadt and was assured that he would be "fair and unbiased."[2]

Army Secretary Royall was much less conciliatory. "The setup of the Hoover Committee to study unification does not impress me," he wrote Forrestal. "It seems to be based on an effort to coordinate and obtain an agreement between the three departments. I believe that our experience to date has shown that this approach . . . will not be successful. Personally, I doubt whether the study is worthwhile . . . and I would be inclined to ask Mr. Hoover not to study unification at all . . ."[3]

Symington may have been conciliatory because from the beginning he had little hope for the work of the committee. He did not prepare formal testimony, but spoke off the cuff in two appearances before the committee. He hit hard on the point that "if a defense bill more on the lines of the Truman–Eisenhower–Army and Air Force ideas rather than the Navy ideas had been enacted into the law," many of the problems they were now facing would not have occurred. The secretary of defense needed "real authority to get the job done." To exercise that authority he would need an undersecretary and a chief of staff, drawn from one of the services, who would serve as chairman of the Joint Chiefs of Staff. He sent a transcript of his testimony to Clifford in the White House, hoping that he would show it to the president—"the problems we have had are invariably the result of not getting the law he wanted."[4]

Royall generally agreed with Symington, but the navy, presaging their all-out attack on the air force and the principle of unification, took a different tack. John Nicholas Brown, assistant secretary for air, presented the navy's case. He was accompanied by an impressive array of navy brass including Nimitz, Denfield, and Radford. Stating, "We have been asked by your chairman to discuss whether the Air Force should absorb Naval Aviation," Brown launched into an impassioned discussion of the navy's role in national defense, larded with invidious comparisons of the navy's carrier-based aircraft and the air force's heavy bombers. Radford added to the denigration of the long-range bomber, commenting, "In view of the Navy's record in the past war, it should not be required at this time to reestablish the right to its own aviation, or to defend the combat utility of the carrier."[5]

Royall at one time had suggested that it might be a good idea to consider incorporating naval aviation into the air force, but no senior officer or civilian in the air force had supported the proposal. John McCloy, a member of the commission, observed that the navy had "offered a defense against a non-existent charge."[6]

Symington made no comment on the navy's tirade until October 25 when he wrote Eberstadt that he "was shocked" by the navy's presentation, and particularly that they had made it at the invitation of the chairman. Asserting that "common sense and justice" would require that the air force be given an opportunity to respond, he was not requesting one: the air force did not want to become party to a public brawl.[7]

Eberstadt responded immediately, and "by hand" so that Symington could have "the maximum available time . . . to determine and advise us whether you . . . are prepared to accept this invitation to appear again before our committee . . . to present any further views . . . on any of the matters referred to in your . . . letter, or on anything else that you desire to put before the committee." Eberstadt seemed hurt that Symington would impugn, even by implication, his motives or those of the committee: "I am sure you do not hold either the Committee members or its Chairman responsible for statements of witnesses . . . I hope that your letter was not intended to convey the impression that, in your opinion, our Committee would fail to do 'what common sense and justice normally would dictate.'" As for the "public brawls" the air force wanted to avoid, "We have dealt with many controversial subjects but our hearings have never been in any sense 'public brawls,' nor have they given rise to any. Whatever 'public brawls' have occurred are not chargeable to our Committee, nor has their occurrence been confined to the time from last June to the present—during which our Committee has been in session."[8]

Symington responded that, of course, his letter "was not intended in any way as criticism of your committee. Our letter was intended primarily as a protest of the Navy's presentation before your committee . . . an unwarranted attack against the Air Force." Nevertheless he had decided not to respond. "I am sure, however, that anybody and everybody will agree that action must be taken to resolve the present conflict resulting from the Navy's continuous attack."[9]

The Eberstadt Committee released its report December 17.[10] It was largely a reprise of Eberstadt's 1945 effort. To be sure, it called for increased authority for the secretary of defense, but again it failed to suggest an organizational structure that would make it possible. As former Secretary of War Patterson, a member of the committee, said in filing a dissent, "The majority of the Committee have looked on the present structure and found it good. It is true that certain changes are recommended, but they strike me as minor in character. The changes recommended will not, in my opinion, stop the waste that is now prevalent."[11] Symington's good friends, McCloy and General Wood, also filed dissents.

Leach wrote Norstad. "The childishness of . . . [the Eberstadt Report] offers the USAF a great opportunity. If I were running public relations I would marshal every resource of press relations in an attack on this document. In the first place you would tie the can once and for all to Eberstadt. In the second place, this document gives an occasion for an effective attack on the deficiencies of the OSD."[12]

Although Symington made no secret of his disappointment with the report,[13] he decided against mounting an all-out attack on Eberstadt or the document. In testimony before the Senate Armed Services Committee, however, on the Tydings bill to reorganize the National Military Establishment, his thinly veiled references to "the apostles of half measures" left little doubt about his opinion of Eberstadt and his report. He said: "They concede the necessity of more centralized authority. . . . They are for it in principle, but they oppose each really significant unifying step which would put the principle into practice."[14]

Symington apparently was giving some thought to making a more public, more direct attack on the Eberstadt report. Leach advised against it, reversing the position he had taken a few months earlier. In a memorandum from Cambridge, "Subject: Ferd.," he warned against getting into a public row with Eberstadt. "Your present testimony and Royall's," he wrote, "have done about as much to shake his standing with the committee as can be done . . . You run the risk of giving Ferd a whole new run of publicity on what he said. Remember what a favor the President did to Drew Pearson in the s.o.b. remark."[15]

Whatever his instincts about going to the mat with Eberstadt, Symington did not pursue the matter, and the amendments to the National Defense Act moved along without much reference to Eberstadt's recommendations, becoming law on August 10.[16]

With the adoption of the 1949 amendments to the National Security Act, Symington found himself in an entirely new position. No longer was he a member of the president's cabinet. No longer did he sit on the National Security Council. Instead of being head of an executive department, with all of the status and independence that implied, he, along with the secretaries of the army and the navy, became the head of a military department, an organization within the Department of Defense.

Although Symington had favored these changes, he soon found his situation quite untenable. What had sounded good in theory didn't work out very well in practice. A superb leader, Symington had never distinguished himself as a willing subordinate—he had been fired from his first job, it will be recalled, because of his penchant for giving the boss unsolicited advice on how to run the company. Although he insisted that his new status had nothing to do with his decision to resign, his protestations were not particularly convincing to those who knew him well. Zuckert, for example, once said, "Symington in theory supported a strong Secretary of Defense. But when he ran up against Louis Johnson who tried to be a strong Secretary of Defense, what did he do? He got out of there."[17]

But there was more to the problem of Louis Johnson than his effort to be a strong secretary of defense. The problem lay in the way he went about it. Zuckert, who was assistant secretary of the air force under both Forrestal and Johnson and secretary under McNamara, characterized Johnson as "probably the worst Secretary of Defense. . . . He ran a highly personal operation. I don't think he understood. That is surprising, because he had been Assistant Secretary of the Army during World War II and had done some damn good things in connection with industrial mobilization. But he didn't act as if he had any concept of how to run the office."[18]

At first Symington seems to have been reasonably optimistic about his new boss. He was aware of Johnson's key role in raising money for the president's re-election campaign. Symington knew that Johnson was a good friend of the president—although not in the poker-playing circle—and he usually took the position that "any friend of the President is a friend of mine." Moreover, it seemed for a while that Johnson would be a much more aggressive and effective friend of air power than Forrestal had been. Symington had told his father-in-law, it will be recalled, that Johnson, he was sure, "would put a stop" to some of the navy's tactics. Without question, Johnson's cancellation of the super carrier *United States* had to be considered a victory for the air force.

At the same time, Symington harbored unsettling doubts about the new secretary of defense. He had never been impressed with Harry Vaughan, Johnson's best friend in the White House, and though Symington himself had not been reticent about criticizing Forrestal in the White House, he did not like the way Vaughan "cut him up" in front of the president. Also, he found it strange that before he became secretary of defense Johnson would frequently come to his office in the Pentagon to talk, saying "you're the only fellow I can trust." Johnson, Symington once said, "always had a chip on his shoulder." When asked to compare Johnson with Forrestal, he replied, "He was not in the same league. Forrestal was a brilliant, attractive man, a tremendous Undersecretary and Secretary of the Navy, who brought in to the Navy all his business experience. . . . People around Forrestal were totally devoted to him. And people around Johnson, except for the cronies he put in, were not devoted to him."[19]

When Johnson assumed office, he announced that he was determined to achieve true unification and keep the defense budget in line with the president's wishes, even if he had to "knock a few heads together."[20] It wasn't long before

Johnson's style began to grate. Early in his tenure, he sent out a directive saying that all invitations to official functions were to be issued by the secretary of defense. He once told Symington that he would have to cancel an off-the-record meeting he had scheduled with a group of newspapermen, because he did not approve of off-the-record talks. Marquis Childs, in reporting the incident, said, "This sounds slightly laughable in retrospect. One of the reasons Johnson finds himself in hot water is his tendency to tell on an off-record basis, or 'use it but don't quote me' so many important decisions."[21]

Johnson was paranoid about leaks to the press. One of the suspected "leakers" was Dean Acheson, then undersecretary of state;[22] another was Symington. Johnson was particularly suspicious of their social relationship with the Alsop brothers, who had been very close to Forrestal. Once when Stewart Alsop was visiting Symington in his office, Johnson appeared at Symington's door. Johnson closed the door and stood there, saying nothing, "nodding his huge bald head up and down with the air of a virtuous husband who has at last caught his erring wife in flagrante delictu." Symington broke the unhappy silence by attempting an introduction. "Yes," Johnson replied, "I know MR. ALSOP," and he pronounced the hated name loud and clear. There was another long, uncomfortable pause, while Johnson continued to nod his head up and down, grinning horribly, before he turned and left. Symington and Alsop thereupon "collapsed into undignified giggles."[23]

But Symington's difficulties with Johnson were based on much more than matters of style. The two men had fundamental differences of opinion regarding the dangers facing the country and the requirements of an adequate defense against them. Johnson was determined to follow the president's mandate to hold down defense spending. Symington was equally sure that an adequate defense was more important than a balanced budget. "What the hell good is it to be the richest man in the graveyard?" he frequently asked.[24]

Adding urgency to the situation was the knowledge that the Russians had the atomic bomb. The sobering news came in through air force intelligence channels. Symington recalled:

> . . . one day General Norstad walked into my office in the fall of 1949 and said, "The Russians have just exploded an atomic bomb." I said, "That's a lot of nonsense." He said, "No, it isn't nonsense." So we called up Vannevar Bush. He said, "It's not possible. They couldn't possibly have done it." I said, "Well, you'd better get down here and find out." So he came down quickly, took a look at the evidence, and said, "No question, they have done it." Then the information was turned over to Secretary Johnson and the President by the Air Force.[25]

The process was a little more complicated than that, but by September 23, Truman had decided that the evidence was so persuasive that he needed to make an announcement. He did so with a simple statement, "We have evidence that within recent weeks an atomic explosion occurred in the U.S.S.R."[26]

Truman deliberately used the term "atomic explosion" rather than "atomic bomb," and there is substantial evidence that he really did not believe the Soviets had the bomb, that he thought the generals and scientists were exaggerating.[27] In any event, with crises breaking out all over—the China debate, the second trial of Alger Hiss, charges of influence peddling, the revolt of the admirals, to name a few—the course of wisdom seemed to lie in trying to avoid too much public discussion. This view prevailed—the Russian explosion was not mentioned, for example, during the October hearings on the struggle between the air force and the navy.

Symington went along with this for a while, but on January 9, 1949, he drafted a memo to Secretary Johnson urging action. "After almost two months of careful consideration of the significance of the Russian atomic explosion," he wrote, "the Air Force realizes that the incident compels us to focus on requirements of the immediate future in fields where heretofore we could look at the indefinite future. With all reasonable effort to avoid exaggeration or overstatement, we must conclude that the survival of the United States may be involved." Prior planning had assumed that the Russians would not be able to produce an atomic bomb before 1952–1953 at the earliest, with some estimates ranging up to 1957–1958 and others predicting that they would never be able to do it. The planned buildup of the air force was simply inadequate, and in addition, Symington pointed out, that plan was being decelerated by current budget proposals. He warned: "Based on the present program, by 1956, when the Russians can be at their strongest in the air, America will be at its weakest."[28]

There is no record that Symington sent this memo, but the next day he had a public confrontation with the secretary of defense on the subject of air force needs. Johnson, "in the spirit of unification," had assembled the service secretaries and the Joint Chiefs of Staff for a press conference on the FY 1951 budget. Johnson opened the conference with a few platitudinous remarks about how well the services were working together and how they all supported the president's budget. He was perfectly comfortable with the president's new $13-billion-dollar ceiling on defense expenditures, and he was sure that the air force could get along with the forty-group structure the budget provided. An alert reporter asked how this statement jibed with Symington's repeated calls for a seventy-group air force as the minimum required for the defense of the country. Johnson, with obvious irritation, replied: "Well, Secretary Symington is saying just what he thinks and there is no effort to gag him or change him."

A reporter then asked Symington, "Mr. Secretary, when the Air Force goes up to the Hill, what are they going to say? Are they going to start out saying they want 48 groups or are they going to say they want 70?" The ensuing exchange dramatized the difficulty Symington had faced almost from the beginning of his tenure as secretary: trying to defend the president's budget while fairly presenting air force needs.

SECRETARY SYMINGTON: Do you want me to answer that question—

THE PRESS: Yes, sir.

SECRETARY SYMINGTON (continuing):—or would you like to have Mr. Johnson answer it?

We've always said we wanted 70 and we're always going to say we believe 70 are necessary. The statement that I made in my prepared statement here says that we recognize at this time . . . that there's not enough money to have 70.

THE PRESS. Mr. Secretary, would it be unfair then to ask why you renewed this 70 group thing at this time if you accepted the other one?

SECRETARY SYMINGTON: I don't understand that. I'd be glad to try to answer if I understood the question.

THE PRESS: If you say you support the President's budget, do you support it or did you say "but"? I just ask it in fairness to you.

SECRETARY SYMINGTON: I think the best thing to do . . . is to read the paragraph we wrote on that, which is fairly short:

"As provided by the administration's budget, the Air Force program for the Fiscal Year 1951 is based upon a 48-group structure. The Air Force supports the administration's budget, because we realize that economic disaster might be equivalent to military disaster. This, however, does not change the conviction of the Air Force; namely, that from a purely military standpoint, we believe 70 groups or its equivalent (now 67 groups) is necessary for the peacetime security of the United States."

That was our testimony before the Finletter Commission. That was our testimony before the Congress in '48, '49, and that would be our testimony in '50. . . .

THE PRESS: Well, Mr. Secretary, on that point, then, I take it that you are at some difference with Secretary Johnson on his statement that all of this provides "sufficiency of defense for the hour."

SECRETARY SYMINGTON: Now don't get me into any trouble with my boss here. He knows how I feel and I know how he feels. I still feel from the standpoint of minimum peacetime security that 70 groups are essential for the security of the United States. I base that on what General Vandenberg and his staff tell me. On the other hand, I feel that we could have an economic disaster by spending too much money, and, if our portion of the joint land, sea, and air distribution comes out to 48 groups, then we support the President's budget on the basis of that decision.

THE PRESS: And you will make no attempt to get Congress to change the 48 groups, sir?

SECRETARY SYMINGTON: No, sir. We will not. . . .

THE PRESS: I want to follow that up, if I could, Mr. Secretary. Then in view of what happened last year about the impounding of the funds that Congress gave to you, would you, this year, say, "No, we don't want you to go above the budget," if Congress again shows similar generosity?

SECRETARY JOHNSON: I don't believe that's a fair question.

SECRETARY SYMINGTON: I'd like to make this very clear—no matter what our position is, we'll never turn down any money given to us! (Laughter) . . .[29]

The next morning a front-page story in the *Washington Post* predicted another congressional drive for increased air power, quoting "congressional leaders" as saying that Symington's statement "would kick off another end run" to go beyond the president's budget for the air force. Scripps-Howard columnist Jim Lucas, a good friend, described Symington as heading "the Administration's loyal opposition," making "no secret of his disagreement with his bosses, Defense Secretary Louis Johnson and President Truman."[30]

Symington did not confine his criticism to Washington, and increasingly he brought into the discussion the threat posed by the Soviet Union. In accepting an honorary degree from Baylor University on February 1, he warned against writing off Russia's growing military might. A few days later he sounded the same theme at a Yale University alumni luncheon. At the same time Johnson was going around the country saying that the United States would "lick hell" out of Stalin if he started anything.[31]

Symington tried to play down his differences with Johnson, but he had difficulty keeping his well-known temper in check. Jim Lucas reported that an "irate" Stuart Symington cornered Steve Early at a cocktail party and demanded bluntly, "What the hell is this all about. I thought we were together on policy. Then Louis gives this speech that makes me look like a fool."[32]

Symington's stance drew wide praise. William Robinson, executive vice president of the *New York Herald Tribune,* called his Baylor speech "the most important declaration made by anybody in this country since the war." He added, "I know it must have taken a lot of prayerful thought to come to a decision to make such a frank and forthright statement of the Russian military strength against our own. Having decided it had to be done, it still took a hell of a lot of courage to do it—in face of the American habit of glib assumption of our superiority." Bernard Baruch, who despite his chilly relations with the president usually tried to see Symington whenever he was in Washington, wired: "Your Baylor University speech makes sound sense." Leach wrote from Harvard that after his Baylor and Yale speeches Symington had become "the embodiment of the crusade for 'defense first, economy second,'" and that he could no longer in good conscience support the president's budget; for him to do so would be interpreted as an admission that "everything must be all right." With his usual flair for hyperbole, Leach concluded: "In summary: you have raised the fiery cross, the clans are falling in line behind you, and you can't throw the cross away now or even lower it."[33]

There was no possibility that Stuart Symington would lead a crusade against the president. He was not the crusading type, and even if he had been, he was intensely loyal to Harry Truman. On March 4 he told the annual convention of the Missouri Young Democrats that he was proud to be associated with the president's appointees from Missouri, that he was "truly honored to be a member of the so-called Missouri Gang."[34]

Although he would not lead a crusade against the president, he had decided that he could no longer continue in the anomalous position of supporting the budget, "but," and he was fed up with trying to work with Johnson. He told the president he wanted out, that he just couldn't take the responsibility for cutting the air force further. He would stay in government if the president so desired; otherwise, he would be happy to return to St. Louis and his job at Emerson.[35]

The president wanted him to stay. Besieged with petty scandals involving several of his appointees, he could ill afford to lose an administrative figure whose reputation for integrity was unblemished. He asked Symington if there was anything he would like to do. Symington replied immediately, "Yes, frankly, and if you want me to stay, I'd like to run this new Atomic Energy Commission because I think this nuclear business is going to get bigger by the minute."[36] Truman replied that he had already promised that to Gordon Dean, a law partner of Brian McMahon (influential Democratic senator from Connecticut and author of the act creating the Atomic Energy Commission).

Later that day Symington received a call from Sidney Souers, a successful businessman from southeast Missouri who was serving as executive secretary of the National Security Council and was a good friend of the president. Souers wondered if he would be interested in being chairman of the National Security Resources Board. "I liked that," Symington recalled, "primarily for one reason. The Secretaries had been moved off, and properly so, of the National Security Council. NSRB would put me back on the Security Council by statute. There I could look in the eyes of those who were constantly cutting the services further down; and also, in discussion, get my thinking over to the President."[37]

Symington agreed to take the job, and Truman announced the appointment from Key West on March 30. The response from around the country could hardly have been more enthusiastic—although the enthusiasm of air power advocates was tempered by dismay at the prospect of losing Symington's leadership for the air force.

The National Security Resources Board, created by the National Security Act of 1947, had never functioned as it was intended. For a year it had been without a chairman while the Senate dawdled over the confirmation of former senator Mon Wallgren of Washington. Symington's appointment, many said, would breathe life into the moribund agency. Syndicated columnist Doris Fleeson wrote, "President Truman has assigned his most difficult selling job to the best salesman in Washington." The *Washington Star* predicted, "Mr. Symington's brilliant accomplishments as Secretary of the Air Force serve in themselves as a guarantee that new life and activity will be injected into the NSRB."[38]

Quick and easy senatorial confirmation seemed assured. James M. Cain, Republican senator from Washington who had led the fight against Wallgren, said he would be happy to vote for Symington's confirmation: "Mr. Symington is favorably known to the entire country as an outstanding administrator and executive. He is the type of man and brain that this job has been crying for." The day after Truman's announcement, Lyndon Johnson praised the appointment, declaring Symington had "one of the finest minds in Government service today. His capacity is virtually limitless. His tireless devotion to duty is equaled by few men; exceeded by no man." He was "an ideal choice." Estes Kefauver, Democratic senator from Tennessee, expressed similar sentiments. Symington was "the highest type of public official."[39]

The confirmation hearing, conducted April 6 by the Senate Armed Services Committee, was a virtual love feast as Republicans and Democrats vied with each other in singing the praises of the nominee. Kenneth S. Wherry, Republican senator from Nebraska and a persistent critic of the Truman administration, came as "an uninvited guest" to express his interest in the nomination: "I just want to say I am here to testify that I am in complete accord with this nomination and I am not always that way with the administration, but in this case I am extraordinarily happy to be here and endorse his nomination. I hope it is approved unanimously."[40]

After a few perfunctory questions and comments about the need to invigorate the NSRB, the committee gave such approval. Four days later, the full Senate, by voice vote, unanimously confirmed the nomination[41]—the fifth time in five years the Senate had unanimously confirmed Symington for an important executive post.

When Symington first told Truman that he wanted to leave the air force, the president asked if he had anybody in mind as a replacement. Symington immediately replied, "Yes, sir, I have somebody, Tom Finletter." In many ways—and certainly in Symington's eyes—Finletter was the logical and best choice. As head of the President's Air Policy Commission, he had forged the report that provided the philosophical justification for the 70-Group program; he understood the role and potential of air power as well as any person in civilian life. A distinguished New York lawyer, he had an impressive record of public service, dating back to 1941 when he was appointed special assistant to Secretary of State Cordell Hull. Like Symington, he moved easily in the Eastern establishment—for Louis Johnson, he was too much like Symington. Johnson let it be known around the White House that he did not want Finletter, that he might resign if the president appointed him. Truman, however, took Symington's advice rather than Johnson's—he told Charles Murphy that he was going to appoint Finletter, and that Johnson could resign if he wished. Johnson came around, and on April 4, in the presence of Symington and Finletter, he called Donald Dawson, executive assistant to the president, who was with Truman in Key West, to say, "It has now been agreed between the President and myself that Mr. Finletter will take this job."[42]

Symington continued, during his last days in office, to sound the alarm over the Soviet Union's growing military might. During a speech in Macon, Georgia, honoring Congressman Vinson, he warned: "Never before has any potential enemy possessed the military means to deal, in a single, swift, surprise attack a possible devastating blow, a blow which would make the farms and factories and front yards of America one gigantic battlefield." In his last speech as secretary of the air force—an address at the centennial banquet of the San Francisco Chamber of Commerce—he delivered one of his most stinging attacks on the Truman-Johnson defense budget. Declaring that the Soviet Union was "far ahead" in the armaments race, he said that he, too, was anxious to see the national budget balanced, but asked, "what is the advantage of a balanced budget if we and more important our children end up in the concentration camp of Slave states."[43]

On Monday, April 24, his last day in office, Symington presented the Air Force Exceptional Service Award to Undersecretary Barrows, who was retiring to return to Sears, Roebuck and Company. Symington held a final press conference in which he reiterated his belief that a seventy-group air force was essential to the defense of the country. Once again he said that he supported the president's final decision on how much will be expended for defense but he emphasized that the combat effectiveness of the air force had declined since Johnson began ordering the economy cuts. Then he went to Johnson's office to watch Thomas Finletter sworn in as the new secretary of the air force. After this he was escorted out of the Pentagon's river entrance by Johnson and Vandenberg to review an honor guard, receive a nineteen-gun salute, and watch a flyover by forty-eight jet fighters, the largest formation of such planes ever to fly over

Washington. Vandenberg capped off the ceremonies with a luncheon in Symington's honor at the Bolling Field Officer's Club.[44]

Laudatory letters, which had been arriving since the president's announcement, continued to pour in. General Eaker wrote from California: "I have often said that the things the great air torch bearers gave their lives for, men like Mitchell and Arnold, without success, you were able to accomplish. Your energies and great political acumen made their dreams come true." McCone wrote: "Sometimes I have felt, as I have so often told you, that you have given too much of yourself. However, the results have been superb, and in leaving your post . . . you must take with you the very greatest feeling of satisfaction in your accomplishments—to say nothing of the devotion of the men in the Air Force who have served under you these trying years." Lovett said: "I know, perhaps better than most, what a tremendous load you have carried and how ably you have fulfilled the responsibilities of your post during most difficult and trying times. You have established a very fine tradition for succeeding Secretaries of Air and that, as you know, lives on endlessly."[45]

In an unusual expression of congressional opinion, Chairman Vinson and Missouri Republican Dewey Short, ranking minority member, wrote on behalf of the House Committee on Armed Services:

> We find it a problem to discuss your contributions to the air power of our nation without becoming fulsome about it. But fulsome though they may be, we know that these remarks quite as accurately reflect the views of this entire Committee as they do our own.
>
> Suffice it to say that we are highly honored to have had your association as Secretary of the Air Force. We know that throughout your career you will be able to look back on your Air Force service with the abiding satisfaction in the knowledge that you, more than any other person in America, have been responsible for the enormous, phenomenal strides made by the new, independent United States Air Force. It is fair to say that you put our Air Force 10 years ahead, through your own efforts.[46]

Half a century later, the judgment of history generally supports the encomiums heaped upon Symington as he left office. To be sure, he was highly controversial. His brusque manner angered many people, and he was accused of being devious, if not unprincipled. His single-minded insistence on the need for seventy air groups irritated even his friends, including the president of the United States. Yet, as George Watson wrote in *The Office of the Secretary of the Air Force, 1947-1965,* Symington "left the Air Force with certain expectations of its civilian leaders, becoming the model against which those leaders would be measured."

Working with two remarkable military leaders—Spaatz and Vandenberg—he established the air force's separate identity. Despite administrative frugalities which prevented him from achieving his goal of a 70-group air force, he built a modern fighting force and created the research facilities to keep it going. He laid the foundations for the Air Force Academy. In building the air force, he distributed contracts in such a way as to maintain the viability of the aviation industry. He integrated the air force, and improved the lot of all enlisted personnel. In short, Stuart Symington was, as Watson asserts, "The kind of leader that the Air Force needed during its imperiled infancy."[47]

16

Frustrated Mobilization Boss

SYMINGTON moved with his usual vigor to breathe life into the moribund National Security Resources Board. He faced a daunting and frustrating task.

The NSRB, created, along with the National Security Council and the Central Intelligence Agency, by Title I of the National Security Act of 1947, had been given the formidable responsibility of advising the president "concerning the coordination of military, industrial and civilian mobilization." This included, among other things, providing advice in the event of war on policies concerning industrial and civilian mobilization and maximum use of the nation's manpower; programs for the effective use of the nation's natural and industrial resources; programs for establishing adequate reserves of strategic and critical materials; and the strategic relocation of industries, services, government, and economic activities.[1] In other words, the NSRB was to advise the president on how to run the country in time of war.

The act further provided that the president should appoint the board from among the various executive departments; the chairman would come from outside the government. Truman initially appointed the secretaries of defense, interior, treasury, commerce, labor, and agriculture; later he added the secretary of state.[2] Arthur M. Hill, chairman of the executive committee of the Greyhound Corporation, became the first chairman. Because all authority rested with the board, the chairman had little power. Moreover, Hill was poorly equipped to provide direction to half a dozen strong-willed cabinet members, each intent on advancing his own agenda. Further complicating life for the chairman was the

Munitions Board, which had been busy with its own mobilization plans. Consequently, the NSRB didn't give the president much advice, and he seemed to have little interest in receiving any. When Hill resigned in frustration in December 1948, Truman appointed his jack-of-all-trades assistant, Dr. John R. Steelman, as acting chairman. Steelman's role essentially was that of a custodian, although he served almost as long as acting chairman as Hill had served as chairman. The president had nominated a former Senate friend and poker-playing crony, Governor Mon Wallgren of Washington, to be chairman, but the Senate, as indicated previously, in an unusual action against one of its own, refused to approve the nomination.

This is where Symington came in. His popularity in Congress assured his quick confirmation; his reputation as an administrator who could get things done blunted criticism that the administration was ignoring an important agency in a time of growing national peril.[3]

Despite the criticism, the administration was not ignoring the agency. While Symington's appointment was being processed, a paper was working its way through the White House that would reorganize the NSRB to provide that the chairman rather than the board would be the final authority in determining which recommendations would go to the president; the board would simply be advisory. This is what happened when Symington became head of the Surplus Property Board in 1945. As in the earlier case, there is no evidence that Symington insisted upon the new arrangement as a condition of his acceptance—the proposed changes were in line with Hoover Commission recommendations—but there is no doubt that it made the position much more attractive. Symington had always been wary of accepting responsibility without authority, and he was never comfortable with simply making recommendations—unless, of course, they were to the president of the United States. Truman submitted the reorganization plan to Congress on May 9, less than two weeks after Symington was sworn in as chairman of the board.[4]

The swearing-in took place on Wednesday morning, April 26, in Symington's new office in the Executive Office Building (Old State), next to the White House. Steelman presided at the brief ceremony and Chief Justice Vinson administered the oath of office.[5] The Wadsworths were all there, as were Symington's brother James and his wife, up from Leesburg, Virginia, for the occasion. Tim and Jim came down from Yale. A Washington society columnist wrote, "The impressive ceremony took place . . . in the presence of a distinguished assembly of diplomats, Supreme Court, and cabinet members (including Secretary of State Acheson and Attorney General McGrath), top ranking military and other Symington friends, quite a few of whom were accompanied by their wives. . . . Beauteous Mrs. Symington, whom Washington circles have known as a debutante as well as official hostess, was present, of course."[6] Despite the gathering of friends and family, there were no post-ceremony festivities—Symington presided at a noon-day meeting of the board.

The new chairman was getting off to a fast start indeed. As had been the case with the Surplus Property Board and the air force, Symington moved quickly to put his imprint on the National Security Resources Board. Hill and Steelman had assembled a good staff, and for the most part he left it intact. He brought Steve Leo over from the Pentagon to handle public relations, and drafted his brother-in-law, Republican Jerry Wadsworth, to work in civil defense.[7] The re-organization scheme authorized a deputy chairman, and Symington appointed C. R. Smith, president of Pioneer Airlines.

As in his other jobs, Symington brought his breezy, informal style to the large old-fashioned office on the second floor of Old State. Raymond Brandt, chief Washington correspondent of the *Post Dispatch,* reported, "Even the dark hall-ways of the Old State Department building . . . seem lighter and NSRB officials and employees walk faster now that the 48-year-old industrialist-turned-public servant has taken over the management of the powerful war-planning group."[8]

At three weeks, Symington knew that he had a tremendous selling job on his hands, that he would need all his highly touted talent as a super-salesman. He had ready and regular access to the Oval Office, but neither the president nor anyone else in the administration—or in Congress—was ready to make the hard decisions necessary to prepare the country for war. Even the Joint Chiefs of Staff did not have a fully developed war plan.

In the absence of such plans, Symington, who always prioritized tasks, turned to planning for civil defense. He, more than most people, had been impressed with the gravity of the news that the Soviets had the atomic bomb, and his last days as secretary of the air force had been devoted to trying to improve the strategic bombing capability that he believed offered the best hope of defense against a possible atomic attack. For several months the NSRB, various other federal agencies, and state and local governments had been working on plans for civilian defense, but relatively little had been accomplished. On the one hand, there were those who insisted that a master plan be adopted immediately; on the other, there was the view that the problem was so overwhelming that the whole effort might just as well be abandoned.[9]

Symington announced that he would have a comprehensive plan to propose by September 1 and went to his home in St. Louis to try to sort out the compli-cated strands of the issue. He interrupted his study to join the president at a reunion of the Thirty-fifth Division, including Battery D, Truman's World War I command. They all gathered at the old federal courthouse overlooking the Mississippi River front where one day Eero Saarinen's magnificent stainless-steel arch would rise to dominate the St. Louis skyline.[10]

Symington knew that whatever plans he and his staff developed regarding civil defense or anything else, his big job would be selling them, and that meant selling the need for any program of mobilization. Despite the fact that the press was full of stories about Soviet rearmament and the spread of communism, the country as a whole was quite complacent. This complacency was shared by many in the administration and in the Congress. Indeed, in the weeks before the Korean War Symington was about the only major figure in government speaking about the danger of war. In his first speech after becoming chairman of the NSRB, he told the Committee for Economic Development, an important business group, that the country was "already in a shooting war"—referring to a navy reconnaissance plane shot down over the Baltic by what the State Department claimed were Soviet fighters—and that the Soviets could escalate it anytime they chose. Should that happen, he warned, the government would have to respond by ordering full mobilization, including a labor draft. On June 26, the day after North Korea invaded the South, he was in Detroit to address the annual convention of the American Red Cross on the subject of civil defense. "In this atomic age," he began, "there is no place to hide." Again, he stressed preparation and deterrence.[11]

Back in Washington, Symington, along with Acheson, Johnson, the three service secretaries, and the Joint Chiefs of Staff, attended the briefing Truman held for congressional leaders on Tuesday morning, June 27, advising them that he had decided to provide American air and naval support to South Korea and to press for immediate United Nations support.[12]

Although Symington had not been present at the earlier war conferences, he soon became much involved in planning the war effort. He was a statutory member of the National Security Council; he had a regular weekly appointment with the president; he was made a member of what Truman called his war cabinet—the regular cabinet plus Symington and Averell Harriman, special assistant to the president for foreign affairs. In making the announcement, Truman said there would be no further additions—"We will not have any WPB or other camp followers at cabinet meetings."[13]

All of this, plus the Senate's approval of the reorganization plan, sparked a blaze of stories about Symington's new importance in the government. Doris Fleeson wrote: "Tossed highest of all by the Korean crisis is W. Stuart Symington, chairman of the National Security Resources Board. A reorganization reform has just established the NSRB chairman as supreme commander of wartime mobilization, almost an Assistant President. It can work because the President likes Mr. Symington and wholly supports him."[14]

The press regularly referred to him as "mobilization czar" and sometimes as "assistant president." In a long and generally glowing cover article, *Life* suggested, "Whether or not President Truman imposes price controls, rationing or wage controls, 'freezes' strategic materials or otherwise tightens the U.S. belt in the next year or so depends to a large extent on the judgments and advice of the handsome man shown on *Life*'s cover this week. W. Stuart Symington is officially chairman of the National Security Resources Board, which means that he is unofficially boss of the home front." The article quoted Clifford as saying, "There are three big jobs in the government now, beside the President's. They are Acheson's, Marshall's and Symington's."[15]

Forbes wrote: "Smooth Stuart Symington has applied his Washington savvy to iron out disagreements with rival agencies, keep sensitive Congressional fur rubbed the right way. If Truman calls him to the White House some day and asks if he can put his accumulated planning to work running the economy, Symington's answer will be snappy, decisive and affirmative."[16]

Despite all the hoopla, Symington knew that to have any chance of succeeding, he needed to get the support of both business and labor. He met frequently with business and labor leaders in an effort to put together advisory committees that he hoped would help sell his program to their respective groups in addition to providing advice. He had a much easier time with labor than he did with business. He had built a solid reputation as a reliable ally of labor during his years at Emerson. With the help of his good friend James Carey, president of the International Electrical Workers Union, he put together a luncheon meeting with the heads of all the major labor organizations. American Federation of Labor President William Green, speaking for the group, pledged "whole-hearted cooperation."[17]

Business was more reserved. They had an ingrained opposition to any kind of controls. Moreover, many business leaders did not approve of the way Symington handled labor at Emerson, and while, as the *Wall Street Journal* reported, businessmen had "no positive objections to him," there was speculation in the business community as to whether "'he's quite up to the job.' Some say Symington is inclined 'to pop off a little too fast,' to make decisions without giving them enough thought." Despite these reservations, however, business went along.[18]

Although he felt that he had to prepare public opinion—and especially influential sectors—for the ultimate acceptance of full mobilization, Symington's real problems were not with the public but within the administration itself. Never one to countenance half measures, he argued from the beginning of the Korean crisis for full mobilization and an aggressive, full-scale prosecution of the war. On July 6, he submitted a memorandum to the National Security Council which argued that the invasion of South Korea "unmasked [the] great and growing combined military strength of Soviet Russia and such of its ambitious and willing satellites as China and North Korea; a strength so great that it will be impossible for the United States to settle this dispute in this little country of Korea for some months; and if additional 'outbreaks' of communist satellite countries force us into further attrition of our own forces, the ramifications of this incident might not be settled for many years." The Korean incident also pointed up the "serious current inadequacy of our own military forces" and the fact that there was no long-range strategic defense plan. He urged that action in response to the invasion of South Korea be based on the premise that the Soviets will attack the United States, "when they believe they are ready," and in the interim, "can be expected to harass the United States through such satellites as North Korea, communist China, and eastern Germany."

"In the light of these two premises," he argued, "we should start now to spend more money instead of less money for our national security." In addition to spending more money, the long-range strategic plan, which the president had called for in 1945, needed to be completed without delay. National survival was "paramount over all other considerations." Symington sent a copy to the president, expressing gratitude "for saying everybody should speak their piece. Please read it when you have time."[19]

It is not clear whether the president read or replied to Symington's memorandum. It soon became clear, however, that Symington's positions had very little support from others in the administration. To be sure, military appropriations went up markedly—the $13 billion figure for FY 1951, which Symington as secretary of the air force had rebelled against, was almost doubled, with the addition of $11.5 billion. Also, the long-range strategic plan that he called for came into being. That plan, known as NSC-68, had been under development since January when Truman, in connection with authorizing work on the hydrogen bomb, directed the secretaries of state and defense to undertake a thorough reexamination of the nation's position in the light of Soviet intentions and capability and to recommend an appropriate strategy. The president approved the document and ordered its implementation in September 1950.[20]

NSC-68, drafted primarily by Paul Nitze, director of the State Department planning staff, with help from Robert Lovett and others, called for "a rapid and sustained buildup of the political, economic, and military strength of the free world, and by means of an affirmative program intended to wrest the initiative from the Soviet Union, confront it with convincing evidence of the determination and ability of the free world to frustrate the Kremlin design of a world dominated by its will."[21]

The document followed closely the gospel Symington had been preaching for months. It was clear, however, that neither the president nor his major advisers were prepared to move as far or as quickly as Symington thought necessary.[22] Moreover, the president knew that selling Congress on anything that smacked of wartime controls would be a monumental task.

Symington favored comprehensive and stringent wartime controls. From the time of his appointment, he had been at work on the draft of an Emergency Powers Act, begun two years earlier, to submit to the president. It developed into a broad document conferring on the president vast powers over the economy. The onset of the Korean War accelerated the timetable, but Truman's decision to avoid all-out mobilization greatly reduced the scope of the proposal. The Defense Production Act of 1950 contained only five of the twenty-one titles in the original draft. Symington testified that these were all that were necessary at the moment, but he held out the prospect that the entire package might be submitted, "in case it was necessary in the interests of security to ask for all-out mobilization." In testifying for the bill, he wanted to make it clear that, from his point of view, the emergency was very serious, and "if this nation is to survive, it must increase promptly its own military stature as well as that of its allies."[23]

For a while it seemed that the president was moving Symington's way. He decided to carry out the powers granted under the Defense Production Act (which passed rather easily) by utilizing existing departments rather than creating a new agency. The NSRB chairman would coordinate their activities; he would also "advise the President on the progress of the defense production program and make such recommendations as he may deem proper."[24]

As was the case when the Senate approved the shift of NSRB authority from the board to the chairman, this was interpreted as giving Symington vast new powers. He was identified as one of the key figures in control of the war effort—the others being Acheson, Marshall, and Harriman. Willard Shelton wrote in the *Nation* that Symington's authority was "very broad." He could lay down policy directives and make sure they were enforced. He could adjudicate interagency disputes over the allocation of resources.[25]

In a long and laudatory article in the *New York Times,* Cabell Phillips described Symington's authority as "about as sweeping as is possible under the constitution." The president had delegated to him "virtually all of the special powers conferred . . . by the Defense Production Act," adding, "What is most important of all, he enjoys along with Dean Acheson and W. Averell Harriman, the full confidence of President Truman."[26]

He did indeed have the president's confidence, and the arrangement worked for a while. In addition to his coordinating functions, Symington was given authority for directing the government's efforts to facilitate the expansion of productive capacity in critical industries. Symington also took the lead in pushing the administration's efforts to increase the stockpiles of critical materials, notably aluminum, rubber, and tin, assuming much of the authority that hitherto had been exercised by the Munitions Board.[27] NSRB staff led the effort to develop the administration's request for increased appropriations, and Symington personally went before Congress to defend the requests. He became recognized on the Hill as the head man in stockpiling.

He took a special interest in aluminum. He knew from his experience with Emerson and the air force how important a healthy, productive aluminum industry was to aircraft production. As surplus property administrator he had been responsible for breaking the Aluminum Company of America's monopolistic grip on aluminum production, and giving both the Kaiser Aluminum and Chemical Company and the Reynolds Metals Company a chance to develop. Now, in an effort to expand production, he worked with Lyndon Johnson, chairman of the Senate Preparedness Subcommittee, to broker a deal whereby the government agreed to take the output of the "Big Three" aluminum producers—ALCOA, Kaiser, and Reynolds—not purchased by civilian industry. To further protect the government, the deal provided that, if necessary, the government could have first call on the three companies' aluminum production.[28]

Symington also moved forward on selling the administration's plan for civil defense, something that had occupied him since his appointment. His speeches usually emphasized the importance of civil defense. He enlisted his good friend, Dr. Howard Rusk, to mobilize the medical community. He contributed an article on the importance of civil defense planning to an issue of the prestigious voice of the scientific community, the *Bulletin of the Atomic Scientists,* devoted entirely to civil defense. On September 8, just a few days after his earlier self-imposed deadline of September 1, he submitted his report on civil defense to the president. Although the report recognized that primary responsibility for civil defense must rest with state and local governments, the federal government needed to be involved. Symington recommended the creation of a Civil Defense Administration to coordinate and direct the effort. He also recognized that a civil defense program to be effective would require the interest and voluntary effort of "hundreds of thousands of our people."[29]

Truman submitted Symington's report to the Congress and recommended the creation of a Civil Defense Administration. Pending action by Congress, he would create a temporary Civil Defense Administration.[30]

Symington continued to stress the importance of civil defense. His interest was a logical outgrowth of the view developed during his years as secretary of the air force, and was greatly influenced by such air force thinkers as Spaatz, Vandenberg, and LeMay that the atomic bomb—albeit overwhelming in its destructive power—was just another weapon. By the same token, partial defense against it was possible with careful, comprehensive planning.[31]

Increasingly, the words, "careful," "comprehensive," and "orderly" came to dominate Symington's speeches on civil defense. He had to face the fact that he, along with others, had probably oversold the immediacy of the emergency.

Illustrative was the sharp questioning he faced from some four hundred mayors and civil defense directors called to Washington for a briefing. The mayors seemed ready to get on with the work, but they wanted to know how much money they were going to get from Washington and when it would arrive. Symington replied that the NSRB would have a proposal for federal support ready for the next Congress, but "the more cities that can do without federal patronage, the better it will be for the country." He called the Korean crisis "a blessing in disguise because it has given us one last chance to face up to the realities of the world in which we live."[32]

He back-pedaled some, too, on the questions of wage and price controls. Some of his early speeches had mentioned the inevitability of wage and price controls as well as the possibility of a labor draft. Nobody wanted to face the specter of a return to World War II controls, and by October Symington was downplaying the immediate need for comprehensive controls, while warning that if they were needed the government would not hesitate to impose them. In a wide-ranging cover interview with the editors of *U.S. News and World Report*, he expressed the hope that the country could "rely heavily on our enormous productive strength, present and potential, to help us carry the increased strains of the increased military program." The dangers of inflation were great, however, because practically all of the income generated by increased military production would go into the hands of the civilian population. "That is why we must have strong credit controls to cut down civilian buying; that is why we must have much higher taxes, on a 'pay-as-you-go' basis, to keep purchasing power down to the level of available civilian goods." He warned: "If we are forced into general price and wage controls . . . it will be because other measures have not been imposed strongly enough, or because business, or labor, or both, have taken advantage of the defense situation to raise prices or wages."[33]

He sounded a similar theme when presiding at the annual *New York Herald Tribune* Forum. He expressed the hope that increased production, higher taxes, and credit controls would do the job, but warned again that if they failed to curb inflation the government would not hesitate to impose price and wage controls.[34]

He was not as much in favor of price controls as he had seemed. Two days after the forum, he urged his colleagues in the cabinet not to indicate that price controls were imminent—"We have not been able to get any qualified price experts to take the administrator's job. They just will not consider it." But he tried to keep the heat on. Within a week, in what was described as "the toughest [speech] he has made since his appointment as mobilizer of defense production," he told the Theater Owners of America, meeting in Houston, that many segments of the business community were not cooperating with the government's effort to increase production and curb inflation. He warned that the government would "impose whatever controls and issue whatever directives are necessary" to win the fight against inflation.[35]

In his public utterances, Symington took a position considerably in advance of that held by the president, who throughout the summer and early fall maintained the hope that voluntary cooperation and modest taxation would do the job. Symington's views were probably closer to those of his good friend Bernard Baruch than to those of the president. Baruch had visited Symington in St. Louis in August, and the two men were in fairly close touch with each other during the fall while Baruch was trying to push Congress toward enacting price and wage controls. Indeed, the Defense Production Act was interpreted as a victory for Baruch over the president.[36]

Symington and most of the press assumed that he would administer the controls provided under the Defense Production Act—recall the spate of articles about "The Assistant President," "No. 3 man in Washington," etc. Truman, however, had other ideas. Instead of turning mobilization authority over to the NSRB, the president created a new agency, the Defense Mobilization Board, and named Charles E. Wilson, president of General Electric, to head it. Truman admired Wilson and remained in his debt for the substantial service he had rendered as chairman of the president's civil rights commission. Wilson was well liked in the business community, whereas Symington had ruffled many business feathers both as secretary of the air force and as NSRB administrator. Many business leaders were suspicious of his close ties to labor.[37]

Symington wanted the appointment, and argued strongly that NSRB could do the job. Up until the last minute, he thought he would get the position. An unsigned memorandum in Symington's personal files details the rather bizarre sequence of events that took it away from him. NSRB staff prepared an executive order that gave Symington control, but Wilson told the president that he would come into the government only if he had full authority to direct mobilization efforts, and Truman agreed to his conditions.[38]

Symington's status changed almost overnight. To be sure, he remained a member of the National Security Council, and he continued to attend cabinet meetings and to meet weekly with the president. He also remained personally close, continuing, for example, as one of the *Williamsburg* regulars. His power and influence, however, all but disappeared. From being the number one man on mobilization, the "Assistant President," he became simply the head of an organization whose authority was limited to long-range planning for mobilization (its original mission). It required no great stretch of the imagination to predict that he would not remain long in such a position.

When word got out that Marshall would soon retire as secretary of defense, there was speculation that Symington would succeed him. Symington scoffed at the idea, saying, "I'm just a country boy, trying to do a job. There's nothing to it."[39]

And to all intents and purposes, he continued to try to do his job. He was particularly concerned with scientific manpower—he tangled with Major General Lewis B. Hershey, director of Selective Service, over plans to draft college students. He established a scientific advisory board with Charles A. Thomas, vice president of the Monsanto Chemical Company, as its chairman. Thomas had been active in efforts to find peaceful uses for atomic energy. The Thomas board reinforced Symington's view that college students should be deferred and then be permitted to enter the labor pool.[40]

In the National Security Council, he continued to push for greater appropriations for defense. As was true in the earlier mobilization discussions,[41] he had little, if any, support. Shortly before he left government, he reflected bitterly:

> The Soviet knew our Security Council had passed a resolution not to defend South Korea if the latter was attacked. So they probably guessed—correctly—that we had no real plan for defending that peninsula.
>
> Even then, June 1950, there was no true recognition of the very great Soviet military power, especially in the air. Nor was there by the following September. We simply would not face up to the truth.
>
> As late as November 1950, General Marshall, in Security Council, requested reduction in the size of the September 1950 recommendations from the Joint Chiefs of Staff for more tanks and planes and men. He said he had been through it all twice before, and therefore knew the American people would not put up with anything but relatively quiet orderly mobilization unless there was an all-out war. It is my considered opinion after working with him over a period of years, in State and War Departments, that he never fully understood either air power or the true nature of the Soviet menace.
>
> The President nodded his agreement as Marshall developed the point. Mine was the sole voice raised in objection to reducing the JCS demand for more power.
>
> I said neither Marshall nor the JCS were recommending enough, but the President, with his great regard for Marshall, kindly but definitely closed the discussion.
>
> At that meeting General Marshall smiled and said, "It would appear Symington is still up in the air." (Referring to my former connection with the Air Force.)
>
> I laughed too. Let the future decide who was in the air.
>
> A few days later the Chinese communists poured into Korea, and Acheson said at the very next meeting of the National Security Council, "I don't know what our ultimate goal is, but if it is 4 million men and 50,000 planes, Mr. President, if we had them today it wouldn't be too soon."

At this meeting of the Security Council, the forces recommended by the JCS rejected at the previous meeting were approved unanimously. Mine again was the sole objection that it wasn't enough. Since then it has all been increased tremendously.

Symington had thought from the beginning that the real enemy in the Korean conflict was not North Korea, or even the Chinese. The real enemy was the Soviet Union. The Chinese and North Koreans were mere puppets. In the long memo just quoted he also wrote: "Stalin probably can now relax. Korea has been his Air University. He has had his Spanish War, has obtained all necessary know-how of what his superlative new jet fighters can do against bomber attack."[42]

In almost every speech he had given since becoming head of the NSRB—and earlier as secretary of the air force—he had tried to warn of the Soviet danger. When the Chinese Communists entered the war, he responded first by urging a greater and more rapid buildup of the armed forces than anyone else among the president's senior advisers thought was necessary. Then, on January 10, he submitted to the president and the NSC a paper which came to be known as NSC-100. It recommended closing down the United Nations effort in Korea, thus releasing air and naval forces to conduct a blockade of China and carry on "an open and sustained attack upon lines of communication in China and Korea; and also upon aggression-supporting industries in Manchuria as considered militarily advisable." This should be combined with "fullest possible support to all anti-Communist elements in the Far East, including Southeast Asia, so they can renew open war and increase guerilla activities against the Chinese Communists in central and south China." Finally, the United Nations should "re-affirm the intent to defend Formosa with air and naval forces to the extent of our military capabilities." Such a course would "regain United States and United Nations prestige in the Far East and throughout the world. . . . [and] establish a United States position of strength in the Far East, thus obtaining an active strategic base against Russia in the event of general war with the Soviets."

If the United Nations refused to go along, the United States should proceed unilaterally, "or with as many allies as it can recruit, on the basis of Article 51 of the United Nations Charter which article states that membership in the United Nations does not prevent any member from defending itself unilaterally in case it is attacked."

Then Symington moved beyond Korea and the Far East. "On the political front," he wrote, "the United States could make the greatest contribution to the defense of Western Europe and other areas of interest to the free nations by announcing, preferably through NATO, that any further Soviet aggression, in areas to be spelled out, would result in the atomic bombardment of Soviet Russia itself."[43]

Symington's views on Korea closely paralleled those being advanced by General Douglas MacArthur, who during the winter was bombarding the Pentagon with demands for heavy reinforcements and changes in strategy that would permit him to carry the war directly to the Chinese. His views also found some support among the Joint Chiefs of Staff, who had recommended blockading China and providing aid to Chiang Kai-shek in an attack on the Chinese. Even so, the Joint Chiefs had relatively little enthusiasm for NSC-100, recommending that the paper merely be referred to the secretaries of state and defense "for information in connection with their joint survey of United States politico-military strategy." Philip Jessup suggested to Acheson that "this might be one way of disposing this paper, at least temporarily, although I imagine we can expect the ideas expressed in this paper to keep coming up until there is a decision by the President."

In the end, Truman, with strong support from Marshall and Acheson, decided against widening the war. As for issuing an ultimatum to the Soviets, such a course was unthinkable. The United States didn't have the firepower to back it up. As secretary of the air force, it will be recalled, Symington had warned that at projected rates of expenditure Soviet air strength would surpass that of the United States by 1956—but apparently he believed that for the immediate future the air force could back up an atomic threat. He continued to accept the air force view (held also by the JCS) that the atomic bomb was just another weapon in the nation's arsenal—a view which the president vehemently rejected.[44]

Symington remained frustrated with the administration's strategy in Korea. That frustration spilled over into his report to the president. In addition to reporting on the activities of the NSRB, he discussed the need for a "positive" foreign policy as a "firm base which the Joint Chiefs of Staff can plan our long-range strategic military defense program." He reminded the president that "Most military and civilian authorities recommended a true Chief of Staff in testimony incident to the passage of the National Security of 1947." He urged the appointment of a chief of staff as essential to the proper functioning of the JCS.[45]

This did not go over at all well in the White House. Robert L. Dennison, who reviewed the report for Steelman, wrote that he saw "no useful purpose" in trying the revive the issue of a single chief of staff. Additionally, he thought it would be particularly unfortunate to "release any criticism of the Joint Chiefs of Staff." He recommended that the report not be released, "certainly not before the conclusion of the MacArthur hearings." Truman wrote across the bottom of the memorandum, "O.K. No release. HST."[46]

Symington's frustration over his inability to influence strategy continued to rankle. He was even more frustrated with his role as chairman of the NSRB. He didn't get along with Wilson, and, always sensitive to press comments, he must have chafed under the stories that talked of his reduced authority. Doris Fleeson, for example, wrote of the "bloodless coup" scored by Wilson at Symington's expense. Robert Donovan, the *New York Herald Tribune* reporter who later would write an impressive biography of the thirty-third president, wrote, "The coordination powers Mr. Symington exercised over mobilization activities in the early days of the program have passed to Mr. Wilson and are now greatly enlarged from what they were." He added, however, that despite the transfer of power to other hands, "Mr. Symington's place in the President's esteem has not diminished."[47]

And indeed it had not. Although by no means as influential as Acheson, Marshall, or Harriman, Symington, despite his frequent disagreements on military matters, remained part of the tight little inner circle around the president, people the president liked and trusted—Clifford, Vinson, Brannan, and Vaughan. When Symington told the president that he was tired of government, that he wanted to get back to Emerson, he received this reply: "If you really do, Stu, okay, but I'll tell you what I wish you'd first do. I've heard there is trouble over at the RFC. If you go over there and straighten it out, I'll promise not to ask you again."[48]

17

Reforming the RFC

HARRY TRUMAN had heard correctly. There *was* trouble at the Reconstruction Finance Corporation—big trouble—and the president had much more than merely "heard" about it. The scandals at the RFC had been in the news for weeks.

The brouhaha started in February 1951, when the Senate Banking and Finance Committee, chaired by Arkansas Democrat J. William Fulbright, issued a preliminary study of the RFC, subtitled *Favoritism and Influence*. It charged two of the directors with favoritism in granting loans and implied the existence of a ring of influence peddlers operating out of or very close to the White House. Among those implicated were Donald Dawson, a White House aide in charge of personnel, William J. Boyle, chairman of the Democratic National Committee, and E. Merl Young, a former RFC examiner whose wife was a White House stenographer.[1] Although Dawson and Boyle were exonerated of all but minor indiscretions, the case of Merl Young was particularly egregious. Young looked a little like Truman and made no effort to correct the impression that he was distantly related, presumably through Truman's grandparents, Solomon and Louisa Young. He had done some Democratic political work in Missouri and was very much a part of the "Missouri Gang"—Dawson and Boyle were also from Missouri. After leaving the RFC, Young had set himself up as an "expediter" of RFC loan applications. It is doubtful that he was as effective as he advertised, but in at least one instance his services were recognized in a fairly spectacular way: he gave his wife Loretta (the White House stenographer) a royal blue pastel mink coat costing $8,540, which, it turned out, had been paid for by Joseph H. Rosenbaum, an attorney who represented applicants for RFC loans.[2]

Although Truman denounced the Fulbright report as "asinine," he was already at work trying to reorganize the RFC. On February 19 he submitted a reorganization plan to Congress, replacing the board of directors with a single administrator. The record is not precise, but Truman's conversations with Symington undoubtedly took place while the reorganization plan was making its way through the Congress. As soon as Congress approved, Truman asked Symington to take the position of administrator. In the letter, which the White House made public, Truman cited Symington's "broad experience in private business and government" as "needed to provide the effective and efficient administration necessary to handle the important responsibilities of the RFC." Symington accepted immediately, although he reminded the president, "As you know, my personal desire since 1949 has been to return to private life."[3]

The announcement elicited relatively little press comment. Symington's appointment had been rumored for weeks, so it was hardly "news." Moreover, the press may have been a little weary of having to comment on Symington's successive appointments, glamour boy though he was. H. I. Phillips summed it up with this:

> All big offices, one by one
> Go to Stuart Symington.[4]

Symington went up for confirmation on April 26. The Senate Committee on Banking and Currency unanimously recommended confirmation, and the Senate for the sixth time unanimously voted to confirm Stuart Symington's appointment to an important administrative post. Despite unanimous action, Symington faced sharper and more intensive questioning than he had in any previous confirmation hearing. Fulbright was blunt and direct. He wanted assurances that Symington would have direct access to the president and that he did not owe his appointment "to Mr. Dawson or Mr. Boyle."[5]

The RFC was no plum. Symington left the cabinet and the National Security Council to head a troubled agency whose future was in doubt.[6] He was doing the president a big favor. His administrative savvy, his reputation for integrity, and his general acceptance by both Republicans and Democrats in Congress were just what the scandal-ridden agency needed. As soon as he was sworn in—and this time the ceremony was relatively simple and low-key—Truman wrote: "I have just received the notice that you have taken the Oath of Office—congratulations! Make that shop over there run as you have everything else."[7]

And Symington did just that.

First, he cleaned house almost from top to bottom. Some of the changes were brought about by the reorganization made possible (and necessary) by the elimination of the board of directors; others resulted from replacing mediocre or incompetent employees with better people. He dismissed a few executives for having approved questionable loans. Probably to show his independence—that, as he had assured Senator Fulbright, he was "not beholden"—he dismissed the wife of Donald Dawson from her secretarial position. In a highly publicized case, he fired the manager of the Minneapolis loan agency for improperly benefiting from property rentals to the federal government. Fulbright applauded the action as showing that "reforms were already under way."[8] Within a few weeks he had his own staff in place, and once again began to demonstrate his ability to select good people and persuade them to come to work for the government.

He knew that he needed an outstanding banker as deputy administrator. The RFC was primarily a lending agency, and aside from serving on the board of the Mississippi Valley Trust Company in St. Louis, Symington had no banking experience, except, as he said at his confirmation hearing, "I am an industrialist . . . and I have borrowed a lot of money from banks." He selected Peter Bukowski, a Republican banker from Chicago who had worked with the Hoover relief administration after World War I. Even though he had assured the Senate Banking and Finance Committee that he would not have to check appointments with anyone, he advised the president that he had checked with Boyle and also with Senator Douglas. Jake Arvey, Democratic boss of Chicago, also was involved in the process.[9]

Of equal importance was a good public relations person. The RFC had no one specifically charged with public relations. Symington, always sensitive to the importance of public relations, knew that had to change. Steve Leo, the brilliant tactician who had handled public relations at the air force and NSRB—and had helped to keep his boss in the limelight for four years—had taken a job with the St. Louis architectural firm of Sverdrup and Parcel and was not available.[10]

One evening shortly after his appointment, Symington gathered a small group of friends for dinner at the Chevy Chase Country Club, including Justice Douglas, Abe Fortas, and Paul Porter. He described the mess at the RFC—"I've seen some bad ones, but this is the worst in my experience"—and then went on: "Look, I've got to get the best public relations man in town, or I can't stay over there, because that place is in real trouble, and I just can't do what has to be done without someone to explain some of the things I've got to do in the best possible light, and give fullest public information on the transactions of the agency."

Fortas said he knew the best public relations man in the country, James Allen, but Symington couldn't get him. He was out on the West Coast and didn't want to come back into government—he had been public information officer for the Securities Exchange Commission and the Department of Justice. This was just the sort of challenge Symington enjoyed. He called Allen and talked him into coming to work for the RFC.[11]

Bukowski and Allen were but two members of a stellar team Symington assembled in a matter of days. Most of them had worked with him in the air force and/or the NSRB: Solis Horowitz, general counsel; Edward C. Welsh, economist; Spencer Shannon, critical materials expert; Don S. Burrows, comptroller; Ramsey Potts, national security matters; Dabney Penick, investments; and George Weaver, labor expert.[12] Symington took great pride in the people he had recruited. Speaking before the National Bankers Association, he said:

> At the RFC we have been lucky. New additions include a young colonel with a superb combat record, once the outstanding scholar at his university; a successful partner in one of your great banking houses, willing to dig in and help; a brilliant prosecutor, recommended unconditionally by a great tax law professor at Harvard; an economist with an outstanding record in occupied Japan; a gifted and penetrating auditor; and the former head of the world's largest group of stores, now again serving his government.[13]

Symington and his new team made an immediate impact at the besieged, scandal-ridden RFC. Internally, morale improved—as it always did when Symington took over an organization. Externally, aided by a few well-publicized dismissals and Symington's announcement that the agency would conduct its business in a fishbowl, that it would "bristle with integrity," its image improved dramatically.

Although Symington's critics charged that he was a publicity hound—Donald Dawson commented that "one could be sure that if Symington did not reform the R.F.C., he would talk about it as though he had"—his reforms were real and lasting. He removed loan authority from the field offices, concentrating it in Washington, so that he could be sure that the loans approved were good business ventures and were concentrated on small businesses—no more big loans to luxury hotels, for example. He provided full disclosure on every approved loan and required all representatives of prospective buyers to register prior to any discussion of their applications. He took pride in the fact that the RFC was "operating with efficiency and dispatch."[14]

In the course of applying his policy, Symington tangled again with his old adversary, Glenn L. Martin, president of the Martin Aircraft Company, who had aligned himself with the navy during the B-36 controversy. Martin had never been able to overcome the stigma of the B-26, dubbed by air force pilots the

"Flying Prostitute" because it had no visible means of support. The company managed to get some commercial business, but when it tried to expand after the outbreak of the Korean War, it soon ran out of cash. As a step of last resort, it applied to the RFC. Symington denied the loan, expressing the view, which he had stated before, that the aircraft industry had too many firms in it. Besides, Glenn Martin was senile and a bad risk. At this juncture, Eddie Rickenbacker, the World War I ace who was president of Eastern Air Lines and a friend of Martin's, accompanied by Laurence Rockefeller, came to see Symington, trying to get him to change his mind. When Symington refused, Rickenbacker called Wilson, head of the Office of Defense Mobilization. Wilson, according to Rickenbacker, "let out a blast at Symington" and promised to see what he could do. With help from the White House, apparently, Wilson brokered a deal whereby the RFC would join with private lenders in advancing the money the company needed to keep going. Martin, however, had to step down from his position as president and CEO.[15]

Despite this rather uncharacteristic compromise, Symington moved ahead to clean up the agency and reform its loan practices. In addition to scrutinizing new loan applications with great care, he canceled existing loans where he found irregularities in the manner in which they had been obtained. A highly publicized case was that of the American Fixture and Manufacturing Company of St. Louis, which had failed to report that it had paid a retainer to Joseph H. Rosenbaum, an influential lawyer who had achieved notoriety as one of the "five percenters"— and who had paid for Loretta Young's highly publicized mink coat. Another was that of Stutts Lumber Industries, Inc., of Thomasville, Alabama, which regularly bought timber from Representative Frank Boykin, Democrat from Alabama. Symington used the crackdown to make the point that "any suspicion of influence is poison to the applicant in this agency today."[16]

When the press reported that Symington had refused an extension on a loan to Carthage Hydrocol, Inc., a company owned by Guy Gabrielson, chairman of the Republican National Committee, Truman wrote long-hand to his crusading administrator:

> This morning's papers have headlines that the Republican National Chairman has been refused an extention [sic] on a loan. Of course I do not know whether the loan is good or bad, but I hope it is a good one. Don't penalize anyone, Stu, because of the present hysteria—even the chairman of the opposition committee. Take a good look and do what would be good business if you were running the 1st National Bank of St. Louis.[17]

Symington's clean-up program pulled the rug out from under the Fulbright committee's investigation of the RFC. He dealt with every instance of wrongdoing or impropriety unearthed by the committee and rooted out several the committee had overlooked. As one historian noted, the committee had been "out-crusaded by Symington." Its final report was something of an anticlimax, reflecting none of the ominous portents hinted at in the preliminary study. Long before the report was issued, Fulbright had spoken approvingly of Symington's reforms.[18]

Symington's vigorous leadership came into play with particular force in the purchase of strategic materials for the government stockpile, a congressionally mandated RFC responsibility. Aluminum, rubber, and tin were all important, but tin provided Symington with his largest challenge.

The world's supply of tin was controlled by a cartel composed of Dutch, British, Belgian, and Bolivian interests. The United States, which produced no tin, constituted the world's largest market. With the outbreak of the Korean War the government greatly accelerated its stockpiling purchases—and the price of tin shot up. On the day before the North Koreans attacked the South, tin sold for 76.4 cents a pound. By February 1951 the price had risen to almost two dollars a pound. It was clear that the tin producers were taking advantage of the situation to gouge the United States. The Preparedness Subcommittee of the Senate Committee on the Armed Services, headed by Lyndon Johnson, recommended in February that, pending the development of an international agreement on tin, the RFC suspend its purchases.[19]

Symington did that. His action brought immediate protests from the tin-producing countries, particularly Bolivia, whose economy was heavily dependent upon tin. *El Diario,* Bolivia's leading newspaper, named Symington as "The Man of the Week, . . . who has managed in a few days to make a pretty bad name for himself among tin producers." The collapse in tin prices, the paper charged, was "due mainly to the handiwork of this personage of sinister reputation." They would "invoke the gypsy curse on Mr. Symington, author of this stab to the Bolivian economy."[20]

The Bolivians were not the only ones who were unhappy with the new man at RFC. Although Acheson remained cordial—and in 1960 would support Symington's bid for the Democratic nomination for president—there were those in the State Department who felt that Symington was undermining their efforts to maintain good relations with the Bolivian government. Indeed, throughout his tenure at the RFC, Symington's relations with the State Department remained prickly. When, for example, he decided to send a mission to Bolivia to try to negotiate a reasonable price for tin, there was objection from the State Department to including George Weaver as a member. Weaver was black. There were no blacks in Bolivia, and the Bolivians might be offended. Symington could hardly believe what he was hearing. At first he tried to kid them out of it, telling a Sam Goldwyn story. Goldwyn wanted to make a film of *The Well of Loneliness,* but was told he couldn't do that because it was about lesbians. Goldwyn answered, "We'll call them Austrians." Symington suggested they call Weaver an Indian. Joking aside, Symington reacted vehemently. "George Weaver is an American citizen," he said, "and a very able one. If the RFC sends a commission to Bolivia, George Weaver is not only going, but he is going as a senior member."[21]

The delegation, as finally put together, included Weaver, Edward Welsh, and Arthur E. de Celles from RFC and representatives of the State Department. They found the Bolivians cordial but anxious to modify the American attitude. Tin exports were Bolivia's only source of foreign exchange, and with the American market gone the flow of foreign currency had dwindled to a trickle. Weaver and de Celles hoped that an interim agreement could be worked out so "the Mission could complete its assignment in a less charged atmosphere." They did not, however, "share the apprehensions of the State Department representatives that an immediate fall of the present government is imminent unless an agreement satisfactory to the Bolivians is immediately consummated." They believed that a price of $1.03 per pound (about the current London and Singapore prices) would be acceptable.[22]

The differences between State and the RFC were more than just matters of perception. In a telephone conversation with Thomas Mann, who had major responsibilities for Latin American Affairs, Symington charged that representatives of the State Department were undermining the RFC's efforts to negotiate a fair price for tin, that the Bolivians had been led to believe that they could get a better deal by working with the State Department than they could through the RFC. Symington accused the State Department of trying to hoodwink Congress by subsidizing the Bolivian government through the price of tin: ". . . do we subsidize the Bolivian government through the price of tin or do we do it through the more direct approach through the Congress."[23]

Symington also had difficulty with the government of Indonesia, second-largest supplier of tin for the American market. The Indonesian embassy forwarded to the State Department an unsigned memorandum, dated June 15, which incorrectly attributed to Symington the comments of Johnson's subcommittee on preparedness that the price of tin was controlled by a cartel and that the cartel was "gouging" the United States. The memorandum flatly denied the existence of a cartel. It charged that Symington's attack on the price of tin was based on unjustifiable economic assumptions and was "worthy of moral disapproval."[24]

Dean Rusk, then assistant secretary of state, forwarded the memo to Symington with a request for comments. Symington fired off a long memorandum, setting the record straight and categorically denying all the charges.[25]

A few days later Symington's problems with the State Department accelerated. Asked to testify again before Johnson's subcommittee, he described in detail the difficulties with both Bolivia and Indonesia. He reported on the findings of the RFC mission to Bolivia. He released the memorandum from the Indonesian embassy, together with his reply to Rusk. He also discussed in some detail the operations of the tin cartel, coming down hard on the Dutch and the British as well as the Bolivians and Indonesians, accusing them of gouging the American taxpayer "when he buys the raw materials necessary to supply the guns, the tanks, and the planes to protect [them] . . . From Soviet communism."[26]

Symington's testimony made a great hit with the committee. Oregon Republican Wayne Morse said, "Mr. Chairman, I simply want to say for the record that I am deeply impressed by this statement Mr. Symington has made to this committee. . . . [it] is not only so unquestionably sound but it is also a very courageous statement. . . . I do not want this record closed this afternoon without my telling him how much he has renewed my faith, as I am sure he will for millions of other American people, in the highest of traditions of public service. Just let the chips fall where they may and call the shots as you see them."[27]

Symington's testimony may have made a hit with the committee, but it did not play well at the State Department. Acheson complained to the president. He was disturbed by Symington's release of the Indonesian memorandum, and also by his discussion of the findings of the group the RFC had sent to Bolivia. Apparently, he was somewhat mollified by Symington's explanation that the RFC had received the Indonesian memorandum several weeks before it had been referred by the State Department and that, indeed, it had been released to the press in Indonesia. As for Bolivia, the committee specifically asked for the team's findings. Truman was not so easily mollified. Matt Connelley, the president's appointments secretary, told Symington at lunch that the president was so incensed that Symington would be well advised not to try to see him for a few days.[28]

Despite his difficulties with the State Department and the White House, Symington was able to get the Bolivians to agree to an interim price of $1.12 per pound, while negotiations continued. Before those negotiations could be completed, however, Symington resigned as administrator of the Reconstruction Finance Corporation. The resignation was hailed as "definitely good news" in the tin-producing countries, with producers predicting a "quick rise" in the price of tin.[29]

Although there were hints that pressure from Acheson had forced Symington out,[30] such was not the case. To be sure, despite his smooth appearance and suave manner, Symington was not very diplomatic. As Senator Morse suggested in his fulsome praise, he called the shots as he saw them and let the chips fall where they may. This he had always done, and in the case of tin, he firmly believed that the tin-producing countries were out to gouge the United States as it sought to rearm the free world. He was determined not to let this happen. If he ruffled a few feathers along the way, so be it. There probably was no moaning in the State Department when Symington announced his resignation, but the decision was his, and it had relatively little to do with his diplomatic difficulties.

When Symington accepted responsibility for the Reconstruction Finance Corporation, he did so with the understanding that he would remain only as long as it took to restore public confidence in the agency. By the end of the year that had been achieved. Symington wrote the president that the agency was in good shape and that it was time to resign, adding: "May I take this opportunity of expressing my very deep appreciation to you in making it possible for me to serve in the Government during the past six and a half years."[31]

In a "Dear Stu" letter, the president replied: "It is difficult to sever official bonds formed during my first months in the White House and I regret that the time for such a step now is approaching." He accepted the resignation, "with utmost reluctance," praising Symington's "long and varied service . . . I say to you well done, and heartily reciprocate your warm personal sentiments."[32]

Despite this cordial exchange, there is some evidence that Truman was not entirely sorry to see his highly publicized troubleshooter depart. He was influenced by State Department attitudes, and he could not help but have been irritated by assertions in the press that Symington was really too good for the administration. Pearson devoted an entire column to contrasting Symington with "the little band of mediocrities around the President" who frustrated Symington's efforts at reform. In response to a letter from New Mexico Democratic Senator Clinton Anderson urging that every effort be made to retain Symington in the administration, Truman wrote: "Stu is in a highly nervous condition, brought about by the major operation he underwent, and I think a rest will help him. I told him he was not parting company with me forever, just as I told you when you ran for the Senate in New Mexico, but I think Stu needs to take some time off and get an objective view of things and it will be good for both of us."[33]

Despite this, relations between the two men remained warm. In writing to express appreciation for Symington's willingness to remain as RFC administrator for a few days after January 15, Truman added, "I understand that Clark Clifford is expecting to have a birthday party for the Chief Justice—maybe I shouldn't say this to you, but I hope you will be there and I hope you will lose," adding in longhand, "Lose only to *me* I mean." The "few days" Truman had requested stretched into several weeks as Harry McDonald, Truman's choice as a successor, had difficulty getting confirmed. Symington remained as titular head of the RFC until February 15, but for all practical purposes, he left office on January 26. That morning, in an impressive Oval Office ceremony, the president awarded him the Distinguished Service Medal "for exceptionally meritorious and distinguished service to the United States of America in positions of great responsibility from January 1946 to January 1952."[34]

The next day the Symingtons returned to their home in St. Louis, "amid recurring reports that many Missourians would like to see him run for the United States Senate."[35] In a wide-ranging interview with the *Post-Dispatch,* he said he was not available. His primary interest now was in getting some rest. He and Eve were going to spend several weeks in Jamaica, where he could "slide away and collect my thoughts."

By the time he had collected his thoughts, he had decided to seek the Democratic nomination for the U.S. Senate.

18

Beating the Odds in Missouri

STUART SYMINGTON, the master of the quick deci-
sion, agonized for days before deciding to enter the quagmire that was Missouri
politics. He had always assumed—and frequently stated—that once he had
completed his government service, he would return to Emerson as chairman
and CEO. If he decided against Emerson, there were many other options. To
quote Clifford, ". . . he had a wide choice of opportunities to acquire really great
wealth as the head of some of the largest and fastest-growing industrial concerns
in the country. . . . phenomenal offers."[1] There was also talk that he might be
offered appointment as commissioner of Major League Baseball. Ardent sports
fan that he was, he could have found this tempting.

Increasingly, however, influential Missourians—Republicans as well as Democrats—were urging him to run for the Senate. The incumbent, James M. Kem,
a prominent Republican lawyer from Kansas City, had done nothing to distin-
guish himself except to oppose the Truman administration at every turn.
Particularly disturbing to those Missouri Republicans who were pushing Eisenhower for president was Kem's die-hard isolationism. He had opposed both
NATO and the Marshall Plan. If he were nominated for a second term, Missouri Republicans would find themselves with a candidate for the Senate who

James C. Olson, "Beating the Odds in Missouri: Stuart Symington's First Campaign
for the Senate, 1952," *Missouri Historical Review* 97 (April 2003): 204–33, is an expanded
version of this chapter. It is published courtesy of The State Historical Society of Missouri.

opposed their candidate for president on many crucial issues. Better to take a Democrat, especially if they could get one who looked like a Republican.

The Democrats, as usual, were in a state of confusion. President Truman was toying with the idea of returning to Missouri and making a run for his old seat in the Senate. Few people in the know expected him to do this, but until he made it clear that he would not run—something he did not do until April 3[2]— potential candidates had to keep the possibility in mind. There were a number of potential candidates, including Governor Forrest Smith, former congressman Roger Slaughter of Kansas City, and William Kemp, reform mayor of Kansas City, but the only person who had filed was Attorney General J. E. ("Buck") Taylor of Chillicothe, one of the "good old boys" who dominated the Democratic party in Missouri. Aside from his record of faithful service in Democratic vineyards, Taylor's only qualifications for the job were his friendship with Harry Truman and the fact that he did not live in St. Louis—for years Missouri had elected one senator from St. Louis and one from the western part of the state, usually Kansas City.

The prospect of Taylor as the only alternative to Kem dismayed many Democrats and some Republicans, particularly in St. Louis. With the consent of his bosses, John R. Hahn, political reporter for the Republican *St. Louis Globe-Democrat,* began to write favorably—one might say "effusively"—about Symington as a possible candidate for the Senate. Hahn's articles made interesting reading, but to the press and even to his friends, Symington insisted that he was not interested in running for the Senate. Then he got a letter from Jacob Lashly, an independent Democrat, one of the leading lawyers in the state, and former president of the American Bar Association. The letter, written January 7, said: "If you should feel the challenge of further public service, I wonder if you would not be interested in running for United States Senator from Missouri. I have talked to some people about it (John Nangle is one), and I believe the prospect for nomination and election is good, so far as can be seen from here. It would be a pleasure for me to get in and try to help, if you would want to do it."[3]

Symington's immediate reply was noncommittal, but he did express "appreciation and pride that a person of your standing would consider me in that connection." He would be in St. Louis within the week and would call.[4]

Back in St. Louis, Symington had lunch with Lashly at the Noonday Club. He reiterated that he was not interested in getting into politics. When Lashly asked if Symington would meet with a few friends at the Chase Park Plaza Hotel that afternoon to discuss the matter further, he replied that there was no need for that, "You know my position." Lashly responded: "Then you will make me look pretty foolish. I've asked these busy men to come meet you." With that,

Symington agreed to the meeting.[5] Among those present were Jack Dwyer, St. Louis Democratic chairman; Russell Dearmont, head of the Missouri Pacific Railroad; Sam Priest, a leading St. Louis businessman, and James H. Meredith, director of finance for Governor Smith and one of the shrewdest political operators in the state.[6] The meeting was pleasant enough, but Symington insisted that he was not interested in running for the Senate, that he planned to go back to Emerson.

That evening he had a call from Sidney Maestre, head of the Mississippi Valley Trust Company on whose board he had served before going to Washington. A friend of his wanted to say hello. The friend was Bill Kemp, mayor of Kansas City. He came on the phone and said, "Mr. Symington, I don't know you or your plans, but believe you could win this race. If you don't run for the Senate, I plan to run; but if you do, I'll support you."

"For the first time," Symington wrote later, "that aroused some interest on my part. Having only moved to St. Louis in 1938, and only living there seven years before coming into the Truman Administration in Washington, obviously I knew few people in the State. But if someone all the way across the State, in Kansas City, felt that way, in this case an able, popular and scrupulously honest officeholder, it did create the first real interest on my part."[7]

Events now moved rapidly. On January 29, Governor Forrest Smith announced that he would not be a candidate for the Senate. This, according to the *Globe-Democrat,* "started an immediate boom for Symington." A few days later, Dr. W. L. Brandon of Poplar Bluff, one of Governor Smith's leading supporters and a powerful political figure in southeast Missouri, endorsed the effort to persuade Symington to run and predicted that he would be "a strong candidate in rural southeast Missouri counties if he decides to enter the race."[8]

It seemed as though the field was opening up, with Truman being the only possible obstacle. He had made no announcement, but the odds were that he would not run. In that case, would he endorse anyone? There were ominous signs that he might be for Taylor: Jim Pendergast in Kansas City and J. V. Conran, a powerful Democratic leader in the Bootheel, had endorsed the Taylor candidacy. Other, lesser figures were falling in behind the attorney general. Lashly began to fear that Taylor had the nomination sewed up. Hahn, who was busy turning out pro-Symington stories for the *Globe-Democrat,* reminded Symington, "Church ain't over 'til the singin's out."[9]

Church wasn't over, but the services were rapidly drawing to a close. It was becoming clear that unless Symington made up his mind soon, other potential candidates—among them, Mayor Kemp of Kansas City—would file.

Symington called the White House to try to set up an appointment with the president. When Truman came on the line, he opened with, "Good morning,

Senator." He seemed a little cool. Symington thought that possibly the president was still miffed because some time earlier he had turned down Truman's request that he consider running for governor. Nevertheless, the president agreed to see him.[10]

When Symington told the press of his appointment with the president, he stated for the first time publicly that he might consider running for the Senate if the president asked him to do so. His appointment, however, was simply to say good-bye as head of the Reconstruction Finance Corporation. "The president and I have never visited about the Senate race," he added, "and I am not going to bring it up."[11]

He was not being completely candid. He had requested the appointment specifically to discuss running for the Senate. Moreover, he had prepared an elaborate set of "talking points" to aid him in his conversation, discussing the indications of support he had received from politicians, editors, and leading citizens from all parts of the state. He was urged to run as a public service, and Democratic leaders felt that he would help Donnell, who was running for reelection, in the cities, and Donnell would help him in the country. He was sure he could win the primary if he had the president's support, and he could beat Kem on the issues: "The consensus of opinion, at all levels and in various categories, is that Taylor cannot beat Kem; also that Kem should not go back to the Senate." The memorandum concluded: "Unless the president himself wants to run for the Senate, therefore, I believe I would like to make the primary race against Taylor, and the election race against Kem."[12]

The arguments that Symington had so carefully laid out apparently did not impress his former boss. The president was unimpressed with his support. Most of the men Symington mentioned "were no good and could not be trusted." Besides, he didn't think Symington could win, because the state would never elect two senators from St. Louis. Most of his friends were for Taylor, and while he had not endorsed Taylor, he probably would vote for him in the primary. When Symington mentioned that everyone he had talked to said Taylor did not have the capacity to be a U.S. senator, the president replied, "I know. He is a drunk and no good, but I am talking politics and not personalities." When Symington asked, "Would it not be fair, with Stalin looking down our throats, to say that we should talk principles, not either personalities or politics?" Truman responded, "Well I will admit that you would be a far better senator than Taylor, but I am not sure you could get the nomination." Near the end of their interview Symington sensed that the president was becoming more sympathetic. He told Symington he could tell the press he was encouraged by their talk, "but don't say I actually asked you to run and don't file now. Maybe we can work out the Taylor business by making him Attorney General."[13]

Symington left the president deeply disappointed. Clifford, who talked to him shortly after the meeting, later said, "I remember Stu coming back after talking to Truman, and Stu was really angry, saying, 'I've given this man five years of loyal service, working as hard as I could, and look what he does . . .'"[14]

Symington denied having said that. Whether he said it or not, it is easy to believe, given his notoriously thin skin, that he was angry. He could also have been disappointed at the low, backwoods, political cunning being exhibited by the president of the United States. That he would even consider supporting a man whom he had described as "a drunk and no good" for the Senate, let alone mention him as a possible attorney general of the United States, was beyond belief. It is not surprising that Symington, ever the loyal lieutenant, filed his memorandum of February 12 in a sealed envelope.[15]

Although Truman had thrown "a lot of cold water" on his plans, Symington told the press that he was "more interested in running . . . than he was before his visit" but right now he was going on a long vacation.[16] This was the vacation he had talked about when he had first arrived back in St. Louis at the end of January. He and Eve rented a house in Jamaica—"Villa Content" in Montego Bay—for a month and settled down to decide about running for the Senate.

He still hoped that he would be able to persuade the president to change his mind. On February 29 he asked Truman if he could visit him at Key West (where the papers said he was going for a short vacation) on March 10, en route to St. Louis.[17]

March 10 wasn't convenient. Mrs. Truman's mother was at the point of death, and the president was not sure when they would get to Key West. He added: "I have not been able to talk to the people in Missouri, as I told you I would when you left here, but I hope to get that done before I go away."[18]

It was becoming clear that Symington would have to make his decision without further consultation with the president. Mayor Kemp called from Kansas City to say that Roger Slaughter—former Democratic congressman from Kansas City whom Truman had helped defeat for reelection—was filing, and unless he heard from Symington very soon that he was going to run, he would file. Symington told him that he would have his answer in twenty-four hours.[19]

This was on March 9. The next day he met with Jacob Lashly, who was vacationing in Florida, at the Congress Hotel in Miami. Sidney Salomon and Jack Dwyer flew down from St. Louis to take part in the meeting. As Symington wrote in "Memories," "We went over various matters and I decided to run, calling Mayor Bill Kemp to that end."[20] Thus, under the pressure of events, Symington rather quickly reached a final decision on the question he had wrestled with for more than a month.

It was a decision that fixed his course for the rest of his active life. When he accepted appointment as chairman of the Surplus Property Board in 1945, he had done so with the firm expectation that he would return to his job at Emerson, and this was his expectation as he accepted successive presidential appointments. Increasingly, however, that became muted as he experienced the charm and challenges of public life on a national scale. He liked to talk about his "poverty" and his need to make some real money, but with what Eve had and his own holdings, he had enough money for the well-to-do lifestyle he enjoyed and practiced with such enthusiasm. Moreover, in public life on a national scale, the horizons were limitless—there was talk around the edges that he should be running for president. Whatever his aspirations, if he were going to remain in public life, his best course was to try to become a senator from Missouri.

There was more to it, however, than raw ambition. When asked why he decided to run, he said: "Why did I decide? This country has been good to me. When I started out in business I didn't have a pot. I owe this country a lot. And the Senate was the place where I felt that I could perform a service."

That, though perhaps a bit disingenuous, was a reasonably accurate reflection of his position. Former Missouri Governor James Blair put it this way: "Why is Stuart in politics? Patriotism. It's almost as simple as that. He really believes he can do a job for his country."[21]

Once he had made his decision—whatever his reasons—he went into action with the whirlwind efficiency that had characterized his career from the beginning. He needed all the energy and skill he could summon. He faced formidable odds.

First, there was Missouri itself, a vastly variegated state with no center of power and no unifying geography. Geographically, the state was divided into a number of distinct sections, with each having little relationship to the others. The fertile lowlands of the southeast, in the region known as the Bootheel, supported some of the state's most productive agriculture, primarily southern—cotton was a leading crop. The Ozark Highlands, which covered most of the state south of the Missouri River, consisted primarily of low, wooded hills, interspersed with deep, twisting canyons. There were significant deposits of lead and zinc in the eastern part of the Ozarks, but for the most part, as Paul Nagel put it in his bicentennial history of Missouri, the region "prospered in little but beauty and the lure of wildlife." By the early 1950s, Lake of the Ozarks, created by the Union Electric Company's Bagnell Dam across the Osage River, had become the state's major vacationland. North and west of the Ozarks were rolling plains that supported both cattle raising and general agriculture, and which were more like Iowa, Kansas, and Oklahoma than the rest of Missouri. Then, as separate sections, there were St. Louis and Kansas City, located on the borders of the state, one looking east, the other west, and, to quote Nagel again, with "a scorn for each other matched only by their disdain for the countryside lying between them."[22]

Exacerbating the geographic divisions were the varied customs, traditions, and attitudes brought to the state by its diverse population. The earliest settlers had come from French Louisiana, but their traditions lingered only in place names and folklore. The principal sources of Missouri's enduring population were Virginia, Kentucky, and Tennessee from the southern borders, the German principalities, and New England. Many of the southerners brought their slaves with them, settling in the eastern and central Missouri River counties in an area that came to be known as "Little Dixie."

The people who settled in Missouri had little in common—their descendants could not even agree on the pronunciation of the state's name. Through the years, sectional animosities had expressed themselves in all aspects of the state's political and cultural life: the state was torn apart during the Civil War, with two rival governments vying for recognition. As the years wore on, many of the old sectional prejudices continued, but most Missourians, particularly in the rural areas, seemed to agree with the Jeffersonian view of government and its distrust of big cities.

The Democratic party generally dominated local politics, except in the southwest and St. Louis County, with its affluent suburbs that had been separated from the city since 1876. The Democrats usually controlled state offices and the legislature. At the national level, however, their control was much less secure— as Senator Kem frequently said, Missouri was a Democratic state in which a good Republican could get elected.

The Democrats were badly divided. For years Tom Pendergast, one of the country's most notorious political bosses, had dominated the party in Missouri as well as in Kansas City.[23] With his imprisonment in 1939, control of the Pendergast machine had passed to his nephew, James Pendergast. Jim, however, was unable to maintain the iron control Uncle Tom had wielded. He was challenged at home by Carl Binaggio, a Kansas City crime figure with reputedly close ties to Al Capone in Chicago. In St. Louis, where Bob Hannegan had worked closely with the Pendergast machine, Sheriff Thomas Callanan was assuming increasing independence. Outstate, J. V. Conran, prosecuting attorney of New Madrid County, deep in the Bootheel, was developing a power base of his own. Both he and the Pendergast machine had endorsed Buck Taylor, which meant that outside of St. Louis Symington's prospects for the nomination were dim indeed.

Aside from the difficulties of making an impact in Missouri and overcoming the power structure of the Democratic party, Symington faced another serious obstacle: himself. He was not a "real" Missourian. He had been a resident of the state only since 1938, and half of that time had been spent in Washington. Moreover, his brief Missouri experience had been confined almost solely to St. Louis. Aside from a hurried trip to Lamar with John Snyder to witness Harry

Truman's notification of his nomination for the vice presidency, he had hardly been out in the state.

In addition to being an outsider, he was an easterner, and a big-city one at that. He was an Ivy Leaguer who had married a rich Republican and whose friends were mostly eastern aristocrats and big businessmen. He knew absolutely nothing about agriculture. He dressed impeccably in well-fitting suits tailored in New York. He neither sounded nor looked like a Missourian, and Missourians tended to reserve their trust for one of their own.

Moreover, he was from St. Louis, and so was Thomas Hennings, who had been elected to the Senate in 1950. In asking the voters to send him to the Senate, Symington was asking them to overturn one of their most cherished political traditions: not more than one senator could come from St. Louis.

The odds, in short, were great—so great that few people thought he had even an outside chance. Richard Nacy, vice president of the Central Trust Company in Jefferson City and one of Missouri's political wise men, told him that his chances of being elected were "less than one in twenty."[24] Most of the politicians agreed. As Jim Meredith put it, "They thought that anyone who got into the race against Buck was just bent on suicide."

Symington recognized the odds, but he was confident that if he threw himself unstintingly into the race, his powers of persuasion would be sufficient to enable him to carry the day. He did just that. Not only did he give the contest all of his restless energy, but Eve and his sons joined in, treating Missourians to a campaign quite unlike anything they had ever experienced.

He assembled a stellar campaign committee, headed by two of the shrewdest political operatives ever to function in Missouri: Jim Meredith and Stanley Fike. Meredith, a young lawyer from the Bootheel, had been president of the Young Democrats of Missouri. He knew every politician in the state and was close to Governor Smith. He had been an FBI agent, and was currently serving as counsel to the state department of insurance. He was thinking of getting out of politics, but, as he later put it, "Stuart impressed me. I took the job." He would continue as Symington's campaign manager until 1962, when, through Symington's influence, he was appointed to the federal bench in St. Louis. Stanley Fike, the other half of the team, was a quiet, unassuming man in his mid-forties. He published a number of small newspapers in western Missouri, had been president of the Missouri Press Association, and knew every small-town newspaper editor in the state. He had worked with Jim Meredith on earlier campaigns, and like Meredith, was thinking of cutting down on his political activity. Like Meredith, however, he was won over by Symington's personality and ideas. After a long talk in the Muehlbach Hotel in Kansas City, he agreed to sign on.[25] He didn't realize it, but he was signing on for life. He accompanied Symington to Washington as his administrative assistant and remained until he retired. He became so influential that he frequently was referred to as "the third senator from Missouri."

Jacob Lashly headed the formal campaign committee. Sidney Salomon, another close friend, who had been treasurer of the Democratic National Committee during Hannegan's chairmanship, took over the fund-raising.

To help with organized labor and the black vote, Symington asked George Weaver, who had worked for him at the NSRB and the RFC, to spend a few weeks in Missouri. Symington didn't need much help with either labor or the African American community—his record at Emerson and the air force spoke for itself—but Weaver's highly visible presence as a member of the campaign team added punch to the record.[26]

Then there was a group of young, liberal, reform-minded lawyers, all graduates of the University of Missouri law school, who had tried to get involved in Democratic politics but found themselves rebuffed by the old guard, men such as John Oliver of Kansas City, William Becker and Warren Welliver of Columbia, D. W. Gilmore of the little Bootheel town of Benton, and Elmo Hunter of Cape Girardeau. They eagerly enlisted under Symington's banner, and, encouraged by Jim Meredith, who was one of them, assumed leadership roles in the campaign. They were particularly effective in Kansas City, where, under John Oliver's leadership, they used the Symington campaign to beat down the remnants of the Pendergast machine.[27]

Symington formally announced his candidacy on March 20 at a press conference in the Hotel Jefferson in St. Louis, thus ending weeks of speculation. For all those who had been hoping he would enter the race, the announcement came like a shot of adrenaline. The *Globe-Democrat,* which had been urging him to run, endorsed him immediately, calling his candidacy "a rare opportunity." He had "a combination of qualifications, experience and performance record not often available to the voters of any state." The *Post-Dispatch* soon followed, dealing at length with two of the most often cited reasons why he should not be senator: he was not born in the state, and his election would give the eastern side of Missouri a second senatorship. Two-thirds of the state's senators had been born elsewhere—"The late speaker Champ Clark, who epitomized political life in Missouri for many years, was born in Kentucky. Carl Schurz, perhaps the most distinguished of Missouri senators, came from Germany." Geographic distribution could be a factor if the candidates were equal, but they were not equal—"They are so unequal the prospect is that Mr. Symington is the only one who can conduct the kind of campaign that would withstand a possible Republican presidential victory." From the western part of the state, the *Kansas City Star* wrote: "The Democrats have an opportunity to rise above routine and petty politics. They can name a man of national stature."[28]

Although Symington had been campaigning steadily since making the decision to run, he formally opened his campaign on April 12 in Paris (population 13,195), the county seat of Monroe County, in the heart of "Little Dixie." He chose Paris in part to counteract the "big city" image, and in part because he knew he would be speaking under favorable conditions. H. J. (Jack) Blanton, publisher of the *Monroe County Appeal* and a member of a well-known Missouri family, had long been urging him to run. Symington and Eve spent the day shaking hands "with hundreds of people" in Paris, Madison, Holliday, Indian Creek, and Monroe City, before returning to Paris "for an evening country ham dinner in Lucille's Cafe," after which the candidate addressed a small audience consisting of members of the Monroe County Democratic Committee and a number of editors from surrounding towns. "Many others who planned to come were detained by unfavorable weather conditions," the *Appeal* explained.[29]

Symington's speech was long and rambling, concentrating on the economy and the need for a strong defense. It may have been a little too pedantic for the audience; it confirmed the fears of those who realized that he was not a particularly powerful orator. Jack Blanton told him the speech was "Rotten. Not Democratic enough."[30]

Symington never developed into a powerful public speaker—but this campaign was not going to be won by oratory. It was going to be won by personal contact with voters in all parts of the state in which he would sell himself and his ideas to individuals alone or in small groups, an activity in which he had few if any peers. So, from that first day in Monroe County, he walked the main streets and courthouse squares of Missouri's small towns. Eve accompanied him everywhere; as the *Columbia Tribune* wrote, "'I just run in and out of stores!' laughed this charming, youthful woman, chic in a navy blue suit and matching shoes complemented by a pearl choker, gold earrings, and a gold bracelet watch."[31]

Eve, who once was listed as one of America's ten best-dressed women, was described as being "dressed as if she had mastered all the rules on proper attire for a candidate's wife. . . . in very good taste, but it wasn't the kind of thing that might excite the envy of any woman she might meet." Lashly, assessing her role in the campaign, said that she made up for Stuart's lack of political experience: "she was brought up in politics, and my, how she knew how to use her charm in politics. We knew that if we could expose the voters to Stuart for a while, they would have a hard time not voting for him. Exposed to both of them, the voters didn't have a chance."[32]

In May, the boys joined the campaign. Jim, studying law at Columbia University, was also making a name for himself as a New York night-club singer. Fortunately, his repertoire included folk songs and country music. He preceded the rest of the family by about an hour in a sound truck. He drew a crowd with his singing, entertaining them until the rest of the entourage arrived, when he would head for the next stop.[33] Sometimes, Symington would make a short speech, but mostly he and Eve just worked the crowd. Stuart, Jr. (Tim), a law student at Harvard, served as chauffeur, put up posters, and researched the issues.

Symington spoke from whatever platform was available, sometimes standing on the back of a pick-up truck or a bale of hay. He abandoned his tailored-in-New York suits for simple seersuckers, not off-the-rack from J. C. Penney, but usually from J. Press of New York and New Haven. He went through several suits a day, frequently changing them in the car between towns. He acknowledged the Missouri heat by removing his jacket, but never his tie. He also acknowledged Missouri's southern heritage by reminding his listeners that his grandfather fought with Pickett during the Civil War. His main theme, however, was that he wanted to go to the Senate to help the country stay strong enough to resist aggression without going broke in the process.[34]

Symington soon learned that the issues which counted were mostly local—roads, bridges, taxes, and farm problems. He knew little about any of them, and was woefully uninformed about agriculture. On his first visit to the Missouri Farmers Association, he asked naively, "What is parity?" That question should have killed his candidacy with this particular group of farm leaders, but Symington so sold them on his sincerity and his ability to learn that MFA became a solid and steady supporter.[35]

Symington mastered the issues—sometimes boning up on them in the car between towns—and he also mastered the art of campaigning in rural Missouri. Herbert Trask, the state political correspondent of the *Post-Dispatch,* wrote from Kennett, deep in the Bootheel, on July 1: "After three months of gathering rural Missouri campaign experience, W. Stuart Symington III, the highly successful industrialist and top governmental official, has now emerged as just plain 'Stu' Symington, a skillful rider of the Missouri political circuit."[36]

In addition to being an effective personal campaigner, Symington exhibited an amazing ability to bring together the divergent and often feuding factions of the Democratic party. He didn't build the standard, run-of-the-mill Democratic organization. Rather, he assembled a campaign team that Edward F. Woods of the *Post-Dispatch* described as "the type of political machine Rube Goldberg could draw cartoons about."

Its components were bankers, labor leaders, battle-scarred ward leaders, country editors, starry-eyed liberals, dyed-in-the-wool reactionaries, Republicans, Democrats, Dixiecrats, dedicated "do-gooders," fugitives from Jim Pendergast's power grab in Kansas City, Sheriff Thomas F. Callanan and those who were out to slit Callanan's throat.[37]

By July, the bandwagon was rolling. Almost every campaign stop added to the groundswell of support as one of the most attractive political families in Missouri's history conducted a campaign quite unlike anything the state had ever seen. The opposition began to fade away. Former Congressman Roger Slaughter of Kansas City withdrew from the race on July 10.[38] A few days later, Governor Smith announced that he was supporting Symington. Buck Taylor, who at the beginning of the campaign appeared to have the election sewed up, was no longer the front-runner—he would not have been in the race at all if he had not had the support of the president of the United States.

Although Truman had told Symington on January 12 that he probably would vote for Buck Taylor, he did not formally announce his support until May 29, when, in response to a question about the Missouri primary, he simply said, "I am going to vote for the Attorney General when it comes my time to vote. I am taking no personal interest in the primary or any activity in it, but I shall support Buck Taylor."[39]

The president's announcement, though not unexpected, created a flurry of comment around the state, most of it negative. Reporters and editorial writers recalled Truman's unsuccessful effort of 1950 to secure the Democratic senatorial nomination for Emory Allison in opposition to Tom Hennings. Many predicted a similar fate for this effort. The *Post-Dispatch* summed it up: "Missouri's most urgent political mission this year is to retire James P. Kem. Stuart Symington is . . . the only candidate who can do it. President Truman's announcement in no way whatever alters the fundamentals of this situation." Lyndon Johnson wrote from Washington: "Just thought I'd tell you that I defeated a Buck Taylor in 1944 and it was easy."[40]

Symington was disappointed in the president and more than a little angry— "It was a pretty unkind cut considering everything," he wrote Johnson—but he leaned over backwards to avoid challenging the president either publicly or in private. He reported occasionally on the progress of the campaign, and while he did not directly criticize the president, he gave him ample opportunity to reflect on what he had done. On one occasion he wrote: "[Taylor] loses ground every day. Most people also know what you told me about him." Later in the campaign he reported, "As you undoubtedly know, Taylor is now slandering thoroughly my wife, my sons and my late father-in-law, as well as myself."[41]

Symington had plenty of ammunition. Taylor conducted a negative campaign from the beginning, and as his prospects worsened, he became more negative. He dredged up the boyish prank in which Symington and a few high school chums had gone joy-riding in a neighbor's car.[42] He charged that Symington was "not a real Democrat," citing his vote for Willkie in 1940. Most of all, though, he sought to draw a contrast between himself, a native Missourian who had worked hard all his life, and his opponent, "a wealthy Eastern industrialist." In July he taped a fifteen-minute talk to be aired on most of the rural radio stations in Missouri—fifteen minutes filled with what he must have thought were invidious comparisons, for example:

> I was educated at the Kansas City, Missouri, School of Law, and did outside work to pay my way through it. Symington was educated at Yale University, where the scions of wealthy families are instructed. I married a legal secretary, a native of Missouri, and a Democrat. He married an Eastern socialite heiress, a Republican, and the daughter of a financial angel of the Republican party for years. Each of us has two sons. My eldest, 17, is a member of the Naval Reserve and is now taking his training at Great Lakes. The younger is fishing, swimming and playing baseball during vacation just as Missouri children have always done. His two sons are attending Eastern colleges . . .[43]

The smear tactics didn't work, and as the campaign wound down, increasing numbers of Democrats came to see that, as the *Kansas City Star* put it, they "had an opportunity to rise above petty politics. They can name a man of national stature."[44]

Missouri Democrats went to the polls in record numbers, and by a two-to-one margin nominated such a man. The final vote was Symington, 368,595; Taylor, 180,849. Symington carried only 59 of the state's 114 counties, but he won big in St. Louis and Kansas City. Bill Becker, the young Columbia lawyer who had worked hard for him, wrote, "I think we could have made it worse, and I think we could have done better out here in the country if we had not exercised such gentlemanly restraint."[45]

The press, both nationally and in Missouri, made much of the fact that Symington had defeated Truman's candidate, pointing with obvious relish to the results in the president's home precinct in Independence, where Symington bested Taylor 114 to 20.[46] There is no doubt that the president's influence had ebbed in his home state—this was the second senatorial primary in two years in which he had backed the loser—but he refused to admit it. "The president has a right to vote for anybody he pleases in a primary, and if the other fellow wins, the president always supports the ticket," he told reporters in response to the suggestion that he had taken a beating in Missouri. "I am just as fond of Symington as I always was, but I was in the frame of mind to vote for the other fellow. . . . and that doesn't affect my standing in the State of Missouri one little bit."[47]

For his part, Symington was prepared to forgive and forget. In response to a telegram of congratulations—the original of which the president had written in longhand—he wrote: "Thank you for your typically gracious wire. After I beat Kem I'll try to give Missouri the same magnificent reputation they received from the chairman of the great Senate War Investigating Committee. Eve joins me in respect and deep affection to you and Mrs. Truman."[48]

Symington was confident that he could beat Senator Kem if he could hold together the "Rube Goldberg" coalition of supporters that had carried him to victory in the primary and gain the support of the Democrats who had voted for Taylor. This was fairly easy to accomplish. Many of Taylor's supporters had been lukewarm at best, and Taylor himself, good Democrat that he was, announced that he would support Symington. Moreover, Democratic candidates all the way from contenders for local offices to the governorship knew that Stuart Symington at the head of the state ticket would pull them all along. He was heavily favored by the Missouri press, and—even though outside opinion doesn't count for much in Missouri—his candidacy was given wide and favorable attention in the national press.[49]

But with the immensely popular General of the Army Dwight D. Eisenhower at the head of the Republican national ticket, the road would be all uphill. Eisenhower's candidacy impinged with particular force on the Missouri senatorial campaign. Kem was a conservative whose position on domestic issues aligned him with the right wing of the Republican party. On foreign affairs he was an extreme isolationist who had vigorously opposed the bipartisan foreign policy that produced such initiatives as the Marshall Plan and the North Atlantic Treaty Organization, which Eisenhower strongly supported and in the months before his nomination had been working to implement. Symington's views were much closer to Eisenhower's than were those of his Republican opponent. Personally, the campaign posed an excruciating dilemma for the two men. They had been close friends since 1946 when Eisenhower as chief of staff and Symington as assistant secretary of war for air had worked together to bring about the unification of the armed services. They were close golfing buddies— Eisenhower had proposed Symington for membership in the Augusta National, and Symington had arranged for Eisenhower to join Burning Tree. With their wives, they frequently had dinner together. Eve's cousin, Jock Whitney, was a leader in the Draft Eisenhower movement and contributed heavily to the campaign. There was even some talk that he might become Ike's running mate. Eisenhower and Symington corresponded regularly in the

months leading up to their decisions to run for office; most of it was social, trying to arrange a vacation together. When Symington indicated that he was
thinking of running for the Senate, Eisenhower wondered if he "would like that
line of work." In response to Symington's letter advising that he was running for
the Senate, Eisenhower responded with a discussion of how busy he was, concluding: "From what you tell me of your own schedule, I know you are busy,
too, so I won't look to you for much sympathy. However, you did have that vacation in Jamaica and I don't know when I might get around to taking one!" He
added a handwritten postscript: "I wish we could have a talk on the whole business of Nat. Defense. It grows tougher by the week."[50]

With that, the correspondence ceased. Politics, in addition to making strange
bedfellows, also strains close friendships. Symington lauded Adlai Stevenson's
nomination. He had campaigned with and for him in 1948 "and found him a
modest and forceful person, a man thoroughly aware of the grave issues which
now face the United States, both externally and internally. . . . He will make a
great president." Eisenhower, campaigning in Kansas City, endorsed Kem "as a
member of the Republican party." This was comparable to his endorsement of
Senator Joe McCarthy in Wisconsin.[51]

After a short golfing vacation in Colorado Springs,[52] the Symingtons went
back on the campaign trail. It was largely a reprise of the primary effort, although Tim returned to law school at Harvard in September and Jim was laid
up for a few weeks with a broken ankle suffered in a fall from a telephone pole
as he tried to put a Symington sign above one of Kem's. George Weaver spent
quite a little time in the state reinforcing the support of labor and blacks.
Lyndon Johnson, newly elected minority leader of the Senate, came up from
Texas to remind Missourians of the importance of defeating Senator Kem and
sending Stuart Symington to Washington. Stevenson supporters complained
that Johnson (who was only lukewarm about the presidential candidate) spent
more time in Missouri campaigning for Symington than he did in Texas speaking for Stevenson.[53]

Symington continued to do what he did best: meeting people and selling
them individually on his sincerity and integrity. He estimated that he met one
hundred thousand people personally, and made friends with most of them.
Early autumn is county fair time in Missouri, and Symington was introduced to
grandstand crowds in almost all of the Democratic counties—requests for appearances frequently were denied in Republican counties. He ate lots of Missouri ham and visited most of the country editors—of the ninety-four
newspapers he visited, ninety-one supported him. It was an exhilarating, ex-
hausting experience. Unlike the primary race, which he feared until near the end

that he might lose, he was confident from the beginning that he would win in the general election.[54]

The campaign against Kem differed from that against Taylor in another important respect: it was a lot dirtier. While Taylor generally had confined his attacks to Symington's eastern origins, big-business background, Republican associations, and St. Louis residence, Kem added accusations of corruption and collusion with Communists, charges that were patently ridiculous. The charge of corruption was based in part on a press interview with Roswell Gilpatric, undersecretary of the air force, in which he mentioned certain subcontracting problems with Emerson Electric Company. Gilpatric wrote Symington that he "intended no reflection" on him in any way: "The records of the Air Force in this matter disclose nothing whatsoever for which you should be criticized. On the contrary, your great efforts to provide necessary and vital air power in the post-war years are matters of national knowledge and widespread commendation." To help with the pro-Communist charge, revolving around Symington's association with William Sentner, Kem brought Joe McCarthy in for a couple of speeches in Kansas City and St. Louis. The *St. Louis Post-Dispatch* blunted McCarthy's thrusts somewhat by publishing a Daniel Fitzpatrick cartoon that showed Kem emerging from the sewer dripping with mud, with the caption, "Well, it paid off for McCarthy in Wisconsin."[55]

Symington generally ignored the charges and rarely attacked Kem personally, preferring instead to confine himself to the issues and Kem's record as a senator. He got personal when the two men met by chance in the little town of Cabool, in the Bootheel, and the candidates took pot-shots at each other from opposite ends of Main Street. Later, during prearranged debates in St. Louis and Kansas City, Symington accused Kem of conducting a smear campaign, "using the tactics of that arch-priest of character assassination in the North in an attempt to destroy my character so he can hide his own pitifully negative voting record in the Senate."[56]

Symington wrote in "Memories" that he received a number of negative letters following the debates, although none are preserved in his papers. Be that as it may, he was uncomfortable with this kind of campaign. He never again publicly attacked an opponent.[57]

Personalities aside, the principal issue in the campaign was Kem's record in the Senate, particularly with respect to foreign affairs. Kem was tied with Senator William Langer of North Dakota for the lowest ranking on support of the bipartisan foreign policy that Eisenhower strongly supported. As the campaign wore on, it became clear that Symington's early belief that he would win was going to be justified. There was some speculation that he might even carry Adlai Stevenson to victory over the tremendously popular Eisenhower.[58]

That was not to be. Eisenhower carried the state by a narrow margin, while Symington and the rest of the Democratic ticket won handsomely. Symington, who proved to be the ticket's best vote-getter, piled up more than a million votes to win in a landslide.

Stuart Symington, the novice in politics who back in February had not been given much of a chance, had beaten the odds to emerge as Missouri's best vote-getter. For the next quarter century he would be the most powerful force in the politics of the Show-Me state.

19

Not Your Ordinary Freshman

WHEN Stuart Symington became the junior senator from Missouri on January 3, 1953, he did so not as some obscure local politician coming to Washington for the first time, but as a national figure who already was being talked about as a possible candidate for president. He had spent six and a half high-profile years as one of Truman's trusted troubleshooters. He had been the first secretary of the air force. He had been unanimously confirmed by the Senate for six important executive positions. He was probably the most widely known member of a freshman class that included such future luminaries as John F. Kennedy (Massachusetts Democrat), John Sherman Cooper (Kentucky Republican and a Yale classmate), Henry M. "Scoop" Jackson (Washington Democrat), and Barry Goldwater (Arizona Republican).

The Symingtons moved in with Eve's widowed mother in her Georgetown house at 3263 N Street. They fit easily into what was called "The Georgetown Set," a coterie of socially and financially influential politicians, journalists, and power brokers of various sorts. As one reporter put it, "The Symingtons' social life is constantly abuzz. Their top-drawer social position, personal attractiveness, friendships reaching back to her days as a senator's daughter and his days as air force secretary have assured them of more Grade-A invitations than they could manage."[1]

Symington probably knew President Eisenhower as well as any Democrat, but politics had put a barrier between them. During his years in the Truman administration he had got along well with many Republicans in the Congress.

Bridges of New Hampshire was particularly close. Symington introduced himself to Goldwater on his first day in the Senate; despite the wide gulf that separated them on many issues, they maintained cordial personal relations of mutual respect. Both were air force partisans. John Hay Whitney, one of Eisenhower's early bankrollers and soon to become his ambassador to the Court of St. James, was Eve's cousin, but wrote on one occasion, "The ties which bind you and us are very close and quite unconnected with relationship and our beloved Eve."[2]

The new senator from Missouri was the only senior member of the Truman administration to remain in government. He did not need to be introduced to any of his Democratic colleagues—and he was a close, longtime friend of the minority leader, Lyndon Johnson.

His friendships extended far beyond the marble walls of the Senate and the borders of Missouri. In 1959 Paul Wellman, who was writing a biography, asked him for a list of his closest friends. He sent twenty-six names. Heading the list, as one would expect, was Clark Clifford. Then came Dr. Lawn Thompson and Eugene Carusi, social friends and golfing companions from Washington. From the Senate were George Smathers, John Cooper, Hubert Humphrey, and Mike Monroney (Lyndon Johnson was no longer close); from the House, Wright Patman of Texas. St. Louisans included Henry Cook; David Calhoun, his banker; Earnest Kirschten of the *Post-Dispatch;* J. W. McAfee, president of Union Electric; Bishop Will Scarlett; and L. V. Sverdup, internationally known engineer. From business there was David O'Brien of Graybar Electric. From air force days were Barton Leach, Thomas G. Lanphier, General Carl Spaatz, and Eugene Zuckert; also included were scientists Edward Teller and Theodore Von Karman and labor leaders James Carey and George Weaver. The list included two women: Anna Rosenberg and Mary Lasker.[3]

But there were many other "good friends," from all walks of life: for example, Juan Trippe, head of Pan American Airways; Bebe Rebozo, the Miami real estate developer who was an even better friend of Richard Nixon; William A. Paley, head of CBS; Bernard Baruch, whom Symington always addressed as "Dear Boss"; and Bob Hope, who wrote, "We got a wonderful kick out of your knocking off that election! One of the few Demos to come around the far turn. We were proud of our Alaskan playmate. I will be in the East the end of February and hope to have a chance to talk to you. Dolores sends her love and I'm sending a detective along with it to investigate the whole thing."[4]

Among the many letters of congratulations and best wishes was a "My dear Symington" letter written in longhand by General George C. Marshall, sending "congratulations on your remarkable triumph in the midst of a general republican victory." He added, "I have done little this winter beyond quail shooting, seldom leaving Pinehurst. Mrs. Marshall has not been well, her only outing was when you saw her in Washington [at the cabinet dinner for President Truman] and that proved too much of an effort. Now she is much better. I go along about the same."[5]

Symington moved quickly to put together a staff. He persuaded Stanley Fike, who had managed his campaign, to come aboard as his administrative assistant. The soft-spoken and unassuming Fike, whose vast knowledge of Missouri politics had contributed importantly to Symington's victory over Kem, remained in his position throughout Symington's years in the Senate. The power and influence of the "third senator from Missouri" was recognized both in Washington and Missouri.[6]

Virginia Laird, who had been Symington's personal secretary since his time as secretary of the air force and whom he described "as one of the best secretaries anywhere," moved to the Senate with him and remained his principal secretary until he retired. Other secretaries in that first group were Catherine Blanton Roberts of Sikeston, a member of a prominent southeast Missouri family and former secretary to Senator Pat Harrison of Mississippi; Reathel Odum, former secretary to Mrs. Truman; and Frances Hallberg of Unionville, former secretary to Congressman Clare Magee. Two attorneys, Frank Cavanaugh of St. Louis and William Kitchen of Kansas City, became legislative aides.[7] As Symington's committee responsibilities and seniority increased, so did the staff. Among those added were Dr. Edward R. Welsh, Ed Braswell and, later, Kathryn Nelson in defense, Ed Jaenke in agriculture, Sandra Moody in education, and John Zentay and Harriett Robnett in state matters. Others were Diane Blair and Toby Godfrey, who had diverse and wide-ranging responsibilities. Among the interns were future Kansas City businessman John Dillingham, future Kansas City lawyer Douglas Curran, and future famous developer of golf courses Robert Trent Jones. (Symington remained an avid golfer, and despite the crippled arm resulting from a boyhood accident, occasionally shot in the low seventies.)[8] Wayland Smith III, one of Symington's pages, rose to prominence as a St. Louis businessman and elected official and became chair of the board of Howard University. It was an exceptional staff. Symington always had surrounded himself with capable assistants, and his senatorial staff continued the tradition.

As had been true during his years in the Truman administration, Symington ran a friendly but tight operation. Staff members all felt like family—and they all knew who was the head of the family. They came early and worked late; "when the senator was in the office, they usually stayed until he left. He liked to have them tell him good night."

A special problem for the office was the heavy burden of constituent mail. Most replies were staff written, but Symington signed many of the letters and frequently added a personal note in longhand. He instructed the staff to keep letters "short and formal." They were not to send "best wishes, or any kind of regards." If he wanted that in the letter, he would add it by hand.[9] Again, he wrote:

> I notice when critical, or fairly critical, letters come into the office, we start off our replies "Thank you—."
>
> I don't see why we should thank anybody for criticism, especially when we do not believe it is justified against us or against the legislation in question.
>
> I would start off a reply "Acknowledging your letter—."[10]

Since his air force days, he had expressed rather strong opinions regarding the use of certain words. He did not like the word "happy." He once told an air force aide, "Occasionally I am glad, but I am never happy." Fike reminded the staff, "Senator Symington does not like to use the word 'help,' much prefers 'service.' "[11]

Because every staff member was made to feel an important part of the team, they worked happily in what were often crowded, uncomfortable quarters. As a freshman senator Symington drew No. 463, Senate Office Building. With an increase in seniority, the office moved to No. 229. There they remained, even though they could have moved into larger quarters.

Symington was accused by some journalists of being "staff driven." The charge was quite unjustified. He depended heavily on his staff, but, for example, he wrote his own speeches, working from drafts prepared by a staff member. As the administrative assistant to Senator Hubert Humphrey once said of Symington: "He always had an ear. He'd listen to his staff groups, not necessarily his own, just anybody he knew."[12]

As Fike told Bill Becker, "We have a great team here in the office, headed by a fine captain. . . . We have only one ambition . . . and that is to serve the people of Missouri and the Nation." He added in longhand, "No presidential race being planned."[13]

Symington made frequent trips back to Missouri, and during his first term, he and Eve usually spent the fall recess at their home in St. Louis. As time wore on they spent less time in St. Louis; they sold their large house in Creve Coeur and purchased a smaller one in Richmond Heights.

Symington established offices in St. Louis, Kansas City, Jefferson City, and Columbia. Fike was the principal direct liaison with the offices, which served as important parts of a highly efficient machine providing superior service to Missourians and particularly Missouri businesses.[14] He did not involve himself in state politics as extensively as many senators did in their home states, but, with Fike's assistance, kept a close eye on political developments and exercised great influence. He maintained cordial relationships with Missouri's governors, particularly with John Dalton and Warren Hearnes. He did likewise with other Democratic members of the Missouri delegation in Washington. With the death of Thomas Hennings in 1960, Symington became the senior senator from Missouri. His position as the undisputed leader of the delegation remained secure throughout his tenure.

As Symington was leaving for Washington to begin his duties as senator, he was asked what committee assignments he wanted. He replied, "I'm very new, with no seniority. I'm anxious to serve the best interests of the country in whatever capacity the Democratic leaders of the Senate decide."[15] He had promised during the campaign he would go on Agriculture, and later he did. There was no question, however, about what he wanted.

All through his campaign for the Senate he had stressed the importance of maintaining an adequate defense against Communist aggression. It was his major nonpersonal issue. Once elected, he wanted above all to be appointed to the Armed Services Committee where he could make his voice heard on what he considered to be the most important issue facing the country. If history were any guide, however, he should have had little hope. Appointment to committees was based strictly on seniority, and there was no way a freshman could expect to land a spot on one of the Senate's most prestigious committees, but, as had been the case frequently in the past, Symington had a friend in a high place.

The minority leader, who controlled Democratic committee assignments, was his good friend Lyndon Johnson. Johnson had overcome the seniority system largely because he had been befriended by Franklin D. Roosevelt and Georgia's powerful Senator Richard Russell. He decided to do the same thing for his good friend Stuart Symington. He really wasn't taking much of a chance. As former secretary of the air force, Symington was an obvious choice for the Armed Services Committee.[16]

The plum came with a price: appointment to the Committee on Government Operations.

The committee, a relatively minor watchdog body created as part of the legislative reorganization act of 1946, had devoted itself to a fairly wide array of subjects, most of them noncontroversial. One of the committee's members, however, Joseph R. McCarthy, junior senator from Wisconsin, had used his membership to conduct a one-man crusade against Communists in government. When the Republicans took control of the Senate in 1953, McCarthy became chairman of the committee and appointed himself chairman of its permanent subcommittee on investigations. The committee had not focused particularly on communists in government—that had been the province of the House Un-American Activities Committee—but with Joe McCarthy at the helm there was no telling what it would look into.

Symington had no interest in serving on the committee, but Minority Leader Johnson wanted him there. Johnson, as was true of almost everyone in the Senate, approached McCarthy very circumspectly. He decided to try to balance McCarthy's power by appointing three new, aggressive senators who represented the liberal wing of the Democratic party and who would not have to face reelection for six years: Jackson, Kennedy, and Symington. All had defeated Republican incumbents despite the Eisenhower landslide; all had impressive credentials: Jackson and Kennedy had served in the House of Representatives, and Symington had been secretary of the air force. It seemed that they might be able to help rein in the freewheeling chairman.[17]

In making the effort, the freshman senator from Missouri moved to the center of a bitter fight that preoccupied the Senate—and the country—for months.

Senatorial campaign, 1952. Stuart Symington Papers, Western Historical Manuscript Collection, Columbia.

"Retail Politics": a typical campaign situation. Courtesy of James W. and Stuart Symington, Jr.

Stuart Symington and Stanley Fike. Courtesy of James W. and Stuart Symington, Jr.

Symington with Lyndon Johnson at the LBJ Ranch. Stuart Symington Papers, Western Historical Manuscript Collection, Columbia.

The McCarthy Committee: Symington, Robert Kennedy, and Senator Henry M. "Scoop" Jackson. Stuart Symington Papers, Western Historical Manuscript Collection, Columbia.

A campaign photo, Senator and Mrs. Stuart Symington, 1960. Courtesy of James W. and Stuart Symington, Jr.

The photogenic Symington family. Senator and Mrs. Symington surrounded by sons Stuart, Jr. (upper left), James W., and grandchildren. In rows with the senior Symington are Janey (left), Tim's wife, and Sylvia, Jim's wife. Courtesy of James W. and Stuart Symington, Jr.

Advice from an old pro: Truman with John F. Kennedy, as Symington looks on, in Kansas City. Courtesy of AP/Wide World Photos.

President Kennedy, Senator Symington, and Bob Hope at the White House.
Courtesy of James W. and Stuart Symington, Jr.

Symington at a helicopter briefing, Da Nang, Vietnam, 1965. Stuart Symington Papers, Western Historical Manuscript Collection, Columbia.

Symington visits with SP4 John Hall of St. Louis in Vietnam, January 2, 1966. Courtesy of King Visual; photo credit, U.S. Army.

Henry Kissinger visits Symington. Stuart Symington Papers, Western Historical Manuscript Collection, Columbia.

Symington with Golda Meir. Courtesy of James W. and Stuart Symington, Jr.

Symington with President Johnson and Senator Ed Long, observing progress of the Jefferson Expansion National Memorial, St. Louis. Courtesy of the National Parks Service.

Father and son in the Congress, Senator Symington and James W. Symington.
Courtesy of James W. and Stuart Symington, Jr.

Symington with Bob Hope and Sidney Solomon at a St. Louis Blues game. Courtesy of James W. and Stuart Symington, Jr.

The "Symington Court": U.S. Circuit Judge Floyd Gibson and U.S. District Judges John Oliver, William Collinson, William Becker, Elmo Hunter, with Senator Symington. Courtesy of James W. and Stuart Symington, Jr.

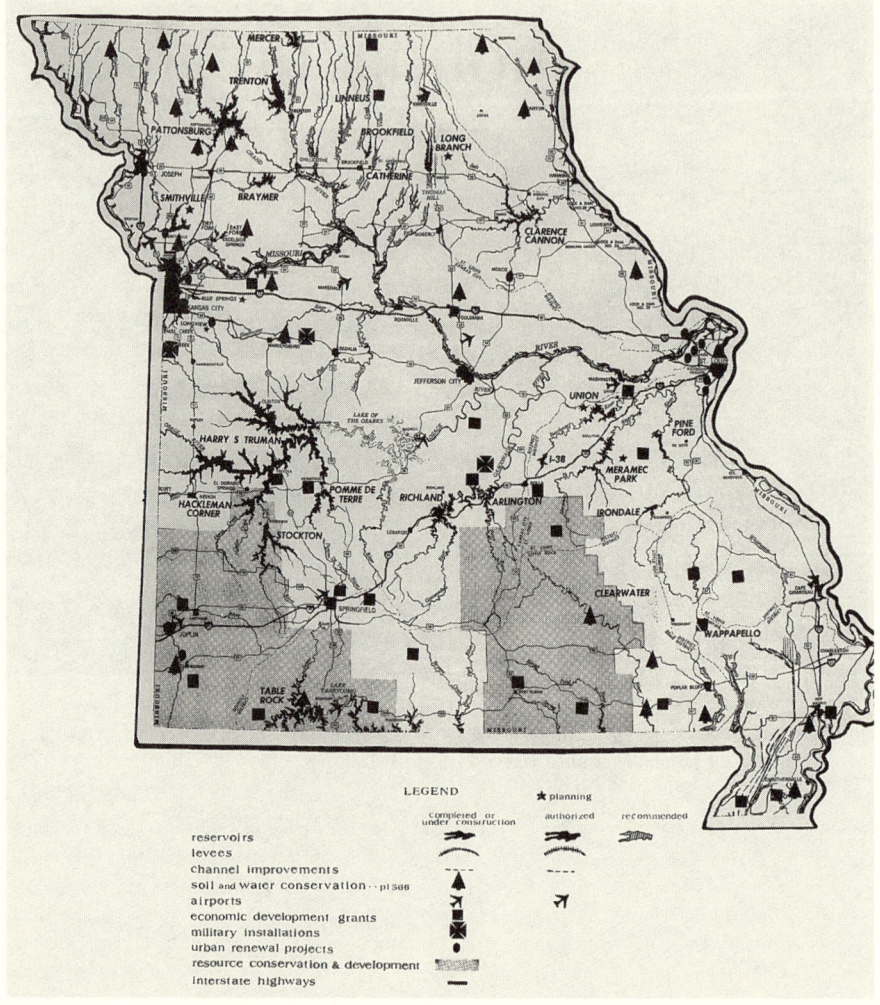

Missouri projects in which Symington's office provided significant assistance.

Symington at the United Nations. Courtesy of James W. and Stuart Symington, Jr.

Stuart and Nancy Watson Symington on their wedding day. Courtesy of James W. and Stuart Symington, Jr.

20

Confronting McCarthyism

SYMINGTON'S first brush with McCarthyism, albeit indirect, occurred in 1950 in connection with the confirmation of Anna Rosenberg as assistant secretary of defense for manpower. During the war Rosenberg had been active in postwar planning, particularly in the field of manpower. Symington got to know her during her service as an adviser to the Office of War Mobilization and Conversion, and along with such a varied group of people as Bernard Baruch, William Benton, Dwight Eisenhower, and George Marshall became one of her staunch admirers. When he took over the National Security Resources Board, he asked her to serve as a consultant on labor matters. In late October 1950, George Marshall, who had recently become secretary of defense, asked her to join him as assistant secretary. The extreme right wing, suspicious of Marshall and hostile to Rosenberg because of her New Deal liberalism, attempted to block the nomination by trying to prove she was a Communist. Although McCarthy was not directly involved, Don Surine of his office actively participated in the plot. Symington was incensed. He wrote the committee on her behalf, and wrote her encouraging letters.[1]

While all this was taking place, Symington watched his good friend Millard Tydings go down to defeat in his bid for reelection to the Senate from Maryland. The defeat had been engineered by the junior senator from Wisconsin, who seemed to be able to run roughshod over all who opposed him. Tydings had won McCarthy's undying enmity by issuing a report highly critical of his methods in investigating various State Department officials in China.[2]

Symington's first direct brush with McCarthy occurred during his campaign for the Senate. McCarthy, then at the height of his powers, made two trips to Missouri to praise his good friend Jim Kem and denounce Symington as a car thief and a Communist sympathizer. The effort may have helped Symington more than it hurt him—at least it reinforced the notion that Kem's campaign had descended to the gutter.

When the Republicans took control of the Senate in 1953, McCarthy became chairman of the Committee on Government Operations, and appointed himself as chairman of the committee's Permanent Subcommittee on Investigations. Other Democrats on the subcommittee in addition to Symington were Scoop Jackson and John McClellan, a conservative from Arkansas. In the beginning, they did not make much impact. The Republicans on the subcommittee were all conservatives and close supporters: Everett Dirksen of Illinois, Karl Mundt of South Dakota, and Charles Potter of Michigan. McCarthy as chairman ran things as a virtual one-man show. He hired the staff, and decided when and where the subcommittee would meet and whom they would investigate.

Symington came very slowly to the point of actually confronting McCarthy. Many of his friends were among McCarthy's strong supporters: Sid Richardson, for example, the Texas oil tycoon who repeatedly bankrolled McCarthy's activities, and Marshall Loeb, the right-wing New Hampshire publisher. George Sokolsky, the conservative columnist who regularly supported McCarthy, wrote: "Stuart Symington is an anti-communist, and when he was appointed a member of the committee on government operations, it was assumed that he would be on McCarthy's side."[3]

For a time it seemed as though he might be. He wrote his mother-in-law during the subcommittee's investigation of the State Department: "The irony of all this McCarthy business is that he has been more right than the State Department to date. Some of their operations have been strictly for the birds (private) but that is the truth and the truth is the main thing in this business."[4]

The State Department investigation, however, marked a turning point in Symington's relations with McCarthy. Initially, he followed the Democratic line that the junior senator from Wisconsin was a Republican problem which should be left to the Republicans. He along with many responsible people in and out of government looked upon McCarthy's antics as broad farce that would soon play itself out. He frequently missed meetings of the subcommittee, giving McClellan or Jackson his proxy, and when he did attend asked only perfunctory questions. When McCarthy launched into an attack on the State Department, however, and particularly on the Voice of America, Symington's attitude began to change.

Symington had brushes with the State Department even when it was headed by his good friend Dean Acheson, and he had little confidence in John Foster Dulles. He sensed a clear danger to the country, however, in McCarthy's continued attacks on the agency responsible for carrying out its foreign policy. Moreover, his innate sense of fair play recoiled at watching innocent people pilloried by the chairman and his chief counsel, Roy Cohn. He objected to the practice of soliciting testimony from disgruntled employees and encouraging them to attack the reputations of their supervisors or associates, usually on the ground that they were Communist or pro-Communist, and then not giving the accused chances to defend themselves. After the hearings had been going for a few days, he spoke up to "express the hope that as . . . people get criticized, they be allowed to come before the committee to defend their name." Jackson voiced his support, and McCarthy, in the patronizing tone he frequently used with staff and other members of the committee, turned to Cohn and said solemnly, "I think, counsel, Senator Symington makes a good point when he says that if there is very damaging evidence presented against John Jones today, and then if John Jones is not called for 2 weeks, it may do him a considerable injustice. So let us have this understood. And I think it has been. . . . If . . . [a witness] says, 'I want to be called immediately to answer this, because I am being embarrassed by the testimony,' then we will call him immediately . . . that will be the modus operandi in the future . . ."[5]

The effort, slight as it was, caught the attention of observers who were unused to seeing any member of the committee make any suggestion for change in the committee's procedures. In his regular broadcast on ABC that night, Elmer Davis said, "McCarthy kept chipping away at the Voice of America today, but there were some notable mitigations in his technique, even though he still offers an open field to all disgruntled employees. Thanks apparently to the pressures of Senators Symington and Jackson, new Democratic members of the committee, a man who is attacked can now answer immediately instead of having to wait the committee's often belated convenience."[6]

Herbert Bayard Swope wrote from New York: "Dear Stu: I thought you handled yourself delightfully in the McCarthy hearing the other day. . . . You'll probably wind up as Pope, or failing that, as President. Neither would be too bad!" Stewart Alsop wrote that Symington was showing "real courage."[7]

McCarthy broadened his attacks on the State Department to include the entire International Information Administration, particularly the overseas libraries created to help foreigners learn about the United States. Conservatives, suspicious of the whole operation, voiced increasing dissatisfaction with what they perceived to be the liberal, left-wing bias of the International Information Agency.

They were concerned that the libraries seemed to be filled with books by liberal and even pro-Communist authors. All this was like manna from heaven for the chairman of the Senate's Permanent Subcommittee on Investigations, and he launched into his task with enthusiasm.

He now had a new helper, a young Harvard graduate named G. David Schine, recently appointed president of a chain of luxury hotels owned by his father. Aside from this evidence of business success, Schine had come to the favorable attention of the right wing by writing a flimsy, error-filled pamphlet entitled "Definition of Communism," which he placed along with the Gideon Bible in all of the Schine hotels. Cohn met him late in 1952 and took an instant liking to him—possibly as much impressed with his suite at the Waldorf, his fancy limousines, and his collection of adoring starlets as with his insights into communism. At Cohn's insistence, McCarthy added Schine to his staff as an unpaid consultant.

With Schine's help, Cohn scattered subpoenas around like leaves in an October breeze. Sometimes Cohn and Schine interrogated witnesses in Schine's apartment; on occasion McCarthy conducted one-man hearings, and somewhat irregularly, the full subcommittee convened. Symington grew increasingly impatient with this procedure, but voiced no public objections. Indeed, he occasionally attended meetings of the subcommittee as the only member besides the chairman who was present, and his interrogation of witnesses was direct to the point of being antagonistic.[8]

Symington came close to an open break with McCarthy over the questioning of James A. Wechsler, editor of the liberal *New York Post*. He knew Wechsler slightly and was fully aware that as a youth he had been a member of the Young Communist League; he knew also that Wechsler had renounced communism and for years had been one of the country's most effective anti-Communist writers. McCarthy subpoenaed Wechsler to appear before his committee shortly after Cohn and Schine returned from a highly publicized tour of Europe in which they wreaked havoc in embassies and United States information libraries in seven countries as they searched for evidence that the libraries contained books by Communists and former Communists.[9] Whether by design or inadvertence, McCarthy did not notify the other members of the committee that Wechsler was to appear. Symington was out of town for the day, and, much to his chagrin, learned about the hearings only when Wechsler called him that evening. McCarthy opened the second day of hearings by announcing that the only remaining evidence the committee sought was a list of persons Wechsler knew who were members of the Communist party or the Young Communist League. Wechsler apparently was prepared to submit the list, but he wanted some assurances that the names would not be released without approval of the full committee. Symington assured him that he would do his best to keep the list confidential as the committee discussed the matter in executive session.

Wechsler saw another problem, and it involved the presence of Howard Rushmore, a former Communist and now an ardent anti-Communist and Hearst reporter, whom McCarthy had hired as a staff member. Wechsler said, "It is a matter of common knowledge in the newspaper business that Mr. Rushmore . . . is a continual source for Mr. [Walter] Winchell." He didn't want Rushmore looking over the list. Symington agreed that this would be bad procedure, getting into an argument with McCarthy as to whether Wechsler or Rushmore was the more credible former Communist. The discussion became personal when Symington called Wechsler "the most forthright witness formerly interested in the Communist Party, or a member of it, that we have had before this committee." When McCarthy responded, "I may say, that perhaps the only reason you say that, Senator, is that you have not been here to hear all of the testimony," Symington shot back, "I have to answer. If you had told me the day before he came that he was to testify, I would have been here."[10] Clearly, Symington's patience with McCarthy was wearing thin.

Symington's relations with McCarthy took another downturn when shortly after the Voice of America hearings concluded, McCarthy garnered more publicity by announcing that he had brokered a deal whereby the Greek owners of 242 cargo vessels had agreed to cease carrying goods to and from Red Chinese and Soviet bloc ports. He trumpeted the deal from the floor of the Senate, with Robert Kennedy, the committee's minority counsel, by his side. The arrangement, worked out by Kennedy, assured the ship owners that they would be spared being called before the committee if they would make the pledge. The deal, which got headlines all around the world, infuriated policy makers in the State Department. Aside from being an obvious infringement upon executive prerogatives, McCarthy's clumsy efforts threatened to upset some delicate negotiations that Harold Stassen, newly appointed director of the Mutual Security Agency, had under way.[11] To complicate matters further, the Defense Department seemed to be supportive of McCarthy's action.

Symington, who already was becoming disenchanted with the Eisenhower administration, suggested that the chairman write the president to inquire just what the administration's policy was. McCarthy thought this was a good idea; he asked Kennedy to draft a letter and hand-deliver it to the White House. McCarthy's letter created great consternation in the administration, still trying to get along with the junior senator from Wisconsin—Secretary Dulles, for example, undercut Stassen, who had been highly critical of McCarthy's actions, by praising McCarthy for "acting in the national interest."

"National interest" or not, White House officials did not want the president to have to deal with the letter. Nixon came to the rescue by calling McCarthy to remind him that Symington's only interest lay in trying to embarrass the administration. He suggested that McCarthy recall the letter before it reached the president "officially." This the senator, still willing to try to get along with the president, agreed to do, irritated that Symington had tried to make a fool of him.[12]

A few days after the letter fiasco, Symington took a step toward publicly distancing himself from McCarthy. Speaking at the Radcliffe College commencement, where Tim's wife, Janey, was taking her Ph.D. in biology, he lashed out at McCarthy's methods, although he didn't mention the senator by name. "There is no place in our democracy for a grand inquisitor," he told the graduates. "There is no place in this country for one-man investigations or for peremptory summons to inquisition. We can, we must search out Communism and fight it to its death—but we must do so with the weapons of democracy—democracy practically applied."[13]

In the summer of 1953, McCarthy was riding high—scheduling hearings, calling witnesses, hiring and firing staff. Symington and the other Democrats on the committee did very little about it. They along with everyone else were uncertain about how far they could go in opposing this man who seemed to have the entire nation in thrall. Then, McCarthy overreached himself. Without consulting anyone on the committee, he hired the Reverend Doctor Joseph Brown Matthews to be staff director of the Permanent Subcommittee on Investigations.

Matthews, a onetime Methodist minister, had been active in a number of communist front organizations in the 1930s, but in 1938 he had renounced his old ties to become staff director for the House Un-American Activities Committee. At the end of the war, he left the committee to become a consultant for the Hearst Corporation. In this capacity, he helped McCarthy produce "evidence" for his attacks on the State Department. He had hardly established himself in his new office when the July issue of the *American Mercury* hit the stands, featuring an article by Matthews, "Reds and Our Churches." The lead sentence declared: "The largest single group supporting the Communist apparatus in the United States today is composed of Protestant clergymen."[14]

The three Democrats on the committee, after a planning session in McClellan's office, stormed into McCarthy's office and demanded that Matthews be fired. When McCarthy refused, they issued a joint statement asserting that Matthews's statement "cannot be supported by the facts" and demanded an immediate closed session to "consider appropriate action." The Fourth of July holiday prevented a meeting until July 7. By that time pressure from the mainline Protestant churches had reached crescendo proportions. Senator Potter, having discussed the matter with the Episcopal Bishop of Michigan, joined the three Democrats in urging that Matthews be fired. McCarthy, however, refused to put the question on the grounds that under the Congressional Reorganization Act of 1946, he had complete authority to hire and fire "non-professional" staff, and he claimed that Matthews was in that category.[15]

Matthews resigned his post on July 10, but the subcommittee voted 4 to 3 to continue to allow the chairman free rein in the hiring and firing of staff. With this, the three Democrats walked out, stating that they had been put in "the impossible position without any voice, right, or authority." McCarthy announced that he would accept the resignations: "If they don't want to take part in uncovering the graft and corruption of the old Truman-Acheson administration, they are, of course, entitled to refuse."[16]

On July 16, McCarthy wrote a two-thousand-word letter to the three Democrats, inviting them to return. The letter, alternately sarcastic and conciliatory, assured the departed Democrats that "the door is open for your return to the committee to share its work and responsibilities." Each of the Democrats, in individual letters, rejected the invitation out of hand. When McCarthy told *Meet the Press* that the Democrats left the subcommittee because they found it "politically embarrassing" to participate in "exposing graft and corruption" in the Truman administration, Symington issued an angry reply, stating that most of McCarthy's recent investigations concerned the Eisenhower administration and that if his concept of politics followed McCarthy's he would have stayed on the committee, "but I resigned because I do not believe he should have such sole authority and because I do not believe certain recent activities of his committee have been in accordance with the tradition of the United States Senate."[17]

Many of Symington's Missouri constituents disapproved of his action, and for the first time in his public career he experienced an avalanche of critical mail. Except for the anonymous letters—and there were quite a few of those—he answered each one. Although each was slightly different—Symington learned early the importance of personalized communications—the burden of all was the same: Matthews's indictment of the Protestant clergy was unfair and dangerous; the Democrats on the committee would not be a part of an arrangement that gave them responsibility without commensurate authority.[18]

The Democrats continued to stay off the subcommittee, despite criticism and pressure for their return. Symington was not at all happy with the situation. In a memo for his files, written December 2, he commented somewhat plaintively, "I do not know what should be done. I would like to go back on the Committee. But I am also certain I do not want to go back unless I have a chance to function properly. . . . After working on this committee for six months, and thinking about it for the last four months, because of the possibility of precedent being involved, I believe the terms under which the Democratic members might return should be a party matter."[19]

It became a party matter, with the leadership on both sides anxious for the return of the three Democrats to restore some sense of regularity to the subcommittee. Finally, after a threat to cut off the subcommittee's funds, McCarthy reluctantly agreed to permit the minority to hire its own counsel and a clerk. He also accepted procedures which provided that if the Democrats on the subcommittee unanimously opposed public hearings on any issue the question would be taken to the full committee for resolution. With these concessions, the three Democrats returned to the subcommittee on February 23, 1954.[20] Within a short time, Symington, who during his first six months on the subcommittee—and in the Senate—had generally deferred to McClellan and Jackson, emerged as the Democrats' principal spokesman, the principal challenger of Joe McCarthy's one-man rule.

McCarthy now was turning his attention to the Department of Defense, and particularly the army. His interest in the army was sparked, in part at least, by Roy Cohn's solicitous concern for his good friend David Schine, who had been drafted into the service. Cohn had tried to get a direct commission for Schine. Failing that, he launched a relentless campaign to secure special favors. He not only badgered Schine's superiors at Fort Dix, where Schine was undergoing basic training, but also took the case all the way to the secretary of the army. The army, trying desperately to get along with McCarthy, made ridiculous concessions—the recruits at Fort Dix complained that Schine was living among them "like a visiting dignitary."[21] Even though the army made itself look ridiculous through its favors to Private Schine, it never yielded on the matter of a direct commission.

Cohn, who was spearheading the investigation, soon zeroed in on the army's signal corps center at Fort Monmouth, New Jersey, the corps' principal research, development, and training center. Monmouth had been the subject of repeated investigations by the FBI, the House Un-American Activities Committee, and the army itself, but nothing credible had been uncovered. Still, the rumors persisted, and no less a person than Major General Kirke B. Lawton, Monmouth commandant, secretly alerted the subcommittee to the possibility of subversives at the fort. The army announced in October that "several employees" had been suspended for security reasons. This was all McCarthy needed. The subcommittee staff, he solemnly announced, had discovered some "extremely dangerous espionage" that dealt "with our entire defense against atomic attack."[22]

While conducting a few low-level—and not very productive—investigations at Monmouth, McCarthy's attention got diverted to the case of Major Irving Peress, an army dentist stationed at Camp Kilmer, New Jersey. Peress had refused to answer questions on an army form regarding any possible subversive associations. In due course, both the army and the FBI began investigating him as a security risk, but, in a classic military SNAFU, promoted him to the rank of major during the course of the investigation and then acceded to his request for an honorable discharge. When summoned before the committee, Peress took the Fifth Amendment in response to virtually every question. McCarthy, enraged, publicly vowed to get to the bottom of the whole mess and let the American people know who was responsible. He started with Brigadier General Ralph Zwicker, commandant at Camp Kilmer.

Zwicker, a native of Wisconsin, was furious over the Peress promotion and had actually tipped McCarthy off to the case. By the time he got to the hearing, however, he had been advised by John Adams, the army's general counsel, that he was not at liberty to discuss personnel matters before the committee. He proved to be a difficult witness, and McCarthy, his temper out of control, subjected Zwicker to a steady stream of invective, declaring him "not fit to command."[23] The spectacle of a decorated combat veteran being humiliated was too much, and the army finally decided it was time to fight back—and this is where Symington came in.

About midafternoon on February 18, Roger Stevens, secretary of the army, accompanied by General Matthew B. Ridgeway, army chief of staff, stopped by Symington's office to talk. Symington had called Stevens earlier to say that he would like to talk to the two of them. Symington had known Stevens since their days together at Yale—Stevens was two classes ahead—and rather liked him. Besides, he was infuriated by what McCarthy was doing to the army. There is no precise record of the conversation, but Stevens later recalled that, "Senator Symington was most helpful in the discussion of Army matters, and stated that if he could be of any assistance to the army, please let him know."[24]

Within twenty-four hours Stevens was asking for help. It turned out that while Stevens and Ridgeway were visiting Symington, McCarthy was humiliating Zwicker in a closed hearing in New York. The next morning Stevens called Symington to report on the Zwicker affair and to ask to see him that afternoon. He also indicated that he was going to try to see other members of the committee. Symington joined Stevens in McClellan's office. Symington was leaving in two days with Senator Styles Bridges for a short trip to Europe on behalf of the Senate Armed Services Committee, and would miss any further hearings unless they were postponed. He wanted very much to be present at any further hearings involving the army, and Stevens wanted it even more. In a rather bizarre exhibit of bipartisanship, a Republican secretary of the army was reaching out to his Democratic friends for help that he seemed unable to get from members of his own party.

McClellan and Symington decided that Symington should write McCarthy requesting postponement of the hearings until he returned from Europe. Symington and Stevens then went to Symington's office, where Symington put in a call to Clifford. Clifford, whom Symington had asked to stand by in his office in case he was needed, came right over. He agreed with Symington that Stevens should stand firm, that he simply could not allow McCarthy to continue to abuse the army's uniformed officers. Stevens and Clifford departed, and Symington dictated his request for postponement of the Zwicker hearings until his return. Fike hand-carried the letter to McCarthy's office. McCarthy was out of town on his celebrated Lincoln Day tour, blasting the administration and the army and generally creating political havoc; Richard O'Melia, McCarthy's administrative assistant, called Symington to say that he had talked to his boss, and that if Symington felt strongly about the matter, the hearing would be postponed.[25]

The next day, Stevens called Symington again. Word had leaked out that he was not going to turn over the names of the officers who had been responsible for promoting Peress, and he had decided he had better call McCarthy. He reported that McCarthy, reached in Albany, had berated him for "coddling Communists" and wound up by telling him that he was subpoenaed for the next Tuesday. Symington talked to Clifford and then called back. He reported that Clifford thought it was a mistake to talk to McCarthy. He then read Stevens a letter that he was writing to McCarthy, thanking him for postponing the hearing on Zwicker, adding: "Secretary Stevens also told me this morning that you were going to subpoena him this next Tuesday, February 23. Because of my great interest in this entire matter, I would greatly appreciate your also postponing any hearing with respect to Secretary Stevens or the Army."[26] Symington, continuing the conversation with Stevens, added:

> I would suggest two things to you, old fellow: 1) Let's counter-punch this stuff and not lead; 2) I think your people over there are pretty harassed and I don't blame them, but maybe some of them can't see the forest for the trees. This boy gets awfully rough."

Stevens admitted that it was "probably poor politics and poor judgment" to call McCarthy, but he didn't want to give him an excuse to "say that we go around his back."

Symington was rapidly assuming the role of protagonist. His friendship for Stevens probably would have put him in that role, but the clincher was his desire to protect the army. When Stevens suggested that talking to McCarthy may have been bad politics, Symington responded with: "It isn't a question of politics at all. It is a question of the integrity and fighting morale of the Army, and, therefore, everybody in my opinion, who has a concept of what is decent will break their back to help you in any way they can. I would never get near him if I could help it."[27]

Symington was on the phone frequently with Stevens before leaving for Europe. Stevens monitored them (with Symington's approval—Symington urged that Stevens monitor all his calls), and their release became a matter of acrimonious controversy during the Army-McCarthy hearings. For the most part, Symington was trying to buck up his beleaguered friend. He suggested that Stevens might consult Abe Fortas or Morris Ernst in addition to Clifford, "good liberal lawyers completely outside the Eisenhower circle." Also, Republican William Rogers. He was on the army's side, and "you can't go wrong with Bill."[28]

On Sunday morning, February 21, just before boarding a plane for Paris, Symington called from New York, considerably agitated over word from Clifford that the *Washington Post* was reporting that Stevens had volunteered to appear before McCarthy. "If you and I are going to work together," he reminded Stevens, "we have got to be on the table with each other." Stevens denied that he had made any such offer, and said that he would appear only if properly subpoenaed. Symington assured him that would not happen: "don't put me in a box by going up there on Tuesday." He reminded the secretary, "If you are going to play with McCarthy, you have got to forget about any of those Marquis of Queensberry Rules."[29]

Later that afternoon, Stevens issued a statement declaring that he had directed General Zwicker not to appear before McCarthy. He cabled the entire statement to Symington at the Hotel Crillon in Paris with this note: "Stu. Issued following public statement Sunday afternoon. Believe it sets the record straight. Appreciate your interest." Symington responded through diplomatic channels: "Many thanks. Very proud of your position. Cabling Senator McClellan that hope any hearing re you or Army can be postponed until my return but leaving decision with him. Achilles."[30]

This seems to have been Symington's last communication with Stevens until he returned. At six o'clock on March 8, two days after he returned from Europe, Symington called Stevens: "Sorry to bother you. I wonder if it would be possible for me to see something. I have heard about it, and somebody has been leaking about it, but I would like to see the report on Schine sometime, if the army is willing to release it."

Stevens doubted that the army would be willing to release it: "Whatever they have got on that would have to be pulled together, and so forth and so on."[31]

Stevens was being less than candid, and Symington knew it. John Adams, the army's general counsel, had compiled a detailed chronology of Cohn's efforts on behalf of Private Schine. Potter, the one Republican on the subcommittee who occasionally objected to McCarthy's excesses, had told him that he had seen a copy in the Pentagon. Two days later, Adams, with the approval of the secretary of defense, sent the document to members of the subcommittee. Symington, now becoming quite disenchanted with Stevens, gave his copy to Phil Potter of the *Baltimore Sun,* who released it to the world.[32]

Whether the army wanted it or not, the gauntlet was down. Cohn's efforts on behalf of Schine clearly constituted an abuse of his position as committee counsel, and the Democrats on the subcommittee, long impatient with his methods, were not going to let him get away with it. McCarthy responded to the army's charges with a five-thousand-word document containing forty-six countercharges against the army. "When placed in proper perspective," he asserted, the army report would be found to have given "greater aid and comfort to Communists and security risks than anything else that could have been designed."[33]

At one point during the run-up to the hearings, Symington told McCarthy, "I can't go along with this, Joe, I'm going to have to take you on." Symington remembered that McCarthy replied, "Don't do it, Stu. I'm fond of you, and if you do, I'll destroy you."[34]

While the administration, the Republican leadership in the Senate, and the Democrats wrestled with the problem of how to handle the row that had erupted between the army and McCarthy, the subcommittee continued to investigate subversion at Fort Monmouth.

McCarthy and Cohn were concentrating on a middle-age black woman named Annie Lee Moss who was serving as a telegraphic typewriter operator for the signal corps. She handled both coded and clear messages, and was in a position that the army described as "sensitive." According to Mary Markward— whom Robert Kennedy described as "an extremely reliable former undercover agent for the FBI"—she had been a member of the Communist party prior to beginning government employment in 1945, although she could not recall ever having seen her at a party meeting.[35] In Kennedy's opinion Moss should never have been given the position she occupied, but there was not "enough evidence to have brought this business out in public. The result has been that Mrs. Moss has been ruined completely without really sufficient information or evidence to warrant it." He added, "The important thing during this whole business was that the army should be embarrassed and she was just the instrument used to do it."

This offended Symington's sense of fair play, and during his question period he gave the witness every chance to prove her innocence. He then went on to show the subcommittee and the nation (watching on television) how Mrs. Moss, who had been suspended from her job, had been abused. She had no savings and if she did not get work soon she would have to "go down to the welfare." She had not applied for work outside the army because she "had been sick in the bed under the doctor."[36]

In a few minutes the hearing came to an end. Symington leaned forward and said, "Mrs. Moss, I want to say something to you, and I may be sticking my neck out and I may be wrong. But I have been listening to you testify this afternoon, and I think you are telling the truth. . . . If you are not taken back into the Army (employment), you come around and see me, and I am going to see that you get a job."[37]

The hearing room resounded with applause, and from around the country, kudos were heaped on Symington, who increasingly was becoming the point man in the effort to rein in McCarthy. Clarence Mitchell, director of the Washington bureau of the NAACP, telegraphed, "Please accept the appreciation of a grateful citizen for your courageous and statesmanlike conduct at the hearing today." NAACP president Walter White followed with, "I send you on behalf of the NAACP this supplemental telegram to Clarence's to tell you how great is our gratitude for the magnificent job you did yesterday in the case of Mrs. Annie Lee Morse [sic]. It was one of the finest jobs of stopping bigotry we have ever seen." Al Capp, the noted cartoonist, wrote: "Your words and deeds yesterday make you a serious candidate for President. All Americans who have been shocked at the UnAmericanism of the Sub-Committee are damn glad you're back and restoring fair play. Keep it up. We're cheering for you."[38]

The hearings, in addition to being televised live, were the subject of a special broadcast of Edward R. Murrow's widely watched program *See It Now.* The radio and television commentator John Crosby, reviewing the program for the *New York Herald Tribune,* wrote: "At the very end, when Senator Symington leaned forward and said to Annie Lee Moss that, if she could not find a job, he would give her one—right there history turned a small but important corner."[39]

Even so, Symington apparently was not sure he had done the right thing. Murray Mauder of the *Washington Post* recalled, "After the scene with Annie Lee Moss, I was walking away from the hearing and Stu came over to me and he said—one of the ironies about Stu was after he made this dramatic stand-up posture before McCarthy, he then came over to me and said, 'Murray, you think I was on good grounds?' and he wasn't really sure. It suddenly dawned on him that maybe he's going to make an ass of himself. I said, 'On the face of it, it looks good. There's always the off-chance that she does turn out to be a Communist.' He says, 'Oh my God! Do you think so?' "[40]

Annie Lee Moss did prove to be something of an embarrassment. The army permitted her to return to work, but on August 4 suspended her again, "on the basis of information which was not previously available and which has not been satisfactorily resolved by an investigation." That evening right-wing commentator Fulton Lewis reminded his national audience of Symington's offer to give Moss a job if the army didn't reinstate her, and said, "It looks as though Senator Symington will have a new employee." Letters, telegrams, and postal cards—some barely legible, some obscene—poured into the office, enquiring about the Senator's new employee. Symington did not bother to answer most of them, but in response to a couple of letters in the *Post-Dispatch* he reminded editor Irving Dilliard that at the hearing he had recognized that there might be additional evidence, and that, if it surfaced, Moss's case should be reopened. He asked McCarthy to do so, but McCarthy, "in accordance with our policy of cooperation," thought it best to let the army conduct its investigation before getting into the matter. The case never got to the committee. On the basis of the army's investigation, Secretary of Defense Charles E. Wilson directed that Moss be restored to duty "in a non-sensitive position." There was some derogatory information from the period prior to 1946, but "the record does not support a conclusion that she is actually subversive or disloyal to the United States." As far as Wilson was concerned, "the case should be closed."[41]

The case had long since been overtaken by the dramatic events of the Army-McCarthy hearings in which Symington and McCarthy traded barbs for thirty-six days before twenty million people.

From the time the army issued its charges, the Senate faced the dilemma of trying to decide who should investigate them. The Permanent Subcommittee on Investigations was the logical body, but McCarthy's role on the committee posed an obvious problem. He agreed to step down temporarily as chairman, but insisted that he remain on the committee. In a press release, Symington said, "The good name of the Senate is involved. I feel confident that Senator McCarthy does not want to appear in the triple role of accusing witness as well as prosecutor and judge. . . . If, however, the Republicans on the Committee insist upon Senator McCarthy filling this triple role. . . . I will recommend that . . . [the hearings] take place before the Senate Armed Services Committee."[42]

McClellan would not comment on the statement, but it was generally assumed that all three Democrats on the committee were in agreement. McCarthy had already agreed to step aside temporarily as chairman of the committee, but was insisting that he remain a member, "to cross examine every witness who appears."[43]

As finally worked out, Senator Herman Welker, a conservative Republican from Idaho, took McCarthy's place on the committee, but McCarthy was permitted to question witnesses and participate in the committee's discussion. Karl Mundt, a bland, somewhat rotund, pipe-smoking conservative from South Dakota, assumed the chairmanship. He didn't want to be chairman, but despite his right-wing background he was determined to make every effort to be fair and reasonable.[44]

After days of jockeying and media hype, the hearings opened on April 12. The large, ornate Senate caucus room was crowded with spectators, reporters, and television cameras there to cover a proceeding that transfixed the nation and drove the soap operas off its television screens.[45]

Symington was probably the most telegenic member of the subcommittee. In recent weeks he had been more visibly hostile to McCarthy than any other committee member. He was frequently mentioned as a likely candidate for president in 1956.[46] He could have been expected to play a dominant role in the hearings.

As it turned out, he was slow to live up to such expectations. He asked relatively few questions, and when he did ask a question, he frequently prefaced it with, "I'm no lawyer." As Mary McGrory, a columnist usually favorable to Symington, wrote: "The matinee idol of the three-man Democratic team, Senator Symington, is tall, blond and handsome. Frequently his blue eyes flashed with fire, but often it seemed misdirected. In the early days, he often said beamingly that he was not a lawyer, as if that were a lovable little shortcoming which should excuse his full participation." Jimmie Allen wrote Symington that his friends and admirers were saying, "Why, oh why, does he hold himself back? Why is he worried that he's not a lawyer? It's his greatest asset."[47]

None of the three Democrats participated extensively in the early stages of the hearings. The Democratic line, after all, was that this was a fight among Republicans and that Jackson, McClellan, and Symington were playing it smart by not intervening. The problem with this approach was that the country got the impression that they were afraid to tackle McCarthy. None of the Democrats on the committee were afraid of McCarthy, but, as Richard Rovere put it, they were hardly "models of valor and eloquent defenders of the faith. They still, sometimes, appeared to be models of discretion and uncertain of what their faith was."[48]

Symington, however, would not long be a "model of discretion." As Michael Straight wrote in the *New Republic* for June 21:

> Symington was neither judicious nor cautious; he was a participant by instinct, and bold—above all in this case. . . . Organization Democrats were privately appalled at . . . his intervention in an internal Republican fight. They felt that it obscured . . . Republican responsibilities, and deprived

the Democrats of the full benefit of the dispute. But Symington was not acting as a party man. To him Army morale and the Subcommittee Chairman were not party affairs. In the drama he became what Stevens could not, and none other would become—the protagonist.[49]

As Symington warmed to the task, his personal hostility to McCarthy became clear. On April 27, while McCarthy and Committee Counsel Joseph Welch were arguing over one of McCarthy's many points of order, Symington, somewhat gratuitously, interjected, "I would like to say that if this is not a point of order, it is out of order. The counsel says it is not a point of order and it is not a point of order, if the counsel says it is not a point of order."

> Senator McCarthy. Oh, be quiet.
> Senator Symington. I haven't the slightest intention of being quiet. Counsel is running this committee and you are not running it.[50]

Characteristically, his participation increased when he felt that McCarthy and Cohn—and for that matter, the army—were trying to keep information from the public. Indeed, his first effort resulted from an attempt by the administration to suppress information regarding high-level conferences concerning ways to handle Cohn and Schine.

Adams had mentioned that such a conference had occurred on January 21, but when pressed for information about the discussions replied that he couldn't divulge such information because a presidential directive prohibited it. This not only gave McCarthy a chance to cry "cover up" but also caused concern among the Democrats on the committee, and even Chairman Mundt. Symington expressed amazement that there would be an effort to bar testimony on such a crucial meeting. When Welch explained that this was a high-level meeting and Adams had been instructed not to discuss the exchange of views, Symington shot back: "Does that mean that we are going to get information about low-level discussions, but not about high-level discussions?"

Welch replied somewhat lamely, "That is only, sir, what I have been informed. It isn't a point of what I like. It is a point of what the witness has been instructed."

The Republicans on the committee wanted to recess the hearings for a week to clear up the matter, and, strangely, McClellan and Jackson went along. Only Symington was opposed.[51]

When the hearings resumed, Symington emerged as McCarthy's principal antagonist. For the first time in the proceedings, he became emotionally involved, and as always when his emotions were aroused, he easily lost his temper. Scoop Jackson, who sat next to Symington at the hearing table, sometimes put his hand on Symington's knee to keep him from getting too excited.[52]

The bad blood between McCarthy and Symington gushed forth frequently, often on points quite irrelevant to the subject of the hearings. For example, on May 26, during an interrogation of Private Schine's company commander, Mc-Carthy brought up the *New York Post,* which had been highly critical of the favors granted Schine, charging that its editor, James Wechsler, "had been one of the top officials of the Communist party." Symington interrupted with a point of order: "Based on the testimony that was given this committee there is no justification, in my opinion, for stating that Mr. Wechsler was a top official in the Communist party."

McCarthy shot back: "Mr. Chairman, could I have the understanding that at least the Senators will not interrupt me half way through a question. If Mr. Symington wants to act as defense counsel for Mr. Wechsler he can do that when my question is finished."[53]

But Wechsler was not the issue. The issue was the fact that former Communists worked for the committee. This, of course, McCarthy did not deny. Indeed, he seemed to be rather proud of it, claiming that they were "helping to send traitors to jail" and were "consistently smeared by the Wechslers who claim to have reformed. . . . I may say to the Senator from Missouri I am deeply disturbed when I find, after he came back to this committee apparently for the purpose of helping us dig out Communists, that the only time I hear him raise his voice at this table is when we appear to be hurting those who defended communism. Let me make it clear—"

And so it went, day after day, with millions watching. Symington and Mc-Carthy were almost constantly at each other's throats.

The hapless Mundt, trying to keep some semblance of control, seemed overwhelmed by the shouting match going on around him.[54] McCarthy repeatedly interrupted the proceedings with "Point of Order, Point of Order." The phrase became the signature piece for the hearings. McCarthy, with his heavy, guttural voice, his heavy beard, and his slumped shoulders became a slightly ludicrous figure. McCarthy occasionally attacked Welch, or Stevens, or, by indirection, Eisenhower, but most of his venom was directed against Symington, who, his emotions thoroughly aroused and his temper flaring, frequently responded in kind. The scene in the hearing room resembled a schoolyard fight, and former Schoolmaster Mundt was hard-pressed to keep the antagonists apart.

Controversy between the two erupted in a particularly virulent form when Symington's monitored calls with Stevens were read into the record. McCarthy demanded that Symington resign from the committee or at least be required to make his statements under oath.

When Symington got the floor, he made a long, impassioned speech, probably his best effort of the entire proceedings. He charged that McCarthy was undermining morale in the armed forces, that "for the first time in history our people have been urged to entertain serious doubts as to the dedication and loyalty of our Armed Forces from top to bottom." He continued, "Millions of Americans have been told by Senator McCarthy that the Eisenhower administration, this Republican administration, has added a year of treason to our proud history. . . . In closing, Mr. Chairman, I am a Democrat. But first and foremost I am an American. It is little comfort to me that these terrible charges are directed against a Republican administration, Republican officials, and our Republican Commander in Chief. It would appear some of us want to end up in this country with just plain anarchy."

McCarthy responded with a sneer: "Mr. Chairman, . . . I may say that I was rather amused to hear Senator Symington worrying about the Republicans, when he has been conniving secretly to get the top political adviser of the Democrats to try to get the Republicans to commit suicide. It may seem very clever to Senator Symington . . . to get Clark Clifford to mislead a fine, naive, not too brilliant Secretary of the Army. But in the end, that is going to be bad for his party and the country, because the two-party system cannot survive if you have the chief political adviser of one calling the shots for the other. . . . Senator Symington made a rather—rather, he read a long speech. Who wrote it, I don't know. He read it rather well today."

He demanded again that Symington permit himself to be questioned under oath—"He shouldn't be afraid to do that, unless he has been guilty of some wrongdoing."

Symington shot back: ". . . You said something about being afraid. I want you to know from the bottom of my heart that I am not afraid of anything about you or anything you got to say, at any time, any place, any where."[55]

McCarthy continued to carry the fight to Symington, insisting that he resign from the committee or permit himself to be interrogated under oath. On a point of personal privilege, Symington said, ". . . I have no objections of any kind to saying anything under oath that I say not under oath, because I tell the truth. I would be glad to go under oath, even though it is a rather extraordinary situation to be a judge in a case of this character and then suddenly to have one of the defendants in the case demand that the judge go to the stand and take an oath and testify."

Back and forth they went. McCarthy used the term "Sanctimonious Stu"; Symington replied, "I object to that reference to my first name, you better go to a psychiatrist."

A frustrated Mundt commented, " . . . this continuing colloquy . . . is ceasing to be as interesting to the rest of us as to the participants in it."[56]

But the colloquy continued. Mundt, in recognizing Symington on a point of personal privilege, commented, "the Chair is going to recognize you, but the Chair would like to say if we are going to continue this mid-morning madness every morning of first you and then Senator McCarthy saying something about the other and then saying, 'I have to have a point of personal privilege,' it is very difficult for the Chair to know how to stop that kind of waste of time as far as the rest of the members of this committee are concerned and the country is concerned."

Symington was willing to call a halt—his points of personal privilege had all been in response to McCarthy-initiated charges—but McCarthy apparently was not. In questioning Cohn, he brought up Symington's relations with Bill Sentner, hinting darkly that the two were in collusion while Symington was president of Emerson. Symington did not rise to a point of order, but when his time came, he said, ". . . these charges presented in a new diversion and a new attack against me by Senator McCarthy, were presented to the people of Missouri in the main on television by Senator McCarthy in the 1952 campaign, and I am reassured by the fact that they will think as little of them now as they did then."

The charges were completely specious. Symington asked that the committee call James Carey, secretary of the CIO, who could answer all of the charges. Mundt replied that if he called every witness requested by him and McCarthy they would be in session well beyond November 4 (the date of the forthcoming congressional elections).[57]

So the hearings dragged on. McCarthy kept insisting that Symington take the stand under oath and that Clifford be subpoenaed. He was determined to show that they had conspired to induce the army to bring charges against him. Symington had sparred with McCarthy over his own participation but as for Clifford, he thought that, as long as he had been indicted before millions of people, he ought to be given an opportunity to clear his name. He would not have to be subpoenaed. The Republican majority on the committee, however, wanted to call no more witnesses; they wanted to get the hearings over as soon as possible.[58]

Before the end, there was still time for additional altercations between the two men who had come to occupy the center ring in the circus. Through close questioning of Francis Carr of the committee's staff, Symington was able to establish that staff members received no clearances even though they handled classified material. Moreover, the committee's files, were, as Symington put it, "the sloppiest and most dangerously handled files that I have ever heard of since I have been in the Government."

McCarthy responded with, "May I say that this is the most dishonest, the most unfounded smear upon some of the most outstanding young men that I have ever seen work to uncover Communists. And before this is over, the American people will have a better picture of it."[59]

The final days of the hearings were occupied with McCarthy's repeated contention that the whole thing had been masterminded by Symington and Clifford, who had taken advantage of Stevens's naïveté to persuade him to file the charges in an effort to embarrass if not destroy the Republican party. Both Stevens and Clifford were willing to testify, but Mundt, backed by the Republican majority, refused to call additional witnesses. Finally, on the last day of the hearings, Mundt allowed a letter from Stevens describing his relationship with Symington and Clifford to be read. It added nothing that had not been learned from earlier testimony. It gave small support to McCarthy's conspiracy charges—McCarthy wondered if the letter had been written by Clifford.[60]

June 17, the last day of the hearings, was occupied with ritualistic concluding remarks. McCarthy acted as though nothing important had happened, that the entire proceeding had been an unfortunate interruption in his important work of rooting Communists out of the government. Mundt regretted that some of the arguments had been "heated and sometimes unhappily personal," but he reminded his colleagues and the television audience, "We settle in America our arguments by an exchange of viewpoints. . . . We don't settle them at pistol point, we don't settle them by brute violence."

McClellan, the ranking Democrat, cast a different light on the proceedings. Calling them "one of the most disagreeable . . . public services that it has ever been my duty to perform," he said, "the series of events, actions, and conduct that precipitated the ugly but serious charges and countercharges that made these lengthy and unpleasant public hearings mandatory, I think will be recognized and long remembered as one of the most disgraceful episodes in the history of our Government."

Symington regretted that Carey and Clifford had not been called. In his opinion the hearings raised a significant issue, "and that is the contention by a member of the legislative branch that he has the right to solicit and that he will continue to solicit employees in the executive branch of the Government secretly to bring him and his staff confidential documents." He agreed with McClellan that the hearings had been most distressing, but "a decision on that important matter, if it comes soon, may have justified these hearings."[61]

The subcommittee did not file a report until September 1, when they issued both a majority and minority report. All agreed that McCarthy was to blame for permitting Cohn to undertake his efforts on behalf of Schine, and that Cohn had exceeded his authority. They also agreed that Stevens and Adams were guilty of trying to appease McCarthy, but that neither was "soft" on communism. Beyond that, however, the Republicans virtually absolved McCarthy of any improper conduct, while the Democrats condemned him for his actions.[62]

The report was something of an anticlimax. The country had already rendered its verdict on Joe McCarthy. As Symington told McCarthy after he was accused of engaging in Communist tactics, "The American people have had a look at you for six weeks. You are not fooling anyone."[63]

And he hadn't. His irresponsible charges, his flailing around from one target to another, his incessant shouting of "point of order," and even his personal appearance—slumped shoulders, heavy whiskers—dramatized for the country that he was little more than a schoolyard bully. Joseph Welch, the army's counsel, contributed to the senator's downfall, particularly when, after McCarthy had tried to attack a young lawyer in Welch's office, he turned to him and asked, "Have you no sense of decency, sir, at long last? Have you left no sense of decency?"[64]

Symington contributed equally to McCarthy's downfall. As Richard Reeves put it, "The clashes with Welch, homespun and witty, and Symington, handsome in his indignation, had been especially ruinous."[65]

Symington talked too much and he lost his temper too often, but he came across to all but die-hard McCarthyites as a man who was willing to sacrifice politics for principle. He did not need to defend a Republican secretary of the army against a Republican senator, but he thought the morale of the army and the security of the country were at stake. He did not need to defend the prerogatives of a Republican administration from encroachment by a Republican senator, but he believed that an important constitutional question was involved. As a newspaper in Ohio commented, "the most salutary thing to come out of the hearings may well be Senator Symington's flat defiance of what Senator McCarthy claims to be the investigative powers of his committee."[66]

There is no doubt that Symington's defiance of McCarthy's investigative powers played a role in dramatizing the dangers of McCarthyism, but his most important contribution to McCarthy's downfall was his willingness to challenge McCarthy without the slightest fear. One of the most dramatic moments in the hearings was when he confronted McCarthy with: "You said something about being afraid. I want you to know from the bottom of my heart that I am not afraid of anything about you or anything you've got to say any time, any place, anywhere." As Michael Straight wrote: "There were few other men in public life . . . who could truthfully say in 1954 that they were not afraid of McCarthy."[67]

Characteristically, once the hearings were over Symington evinced little interest in pursuing McCarthy further. He was not enthusiastic about the censure resolution introduced by Senator Ralph Flanders of Vermont. He was reported as "being all over the lot" on the issue. Pearson wrote in his diary after a dinner at the Abe Fortases': "Stuart Symington and his wife were there . . . Stuart talked about ducking out on the Flanders resolution against McCarthy. I was interested in the fact that his wife, who I have always thought was pretty much to the right of center, chided him. 'You can never do that,' she said. 'You have taken a stand against McCarthy and you can't possibly duck a vote on him.' Stuart, however, is hoping they will postpone any vote on the Flanders resolution."[68]

Symington did not participate in the debate on the resolution, although he voted for it, as did all the Democrats in the Senate except Kennedy, who was in the hospital. Aside from this, he seemed to want to distance himself from the ugliness of the hearings as much as possible. As Clifford put it, "Symington, true to his character, never saw the battle with McCarthy as a personal vendetta. He never felt personally hostile toward the Senator despite the harsh words they had exchanged at the hearings."[69]

Symington was always gracious in victory, and as his star ascended—people were talking about him as a possible candidate for the presidency—and McCarthy slid into oblivion, he couldn't resist the gracious gesture. One day, in a hearing room, he spotted Jean McCarthy looking for her husband. He stopped the hearing, got up, and escorted her to a seat. That evening he had a call from McCarthy, thanking him for the courtesy, and wondering if the Symingtons would care to join the McCarthys for a barbecue dinner some evening. Clifford, who reported the incident, wrote: "I am not sure whether or not Stuart would have accepted the invitation out of sympathy for McCarthy's personal decline, but Evie Symington ended the issue swiftly: under no circumstances would she dine with Joe McCarthy."[70]

Symington was tired of the whole business. As the Democrats, victorious in the 1954 elections, were preparing to organize the new Senate, Symington wanted to get off the Government Operations Committee, but recognized that it would be difficult to do so without looking as though he was running away.[71] He stayed on the committee, but under McClellan, who succeeded McCarthy as chairman, the agenda was much less controversial. Symington was able to devote himself more fully to the work of the Armed Services Committee, his first love.

21

Defense—A Voice in the Wilderness

SYMINGTON enjoyed membership on the powerful Armed Services Committee throughout his years in the Senate. He received his initial appointment, "almost unheard of for a freshman," because of his good friend Lyndon Johnson, the minority leader. Gradually their friendship cooled, and during the Vietnam War they came to an open break. As Johnson's friend Bobby Baker put it, "Symington was an independent loner who refused to let LBJ get a grip on him."[1]

Almost from the beginning Symington found himself in conflict with another old friend, Dwight Eisenhower, the newly elected president of the United States. They had worked closely together to bring about the unification of the armed services, and they had become close golfing and bridge-playing friends. When Eisenhower moved into the White House he decided that he would have to quit playing with Symington and other Democrats whose company he enjoyed.[2] But there was more to it than that. Symington became such a vociferous critic of Eisenhower's defense policies that the two men could hardly have been comfortable with each other around a bridge table or anywhere else.

The controversy began as soon as the president submitted his first budget, substantially reducing the amounts for defense in Truman's last budget and specifically cutting the air force by $5 billion. Symington reacted even before the Armed Services Committee had an opportunity to take up the new budget. Speaking before a capacity crowd at the annual *Philadelphia Bulletin* Forum, he said that while he did not want his listeners "to construe his position as criticism of the new Administration," and without specifically mentioning the president's budget, he charged that the people of the United States were not being told the truth about the country's relative strength vis-à-vis the Soviet Union. This, he said, had been the case ever since the Soviets exploded an atomic bomb in 1949, and with the new administration the policy had not changed. The American people were still being lulled into believing that they could have an adequate defense without paying the price, that they could have both guns and butter.[3]

Eisenhower, obviously nettled, told a group of congressmen that the Soviet threat was "a figment of Stuart Symington's imagination." This was in a private meeting, but he went public with his criticism of those who questioned his judgment, reminding the country of his role in defeating the Nazis.[4]

There was no questioning the immensely popular president's military credentials, and for a time Symington, who soon emerged as the Senate's most vociferous critic of the administration's defense policies, carefully avoided direct criticism of the president himself. Rather, he directed his fire at the president's subordinates, particularly Charles E. Wilson, former head of General Motors, whom Eisenhower had appointed secretary of defense.

Symington tangled with Wilson during the confirmation process. Wilson had given the impression that there was no need for him to dispose of his General Motors stock, that there was no conflict of interest. After all, what was good for General Motors was good for the country. At Wilson's first hearing, Symington declined to comment on the grounds that he was a new member of the committee, but he told the press that he had sold all of his holdings in Emerson before taking office in the Pentagon.[5] When Wilson came back for a second hearing, he announced that he had disposed of his General Motors stock. Symington wanted to carry the questioning further. Prefacing his remarks with, "Mr. Chairman, I would like to have the record show that I think that Mr. Wilson has had both the training and experience to be a fine Secretary of Defense," he brought up an earlier investigation of apparent bid rigging by automobile parts suppliers. He realized that Wilson could not be expected to be familiar with the matter, but asked that he look into it and comment on the industry's practices. Wilson responded with obvious irritation, "for me to study those records . . . and try to tell you what I am going to do about the past seems to me to be sort of an unnecessary burden on me."

Leverett Saltonstall, the Massachusetts Republican who was chairman of the committee, intervened to remind Wilson that Symington had sat in the seat Wilson was occupying many times, "and he knows as a former executive that many questions are asked that may be material, may seem very immaterial, may seem to be all in the past and utterly unnecessary." He was sure that "the Senator from Missouri would not ask it if he did not think it is pertinent."

Wilson recognized that "those are pertinent questions." Symington, obviously irritated, responded, "Mr. Chairman, I will not yet yield to the witness. I was trying to help the witness because these questions were given to me."[6] Symington voted for Wilson's confirmation, but relations between the two men remained strained, and in the weeks ahead, Symington directed most of his fire to the secretary of defense rather than the president.

And there was plenty of fire.

Since his time as secretary of the air force, Symington had maintained that an adequate defense should not be sacrificed to a balanced budget. "What's the good of being the richest man in the graveyard?" he frequently asked. Eisenhower, on the other hand, had been elected on a pledge to reduce spending and balance the budget. The most obvious target was the Department of Defense, where, Eisenhower knew from experience, there was both waste and inefficiency. There would have to be more, however, than simply trimming the fat; there would have to be radical surgery. As Secretary of the Treasury George Humphrey, the leading cabinet proponent of a balanced budget, told Wilson, in language that he thought the former General Motors executive could understand, "Charlie, . . . You just got to get out the best damn streamlined model you ever did in your life. . . . This means a brand-new model . . . we can't just patch up the old jalopy . . ."[7]

When Wilson unveiled his "new model," a budget calling for a $10 billion decrease in the defense appropriation, $5 billion of which would come from the air force, Symington jumped to the attack. This budget, he told the Senate, was wholly inadequate to prepare the country against a rising Soviet menace in "a period of total danger." Moreover—making specific the generalized charges he had made in Philadelphia—he accused the administration of trying to explain its policy with slogans, and of not telling the American people "all the truth."[8]

He sounded a similar theme on April 17 before the American Society of Newspaper Editors, stating that in the past three years the Soviets had increased their lead over the United States in all military categories, "and based on our Intelligence, as well as that of our Allies, tomorrow the Soviet advantage in these categories will be greater than it is today."[9]

A few days later, he went to Charlottesville, Virginia, at the request of Senator Willis Robertson to speak before the Albemarle County Historical Society. A few hours before he spoke, the president had announced his intention to cut federal appropriations by about $8.5 billion, less than the $10 billion Wilson had talked about, but still, in Symington's views, way too much. He called the recommendation the result of a policy aimed "to pay less and hope more," adding, "There is no justification in the world picture for such a policy."[10]

Symington had nothing but contempt for the administration's contention that they were not reducing air force strength, they were simply "stretching out" the rate of buildup. Speaking at Armed Forces Day ceremonies in Enid, Oklahoma, he charged that Eisenhower was putting fiscal policies ahead of military strategy. "President Eisenhower criticized that policy in his campaign," he said. "I was hoping that his Administration would not follow the advice of those who would cut down the flow of planes, funds, materials and men which must build tomorrow's Air Force today. But what did the Administration offer us last week, more stretchout, more soothing syrup, more cars, more fat, less muscle."[11]

In what *Time* described as "his most somber warning yet," Symington charged on NBC's *Meet the Press* that the Soviets had—or surely would have in the next twelve months—the ability to destroy one-third of the nation's industrial capacity and "kill around 13 million people" in a first attack. When asked what he and other air power advocates would do if they failed in their efforts to override Wilson's recommendations, he said, "We're just going to keep on trying to give the American people the facts about the American air force as compared to the Russian air force. We may lose this battle, but we won't lose the war. If we do lose the war, then we've lost the country."[12]

On June 25, in his maiden speech as a senator, he took his case to the full Senate. He had not planned to speak on the floor during his first year as a member, "But because of recent further reductions, and postponements, in our defense strength," he "desired now to discuss the tragic implications of these reductions." Money rather than national security was the principal consideration in a decision made by new and inexperienced civilian heads, without the concurrence of a single top military expert, he said.[13]

He launched into a frontal attack on those "new and inexperienced civilian heads," particularly Secretary of Defense Charles E. Wilson. He lashed out at Wilson not only for his errors in judgment but also for the way in which he criticized former secretaries of defense, particularly his immediate predecessor, Robert Lovett: "I have known Bob Lovett for a long time, before either he or I came into Government service. After 12 years' association with the Government, if I had to make a choice as to who . . . had been the outstanding public servant on the executive side during that period, I might well pick Bob Lovett. He is a true American patriot—intelligent, experienced, and hard working."

As for Wilson's own performance, he had simply turned the process over to the "money men." At no point was there any indication that "the effect of this cut on the military strategy of this Nation, and hence upon its national security, was thoughtfully considered." Amazingly, the cut seemed to have been made without the concurrence of a single military leader. "And what of the President? Did he really decide this budget as a military matter, or did he merely decide that he was going to have to back up the Secretary of Defense?"[14]

A few days after his maiden speech he got into a controversy with New York Republican John Taber, chairman of the House Appropriations Committee. Taber had written a letter to the *Boston Herald* complaining about the paper's criticism of the administration's defense budget, pointing out that the paper did not have all the facts. If it had, it "would begin to realize what kind of sabotage Mr. Wilson was up against from Vandenberg and the crew that is trying to cover up their own iniquities by making false statements about what the situation is." This was all Symington needed. No one could criticize Hoyt Vandenberg and get away with it. Reciting Vandenberg's thirty-year service and his many decorations for gallantry in action, he said, "His reward, as he now leaves his country's services, is to be accused of making false statements, of being a 'saboteur' against his country's interest."

More was at stake, however, than the defamation of an individual. The larger issue was whether uniformed officers could "come before Congress and give their best professional judgment without being subjected to bitter personal attack." "Mr. President," he concluded, "this is a subject to which the Senate should give serious consideration—because it has much to do with the security of our country, and therefore with the freedom of every citizen."[15]

This, for all the action it produced, was simply more "crying in the wilderness." Nevertheless, he continued.

He wrote an article for the *New Republic* on "Wilson's Gamble With Defense"; he tangled with Michigan Republican Senator Homer Ferguson on NBC's *American Forum of the Air,* criticizing Ferguson for not allowing him to testify before the Senate Appropriations Committee. During a twelve-hour debate on the defense budget, Symington led the attack on what he called "the incredible and radical cuts" in the air force budget. He clashed repeatedly with Ferguson, who was presenting the budget for the Appropriations Committee, and at times the argument descended to personalities. Symington carefully avoided direct criticism of the president, but was unsparing in his attacks on Wilson. Ferguson, increasingly impatient with Symington's interruptions, suggested that the "waste" in air force expenditures that Wilson's people had uncovered was nothing new, that it went back to Symington's years as secretary.[16]

The long, inconclusive debate changed no minds. In the end, the administration's budget was approved. There was simply no way that the Democrats could prevail against the prestige of the man who had led the Allied forces to victory in Europe. The country was perfectly content to accept his view of what was needed for an adequate defense—particularly when it appeared to save the taxpayers money.

After a short trip to France and England with New Hampshire Republican Senator Styles Bridges, Symington continued his attack on Secretary Wilson and the Department of Defense. His resolve had been strengthened, if that could have been possible, by his visit with Winston Churchill. Always impressed by the dramatic incident, he carried with him throughout his life the memory of the aged warrior pleading as they parted, "Don't forget; think of us all." The message, in Symington's view, was clear. Twice in the century Britain had given up the flower of its youth and the bulk of its resources to preserve freedom, but if freedom had to be defended again it would be up to the United States.[17] That is why he repeatedly inveighed against a policy which he felt weakened the nation's capability.

On March 30 he rose in the Senate "to protest certain aspects of the so-called New Look in military planning and the military budget." He charged that military planning was in the hands of "inexperienced money first men" who were not heeding the advice of seasoned military leaders, that the Senate, and particularly the Armed Services Committee, was not being given sufficient information on which to base sound judgments. When Saltonstall interrupted to remind him that the committee had received assurances during the past year by military authorities and that Symington had been present at each one of them, he retorted: "Representing the good people of Missouri, I do not think they sent me to the Senate to accept soothing sirup of any kind from the military without any investigation of their statements."[18]

Such investigation, Symington was confident, would reveal that current planning did not take into account the "facts and implications of the atomic armaments race between the United States and the U.S.S.R." If it had, the administration would be recommending increases for the air force rather than reductions. He acknowledged that the administration claimed that it was adequately supporting the air force, but charged that these were simply accounting maneuvers. There ensued an extended colloquy with Saltonstall over the adequacy of air force support and the quality of the information received from the military as well as the Defense Department's civilian leaders. Symington expressed irritation with Wilson's cavalier responses to his requests for information.[19] Moreover, he clearly was not as comfortable with the new military leaders as he had been with the veterans he had worked with during his years as secretary of the air force. They did not express their own views, they simply parroted the administration line. Wayne Morse, an independent from Oregon, joined the debate to declare, "Unfortunately, there are not very many Bradleys or Shermans in the Military Establishment. When those two great men were in uniform, many times they came before the committee and volunteered information which, as representatives of a free people the members of the committee should have had. But with respect to most of the brass, unless we dig it out we shall not get it at all. We should not have to rely on newspapers and periodicals."[20]

All the arguments about figures aside, the simple fact was that the American people were not being told the truth. Symington concluded, "I believe it is time we started telling the truth to the American people about the whole question of airpower, and our relative strength against the Soviets."[21]

On April 5, Symington, along with Lyndon Johnson, attended the funeral of General Hoyt Vandenberg, "another officer who retired with a cloud because he had the courage to tell the American people the truth." Four days later he resumed the struggle again, this time to defend previous air force administrations (his own included) and to eulogize Vandenberg ("a true prophet of airpower"). He argued that had the plans developed by Vandenberg been carried out, the nation's defenses would be in good order. Senator Ferguson had argued that the plans were impractical and could not have been carried out as projected. "It is a source of regret to me," Symington lamented, "that people currently running the Pentagon, or representatives of those who do, appear to take delight in criticizing the past administration of the armed services."[22]

In a major speech on July 21, Symington broadened his attack on the administration. Calling attention to "two major developments which threaten the security of the United States as it has never been threatened before"—the growing supply of fissionable material and the development of long-range, intercontinental ballistic missiles—he warned that the United States faced destruction if the Soviets were allowed to improve their relative position in armaments.

> If we are to continue to exist as a free people [he warned] America must lead in weapons: first, with superior bombers and fighters, naval task forces and mobile ground forces; second, and as soon as possible, with superior long-range missiles. . . . If we adequately increase our efforts toward such preparation, and stand firm against all threats, we can hold these power-drunk Communists in check.[23]

In retrospect, this speech might be looked upon as the first step in building the "missile gap," which Symington by 1960 would have developed into a major political issue. He acknowledged that "we are increasing the strength and striking power of our own Armed Forces," but that was not the question. "The important question," he insisted, was whether "our ability to handle the Communists in case of attack grows more rapidly than their ability to successfully deliver such an attack?" The answer was "probably not," and the administration was doing nothing to alert the American people to the dangers they faced.

The discussion moved to other issues. The night before Symington spoke, the French had agreed to a truce in Indo-China that gave the Communists virtually everything they were seeking. Senator Jackson, strongly supporting Symington's views, asked whether "with the tragic loss suffered in Indo-China," the Defense budget approved for fiscal 1955 could be considered adequate. The answer was an obvious and unequivocal "No." At this juncture, William Knowland, California

Republican and the majority leader, entered the colloquy. Taking a position somewhat independent of the administration's, he was concerned about the dangers of appeasement and the importance of giving realistic hope to the millions of innocent people living under Communist domination. Symington, of course, agreed, and argued that this was just another reason for providing an adequate defense budget.

A number of Democrats in addition to Jackson—Lister Hill, Mike Monroney, John Stennis, Albert Gore, Herbert Lehman—rose to compliment Symington on his effort and to urge him to continue. The only voice raised in opposition was that of Saltonstall, who somewhat tepidly suggested that Symington was engaging in scare tactics, that the administration was fully aware of Soviet activities and was taking appropriate steps to deal with them.[24]

Symington's speech received wide attention. *U.S. News & World Report* reprinted most of the text under the heading, "U.S. Chances in a War with Reds Getting Worse and Worse." *Time,* referring to Symington as "the Senate's most informed man on air power," wrote that Symington had "brought up a problem which hardly anyone else was thinking about: intercontinental ballistic missiles." The conservative journal *America* was less laudatory. Writing about "Senator Symington's IBM," it accused him of drawing conclusions unwarranted by the facts, adding: "If these conclusions follow, a preventative showdown seems to be the only alternative to slavery or annihilation. Rather than accuse the Senator of advocating such a self-defeating course, we prefer to believe that in his eagerness to keep the United States ahead in the race for IBM superiority he proved too much."[25]

Saltonstall took a similar line in a speech on the floor of the Senate. Symington was politicking in Tennessee, but on August 14 he took the Senate floor to respond. Referring to Saltonstall's statement that his appraisal of the nation's air power program would be "calm and objective," Symington said, "It was calm—so calm, in fact, I was reminded of the rosy optimism which prevailed in 1950, just prior to the outbreak of the Korean war." Moreover, the appraisal was far from objective: "Most of it was designed to criticize the previous administration, which called for a rapid buildup, and to praise the present administration's program of a slow and leisurely buildup."

Kennedy and Morse endorsed Symington's views and praised his understanding of air power. Morse doubted that any person in the country knew more about air force problems than Symington; Kennedy called him "the strongest voice in the United States in favor of building up our air strength and in opposition to the idea of a stretchout."[26]

Although Symington received favorable comments for his efforts, he achieved very little. He remained "a voice in the wilderness."

Into the Mainstream

THE ELECTION of 1954, which converted a narrow Republican majority in the Senate to a narrow Democratic majority, markedly changed Symington's status in the defense debate. He was transformed from a minority gadfly into a leading spokesman for the majority. His voice was no longer lost in the wilderness.

Richard Russell of Georgia, who replaced Saltonstall as chairman of the Armed Services Committee, believed firmly in a strong defense and seemed perfectly willing to let Symington dominate the discussion, at least insofar as the air force was concerned. Almost all of the other Democrats on the committee represented the Senate's senior establishment: Harry Byrd of Virginia, Majority Leader Johnson of Texas, Estes Kefauver of Tennessee, John Stennis of Mississippi, and Sam Ervin of North Carolina; the exception was Scoop Jackson, who, along with Symington, was one of the party's rising stars. Although not united in their willingness to take on the president, with the exception of Kefauver they were all hard-liners on defense.

Symington used every opportunity to criticize the administration's defense efforts in their specifics and increasingly challenged its lack of candor in discussing the Communist threat. In announcing, for example, that he would support the president's request for a resolution on the defense of Formosa, he observed that the letters and telegrams coming into his office were running heavily against granting the request. "I do not believe that would be the case," Symington noted, "if the people knew the truth about the danger which now literally hangs over this country as the result of the possession, by the Communists, of both the atomic bomb and the hydrogen bomb, and also of the means of delivering them."

The president's 1956 budget, he argued, while "partially atoning" for the mistakes of 1953 by restoring part of the cut in air force funds, now proposed to reduce funding for the army and the marines. "How can this administration expect the American people to really get behind this unprecedented request . . . unless the facts are known?" he asked. "And how can the administration justify at this time a further reduction in some of our armed forces?"[1] On *Meet the Press* April 24, Symington not only criticized the administration's defense program but also directly challenged the president's ability as a strategist. Lawrence Spivak said, "With all due respect to your record and everything else, I'd like to know why we should listen to you rather than Gen. Eisenhower, who led this country to victory in the last war?" Symington replied:

> I have great respect for Gen. Eisenhower but he has certainly been no prophet when it comes to what we need from the standpoint of defense. He is just as identified with our position before Korea as either Mr. Truman and [*sic*] Gen. Marshall and the facts speak for themselves. In an open hearing on March 29, 1950 he said under no circumstances should we have more than 15 billion dollars in our military budget. Within a short time we were asking for sixty billion. He said 48 groups was plenty. Within a short time we were asking for 143; so think that inasmuch as he at that time was one of the principal advisors to the President it shows that he could be wrong just like anybody else.[2]

Then he went on to Wilson and the secretary's lack of candor in dealing with Congress and the public. May Craig mentioned an order that Wilson had just issued expanding the range of material that could be withheld from the press beyond national security to include what was "improper" for them to have. Had Symington seen the order, and what did he think of it? Yes, he had seen the order. As to what he thought of it: "I read the Goebbels Diaries; on page 40 is the same kind of order. I don't see any difference between the order of Wilson and Goebbels except the date."[3]

A few days later he seized on a Defense Department release that called attention to a new B-52-type bomber and an all-weather fighter developed by the Soviets as evidence that Wilson had misled the public a year earlier when he had assured people that the Soviets were "building primarily a defensive force." He introduced a resolution asking the Senate "to investigate this announcement, . . . and take appropriate steps to determine the relative strength of the Communist forces as against the forces of the free world in all military categories, and with respect to all weapons systems."[4] Eisenhower, who had refrained from responding directly to Symington's attacks, called a press conference to assure the country that the United States had not lost control of the air to the Soviets. He conceded that the Russians had "progressed faster than anticipated in aircraft, science and other lines of endeavor in which the United States usually considers itself foremost. . . . [but] to say that we have lost in a twinkling all this great technical development and technical excellence as well as the numbers in our total aircraft is just not true."[5]

Despite the president's status, Symington was getting the better of the argument. His old nemesis, Hanson W. Baldwin of the *New York Times,* wrote that the Defense Department's press release contained nothing that was not well known and was but a clumsy attempt to forestall Senator Symington's inquiry. It might have blunted that attack a little, but it "provided political fuel for the Democratic opposition instead of quenching the fire."[6]

Symington won a minor victory when the Senate approved, 40 to 39, his motion to prevent a cut in Marine Corps strength as the administration's budget had provided, but he dropped efforts to prevent a cut in the army's appropriation and to increase funds for the air force when it became apparent that they would not succeed.[7] In the debate on the Formosa Resolution, Symington, the quintessential air power apologist, had made it clear that his concerns extended to the army and the navy as well as the air force. "If there now is atomic stalemate," he argued, "then it is certain that any new hostilities will result in fighting on land—and I for one have always believed that any war of any kind will involve fighting on land. They always have, and they always will." He thought it entirely possible that Communist aggression was tied directly to our weakened military capabilities. "The Communists were not afraid of us when we had the atomic deterrent," he said. "Why should they be afraid when we have not? And if that is a fair premise, why should we not build up our Army and Marines, instead of continuing to tear them down?"[8]

Meanwhile, the Symington-Wilson exchange grew hotter. Testifying in executive session before the House Appropriations Committee, Wilson commented that he would like to clamp down on Symington's sources. It was commonly assumed that Symington had a direct line to sources within the air force, but when Wilson's comments were made public, Symington promptly retorted that his information came "from proper sources, primarily trade magazines and so forth." There ensued an exchange of letters in which the two men argued about who was entitled to what information and whose facts were accurate. Nothing came of it except to exacerbate the ill-feeling between the two men.[9]

Meanwhile, Symington injected a new idea into the defense debate: economic disarmament.

He used the failures of the London Conference on Disarmament as the basis for introducing a resolution in the Senate calling upon the president to submit to the United Nations a proposal "to explore the possibility of limiting the proportion of every nation's resources devoted to military purposes . . . so as to increase steadily the proportion devoted to improving the living levels of the people." The resolution argued that the way in which a government divided its resources could be used as a guide to its potential for aggression against world security. It proposed the ultimate establishment of ceilings on the percentage of a nation's resources that could be spent on armaments and the devising of an adequate inspection system to assure that the ceilings were observed.[10]

Symington apparently got the idea from an article by the noted economist Samuel Lubell, a close associate of Baruch, proposing a disarmament plan based on the principle of "guns over butter." The proposal was not put forward with any thought that it could stand alone. Rather, it was advanced "as an integral part of any enforceable proposal to achieve a balanced reduction of all arms and armaments." By no means should it be considered "as a substitute for our capacity to wage conventional war—or for our capability for instant retaliation with nuclear weapons in case of all-out attack." In its essentials it was designed to curb the ability of the Soviet Union to conduct aggressive warfare, but because the plan was applicable to all nations "it would offer the Soviet leaders a means of preventing any effective invasion of Russia."[11]

The plan received a substantial amount of attention. Forty-seven senators representing both parties joined as cosponsors. When Eisenhower was asked at a press conference what he thought of it, he replied, "I find here recently more and more occasions to referring to my favorite author. I think you might find the same idea in a speech I delivered I believe on April 16, 1953."[12] The Senate unanimously adopted the resolution on July 28.

It is hard to say what impact, if any, the resolution exerted. A few days after Symington introduced it, Eisenhower created the post of special assistant on disarmament; a few days before passing the resolution the Senate created a Disarmament subcommittee under the chairmanship of Hubert Humphrey. Symington became a member of the subcommittee and worked closely with Humphrey as they considered ways to slow down the arms race.[13]

Symington's principal efforts, however, continued to center on the Communist threat and the nation's ability to meet it. In a speech before the Executives Club of Chicago on September 30, he summarized all of his complaints against the Defense Department: inefficiency, a growing bureaucracy, neglect of research, and, above all, failure to tell the truth about the relative strength of the Soviet Union and the United States, particularly in the air. By whittling away at our strength, the administration, in addition to endangering the nation's immediate security, was weakening its position in disarmament efforts. He spoke of his disarmament resolution—"a practical method for approaching this complex problem"—but the United States could not take the lead in disarmament discussions unless it could do so from a position of strength, "because if we have learned anything from history, it is that the Communists respect power—and power only."[14]

A few days later, in an address celebrating the centennial of the *Mexico* (Missouri) *Ledger,* he excoriated the administration again for its lack of candor with the American people; he sounded the same theme in an address before the Jefferson–Jackson Day dinner in Baltimore.[15] He sent a copy of the speech to Lyndon Johnson, saying that he was taking on defense because "For many years I have felt it was the great over-riding issue of our time—and putting it mildly, the predictions I made when you were good enough to set up that great honor for me at Baylor, February 1950, have come true."[16]

But Symington wanted to do much more than travel around the country making speeches. In a memo for his files, he vented his frustration. As he saw it, the Soviets were ahead, "on the land and under the sea . . . and they are overtaking us in piloted combat planes and they are well ahead of us in long range missiles." The American people were not getting the truth, and "because of their blind faith in the man now in the White House (comparable to the fatal British trust of Baldwin) they will not move unless the truth is brought to light." The only way to do that was through "a careful intelligent non-partisan investigation." He had introduced resolutions calling for an investigation in each session of Congress. The Republicans had done nothing. He hoped for better from the Democrats.[17]

In September Symington had a long talk with Johnson at the LBJ ranch. The majority leader agreed that there should be an investigation, but wasn't sure just how to set it up. Symington thought Russell would be an ideal chairman, but if that were not possible, he was confident that he could handle it himself. To be sure, he was sixth in seniority among the eight Democratic members of the Armed Services Committee, but he had been in the Senate for three years and had been secretary of the air force. Johnson, he reasoned, had been named chairman of a subcommittee when he was the fifth-ranking man of the seven and had been in the Senate only two years.[18]

Early in the new session of Congress, Symington led a Democratic attack on the administration's defense policies. He had criticized Eisenhower in speeches and on television, but this was the first time he attacked him from the Senate floor. He focused on a recent press conference in which the president had sought to rebut criticism of the administration's missile development program. Noting that the president had said that while in certain fields of missile development the Russians were probably ahead of the United States, they were behind in others and that overall there was "no reason to believe that we are not doing everything that human science and brains and resources can do to keep our position in proper posture." Symington commented, "This statement might lead some people to believe that our being ahead in some missiles and the Communists being ahead in others is nothing to worry about—sort of a balance."

"The facts are," he added, "that our missile development may be ahead in the short-range area, but their missile development is ahead in the area that counts by far the most—the long range area." If the president thought otherwise, he was misinformed. Perhaps he was relying too heavily on the secretary of defense, "who not so long ago expressed himself as believing the development of an atomic airplane was comparable to finding out why potatoes turned brown when fried."[19]

There was no Republican reply to Symington's charges—most Republican senators were away for Lincoln Day speeches—but it was clear that Symington's efforts were beginning to have an impact. Influential newspapers from around the country had begun to question the administration's position.[20] Scoop Jackson, who was almost as aggressive as Symington, announced that Trevor Gardner, who had recently resigned as an assistant secretary of the air force for research in part as a protest against administration policies, would be called before the Military Atomic Energy Subcommittee. At the same time, Texas Democratic Representative George H. Mahon disclosed that the House Appropriations Committee would back a missile inquiry. Most important, Saltonstall told William S. White of the *New York Times* that there should be an inquiry into whether enough money was being spent on missile research.[21]

On February 18, Symington, getting impatient, wrote urging Johnson to act.[22] Johnson, who had remained at his Texas ranch until mid February, now moved to get the inquiry under way, and Symington was chosen to head it. Russell established a five-person temporary subcommittee on the air force, with Symington as chairman. He was joined by Democrats Jackson and Ervin and Republicans Saltonstall and James Duff (Pennsylvania). Their mission was to "examine into the condition and progress of the Department of the Air Force and ascertain if present policies, legislative authority and appropriations are adequate to maintain a force capable of carrying out its assigned mission." They were to report not later than July 1.[23]

Symington opened the hearings with an executive session on March 5. Only Jackson and Saltonstall were present at the meeting, which was largely organizational. The proceedings exuded goodwill and senatorial courtesy, with Symington particularly solicitous of Saltonstall's wishes on schedules and staff. All agreed that the position of counsel was important if the investigation were to proceed on a high-level, nonpartisan basis. Symington had proposed Fowler Hamilton, a Kansas City native who had attended the University of Missouri and Oxford. A New York lawyer, he had been a special assistant to the attorney general for antitrust prosecution. During World War II he had been an air force intelligence officer and had served on the U.S. Strategic Bombing Survey.[24] Saltonstall said that he had checked him out with a number of people in whom he had great confidence—including former Senator James Kem!—and he thought he would be ideal for the job. So they agreed to hire Hamilton as a person who could help keep the investigation on a high level. Symington was concerned that the investigation not "in any way or sense" appear to be a partisan effort. If that were to happen, the whole effort would be a failure. Jackson agreed: "We all realize that once it becomes a political football, why, then, the whole thing will blow up in smoke and confusion."[25]

There was ample reason for concern about perceptions of partisanship. Symington and Jackson, from St. Louis and Seattle, the nation's leading producers of military aircraft, had emerged as the Senate's leading critics of the administration's defense policies. Both were being discussed as possible candidates for national office, and no matter how much they might protest, they could hardly present themselves as credible nonpartisans in an election year. Symington was being much discussed as a possible compromise candidate for the Democratic presidential nomination, and Jackson probably was going to be advanced as a candidate for the vice presidency. Symington even expressed public concern that talk of his possible presidential candidacy could harm his committee efforts. He repeated his oft-expressed statement that he was not a candidate and announced that he would refrain from criticizing the administration until the committee had completed its work.[26] Try as they might, however, there was no way that Symington or Jackson could keep politics out of their probe. Doris Fleeson, for example, wrote a column on the probe headed, "In Election Year, Issues Become Sticks With Which to Beat the Other Side."[27]

Symington made a great public show of being nonpartisan—he even announced that he would delay the publication of the committee's report until after the presidential election. It is obvious that he sincerely believed he was acting in the national interest, but he also was sure that his findings could be of great political value. Shortly after the hearings began, he wrote Johnson: "Incidentally, although the party comes second to the country, I do believe we are developing a real issue for the party. 'Peace and Prosperity' will be hard to beat. . . . But I believe the people are already beginning to realize that something is wrong about defense, lack of it and disorganization, especially when considering the rapidly growing Communist menace."[28]

The hearings began unpropitiously on Monday, April 16, in the Old Supreme Court room of the capitol. The small room was only about half full. There seemed to be too many distractions. The president had muffled the committee's thunder by requesting an additional $500 million for new bombers, and he had created a Washington uproar by vetoing a Democratic farm bill. Moreover, implicit in the committee's creation was the need for more military spending, and spending was anathema to Congress and most of the public. As Doris Fleeson commented: "A certain lack of political savvy was evident too in the choice of the opening date—the day of the Federal income tax deadline. No Tammany ward heeler would even mention spending to the customers on such a day."[29]

Symington opened the hearing with a long and carefully crafted statement setting forth the purpose of the hearings and the procedures the committee intended to follow. The primary purpose of the hearings was to "further the cause of world peace," something that could be achieved only through total disarmament, which the United States could negotiate only from a position of relative strength. The committee's duty was "to examine into the condition and progress of the Department of the Air Force and ascertain if present policies, legislative authority and appropriations are adequate to maintain a force capable of carrying out its assigned mission."[30]

He then called as the first witness General Omar N. Bradley. The highly respected former chief of staff set the tone of the hearings by reminding the subcommittee that the United States could no longer rely on its ocean barriers to protect it from sudden attack, that the only defense would be air power, and to be effective it must be "airpower in being." Unlike earlier wars, there would be no time to prepare after hostilities had begun. Bradley was followed by a parade of high-ranking army, navy, and air force officers—the Republicans had insisted that the hearings be broadened to include the army and navy. The officers were in a difficult position. They could hardly speak out against their civilian superiors, but under skillful questioning by Symington, and to a lesser degree by Jackson, they were led to assert that they were not receiving adequate support and that the Soviets, if present policies continued, would soon be superior to the United States. Symington insisted that all testimony be under oath, which he had learned from his days as secretary of the air force provided a shield for subordinates who disagreed with their superiors.

The testimony of General Nathan F. Twining, air force chief of staff, was particularly compelling. He visited the Soviet Union while the hearings were in process, and Symington was anxious that he add to his earlier testimony, in which he had asserted that the Soviets had "thousands" more combat aircraft than the United States. When Twining came back before the subcommittee, the following exchange took place:

> Senator Symington. You indicated at that time [in earlier testimony] the quantitative advantage of the Soviet Air Force over the United States Air Force was numbered in thousands of combat aircraft. Is that still your view?

General Twining. That is correct. The Soviet Air Force has thousands more aircraft in combat units than the United States Air Force. . . .

Senator Symington. . . . Every day that goes by, based on present production that national intelligence gives us . . . the Communists are closing the gap with respect to their strategic airpower as against ours?

General Twining. Well, they are certainly improving their position, there is no question about that. . . .

Senator Symington. Do you have any question in your mind that the Soviets have in the past three years outproduced the United States in numbers of combat aircraft.

General Twining. According to our estimates, that is true. They have outproduced us.

With the uniformed officers, Symington's attitude was one of seeking information. He knew most of them well, and his questions were universally friendly. With the civilian heads of the services, however, his questions became increasingly confrontational. This was particularly true of Secretary Wilson. He repeatedly asked Wilson to comment on statements by high-ranking officers in speeches or in testimony before the subcommittee. Wilson tried to deflect the questions or give his interpretation of the facts. Occasionally, he refused to comment, but at times he flatly contradicted the statements. Symington relentlessly pursued the contradictions. When, for example, Wilson said, "We deplore efforts to belittle the capacity and resolve of this Government," it produced the following exchange:

Senator Symington. If the Chief of Staff of the Air Force [Twining] makes a speech saying: If being ahead is related to the number of aircraft and combat units we are not ahead.

The Communists have thousands more combat airplanes than we do. If being ahead is related to aircraft production, we are again only second best. The Communists are producing far more combat planes than we are.

If he makes that speech, and he confirms that statement under oath before this committee, he has probably done more to create that impression than anybody; wouldn't you say?

Secretary Wilson. Well, I think the military people to some degree have contributed to it. I think that is right. And I think we can properly be criticized for it.

And I wish it would stop.

Senator Symington. But General Twining's speech was cleared by your Department.

Secretary Wilson. I have not tried to censor the speeches of individuals beyond the security business.

I think a man is entitled to make his own mistakes, but the difficulty really comes in when some eager beaver in the Air staff or something trying to over promote the Air Forces or the Army or the Navy, and that is where it comes from and it is a very deplorable business and I don't like it.

Senator Symington. Do you think General Twining comes under the category of "eager beaver?"

Secretary Wilson. Not intentionally, no. No, the man that wrote the speech for him did it. [Laughter.]

Senator Jackson. But the fellow who says it is not the eager beaver?

Secretary Wilson. Oh, no. [Laughter.]

At the conclusion of Wilson's testimony, Symington read a statement in which he told the secretary that his testimony was "inconsistent with the sworn testimony of leading military officers of the United States." He accused Wilson of refusing to spend money that had been appropriated for the modernization of the air force, specifically for the new B-52 long-range bomber, adding: "Two conclusions are now inescapable: (1) You are considering going against the expressed will of the Congress by refusing to increase B-52 production as promptly as practicable; (2) either you are misleading the American people, or responsible military officials of the Defense Department are misleading the American people as to the relative military strength of the United States vis-a-vis the Communists."

Wilson, after determining that Symington's statement reflected his personal views and not those of the committee, responded by letter. He categorically denied that he was going against the will of Congress regarding the B-52. With regard to the relative air power of the United States vis-à-vis that of the Soviet Union, he wrote, "Depending upon how such a question is phrased, any one of a number of assumptions could be proven by the best intelligence estimates available. I merely wish to emphasize my belief, based upon evaluations of the facts, that in our overall air strength we are ahead of the Russians today and we intend in the future to build and maintain total air strength capable of preserving the security of the United States, and as a visible deterrent to wars of any kind."

Symington's handling of the hearings did not sit at all well with the Republicans on the subcommittee. At one point Senator Duff remarked: "I am getting sick of this business of listening all the time to how good the Soviets are: their putting out the propaganda and our saying how good we think they are." Saltonstall, though more diplomatic, made it a point to defend the integrity and competence of the administration. After Symington had delivered his charges against Wilson, for example, he praised the secretary as one who "will do his utmost to carry out efficiently the mandates of Congress so far as he can carry them out in the best interests of the defense of our country."[31]

The hearings ended on July 3. Symington earlier had announced that to void injecting partisan politics into the subcommittee's activities he would not issue his report until after the presidential election. It was fairly clear, however, that the subcommittee's activities had become tainted with partisanship. Symington gave further partisan color to the hearings on July 12 when he spoke on the Senate floor about his statement to Wilson, adding, "Mr. President, if this country does not start promptly to create a Defense Department which is based on progress, instead of one which is based on tradition, the danger to our economy will steadily increase."[32]

He said no more about the hearings.[33] When Congress adjourned, he joined Eve on Nantucket, where, interspersed with rest and golf, he kept a close, if officially disinterested, eye on the efforts of his fellow Missourians to promote him as a favorite-son candidate for the presidency.

23

Reluctant Favorite Son

SYMINGTON had hardly settled in his Senate office when his name began to surface as a possible Democratic nominee for president in 1956.

The talk had begun among some of his friends in Missouri even while he was making his first try for an elective office. His stunning victory in 1952 intensified the talk and extended it beyond Missouri. It is not difficult to see why.

Adlai Stevenson had been soundly trounced in 1952, and losers seldom get a second chance. Moreover, Stevenson was not particularly popular, especially in the South, where many people were put off by his liberal views and egghead demeanor. Symington, in contrast, had deep southern roots—his grandfather, he was fond of reminding southern audiences, had fought in the Confederate army and his strong pro-defense views were popular in the South. His principal mentors in the Senate, Russell, Stennis, and Johnson, were all from the South. At the same time, his liberal voting record made him popular in the North, particularly with labor. In a few months he was being called the "Senate rookie of the year"—no mean feat in a class that included such rising stars as Kennedy and Jackson. Doris Fleeson wrote that despite his denials, his friends kept talk of the presidency alive, adding, "Candidate or not, Senator Symington is leading for his party in its first real attack on the Eisenhower policies." She noted, however, "Fast and picturesque in personal conversation, Mr. Symington has not yet mastered the formal Senate speech. His remarks are written with care and studded with telling phrases but his delivery is monotonous. So far, he has not been under harsh attack by Republicans, so it remains to be seen what he can do in debate."[1]

Whenever the question of his candidacy arose, Symington issued a flat denial of interest. For example, on a trip to Omaha to inspect the Strategic Air Command and visit with General LeMay, he told a press conference, "I am not interested and I am not available. My ambitions are to be a Senator and ably represent the people of my state."[2]

The rumors, nevertheless, continued to grow, fed in part by the poorly disguised coolness with which the southern patriarchs of the party in the Senate—notably Russell and Johnson—greeted the prospect of another Stevenson candidacy. That attitude, the *New York Times* reported, was considered by the Stevenson people to be "back of a plan, now some months in progress, to 'build up' Senator Stuart Symington of Missouri, with or without his participation, as a possible Presidential nominee for 1956."[3]

Symington undoubtedly was sincere in his protestations of noncandidacy, but few people took him at his word. *Time* observed that his assertion that his ambition was to be the best Senator possible for the people of Missouri "did nothing to keep his hat out of the ring."[4]

And Symington, while insisting all along that he was not a candidate, busied himself with the kinds of activities a presidential hopeful might be expected to perform. He accepted the chairmanship of the finance committee of the Senate Democratic campaign committee, headed by Earle Clements of Kentucky. Some of the press interpreted this as part of Symington's presidential strategy. Robert S. Allen, Drew Pearson's former associate, wrote, for example, on August 27: "One of the first pieces of news heard by Stevenson [when he returned from an extended trip abroad] was about a 'secret National Committee' set up for the purpose of pushing the ardent Presidential yearnings of Sen. Stuart Symington." According to Allen, the committee, headed by Leslie Biffle, retired secretary of the Senate and a Democratic powerhouse, was also designed to oust Steve Mitchell as chairman of the Democratic National Committee and replace him with Biffle, who would support Symington.[5]

Symington was furious. He tried to phone Clements from his home in Creve Coeur but couldn't reach him before he had to leave for speeches in southern Missouri and Arkansas, so he sent a copy of the clipping to Clements with an indignant yet almost plaintive letter. He had done everything "except jump out the window" to discourage talk about 1956. He did not want the fund-raising job, "and did it because you and Lyndon wanted me to." Before going ahead, he should have letters from Stevenson and Mitchell.[6]

Although there is no record of letters from Stevenson or Mitchell, or, indeed, of a response from Clements, Symington went ahead with his fund-raising chores—and most successfully.[7] In addition, he campaigned tirelessly for Democrats in all parts of the country, working particularly hard for Hubert Humphrey in Minnesota and Paul Douglas in Illinois. When it was all over, the Democrats wound up with a 49 to 47 margin in the Senate—48 Democrats plus Independent Wayne Morse of Oregon, who had announced he would vote with the Democrats. After the election, Lyndon Johnson, who would become Senate majority leader in the new Congress, wrote, "I don't know of anyone who worked harder than Stu Symington or anyone who was more effective. It took days and nights of sustained effort, and you came through with a top-notch performance that meant the difference between victory and defeat in many states."[8]

Shortly before Christmas, Stuart and Eve visited the Johnsons at the LBJ ranch. Although the two men talked politics, the visit was primarily social. Lyndon regaled them about the history of the Texas hill country, and they went on a wild turkey shoot. They had never shot wild turkey before, and it was "a real thrill."[9] Eve, it will be remembered, was an expert markswoman.

When the new Congress convened, Symington, now part of the majority, continued his unrelenting attack on the administration's defense budgets and what he termed as its failure to level with the American people on Soviet air strength, solidifying his position as the Democrats' most vociferous critic of the administration. This, of course, enhanced his visibility and viability as a potential challenger to Eisenhower's probable bid for reelection. When the subject came up, however, he treated it as he had in the past: "not interested, not available."

During a New Orleans television discussion of air power with Louisiana representatives Hale Boggs and Edward Hebert, both men wanted to discuss Symington's availability as a candidate. He repeated his "not interested, not available" statement, then added, "Let's get back to talking about air power." They did, but before that happened Boggs said, "A great many people would be pleased if you were the nominee." Hebert agreed, saying, "I'm all for you, Stu."[10]

A few weeks later, Clarence Cannon, dean of Missouri's Democratic delegation in Congress, endorsed Symington for president and predicted that he would be nominated. Cannon, a power in Missouri politics, also had great influence nationally: he had served as parliamentarian for every Democratic national convention since 1912. He expressed great admiration for Stevenson, but ruled him out "because we can't put a loser on the ticket." Symington, on the other hand, had "a talent for winning." He acknowledged that Symington's protestations were sincere, but didn't think the party would pay much attention to them.[11]

All the while, Symington stayed close to the center of power, particularly as it was manifested in the person of Majority Leader Lyndon Johnson, who was an even more active noncandidate. Symington and Johnson had dinner with Sam Rayburn the night before Johnson started feeling symptoms of his massive heart attack. Symington kept in close touch with Lady Bird, and was among the various dignitaries who visited the senator in his room at the Bethesda Naval Hospital. On August 2, as Congress was adjourning, he introduced into the *Congressional Record* a compilation of newspaper editorials from around the country praising Johnson's leadership.[12]

When Congress adjourned, Symington joined Eve on Nantucket, although he interrupted his time there with frequent trips to Missouri—he visited 80 of the state's 114 counties during the last half of 1955 and made some two hundred speeches. Johnson, now at the ranch, wrote to urge a visit: "The stormy New England coast cannot compare with the restful Pedernales Valley." Symington responded with an uncharacteristically long, rambling letter touching everything from family visits to politics to golf. His fall schedule was fairly full, but he could come down in mid October or mid November. Either time was OK with the Johnsons, "but if you leave the decision to me, I will say the sooner the better." They finally got it worked out for the weekend of October 21. Both men described the visit as "purely social," and they did have fun, swimming in Johnson's new pool and taking a turn in the Pedernales River. They attended a black-tie dinner in Austin honoring former Secretary of Health, Education, and Welfare Secretary Oveta Culp Hobby as "Texas Woman of the Year." Symington also paid a call on Governor Allan Shivers. The press challenged the "purely social" nature of the visit, pointing out that the Johnson ranch had been the scene of numerous visits by high-ranking Democrats, including Stevenson and Rayburn. Symington, interviewed between planes in Dallas en route to St. Louis, repeated his "not interested, not available," phrase. He said he wouldn't be surprised if Johnson decided to run: "He looked better than I've ever seen him. I'm sure he'll make a complete recovery."[13]

Meanwhile, the presidential pot continued to bubble. Before going to Texas, Symington had quashed a move by Kansas City attorney D. W. Gilmore to try to start a "Symington for President" movement, but at a press conference in Washington on November 28, he said that while he was not a candidate for the presidency, he would accept a "favorite son" designation by the Missouri delegation at next year's convention. He also went out of his way to praise Stevenson, "a fine fellow . . . a great credit to his party. . . . [He] ran like a thoroughbred in his last campaign and acted like a thoroughbred in defeat."[14]

In the weeks leading up to the Democratic state convention Gilmore and Meredith busied themselves with making sure that Symington would be designated as a favorite-son candidate. It is clear that they were impatient with the limitations Symington had forced on them; they wanted to make an all-out campaign. Stanley Fike, who was helping them, said that if the boss would just give the word, he would be prepared to try to go all the way.[15]

Clifford sent an article from the *Christian Science Monitor* discussing Symington's favorite-son status: "There are many Missourians, including veteran Representative Clarence Cannon, who say that Senator Symington will be nominated. The senator himself has made a brave show of reluctance, but he is, in the opinion of many, a serious contender for the nation's highest office." Clifford's handwritten note, enclosing the article, gives some indication that he was among those who held that view: "this type of article which emphasizes your career has the most appeal, in my opinion."[16]

On the eve of the Springfield convention, Symington drafted a statement expressing appreciation for the efforts of those who wanted to run him as a favorite son, but requesting that they not go forward. He had accepted appointment as chairman of the Senate Democratic Campaign Committee for 1956. That would be a time-consuming job, and "any assistance I might render various Democratic senatorial candidates. . . . would be less effective if people felt that I was also talking as a possible candidate myself."[17]

There is no record that the memo was ever sent, but if it was, no one paid much attention to it. Meredith, Fike, and others busied themselves among the delegates in Springfield. When it was all over, Meredith was sure that virtually all of the Democrats at the convention were in favor of Symington as a favorite-son candidate.[18]

This posed a problem for the Stevenson forces in Missouri. Congressman Richard Bolling of Kansas City, a strong Stevenson supporter, refused to join the state's other Democratic congressmen in urging Symington as a favorite son, saying that while he had "great admiration for Senator Symington" and thought he was "fully qualified to be President," he felt that such a decision should be made by the Democratic state convention. John Oliver, a young Kansas City attorney who had supported Symington in 1952 and would continue to be a strong supporter, was also worried about what effect the favorite-son movement would have on the Stevenson campaign. He wrote Meredith that in response to a call from the Stevenson people in Chicago, he told them that "they could take the reports of the Senator's public statements at full value and that he could no more control the activity of his staunch supporters than Governor Stevenson could do that sort of thing back in 1952. That seemed to satisfy everyone."[19]

Estes Kefauver's upset victory in the Minnesota primary was widely interpreted as giving a boost to Symington as a dark-horse candidate. The results underscored fears, held by many in the party, that Stevenson was not a good vote-getter and would do no better against Eisenhower in 1956 than in 1952.

The party regulars would never accept Kefauver, so the reasoning went, and if Stevenson showed continued weakness, the convention would turn to Symington as someone all could agree on. Symington's growing prominence as a possible dark horse inspired political commentators to try to analyze the basis of his popularity. He looked like a president and he had powerful friends in all parts of the country. Coming from an important border state, he possessed a heritage that included birth in Massachusetts of parents with deep southern roots, a boyhood in Baltimore, and a business career in New York and St. Louis. As Earl Mazo wrote in the *New York Herald Tribune,* "From a geographical standpoint . . . [he was] the most richly endowed Presidential possibility of them all."[20]

But there had to be more to it than good looks, powerful friends, and geography—and when the press started analyzing his record they confronted a dilemma. His "big bomber" reputation appealed to southern Democrats, and his opposition to Eisenhower's farm policies also won southern approval. Yet on other important issues, his record and views should have been anathema in the South. He had one of the Senate's most liberal voting records. He was strongly pro-labor. Victor Riesel, a labor—but not pro-labor—columnist, wrote: "Symington is a natural for the labor chiefs. He's been close to them for years. From their point of view, he has the best pro-labor record of all the prominent possibilities."[21] Symington seemed to be in the best position to consolidate the southern and northern big-city wings of the Democratic party.

Symington's friends in Missouri continued to push his candidacy. Meredith and Fike lined up endorsements from virtually every county, and when the Democratic convention met in Jefferson City on May 28, the delegates enthusiastically endorsed him, not as a favorite son, but as a bona fide candidate for president.[22] He still insisted that he was not a candidate—he complained in Washington that all of the presidential talk would impede his investigation of air force funding just getting under way—but the entire family was in Jefferson City for the occasion. Doris Fleeson wrote:

> A whole charm school of handsome Symingtons was on the platform smiling and waving at the Missouri State Convention which has launched Senator Symington's presidential boom. It included the Senator, his wife, their two sons and the sons' wives—and there are some photogenic grandchildren left over for later pictures.
>
> Such wholesale charm is an asset in politics as elsewhere and it is not the Senator's only asset. But his boom depends nevertheless on events outside the control of its participants.
>
> Only as and if Adlai Stevenson takes a real tumble in Florida today and in California a week later can it get off the ground.[23]

Stevenson's victories in both Florida and California considerably darkened Symington's "dark horse" prospects. Yet as far as the press was concerned, he remained in the race. Many Democratic regulars, especially in the South, were cool to a Stevenson candidacy and froze up when they contemplated Kefauver, who had adopted an independent course too often to be considered reliable. Johnson, who was put forth by the Texas delegation as a favorite son, would have commanded considerable support, but his heart attack ruled him out. New York Governor Averell Harriman had also entered the race, reportedly with the encouragement of Harry Truman. Harriman was perceived as far too liberal for the South. Symington seemed the best bet, even though he was as liberal as Harriman on most issues.[24]

Stevenson did not stumble, but steadily gained strength as the convention approached. Kefauver withdrew from the race on July 30 and urged his followers to support Stevenson. Some of Missouri's Democratic leaders, including National Committeeman Mark Halloran, felt that it was important for Missouri to get behind Stevenson. Missouri's delegates were pledged to Symington under the unit rule unless they were released by the candidate or a majority decided to switch. Symington, contacted by the press just before leaving Washington for a short vacation on Nantucket, gave no indication that he intended to release them. He simply said that any decision to switch was "entirely up to the delegation"[25] and went off to Nantucket to be with Eve and to play golf.

Symington, like most of the country, believed that Stevenson had the nomination sewed up and that the convention would be a rather dull ratification ceremony. Then, two days before the convention was to open, Harry Truman arrived in Chicago. In a well-staged press conference, he announced that he was endorsing Harriman for the nomination. Despite the fact that Truman's endorsements had not proven to be worth much in the recent past,[26] the announcement was seen as slowing the Stevenson bandwagon and opening up the convention. It was also perceived as breathing life into Symington's "non campaign." Harriman was even less popular in the South than Stevenson; if it appeared that he might have a chance, the South would seek an alternative—and that alternative could well be Symington.

Fike and Meredith went to Chicago a couple of days in advance of the convention. They had no headquarters and no literature. As they milled around among the delegates, they picked up considerable evidence that Symington had strong "second-choice" support among both Stevenson and Harriman delegates. Truman, apparently sensing this, urged Symington to come to Chicago as soon as possible. Fike also tried to persuade him to hurry up, but to no avail.[27]

Stuart and Eve arrived at Chicago's Midway airport at 2:14 the afternoon of August 12. Much to their surprise, the terminal was packed with Missourians, chanting and waving banners. Meredith, Fike, and Company had organized a seventy-five-car motorcade to escort the Symingtons to their hotel. In a crowded press conference at the Conrad Hilton, Symington reiterated that he was "entirely in the hands of the Missouri delegation." When asked if he would accept the nomination, he replied, "This is a great country, and that's a great honor, and of course I would accept it." He wanted to make it clear, however, that he had not been asked to join in any Stop Stevenson movement, and that he would not participate in any such activity.[28]

As the nominations approached, it was clear that Truman's efforts to promote Harriman had fizzled and that Stevenson would be nominated, probably on the first ballot. Nevertheless, the Missouri delegation decided to go through with the formality of placing Symington's name in nomination. Senator Hennings delivered the nominating speech, calling Symington "a valiant fighter for the rights of the people." Former Mayor William E. Kemp of Kansas City, Congresswoman Leonor Sullivan, and Calvin Rampton, a Democratic leader from Utah, made seconding speeches. The obligatory demonstration took up the twenty minutes allotted.[29]

Stevenson swept to an overwhelming victory on the first ballot, garnering 905.5 votes to 210 for Harriman, his principal challenger. Johnson received 80 votes, and Symington, 45.5. Six additional favorite sons each received a few. The Missouri delegation tried to shift its votes to Stevenson, but couldn't get the chairman's attention before he called for a vote to make the decision unanimous.[30] Symington, who was watching the proceedings from his suite in the Sherman Hotel, immediately issued a brief statement:

> The thing that pleased me most in Chicago was the esteem in which the Missouri delegation was held by people from all over America.
>
> The pride that I felt in having the Missourians select me as their candidate has only been accentuated by their conduct here.
>
> I have never been so proud of being a Missourian as I am tonight.
>
> I am very glad to support Adlai Stevenson and I am convinced the party will unite behind him. I believe he will very effectively present the issues in this campaign.[31]

It is astonishing that the favorite-son campaign got as far as it did. Symington did virtually nothing to forward it, and his friends spent very little money. No one could have thought that he had a ghost of a chance, but as Meredith wrote to Jimmy Allen, who had helped Symington in his 1952 campaign and who had come to Chicago to be helpful, "It was a good experience for Stuart and, if Stevenson loses in 1956, we will crank him up for 1960."[32]

Symington would make a much more serious effort in 1960, but for the time being he concentrated on helping Stevenson. There was never any great warmth between the two men, and many of the young liberals around Stevenson were openly critical of both Symington's ability and his liberal credentials. They tended to ignore his solid liberal voting record and concentrate instead on his refusal to join their crusades. They didn't like his hawkishness on defense and were suspicious of his strong southern support. They particularly irritated him with the charge that he was "a light weight." Symington wrote Bill Becker: "The so-called liberal press went to work on me, even some of my friends, but I hold no basic ill will against them because they were determined that Stevenson should get the job."[33]

Relations between Symington and Stevenson warmed considerably after the convention. Stevenson wrote Symington an anguished letter over a *Time* story to the effect that he had "vetoed" him for vice president at a meeting of party leaders:

> . . . I am distressed by this report, but not surprised as it is but one of several inaccuracies in the piece.
>
> Actually, as I think you know, I have had not only the warmest personal regard for you for many years, but also the utmost admiration for your record in the many capacities in which you have served our country.
>
> I am sure you put no credence in this absurd story, but I wanted to take this means to deny that I ever said such a thing or had such an idea, and I hope to have an early opportunity to repeat this denial in person. . . .
>
> P.S. Perhaps I'm also a little indignant because to say such a thing in a large meeting (I think there were 12 or more present) hardly credits me with normal intelligence![34]

Symington responded with equal grace: "Your kind thoughts are more than reciprocated. I was very proud of you in Chicago. . . . And of course, in every talk I intend to give the facts as to why it will be better for the people of this country and the free world when you replace the present incumbent in the White House."[35]

Following the convention, Symington returned to Nantucket, where he remained until after Labor Day. He then threw himself into the campaign. He had Senators Hubert Humphrey and George Smathers as his guests at the Democratic state convention in Jefferson City—which didn't do him any harm with the home folks—then he and Smathers headed west on a fund-raising trip. He campaigned extensively in Missouri, working for both Stevenson and Hennings, who was facing reelection. He and Eve went to Abilene, Texas, to help Lyndon and Lady Bird Johnson kick off a series of Democratic fund-raising dinners.[36]

One of his more important efforts was to join Senator Clinton Anderson of New Mexico in a television broadcast from Chicago designed to dampen the furor created by Stevenson's statement on the campaign trail in California that he would end the draft and give nuclear materials to other nations. This gave the Republicans an easy issue and infuriated the hard-liners in the Democratic party, including Russell, who confided to friends that he was through with Stevenson and boarded a steamer for Europe. Symington, along with Anderson, thought that Stevenson had "blown it," but he agreed to go to Chicago to try to salvage something. Symington assured the country that Stevenson's proposal would not weaken our defenses. Then he launched into his standard anti-Eisenhower speech on defense, charging that the Republicans had weakened the country's defenses by cutting the air force budget.[37] The effort was not particularly successful.

Johnson suggested that Stuart and Eve go to Paris with Lady Bird and him after the election to attend a NATO meeting. It was tempting, but he simply was too tired to contemplate it. Actually, he was planning to meet Ed Welsh in Florida, "to draft up the report on airpower in the mornings and swim or golf in the afternoon."[38]

Symington had held his report on air power until after the election, "to avoid making a partisan issue of it," and he was now anxious to get at it. The hearings had been tinged with partisanship. With the issuance of the report, the issue became eminently partisan, and Symington became even more a central figure in the defense controversy.

24

The Missile Gap

SHORTLY after the Eighty-fourth Congress convened, Symington issued his long-awaited Report on Air Power. The conclusions contained little that was new; they simply codified the charges Symington had been making since he first arrived in the Senate. Buttressed, however, by testimony from the nation's leading military thinkers and set forth in an official document, they dramatized an air force steadily falling behind its Soviet counterpart. Conceding that "The United States has a strong strategic striking force at this time," the report reminded the public that this was due, in large measure, "to weapons designed, money appropriated, and contracts let many years ago; and even this strength is declining relatively as against the steadily growing striking capacity of the Soviets."

This was followed by a twenty-point indictment of the Eisenhower administration both as to its support of air power forces in being and its preparation for the future. The report did not mention a "missile gap" as such, but it criticized the Department of Defense for its failures in the development of missiles, with the result that "there has been a serious loss of time as compared with the rapid progress of the Soviets."[1]

Jackson and Ervin joined Symington in the report, but Saltonstall filed a minority report. (Duff was no longer in the Senate, but he assured Saltonstall that if he were, he would join in a minority report.) Saltonstall refused to sign the majority report because it was "unduly pessimistic"; it was "not sufficiently objective"; it did not "give sufficient weight to the testimony of the civilian heads of the Department of Defense"; and it confined its analysis almost exclusively to the four years following 1953, whereas "the present military effort cannot properly be evaluated without considering our position at the close of World War II, the speedy demobilization after that war, and the build up for the Korean War, which determined the composition and capabilities of our defense forces in 1953."

Saltonstall was not going to let the Democrats put all the blame on the Eisenhower administration. Moreover, he was far from sure that any blame should be assessed. "Our airpower and our naval strength, together with our ground forces, make us superior to the Soviet Union today," he wrote. He was confident that those responsible for our defense would "continue to plan and provide adequate military strength, of which airpower is the most vital segment, for the Nation in years to come. We can never engage in a numbers race with Russia. We do not want to do so. What we do want are balanced land, sea, and air forces which give us a visible deterrent and such power to retaliate quickly and devastatingly that no enemy would dare to attack us. . . . The task then is to press forward with those programs which, in our judgment, will provide for such modernization of our forces as is essential for the security needs of our country."[2]

The report received wide coverage, with a number of major publications reprinting its recommendations in their entirety. Outside the air force and the aeronautics industry, however, it received little favorable comment. Most commentators dismissed it as a partisan, political document. On *Meet the Press* on February 3, Lawrence Spivak began with the charge that the report was purely political. Symington responded that Republican efforts to defend the administration made it clear that there would be a minority report. The answer as to whether or not the report was political lay in the report itself. He urged all who were interested to read it.

Symington spent most of the rest of the program criticizing the administration and defending the military. When Spivak suggested that Symington surely knew from experience that military men "ask for as much as possible, hoping to get as much as they want," Symington retorted: "I don't think that's a fair statement. When General Eisenhower was Chief of Staff of the Army, I always felt that he came in and asked for what the Army needed, and the same was true of General Spaatz and General Vandenberg."[3]

Reading the transcript, one is impressed that Symington made a strong case for the report. Symington, too, felt that he had done well. He wrote Spivak: "Putting it mildly, we got a better reaction to this program than any I ever did before and I am grateful to you because it gives a chance to put across a story that is not carried in many newspapers."[4]

Symington was correct about the newspapers. As indicated, the report received wide notice when it was issued, but it generated relatively little editorial comment. Symington's papers contain only two editorials relating to the report, both favorable, from the *New York Herald Tribune* and the *St. Louis Globe-Democrat*, both, as Symington reminded Johnson, "Republican papers which are ardent supporters of President Eisenhower and his administration."[5]

In mid April he took Ed Welsh and several members of the staff of the Armed Service Committee for a quick inspection of American and NATO installations in Western Europe. It was a time for renewing old friendships: General Lauris Norstad, commanding SHAPE, in Paris; Ambassador David Bruce in Bonn; and in London, Ambassador J. H. Whitney (Eve's cousin), former Secretary of the Air Force Thomas Finletter, and former Air Marshals John Slessor and William Elliott. Whitney took him out to Chequers for the weekend. Churchill was not at home and had turned the house over to Foreign Minister Selwyn Lloyd, with whom they had "much discussion."[6]

The trip strengthened Symington's belief in the importance of achieving greater unification of the armed services. "After a trip abroad last week," he wrote Johnson, "I am more worried about our security than ever before." The country could not continue "to pay so heavily for the duplication and waste this Administration is levying against the taxpayer in order to maintain our Department of Defense with its foreign military aid." He urged a thorough investigation. It would help the Democratic party, but "far more important, it would help the security of our country."[7]

He sounded the same theme in a speech before the Wilkes-Barre (Pennsylvania) Chamber of Commerce. Although he insisted that his position had not changed,[8] he was beginning to moderate his "defense first, the economy second," attitude in favor of insisting that an adequate defense could be achieved if only the enterprise were well managed, frequently citing the Cordiner report, the result of a study of the Defense Department conducted at the president's request by Ralph Cordiner, president of General Electric. His increasing pessimism over the efficacy of foreign aid presaged the development of active hostility to the whole concept, particularly as it impinged on the military budget. He seems to have been influenced by an article that Henry Kissinger, then a professor at Harvard, wrote for the April 1956 issue of *Foreign Affairs,* in which he argued that "an adequate strategic doctrine" was a basic requirement of American security and that no amount of spending would substitute for its absence.[9]

During the summer of 1956 he occasionally lobbed criticism at the administration, but without much effect. He was particularly critical of the mixed signals on defense emanating from the administration. He charged that Wilson's directive to the air force to cancel or slow down orders for certain aircraft ran counter to the president's assurances that air force funds would be increased. He characterized defense planning as "Alice in Wonderland." In an extended discussion of the military budget, he bemoaned the steady decline in the defense budget as a percentage of the gross national product during the Eisenhower presidency. "The Communists," he observed, "have every right to believe . . . that figures are more important to this Government than forces; and to set their foreign policy plans and programs accordingly." He created a minor stir in July by accusing the president of "vacillation" to the point of "incredible irresponsibility," but nothing much came of it. James Hagerty, Eisenhower's press secretary, countered by telling reporters, "Mr. Symington ought to get his facts straight."[10]

The verbal exchange with Hagerty served to keep the issue before the public, but Symington was frustrated in his effort to launch another investigation of the Defense Department. Johnson had appointed him chairman of a task force of the Preparedness Investigating Subcommittee to conduct a study on aircraft procurement, maintenance, operations, and training. Johnson and Bridges would be the other members. The task force filed a few routine reports, but nothing much happened until Jackson charged that the air force was planning to transfer a contract training program from Tillinghook, Oregon, to the Amarillo (Texas) Air Force Base at much higher costs. He wanted the task force to investigate. Symington agreed that the matter should be investigated and called a hearing. Johnson, for obvious reasons, wanted no hearing and insisted that it be called off. Symington did so, but then, exhibiting an uncharacteristic lack of political savvy, agreed to a conference in his office with Air Force Secretary Douglas, Jackson, Oregon senators Morse and Neuberger, plus various staff people. When Johnson heard about it, he was furious. He reminded Symington of their agreement that there would be no task force hearings relating to Texas. Symington's first reaction was to ask to be relieved of the chairmanship of the task force, but in the end he decided to go along with the majority leader and drop the whole matter.[11]

When Congress recessed in September, Symington, instead of vacationing as usual on Nantucket, launched into an ambitious sixty-day speaking schedule that would take him to all parts of Missouri. Most of his appearances were "nonpolitical"—crowning the centennial queen at Kahoka, speaking to an Italian social club in Kansas City, etc.—but many observers looked on the tour as the opening of his campaign for reelection in 1958. The tour went well. Symington had devoted considerable energy over the past several months to agricultural problems—his attacks on Secretary of Agriculture Ezra Benson were exceeded in vigor only by those on the secretary of defense—and it was good to meet with groups of farmers and farm leaders from various parts of the state. He also found time to make a few out-of-state speeches, including one at the National Corn

Picking Contest in Sioux Falls, South Dakota, where he continued his attack on Benson and praised Congressman George McGovern, who introduced him as "a great farm leader."[12]

Then, the Soviets launched Sputnik. For Symington, it was a dramatic—and alarming—confirmation of what he had been saying for years. From his home in Creve Coeur, he called for a complete investigation by the Senate Armed Services Committee.[13] He followed this with a long letter to the president urging a special session of Congress. He wondered if the president was aware of the danger posed by the Defense Department's policy of "cutbacks and slowdowns." He wrote almost plaintively,

> When ten years ago we were together in the Pentagon, you as Chief of Staff and I as Assistant Secretary of War, our thoughts as to what was necessary for the defense of our country were in close agreement.
>
> Therefore I do not understand what is now going on; and that is particularly true in light of the events of the past few weeks.[14]

The president responded on October 29—very formally, enclosing a memorandum from the secretary of defense, "which I trust you will find adequately responsive." He saw no need to call a special session of Congress.[15]

Even before the president had a chance to respond, however, Symington issued a long statement, "to bring into focus what the successful launching of this Russian satellite means to the defense policies and programs of the United States." To do so, he gave a scathing, richly detailed denunciation of the administration's past policies, which, he charged, were directly responsible for the lag in missile development dramatized by Sputnik. He heaped particular scorn on Eisenhower's post-Sputnik statement that he didn't know what more could have been done. "How can the President tell the American people," he asked, "and the people of the free world, and the Communists, that he 'doesn't know what could have been done more,' when for purely fiscal reasons, he has recently approved cutbacks and slowdowns and fiscal limitations in all fields of our national defense, including missiles." As for the president's statement that the Soviet's satellite success did not increase his apprehension over the security of the country "by one iota," Symington said, "This statement is either a chilling hint that the President does not understand the true import of the Communist satellite, or it is an attempt to maintain a calm front, behind which emergency action is presumably being undertaken to meet this critical Soviet challenge." He hoped the latter was the case, but considering the duplication in the Department of Defense and the mind-set of its leaders, he was not optimistic. He called for a special session of Congress.[16]

Eisenhower did not respond publicly to Symington's charges, but he warned Johnson that if Symington continued to push the matter for partisan purposes, the Democrats could be blamed for the small amounts spent by the Truman administration on missile research.[17]

With Eisenhower seemingly out of reach, Symington took on Vice President Nixon. Ten days after the Sputnik launch, Nixon, speaking to a group of businessmen in San Francisco, disassociated himself from earlier administration statements downplaying its significance. "Militarily the Soviet Union is not one bit stronger today than it was before the satellite was launched," he said. "But we could make no greater mistake than to brush off this event as a scientific event of more significance to the man in the moon than to men on earth." He insisted, however, that the United States had the capacity to meet any challenge the Soviets might pose, and outlined a program based on American private capital to meet the challenge. Symington's good friend Arthur Krock praised Nixon's proposal as "an intelligent and feasible counter play."[18]

The next day Krock published a summary of Symington's news conference in the *New York Times,* characterizing him as "the outstanding challenger of the soldier-President's evaluation of our military capacity vis-a-vis that of the Soviet Union." On October 24, Krock published a memorandum from Nixon that, while praising Symington's service as secretary of the air force and his efforts "to promote a full public discussion . . . of issues on which our survival depends," contradicted his major points. He was particularly critical of Symington's charge that the administration had vacillated on the defense budget. Symington sent a memorandum correcting Nixon's "misstatements,"[19] but Krock chose not to publish it. The debate ended in a stalemate.

Symington hoped for much more from the hearings about to get under way with the Preparedness Subcommittee of the Armed Forces Committee.[20] He wrote Johnson a long letter suggesting procedures—"all testimony [should] be taken under oath"—and discussing the scope of the inquiry. The hearings should not be limited to missiles and satellites: "otherwise we will not find out how these developments fit into the overall defense picture." He urged comprehensive hearings dealing with all aspects of defense, including education and the organization of the Department of Defense. The subcommittee had a great opportunity "to get the truth out to the people."[21]

Symington clearly wanted a hard-hitting, partisan investigation. Johnson had other ideas. He took seriously Eisenhower's threat to turn the light on Democratic failures to support missile development during the Truman administration if the investigation became too partisan. He did not want to endanger his cordial relationship with the president, and he was convinced that a less partisan investigation than Symington had in mind would better serve the country and his own presidential ambitions. Moreover, he was not about to give Symington an opportunity to further enhance his reputation as an authority on defense.[22] To that end, he sought the cooperation of the Defense Department and urged his colleagues on the subcommittee (Democrats Kefauver, Stennis, and Symington and Republicans Bridges, Flanders, and Saltonstall) to avoid partisanship.

Johnson established his intentions when he opened the hearings on November 25 with a strong disavowal of partisanship and a determination to get at the facts. "Our goal is to find out what is to be done," he said. "We will not reach that goal by wandering up any blind alleys of partisanship."[23]

Despite Johnson's hope to avoid partisanship, Symington, who had hoped to be chairman of the subcommittee,[24] relentlessly pursued two themes: the administration had sacrificed an adequate defense on the altar of the economy, and improper organization of the Department of Defense was costing the taxpayers vast sums—"billions"—and endangering national security.

Symington fanned the flames by criticizing the quality of preparedness planning and repeatedly expressing concern that the administration, in the interests of economy, was not providing adequate support for forces in being. For example, in questioning Dr. Edward Teller, head of the Radiation Laboratory at the University of California at Berkeley and widely known as "Father of the H-Bomb," he said (and this was typical of his questioning):

> Since sputnik, we have had a great many pages about ballistic missiles, and other weapons of the future, in the press.
>
> But we have not had very much about the importance of existing forces; and inasmuch as we both know we won't have ICBM's operational for some years, if we are forced into defending ourselves, of course, we must use existing forces.
>
> As I understand it you are not one who thinks that today, or for years to come, the manned bomber is obsolete. Is that correct?

Teller responded predictably: "I am convinced that the manned bomber is not obsolete. . . . I furthermore believe that even after we get a rocket capability, the manned bomber will still not be obsolete. A rocket can hit a target, of which you know. A bomber can fly out and look for the target, for targets which you may not know of right now or whose location is not exactly available or even targets of opportunity."[25]

When Neil McElroy, the new secretary of defense, took the stand, Symington said that he wanted to discuss the memorandum which the secretary had prepared in response to his letter to the president following Sputnik. He wondered whether, after the testimony of Dr. Teller, McElroy still felt that the United States was ahead of Russia. McElroy responded that "on an overall basis" the United States remained superior to the Soviet Union. Symington wanted to explore the question in detail. Indeed, he wanted to go over McElroy's memorandum point by point. The hour was late, and the committee members became restless. Finally, Johnson broke in to remind Symington that he had run over his time, that "We do have plans to conclude the hearings." Symington, obviously miffed, said, "All I would like to do is get a chance to ask my questions. The President sent me this long memorandum from Secretary McElroy; and I have been working on my analysis of it for some days now, and have covered . . . 5 pages of the analysis, and still have 6. I believe this analysis is important to national security." Through the good offices of South Dakota Republican Francis Case, who volunteered to yield his time, Symington was permitted to continue until eight o'clock when the committee had agreed it would recess for dinner, and Symington continued his not particularly productive analysis of McElroy's memorandum.

Symington's interrogation of the military brought out the sad state of the country's defenses in being. The most startling testimony came from General LeMay, commanding general of the Strategic Air Command. Through a series of leading questions Symington drew from LeMay that SAC's fleet contained "obsolete and obsolescent" planes, that for a time the SAC fleet was grounded for lack of money, that it was doubtful that the United States could catch up with the Soviets at its present rate of improvement.[26]

Although Symington pushed to the end for a hard-hitting attack on the administration's failures, he found no support in the committee. Johnson was fully in charge, and from the beginning he was determined that the best course—for his own political advantage as well as for the welfare of the country—was to avoid a partisan attack and to concentrate on the future. Thus, while acknowledging that the Soviets were ahead of the United States in missile development, the report made no effort to assign blame. Rather, it complimented the administration on steps that had been taken since Sputnik—all with the subtle implication that they had been taken largely in response to Democratic prodding—and advanced a seventeen-point program (most of it short on specifics) to enable the United States to regain leadership in space. The report was a major step in establishing Johnson's position as the leader in space, and though it did nothing to slow the widening of the missile gap, Symington, as one of its principal architects, came out of the hearings more as a partisan scold than a thoughtful leader.[27]

He was soon able to recoup his position as one of the Senate's leading authorities on defense—and he did it by providing strong support for a major presidential initiative.

In his State of the Union address, Eisenhower listed defense reorganization as the first of eight priority tasks. On April 3 he transmitted to Congress recommendations for substantially increasing the authority of the secretary of defense, particularly in the development of new weapons, and providing for a unified command structure.[28]

Although the president's recommendations did not go as far as Symington might have liked, he immediately came out in support of them.[29] After all, he had been preaching the need for reorganization of the Department of Defense since his days as secretary of the air force, and in all of his criticism of the Eisenhower administration's defense efforts, the inefficiencies of the Department of Defense stood high on his list of complaints. An effective organization had never been achieved, and it was not going to be easy now. Even before hearings were held, members of both parties were criticizing the president's proposal,[30] and the bill passed by the House of Representatives was much less sweeping than the president wanted. The secretary of defense would still exercise control of the military departments through the service secretaries, a single member of the Joint Chiefs of Staff could block major command changes, and the services were still able to report directly to Congress.[31] In short, the House bill read a lot like "business as usual."

The Senate Armed Services Committee held extensive hearings on the bill in June and July. A leading witness was Symington's old nemesis, Ferdinand Eberstadt, Forrestal's principal adviser from the days when the Congress was considering the establishment of the Department of Defense. He had not modified his opposition to strong central control. He favored passage of the House bill. Symington interrogated Eberstadt at length—not so much an interrogation as a colloquy between two longtime acquaintances who had never agreed on the issue. Eberstadt agreed with Symington about the need for strength and efficiency in the Department of Defense, but he would not admit that the degree of centralization proposed by the president was necessary.[32]

Symington found much more support from another old nemesis, Admiral Arthur W. Radford, former chairman of the Joint Chiefs of Staff. Radford, the final witness, unreservedly supported the president's position. He also reinforced Symington's view that the country was in much greater danger than was generally realized. The country was not in a shooting war, but because of the nature of the Soviet-Sino threat, "this Nation is really in more danger today than it ever has been in its history."[33]

Although few if any members of the committee seemed to share Symington's cataclysmic view of the world situation, they all agreed that the provisions in the House bill to which the president objected should be eliminated. Symington argued in executive session that the bill was not strong enough in setting forth the authority of the secretary of defense, that it was too solicitous of navy and Marine

Corps sensibilities. The navy, he reminded his colleagues, had always been opposed to unification, and, while he would not oppose the bill, he would like the language to be more direct in asserting the authority of the secretary of defense over the service secretaries.[34]

Despite the fact that his views did not prevail in the committee, Symington made a long speech on the floor of the Senate urging adoption of the bill as reported. "As many of my colleagues know," he said, "I do not believe the bill goes far enough from the standpoint of basing our Department of Defense on progress rather than continuing to base it on tradition. But I do not see how it would have been possible to pass a bill which went beyond what the President recommended."

Colleagues, both Republicans and Democrats, rushed to compliment Symington on his leadership and his speech. Connecticut Republican Prescott Bush, who also served on the Armed Services Committee, spoke for many in both parties when he said: "I believe that no member of the Senate has . . . devoted as much time and study to this subject as has the Senator from Missouri, because of his long service as Secretary of the Air Force and his long study after he left the service of the Air Force. Certainly no one could more ably have done so. . . . I think the Senate should know that he deserves our respect and our gratitude for the time, the effort, and the intelligent work he has devoted to the bill."[35]

When the committee's bill and the report of the conference committee, adopting most of the Senate's language, passed unanimously,[36] the action was interpreted as a victory for Symington. The *St. Louis Globe-Democrat,* noting this, editorialized:

> . . . The vote on the Defense Bill marks full cycle in Senator Symington's distinguished service in the defense field.
>
> In his earlier career in the Senate, perhaps because he had served as first Secretary of the Air Force, Mr. Symington was the most outspoken proponent of this branch of the service, and his extreme partisanship for the Air Forces was criticized in some circles.
>
> Whether or not this comment was valid, Missouri's junior senator has vastly broadened his concept of strength for America since those early days. . . .
>
> No Senator has more fully understood the complexities of the entire Defense establishment . . . than has Senator Symington. The Administration and the American people have great cause for gratitude for Senator Symington's untiring efforts for national defense.[37]

If the administration was grateful for Symington's efforts on its behalf, it gave no indication, probably because his support of the reorganization bill represented only a brief hiatus in his criticism of the administration's defense efforts. Indeed, on the same day that the Senate agreed to the conference report, Symington complained on the floor of the Senate that the army was being poorly supported, and went on to introduce a column by Joseph Alsop entitled "The 'Gap,' " which described in chilling detail the nation's shortcomings in missile development. Alsop charged that by 1960, "The American government will flaccidly permit the Kremlin to gain an almost unchallengeable superiority in the nuclear striking power that was once our specialty." The column had nothing to do with the speech Symington was making (unsuccessfully) on behalf of a larger appropriation for the army. It was current, having appeared in the *Washington Post* that morning. Symington could well have put it in the *Record* to keep the issue alive.[38]

In this he was successful. The missile gap was much discussed during the summer and late fall of 1958. The issue gained strength when Kennedy, already looming as a formidable contender for the Democratic presidential nomination, told his colleagues in the Senate that he wished to "associate himself with Senators Symington, Johnson and Jackson" with respect to the missile gap. Joseph Alsop devoted two columns to the speech, and Symington placed them in the *Congressional Record*, with praise for both Kennedy and Alsop.[39]

Symington created a short-lived contretemps when he also placed in the *Congressional Record* an article that retired Brigadier General Thomas Phillips had written for the *Post-Dispatch* describing the conditions under which the United States should consider surrendering in an all-out nuclear attack. Not surprisingly, the revelation created an instant uproar. Eisenhower was reported to have "blown his top" at the news, ordering a "top to bottom" investigation. Symington fanned the flames by introducing a second article from the pen of General Phillips, in which he asserted that "the best informed military experts in the Pentagon" considered the United States' missile program "shockingly inadequate." This touched off a two-day debate that concluded with the Senate adopting an amendment to the Department of Defense appropriation which prohibited the use of public funds for any study dealing with the possibility of an American surrender "under any circumstances."[40]

But Symington did more than just speak for political effect. He became convinced that the president was not receiving adequate intelligence regarding Soviet missile development. Near the end of July, Symington received a private briefing from Allen Dulles, director of the CIA, on Soviet missile development.[41] Subsequent information led him to believe that Dulles's figures were too low. He arranged a second meeting on August 6, this time accompanied by his good friend Thomas Lanphier, vice president of Convair, a much-decorated World War II fighter pilot who had been his assistant in the air force and at the

National Security Resources Board. They presented figures considerably higher than those Dulles had given out in July. When Dulles briefed the Senate subcommittee on the CIA, however, he reverted to his earlier figures. As he thought about this, Symington's sense of apprehension increased to the point where he sought an interview with the president. Eisenhower was cordial—after all, the two men had been close friends before they ran for office—but he seemed defensive and a little tense. He reminded Symington that if the Russians were ahead it was because they had an earlier start, and that we were using the maximum amount of money that could be spent effectively. He asserted that he had complete confidence in Dulles, but added, much to Symington's surprise, that the Intelligence Advisory Board and Secretary McElroy were above the CIA in intelligence matters, and that Symington might want to get a briefing from McElroy. He thought the CIA might have been overestimating Soviet missile strength, but he assured Symington that he would carefully review his letter requesting the interview. Symington wrote, "I thanked him for that and I said that in itself made my visit worthwhile and I would hold myself at his command anytime he wanted to discuss it further."[42]

Eisenhower exhibited no interest in discussing the matter further. In preparation for the off-year elections, he tried to buck up a dispirited Republican party. His generalized words of assurance, however, seemed to have had little effect. The Democrats, with Symington and Kennedy in the vanguard, kept hammering away at the inadequacy of the nation's defenses, particularly vis-à-vis the power of the Soviets. "Missile gap" was something of a code descriptor, even though Symington generally referred to long-range intercontinental ballistic missiles (ICBMs) when he used the term. However described, defense was a major factor in the overwhelming Democratic victory on November 4, 1958.[43]

Symington participated in the victory, winning reelection by the largest margin ever amassed by a candidate for statewide office in Missouri. Defense was an issue in Symington's victory, but of equal importance was agriculture, Missouri's largest industry.

25

Agriculture—The Other Big Issue

ALTHOUGH Symington seemed to be preoccupied with the problems of defense, he recognized that for many of his constituents, the problems of agriculture were of equal or greater importance. Nothing in his experience equipped him to understand the lives led by most Missouri farmers—the only "farmhouses" in which he had spent a night were the Wadsworth mansions in New York and the Johnson ranch in Texas. He and his brother Charles had owned a cattle ranch in Arizona, but he had had no part in its operation. In short, when he first ran for the Senate, he knew virtually nothing about agriculture, Missouri's leading industry. In visiting with leaders of the Missouri Farmers Association, for example, he asked, "What is parity?"

He may not have known much in the beginning, but he was a quick learner. He was a good listener, and while Missouri farmers may have been put off a bit in the beginning by his elegant attire, his eastern accent, and his big-city ways, they soon came to respect his sincerity and to feel comfortable in his presence. From the beginning, he kept in close touch with the state's farmers and farm leaders. He learned a lot by just listening.

He learned most importantly that Missouri's farmers did not speak with one voice, that their interests were as varied as the state itself, that the cotton producers in the Bootheel had little in common with the corn and soybean growers of the northwestern counties, and that neither had quite the same interests as the dairy and livestock producers of the state. Each of these interests had its own association, most of them with a full-time professional staff. In addition, two large, competing organizations sought to speak for Missouri agriculture: the

Missouri Farm Bureau Federation and the Missouri Farmers Association.[1] The National Farmers Union also had a presence in Missouri, its membership increasing in times of agricultural depression, but the Farm Bureau and the Missouri Farmers Association dominated agricultural politics in the state.

Symington maintained cordial relations with the leaders of both organizations, but increasingly he turned to the Missouri Farmers Association for advice and support, becoming particularly close to Fred Heinkel, its longtime president.[2] Although both organizations were ostensibly nonpartisan, the leadership of the MFA was essentially Democratic, while that of the Farm Bureau was essentially Republican. For that reason alone, Symington would gravitate to the MFA, but there was more to it than simple party affiliation. As he wrote Meredith: "I cannot feel in my mind and heart that the Farm Bureau policy is the right policy, at least for the farmers of Missouri. It may be right for the 'factory farm' but it just isn't right for the family farm and the fact that we are losing that type of farm worries me as much as anything, except the Communist menace."[3]

Symington early became convinced that the Eisenhower farm program was as bad for the country as were his defense policies, and he became an aggressive, articulate critic. Eisenhower's major goal for agriculture was to get the government out of farming, and this meant dismantling the New Deal program of fixed price supports and production controls in favor of allowing the market to find a solution to the problem of overproduction, which was responsible for low farm prices. To ease the transition to a free market, the administration proposed for the immediate future replacing the long-established Democratic policy of fixed supports at 90 percent of parity with a system of flexible or sliding price supports, ranging from 75 percent to 90 percent. Farmers frequently grumbled about government controls, but many were fearful of a future without high price supports.[4]

Symington understood the farm dilemma, and he made no apology for advocating government supports for agriculture. The strength of agriculture was central to the strength of the economy, and a strong economy was as essential a bulwark against communism as was a strong military. Moreover, he was fond of reminding his audiences that talk about the farmer being the only beneficiary of government support was wholly incorrect. "What about the minimum wage?" he asked. "What about subsidies for business and industry?" He hastened to say that he strongly favored the minimum wage—"it increases the personal dignity of human beings; it also increases purchasing power at the base"—and he did not oppose other subsidies, "especially if they are incident to a build up in our national defense structure." They were, however, subsidies, just as direct as farm price supports.

From the beginning of his senatorial career, Symington emerged as a major critic of the Eisenhower farm program. He frequently carried the fight to the president himself, but his usual target was the man Eisenhower had chosen to carry out his program: Secretary of Agriculture Ezra Taft Benson. A devout Mormon, Benson was a member of the Council of Twelve, the supreme governing body of the Mormon Church. He looked upon public service as a means of serving God by serving man and was convinced that his views were morally as well as economically right. Rigid in the extreme, he made an easy target.[5]

An early confrontation occurred over Department of Agriculture practices in Missouri. During his first presidential campaign, Eisenhower promised that farmers would be given more control over the administration of federal farm programs. Early in his tenure, however, Secretary Benson announced that in the interest of "greater uniformity, efficiency and economy," control of policies and administration of the production and marketing programs (soon to be known as agricultural stabilization and conservation programs, or ASC) was transferred from county committees whose members were elected by local farmers to state committees whose members were appointed by the secretary of agriculture.

In Missouri, the process became riddled with politics. Murray Colbert, chairman of the state ASC committee, created an uproar by suspending or dismissing a number of county committeemen, most of whom were Democrats, for what seemed to be political reasons. Senator Hennings first raised the issue, but Symington picked it up and took the lead in pursuing it. He joined with Hennings and Tenth District Congressman Paul Jones in demanding a full report from Benson.[6] When none was forthcoming, the Senate Committee on Agriculture and Forestry appointed Senator Humphrey chairman of a subcommittee to investigate the matter. Symington, though not a member of the committee, was invited to participate.[7]

The hearings, held in November 1955 in a large conference room on the fourteenth floor of the new Jefferson state office building in Jefferson City, opened to an overflow crowd and immediate controversy. Humphrey and Republican Senator Andrew Schoeppel of Kansas, the other committee member, both gave assurances that the two-day hearings would be conducted on a nonpartisan basis. "We're not here on any fishing expedition," Humphrey said. They had come in response to the many complaints of unjustifiable dismissals forwarded to the Senate Agriculture and Forestry Committee by Senators Hennings and Symington, complaints which had elicited no response from the Department of Agriculture. He noted that of 191 such complaints received from the entire country, 49 were from Missouri. He thought the situation merited a careful look.

But even before the first witness was called, Republican Congressman Thomas B. Curtis of St. Louis spoke up to charge that the trouble came "from the attempt to get politics out of the program," and that Democrats, reluctant to lose their jobs, were at the root of the uproar. Symington countered by saying that some of the harshest criticism of the program had come from strong Republican counties.

Humphrey conducted the two-day hearing almost on an around-the-clock basis, going from 9 A.M. until after midnight, with short breaks for lunch and dinner. The 250,000 words of testimony produced mixed results. It was clear that the state committee had been heavy-handed in many of its dealings, and that some of the dismissals had been for purely political reasons—"in open violation of the law," according to Humphrey—but there was no evidence of fiscal wrongdoing or inefficiency by the new administration. Humphrey said at the end that centralized control in the state office was "definitely the wrong philosophy," but, he added, "There seems at times to have been a great deal of fuss over gnats and details." In any event, he would report the proceedings to the full Senate Committee on Agriculture and Forestry. But back in Washington, he wrote Benson that he was "shocked" by the operation of the ASC committee system in Missouri, and that "This is a matter of such grave concern that it requires your personal attention."[8]

Symington, too, was "shocked" by the findings. In speech after speech before Missouri farm audiences, he criticized the operation of the state ASC office. He and Hennings joined in asking Benson for a full review. The secretary not only rejected this request but also reappointed Murray Colbert, whose actions as chairman of the state committee had been central to complaints against the ASC administration. Seemingly to add insult to injury, the Department of Agriculture issued new regulations increasing the authority of the office managers in each county as opposed to that of the elected county commissioners, further indication of a trend toward more centralized control. Symington issued a statement saying, "The farmers in Missouri have repeatedly reported to us that they do not approve of this trend." He hinted that the Agriculture and Forestry Committee might hold hearings, but nothing came of it.[9] It seemed that there was little he could do but complain.

Symington's ability to represent Missouri farmers greatly improved when he was appointed to the Senate Committee on Agriculture and Forestry, replacing Clinton Anderson of New Mexico, who transferred to the Senate Finance Committee. Symington gave up membership on the Public Works Committee, whose activities were of considerably less interest to Missourians than those of Agriculture and Forestry. Missouri farmers and farm leaders greeted the appointment with enthusiasm;[10] they were sure that Symington would be an active and effective member of the committee. They were correct.

Symington's appointment came too late for him to have much impact on the farm bill working its way through the Congress, but he strongly supported the

Democratic amendments attached to the administration's proposal. The bill provided for the establishment of a "soil bank," a conservation measure that had broad bipartisan support. Attached to it, however, were flexible price supports, opposed by most Democrats and Midwest Republicans. This combination was able to restore the system of rigid supports at 90 percent of parity. Symington hailed the legislation as "A major victory for the American farmer." Eisenhower and Benson thought otherwise, and Eisenhower vetoed the bill.[11] The Democrats were unable to override the veto, but they had an issue for the 1956 campaign that worked well in the farm states.

During much of his time on the committee, Symington concentrated on Missouri issues. He obtained appointment to Humphrey's subcommittee on the operation of county committees and pushed for the renewal of the investigation of ASC operations in Missouri. Humphrey was glad to oblige, setting up a hearing in Washington for June 11. Declaring, "We are heading for a showdown on this issue," he asked Benson and other top agricultural department officials to appear. Benson did not attend—he was at his daughter's wedding—and Undersecretary True Morse, a Missourian, represented the department. Benson asserted that Missouri farmers were receiving efficient service from the ASC. He also reminded the committee that the Department of Agriculture had distributed more drought aid in Missouri than in any other state except Texas. This satisfied neither Humphrey nor Symington. Humphrey complained about the "high-handed" manner in which the ASC operated in Missouri; Symington contested Morse's statement that the ASC was working well in Missouri. He also criticized Benson for not attending the hearing, "which was arranged for his convenience." As a follow-up to the hearings, Symington and eight other Democratic senators cosponsored a bill introduced by Humphrey to revamp the selection and operation of the ASC committees. Benson opposed the bill, and his position prevailed.[12]

Symington repeatedly criticized Benson's handling of drought aid for Missouri. Despite Morse's assertions, Symington charged that for 1956—the worst year for Missouri in the prolonged drought that ravaged the Midwest and West during the 1950s—the Department of Agriculture consistently ignored pleas for help from Missouri farmers. At times, his argument descended to the ad hominem level, as when he reported that he had been told "by a high official of the Missouri farm effort" that Benson had passed the word through the department to slight Missouri "because he feels he was insulted by the Missouri State Commissioner of Agriculture." He added, "If that is true I am truly sorry, but on the other hand, if Mr. Benson is taking out his personal pique against one Missourian on hundreds of thousands of Missouri farmers, then he is unfit for the high office he holds, and he should resign."[13]

Symington's barrage of criticism extended over several days in January and February of 1957. In all of it he was cheered on by Humphrey, but Republican Barry Goldwater of Arizona was not so enthusiastic. He challenged Symington's figures on drought relief in Missouri. An extended colloquy between the two men—normally quite good friends because they saw eye-to-eye on defense matters—only revealed that they were talking about different years.

Benson entered the fray by issuing a press release defending the department's treatment of Missouri, pointing out that the state generally had enjoyed good crops the year before. He added fuel to the flames by charging that Missouri officials had done very little to help the farmers of the state. "Surely," he said, "Senator Symington can hardly be serious." Predictably, Symington did not let the comment go unnoticed. He challenged Benson in a meeting of the Agriculture and Forestry Committee and on the floor of the Senate. He pointed to the plight of Missouri farmers and the government's failure to provide commensurate aid, adding, "I want to assure Mr. Benson that I am very serious about this matter."

In fact, the two men were talking about two different things. Benson's figures dealt with the state as a whole, whereas Symington was referring only to twenty-eight southwestern counties severely hit by the drought that ravaged the Plains. Be that as it may, Benson sent an inspector to Jefferson City to meet with Governor Blair and state agriculture officials. At Blair's invitation, Symington also attended. As a result of this meeting, farmers in the stricken counties were given access to emergency credit, "but," Symington lamented, "neither this nor hay can be of much help at this time."[14]

Symington continued his attack. He charged that Benson's assertion that farm income was running 7 percent above the previous year "was another misleading presentation." Benson had used only one month in each of the years. If he had used the entire year, "he would have said that prices for the year 1956 would have averaged exactly the same as in 1955." A few days later, he joined Humphrey in a further attack on Benson's credibility, charging that, as in the case of defense, "we are not being given all the facts about our agricultural position."[15]

Apparently, Symington's constant criticism was beginning to get under Benson's skin. He told a group of Republican women, "You know, we have let the opposition get away with too much loose talk. We let rich Democrats like Harriman, Symington and Stevenson pin the 'party of wealth' tag on us without returning the fire."[16]

The two men remained at loggerheads, with Symington's criticism of Benson and the Department of Agriculture being second only to that which he leveled against Wilson and the Department of Defense. This criticism extended to one of Benson's principal assistants, Don Paarlberg, a widely known professor of economics at Purdue University who had spoken extensively in support of Eisenhower's farm policy. During Paarlberg's confirmation hearing Symington questioned him closely on certain of his views, frequently interrupting his replies with a request for "Yes or No." Finally, Democrat Spessard Holland of Florida, who was presiding, told Symington that Paarlberg could answer the questions in his own words. "We are never going to bully a witness into answering before this committee," he declared.[17]

Symington continued to make Benson the issue, and Benson came under bipartisan attack as Midwest Republicans with an eye on the midterm elections came to view the secretary of agriculture as a serious liability. Dramatic evidence of Benson's unpopularity, and by coincidence Symington's popularity, came during the national corn-picking contest in South Dakota. Speaking to an audience of thousands, Symington drew cheers as he excoriated Benson and "his theoreticians" for their unsound and unrealistic policies. In contrast, Benson had been greeted the day before by a shower of eggs.[18]

The South Dakota speech came as an interruption to an extended tour of Missouri in which he met with farmers and farm groups in all parts of the state. These meetings convinced him that his attacks on Benson and his policies were resonating among Missouri farmers. He continued his criticism and extended it to the president. At the same time, he worked with Humphrey and others to retain as much as possible of the New Deal system of high price supports. For example, he cosponsored with Humphrey a joint resolution to prevent the secretary of agriculture from reducing price supports and acreage allotments below 1957 levels. This, as he explained to a farmer in Missouri, "would give Congress additional time to work out a sound long-range program."[19]

There was little hope, however, that such a program could be developed. The Democrats had a majority in both houses, but it was by no means veto-proof. Eisenhower vetoed the resolution and they were unable to override.[20]

During consideration of the farm bill of 1958 Symington joined with Humphrey and Wisconsin Democrat William Proxmire in dissenting from the action of the Committee on Agriculture and Forestry supporting a modified version of the administration's proposal. They expressed the view that a majority of the committee "would support and report more effective legislation for corn and feed grain producers, for wheat growers and for dairy farmers—if it were not for the constantly repeated threat of a veto, and the fear that even the compromise cotton and rice provisions would be rejected if the committee took any action on these other commodities of which the Secretary did not approve."[21]

Symington spoke frequently and at length against the bill, but to little avail. He offered amendments on the Senate floor to improve the bill for dairy farmers and corn and feed grain producers, but they received little support. The leadership was determined to enact the committee's compromise. Humphrey provided steady and highly vocal support, but few others spoke in favor of Symington's amendments. William Langer, the maverick Independent from North Dakota, in announcing his support declared, "The farmers have no more able friend fighting for them than the distinguished Senator from Missouri."[22]

Symington enjoyed one minor bit of success when the Senate adopted, by voice vote, his amendment to maintain the principle of parity with respect to the cotton program—but without changing the level of support.[23] For the most part, though, as in the early stages of his efforts to increase defense expenditures, Symington was something of a voice in the wilderness.

Following enactment of the farm bill, Symington gave a long speech in the Senate entitled "A Prophecy on Agriculture." He feared that the country was "planning disaster" by eliminating the system of price supports upon which farmers had depended. "This is a serious matter," he declared, "not only to the millions who now live on our farms, but also to the Nation as a whole. Unless the agricultural policies characteristic of this Administration are altered, there is grave danger that agriculture will ultimately drag down the rest of our economy."

"Fortunately," he continued, "there are other alternatives if farmers decide they do not want to continue in the present direction." He was not proposing a specific program, but he suggested three possibilities: (1) producers could develop a cooperative program of adjustment that would balance production and demand; (2) the government could develop supplementary surplus distribution programs, both at home and abroad, to help maintain prices; (3) the government could adopt a compensatory payment program that would allow prices to seek their own level in the market but would provide a degree of protection for the farmer. He concluded: "Once given the facts and the opportunity to choose, I believe farmers will work out a program that will bring to them returns reasonably comparable to those received in other segments of the economy."[24]

This was hardly a call to action. Indeed, it seems somewhat anticlimactic when read in the context of Symington's earlier criticism of Benson and the Department of Agriculture. It may have represented a recognition that it was no longer possible to preserve the New Deal program of high price supports and rigid production controls. Symington remained an activist insofar as government's responsibility to support agriculture was concerned. He recognized the speciousness of the notion that government should "free the farmer to farm." As long as government supported other segments of the economy, he passionately believed that it must continue to support agriculture. In the years ahead, he would seek ways to provide that support, but first he had to be reelected.

Three days after Christmas, at home in Creve Coeur, Symington announced that he would seek a second term in the Senate.[25] The announcement surprised virtually no one, and everyone—except possibly the candidate himself—thought he easily would be reelected. But more was needed than simple reelection. To keep in contention for a presidential nomination in 1960, he would have to win by a convincing margin.

Meredith signed on again as campaign manager, and Fike ran things from Washington. Prominent business leaders Sam Cook of Jefferson City, Lester Cox of Springfield, Charles Curry of Kansas City, and Sidney Salomon of St. Louis served as fund raisers. The young lawyers who had been helpful in 1952—John Oliver and D. W. Gilmore of Kansas City, and William Becker of Columbia—remained active. Son Jim, then practicing law in St. Louis, entertained audiences with folk songs during the early stages of the campaign, but left for London before the primary to serve as an aide to his uncle, John Hay "Jock" Whitney, Eisenhower's ambassador to the Court of St. James.[26]

Symington himself did relatively little campaigning before the primary. He had only token opposition and felt that it was best to remain in Washington to work on defense and the farm bill. A minor brouhaha developed over campaign billboards that carried only a large portrait and the message, "Re-Elect Senator Symington," without mentioning his party affiliation. Some of the bosses in St. Louis complained about "Democratic candidates not wanting to run as Democrats," but no significant defection developed. Meredith explained that the campaign staff wanted the message to be as succinct as possible so that it could be easily read by passing motorists. He expressed surprise at the protests. "I thought everyone in Missouri knows that Senator Symington is a Democrat," he said. "Besides these signs are for the primary and only Democrats can vote for him in the primary."[27]

Despite these distractions and the fact that he spent only seventy-eight thousand dollars on the campaign—most of which went to ward leaders in St. Louis to help them get out the vote—Symington swept to an overwhelming ten-to-one victory, carrying every precinct. His opponent in the general election was Hazel Palmer, a Sedalia attorney who had established some statewide reputation as a leader in business and professional women's clubs but otherwise was a political unknown. She had been nominated almost by default; no prominent Republican had any interest in sacrificing himself in a race against the state's best vote-getter.[28]

Following the example of 1952, Symington officially opened his campaign in the little Monroe county seat town of Paris. Speaking to about 250 people in the Mark Twain cafe, he said he had come back "to report . . . to you on my work as your Senator in the past six years." After a short review of the accomplishments of the Democratic-controlled Congress, he devoted most of his remarks to an attack on the Eisenhower administration's record in national defense, foreign affairs, and agriculture, particularly stressing the president's lack of leadership. He followed this pattern throughout the campaign, seldom mentioning his opponent as he stumped the state from one end to the other. Although he did not maintain the hectic pace of 1952, his voice gave out and he returned home.[29]

It really didn't matter. He had the election sewed up. Every major newspaper in the state endorsed him, even the *Post-Dispatch,* his most regular editorial critic. Although the *Post-Dispatch,* in common with many liberals, criticized Symington for his preoccupation with defense and "a certain tendency not to commit himself on close controversial questions until late in the game," it praised his voting record as "thoroughly progressive." It also spoke approvingly of his support of Missouri causes and his "excellent staff which renders first-class service to his constituents." The Republican *Globe-Democrat* praised his national leadership and called him "The most effective Senator for Missouri this state has had since Thomas Hart Benton's time." Across the state, the Republican *Kansas City Star,* while criticizing Symington for being "overpartisan or political in some of his stands—on the farm question for instance," praised his "broad understanding of the times which enables him to make his particular contribution to the national defense." The times were "too perilous to put partisan considerations above an obvious contrast in the choice before Missouri." As for the fact that both senators lived in St. Louis, "On the many problems that arise from Kansas City and Western Missouri in Washington . . . few men have served the interests of this immediate territory more diligently and sincerely than have Symington and his able administrative assistant Stanley Fike." Even Hazel Palmer's hometown newspaper urged that "Nothing short of an overwhelming endorsement should be accorded Senator Stuart Symington."[30]

The voters gave Symington the "overwhelming endorsement" that the *Sedalia Democrat* and other papers had called for. His margin of victory was the largest ever given a candidate in Missouri in an off-year election; his margin increased from the 54 percent received in 1952 to 67 percent in 1958.

As the *Globe-Democrat* put it, he could "well read the election results with justifiable pride."[31] The *Globe-Democrat* capped his year by giving him its prestigious "Man of the Year" award, the first time it had honored a public official. David Brown's fulsome biographical sketch, complete with pictures of the glamorous Eve and the photogenic family, which filled the paper's magazine section the Sunday after Christmas, would be an admirable promotion piece should he decide to seek higher office.

26

Half-Hearted Run for the Presidency

EVEN BEFORE his reelection in 1958, Symington had been widely discussed as a possible presidential candidate in 1960. In November 1957, Harry Truman told a Democratic dinner in St. Louis that Missouri should reelect Symington by a large majority because "greater things were in store for him."[1] Symington's friends in Missouri did not need to be told about the importance of the senator's reelection. They worked assiduously to bring it about—and by a large margin—to improve his prospects for 1960.

The prospects looked fairly good. As Marquis Childs wrote in the *Washington Post,* Symington was the only one "of the eight or ten eligibles who figure on most lists" against whom some objection could not be raised. His voting record was one "with which no liberal Democrat could quarrel. Yet with his genial Ivy League manner and his 'old family' background," he was not considered "a shouting liberal." He would be more acceptable to the South than any other northerner. Moreover, tall and handsome, he looked like a president. On the surface, at least, he seemed to be an almost ideal candidate.[2]

Symington's impressive victory in 1958 catapulted him into the front rank of Democratic hopefuls, second only to Kennedy, who had been actively campaigning for months and who had won an even more impressive reelection victory.[3] This was good news for Symington's friends, and undoubtedly it was for the senator, too. Symington, however, continued to insist that he had "no plans" to seek the nomination. Returning to Washington from a four-week vacation in

Puerto Rico, he told reporters who were pressing him for word of his intentions that he was aware that his two-to-one reelection victory had increased discussion of his possible candidacy. "Naturally," he said, "One is always pleased and gratified when one's friends think well of you." As of the moment, however, he had made "no changes in any plans I have. I want to be a good senator."[4]

Throughout 1959 he actively participated in the work of his two major committees, Agriculture and Defense, becoming steadily more partisan in his attacks on the Eisenhower administration. He persuaded Johnson to let him drop the Committee on Government Operations for a place on the Space Committee. This, he told Johnson, would let him function more effectively as a member of the Armed Services Committee and would be "to the interest of myself, my party and the country."[5]

The Space Committee's jurisdiction included the newly created National Aeronautics and Space Administration. Symington's principal interest, as might have been expected, was in the military uses of space. He was critical of the administration's failure to coordinate military and civilian uses. As chairman of a subcommittee to study the operations of the space agency, he urged such coordination, and he also declared that adequate coordination of the military uses of space "could be achieved only as an integrated part of further unification of services within the Department of Defense."[6] This was in line with Symington's continuing efforts to bring about greater unification in the Defense Department.

Symington generally refrained from criticism of the space agency despite a fairly low opinion of T. Keith Glennan, the first NASA administrator.[7] He exercised no such restraint with respect to the Departments of Agriculture and Defense.

He greeted the administration's new farm bill with scathing comments on Secretary Benson's policies and administration. On July 13 he spoke at length on the farm problem. After reciting the department's failures to deal with the problem, he concluded: "I have come reluctantly to the conclusion that the Secretary of Agriculture is either unwilling, or unable, to tell the Congress what he thinks should be done to deal with this growing farm problem."

At year's end, in a speech before the annual convention of the National Grange, Symington summarized his indictment of Benson and the administration's farm policy, and presented a program of his own. Basically, he would give farmers more control over the formulation and administration of farm programs, establish a "realistic" system of price supports and production controls, make use of surpluses to feed the hungry around the world, and establish a "special agency" within the Department of Agriculture to deal with the needs of low-income farmers.[8]

This was a campaign policy speech. Symington could assure the farmers of the country that his thinking on agriculture followed established Democratic doctrine.

Regarding defense, Symington continued to be the Senate's principal critic of administration policies, although Kennedy took essentially the same position: the United States continued to fall dangerously behind the Soviet Union, a condition summed up by the term "missile gap." Symington pursued the gap both on and off the Senate floor. As his arguments became more intense—and as they seemed to be gaining wider acceptance—the Republicans moved to counter them. When he challenged an assertion by Vice President Nixon that the United States was closing the missile gap "at a fairly rapid pace,"[9] the Senate minority leader, Everett Dirksen of Illinois, praised Symington's "truly impressive record in the cause of our national security" as a member of the Truman administration. With his best tongue-in-cheek manner, however, he asked: "Instead of downgrading our deterrent power or threatening to release figures which might be classified and constitute an unwarranted disclosure, would the distinguished senator from Missouri, whose competence and concern are freely conceded, not better serve the cause of security by telling the country that despite the irretrievable loss of time in the Truman era, we have under Eisenhower made amazing strides in the missile field of which all can be proud?"

Symington responded that the whole discussion had been initiated by the vice president, and he should clarify his position and that of the administration: "Does he believe we are now 'closing the gap at a fairly rapid pace,' or that the gap continues the same, or that we are losing ground, or that there is no gap?" As for the charges made "by the able minority leader, my friend from Illinois," he would have to study the matter before answering. There is no record that Symington responded directly to Dirksen's questions or to a charge by the Republican National Committee that he had been a "failure" as secretary of the air force and was now posing as an "expert."[10]

Symington did not need to respond. His friends did it for him. The *Washington Star* declared that the Republican effort to downgrade Symington as a prospective presidential candidate had "soared to such heights of massive misrepresentation as to compel a sort of grudging, though perverse, admiration." Majority Leader Johnson announced that he was going to conduct another investigation of defense policy and was appointing Symington a member of the subcommittee. "If ever there was a man who fought to strengthen America," he said, "it was the Secretary of the Air Force, Stuart Symington." Lister Hill of Alabama echoed Johnson's words of praise. He paid tribute to Symington as "the builder of America's air power, as the man who has fought the greatest battles, the greatest number of battles, and the most effective battles for the strength of

America in the air." Acheson and Truman wrote letters of encouragement. Acheson said that the attack was "A good example of the tactics of deception and smear which the party of Lincoln adopted when it became the party of Nixon." Truman wrote that the attack was "the best thing that could happen to you."[11]

Symington, as if energized by the furor, continued his attack on the administration's defense policies. His basic position was one he had espoused for years: the Eisenhower administration placed the budget ahead of defense, and it compounded the evil by refusing to level with the American people about the country's relative strength vis-à-vis that of the Soviets—the "missile gap." He greeted the president's 1960 defense budget with skepticism, especially in its provision for intercontinental ballistic missiles. He assailed Defense Secretary McElroy for asserting that there was "no positive evidence" that the Soviets actually possessed operational ICBMs or that they would develop one ahead of the United States. He was certain that the Soviets did have such a missile, and by 1961 would have "a four-to-one lead" over the United States. As the debate raged, with numbers tossed around with abandon, the country became thoroughly confused. Walter Lippmann, in a column stating that Symington was right and McElroy was wrong, suggested, "At bottom the argument between the administration and Senator Symington is whether the balance of power should be calculated in terms of intercontinental missiles or whether it shall be judged in terms of the whole complex of armaments and of the international political situation." Symington was quick to point out that his argument with McElroy was not just about missiles, that it was about defense in the broadest sense: the administration was allowing the nation's "overall retaliatory capacity to deteriorate . . . [and] is not being candid in its presentation of this deterioration to the people."[12]

Symington was absolutely correct. His criticism of Eisenhower's defense policy was not confined to missiles, it was total. The "missile gap," however, was the term used by the press and frequently by Symington himself, to describe the argument that became central to the presidential campaign. To paraphrase a political strategist of a later generation, the "missile gap" became the horse Symington "almost rode in on."

Symington's chances for the presidency never were higher than they seemed at the height of his debate on defense. Most Democrats in Congress rated him as the party's strongest candidate. Kennedy supporters told the *New York Times* that Symington probably was their strongest opponent. They recognized his strength among the professional politicians, as evidenced in a *Congressional Quarterly* poll, and admitted that he had "all the external virtues" politicians like to see in a presidential candidate: "These include his coming from a strategic state, his Protestantism, his experience with business and government and his identification with a virtuous issue—national defense. He also resembles a popular image of a presidential candidate." The Kennedy people had reason for concern. Added to the *CQ* survey of congressional Democrats, a national poll conducted by *U.S. News & World Report* showed Symington, "surprise man of the front runners," as the first choice of more key party leaders than any other potential candidate.[13]

Symington kept insisting that he was not a candidate, but he was not very convincing. Ed Korterba, for example, reported that the senator arrived for a speech at the National Press Club, in which he denied once again that he was a candidate, "sniffling, watery-eyed and raw-throated from a cold he got from working up a sweat from running so hard from the Presidency." Robert Novak reported in the *Wall Street Journal* that Symington had "mastered the art of being a Senator and running for President at the same time."[14]

There is no question but that he was running, his disavowals notwithstanding. A run for the presidency had been in the back of his mind since his first election to the Senate in 1952. Fike and Meredith worked, with his acquiescence, to promote his "favorite son" candidacy in 1956. When running for reelection in 1958, he did nothing to discourage the national importance of a big victory. With that and the national attention that followed, he began to shape his plans.

One night early in January 1959 while he and Eve were having dinner at the Clark Cliffords', as they often did, he told Clifford that he was seriously considering a run for the presidency. They talked until after midnight. The conversation was purely exploratory, but the campaign was probably launched that night.[15]

At first, the prospects seemed bright. The polls were encouraging, and as Symington went around the country, he found large reservoirs of support. The reservoirs, however, were shallow. Most people liked him, and he got along well with the professional politicians, but he didn't inspire much enthusiasm among the rank and file or the liberal press. The liberal pundits were leery of his concentration on defense, his reputation as a "big bomber" man; they charged that even though his voting record was almost 100 percent liberal, he was really a closet Republican; most devastating of all, they charged that he was a "light weight" who was not up to the job. The charges hurt, coming as they did from people he thought were friends, but they did not cause him to alter his course. He wrote a friend in St. Louis, who had commiserated with him about the attacks, "It is hard to win around here—but all one can do is keep on trying."[16]

He continued his attacks in the Senate on the administration's defense and farm programs. He made an effort to add $240 million to the defense budget to modernize army equipment, but it failed by five votes. To strengthen the nation's diplomacy, which he always felt was closely aligned to the nation's military strength, he proposed the establishment of a Foreign Service Academy, similar to the military service academies, for training young diplomats; the proposal received wide acclaim but no action. He continued to visit Democratic leaders in all parts of the country. Friends in Missouri did the same thing, among them Governor James Blair, Congressman Charles Brown, William Becker of Columbia, Charles Curry of Kansas City, William Nacy of Springfield, and James Meredith of St. Louis. D. W. Gilmore of Kansas City was busy organizing "Symington for President Clubs," and Jerry Litton, a student at the University of Missouri, mobilized college students. Clifford, who visited the delegate-rich state of California in August, found the atmosphere most encouraging.[17]

By fall, the strategy was worked out, and a campaign team was beginning to take shape. Clifford dominated the effort, and it was he who made the central strategic decisions. The most important of these was that Symington would stay out of the primaries. Clifford had discovered that while Symington was well liked by those who knew him, outside of Washington and Missouri he was not well known. "Everyone liked Stuart," Clifford later wrote, "but he was not the sort of person who commanded intense loyalty, like Kennedy, or controlled people through raw power, like Johnson. Traveling around the country, he found most people wishing him well, telling him that he had a lot of unfocused secondary support, and offering to back him if the front-runners faltered or deadlocked."[18]

So Symington spent his time speaking at Democratic conclaves and meeting with party leaders who could be expected to control their delegations at the Los Angeles convention, men such as Carmine de Sapio of New York, Jacob Arvey of Chicago, Frank McKinney of Indiana, and Governor Pat Brown of California. He spoke whenever the opportunity presented itself—between the time Congress adjourned in September until Thanksgiving, he was in twenty states[19]—and observers noted that his oratorical powers seemed to be improving. Russell Baker, for example, wrote in the *New York Times* that Symington completely confounded twenty-five hundred party leaders meeting in Washington: "Among his competitors 'Stu' was known as the candidate who looked most formidable until he opened his mouth. 'He can't think on his feet' was the standard Washington summation of his major flaw as a Presidential candidate. . . . What happened before the 2,500 party leaders when his chance finally came, has astonished the pundits and confounded the opposition. The Symington speech was one of the evening's smashes." Symington "memorized his speech and reeled it off without encumbering text. It sounded fresh and spontaneous and the party pros apparently loved it."[20]

Not everyone on the team approved of Clifford's strategy. Symington's two sons, who were devoting themselves full-time to the campaign,[21] believed that precisely because he was not well known he should enter at least those primaries where he might have a chance to win. Others in the campaign felt the same way. Indiana, a state somewhat like Missouri, seemed a likely bet, as did Maryland, Symington's boyhood home. The candidate would have none of it. Primary campaigns would require large sums of money, and there was no way Symington could raise enough to match the huge sums Kennedy had at his disposal. Moreover, he had little stomach for the struggle itself. He would rely on Clifford, whose views were reinforced by Truman. "You young men had better understand something," Symington told his sons. "Mr. Clifford and Mr. Truman knew [*sic*] something about winning elections."[22]

When Kennedy officially entered the race on January 1, 1960, he challenged Symington to meet him in the primaries, but Symington refused to accept the challenge. In all but formally announcing his candidacy, he said on *Meet the Press* that he would "certainly like to be President," but that he had no intention of entering any presidential primaries. He noted that few states had them and questioned their significance.[23]

Although there was some support for Symington's position,[24] events soon dramatized the folly of the decision. Kennedy's campaign, winging along on the *Caroline*—it was the first time a presidential candidate enjoyed the luxury of a private plane—and fueled by unlimited funds, was rolling to an overwhelming lead. Victory in primary after primary demonstrated Kennedy's vote-getting ability, and when he defeated Humphrey in heavily Protestant West Virginia, he effectively quashed the myth that a Roman Catholic could not be elected president.

The Symington-for-President committee established campaign headquarters in Washington, just a few blocks from the White House, on February 11. William H. Perkins, Jr., a Chicago insurance executive who had been active in Stevenson's campaigns, came on as full-time administrator of the office. Congressman Charles Brown, who had headed the effort from the beginning, continued as overall campaign manager. Fike directed the whole effort from his Senate office. Campaign headquarters buzzed with activity, but everyone freely admitted that "working for a candidate who will not say whether he is a candidate is something of a handicap."[25]

Symington's decision to stay out of the primaries deprived his supporters of an opportunity to showcase their candidate around the country. It also required them to refute charges that their candidate was afraid of defeat. Kennedy repeatedly challenged Symington to put himself before the voters, but Symington consistently refused to touch the bait. Instead, he continued to campaign from the Senate, engaging in high-profile debates on defense, the subject he knew best.[26] Symington was sure that defense would be a major issue in the campaign—as, indeed, it was—but his continuing emphasis on the subject reinforced the view that he was a one-issue candidate. He tried to defuse this in speeches around the country, but with only modest success. The liberals in the party, generally committed to Kennedy, grudgingly admitted that Symington's voting record was 100 percent perfect, but argued that he was not aggressive enough in pushing liberal causes. He seemed to be ambivalent on civil rights, which was becoming a litmus-test issue among northern liberals, who chose to ignore the fact that he had a better record in support of civil rights than any of the other candidates. He had risked alienating the South by canceling an appearance at a Democratic dinner in Little Rock when he learned that Negroes would not be seated at tables with whites.[27] At the same time, he spoke in generalities when confronted with a question on civil rights. On the other hand, he left no doubt about where he stood on the controversial proposal to provide birth-control information. Kennedy was opposed, and Humphrey ducked the issue, but Symington, declaring that the poverty and disease which were characteristic of many overpopulated countries were "two of the foremost allies of communism," strongly supported the practice.[28]

Although there was little of substance in Symington's record with which Democratic liberals could find fault, his candidacy failed to generate much enthusiasm in liberal circles. There was continued talk—covertly encouraged by Kennedy—that he was not quite up to the job. The innuendo was patently unfair. Most of all, it reflected a fear in the Kennedy camp that if anyone could stop them it would be Symington.[29]

The Kennedy fears were justified. Symington had significant strength in the big states—California, New York, Pennsylvania—organized labor was generally supportive, and the titular head of the Democratic party, former president Truman, had made it clear to his friends that Symington was his first choice for the nomination, although he had not issued a formal endorsement. This, however, brought into the fold such luminaries as Harriman and Acheson.[30]

Symington had intended to withhold a formal announcement of his candidacy until the convention. His staff, however, chafing under the difficulty of trying to promote an unannounced candidate, finally convinced him that if he waited until the convention it would be too late. On March 24, at a crowded press conference in the Caucus Room of the Old Senate Office Building, he announced that he was a candidate for President of the United States. Looking every bit a president, and flanked by his extraordinarily attractive family, he declared that he was in the race to win. Citing his extensive management experience in both business and government and his seven years in the Senate, he offered a four-point program to unite the country and move it forward in the world:

1. A positive program for peace through negotiation from a position of relative strength, including a worldwide "good-trader, good-neighbor" policy. . . .

2. A sound public investment program in such fields as education, health, slum clearance, highways, water control, and more realistic benefits for the elderly and disabled.

3. A sound program to reverse the present trend toward the elimination of the family-sized farmer and help him attain a standard of living comparable to other Americans.

4. Policies and programs which would guarantee to every citizen equal rights and equal opportunity.

He would pay for the programs with savings achieved through the elimination of government waste, a favorite theme. He didn't mention the missile gap, but it was surely implicit in his first point. As for the primaries, he reiterated and elaborated upon his refusal to participate in the primary system. There were only five states in which there were contested primaries with less than 7 percent of the convention votes. He believed that all delegates should have a voice in selecting the nominee. He freely recognized that Kennedy was in the lead, but he emphasized again and again that he was in the race to win, even though he inadvertently omitted that statement in his formal announcement.[31]

The omission may have been a portent. Even before Symington announced, his trusted aide Stanley Fike began to have doubts that Kennedy could be stopped. When Kennedy won the Wisconsin and West Virginia primaries, the politicians who originally had believed that Kennedy would not be nominated on the first ballot, and that Symington, everybody's second choice, would prevail, began to have second thoughts. The folly of the Truman-Clifford strategy daily became more apparent. When Kennedy won the Indiana primary, Larry O'Brien publicly offered thanks to Symington, who, he said, had chosen not to enter the Indiana primary, "for reasons known only to God." Charlie Brown blamed "that goddamned Clifford. His advice was just so bad."[32]

In any event, by the time the delegates began to assemble in Los Angeles for the national convention it was clear that Kennedy would be nominated, probably on the first ballot. Symington still enjoyed some support among the politicians—Senator George Smathers, in introducing him to the Florida delegation, said that he was the only candidate who knew all the words to "Dixie"—but his most important supporter, the former president, had announced somewhat peevishly that he would not attend the convention because the Kennedy forces had it rigged.[33]

Although Symington gamely asserted that the president's decision had no effect on his candidacy,[34] it cast a pall over the proceedings. Symington felt obliged to contradict the president's assertion that the convention was rigged for Kennedy. At the same time, he had to deny that he was joining Johnson, who had formally announced his candidacy on July 5, in a "stop Kennedy" move.[35]

Johnson's formal announcement only confirmed what people had known for months, but it refocused attention on Johnson as Kennedy's principal opponent.[36] Symington's campaign had been predicated on the notion that his chance would come when the leading contenders canceled each other. By the time that the convention opened, however, there was no prospect that this would happen.

Symington refused to give up, or at least to give the impression that he was giving up. He and Eve moved into a spacious corner suite in the Biltmore Hotel—a floor below the Kennedys and one above the Johnsons—and his supporters did what they could to hold his pledged votes and round up new ones. Governor Blair stuttered through a nominating speech, and the candidate's supporters conducted what was described by the obviously partisan *St. Louis Globe-Democrat* as "one of the best organized and most colorful of all in the battle of balloons" that preceded the voting.[37]

The demonstration was the last gasp of a dying campaign. Kennedy swept to victory with 806 votes on the first ballot; Johnson was a poor second with 409 votes; Symington placed a distant third with 86 votes, 45 of which were from Missouri, whose delegates were bound by the unit rule to vote for Symington until he released them.[38]

When Symington was asked why Kennedy had won, he replied simply, "He worked harder than the rest of us." That certainly was true. Robert Novak, writing in the *Wall Street Journal,* described the Symington campaign as an "island of tranquility" amid the election-year turbulence. The campaign had "a somnambulistic air, a feeling that the Senator and his aides are going through the motions of the social convention that requires every candidate to campaign." The reason, Novak accurately surmised, was "the lack of a demon within the urbane Missourian driving him irresistibly toward the White House. . . . Mr. Symington gives the impression that life would go on for him much as it has before even if he never becomes President of the United States."[39]

There is no question that Kennedy worked harder and more purposefully. Almost from the beginning there was an uneasy feeling in the Symington camp that the Truman-Clifford strategy of letting the other candidates slug it out in the primaries and on the hustings while Symington stood above the fray, making no enemies and being ready to come forward when the other candidates had fought to a draw, would not succeed. For it to have had a chance, especially after the West Virginia and Wisconsin primaries, when it became clear that Kennedy would go to the convention with a commanding lead, Symington would have had to join with Johnson in a "Stop Kennedy" effort. That he refused to do. "I have never been interested in stopping anyone," he told a reporter in St. Louis as he and Eve departed for Los Angeles.[40]

In the last analysis, Symington's failure resulted from the fact that neither he, Truman, Clifford, nor the many other old-line politicians who advised them realized that the day when presidential politics were decided by the professional politicians was largely over. In the new day, candidates could go over the heads of the professionals directly to the people. Jack Kennedy, with his youth and his unparalleled charisma, was the harbinger of the new day, and he was not to be denied.

After the voting was over, Symington, who had been watching the proceedings on television with Eve and the Cliffords, emerged to face the press. He congratulated "my friend and colleague" and pledged to do everything possible to help him get elected. George Reasons of the *Los Angeles Times* commented, "As he emerged from the darkened suite he looked every inch the gentleman. That's the way he fought, too."[41]

Even before the balloting for president began, the press and most of the delegates shifted their interest to the selection of a nominee for vice president. The common wisdom around Los Angeles held that the nominee would be Symington—the Los Angeles papers on July 14 carried banner headlines declaring the ticket to be Kennedy and Symington. By the next afternoon, the ticket had become Kennedy and Johnson. The full story of the switch—why and how it happened—may never be known, despite the reams that have been written about it. This much, however, seems clear: Kennedy offered the vice presidency to Symington, and then changed his mind.

Clifford tells the story in his memoirs. Late on the afternoon of July 14, Evelyn Lincoln, Kennedy's personal secretary, called Clifford to say that the senator wanted to see him as soon as possible. When he arrived in the senator's "hideaway suite," he found Kennedy "relaxing with a drink, acting as though he did not have a care in the world." He wanted to offer Symington the vice-presidential nomination. Clifford was to find out if he would accept and let him know right away. Symington said he wanted to talk it over with his family before giving his answer. That evening over dinner in the Symington suite, the Cliffords, the two sons and their wives, and Stuart and Eve thrashed out the matter. Tim and Jim were vehemently opposed; Marny Clifford and Eve also expressed reservations. Their reasoning was simple: Why give up a safe Senate seat with growing seniority and influence for an uncertain shot at the vice presidency, which in 1960 was a relatively unimportant ceremonial office? As Clifford observed, "Of course, no one in the room even considered the possibility that the youngest man to run for the Presidency in over half a century might not survive his first term." Clifford argued strongly for acceptance. Symington, who had said little during the discussion, asked Clifford to step into the bedroom with him. He said he could accept, but added, "But I will bet you a hundred dollars that no matter what he says, Jack will not make me his running mate. He will have to pick Lyndon."

And that, of course, was what he did. The next morning Clifford was summoned again to the Kennedy suite, where Kennedy told him: "Clark, I must do something I have never done before in my political career. I must renege on an offer made in good faith. During the night I have been persuaded that I cannot win without Lyndon on the ticket. I have offered the Vice Presidency to him— and he has accepted. Tell Stuart that I am sorry. I would greatly appreciate his and your understanding. I hope to call on both of you for help during the campaign."[42]

It is impossible to determine just what happened during that fateful night. Most northern liberals and most of the labor leaders were vehemently opposed to Johnson, but that opposition did not translate into active support for Symington.[43] Many northern liberals had never supported Symington, despite his almost impeccable voting record. He was too much a "big bomber" man, and some of them—possibly including Kennedy himself—did not think he was up to the job.[44] On the other hand, Robert Kennedy and many members of the inner circle, opposed to Johnson, would have been comfortable with Symington.[45] Robert Kennedy, the key actor in the drama, told John Barlow Martin that the selection of the vice president "was the most indecisive time we ever had." They "changed and re-changed" their minds "probably seven times." "We thought either Jackson or Symington. I don't know whether we concentrated, but I think Symington probably at that time."[46]

It had become clear to the nominee, however, that Johnson would bring greater strength to the ticket than Symington. Texas was more important than Missouri. Kennedy was sure that he had to have Texas to win, and he could not carry Texas without Johnson on the ticket. Moreover, he was convinced that, despite his earlier posturing, Johnson wanted to run for the vice presidency. However he arrived at the decision, Jack Kennedy decided in the early morning hours of July 15 that he would go with Lyndon.[47]

Symington took the news with his usual good grace. Clifford, who had been the go-between and who remained Symington's closest friend, wrote: "Stuart . . . never complained about the might-have-beens of history. Not once in the remaining twenty-nine years of his life did I hear him talk about how close he had come, through succession, to the Presidency. . . . Later Stuart laughed about the evening he almost became Vice President. 'At least I made a hundred dollars out of it,' he said, after I had paid off on our wager."[48]

Symington introduced Johnson for his acceptance speech, calling him "a great leader of and for America." Before getting to his prepared text he spoke extemporaneously for a moment:

> I've watched the American people, slowly at first and then with ever increasing crescendo, take to their minds and hearts the leading Democrat, the leading American of this day, John F. Kennedy of Massachusetts. People ask, how did he do it? Well, I will tell you how. He did it because he had just a little more courage, just a little more stamina, just a little more wisdom, and just a little more character than any of the rest of us.[49]

Stanley Fike, who took down the words, said, "I would agree as far as the campaign was concerned. I wouldn't agree about 'the little more character,' . . . nobody could have had more character in this campaign than Stuart Symington did."[50]

The campaign of 1960 put an end to any presidential ambitions Symington may have had. Those ambitions had been in the background of his first eight years in the Senate—ever since his initial election. He would spend the next sixteen years being just a senator—growing steadily in influence and prestige.

27

The Kennedy Years

SYMINGTON'S laudatory comments about Kennedy at the end of the Los Angeles convention represented more than an effort to strengthen party unity. They represented a sincere expression of Symington's high regard for the man who had defeated him for the Democratic presidential nomination and who had disappointed him in the selection of a running mate.

Despite their difference in age, Symington and Kennedy, to all appearances, were good friends. They came into the Senate together, and their slight prior acquaintance grew into solid friendship. As Symington told an interviewer from the Kennedy Library, ". . . our relationships . . . were very fine from the standpoint of friendship, and all the years we served together, I can't remember a single difference that we had. Most of the time we voted together and, of course, that always makes it easier to get along."[1]

Both were close to Senator Smathers, one of Symington's favorite golfing companions. Symington and Smathers sponsored Kennedy for membership in the Burning Tree Country Club. Because of back problems, Kennedy played sporadically, but even as president he played golf at least twice with his two former colleagues in a foursome that included Undersecretary of the Navy Paul Fay, Symington's distant relative by marriage. At a dinner dance in the spring of 1953, Kennedy introduced Symington to "a very lovely girl who, he told me, he was going to marry." It turned out that Symington had known Jacqueline Bouvier's parents for many years—they had both enjoyed summer sojourns in the Hamptons—and he also knew Hugh Auchinloss, whom Jackie's mother had married after her divorce from John Bouvier. The Kennedys lived just four doors from the Symingtons on N Street, and the families saw each other frequently. Both were part of the "Georgetown set" that dominated capital society. Despite the difference in their ages, Eve Symington and Jackie Kennedy became close friends. At one time, Jackie wrote to Eve, "It would have been such fun if it had been you and Stu."[2]

Never one to look back, Symington moved easily from being a competitor to being an enthusiastic supporter. The transition was easy because during the fight for the nomination, Symington, unlike Johnson, had never attacked Kennedy personally.[3]

Shortly after the convention he asked Fike to furnish the Kennedy people with names of his supporters who might be helpful in the general election. Early in August Symington spent two days with Kennedy in Kansas City, Omaha, and Des Moines. Reporting on the trip, which included a visit to the Strategic Air Command, he told a friend, "[I] believe America may have a real opportunity under him." On October 2 he introduced Kennedy at a large fund-raising dinner in St. Louis.[4]

As he did in almost every campaign speech, Kennedy in St. Louis hit hard on the Republican defense record. Speaking directly to and about Symington, he said: "But I have great confidence in this Nation and in the American people. . . . I have confidence in our ability to close the missile gap, to modernize our conventional forces, and to give this country the kind of defensive strength that Stuart Symington has been warning for years we will need if we are going to remain free at the end of the next years."[5] Symington's most important role in the campaign was the chairmanship of a special committee to prepare a plan for the reorganization of the Department of Defense.

The Symingtons spent the night of August 6 as the Kennedys' guests at Hyannisport. At noon on August 7, Kennedy, with Symington at his side, announced that he was asking his former rival to head up a committee to study "how to strengthen the Defense Department and make it more efficient and more responsive to the needs of our time." Symington would select members of the committee, and, in the event of a Democratic victory, have a report ready by January. During the afternoon Kennedy took his guests sailing on Nantucket Sound, and they all flew back to Washington that evening on the *Caroline* to be ready for the opening of Congress the next day.[6]

The appointment created a great deal of interest and fueled talk that Symington might be in line for appointment as secretary of defense. In response to a question, Kennedy simply stated that the matter had not been discussed,[7] and Symington, contrary to earlier interest he might have had in the position, was quite uninterested in leaving the Senate for a post in the administration.

As committee members, Symington turned to old friends and former associates from the Truman administration: Clifford; Thomas K. Finletter, who had succeeded Symington as secretary of the air force; Roswell L. Gilpatric, Finletter's undersecretary of the air force; Fowler Hamilton, general counsel to Symington's earlier study of air power; and Marx Leva, who had been Secretary of Defense James Forrestal's general counsel. Dr. Edward C. Welsh, Symington's trusted assistant for defense matters, headed the staff. In approving the appointments, Kennedy said that the committee would not make a sweeping study of the nation's defense, but would make use of the work of numerous prior studies to determine what legislative or executive action was needed to obtain a defense adequate to protect the nation and to enable it to discharge its international responsibilities, and to obtain such a defense within the framework of a free and solvent economic system.[8]

The committee went to work immediately, meeting in both New York and Washington. On the whole, the members worked well together. Symington consulted closely with Jerome Wiesner of the Massachusetts Institute of Technology who was heading up a committee on space problems. Shortly after the election, Symington, who had been vacationing at Key Biscayne, spent two days with the president-elect at the Kennedy home in Palm Beach, playing golf and discussing the report. Kennedy asked that the report's submission be advanced from December 31 to the end of November. Symington, meeting with reporters, repeated his earlier assertion that he was not interested in being appointed secretary of defense. He would rather push the Kennedy legislative program in the Senate.[9]

Symington returned to Palm Beach on December 5 to submit the long-awaited report. He and Kennedy then flew to Washington together. The report, reflecting views that Symington had advanced since his days as secretary of the air force, called for a complete overhaul of the Department of Defense to remove any doubt that might exist with respect to the authority of the secretary. The services would continue to exist, but the service secretaries were to be replaced by undersecretaries of defense for the army, navy, and air force. The Joint Chiefs of Staff were to be dissolved in favor of a single chief of staff to whom the service commanders would report, although they would retain full operational control of their various units. The scope of their authority, however, would be narrowed through the establishment of three unified commands—strategic, tactical, and defense—whose commanders would report directly to the secretary of defense. Research and development would be under the direct control of the secretary of defense, and a special assistant for arms control would be established.[10]

The report engendered much discussion but little support. The services—especially the navy, which had a long history of opposing any move toward unification and, to a lesser degree, the army—made no secret of their opposition. The air force, usually supportive of unification, while not openly hostile, was muted in its support.[11] Editorial comment ran so heavily against the report that Symington charged in the Senate that the opposition was coming from "a group which invariably opposes any change of any kind in the current structure of the Defense Department. . . . As a result of this governmental and privately financed effort, anyone who was uninformed or uninterested might conclude that there was little public approval of the recommendations in the report." As illustrations, he included editorials from nineteen newspapers from around the country.[12]

The president-elect commented only that he would "study" the report—and that was the last official reference to it. Robert McNamara, the new secretary of defense, never mentioned it. This report appeared destined for a place in the archives alongside Symington's earlier controversial report on air power.

Appearances, however, were misleading. Gilpatric, a member of the Symington committee, became deputy secretary of defense, and even though he did not mention the report by name, McNamara moved to implement many of its recommendations. The service secretaries remained in place, but their power and influence was much reduced. Eugene Zuckert, appointed secretary of the air force, once said that he had as much or more authority as an assistant secretary under Symington than he had as secretary under McNamara.[13] The Joint Chiefs of Staff met a similar fate as McNamara, and an unusually competent corps of assistants moved to concentrate technical services, including ordnance, supply services, and intelligence, in the office of the secretary of defense.

Even though McNamara put his own stamp on the changes, Symington's influence was felt throughout the sprawling bureaucracy.[14] *The Army Navy Air Force Journal* observed: "Perhaps the most convincing evidence that the Symington Report has not been abandoned, some military men say, is the fact that the Missouri Senator himself has neither demanded action on the recommendations of his Committee, nor denounced present Pentagon reorganization moves. The former Air Force Secretary is not in the habit of shrugging off Defense Department indifference or delay in instituting reforms he considers vital to the nation's security." Indeed, Symington seemed completely satisfied with McNamara's response to his report, calling his accomplishments "The greatest in Defense Department history."[15]

Another carryover from the campaign was the missile gap. Symington did not invent the term, but because of his role as the Senate's leading critic of the Eisenhower administration's defense policies he was generally credited with being its leading proponent. Kennedy had associated himself with Symington's position on defense as early as 1958 and during his campaign for the presidency campaigned vigorously on the issue of the missile gap. Shortly after being sworn in, the new president asked his secretary of defense to study the relative strength in missiles possessed by the United States and the Soviet Union. McNamara set off the first public relations crisis of the new administration on February 6 when, during a background briefing for members of the press in response to reporters' questioning, he commented that he did not believe the Soviets led the United States in operational missiles. Although McNamara later hedged and then denied the statement, it created an uproar in the press and in Congress.[16]

On February 9, Senator Dirksen, the minority leader, noted with obvious relish the newspaper discussion and hoped that the Defense Department's investigation would soon be completed. He went on, "All I wish to say, Mr. President, is, Let us hope and pray there is no missile gap."[17]

Symington immediately rose in rebuttal. He hoped that "this missile gap discussion will not be made a partisan matter." He thought it most unfortunate that so much was being read into Secretary McNamara's presumed comments. "The whole subject of the missile gap," he reminded his colleagues, arose "when the then Secretary of Defense, Mr. McElroy, was candid enough to state that at that time we were planning to allow the Russians to obtain a three-to-one lead in long-range missiles. . . . I have checked, and as of the next due date that lead will be more than 3 to 1." The new president was trying hard to get at the truth of the matter, but was handicapped "by a calculated and deliberate effort on the part of the previous administration" to prevent him as a candidate from receiving adequate information on the nation's security.[18]

Symington carried the argument forward with an article in the *Reporter* for February 15, "Where the Missile Gap Went." Replying to those who charged that the gap was a synthetic issue from the beginning and that the president as candidate had never emphasized the missile gap issue, he pointed out that he had discussed it in at least nine major campaign speeches: "Whether or not there was a missile gap, it is clear that President Kennedy believed there was." Additionally, Secretary McElroy and his successor, Thomas Gates, both believed that the United States lagged behind the Soviets at least in the development of long-range missiles. The problem was with intelligence and its interpretation. When the Eisenhower administration made the decision to base estimates of relative strength on probable intent rather than capability, "we immediately made an immense and costless advance in the missile race—without actually moving." However the numbers were calculated, the dangers of underestimating the Soviet Union's ICBM strength were self-evident. "Fortunately," he added, "there is no reason to believe that President Kennedy has underestimated." In accordance with his campaign statements, he had ordered substantial increases in defense spending.[19]

In further response to Dirksen's taunts, Symington said, "I hope that the gap is not one missile larger than the very minimum that is now admitted. . . . But even if our fondest hopes are true, the gap is still there. It is real and it will be there for some time to come. . . . Let us finally dispose of the semantic talk . . . and get around to carrying out the corrective actions that President Kennedy has already begun."[20]

Symington continued to support Kennedy's efforts to strengthen the country's defenses, and for the most part he went along with the administration's initiatives in foreign relations. He was in an excellent position to make his influence felt in both areas.

As a member of the Senate committees on Armed Services and Space, Symington had been the Senate's principal critic of the Eisenhower administration in both areas.[21] With the election of Kennedy and Johnson, Symington's relative importance in the Senate increased, and he was anxious to strengthen his position even further. His first effort was to seek a spot on the Appropriations Committee, but Senator Fulbright, chairman of the Committee on Foreign Relations, asked him to fill a vacancy there—an offer too tempting to refuse.[22]

Symington and Fulbright had been friends since Symington's time as head of the Reconstruction Finance Corporation. They were occasional golfing companions, and at least on one occasion the Symingtons and the Fulbrights spent a weekend together at the Greenbrier in White Sulphur Springs. Despite their personal friendship, however, they frequently differed on the issues. Symington was one of the Senate's most hawkish members, Fulbright one of its most dovish, but Fulbright wanted the strength Symington would bring to the committee.[23]

Membership on the Foreign Relations Committee meant that Symington had to relinquish his post on the Committee on Agriculture and Forestry, where he could look after the interests of Missouri's most important industry. He assured his constituents that he would stay in close touch with the farm problem. His son Jim was being appointed deputy director of the Food for Peace program headed by George McGovern, and Ed Jaenke of his staff was going to be associate administrator of the Commodity Stabilization Service. Moreover, in Orville Freeman farmers had a friend as secretary of agriculture. As the only senator whose committee assignments included Armed Services, Foreign Relations, and Space, he would be dealing with "the overriding question of our time. How to maintain world peace by establishing some form of mutually agreed on arms control, with the hope that success in this field could lead ultimately to world disarmament."[24]

Symington used his position on all three committees to support the Kennedy administration's efforts to strengthen the space program, build up armaments, and search for some kind of effective arms control. When the president an-

nounced a space program that would put a man on the moon before the end of
the decade, Symington moved immediately to support it. In his view, leadership
in space was key to the nation's security; his criticism of the Eisenhower space
program was part of his general criticism of the former administration's defense
efforts. In a long speech shortly after Kennedy's call for a renewed effort in
space, he lamented the "waste and delay" that had characterized the previous administration's efforts, the results of "a starvation budget" and "an antique organization structure." He continued to emphasize the defense aspects of the space
program, but he also supported the creation of NASA and continued to push
for ever-increasing appropriations for the new agency. He did not always agree
with McNamara's relative priorities, as for example, the decision to cut back on
the B-70 and the Skybolt missile, but he supported continuing increases in the
Defense Department's missile budget as well as increases for NASA. To those
who complained that too much money was being devoted to the moon landing
project while military efforts in space appeared to be neglected, he said, "The
moon is no finish line in a race. It is but a proving ground, where we will test
and demonstrate that competence in space technology which our security
should insure."[25]

Symington's efforts played well in Missouri, which was second only to California as a beneficiary of NASA expenditures, largely a result of advances in cap-
sule research and construction by McDonnell Aircraft.[26]

A defense-related issue in which Symington became the central figure concerned the national stockpile of strategic and critical materials. Congress established the stockpile in 1946 to assure that the country would have access to raw
materials needed for industrial—and particularly defense—production in time
of war or national emergency. The United States, despite its vast resources, depended upon imports for about a third of the minerals used by industry. During
his time as head of the Reconstruction Finance Corporation Symington had su-
pervised purchases to build the stockpile. There is no record that he thought
much about it until he became chairman of the Subcommittee on the National
Stockpile and Naval Petroleum Reserves of the Senate Armed Services Committee. Indeed, nobody seemed to be paying much attention. As the leading
historian of stockpiling put it: " . . . stockpiling, once under way, tended to per-
petuate itself . . . more or less in blissful isolation from changing defense concepts and capabilities. . . . Stockpiling might be described as a 'middle-level'
program, the kind of program which was not important enough to appear very
often on the desk of the President or even on the desks of the highest officials of
the agencies concerned."[27]

Symington put the issue on the desk of the president. From the beginning of
his time on the subcommittee Symington had been frustrated by the fact that

the stockpile was classified—it dealt with national security, therefore it must be kept secret. Symington had raised the issue with Eisenhower's director of the Office of Defense Mobilization, Arthur Flemming, but got no response. He did not pursue the issue during the Eisenhower administration, but when Kennedy took office he began to pressure the administration to look into the stockpile and declassify much of it. On January 31, 1962, Kennedy called for a congressional investigation. The stockpiling program was overgrown and "a potential source of excessive and unconscionable profits." He said that he had discussed the matter with Senator Symington, who agreed that "the program should be completely explored, and without delay."[28]

As Tom Wicker reported in the *New York Times,* "For a President to take the unusual step of requesting a Congressional investigation was considered significant. It reinforced the belief that Mr. Kennedy sought the disclosure of past events and policies rather than anything that might touch his administration."[29]

The announcement caught the other members of the subcommittee—Strom Thurmond of South Carolina, then still a Democrat, and Republican Francis Case of South Dakota—off guard. This contributed to the impression that the investigation was politically motivated. Dirksen and Saltonstall thought that the investigation should be conducted by the Joint Committee on the Reduction of Nonessential Federal Expenses, headed by Senator Harry F. Byrd of Virginia, who seemed perfectly willing to take it on.[30] The Senate nevertheless authorized Symington's subcommittee to proceed, augmenting its membership by the addition of Democrats Clair Engle of California and Howard Cannon of Nevada, plus Republicans Prescott Bush of Connecticut and J. Glenn Beall of Maryland. Francis Case died during the course of the investigation and was replaced by Clifford P. Case of New Jersey.

Symington sought to blunt charges of partisanship by appointing Richmond Coburn, prominent Republican lawyer from St. Louis, as chief counsel, but in a highly unusual arrangement, Timothy May of the White House staff was appointed assistant counsel. In a long press conference held before the hearings began, Symington praised the president for declassifying most of the stockpile documents and pledged that the "controlling purpose" of the investigation would be "the development of the facts, without concern to what person, interest or group may be affected."[31]

The subcommittee met sixty-three times between February 23, 1962, and January 30, 1963, producing a record that totaled thirty-nine hundred pages. Symington dominated the proceedings throughout—on some occasions he was the only senator present—and he made frequent headlines with charges against former officials of the Eisenhower administration. He was highly critical of

Flemming for administrative laxity, but his prime target was former Secretary of the Treasury George M. Humphrey, whom he accused of conflict of interest in the administration of the stockpile.

At the time he was appointed secretary of the treasury Humphrey was serving as president of the Hanna Mining Company. Testimony from government witnesses revealed that after Humphrey's appointment had been announced, and just hours before he was sworn in, the General Services Administration entered into contracts with Hanna to purchase millions of pounds of nickel at inflated prices in addition to building a smelter that would become Hanna's property. Humphrey told the *Christian Science Monitor* that the hearings were "beginning to look like a personal vendetta against me" and demanded an opportunity to appear before the committee. On August 16, flanked by lawyers and accountants, Humphrey testified from ten in the morning until five in the afternoon. He disputed the government's figures and denied any impropriety. When the committee recessed until the next day, Symington said, "Mr. Secretary, you have been a tolerant and understanding witness."

The next morning, however, Symington quoted a story in the *Christian Science Monitor* of the day before in which Humphrey had said, "They don't dare attack Ike direct so they are attacking me. This is a stab in the back." Symington added: "In other words, since these hearings started, Mr. Humphrey not only disagrees with the figures as to his own and his company's profits, but now impugns the motives of the Senate and this subcommittee." He wanted to hear no more; he was going to adjourn the committee. Bush, who had defended Humphrey, demanded a vote, but Symington declared that the chairman had authority to adjourn a meeting and that he proposed to exercise it. Humphrey then said, "You cannot stop me from making a statement and adjourn this. You don't dare."

Symington responded, "This hearing is adjourned. Don't ever tell me as a U.S. Senator and chairman of the committee what I dare or dare not do."[32]

Symington's encounter with Humphrey and his abrupt adjournment of the hearings dominated press coverage of the hearings—one columnist called his action "a fantastic abuse of senatorial powers"—and the hearings concluded on an intensely partisan note. Bush's term expired before the committee's report was issued, but he indicated that he would have refused to sign it. Case and Beall, the other Republicans on the committee, issued minority reports, as did Strom Thurmond. Only Cannon and Engle joined Symington in approving the report.[33]

Of all the issues to come before the Senate, none concerned Symington more than arms control. He had served on Hubert Humphrey's special subcommittee on disarmament. His speeches frequently urged the importance of arms control, looking to the prospect of eventual disarmament. During their golfing weekend in Palm Beach, he had urged the president-elect to concentrate on international arms control to meet the nuclear and space-age threats of war.[34]

With all of his emphasis on arms control, however, he continued to advocate ever greater expenditures for defense. He saw no inconsistency in this position. As a preeminent Cold Warrior, he had a profound distrust of the Soviets and argued repeatedly that the United States could not conduct disarmament negotiations except from a position of strength. For the most part, his views coincided with those of the new administration, which moved forward simultaneously on a large buildup in defense and efforts to achieve disarmament.[35]

Although he supported the administration's principal thrusts, Symington by no means approved all of their decisions. Most notably, he strenuously objected to cancellation of the B-70, a high-speed, missile-carrying manned bomber, along with the decision to halt production of the B-52 and B-58 long-range bombers, and particularly the Skybolt missile, which could be launched from a B-52. These planes were dear to the hearts of the air force generals. They would work to develop the country's missile capacity—although they had little enthusiasm for the highly touted Polaris missile (supported, however, by Symington) that could be launched from the navy's submarines—but in their eyes the manned bomber remained central to the nation's defense. They mounted a heavy campaign against the proposed cuts, and Congress, in an action similar to that of 1948, when Symington was secretary of the air force, appropriated more than the administration had requested. McNamara, like Forrestal earlier, refused to spend the money.[36]

Symington joined the leadership of the Senate Armed Services Committee, especially Russell and Stennis, in criticizing the decision. "No member of this body has supported more completely the new Secretary of Defense than have I," he reminded his colleagues. "He is an able and intelligent man, but he has been on this job only a few months." The members of the Armed Services Committee had "worked for many years on these matters. . . . we should respect their opinion as much as we respected the opinion of the Secretary of Defense."[37]

Symington found it particularly incongruous that the administration's budget contained an item to subsidize the development of a super-sonic commercial transport while denying the air force the authority to develop a super-sonic bomber. He offered an amendment to delete the commercial transport subsidy; it failed on a tie vote.[38]

He remained uneasy with some of the ideas emanating from the Defense Department. He wrote Russell: "More and more people I respect in the Air Force and Navy tell me quietly that they are very worried about the 'degree' we seemed to have gone overboard on missiles."[39]

On disarmament, he distrusted the Democratic liberals in the administration who felt that the United States, having used the atomic bomb, should lead the world in eliminating nuclear weapons. He welcomed Kennedy's resumption of test ban talks in Geneva, but he was reluctant to support specific recommendations. In May he addressed twenty questions, largely procedural and technical, to John J. McCloy, the president's adviser in the negotiations (and one of Symington's longtime friends). In responding, McCloy expressed grave doubts that anything would come of the negotiations. The Soviets insisted on a three-man inspection team with a right of veto on any enforcement action. This, of course, was wholly unacceptable. Symington inserted McCloy's answers to his twenty questions in the *Congressional Record,* along with testimony that Zbigniew Brzezinski, the Columbia University political scientist well known for his hard-line approach to the Soviet Union, had given the Foreign Relations Committee. Although he did not say so directly, Symington left the clear impression that the American response to the impasse at Geneva should be the resumption of nuclear testing. "Would it not be ironical," he asked, "to find out on some unfortunate day that . . . [the Soviets] had decided not to come to any test cessation agreement because of the tremendous unilateral advantage we had passed over to them voluntarily . . . by refusing to test for a long period of time."[40]

When Senator Humphrey, at the president's request, introduced legislation to establish a U.S. Disarmament Agency for World Peace and Security, Symington, while protesting that he endorsed the general objectives of the bill, found much fault with the details. He was particularly concerned about the ambiguous reporting arrangements; the director of the new agency would report to the president and the secretary of state. Despite assurances from his friends McCloy and Gilpatric, as well as from Secretary of State Dean Rusk, that dual reporting would work out, he remained unconvinced. Also, he was concerned that an agency such as was being proposed would attract too many pacifists who might use it to increase support for reductions in the country's defense capability.[41] Despite these reservations, he voted for the bill.

Symington continued to express the belief that the Soviets were conducting clandestine underground nuclear tests. When, at the end of August, Soviet Premier Nikita Khrushchev announced that the Soviet Union would resume atmospheric testing, Symington called on the United States to do the same. He applauded Kennedy's decision to resume testing, and he had little patience with the scientists and others around Kennedy who opposed any resumption. These were the same people who had continually opposed the development of nuclear weapons, and especially the hydrogen bomb. "If any of these scientists had been successful," he declared, "the country would be defenseless today."[42]

Fearing the influence of those who opposed any development of nuclear weapons, Symington opposed the president's efforts, shortly after he announced the resumption of testing, to negotiate a comprehensive test ban treaty with the Soviets. On March 21 he wrote Russell, " . . . some of the stories now coming out of Geneva give me grave apprehension." He urged that the Senate Preparedness Subcommittee hold hearings on the subject. When the U.S. delegation to Geneva, in an effort to bring the Soviets around, proposed a reduction in the levels of testing and in the number of inspections, Symington's fears were realized. He wrote his friend, John Foster, director of the newly established Arms Control and Disarmament Agency, that the offer "represented a grave danger to the security of the United States."[43]

To support his position, Symington turned to Dr. Edward Teller, "father" of the H-bomb and director of the University of California's Lawrence Radiation Laboratory. He took Teller to see Stennis, to urge the importance of holding hearings on the impending treaty. At his request Teller prepared a memo for Stennis discussing the dangers of further concessions to the Russians. Symington had to remove himself temporarily from the discussions for a hernia operation, but Teller kept him supplied with letters. He was particularly concerned with talk, including comments from Foster, that new technological developments made it possible to detect test explosions from a distance, thus making it unnecessary to have test sites inside the Soviet Union. Symington believed that public hearings "might be vital in forestalling our next mistake."[44]

Although Symington ultimately would disagree with Teller, during the winter he retained his skepticism. On February 25, 1963, he joined with Russell and Jackson in a letter to the president expressing alarm that the administration was "apparently ready to accept an agreement which does not, in our judgment, provide for an adequate inspection system." They reminded the president that they had always tried to maintain Democratic unity on national security matters, but they wished to warn in advance "that we have no alternative but to oppose vigorously the reaching of an agreement on anything like the basis now being offered by our side."[45]

Symington participated actively—and aggressively—in the hearings before the Preparedness Investigating Subcommittee. At times, in Stennis's absence, he chaired the hearings. He was relentless in his questioning of administration witnesses—so relentless that one could assume from reading the transcript that he was opposed to any test ban treaty. He may have sensed this. At one point in the hearings, he recited his long history of involvement in efforts to achieve disarmament and added: "No one has a right to think, for a minute, because of the questions being asked, that I am not just as anxious as anybody in the world to achieve a nuclear test ban agreement." He just did not trust the Russians, and he would not support an agreement that would let them cheat.[46]

Symington joined a majority of the Preparedness Investigating Subcommittee in expressing "grave concern" about the treaty. He joined the majority of the Foreign Relations Committee, however, in recommending ratification. To the press and many others, this represented a blatant straddle.[47] Symington saw no inconsistency in his seemingly contradictory positions. As the only senator who sat on both committees, he had listened to all of the testimony. He believed the data contained in the Preparedness Subcommittee's report was correct, but the findings and conclusions were overly pessimistic. On the other hand, testimony before the Foreign Relations Committee had convinced him that "our national security would be adequately protected under the terms of the treaty."[48]

Symington was comforted by the fact that the treaty would allow the United States to continue underground testing, and also by assurances from McNamara that adequate detection systems were provided for and that the United States would resume atmospheric testing if the Russians were caught cheating. Symington also may have been influenced by pressure from the president. He and Senator Albert Gore of Tennessee were invited to the White House the evening of July 23 for a private briefing that apparently was effective. Mike Manatos reported to Larry O'Brien: ". . . Symington said he was against a treaty of this kind, but after talking to the President he was very much impressed. He thinks it will be a momentous event and that the Senate will ratify it. Ratification will be much easier, in Senator Symington's estimation, if the President consults Stennis and Russell."[49]

Symington played a leading role in the fight on the Senate floor over ratification. His position as the only senator to serve on both the Armed Services and Foreign Relations Committees, combined with his experience in the Pentagon and his unassailable pro-defense credentials, made his a particularly convincing voice. Fulbright, who was handling the effort, thought his statement "most very reassuring, not only to the Senate, but also to the country as a whole." Not everyone felt the same way. Many air force supporters strongly opposed the treaty, and in Missouri, where Symington faced a reelection campaign in a year, opinion was sharply divided.[50]

Looked at from the perspective of Symington's subsequent career, his struggle with the test ban treaty may be seen as the beginning of a change in his attitude regarding defense. Since his days as secretary of the air force he had been for defense first and economy second, if at all. While he still remained one of the country's preeminent Cold Warriors, during the Foreign Relations Committee's hearings he began not only to question Pentagon waste and inefficiency—which had long been favorite targets—but also to ask whether the United States was acquiring too much defensive capability. Referring to a report that the United States had ten times as many nuclear weapons as the Soviet Union, he suggested, "Maybe we could make some savings for the taxpayer and put the money . . .

into education, instead of building a lot more weapons when we already have more than enough."[51]

Symington generally supported the administration on foreign aid, which in his view was important to national security. Moreover, foreign aid, which involved the purchase of large quantities of agricultural products, was popular in Missouri.[52] His principal reason for supporting foreign aid, however, remained its importance in halting the spread of communism. Strengthening free-world economies reduced the appeal of communism; direct military aid increased the ability of free-world countries to fight local wars fomented by the Russians, and, increasingly, the Chinese.

Symington was particularly concerned with the adequacy of the country's representation abroad, especially in the new missions such as the Agency for International Development. This had long been a concern. During his frequent trips abroad, he had been impressed that the United States in many instances was represented by amateurs who did not speak the language of the country in which they were working and knew little of its history and culture. He introduced bills in 1959 and 1961 to establish a foreign service academy modeled after the armed services academies. "The basic idea," he told his colleagues in the Senate, "was that if the United States could afford three academies to train its youth for the hot war we all pray will never come, surely it could afford one Academy to train its youth . . . for the cold war in which we are now engaged." The proposal failed to gain much support. Kennedy favored the idea, but along with many in the administration, he had little enthusiasm for an academy narrowly focused on training young Cold War warriors. He persuaded Symington to introduce a modified bill to establish a graduate school of foreign affairs. The bill had twenty-seven cosponsors, but even with presidential support it failed to generate much enthusiasm. Fulbright saw little merit in the idea, and former Secretary of State Acheson leveled a slashing attack against it.[53]

Although Symington reluctantly cooperated with Kennedy in the matter of the foreign service academy, he refused to support the administration on aid to India. He early became disenchanted with India's prime minister, Jawaharlal Nehru, whose efforts to keep India nonaligned in the Cold War struggle made him an unpromising recipient of American dollars as far as Symington was concerned. His efforts to reduce aid to India caused Kennedy to intervene personally to save the appropriation.[54]

Symington's belief that giving aid to India was a waste of money was part of his growing concern that the country's commitments abroad constituted an unnecessary drain on the economy that ultimately would weaken U.S. defenses. He called for a major reduction in U.S. troops stationed overseas. The countries of Western Europe were enjoying unprecedented prosperity, thanks largely to

American aid, and there was no reason why they should not assume greater responsibility for their own defense. Moreover, the development of the very long-range bomber, the intercontinental ballistic missile, and the Polaris submarine reduced the need for bases in Europe. In urging troop reduction, Symington was merely joining the Democratic leadership in the Senate, headed by Mike Mansfield of Montana, which broke with the administration on the issue.[55]

For Symington, the principal reason for reducing troop commitments abroad was that they contributed heavily to the unfavorable balance of payments that was turning the United States from a creditor to a debtor nation. During November and December 1963 he delivered five long speeches in the Senate on the issue. Each year the country was spending abroad more than it took in. To prevent disaster, the United States would have to reduce the amount it was spending on foreign aid and troops abroad as well as change the way it negotiated trade agreements.[56]

The highly conservative Washington Daily News expressed the hope that "Congress has been listening to the Senator from Missouri." The speeches elicited some favorable comment from Senate colleagues, but no action. Symington wrote a friend from St. Louis, "Now that I am in this balance of payments situation I am going to ride it."[57] He expressed concern about the problem from time to time, and in his later years became preoccupied with protecting the value of the dollar. He remained wary of foreign aid expenditures, but generally he supported the administration's positions.

Indeed, Symington almost always sided with the young president, and at times went out of his way to praise Kennedy's administration. When former President Eisenhower criticized Kennedy's handling of the Cuban missile crisis, Symington said, "No one is proud of Cuba. But I was proud of the willingness of President Kennedy to accept full responsibility" for mistakes that were made partially on the advice of persons appointed by the previous administration. At the end of the administration's first year, he praised McNamara's accomplishments as "greater than in any period since the Defense Department was organized." He enthusiastically embraced the Peace Corps, telling Sargent Shriver, its director: "I am confident many people in many countries will be grateful to you and your organization, and will think more of America as a result of the effort you are making." On domestic policy, he frequently praised both the president and Secretary of Agriculture Orville Freeman for their approach to the farm problem. As he told the Jackson County Democratic Central Committee, "How proud we can all be that we have a man of proved courage, capable of . . . vision and foresight, guiding the destinies of this Nation at this time."[58]

When the awful news came from Dallas, Symington issued the following brief statement:

Once again the former Naval lieutenant, now President John F. Kennedy, has offered his life for his country. This time he lost. All free people in turn have lost a gallant and dedicated leader.

It was impossible to know him well without having deep respect for him and devotion to him.

To Mrs. Kennedy and the family, my wife and I send deepest sympathy.[59]

That night, unable to sleep and not knowing what to do, he went to a church and lit a candle.[60]

28

Vietnam—From Hawk to Dove

ON APRIL 7, 1969, the *Washington Post* published a long article by Ward Just entitled, "Stu Symington: The Path of a High-Level 'Defector.'"

"When a major political figure *actually changes his mind,*" he wrote, "and shifts a position, and does so moreover not from outside pressure but from hard thought, it is an event, a high-level defection. A priest leaves the church, and neither is ever quite the same again." Symington, who used to be part of the military-industrial establishment, "now opposes the war in Vietnam, is a leader in the fight to defeat the Administration's anti-ballistic missile program." Symington's road from advocate to critic was "not an easy one to map." It was full of "eccentric twists and turns, dead-ends, false starts and inconsistencies; all of that along with . . . good sense. There is almost a schizophrenia about the position—until it is understood that Symington is unique among Senators, a senior member of both the Senate Armed Services Committee and the Senate Foreign Relations Committee. He is the only man in Congress who hears all the arguments pro and con from both sides of the street, can go from a closed session with Secretary Rogers in the morning to one with Secretary Laird in the afternoon—or, sometimes more interesting, back to back sessions with Richard Helms of the CIA, the one relating to diplomacy, the other relating to war."[1]

In the beginning, Symington had no reservations about the importance of confronting communism in Vietnam if the free world was to prevent a Communist takeover in all the countries of southeast Asia. As the newly appointed chairman of the Subcommittee on the Middle East and South Asia of the Senate

Foreign Relations Committee, Symington visited South Vietnam in October 1961. While there he met with General Maxwell Taylor and Walt W. Rostow, who were heading a mission for the president to determine what, if anything, the United States might do to prop up the shaky Diem government.[2] Also, at the request of Ambassador Frederick Nolting, he visited with Diem. The Vietnamese had been pushing for a mutual defense treaty with the United States, something that the State Department, for obvious reasons, was resisting. Nolting hoped that Symington could discourage Diem from pursuing the matter by emphasizing the complications of getting a treaty approved by the Senate. Apparently, Symington was successful. Nolting reported, "Senator Symington's handling of this question cooled considerably the previous interest of Diem and Nhu [Ngo Dinh Nhu, Diem's younger brother, who was head of the secret police] in a bilateral treaty." Symington, who could speak with authority on the Senate, assured Diem that once the president had committed forces, "no responsible member of Congress would rise to ask that we back down." He cabled President Kennedy from Saigon: "It seems to me we ought to try to hold this place. Otherwise this part of the world is sure to go down the drain." He added: "If you so decide, it will be my privilege to support your position to the best of my ability."[3]

Symington's memorandum, coming on the heels of the Taylor-Rostow report, reinforced Kennedy's determination to support the faltering government of South Vietnam with additional military advisers. Although some influential Democrats, including the hawkish Richard Russell and the dovish John Kenneth Galbraith, ambassador to India, began to question the policy, Symington remained firmly committed to it, a position taken by most of the members of the Senate Foreign Relations Committee, including Chairman J. William Fulbright. Possibly, as William Gibbons suggests, they "were either co-opted by the administration or were privy to sensitive information that they refrained from discussing or acting upon."[4]

Symington, along with Fulbright and Idaho Democrat Frank Church, met privately with the president during the Foreign Relations Committee's executive hearings on Vietnam in October 1963. Symington was absent during the questioning of Taylor and McNamara, who had just returned from a trip to Vietnam. He was present, however, when Secretary of State Dean Rusk came before the committee. To the obvious irritation of Chairman Fulbright, Symington used his time to criticize the administration of foreign aid in Vietnam and to bemoan the failure of his efforts to establish a foreign service academy. As part of the same hearings, the committee also queried McCone on the role of the CIA in Vietnam. Symington repeated his point about the need for a foreign service academy to avoid the "sickening sequence of blunders" characterizing the country's operations in the area.[5]

Less than a month after the hearings ended, the problem of Vietnam passed from John F. Kennedy to Lyndon Johnson. Symington readily transferred his support from one to the other. Early in February he sent the new president a copy of his 1961 memorandum to Kennedy. Johnson replied: "Dear Stu: . . . I would say that much of what you wrote then remains valid today. . . . The importance of South Vietnam . . . remains unchanged. As you say, its loss would jeopardize the remainder of Southeast Asia and other adjacent countries. I am determined not to accept that loss." The president could have assumed from Symington's reply that he would support an escalation of the American effort. Symington wrote: "In that the people out my way are becoming restless about this matter, I will do my best to have them understand that the two alternatives to the current status quo are (1) more aggressive military action, or (2) abandonment."[6]

As Vietnam fell into chaos, with one coup after another toppling successive governments in South Vietnam and the Vietcong threatening to take over the entire country, Symington remained supportive of Johnson's efforts to hold South Vietnam, but he began publicly to express doubts that they would be successful. Speaking to the St. Louis Council on World Affairs, he admitted that the war was going badly. The South Vietnamese seemed unable or unwilling to defend themselves. Moreover, our allies, in whose defense against communism we were spending billions, seemed to have no interest in coming to the defense of freedom in Asia. He put particular blame on Charles DeGaulle, who had weakened the Western alliance by pulling France out of NATO, recognizing the People's Republic of China, and recommending neutrality in Vietnam. Nevertheless, he did not see "how we can simply give up as is recommended by some of my colleagues—not more than two or three, at least at this time—and leave." If we did, we would surely lose Laos, "which is far gone already," plus Cambodia and Thailand. We might lose India, and there would be serious repercussions in Pakistan and Afghanistan. "Beyond that, it would seriously affect our defense line . . . from Japan through Okinawa to the Philippines." The president's position was sound. He should try to persuade some of our allies to join, "and if they don't—if I were in his position I would take another look."[7]

Despite the emerging doubt evident in his St. Louis speech, Symington remained strong in his support of the president's policies. He voted for the Gulf of Tonkin resolution, which in effect gave congressional approval of any action that the president might deem necessary, "now and in the future," to restrain Communist aggression in southeast Asia. Speaking in support of the resolution, he said, "If we allow these attacks to proceed without any response, the position . . . of the United States . . . would suffer a serious loss of respect." He was proud to join Fulbright in support of the resolution."[8]

With the passage of the Gulf of Tonkin resolution, Vietnam temporarily slipped from the top of the public agenda. Johnson, though secretly escalating the country's commitment, desperately sought to keep Vietnam from becoming a campaign issue that might interfere with his reelection. Even those Democrats who were beginning to have serious doubts about the president's policies—most notably Fulbright—refrained from criticism for fear it might help Goldwater, whose possible election was viewed as an unmitigated disaster.[9]

Symington, seeking a third term, concentrated on domestic issues. His strong pro-labor, pro-farmer, pro–civil rights record won him support in both the cities and outstate. His reputation as someone who could get things done for Missouri spoke persuasively to the importance of increasing his seniority so that he could accomplish even more for the state. His campaign, starting with the celebratory picnic in the little town of Paris, where as twice before he opened his campaign, was little short of a victory parade. His opponent, Jean Paul Bradshaw, a prosecuting attorney from Springfield, seemed unable to find an issue. Finally Bradshaw resorted to a smear campaign. He tried to link Symington to Bobby Baker, Johnson's freewheeling associate who would ultimately wind up in prison.[10] He also hinted ominously that some of Symington's supporters in St. Louis were "unsavory characters." Bradshaw's charges had no effect on the campaign; if anything, they backfired. On election day, Symington piled up the largest majority in Missouri's history, winning 66.55 percent of the vote and in effect carrying Missouri for President Johnson and the rest of the Democratic ticket.[11]

After the election, Vietnam soon moved to the top of the nation's agenda.

Johnson continued to hope that his policy of standing firm and gradually increasing aid to South Vietnam would stabilize the government and make it possible for it to defend itself against the Vietcong. That hope proved illusory. Top officials in Saigon, preoccupied with personal prerogatives, seemed unable to provide any kind of defense. A Christmas Eve attack on a Marine barracks, killing two U.S. servicemen and wounding thirty-eight, dramatized the futility of depending on the South Vietnamese. The administration responded to this and an attack on the marine barracks at Pleiku, which killed eight Americans and wounded 126, with a sustained bombing campaign against North Vietnam, code-named Rolling Thunder. This was followed by the introduction of one hundred thousand troops in addition to the twenty-three thousand already stationed there. In contrast to some leading Democrats, including Majority Leader Mike Mansfield, Fulbright, and Russell, who were beginning to express doubts, Symington remained silent on the deepening crisis.[12] He seems to have had little or no contact with administrative leaders as they moved to escalate the war. In a sense, his silence is reminiscent of the caution he exhibited in the early stages of the McCarthy hearings. If he did not speak much, he worried a great deal. Shortly after Johnson announced that he was sending one hundred thousand additional troops to Vietnam, Symington wrote a memorandum to himself that clearly expressed his frustrations.

"The American people would not accept quitting in South Vietnam," he wrote. But he thought that there was little likelihood the United States could prevail with its present tactics. The only hope for success was through more effective use of naval and air power. "Why don't we use our forces that are relatively strong, rather than continue to plod along in a ground war, where we are relatively weak." These private thoughts would find public expression in the months ahead as Symington turned from supporter to critic, but throughout 1965 he continued to support the president without reservations.[13]

Beginning with Thanksgiving, Symington spent six weeks in the Pacific and the Far East, concluding with ten days in South Vietnam. He had long talks with Ambassador Lodge, General Westmoreland, and key commanders in the field. He visited combat troops and combat support units. He visited servicemen in hospitals, on one occasion pinning Purple Hearts on two young men who had been wounded the previous day. He came back with high praise for all: "Cooperation and understanding between the Services is excellent. Representation of this country by Ambassador Lodge is of the highest caliber.... General Westmoreland is handling the military operations in the highest tradition of the Armed Services.... Morale in the military is high."

He expressed serious reservations, however, about the conduct of the war. Rolling Thunder had been largely ineffective because the air force had not been permitted to hit significant military targets such as power plants, oil stores, and docks. The president had ordered a pause in the bombing on December 24. Symington recommended that bombing not be resumed unless the air force were given license to hit significant targets. He continued:

> If South Vietnam is not the right place to defend the Free World against totalitarian aggression, we should retire from that country on the best possible terms. This would probably result in a Communist takeover of additional countries and would damage seriously the world position and status of the United States.
>
> If South Vietnam is the right place to defend the Free World against totalitarian aggression, then that fact should be recognized in more practical fashion. We cannot continue indefinitely the plans and programs incident to the current holding operation.[14]

When the president decided to renew air attacks on North Vietnam, Symington expressed the hope that "they would be undertaken against more meaningful targets." He agreed with "some leading military authorities that a real air effort to knock out important military targets, instead of periodic attacks on targets of far less importance, such as bridges, barracks, and buses, might eliminate the necessity of sending hundreds of thousands of additional ground troops to South Vietnam."[15]

Symington's views received fairly widespread approval,[16] but the White House was not impressed. Writing to Congressman Paul C. Jones, veteran representative from Missouri's Tenth District, McGeorge Bundy, the president's national security adviser, denied that the bombing so far had been ineffective, and suggested that "there is some question whether the weight of military judgment is in agreement with Stuart Symington's conclusions."[17]

Symington, nevertheless, continued to urge a more aggressive and effective air campaign. He also declared that the United States should blockade and mine the port of Haiphong. Reflecting his growing disillusionment with America's allies, he told the Mississippi Valley Association, meeting in Washington, "One thing that turns my stomach is the way some of our friends and allies continue to move supplies into Haiphong, which are used in support of the North Vietnamese attacks."[18]

As the country's division between "hawks" and "doves," as they were now being categorized, became ever sharper, Symington became more hawkish. On his return from Vietnam he had criticized the conduct of the war, particularly the failure to carry the air war to the north. Air power was not effective, he insisted, because it was not being used properly. He frequently referred to the successful air attacks of World War II as models for Vietnam. While interrogating McNamara during an Armed Forces Committee hearing in January, he said: "No one has ever explained to my satisfaction why it was urgent and appropriate to destroy Hitler's Nazis with bombs . . . and to blast Japanese factories, harbors and cities with Navy and air power, while another menace, Communist aggression, is now spared this effective treatment."

"They have taken the Air Force," he charged, "put it in the ring, said make a good fight, then tied one of its arms, then criticized it. . . . It isn't right to send these men out to risk their lives in an expensive airplane to bomb just an empty barracks or a bus."[19]

Symington's reaction to resumption of the bombing was the direct opposite of Fulbright's, who had become convinced that Johnson had misled him, and whose suspicions were confirmed by the renewed bombing. Fulbright went on national television to declare the war morally wrong and against the country's best interests. He expressed deep regret that he had shepherded the Gulf of Tonkin resolution through Congress. He began to make plans to hold public— indeed televised—hearings on Vietnam.[20]

At this point, Symington parted ways with his longtime friend. His concerns were based not on the morality of American attacks, but, as he frequently stated, on whether South Vietnam was the proper place to defend the free world against the spread of communism. Regardless of the answer to that question, the administration had committed the country's honor and prestige to the effort, and there was no acceptable alternative to winning. His quarrel with the president was not over the acceleration of the conflict, but rather the ineffective manner in which Johnson was going about it. "The truth of the matter," he said in a national radio interview, "is the Free World is held together in many ways by the honor of the United States. . . . I don't see how ever again the people of the world could respect the word of honor of the United States if we just walked out."[21]

Johnson reacted angrily to the proposed hearings, asserting they would only benefit the Communists. He directed his aides to do everything they could to sabotage them and sought to divert the nation's attention by flying out to Honolulu for an impromptu, highly publicized conference with General Westmoreland and South Vietnam strongman Nguyen Cao Ky.[22]

Symington, despite the chill that had developed in his relations with Johnson, worked to assure that the administration's witnesses made the best case possible for continuing the war. Along with Republicans Dirksen and Bourke Hickenlooper and Democrat Russell Long, he met with Johnson to persuade him to permit General Taylor and Secretary Rusk to testify. He even coached Taylor prior to the hearings.[23]

When his turn came at the hearings, Symington opened his questioning by praising Taylor as "a native son of Missouri. . . . one of the highest decorated officers in the Army." He recited the general's long military career, his service as presidential adviser and as ambassador to South Vietnam. He recalled their visit to Vietnam in 1961. "So, in my opinion," he concluded, "combining the military and political, you have as much experience and therefore as much right to speak on this as any American." He then asked a series of leading questions. For example, he quoted Winston Churchill on early efforts to appease the Nazis before World War II: "The belief that security can be obtained by throwing a small state to the wolves is a fatal delusion," then asked, "Would you say that has some application here?" The general dutifully replied, "I would say yes." With regard to bombing, Symington noted that Taylor had opposed massive air attacks on North Vietnam, but he wondered whether he had objections to attacking "military targets of any type" in North Vietnam. Taylor assured him that he did not, "and I would favor a gradually increasing scale of attack."[24]

Symington was equally gentle with Secretary of State Rusk,[25] but less so with a longtime friend, retired General James M. Gavin, wartime commander of the

Eighty-second Airborne Division. Gavin had created a mild sensation by writing a letter to *Harper's* that the editors interpreted as advocating withdrawal from Vietnam. During close questioning, Gavin asserted that this was not the case, that what he advocated was fighting a limited war to defend a South Vietnam enclave while the larger political issues were negotiated through the United Nations. Symington did not believe the "enclave" theory would work, but confined himself to getting an admission from Gavin that an accelerated use of air power against military targets in the north was required if there was any hope of success.[26]

When George Kennan took the stand, Symington's questioning became aggressive and hostile. Kennan was Fulbright's star witness. He possessed impeccable credentials. A distinguished scholar and former ambassador to Yugoslavia and the Soviet Union, he was widely credited with being the "father" of the Cold War containment doctrine. He had provided much of the philosophical underpinning for the Cold War arms buildup. When he suggested, therefore, that no strategic purpose could be served by escalating the war in Vietnam, his words carried weight.[27]

Symington's questions were designed to undermine both Kennan's views and his credibility. Kennan supported the position that the United States should cease its attacks on the north and withdraw to the south, letting the Vietnamese work out their own problems. Symington charged that this would sentence the South Vietnamese to the unspeakable horrors of domination by the Vietcong. "When were you in Vietnam?" he asked. When Kennan replied that he had never been there, Symington said, "Never been there." Later he said, "I wish at some time as long as you feel so definite about these things, that you would take a little time off and go out there and visit in South Vietnam, not with the leaders but with the people in the villages and the political action teams and the young men we are training by the thousands to try to go back and be good citizens in the villages. I think, if I may respectfully say so, you would change your opinion some."[28]

Fulbright tried to rescue the witness by observing that he did not understand Kennan to advocate retirement from Vietnam but rather that the United States should recognize that its interests in Vietnam were limited and should content itself with maintaining a defensive enclave in South Vietnam, a view also held by General Gavin and given a certain immediacy by Walter Lippmann in a column published the morning of the hearing, advocating what was coming to be known as the "enclave strategy."[29] Kennan, answering Fulbright, said he would "gladly identify" himself with Lippmann's position.

Symington responded: "I want to get out. But I do not see how we can get out, and the only way to stay in there, in my opinion, without very heavy additional loss of American life is to utilize where we are strong, sea air power and air power, and not fight on the ground."[30]

Symington continued to support the president's policies, but his insistence on accelerating the air campaign put him at odds with the administration. During hearings of the Senate Preparedness Subcommittee he accused Defense Department officials of "deliberately misleading" Congress and the public on the progress of the war. He warned that the people "are getting wise to just what is going on" and attributed the administration's decline in public opinion polls largely to this. When Johnson escalated the war in June by authorizing air strikes against oil storage facilities at Haiphong and Hanoi, Symington rushed to his defense. Accelerated bombing of military targets in the north was the only feasible way of ending the war in a way that upheld American honor.[31]

This view was becoming increasingly unpopular, particularly on college and university campuses where opposition to what was perceived as an immoral war was joined to the free speech and civil rights movements. This created a dilemma for Symington. He was a strong supporter of civil rights, but opposed anything that might interfere with winning the war. While in Vietnam, for example, he said that three Americans who were visiting Hanoi at that time were "probably guilty of a criminal offense." Again, he proudly called the Senate's attention to the fact that while only ten students showed up at an antiwar rally at the University of Missouri–Columbia, 1,125 signed petitions supporting the administration's policies in Vietnam. Refusing a request from the St. Louis chapter of the Women's International League for Peace and Freedom that he send a telegram to the president urging him to halt the bombing, he wrote: "No one wants peace more than I, but it is not understood how a halt in air attacks, with a unilateral withdrawal of American troops, would bring peace to the South Vietnamese and Americans remaining under attack on the ground."[32]

A trip to Geneva to attend the disarmament conference reinforced his earlier views about the importance of Vietnam in the struggle against communism. It also increased his disappointment with America's European allies, particularly France, for their failure to come to the aid of the United States in Vietnam.[33]

Symington visited Vietnam over the 1966 Christmas holidays as part of a month-long trip which took him around the world. Conversations with leaders in the Middle East—including his old friend Moshe Dayan—and in Europe reinforced his views about the conduct of the war: "They simply cannot understand how this nation . . . continues to have so much trouble in . . . a war against an undeveloped country." The problem, he was convinced, lay in "too much detailed instruction . . . sent out by civilians in Washington." He asked about a Colonel Smith whom he had visited a year earlier and was told, "He got his going after a truck." Reporting all this to Fulbright and Russell, he wrote that he still held the views he had expressed a year earlier, that the United States should either move forward or move out.[34] Talking to John Cauley of the *Kansas City Star,* however, he said he "was now more favorably inclined toward a political settlement for ending the war in Vietnam than he was a year ago." The war was going to be "long and expensive . . . I am not as optimistic on the long pull as I was last year."

Despite his growing concerns, during 1967 Symington continued to call for more effective use of air and sea power. He asked Stennis to conduct hearings on the air war,[35] and the Mississippian promptly obliged. The closed-door hearings, frequently referred to as the "Stennis-Symington" hearings, opened on August 9. After listening to a parade of beribboned admirals and generals declare that they could win the war if only the military were "unshackled," the subcommittee called McNamara. When the hearings broke for lunch during the first day of McNamara's testimony, McNamara met with the press. A reporter said, "Senator Symington charges your policy differs from the military commanders. . . . [and that] if you are right, we should get out of Vietnam." McNamara responded: "Symington . . . is completely wrong. My policies don't differ with those of the Joint Chiefs and I think they would be the first to say it."

McNamara was wrong about the Joint Chiefs, who considered resigning en masse over McNamara's statement. They didn't, but McNamara's days as secretary of defense were clearly numbered as a result of his testimony.[36]

For his part, Symington continued to press for accelerated air attacks on North Vietnam and stepped up his criticism of McNamara. He continued to oppose suggestions that the United States try to influence the North Vietnamese by another halt in the bombing, but even before the Preparedness Subcommittee's hearings began, he proposed that rather than follow McNamara's policies, the United States, "as a preliminary to negotiation," should offer "not only to stop the fighting in North Vietnam, but also the fighting in South Vietnam." He reluctantly supported Johnson's request for a tax increase to support the war, but stated that he could not support a decision to send additional ground troops to Vietnam. "For over two years," he said, "it has been my considered opinion that we would have far more success in Vietnam . . . if we would take the shackles off our sea and air power so they could both attack the scores of meaningful military targets in North Vietnam which . . . remain untouched." When, a few days later, Johnson authorized broadening the target list, Symington wrote a letter of fulsome praise.[37]

But he continued his public criticism of the administration's management of the war. There had been an increase in the number of targets authorized, but the effort was halfhearted. Symington would be satisfied only with an all-out air attack on North Vietnam, and that wasn't happening. The president, it seemed, had delegated the conduct of the war to the secretary of defense, and he persisted in following a strategy that was in conflict with his best military advice.[38]

As the conflict intensified, Symington decided to take advantage of the September recess to make another visit to Vietnam. Again, it was an around-the-world trip, with visits to the Middle East and Europe as well as Southeast Asia. As on earlier trips, he made special efforts to visit with the pilots who flew the missions. They were permitted a broader range of targets than in the past, but were severely restricted in the tactics they could use. He discussed strike tactics with pilots on the aircraft carrier *Coral Sea*. He learned that the method of attack and the direction of retirement were not the ones these pilots would have chosen. "This they quietly resented," he reported, "because (1) it increased danger to their own lives, and (2) gave less chance for successful performance of their mission." He added: "We were told that the rules which resulted in the above unfortunate condition resulted from desire by higher authority to hold North Vietnamese casualties to a minimum."

In short, the United States still was not making proper use of its air and sea power, something Symington had been urging since the war began. He contrasted the country's Vietnam performance with that of the Israelis in the Seven Days War with Egypt. Reporting on his stopover in Tel Aviv, he wrote, "The accuracy and effectiveness of the bombing of the Israeli Air Force has to be seen to be believed. Once again, this campaign demonstrated the tremendously effective potential of modern strategic air when used properly."[39]

Symington returned to Washington convinced that the war was no longer winnable. General Westmoreland and Admiral Sharpe were providing "superb leadership," but they were severely hampered by: "(1) unprecedented restrictive regulations on the war, (2) division in this country re the war, (3) differences in Congress re same, and (4) basic differences between civilian Pentagon leadership and military as to how the war should be fought." Moreover, the South Vietnamese government had lost the respect of its own people, who were becoming bitter toward it and the United States. The war was a serious drain on the U.S. economy and threatened the country's ability to meet its commitments elsewhere in the world. In sum, the Vietnam War was "expensive in prestige, in military posture, in growing cost, and above all, in the taking of the lives of so many of the best of our youth."[40]

On October 3, Symington presented "A Proposal Looking Toward Peace in Vietnam."

> . . . I propose that this Government announce, as of a certain date, the cessation of all military action in South Vietnam as well as over North Vietnam; and also announce that there will be no reinforcements into the theater.

The Government would announce that these policies were being undertaken in earnest hope that their adoption would result in prompt and meaningful negotiations in the interests of a just peace.

At the same time, the United States should also announce that, if after this cessation of all military action . . . the North Vietnamese and Vietcong nevertheless continued hostilities, then the United States would feel free to pursue this war in any manner of its own choosing.

Concurrently with the above proposed announcement of U.S. policy, the Government of South Vietnam should announce its willingness to negotiate with anybody, and offer amnesty to members of the Vietcong.[41]

The proposal drew wide discussion but in the end little support. Administration officials privately expressed the view that the plan would have no chance of bringing North Vietnam to the peace table because Hanoi would not negotiate under a threat of renewed attack. Johnson, distressed that he was losing the support even of Democratic hawks, was portrayed as treating Symington's announcement as a stab in the back. Fulbright applauded his colleague's call for a cessation of hostilities, but was unhappy with his call for resuming the war if the peace effort failed. Almost alone among the country's major newspapers, the *Washington Star* supported his proposal, and in the Senate George McGovern, who inserted the *Star*'s editorial in the *Congressional Record,* was a lone voice of support. In Missouri, the proposal received mixed reviews. The mail ran heavily against it, and while the *Kansas City Star* gave it lukewarm support, both the *St. Louis Globe-Democrat* and the *Post-Dispatch* were critical.[42]

In an effort to explain his position, Symington went on the TV talk shows and distributed his position paper on Vietnam to Missouri editors and members of the Senate. He told the Senate that the charge by James Reston of the *New York Times* that Symington's proposal could well make things "worse than they are now" by "[gambling] on a one-way cease fire, and, if it didn't work, on a bigger and riskier war," was "an inaccurate deduction." He reminded his colleagues that the bombing halts, which Reston and the *Times* favored, had been counterproductive. His proposal would provide the time and opportunity to see if negotiations were possible. If they were not, the United States could assess its options, and they "by no means should be strictly limited to an escalation of the war."[43]

As he sought to explain his position, it is clear that Symington was moving toward a complete abandonment of the military effort in Vietnam. It caused too great a drain on the country's resources and was inhibiting our ability to meet commitments in other parts of the world. Moreover, the loss of young American lives was becoming too great for the nation to bear. From the beginning of the conflict, Symington and Eve had written a personal letter to the family of each

Missourian killed in the war. At the time he called for a cease-fire, the number had reached 429.[44]

From the beginning, Symington had prefaced his support of the war on the assumption that Vietnam was the right place to defend the free world against global communism. He was coming to the conclusion that it was not. More significantly, Stuart Symington, the preeminent Cold Warrior who for three decades had preached the necessity of large defense expenditures to contain communism, was coming to the conclusion that global communism was no longer a serious threat. Richard Dudman of the *Post-Dispatch* reported: "He [Symington] believes that Rusk and others have oversold the country on the threat of international communism."[45]

Reminded during hostile questioning on *Meet the Press* of his earlier statements urging the importance of standing firm in Vietnam, he said, "the world changes every day. . . . One changes one's opinion when one goes around the world. I've always come back through Europe, and I believe we have to recognize that the world is changing in this nuclear space age."[46]

Symington was disappointed that his cease-fire proposal received so little favorable response. During a hearing on the Foreign Assistance Act of 1968, he complained to Rusk that no one in the administration had ever talked to him about it. Rusk replied: "Well, Senator, although it might not have been discussed with you in detail, it was examined in detail. We continue to examine all possibilities and all variations and I would be glad to go into certain aspects of this in private session."[47]

There is no record that such a discussion ever took place, with Rusk or any other member of the administration. Symington seemed to be completely cut off from the president and his associates, even after his close friend Clifford became secretary of defense. It is hard to believe, however, that the two men did not discuss Vietnam. They saw each other frequently and talked almost every day on the phone. Symington was among a small group of "influential" senators with whom Clifford and General Earle Wheeler, chairman of the Joint Chiefs of Staff, met on March 8, 1968, to discuss Westmoreland's call for two hundred thousand additional troops in response to the so-called Tet offensive. None of them supported the idea. Symington had suggested in other contexts that if more troops were needed in Vietnam, they should be transferred from Europe, where he had argued they were no longer needed.[48]

In domestic policy, Symington refused to classify himself as a liberal while establishing one of the most liberal voting records in the Senate. Likewise, he resisted being called a dove while refusing to support the administration's efforts to continue the war. He did not join the students in the streets, although he sympathized with them and was always willing to talk to student delegations from Missouri who visited his office. He was yet another Cold Warrior who had given up on Vietnam. One evening during cocktails at a dinner given by the Lucius Battles, Symington and Acheson, who still supported the war effort, got into such a heated argument that they repeatedly ignored their host's entreaties to sit down for dinner.[49] Whether he liked the characterization or not, Symington by the early part of 1968 had become a dove on Vietnam.

This was clear during hearings in the Foreign Relations Committee on March 20. The committee was hearing testimony from General David M. Shoup, retired commandant of the Marine Corps. General Shoup had been critical of the war effort, and Symington, after saying, "Of all military, there is none that I admire more than you," asked leading questions that enabled the general to vent his frustrations. Despairing of an effective air campaign against North Vietnam, Symington had turned his attention to U.S. efforts to create stability in South Vietnam. He asked Shoup why those efforts had not been more successful. The general replied: "I think that while we have tried hard . . . instead of winning the minds and hearts of their people, we have rather closed their minds and broken their hearts. . . . And then I don't think the South Vietnamese people . . . like us, and they don't like us meddling in their business and they don't like us trying to tell them what kind of house they ought to live in, what kind of bandage they ought to put on their foot, and all the rest of it. They would like to live the way they want to live."

Symington responded by quoting Moshe Dayan. Dayan had told him that if the Vietnamese reverted to guerrilla warfare the United States could never defeat them, and also that "No American was ever going to sell his choice for village chief to the villagers." Then he asked Shoup: "Is that, in effect, what you are implying in your answer?" Shoup replied, "I think so. I don't think I said it as well."

The colloquy continued. The two men agreed that success in Vietnam was unachievable without a clear statement from the president of the country's objective, something they did not have and probably would not get. Finally, Symington asked Shoup, "As a former respected member of the Joint Chiefs of Staff, don't you have some apprehension, about not only the nature, but the degree, of the military and economic commitments we have made in this little country in Southeast Asia?"

Shoup replied, "Senator, it is a serious thing to me considering all the treaty commitments we have and all the promises that we have made that this great Nation can be so shaken by such a little nation with such a few people, with such unsophisticated weapons."

Finally, Symington asked General Shoup about the cost of the war. Did he agree with Secretary McNamara that the United States could continue forever to spend two and a half billion dollars a month "chasing people around the jungles over there?" Shoup did not agree, and he seconded Symington's concern that the country was overcommitted and could no longer afford the adventure in Vietnam.[50]

The colloquy with General Shoup dramatized the change that occurred in Symington's attitudes toward the Vietnam War. He no longer talked about developing a winning strategy. He had given up any hope of "winning," however that was defined. He simply wanted to get out. He applauded Johnson for "[putting] his country ahead of anything else" when in an effort to obtain national unity Johnson announced that he would not seek another term of office, and he expressed cautious optimism that his two longtime friends Averell Harriman and Cyrus Vance would succeed in their efforts to bring Hanoi to the negotiating table in Paris. He had no confidence in the government of South Vietnam, calling Saigon a "center of corruption." He had observed the black markets in American goods in streets around the American embassy, with neither the Americans nor the South Vietnamese doing much about it.[51] Symbolizing the corruption for Symington was a chance encounter at the Saigon airport with a high government official leaving for his condominium on the Riviera.

Aside from making a few speeches for Democratic candidates in Missouri, Symington took no part in the campaign of 1968. He favored Humphrey for the Democratic nomination, but told him, "if the war is not settled soon, the question of who will be our nominee in June will be pretty theoretical." On August 15 he wrote Humphrey that he was "distressed" to hear him say on the *Today* show that it was in the best interest of the United States to be in Vietnam. "If I know anything," he wrote, "and this especially with respect to my own constituents in Missouri, the people are steadily more fed up with this undeclared war, the coupling of shackles on our military with the heavy and tragic casualty lists."[52]

Symington renewed his call for a cease-fire in Vietnam made a year earlier. Since then, he said on the floor of the Senate, "Our casualties have more than doubled. . . . And 30 billion additional dollars which might have gone into worthwhile domestic and international programs have instead gone down the drain. What is there to show for this high cost in lives and treasure except further loss in the political, military, and economic prestige of the United States?"[53]

A few days later, during a colloquy with Russell on a defense appropriation bill, he said, "It is becoming increasingly difficult for the American people to understand why, despite this gigantic loss in treasure and lives, we have made little progress. It is one reason why so many of us have changed our position with respect to the whole question of this Vietnam war."[54]

Symington had changed his mind not only about the Vietnam War. He had changed it about the importance of defense expenditures as well, and the wisdom of America's historic role as the defender of the free world.

29

Laos, Cambodia, and the CIA

AS LYNDON Johnson prepared to leave office, the chill that had developed in his relations with Symington began to thaw a bit. The Symingtons, who earlier had been stricken from the White House invitation list, were among ninety guests invited on January 4 to view the official portraits of the Johnsons. A few days later Symington joined in the Senate eulogy of the departing president, praising his leadership in the areas of education, civil liberties, and civil rights. Carefully avoiding any mention of Vietnam, he spoke of Johnson's "great ability, . . . tireless energy, and . . . strong desire to maintain a prosperous and secure nation." Johnson responded that it "meant a great deal to Lady Bird and me that you would think well of us, and that you spoke as you did."[1]

With Nixon, everything was different. Symington had never liked him, had never trusted him. His criticism of Johnson's conduct of the war in Vietnam had been more in sorrow than in anger, but with Nixon there was nothing to be sorry about. To be sure, William Rogers, secretary of state, and Henry Kissinger, national security adviser, were longtime friends. Symington was among a small group of senators whom Kissinger periodically invited to his home for private, informal conversations on foreign policy. The practice was stopped when the new president objected.

In criticizing the administration's foreign policies, Symington tended to put the blame on the president rather than on Rogers or Kissinger. He worried, though, about Kissinger's growing power at the expense of the secretary of state. This, in his view, created a major problem for congressional committees. Rogers, as secretary of state, had no choice but to appear before congressional committees, but Kissinger, who had the real power, could plead executive privilege and refuse to testify. Symington roused the president's ire by declaring that Kissinger had become "Secretary of State in everything but title," and that Rogers "had become a laughing-stock in Washington." Nixon accused Symington of taking "a cheap shot" at the secretary of state, and went out of his way to praise Rogers as his "oldest and closest friend in the cabinet." At the same time he outlined a role for Kissinger that seemed to some observers to give him a broader mandate than that exercised by Secretary Rogers.[2]

Symington's sense of the relative roles of the two men proved to be prescient. In September 1973, Kissinger became secretary of state in name as well as in fact. Symington told him that he would support his nomination if he would agree not to plead executive privilege before the Foreign Relations Committee. Kissinger agreed except with respect to private conversations with the president.[3]

By the time Kissinger became secretary of state, Symington had emerged as a central figure in the struggle between Congress and the executive over control of the nation's foreign policy.

On February 3, 1969, Fulbright announced the establishment of a subcommittee on U.S. security agreements and commitments abroad. He had asked Symington to chair the subcommittee, and he was appointing himself a member.[4] Other Democrats on the subcommittee were John Sparkman of Alabama and Mansfield of Montana (the majority leader). George Aiken of Vermont, John Sherman Cooper of Kentucky, and Jacob K. Javits of New York represented the Republicans. It was a powerful subcommittee, and, with the exception of Sparkman, all of its members had been critical of American involvement in Vietnam.[5]

Symington accepted his new assignment with enthusiasm. He frequently had expressed concern over the extent of American military and economic commitments around the world; fear of overcommitment had played a role in his call for a cessation of hostilities in Vietnam.[6]

Vietnam was specifically excluded from the subcommittee's purview, because, as Fulbright explained, the situation there raised "a number of complicated and unique questions which will continue to receive the close attention of the full committee."[7] Even so, the subcommittee's creation had its roots in the Vietnam War, and the shadow of Vietnam hung over most of its deliberations.

Symington, as was the case with all of his efforts, surrounded himself with an excellent staff. He hired Walter Pincus, a reporter for the *Washington Post,* as chief consultant, and Roland Paul, who had worked for the Department of Defense in the Johnson administration, as counsel. Pat Holt of his own staff became staff assistant. In addition, Fulbright made available the services of Richard Moose and James Lowenstein, two highly competent, experienced Senate investigators.

The subcommittee did not complete its work until November 24, 1970. It held thirty-seven days of country-by-country hearings, all in executive session, on NATO and thirteen specific countries. Although there was a constant struggle with the Departments of State and Defense—occasionally involving the White House—the subcommittee released more than two thousand pages of testimony.[8] The releases revealed a worldwide network of clandestine activities abroad and provoked wide editorial comment, most of it reflecting unfavorably on the administration.

As John Lehman suggests in his perceptive study of the Nixon administration's relations with Congress, the Symington investigation "Provided the first test of the proclamation by the Nixon administration that it would be an 'open administration,' and that Congress would have full access to information in the executive branch."[9]

Nixon, trying to capitalize on the excessive secrecy that had characterized the Johnson administration, pledged that his would be an "open administration," and initially he gave every indication that he tended to honor his pledge. Executive departments were instructed to provide all information requested by Congress; exceptions had to be approved by the White House.

Taking the president at his word, Symington wrote Secretary of Defense Melvin Laird requesting a copy of a report on U.S. bases around the world prepared for the Johnson administration by General Robert Wood and Ambassador Robert McClintock. This would seem to have been a legitimate request from a subcommittee charged with investigating security agreements and commitments abroad, but the report contained much highly classified material. The Defense Department balked at releasing it. Finally, Pincus and Paul were permitted to read the report in the Pentagon and take notes. Symington followed up with a second letter to Laird requesting details of U.S. activities in all parts of the world, including southeast Asia. Even though Vietnam had been specifically excluded from the subcommittee's purview, it was clear that the war in Vietnam was much on Symington's mind. For a host of reasons—not the least being its impact on negotiations with North Vietnam under way in Paris—neither Defense nor State wanted to accede fully to Symington's request. They had concluded that the subcommittee could not be trusted with sensitive material. It seemed to officials at State, for example, that it was no mere coincidence that a few days after Pincus and Paul had examined the Wood-McClintock report, the *New York Times* published a long story discussing its contents.[10]

Symington spent the summer of 1969 sparring with the administration over the committee's right to access. As the announced date for the hearings, September

30, approached, the administration developed something of a siege mentality. The president, who at this time was still wanting to cooperate with Congress, asked Symington to meet with him in the Oval Office, where Symington agreed that the subcommittee would not take up nuclear weapons deployment or contingency plans, and the president indicated his willingness to permit the director of the CIA to testify. These generalized agreements left many questions unresolved. The hearings all were conducted in executive session. Symington pushed for the early release of the transcripts; the administration, genuinely concerned that disclosure would damage the country's foreign policy and fearful that the Democratic-controlled subcommittee would try to build a campaign issue, resisted.[11]

The administration had ample cause for concern. Testimony, wrung from reluctant witnesses by Symington and others on the subcommittee, revealed the extent to which America's war in Vietnam secretly had spread to virtually all of southeast Asia. The initial hearings, devoted to the Republic of the Philippines, brought out the disturbing fact that the United States was paying the full cost of Philippine operations in Vietnam—operations that had been trumpeted in both Washington and Manila as volunteer efforts. Although the hearings were in executive session, word of their contents soon leaked out, despite the administration's efforts to keep them secret. As Symington negotiated with the State and Defense Departments, the goodwill that had issued from the Oval Office conference began to evaporate. The administration decided that "Symington was really out for blood," and that the cooperation hoped for at the beginning of the hearings would be impossible. Symington was not "out for blood," but he sensed a major constitutional issue and was determined to give no quarter. He released the Philippine transcript on November 18. He had agreed to some deletions, but not as many as the administration wanted.[12]

The release precipitated a domestic uproar and something of an international crisis. It was revealed that in 1966 the United States had spent $13 million to send a small construction battalion to Vietnam, and continued to subsidize Filipino operations there. The Filipinos were supposed to be in Vietnam as volunteers, helping to roll back communism. Instead, they were little more than mercenaries. The Philippine government reacted angrily to this characterization of its troops, threatening to withdraw them from Vietnam and demand the dismantling of U.S. bases in the Philippines. As John Lehman put it, "The Symington subcommittee had drawn its first blood."[13]

For Symington, the issue was executive secrecy, which, he asserted repeatedly, undermined constitutional government. In announcing the subcommittee's intent to hold hearings on Laos, he said, "We have been at war in Laos for years and it is time the American people knew the facts." The hearings would be secret, but he would undertake to release the information as soon as possible. "For too long," he said, "we have permitted our activities abroad to be carried on under a cloak of secrecy—and often that secrecy veils such activity from the people of this country and their elected representatives, not from the enemy."[14]

The "secret war in Laos" became something of a cause celebre for Symington. His committee held four days of secret hearings late in October. Despite his experience with the Philippine hearings, Symington cooperated fully with the State Department's desire for confidentiality; he even refused to release the names and number of the witnesses. He soon became disenchanted with the State Department, however, because of its refusal to authorize release of the transcripts. "You cannot expect the public to stand by unquestioning," he said, "as the silent war in Laos escalates, while the public war in Vietnam is being de-escalated with great fanfare." On March 26 he complained in the Senate about the delay. "We want it to be clear . . . ," he said, "that we have never suggested the entire record be published. I agree it contains some material which should not be published. But it contains a great deal of material which should be published if the American people are to maintain . . . proper confidence in their Government." The newspapers almost daily were revealing new facts or asking new questions. It was high time the government gave the American people the facts.[15]

Kissinger, who was at the center of the controversy, saw the problem primarily as one of executive privilege. As he explained it to the president, by releasing the Laos testimony they "might kill two birds with one stone: placate Symington, Fulbright, et al, and show the public what we are really doing."

"On the other hand," he cautioned, "it is doubtful whether the release . . . will placate the Senators. They *know* what is going on in Laos and why. . . . Releasing the testimony would help North Vietnam document its case that we are violating the Geneva Accords, without admitting that it is violating them, and thus seriously undermine the real basis for our action. . . . Furthermore, by giving in on Laos . . . we might be opening a real Pandora's box for ourselves, not only domestically, but in our relations with other countries."[16]

Symington and the administration remained at odds over the transcripts. Nixon offered to release a heavily censored version, but Symington refused to accept on the grounds that it would be misleading. Nixon, vacationing on Key Biscayne, tried to stem the flow of criticism by issuing a long statement. In a veiled reference to Symington, he said that he had not thought it in the national interest to discuss U.S. activities in Laos, but was doing so now because of "the intense public speculation" and the issuance of so many "grossly inaccurate" statements about the situation. He discussed American involvement in Laos, going back to the Kennedy administration. He admitted that the United States was bombing that part of the Ho Chi Minh Trail which crossed the northern part of Laos, and, "at the request of the Royal Laotian Government," was providing logistic support and was "engaged in some other activities." He assured the nation that the United States had no ground troops in Laos.[17]

Symington, interviewed in Clayton by John Dancy of NBC, said, "Everything the President said was accurate. Unfortunately, he only gave the ground part . . . of the story. He didn't give the full story based on my knowledge of the matter. . . . But if you're fighting in the air, you're fighting. Whether it's under the sea, or on the sea, or on the ground or in the air, there's a major war going on in north Laos."[18]

Finally, on April 19, the subcommittee released a (still heavily censored) transcript of the hearings. The information, partial though it was, provided ample documentation for Symington's repeated references to "the war in Laos." As Murray Marder wrote in the *Washington Post*, "For more than six years, the Symington Subcommittee's report on Laos shows, the United States practiced a policy of official deception about its extremely extensive military operations in Laos. . . . Sen. Stuart Symington, who is anything but anti-military, and who knew from visits to Laos as much as any Senator about the U.S. role there, raises the matter in blunt terms:

> We incur hundreds of thousands of U.S. casualties because we are opposed to a closed society. We say we are an open society and the enemy is a closed society. . . .
> Here we are telling Americans we must fight and die to maintain an open society but not telling our people what we are doing. That would seem the characteristic of a closed society.

Marder concluded his piece with: "Those who express bafflement about why a younger generation loses faith in the words of its leaders will find some answers in the Laos transcript." Nearer to home, the *Post-Dispatch* wrote that even the sanitized version was "extremely valuable" for the information it contained, adding, "Mr. Symington has performed a notable service in tearing the veil of secrecy from the reprehensible U.S. involvement in Laos."[19]

Symington continued his efforts to pierce the veil of secrecy that the administration tried to keep over operations in southeast Asia. The story in Laos was repeated in Cambodia, and, to a degree, in Thailand. The bombing and later invasion of Cambodia provided Symington with further ammunition for his struggle with the administration. He decried the bombing as "wasteful, immoral, and illegal." President Nixon's highly publicized withdrawal of American forces from Vietnam—"Vietnamization"—was in Symington's view little more than a smoke screen to cover secret efforts to widen the war.[20]

Symington's opposition to the Cambodian incursion placed him in the majority on the Foreign Relations Committee, but put him definitely in the minority on the Armed Services Committee. For example, following a meeting of the Armed Services Committee with the president just after the Cambodian invasion was announced, Symington, alone among members of the committee, expressed doubt that the president could keep his optimistic promise that the United States would be out of Cambodia in "three to seven weeks."[21]

Along with most of the other doves in the Senate—and their number was growing—Symington believed that the most effective tactic against the administration was to work through the budget. He supported an amendment to a foreign military sales bill offered by Cooper and Idaho Democrat Frank Church severely limiting the president's ability to act in Cambodia without congressional approval.[22]

As the war dragged on, Symington continued his efforts to restrict funding. He joined with New Jersey Republican Clifford Case in offering an amendment to impose a ceiling of $250 million on military and economic aid to Cambodia during fiscal year 1971. The amendment, adopted by the Foreign Relations Committee 10-3 over strenuous administration objections, also limited to two hundred the number of American civilian and military personnel that could be stationed in Cambodia. The Joint Chiefs of Staff wanted a higher figure. Symington, who in earlier years would have almost automatically approved a JCS recommendation, expressed the fear that "the real intention" of the JCS was to establish positions of strength in Cambodia and Laos, "where we could remain indefinitely."[23]

And "indefinitely" seemed to be an accurate predictor. Nixon, preoccupied with his 1972 reelection, played down the war in southeast Asia. He hoped that his triumphs in Beijing and Moscow would overshadow his failures in Vietnam. Kissinger's failure to nail down an agreement in Paris blunted his effort to contrast his "peace with honor" with Democratic candidate George McGovern's "peace by surrender." Blunted or not, the message got across. Nixon won reelection by one of the largest margins in history.[24]

Symington supported McGovern as a matter of course, although initially he had favored Senator Edmund Muskie of Maine. He campaigned for the Democratic ticket, but his efforts were curtailed by a bronchial infection. He had little hope of victory. He wrote Flora Lewis, *New York Times* correspondent in Paris, " . . . this is not the best of all years for Democrats." His principal concern was the effort (successful) of his son Jim to win a third term in Congress from Missouri's Second District. After the election Symington, accompanied by Eve, headed an American delegation to the North Atlantic Assembly in Bonn, Germany. After that, they toured Yugoslavia, Bulgaria, Romania, and Czechoslovakia. They were planning to take a personal trip to Ireland, but Stuart's continuing bronchial trouble caused them to cancel it in favor of a few days in the Florida sun.[25]

Back in Washington on Christmas Eve 1972, tragedy struck.

Stuart and Eve, accompanied by Senator and Mrs. Howard Cannon of Nevada, attended the NFL playoff game between the Washington Redskins and the Green Bay Packers. Eve apparently had her usual good time and gave no sign that she was having any difficulty. The Symingtons were planning to fly to St. Louis after the game to spend Christmas with Tim and his family. Returning home, Stuart put the car in the garage while Eve went into the house to make preparations to go to the airport. When Stuart came into the house, he found his wife collapsed on the floor. She had suffered a dissective cardiac aneurysm and died an hour later at the George Washington University Hospital. She was sixty-nine. On December 28, hundreds of mourners listened as the Right Reverend Francis B. Sayre, dean of the National Cathedral, eulogized her for her life of love and service. Jim, speaking for the family, said, " . . . she was the cement that held us together and kept us at the task." Ruth Spaatz, wife of the former air force chief of staff, praised her concern for air force wives and families in installations all around the world.[26]

Symington was devastated. He wrote Eve's cousin, Jock Whitney, "We were having a lot of fun living—she was so interested in, and sympathetic about everything. I never knew this much loneliness could be around."[27]

He went on the annual Fort Lauderdale golfing excursion organized by Clifford in January, but for the most part he immersed himself in his work. The work was varied and heavy, but the central focus remained the effort to penetrate the veil of secrecy that shrouded American activities in southeast Asia and particularly Cambodia. His opposition to the war intensified. In what was described as "one of the most impassioned speeches of his career," he urged the Democratic Policy Committee to oppose further funds for continuing the war. He was particularly distressed at the resumption of bombing over North Vietnam. "My grandchildren ask me why we are doing this," he said, "and I have to tell them I don't know." He sat down and buried his head in his hands.[28]

Symington's responsibilities and opportunities increased when John Stennis was seriously wounded during a sidewalk robbery attempt in Washington. Symington as the senior Democrat on the committee became acting chairman. Normally this would have caused little comment. But now that he was looked upon as one of the Senate's leading doves, some observers expected a change in direction for the Armed Services Committee. There was some change, but not as much as expected. Although Symington and Stennis were described as "poles apart" on major issues, Symington remained personally close to Stennis and tried hard to represent his interests. Moreover, it was clear that if Symington made any effort to induce the committee to retreat from its hard-line views, he would have a fight on his hands. With the exception of Iowa Democrat Harold Hughes and Ohio Republican William B. Saxbe, the members were all hard-liners.[29]

His principal venue continued to be the Subcommittee on U.S. Security Agreements and Commitments Abroad. At his request, the committee's two most experienced investigators, James Lowenstein and Richard Moose, spent the month of April in Cambodia. Their report showed that American air operations were not directed against the North Vietnamese as the administration had asserted, but rather against Cambodian insurgents in support of the tottering government of Lon Nol. The report described a Byzantine arrangement whereby target decisions were made by a young embassy air attaché working with Cambodian defense officials. All of this, Symington charged, violated the "clear intent" of Congress to limit American involvement in Cambodia. He released the report with a blistering statement about "the continuing destruction of this little country" by American air power in support of the weak and ineffective government of Lon Nol.[30]

It got no response from the administration, and very little from Symington's colleagues in the Senate. The nation seemed to have wearied of the whole business. When General George Brown came before the Armed Services Committee for confirmation as air force chief of staff, Harold Hughes, about the only other member of the committee who felt as strongly as Symington about the war, asked him specifically about air strikes in Cambodia prior to May 1970, the date that had been given the committee for the onset of the Cambodian campaign. Brown's evasive answers prompted Symington to call hearings that produced, as one observer wrote, "a public response of excuses and lies that were perhaps more alarming than anything that was coming from the Ervin Committee."[31]

Throughout the summer Symington used his position as acting chairman of the Armed Services Committee to try to ferret out the history of the Cambodian operations, something Stennis probably would not have done. The committee, however, generally supported him. Hughes asserted that the Department of Defense "deliberately deceived" the Armed Services Committee about the early B-52 strikes in Cambodia and praised Symington for his willingness to take on the subject. Even Goldwater, while urging caution, wrote that Symington should "by all means proceed to get at the bottom of who ordered these raids which in my opinion came from the only proper source, the President himself." For his part, Symington wrote that "never during my career in government have I been as distressed as I am now with respect to the consistently false information that has been given to Congress about the bombing of Cambodia. . . . It is now clear that it is our duty to the end."[32]

On July 24, Symington announced that the Armed Services Committee would hold hearings on the Cambodia bombing. He set the tone by charging that the Defense Department had "deliberately deceived" Congress and the American people and that the goal of the hearings would be to determine who was responsible.[33]

The hearings, held in the shadow of Watergate, were tumultuous affairs. The country was treated to the sorry spectacle of junior officers describing orders to falsify reports and their superiors seeking to deny that any such orders were given. Symington opened the hearings with the belief that responsibility lay at the highest levels of government. Through days of detailed questioning, however, the committee was unable to fix responsibility. It became clear, nevertheless, that the cover-up originated in the White House, and probably with the president himself. On August 20, speaking before a Veterans of Foreign Wars convention in New Orleans, Nixon acknowledged that he had approved the secret bombing of Cambodia, vigorously justifying it as being necessary to protect American lives.[34]

In the midst of all this, Nixon nominated Kissinger to be secretary of state. As has been indicated, Symington had known Kissinger since Kissinger was an obscure professor at Harvard, and thought highly of his ability. He was concerned, however, about Kissinger's penchant for secret negotiations. Above all, he wanted to use the confirmation hearings to ferret out Kissinger's role in the Cambodian mess. He was not particularly successful.

In response to a direct question on whether he approved withholding information, Kissinger replied that he was new to the administration and it was not his role to "approve or disapprove" such action. He added, however, "I do not want to mislead the committee. I was in agreement with the policy." When Symington asked, " . . . who directed the secrecy with respect to the bombing and the bombing itself?" Kissinger referred to earlier testimony by General Earle Wheeler, chairman of the Joint Chiefs of Staff. Wheeler had admitted that he carried out the policy at the direction of the president. Again, Kissinger admitted that he was in agreement with the policy, but he added that if a similar circumstance should arise again, "a procedure must be found by which the proper Congressional committees are informed."[35]

Symington spoke on the Senate floor in favor of Kissinger's confirmation. Calling him "able, with a brilliant mind," he said, "I know of no one who has had more experience in the field of foreign policy." Still, he remained troubled by Kissinger's penchant for secrecy and his role in determining national policy.

He thought it particularly unfortunate that Kissinger would retain his position as national security adviser while serving as secretary of state.[36]

But Symington was troubled by much more than Henry Kissinger's activities. He was becoming deeply concerned by the uses to which the Nixon administration was putting the CIA.

Symington was one of the architects of the National Security Act of 1947, which had created the CIA. His good friend Hoyt Vandenberg had been detached from the air force to serve as the agency's first director. Symington brought him back to the air force in 1948 to serve as chief of staff. Symington knew most of the men who served as head of the agency and was a friend of a number of them. His membership on the CIA oversight subcommittee of the Senate Armed Forces Committee enabled him to be closely informed about the agency's activities. In general he was supportive. With the widening of the war to Laos and Cambodia, however, and disquieting rumors about the administration's use of the CIA, he began to raise serious questions.

Traditionally, Congress appropriated funds for the CIA with few if any questions asked. Indeed, many in Congress were reluctant even to know about intelligence operations. There was no way they could use their information, and knowledge could make them vulnerable to the charge that they had leaked secrets or mishandled their responsibilities.[37] Neither Russell nor Stennis evinced much interest in probing into CIA operations. Stennis didn't even bother to call meetings of the subcommittee on the CIA.

On December 21, 1970, Symington's Subcommittee on Security Agreements and Commitments Abroad recommended "an in-depth and continuing study of our intelligence activities." Stennis apparently was not interested, but Symington kept at it. He charged that "many of the unfortunate developments incident to our operations in Indochina, especially those in Laos, have occurred as the result of a general lack of adequate information on the part of the proper committees of the Congress about the operations of the Central Intelligence Agency." He urged an investigation.[38] In the interim, he introduced an amendment to the Defense Department's appropriation bill to place a ceiling of $4 billion on all intelligence operations, which, after considerable discussion, was defeated.

Symington normally got along very well with Stennis, but when he could not get him to call a meeting he complained on the Senate floor that "As a longtime member of the Committee on Foreign Relations, as an ad hoc member of the Appropriations Committee and the ranking member of Armed Services" he was unable to get "enough intelligence information to . . . form an intelligent judgment on matters which so vitally affect our security."[39]

He continued to push for open information. Moreover, though he was not yet prepared to say so publicly, he was becoming concerned that the president, in addition to using the CIA to conduct secret wars in southeast Asia, was about to politicize the organization. He expressed serious misgivings about the reorganization announced by the White House in November 1971. His misgivings were reinforced when Nixon replaced Richard Helms as director of the CIA with James R. Schlesinger. Helms and Symington had been rather close friends for many years.[40] Symington and Schlesinger were well acquainted, but their relationship, while cordial, was never close. In any event, Symington thought Schlesinger's confirmation hearing should be public. Stennis thought otherwise. Disappointed, Symington wrote: "In that, in effect, Mr. Schlesinger will head up an organization of thousands of men which in at least one country has been directing United States activity in a war over a period of years, . . . I believe the American people should have the right to have a look at the man now nominated to head up that . . . [organization]; otherwise there can only be further disrespect for the true role of the Senate, and a further lack of confidence in Government in general."[41]

When Symington became acting chairman of the Senate Armed Forces Committee, he found a way to investigate the CIA in a manner that Stennis approved. On May 8, Symington and Schlesinger visited Stennis in his hospital room to discuss the rumors rife in Washington that the CIA had acted illegally. Stennis agreed that an investigation should go forward. The immediate problem was to determine whether and to what extent the CIA had been involved in surveillance of Daniel Ellsberg, the Department of Defense employee who had released what had come to be known as the Pentagon Papers, a detailed chronicle of Vietnam War planning. Also, had the CIA been part of the bungled attempt to burglarize the office of Dr. Lewis Fielding of Los Angeles, a psychiatrist who had been consulted by Ellsberg? Schlesinger had stated that he was "glad there was no Watergate aspect."[42]

The next morning the *New York Times* published a memorandum that James W. McCord had submitted to the Senate Watergate Committee, outlining a bizarre plot to blame the CIA and former director Richard Helms for the Watergate operation. Symington called Helms, then serving as ambassador to Iran, to urge him to come back immediately to protect his position and his good name.[43]

As he opened the hearings on May 11, Symington in a long statement recited the history of the legislation creating the CIA. He also spoke approvingly of Helms's stewardship of the agency and of his scrupulous avoidance of any domestic activity. The rumors regarding the CIA's involvement in the Ellsberg case struck at the very foundation of the nation's legal system. "In the last analysis," he concluded, "the question before us in these hearings is whether or not it is proper for the employees of one of our most important government agencies to assume that instructions from a building called the 'White House' need not be within the law. Whatever the circumstances, any assumption which places White House employees, including the top White House employee, beyond the law, is intolerable."[44]

The hearings were in executive session, but Symington, in an effort to slow down the rumor mill, regularly briefed the press.[45] The briefings firmly established what had been rumored for months: the White House, and by direct implication the president himself, not only was aware of the Watergate break-in but had engineered the whole thing and the effort to cover it up. The testimony, particularly that from Lieutenant General Vernon Walters, CIA deputy director, clearly implicated top White House aides—H. R. Haldeman, chief of staff; John D. Ehrlichman, former chief domestic adviser; and John W. Dean III, former White House counsel—in efforts to involve the CIA. "What I learned . . . that I didn't know before," Symington said, "was how deeply involved Haldeman was as well as Ehrlichman and Dean." He added, "Ehrlichman and Haldeman—particularly Haldeman, were up to their ears in this, along with Dean, in trying to involve the CIA in this whole Watergate mess."[46]

The Symington hearings occurred just before North Carolina Democratic Senator Sam Ervin began his televised Watergate hearings. In a sense, Symington, without intending to, had stolen some of Ervin's thunder by calling attention to the role of the White House. At one point, at the suggestion of his legislative aide, Kathie Nelson, he asked Walters if he had kept any memos of his White House conversations. Walters had, and at Symington's request produced eleven, which, Symington told the press, documented White House involvement. He added, "It is difficult for me to visualize that the President knew nothing about it."[47]

The president responded with a statement categorically denying that he had any prior knowledge of the Watergate operation and specifically that he was involved in any attempt to implicate the CIA. He suggested that continuing the investigations "could lead to further compromise of sensitive national security information." Symington responded by saying that it was "more a case of national embarrassment than . . . of national security."[48]

He remained critical of the president. The appointment of General Alexander M. Haig as White House chief of staff to replace the discredited Haldeman, who had resigned, caused him particular concern. Haig apparently was going to retain his military rank, which in Symington's view clearly violated the legal prohibition of an officer on active duty accepting a civilian appointment. He asked Elliot Richardson, then serving briefly as secretary of defense, for an explanation. It was more than a technical problem. "In the wake of recent disclosures," he reminded Richardson, "our citizens are seriously disturbed about a seeming disregard for the standards of conduct that our laws seek to enforce." There followed a long and somewhat involved correspondence between Symington and Department of Defense lawyers that settled nothing.[49]

When the revelations of the Cambodia hearings were added to all of this, there remained no question but that the administration had been engaged in a systematic effort to mislead Congress and the public.

In his own mind, Symington had long been convinced that the president had committed impeachable offenses. Characteristically, he refused to be drawn into a public statement, arguing that as a member of the Senate he would be called on to sit as a judge. On October 21, however, following Richardson's resignation as attorney general, he told the press, "I have been quiet until now about Watergate and other scandals that have surfaced in recent months in this Administration. I can no longer remain quiet."

Richardson, who had moved from the Department of Defense to Justice in May 1973, resigned rather than yield to Nixon's demand that he fire Archibald Cox, the special prosecutor in the Watergate case. The president, in Symington's view, had "violated his solemn pledge" with respect to the independence of the attorney general and the special counsel. Moreover, he was in contempt of court by refusing to turn over the tapes of his Oval Office conversations. "For these reasons," he concluded, "there is no question that, whatever the chances for impeachment were before, they have now been substantially increased."[50]

As the House of Representatives moved toward impeachment, Symington, asked by the *Post-Dispatch* for an opinion, issued only a brief statement reiterating his earlier position: "In case the President is impeached, the Senate will act as jurors in his trial. For this reason, as a possible juror, I have consistently refrained from commenting on the President's actions in his defense, the one exception being my criticism of his summary firing of his special investigator, Mr. Cox."[51]

The president's resignation made the issue moot. For Symington, the issues of trust in government and executive secrecy were at the core of his problem with the Nixon administration. He continued to press for openness in the administration of Gerald R. Ford, with whom he generally got along. His major concern now, in the last years of his Senate career, was with disarmament and preventing the spread of nuclear weapons, both of which, in his view, were essential to achieving any kind of peaceful world.

30

Meanwhile, Back in Missouri

STUART SYMINGTON was one of the most powerful and popular political figures in the recent history of Missouri, second perhaps only to Harry Truman. Yet he never was comfortably at home in Missouri. He never lost his Maryland accent or his urbane appearance. To many Missourians he seemed distant and aloof. To some he gave the impression that he would rather be anywhere in the world than in Missouri.[1] An exaggeration, perhaps, but there is little evidence that the Symingtons had strong emotional ties to their adopted state. They spent their summer vacations on Nantucket Island and in the winter sought out resorts in Florida or the Caribbean. Most of their early contemporaries in St. Louis had passed from the scene. The social/business community had changed. Many prominent St. Louisans were Democrats when Symington's career was beginning; in his later years few were. Their friends were national and international rather than local. They had more friends in Washington and New York than in St. Louis. During his years in the Truman administration Symington frequently talked about returning to St. Louis to resume his business career, but there is no evidence that he seriously considered it. In 1966 the Symingtons sold their large house in Ladue and purchased a much smaller one in Richmond Heights. "Home" was the Georgetown house that had once belonged to Eve's parents. After Eve's death, Stuart sold the house and took an apartment in the fashionable Watergate complex. He never considered returning to St. Louis after retiring from the Senate.[2] With Eve gone, the only support group in St. Louis was Tim's family. He visited them frequently and enjoyed such old friends as were still around, and each fall he managed to see a Missouri football game or two.

In the Senate, Symington devoted most of his attention to national and international issues. Except for a term early in his career as a member of the Committee on Agriculture and Forestry, his major committee assignments—Atomic Energy, Armed Services, Foreign Relations, Space—dealt with broad issues. To be sure, he used his position, particularly as a member of the Armed Services Committee, to advance the aerospace industry in St. Louis and the development of military installations in Missouri, but in general he was concerned with national and international questions. Moreover, as he became disillusioned with the Vietnam War, he took positions that were opposed by many Missourians.

In short, Symington was from Missouri, but he was by no means of it. Why then was he so popular?

An important reason was that he effectively looked after Missouri's interests, using his great influence for the benefit of the state and, frequently, of its individual citizens. He was aided by an unusually competent staff headed by Stanley Fike, "the third senator from Missouri." Indeed, while visiting Missourians liked to have a chance to talk to the senator—and his door was always open to them—they knew that as far as the success of their mission was concerned, talking with Fike was as good as talking to the senator himself.

Despite his heavy committee schedule and extensive foreign travel, Symington made frequent trips back to Missouri. These trips, carefully orchestrated by Fike, were filled with speeches to service clubs and chambers of commerce. They gave him an opportunity to do what he did best: carry on informal conversations with individuals and small groups. His presence in an office always created a stir, particularly among female employees. For many, he was "the sexiest man I've ever met." He set hearts aflutter as he stopped at each desk for a brief chat or a pat on the shoulder. During the 1960 presidential campaign, one woman remarked, "Women want to mother Jack Kennedy, but with Stu they feel illicit."[3]

Every letter from Missouri received a personal reply. Many letters were produced by what was known as a robotype, a precomputer device that individualized form letters. Most of the others were written by the staff. Symington signed them all, however, and frequently added a handwritten note such as "give my love to that sweet Mary."

During the Kennedy and Johnson administrations Symington virtually controlled federal appointments in Missouri. His influence was felt with special force in the judiciary, where a number of vacancies on the federal bench were filled with bright young lawyers who had been active in his campaigns: William H. Becker, Elmo Hunter, James Meredith, and John W. Oliver, all graduates of the University of Missouri School of Law.[4] Symington also was instrumental in the appointment of Charles Whitaker to the Supreme Court.

On occasion, Symington did legislative favors for individual Missourians. For example, he introduced a "private bill" granting citizenship to Dr. Felix Sabates, a prominent Kansas City ophthalmologist fleeing Castro's Cuba. He did the same thing for Sandy Gellhorn, the adopted son of the noted journalist Martha Gellhorn, who had been born and reared in St. Louis. An effort that did not particularly please one prominent Missourian was his push to persuade Congress to appoint General Douglas MacArthur General of the Armies, thus giving him a sixth star. Former President Harry Truman is supposed to have said that "if he had anything to do with it, he would demote General MacArthur from five to four stars." Symington garnered considerable bipartisan support for what originally had been primarily a Republican effort, but nothing came of it. MacArthur's name kindled too much partisan passion; the Pentagon opposed the elevation because it would not be fair to other five-star generals.[5]

For communities in all parts of the state Symington supported efforts to secure federal funds; the results were evident throughout Missouri in park improvements, conservation projects, post offices and other public buildings, Head Start programs, low-income housing—anything for which federal funds could be obtained. He used his membership on the Public Works Committee to steer federal highway funds to Missouri; the first Interstate highway system contracts were let in Missouri. His influence was crucial in bringing about the appointment of Rex Whitten, Missouri state highway engineer, as director of the federal highway program.

Symington also became heavily involved in promoting three major projects of the National Park Service in Missouri: the Jefferson National Expansion Memorial in St. Louis, the Ozark National Scenic Riverways, and the Wilson's Creek National Battlefield, site of a Civil War battle in southwest Missouri. The Jefferson National Expansion Memorial, usually referred to as the Gateway Arch in recognition of Eero Saarinen's soaring steel masterpiece, had been in progress since the 1930s.[6] The memorial was the first national historic site established under the Historic Sites Act of 1935. Using federal and local money, the National Park Service bought and demolished buildings covering forty blocks of land between the old federal courthouse and the Mississippi River, sparing only the Old Cathedral, which dated from 1834. The project lay dormant during World War II, with the cleared land serving as a parking lot. After the war the Jefferson National Expansion Memorial Association, led by Luther Ely Smith, who had shepherded the project from the beginning, conducted the architectural competition that resulted in Saarinen's design. Despite excitement over Saarinen's breathtaking design, the project languished. The railroads, which would have to relocate elevated tracks along the base of the monument, lobbied so effectively against the project that it appeared that the federal share of the construction money would not become available.

This is where Symington came in. As a member of the Missouri delegation, he had supported the project as a matter of course, but he had not taken a leadership position in the effort. That had been left to Senator Hennings and Congresswoman Leonor Sullivan, in whose district the memorial was located. Both Hennings and Sullivan had worked hard and achieved some success, but much more needed to be done in both St. Louis and Washington. In Washington, the most serious opposition came from Senator Theodore Francis Green, aged bachelor from Rhode Island, the oldest man in the Senate. Green, handling the authorization bill, considered the project nothing but a boondoggle. Harry Byrd of Virginia, who favored the project, suggested that Symington bring Green out to his home in Berryville for lunch. On a beautiful spring Sunday, Stuart, Eve, and Green drove out to Berryville in the Symingtons' Pontiac convertible. Apparently, the Symington charm worked again. Tim was along as well. Green sat in the back seat and slept most of the way, but at lunch and also during a visit with Eve's aunt and uncle, the Fletcher Harpers, of the plains in Virginia, he was the life of the party. They discussed the arch, and somehow Green was persuaded to change his mind.[7]

Although he had been able to convert Senator Green, Symington remained pessimistic. The reason: the people of St. Louis did not seem to be solidly behind the project. A number of downtown businessmen had joined the railroads in opposition; most important, the influential *Globe-Democrat* was less than enthusiastic. Symington warned the project's promoters that unless they could show solid support from St. Louis they didn't have a chance in Washington.[8] Finally, the opposition faded away, and the city's civic leadership united in solid, if not completely enthusiastic, support. Symington was given credit for major help in the effort, and his influence appears to have been crucial in goading the civic leaders into action and in furthering the project's interests in Washington.[9]

Another major project involving the National Park Service was the Ozark National Scenic Riverways. The Ozark Highlands, occupying most of the southern half of Missouri—an area of rare beauty—cried out for protection. The problem was that many people living in the area wanted nothing to do with federal protection. Suspicious of government in general, they were sure that if the feds had anything to do with the region they would lose their rights to hunt and fish. Symington recognized this, but once preservationists had developed some strength, he joined with Senator Edward Long, who had replaced Hennings, in sponsoring a bill in the Senate to create the Ozark Rivers National Monument. Representative Richard Ichord, the project's leading advocate in Washington, had introduced a similar bill in the House. This was pioneering legislation. In addition to the normal skepticism that attaches to something new, the proposal faced highly vocal opposition from hunters in the area. It was clear that unless that opposition could be muffled, the bill would not have a chance. Finally, the National Park Service was persuaded to approve closely controlled hunting in the area, and the bill went through. Symington and Ichord received most of the credit.[10]

Symington also gave vigorous support to the establishment and funding of Wilson's Creek National Battlefield, an important Civil War site. Wilson's Creek was another Missouri project of the National Park Service.

Symington exerted major effort on behalf of water projects in all parts of the state; his papers contain voluminous files of correspondence and reports. Among the most important and protracted of these projects was the Kaysinger Bluff reservoir in western Missouri. Symington, through Fike, worked with the project from the beginning. In particular, when it seemed in danger of falling through the cracks in the Washington bureaucracy, he moved to rescue it. When he learned that the Bureau of the Budget had not included funds for Kaysinger construction in the 1965 budget, he went straight to the White House, with the result that $1 million to begin construction was included in the president's supplementary budget.[11]

An avid sports fan, Symington took great interest in the professional athletic teams in the two major cities. He helped his good friend Sidney Salomon bring the Blues professional hockey team to St. Louis and became a member of the board of the Blues organization. When the Blues played for the Stanley Cup in their first year of competition, he took the floor of the Senate to announce: "St. Louis is now mighty proud of its new champions, a team of character and indomitable courage, a gathering of determined athletes who fill out a worthy triumvirate along with the baseball and football St. Louis Cardinals."[12]

Symington took a special interest in the football Cardinals. The team, moved from Chicago in 1960, never quite caught on in St. Louis. It always played in the shadow of the more established baseball Cardinals. William and Charles Bidwill, the team's owners, were generally unpopular, and rumors that they were thinking of moving the team to Atlanta did nothing to improve their standing. Symington wrote the Bidwills a sharp letter, threatening congressional action if they moved the team. This, along with pressure from the civic leadership, apparently was persuasive; the Big Red remained in St. Louis, at least for a time.[13]

Although important in the St. Louis sports world, Symington, as Bob Broeg, sports editor of the *Post-Dispatch*, put it, was "an even bigger man in Kansas City sports." The issue in Kansas City was professional baseball. Charles O. Finley, owner of the Athletics, was even more unpopular in Kansas City than the Bidwills were in St. Louis. When he persuaded the American League to approve moving the Athletics to Oakland, Kansas City, aghast at the prospect of being without professional baseball, called for help. Symington responded with a vigorous assault on Finley, whom he called "a disgrace," and the American League owners, whom he threatened with a congressional investigation. Unlike many

Missouri projects that were largely turned over to Fike or another staff member, he handled this one himself. At issue was the location of two expansion teams being proposed by the league. Symington insisted that one of them must be in Kansas City. He joined Mayor Ilus Davis and a group of civic leaders at a meeting of league owners in Chicago. As Mayor Davis wrote later, "The most distinguished, persuasive and wrathful of the Kansas City delegation was Senator Stuart Symington. There can be no doubt that his presence and his active participation in Kansas City's case to the owners caused them . . . to grant Kansas City an expansion team franchise . . . to replace the departing Athletics."[14]

Ewing Kauffman, the legendary Kansas City entrepreneur who had built Marion Laboratories into a major drug manufacturer, stepped forward to establish the franchise and bring the Kansas City Royals into being. Opening day, April 8, 1969, was a day of great celebration in Kansas City, and it was a great day for Symington. He was greeted with a standing ovation when Mayor Davis introduced him to throw out the first ball; his pitch was a little weak, but the crowd applauded anyway. Symington then joined Ewing and Muriel Kauffman to watch the Royals defeat the Minnesota Twins, 4 to 3.[15]

All of this provided an auspicious run-up for what proved to be the most difficult campaign of Symington's entire career.

With his stunning upset victory over Kem in 1952, Symington emerged as Missouri's best vote-getter. He was reelected in 1958 with only token opposition; when the Republicans put up a much stronger candidate in 1964, Symington still won easily. He seemingly was invincible. Even so, there were ominous signs on the horizon. The Democrats, who since the days of the New Deal had ruled Missouri virtually as a one-party state, were beginning to lose their hold on the electorate. Eisenhower carried the state in 1952 and 1956, Nixon in 1968. The Democrats were viewed by many as old, tired, and fractious. Governor Warren Hearnes, whose election in 1964 had been applauded by many urban liberals, seemed to be reverting to his Bootheel origins. He and Symington, however, remained close political allies. Jack Flach, a widely read political columnist, described them as constituting a "mutual admiration society."[16] The Republicans, by contrast, were developing a number of attractive young leaders. Chief among them were Christopher (Kit) Bond of Mexico, whose mother was a member of the rich and influential A. P. Green family, and John H. (Jack) Danforth of St. Louis, an heir to the vast Ralston-Purina fortune. Bond was elected state auditor in 1970; Danforth, attorney general in 1968. Both positions were looked upon as stepping stones to higher office, and both Bond and Danforth were obviously ambitious.

Symington for some time had been pessimistic about the Democratic party in Missouri. As early as 1961 he wrote Larry O'Brien, special assistant to Kennedy:

"In Missouri, four of the five largest dailies are Republican. We have two Republican congressmen and—except for farm issues—four Democratic congressmen who could be classed as conservatives."[17]

Despite his gloomy assessment of the Democratic party in Missouri, Symington remained strong in all parts of the state. As 1970 approached, there was never a question but that Symington would run for a fourth term.

In February 1970 the *Post-Dispatch* published a series of four articles on Symington by Washington correspondent Thomas W. Ottenad. Taken together, they provide a good brief biography. The headlines summarize the major themes: "Senator Symington: At Peak Or Near End of Career," "Few Setbacks for Symington," "Symington's Reversal on Military Spending," "Symington Odyssey: From Hawk to Dove." The articles were by no means paeans of praise, but they were basically fair and objective. Early in the series, Ottenad wrote:

> Symington now stands near either the peak or near the end of his career. His influence and stature have been rising in recent years. . . . Whether he will have the chance to climb the mountain is up to the voters of Missouri. In November they will decide whether Symington will have his fourth consecutive term in the United States Senate.[18]

Long before Ottenad's articles were published, Jack Danforth had emerged as the principal threat to Symington's continued career in the Senate. As a popular young attorney general, Danforth was threatening the Hearnes machine in Jefferson City. He spoke in all parts of the state and was universally well received. Tall and somewhat Lincolnesque in appearance, he was a moderate Republican who appealed to many independents who had supported Symington over the years. He had unlimited financial resources. He could be a formidable opponent. In February, while at a meeting in Washington, he told David Bowes, Washington correspondent of the *St. Louis Globe-Democrat*, that he "would love to be in the Senate." When asked about his chances against Symington, he replied, "He's really an unknown quantity. He's never been tested."[19]

Both men easily won nomination in the August 4 primary, and the stage was set for what would be the costliest campaign (to that date) in Missouri's history. The *St. Louis Globe-Democrat* ran a story headed "How Millionaires Campaign." The Symington campaign had plenty of money, but it was an exaggeration to put his resources in the same league with Danforth's. Symington expected that Danforth, in addition to his own money, would have the help of many traditionally Republican business leaders as well as the Republican National Committee.[20] He was disappointed, however, when Donald Douglas, vice president of McDonnell Douglas and Danforth's fund-raising chairman, sent "thousands" of letters to Missouri businessmen soliciting contributions for the Danforth campaign. They began with, "If you are like a lot of other Missouri businessmen I know, you probably feel like a forgotten man most of the time. Forgotten by those who are supposed to represent your interests in Washington." Without mentioning Symington by name, the letter was a thinly veiled attack on Symington's record. Symington was shocked, hurt, and angry, but he didn't reply.[21] He had no need to. His longtime friend Eugene Zuckert, who had been secretary of the air force in both the Kennedy and Johnson administrations, published a vigorous defense of the senator and his staff. He gave Symington much credit for the air force decision to purchase the F-4 Phantom jet, up to that time used only by the navy. He continued: "I know of my own knowledge how vigorous were his representations to me personally and in Senate committee hearings. He was an effective advocate in the lengthy debate out of which resulted the purchase by the Air Force of over 2,000 of the F-4 and reconnaissance version of the airplane." Zuckert also disclosed that Symington had successfully opposed the establishment of a new F-4 plant in another state.[22] Zuckert's letter blunted Douglas's appeal, but Symington, ever sensitive to what he perceived as unfair criticism, never forgot the incident, even though he continued to push the interests of McDonnell Douglas in Washington.

Danforth opened his campaign by calling Symington's record "a disgrace." He challenged Symington to a series of debates, "so the voters will clearly know how we stand on the vital issues facing this country."[23] Symington, running on his record, not only refused the challenge, he rarely mentioned Danforth's name. Jim Symington, running for reelection from Missouri's Second District, felt no such inhibitions. He frequently challenged the veracity of Danforth's charges, and in a hard-hitting, much-quoted speech before the Springfield Kiwanis Club, contrasted Danforth's record with that of his father, concluding with:

> Gentlemen, the question comes down to this: Which candidate can best carry the load for Missouri over the next six mountainous years? As you ponder the matter, bear in mind the scripture "Be ye doers of the word and not hearers only, lest ye deceive yourselves." The choice is clearly between a proven doer of your words and a latter day hearer only. Let's not deceive ourselves.[24]

Danforth's problem, as frequently mentioned in the press, was that he had no real issues. There was little discernible difference in Symington's and Danforth's views on basic issues of interest to Missourians: agriculture, economy in government, federal expenditures in Missouri, the war in Vietnam, to name a few. In addition, both were Yale men, both Episcopalians, and both from St. Louis County. As a result, Danforth resorted increasingly to ad hominem attacks, calling Symington a "do-nothing senator," a "modern Rip Van Winkle, asleep for 18 years." He charged that Symington had missed eighty-six roll calls in the current session of Congress. This was technically true, but it did not get very far. The Symington campaign made public a letter from Mike Mansfield, the Senate majority leader, lamenting the "partisan attack" on Symington's voting record. Mansfield pointed out that an unusual number of votes had occurred during December when Symington had been absent with Eve, who had undergone two serious operations. Mansfield noted that none of the votes were on major issues, and Symington had arranged for pairs on most of them. He wrote: "I am disturbed and distressed at this attack. . . . It is ironic, indeed, that you, more than any other senator I can recall, have been most insistent about being present to vote on matters affecting the State of Missouri and the Nation as a whole."[25]

As the campaign wore on, Danforth's attacks became more strident, and on some issues he moved to the right. On the Vietnam War, for example, he insisted that he still favored an early withdrawal, but he opposed both the McGovern-Hatfield and Cooper-Church amendments for ending the war (which Symington supported) as being "Anti-Nixon." He made a point of endorsing Nixon's economic program and in other ways sought to identify himself with the president, who made a trip to the state to support his campaign, but nothing seemed to take hold. The Danforth camp made an effort to link Symington with the Democratic machine that had controlled state politics for years and that had become increasingly vulnerable to charges of corruption. The trouble with this, as R. W. Apple suggested in the *New York Times,* was that "Mr. Symington has no direct connection with any of this—indeed, he has held himself more aloof from state politics than most three-term senators."[26]

Danforth's campaign took on some of the attributes of a crusade—some cynics called it "the children's crusade"—but to slight avail. As the calendar moved toward election day, the polls showed Symington with a comfortable lead. The majority of the state's newspapers, including all of the big-city dailies, urged his reelection. The *Post-Dispatch,* a frequent critic, wrote, "To replace Senator Symington with Mr. Danforth would be to exchange a man with important power in the most critical areas of national policy for one who, whatever his merits, would have but minor impact on the course of events." The *Globe-Democrat* called Symington "One of the most distinguished, esteemed and knowledgeable members of the United States Senate." Across the state, the *Kansas City Star* wrote: "Although the choice is a difficult one, The Star believes that Senator Symington has earned the right to a fourth term. In the Senate, he has addressed himself to many of the critical issues facing the nation, while at the same time he has been an effective representative of his home state. His seniority on three powerful Senate committees (armed forces, foreign affairs, and space) cannot be overlooked." Many television and radio stations joined the chorus, as did most of the smaller dailies and country weeklies.[27]

Symington won reelection by forty-three thousand votes, a comfortable margin, but far from the landslide he had achieved in earlier contests. Symington's age may have been a factor—his sixty-nine years stood in marked contrast to Danforth's thirty-four—and the perceived decline of the Democratic party may have contributed as well. The most important factor probably was resurgent Republicanism, led by extremely attractive young candidates. Kit Bond, who would become governor and, later, senator, defeated Haskell Holman, who in the minds of many voters epitomized the Democratic machine, for the position of state auditor. For Symington, the campaign had been but an interruption in his effort to uncover the story of American military commitments abroad. He resumed that effort with renewed enthusiasm.

31

The Search for Peace

DURING HIS last term in the Senate, Symington was almost wholly preoccupied with efforts to reduce armaments and achieve a degree of international stability. During his first term he had been recognized as a superhawk; in his last he was a leading Senate dove. "It's not that you switch; it's that you learn," he told the noted foreign correspondent Flora Lewis. She added: "What Symington . . . learned . . . changed him from an ardent advocate of military supremacy to an advocate of retrenchment, from a cold warrior to a critic of over commitment, from a hawk to a dove."[1]

Symington was by no means a pacifist and he was hardly an internationalist, but as he had become disillusioned with the war in Vietnam he had lost faith in the ability of the United States to work its way in the world. The country could not afford the effort. He used to complain that Eisenhower and even his old boss Harry Truman were sacrificing defense to the budget. Now he argued that a truly adequate defense depended on a sound economy. He scrutinized defense budgets as never before, particularly requests for new weapons systems, and his long-held fears that the dollar drain resulting from trying to defend the free world would bankrupt the country frequently surfaced in his thinking. At the same time, he remained solicitous of the armed forces, and particularly of the air force. In 1972 he was described as "still . . . [the air force's] most influential booster."[2]

He frequently reminded listeners that while an adequate defense structure was of prime importance, true national security required, in addition, a viable economy with a sound dollar, and "credibility, faith of the people in their government."[3] The latter two were undermined in Vietnam, and the Nixon administration, with its penchant for secrecy, continued the erosion.

Symington's views were informed by extensive travel. Indeed, as a traveling senator he had few peers. Fairly early in his last term, "because of conflicting reports about United States economic, political and military activities abroad, plus some disturbing rumors about how we were handling the stockpiling of nuclear weapons . . . ,"[4] he decided to take a trip around the world. It was almost a solo adventure. Eve was with him most of the way; they were accompanied by Arthur Kuhl, chief clerk of the Senate Foreign Relations Committee, and Colonel H. J. Anderson of the air force. They visited thirteen countries in the Far East, the Middle East, and Europe, beginning in Japan and ending in Germany. In each country he visited with senior American military and diplomatic officials and with heads of state, most of whom he knew.[5] He had high praise for the Americans he encountered, but severe criticism for some of the policies they were forced to try to implement. The renewed bombing of North Vietnam, under way while he was in Saigon, was destroying "the single remaining hope for successful outcome, . . . the return of our POW's . . ." He reported with regret that "the political, economic and military posture of the United States has never been lower around the world than it is today. Our friends are few indeed, at a time when we find ourselves increasingly in need of friends; and those in open opposition to our policies, already many, are increasing in number."[6]

Reducing the number of U.S. troops in Europe offered an effective way to help redirect expenditures. Symington had long advocated such a course. Indeed, he had become its leading proponent in the Senate. In 1966 he initiated an effort in the Democratic policy committee that resulted in a motion introduced by Majority Leader Mansfield for a "sense of the Senate" resolution that there should be a "substantial reduction" in the number of U.S. troops under NATO. The Johnson administration immediately signaled its opposition. Republicans and many Democrats, irritated by the action of the policy committee in bringing the resolution directly to the Senate rather than giving it to a committee, spoke out in opposition. Mansfield did not push the matter, and it was left to Symington to keep the issue alive. Instead of a resolution expressing the sense of the Senate, he introduced an amendment to the defense procurement bill that would prohibit use of the funds after December 31, 1968, to support troops in Europe. This effort, though it had the support of such diverse members of the Senate as James Pearson of Kansas and Frank Church of Idaho, attracted little general support. To many it seemed too drastic; the Soviet intervention in Czechoslovakia in August dramatized the need to maintain a strong position in Europe. Moreover, as Symington himself admitted, the procurement bill was not a good place to discuss the issue. He withdrew the amendment, but served notice that he did not consider the issue dead. He offered an amendment to the defense appropriation bill providing that after December 31, 1968, funds could not be used to support more than fifty thousand troops in Europe. This, like his earlier effort, won praise but little support. Despite these setbacks, Symington continued to oppose expansion of the country's European effort.[7]

For Symington, the issue was cost and the impact of American commitments on the nation's economy. He had long worried about the balance of payments problem and the impact of a constantly growing unfavorable balance on the nation's economy. This was a major reason for his opposition to continuing the war in Vietnam, and would become the focus of his hearings on U.S. commitments abroad. He came to be recognized as the "most representative" of that group of anti-European senators who were motivated primarily by the cost of European involvement.[8]

The issue did not win Symington many friends in Missouri. The agricultural and aerospace interests in the state favored measures that would create markets; most Missourians were indifferent. Additionally, many of his friends in the "Eastern Establishment" viewed his efforts with dismay. John J. McCloy wrote that while he had "the greatest respect and admiration" for Symington's "patriotism and knowledge of military affairs," his efforts were "ignoring forces and risking dangers that are threatening our security and that of the free world." Symington, responding with obvious irritation, reminded McCloy that when he and others were "directing things down here some years ago, America's physical condition was impregnable . . . ," but now things were different. Russia had the bomb, and the war in Vietnam was costing "over two and a half billion dollars a month." Moreover, and "perhaps saddest of all . . . Vietnam is preventing us from achieving a better relationship with the Soviet Union, the only nation in the world of today that could destroy the United States." He had "the greatest affection" for Europe, "once went to school there . . . , but if the value of the dollar is destroyed because of Federal spending, nothing could be worse for . . . Europe as well as ourselves."[9]

In November 1972, Symington attended a NATO session in Bonn, after which he joined a bipartisan group of senators on a visit to Yugoslavia, Bulgaria, Romania, and Czechoslovakia. His report did not mention the question of troops in Europe except by implication. He thought the prospect bright for détente between East and West, and this, of course, would reduce the need for U.S. troops on the continent. As American military involvement in southeast Asia finally appeared to be ending, he suggested that the time was ripe for the Senate to study the relationship between military and economic questions in Europe. He persuaded Fulbright to authorize the despatch of Lowenstein and Moose to Europe for an on-the-spot study.[10]

The two men returned with startling news: the United States not only had a large stock of nuclear weapons deployed in Europe (a fact which in itself had been only vaguely understood in the United States, even in Congress) but also had agreed on a strategy that would coordinate the use of nuclear weapons in Europe with those of the United States stationed outside Europe. Symington, in releasing a heavily censored version of the report, said, "The relationship of the United States with its European allies is presently under greater stress than at any time in the recent past." Differences over burden-sharing were exacerbated by the very existence of nuclear weapons. At the request of Maryland Democrat Charles Mathais, a supporter of troop reduction, the report's conclusions were printed in the *Congressional Record*.[11] Symington scheduled hearings for the second and third week in February, inviting both Kissinger and Schlesinger to appear. For some reason, the hearings were not held.

Symington's concern about the cost of maintaining troops in Europe extended to the whole field of foreign aid. He had long been uneasy about the cost of foreign aid and its impact on domestic needs. He had gone along, albeit reluctantly, with the Kennedy foreign aid program. He was less supportive of Johnson's efforts. Foreign aid was an integral part of the nation's effort in Vietnam, and a significant component of its cost. As he became increasingly preoccupied with the deficit, he increased his opposition to foreign aid in general. In 1972, for example, he offered strong support to an effort by West Virginia Democrat Robert Byrd to reduce an appropriation that would enable the Export-Import Bank to increase its loans to Latin American countries. His argument reflected the evolution of his opposition to any kind of foreign aid, opposition grounded in the growing deficit. He said, "The past is past, but now we have a different position . . . , which nevertheless would appear to be ignored by those who propose this bill." The "different position" resulted from the growing deficit. In the past two decades there had been "16 years of deficits and 4 years of surpluses, . . . a total red ink net of $159.8 billion." These, he argued, "were terrifying figures. . . . We now know that our central cities, our urban, suburban and rural areas are badly in need of money to maintain a decent standard of living. . . . I would earnestly hope that . . . we would pay less attention to the problems of other nations . . . and more attention to the problems of the people of the United States."[12]

Byrd's amendment was defeated by a substantial bipartisan majority.[13] Symington maintained his opposition to increases in foreign aid throughout the remainder of his term. The single exception was Israel. Symington frequently reminded people that he had been secretary of the air force when President Truman recognized the State of Israel, thus making possible its existence, and the United States had an obligation to help Israel defend itself.[14] He saw Israel as the bastion of democracy in the Middle East, and a protector of America's access to oil. As chairman of the Subcommittee on Near Eastern and South Asian Affairs of the Senate Foreign Relations Committee, he usually visited Israel on his return from the Far East. He developed cordial relationships with various Israeli leaders, especially Golda Meier, Moshe Dayan, and Rabbi Chaim Herzog. He had great admiration for the tiny nation's fierce independence and fighting spirit. He was unstinting in his praise of the Israeli air force.

Symington became closely involved in the controversy over selling planes to Israel during the troubles with Egypt, joining Senators Jacob Javits and Abraham Ribicoff in protesting the Nixon administration's refusal to continue the sale of Phantom jets to Israel. He defended Israel as "one of the few countries in the world today resisting successfully Communist arms and Communist satellite aggression without the support of American troops." The administration's refusal to supply Israel with the planes it needed was "incredible."[15] The Javits resolution passed by an overwhelming majority, but it did not change American policy.

In addition to his leading role in trying to push the Javits resolution, Symington remained much in the news because of his charge that Kissinger had replaced Rogers as de facto secretary of state. Seymour Hersh suggests that "Symington's criticism of Rogers, which was really an indictment of the administration's foreign policy procedures, undoubtedly was a factor in Nixon's decision to see—for at least a few weeks—whether a Middle East compromise was possible."[16]

Despite his disenchantment with foreign aid, Symington remained supportive of the United Nations. Two terms as a member of the U.S. delegation to the General Assembly (the twenty-third session in 1968, and the twenty-ninth in 1974) enhanced his understanding and appreciation of the work of the international body. He enjoyed the social life, particularly in 1974 when Henry Kissinger was secretary of state, but the experience was much more than a round of parties. He took seriously the work of the committees to which he was assigned and did not hesitate to express his own views. He criticized, for example, the United States' opposition to the admission of the People's Republic of China, which he called "unrealistic." In his report on the twenty-third session, he wrote that "a change in our China policy is long overdue. . . . there is an aspect of incredibility in going on, year after year, decade after decade, without having any relationship of any kind with the world's largest populated country."[17]

Speaking before the "First Committee" in 1974, he took a position on nuclear proliferation considerably in advance of the official U.S. position. Charles Yost, president of the National Committee on United States–China Relations, wrote, "I personally think that it is important, from every point of view, that our public members occasionally take an independent stand, particularly when it is so thoroughly justified as it was in the present case." Kissinger apparently felt the same way. In a "Dear Stu" letter of thanks for his service, he wrote, "Your work on the First Committee during the disarmament debates was particularly creative and well-received."[18]

Symington's growing disillusionment with the military expressed itself with particular force in the debate over the anti-ballistic missile (ABM). Department of Defense Secretary McNamara had become intrigued with the idea of building a nuclear shield to defend the United States from a Soviet missile attack. Initially the thought was to protect the major cities, but when this appeared to be technologically impracticable, Department of Defense strategists shifted their emphasis to protecting the ICBM sites in various parts of the country. One of these sites was operated by troops from Whiteman Air Force Base near Sedalia, Missouri. Symington's influence had been important in the air force decision to locate an ICBM site at Whiteman, and he might have been expected to favor anything that would protect the site. By 1968, however, largely through discussions with Wolfgang Panofsky of Stanford University and Jerome Wiesner of MIT, he had become convinced that the ABM would not work, that it was little more than a multi-billion-dollar boondoggle.[19] He joined a bipartisan group of antiwar senators in trying to develop a strategy to derail what seemed to be a headlong rush to develop an ABM.[20]

By the time McNamara left office he had lost much of his enthusiasm for the ABM, and Clifford, possibly because of Symington's influence, gave it little support. With Nixon, however, everything changed. Shortly after taking office, he made it clear that his administration would push to develop an improved ABM, with particular emphasis on protecting ICBM sites, such as the one at Whiteman. Close examination, however, revealed that Safeguard, the proposed new version, was physically the same system as the old Sentinel.[21]

Symington helped lead the attack on Safeguard. He told Secretary of Defense Melvin Laird, who had argued before the Senate Armed Services Committee that Safeguard was necessary to preserve the nuclear balance of power, that deployment of the system would be "a grave mistake." He was not impressed with the argument that Safeguard was needed as protection against a Soviet threat when it had been put forward initially to counter a possible threat from the Chinese. Symington's position was supported by a bipartisan minority, but the Armed Services Committee approved going forward with Safeguard by a vote of 10 to 7.[22]

Symington nevertheless continued to press the attack—in committees, on the Senate floor, on television, and in newspapers and magazines. His efforts disturbed many of his supporters. The usually supportive *St. Louis Globe-Democrat* accused Symington, along with Senator Fulbright, of waging a "Reckless

Anti-ABM Campaign." On the other hand, the *Post-Dispatch* commented, "Senator Symington, one of the most knowledgeable men in the Senate when it comes to missiles, is not fooled by this [Pentagon] propaganda."[23]

The ABM did not figure much in the 1970 campaign that gave Symington a fourth term. After the election Symington promised to take a more active lead in the ABM opposition in the Senate, but as John Finney observed in the *New York Times,* the opposition was unorganized, and there was "a notable lack of enthusiasm over the prospect of going through another prolonged, bruising debate, repeating many of the same arguments and then probably once again going down to defeat."[24]

Symington might have taken an active part in organizing the opposition. Instead, he chose to continue largely on his own, while working closely with other ABM opponents on both sides of the aisle, notably Democrats Philip Hart of Michigan, Frank Church of Idaho, and George McGovern of South Dakota, and Republicans John Sherman Cooper of Kentucky and Charles Percy of Illinois. He continued to speak out. On June 30, 1971, he told the Senate that the ABM was "the greatest single boondoggle that I have seen since I have been in government—and that is saying a lot." The United States was trying to defend itself "by getting behind a modern technological Maginot line, the same thing could well happen to this country as happened to France." He tried to persuade Stennis that Safeguard was a poor investment, particularly as a means of defending SAC's bomber bases. He wrote Stennis that he had specifically asked the air force and had been told that "so far as SAC is concerned, Safeguard is not necessary." Seeking a compromise, Symington introduced an amendment limiting the expansion of ABM to two sites as something that might have a chance of adoption and would have no adverse effect on the Strategic Arms Limitation Talks (SALT) being pursued by the administration.[25]

Symington, as much as any member of the Senate, remained alert to the nation's total defense needs. Had he thought the ABM system would work and would contribute to getting an arms limitation treaty, he might have gone along with it, despite its staggering costs. He was convinced, however, that it would do neither. He became one of the leading supporters of the anti-ABM treaty that grew out of the strategic arms limitations talks.

Similarly, as he worked through Defense Department requests in the early 1970s, he rigorously applied a cost-benefit test to each proposed new weapons system. He remained particularly alert to competing requests from the services. A case in point involved the navy's F-14 fighter, manufactured by the Lockheed Corporation of California, and the air force's F-15, produced by McDonnell Douglas in St. Louis. His air force loyalties and his concern for St. Louis industry aside, conversations with "scores of pilots in Southeast Asia" had convinced him that "the F-14 just can't hack it as a fighter."[26]

Overall, he persisted in his efforts to keep the defense budgets in check, particularly in the area of new weapons development. He tried unsuccessfully to slow the development of TRIDENT, the navy's new submarine program being put forward as a replacement for POLARIS, the missile-carrying vessel that was the backbone of the navy's submarine fleet. In his air force days, Symington would almost automatically have questioned large new expenditures requested by the navy, but in the 1970s he could speak as one "who for many years has been a strong proponent of this nation's submarine program." He was prepared to do what was necessary to develop the submarine fleet and could envision that the time might come when he could support the development of TRIDENT, but that time had not arrived. The navy had not convinced him and other skeptics that it was prepared to spend development money wisely. Admiral Elmo Zumwalt, chief of naval operations, who was pushing hard for TRIDENT, did not make a particularly convincing case for rapidly accelerating the program.[27]

Symington argued vigorously for an amendment introduced by Senator Lloyd Bentsen of Texas to slow down the development of TRIDENT. When that failed on a tie vote, Bentsen tried to amend the appropriations bill on the Senate floor, but that also failed, 47 to 39. Symington argued vigorously for the amendment. He praised Department of Defense Secretary Melvin Laird for his policy of "fly before buy" with respect to new weapons systems and warned that the decision to accelerate the development of TRIDENT represented "a major violation" of that policy. Bentsen, in thanking Symington for his "tremendous help," wrote, "Your experience and advice were invaluable and made a significant difference, I am sure, in achieving such a close vote." After the vote, Symington charged that the Senate, by refusing to support the Bentsen amendment, had "repudiated an in-depth study by one of its own subcommittees [whose recommendations] . . . were countered by a telephone call, several letters and some personal visits to key members of the Senate from outside officials with an axe to grind." Characteristically, Symington did not name names, but he probably was referring to David Packard, former deputy secretary of defense, and Admiral Hyman Rickover, "father" of the nuclear submarine.[28]

Symington agreed with the minority of the Senate Armed Services Committee that "A more orderly development of TRIDENT enhances our bargaining position at SALT. The Soviets must be more concerned about a reliable and more thoroughly proven TRIDENT that will result from the careful development of the system than they will be by the folly of massive monies spent helter skelter." The result of the minority plan would be "an imposing, dynamic TRIDENT program" that would "insure that our military position at SALT II will be a powerful incentive for the Soviets to come to a serious and secure agreement."[29]

Central to Symington's thinking about defense and disarmament was his fear of nuclear proliferation. He had been involved with nuclear weapons almost from the end of World War II. As assistant secretary of war for air, he had observed the overpowering effectiveness of the atomic bomb in the Bikini tests; as secretary of the air force, he had played a key role in decisions regarding the atomic bomb; as a member of the Senate Committee on Aeronautics and Space Sciences, he had participated in formulating legislative policy involving space and nuclear weapons, and beginning in 1973 he served on the joint Senate and House Committee. His views on nuclear weapons evolved along with his overall views on disarmament and defense.

By his last term Symington was firmly convinced that the overriding need of the country was to stop or at least slow the proliferation of nuclear weapons. At the same time, as a member of the Aeronautics and Space Committee, he gave strong support to NASA initiatives. He was particularly enthusiastic about the space shuttle.[30]

But his attention increasingly focused on nuclear weapons; he used his chairmanship of the Subcommittee on Security Agreements and Commitments Abroad to probe nuclear development and specifically the deployment abroad of nuclear weapons. This had been a central purpose of his 1971 trip around the world, and it continued to be a major preoccupation.

Always suspicious of executive secrecy, he felt that the "excessive" secrecy which shrouded nuclear developments seriously impeded congressional oversight and was not in the nation's best interests.[31] As chairman of the Subcommittee on Military Applications of the Joint Committee on Atomic Energy, he asked the Atomic Energy Commission to declassify as much of the subcommittee's hearings as possible. In doing so, he said, "Although this is the first time information of this character has been released to the public, we believe additional data should have been declassified for publication." When he released the second part of the hearing, he said, "Although some vital information is deleted which should be made public, we believe said hearings are another important step toward educating the American public to this new and relatively unknown force which is bound to affect the future of civilization—the nuclear force."[32]

Symington also used the Foreign Relations Subcommittee on U.S. Security Agreements and Commitments Abroad to try to educate his colleagues and the country at large on nuclear weapons and their effect on foreign policy. In the spring of 1974 his subcommittee and the Subcommittee on Arms Control, International Law and Organizations chaired by Edmund Muskie held a series of open joint hearings on "Nuclear Weapons and Foreign Policy." "The ever present danger to the world of a nuclear holocaust," Symington said, "is so horrendous that few of us can bring ourselves to think about it. Meanwhile, we go on developing and deploying more nuclear weapons—this despite the fact that we already have enough intercontinental nuclear warheads to deliver 150 missiles or bombs on the fifty leading Soviet cities while the Soviets can deliver only fifty warheads on each of our fifty leading cities."[33]

The subcommittee called a number of academic experts and foreign officials, Lowenstein and Moose described what they had found on earlier visits, and the hearings concluded with Secretary of Defense James Schlesinger. Symington pushed Schlesinger on the number and kind of nuclear weapons the United States had in Europe, but could not get him to agree that the nation was overcommitted.[34]

As much as he worried about the nation's commitments and the security of its atomic stockpile, Symington worried even more about the proliferation of nuclear weapons. Indeed, he saw it as "the greatest danger facing the world today."[35] He consistently supported international efforts to restrict the spread of nuclear weapons. The SALT negotiations between the United States and the Soviet Union began in 1969 and resulted in an accord, signed on May 26, 1972, consisting of an ABM treaty and an interim agreement on the limitation of strategic offensive arms.

Symington supported the basic objectives of SALT regarding ABM. After all, he had long opposed the program. He was not at all pleased, however, with the way in which the Nixon administration was conducting the negotiations. In April of 1971 he visited the American delegation in Vienna, site of the talks. When he returned, he said that he had "lost all hope" for an agreement. He charged the administration was "planning deliberately not to have any arms control agreement at all." While supportive of efforts to achieve arms control, Symington had trouble with the secrecy that characterized the actions of the Nixon and Ford administrations. He expressed dismay when the United States entered into a secret agreement with the Soviet Union, Britain, France, Canada, West Germany, and Japan intended to retard the spread of nuclear weapons. In two days of hearings before the Arms Control Subcommittee of the Senate Foreign Relations Committee, he tried without success to pry out of representatives of the State Department the terms of the agreement or even the precise identity of the signatories.[36]

A few weeks later he spoke in the Senate on "The Nuclear March to Armageddon." Calling attention to the fact that for some years he had been reminding the Senate that "the greatest security problem facing the United States and the world today" was "the steady increase in the number of nations capable of building nuclear weapons." Unless something were done there would soon be many more.

The basic problem lay with the exporting nations. Under the atoms-for-peace initiative, "nuclear know-how and equipment . . . [had] been spread throughout the world. Many of the nations we have helped are today themselves nuclear exporters; and unfortunately some of their policies . . . have not been as restrictive as ours." The only hope for a solution lay in open discussion of the issues involved. "All we hear about today, however, are secret nuclear meetings, secret nuclear deals, inadequate controls—policies which, in themselves, would appear to defeat the very purpose of preventing further nuclear proliferation."[37]

As one of his last legislative efforts, Symington introduced an amendment to the 1976 foreign aid bill that would cut off all aid to any country which sold or bought facilities for enriching or reprocessing nuclear fuel unless it agreed to submit the facilities to inspection by the International Atomic Energy Agency and to subject them "to any multi-national controls that may come into being in the future." The Ford administration opposed the amendment on the grounds that more could be achieved with quiet (presumably secret) diplomacy. Despite this, the amendment passed, and it seems to have contributed to modifying administration behavior. In response to a letter from Symington and members of the Arms Control Subcommittee (both Republicans and Democrats) expressing concern about the negotiations between the Federal Republic of Germany and Iran to conclude a nuclear cooperation agreement, Secretary of State Kissinger assured Symington that the concerns he and his colleagues had expressed were being dealt with.[38]

Symington supported a plan proposed by Harold Agnew, director of Los Alamos Scientific Laboratory, to lease rather than sell nuclear fuel, thus keeping control of it. "Taking the lead in curbing nuclear proliferation is a difficult task," he said in the Senate, "but inasmuch as we, in effect, originated the current spread of nuclear power throughout the world, it would seem we have a special responsibility to insure that this unprecedented new power will be used for peaceful purposes only."[39]

Symington made no effort to advance the idea through legislation. Indeed, he did not speak again in the Senate on the issue. In October of 1976 he gave a talk to the arms control seminar at the program for science and international affairs at Harvard, "The Washington Nuclear Mess." It summed up the failure of a generation:

> When I first came to the Senate back in 1953 and was placed on the Armed Services Committee, I observed to the Chairman . . . that my years in the Pentagon as Secretary of the Air Force had convinced me that nuclear power would be important if not decisive to America's future security. The Chairman's reply just about summed up much of why we face an incredible disorganization and lack of control in the nuclear field today. He said, "That subject is so secret I do not want to know anything about it."

. . . this has been that committee's attitude over the years, and it could well have cost the American taxpayer many billions of dollars. . . .

Control over nuclear energy is slipping at both the national and international levels. Now and then we hear of a plan proposed, agencies reshuffled, meetings held, speeches made—all of which give the illusion of progress. We know of secret meetings held among several nuclear supplier nations, and of vague "principles" of nuclear commerce they have presumably agreed upon; but it is a fact that no one has signed any concrete agreement addressing itself to the fundamental question of who is to control the nuclear fuel cycle and how. . . .

The problem of nuclear proliferation which now confronts us will not be easily solved. It is now all too clear, however, that we must do our best to find solutions. If we do not, the arrival of Armageddon is only a question of time.[40]

32

The Final Years

ON APRIL 22, 1975, Stuart Symington told a hastily organized press conference in the Chase–Park Plaza Hotel in St. Louis that he would not be a candidate for reelection in 1976. Typically, he did not give many reasons. He said, "It is a sad day . . . but a realistic day for me." He continued:

> As the people of my state well know, during all of my previous campaigns, as well as in subsequent Senate operations, my wife Eve was my political partner, her efforts and wise counsel being of very great assistance to me; and it is no secret to my friends that her loss has had a major impact on my desire to continue in the Senate.

He paid tribute to Stanley Fike and his "superb staff" and sat down.[1]

The announcement took almost everyone by surprise—his staff, his close associates, and even his family.[2] He had repeatedly responded in the affirmative to questions about his candidacy in 1976. Why this sudden change?

Eve's death, as he stated, surely was an important factor, but there were other reasons. The Symington tide in the state's Democratic party was beginning to ebb, and with the announcement by former Governor Warren Hearnes that he would be a candidate, Symington would face serious opposition in the primary for the first time since 1952. Even if he won the nomination, reelection was far from certain. Attorney General Jack Danforth, who had come close to unseating Symington in 1970, was almost sure to run; buoyed by resurgent Republicanism in the state, he could well emerge the victor this time. Finally, Symington, if re-elected, would be eighty years old by the time his fifth term ended, and his health was not the best. It was understandable that he did not want to go through another grueling campaign.[3]

The press, looking ahead, immediately started to speculate on possible Democratic candidates. Jim Symington, in his fourth term as representative from the Second District, was almost sure to file, as was Jerry Litton, the young second-term congressman from the Sixth District in northwest Missouri who had been active in Symington's presidential campaign. Both men filed, as did Mayor Charles Wheeler of Kansas City. Jim, outspent by both Litton and Hearnes, ran third, being narrowly bested by Hearnes, who lost to Litton by al-most a two-to-one margin.[4]

Newspapers large and small, from across the state and nation, noted Syming-ton's decision and wrote generally favorable editorials on his career. Letters from high government and business officials, celebrities, and common folk poured in. A poorly typed letter from St. Louis helps explain Symington's longtime hold on Missouri voters:

> I know I speak for all the poor, the disable [*sic*] and all the little people of our State when I say that all our hearts are sadden [*sic*] as well as bewil-dered at your announcement of your retirement.
> It will be a great loss, not only to the old and poor, but to all the people of Missouri when your term is ended.

On the morning after Symington's announcement, Fike typed out a memo to his boss: "Senator: This morning begins a new chapter in your life, and also in mine. For the first time in more than 24 years we don't have to be conscious of your (our) next election." He detailed some of Symington's accomplishments in Missouri and the nation. "What a magnificent career you have had," he wrote, "but your greatest contributions, of most lasting value could be ahead. And I be-lieve they will be."[5]

Although his final year in the Senate hardly lived up to Fike's prophecy, Symington continued his energetic interest in the search for peace, and particu-larly in preventing the spread of nuclear weapons. As chairman of the Arms Control Subcommittee of the Senate Foreign Relations Committee, he focused much of his attention on negotiations between various nuclear powers and non-nuclear nations regarding the transfer of nuclear technology. Such transfers, sanctioned by the "Atoms for Peace" program, could, Symington felt, result in the transfer, inadvertently or deliberately, of sensitive technologies such as ura-nium enrichment or chemical reprocessing. He expressed dissatisfaction with what he knew about the provisions of a "secret" pact that the United States worked out with the other nuclear powers after eight months of closed-door discussions in London. He did not like the cloak of secrecy thrown over the whole matter, and from what he knew he doubted the efficacy of the pact.[6]

As what was described as his "swan song," Symington called a special meeting of the Arms Control Subcommittee of the Senate Foreign Relations Committee on November 8 to consider "by far the most important subject in the world today," the worldwide arms race. Gunnar Myrdal, the famous Swedish writer and advocate of disarmament, was the only witness. Despite Myrdal's fame, the hearing received little notice. Congress was not in session, New Jersey Republican Clifford Case was the only other lawmaker present, and very few reporters were around. The hearing provided Symington a final chance to air his views in an official context and to explain once again his conversion from a big-bomber man to the Senate's most vocal advocate of disarmament. He had become disillusioned with SALT, and applauded Myrdal's description of it as "not much but an institutionalization of the arms race."[7]

In another area, Symington took the lead in the successful effort, initiated by former Secretary of the Treasury Snyder, to establish and fund the Harry S. Truman Scholarship Foundation to provide graduate or professional scholarships to one person from each state who intended to engage in some sort of public service after graduation. Indeed, it was Symington who first suggested the scholarship idea to Snyder. Also, in a typically gracious gesture, Symington introduced and supported Rosemary Ginn, Republican national committeewoman for Missouri, whom President Ford had nominated to be ambassador to Luxembourg.[8]

As the second session of the Ninety-fourth Congress came to a close, the tributes began pouring in. Thomas Eagleton and Clifford organized an informal luncheon in Symington's honor, held in "a historic Senate hideaway" near the office of Senator Warren Magnuson. As Dean Reed described it in the *St. Louis Globe-Democrat*:

> They started arriving a few minutes after noon Wednesday, those giants of the U.S. Senate.
> They were Jackson and Stennis, Humphrey and Scott, Church, Sparkman, Case, Byrd, Magnuson, and other ranking leaders—all members not only of what Clark Clifford called "the world's greatest deliberative body," but of the Senate's heart, its establishment.
> . . . they were gathering not so much to bid farewell but to salute personally one of their own stalwarts. . . .

It was a convivial affair, with the wine flowing freely. Eagleton had said that there should be no speeches, except, perhaps, by Symington. All present appeared to be observing Eagleton's injunction except Hubert Humphrey, who arrived late. With Humphrey leading the way, "there began a flow of praise that . . . [was] expected to last at least two days."[9]

Because so many dignitaries not members of the Senate wished to participate either in person or by letter, the opening session of the Senate on Thursday, September 27, was advanced from 10 A.M. to 8:30. The chamber resounded with high-flown oratory as senator after senator, from both sides of the aisle, rose to pay tribute to their departing colleague. Many cited the importance of his prior experience in business and government, and of his unique role as the only senator to serve on both the Committees on Armed Services and International Relations; others, his efforts to end the war in Vietnam, to eliminate secrecy in government, and to maintain a strong economy. A few mentioned his fight against McCarthyism. Almost all spoke of his hard work, his gracious manner, and his integrity.

Democratic members of the House of Representatives from Missouri heaped praise on the senior member of the state's delegation. Senator Eagleton read into the record letters from senators who could not be present, and from important people outside the Senate: President Ford, Presidential Candidate Jimmy Carter, Vice President Nelson Rockefeller, Secretary of State Henry Kissinger, former Secretaries of State William Rogers and Dean Rusk, the Missouri federal judges who owed their appointments primarily to Senator Symington, and many others.

In a short response, Symington expressed thanks for "these undeserved but kind remarks" and went on to say:

> I am especially grateful to my colleague from Missouri, Senator Tom Eagleton. Our relationship in the 8 years he has been in the Senate has been that of a younger brother. I could not wish for more friendship and understanding than he has given me. . . .
>
> I would also express deep gratitude to my staff, above all to Stanley Fike, possibly the most popular man in Missouri, my administrative assistant for every day I have been in the Senate; and to his superb wife, Mildred, for putting up with his consistent long hours in the office. Stan has brought together something that really is not an organization, rather what might appropriately be called a happy family. . . . The respect and admiration for Stan back in my state have made it possible for me to do much more work in committees that have been mentioned, because all Missourians knew that when they talked to him they were, in effect talking to me. . . .
>
> Much of the interest in continuing my political life left when I lost the gracious lady many people have been so kind as to mention this morning; and in any case, as our majority leader, Senator Mansfield, recently said, "There is a time to stay and a time to go." I feel my time has come.[10]

Symington resigned from the Senate on December 27, to give his successor, Jack Danforth, a few days of seniority over others who had been elected for the first time in 1976. Danforth appreciated this gracious, wholly unnecessary gesture, which erased the memories of the rather bitter campaign of 1970. Senior Washington bureau reporters from both the *Globe-Democrat* and the *Post-Dispatch* were present as Symington was cleaning out his office, and moving crews were packing the extensive collection of records being sent to the University of Missouri.[11] Though it was a time for remembrance, the reporters found Symington's thoughts "on the present and the future." He sounded familiar themes, jumping from one topic to another as thoughts occurred to him: the economy, the importance of a balanced budget, arms control, and the dangers of nuclear proliferation.

> What will bring this country down more than anything else is the long failure to balance the government budget. The greater danger to this country is from inside.

This was a familiar theme, as was his support of the missile program. This might have seemed to contradict his commitment to arms control, but in Symington's eyes there was no contradiction. He was by no means a pacifist; his goal was to maintain military strength without bankrupting the country. Missiles, in his view, had simply replaced the big bombers as the most cost-effective strategic weapon: "The B-1 bomber will cost $100 million apiece and it can be shot down by $1 million missiles. Where is the cost effectiveness in that . . . program?"

He was mellow and nonpartisan. He had nothing against Republicans as such. After all, he had married one. He thought that some of the differences between Democrats and Republicans were "geographic." Likewise, he didn't care for the terms liberal, moderate, and conservative. "There are no senators more liberal than some Republicans," he said. "There are no senators more conservative than some Democrats. The words don't mean anything. . . . The word that means the most to me is the word realistic. I would like to think I am liberal about people and conservative about money."

He said his political philosophy was in line with three points expressed by Walter Lippmann. He paraphrased them this way:

1. No man has given the United States a mandate to police the world.

2. It's about time we stopped worrying so much about people in other countries and started worrying more about people of America.

3. It's time for old men to quit passing laws resulting in young men dying in battles not essential to the security of the United States.

When Symington was asked what he planned to do in retirement, he said that he had no plans, but if he decided to take up anything, it would be in the field of disarmament.[12]

Upon retirement, Symington occupied an office with the Washington law firm of Smathers, Symington, and Herlong—he did not consider returning to St. Louis. Son Jim, who had retired from Congress after four terms, was a member of the firm. George Smathers, former senator from Florida, was a longtime friend. Symington did no work for the firm, but the office provided a convenient place from which to keep up with national events and carry on an active correspondence with old friends.[13] He also worked sporadically on his memoirs, a project in which he seemed to have had relatively little interest, and which was never finished.[14]

His public services continued to be recognized. His friends from the air force and the aerospace industry were particularly generous in their recognition. The Air Force Association honored him with its "Jimmy Doolittle" award, with longtime friend (and political rival) Barry Goldwater making the presentation.[15] The association also established an award in his name; the first award went to Secretary of Defense Casper Weinberger.[16] In recognition of his role in establishing the Air Force Academy, a bust was placed in the academy's library.

Symington's closest brush with gainful employment came as a result of his friendship with Clifford, who was involved in efforts of a number of Middle Eastern potentates to get control of Financial General Bankshares, one of Washington's largest bank holding companies. Initially, Financial General fought the takeover, but Clifford brokered a deal whereby the company dropped its opposition. A key element in the deal was the appointment of Symington to the board of Financial General to represent Arab interests.

The deal raised eyebrows throughout Washington and the financial community. Symington, it was alleged, was being used as a "Mr. Clean," to put an honest face on machinations of a group of wealthy Arabs of dubious reputations. This Symington and the Arabs hotly denied. Symington, who did not know how much compensation he would receive, told the *Post-Dispatch,* "I don't mean to be corny, but I think there's an aspect of public service in this."[17]

As it turned out, there was none.

Symington served as a fairly active member of the board of Financial General and helped to negotiate the bank's entry into New York City, but he was blissfully unaware of the Byzantine negotiations being carried out by Clifford and his new partner, Robert Altman,[18] to effect the takeover of Financial General by the Bank of Credit and Commerce International (BCCI), an Arab-owned bank holding company with headquarters in Brussels.

Shortly after consummating the takeover, Clifford changed the name of Financial General to First American Bankshares, with headquarters in Washington.

He became chairman of the board and named Altman president. He named Symington to the board along with retired generals Elwood (Pete) Quesada, celebrated fighter pilot, and James M. Gavin, famous World War II commanding officer of the Eighty-second Airborne Division.[19] As far as basic negotiations were concerned, the three men were primarily figureheads. Clifford and Altman kept the outside directors totally in the dark regarding their dealings with BCCI. Mercifully, Symington died before he had to witness the humiliation suffered by his best friend.[20]

Symington continued to live in the Watergate apartment he had purchased after Eve's death. He made an occasional trip to St. Louis to see Tim and his family, and to visit old friends. He was solicitous of his grandchildren's progress in school and in athletics. He remained on the board of the Truman Scholarship Foundation and made an annual trip to Kansas City to attend the regular meeting of the board of the Harry S. Truman Library Institute and (while she lived) to see Mrs. Truman.

In Washington, he carried on an active social life—he was a great addition to any party. Also, rumors had it, he was being pursued by a number of eligible widows.

Symington put aside all speculation by announcing that he was going to marry Mrs. Ann Hemenway Watson, widow of Arthur K. Watson, chairman of the IBM World Trade Corporation and former ambassador to France. Nancy, as her friends called her, was rich (very rich), but she was not "one of those rich dames who had been chasing" Symington. The two met at the Palm Springs home of Bob and Delores Hope while attending a golf tournament.[21] They were married on June 16, 1978, at Nancy's home in New Canaan, Connecticut.

Marriage to Nancy Watson enlarged Symington's social life and travel schedule—if such were possible. They spent time in Nancy's homes in New Canaan and Camden, Maine. They bought a new condominium in Palm Coast, Florida. Symington kept his Watergate apartment, and they stayed there when in Washington.

Symington's health began to decline, and he and Nancy spent more and more time in New Canaan. His mind remained clear, and he maintained a keen interest in public affairs. However, a series of illnesses (hip replacements, cardiovascular problems, and a particularly severe attack of shingles) gradually weakened him, and he was bedfast for the last weeks of his life.

He died in his sleep on December 14, 1988.

There were two memorial services, both in Washington. The first, a family service, was held December 17 in a small chapel in the National Cathedral in Washington. About 150 persons attended, including, in addition to the family, a number of senators and other dignitaries. After the services, Symington's cremated remains were placed in a crypt beside Eve's in the National Cathedral. The second service, held January 10 in the National Cathedral, attracted more than 700, including, as the *Post-Dispatch* described it, "a former president's widow, several former presidential hopefuls, numerous senators and other dignitaries." The full Episcopal service, conducted by the Right Reverend John T. Walker, Bishop of Washington and Dean of the National Cathedral, was preceded by a prelude played by the brass quintet of the air force band; an air force honor guard presented the colors; James W. Symington, David C. Acheson (son of former Secretary of State Dean Acheson), South Carolina Democratic Senator Ernest F. Hollings, and Clark Clifford delivered eulogies. Clifford, who described Symington as "my best friend," praised his "unique and rare quality of courage in public life. I saw it again and again. It was an important thread that wove throughout his life."[22]

Clifford had it just right. Despite the suave, gracious affability which gave the impression that nothing mattered quite so much as getting along, time and again Symington exhibited plain, old-fashioned "to hell with the consequences" courage. His life story yields many examples: a young businessman taking on a powerful RCA; a newcomer in conservative, segregated St. Louis integrating the workforce at Emerson and agreeing to a union shop; an inexperienced surplus property administrator breaking the aluminum monopoly; a secretary of the air force defying the secretary of defense and even the president over the budget; a freshman senator taking on Joseph McCarthy; a relatively new senator defying a popular president in the interest of a strong defense; a senator defying his constituents and his president over the Vietnam War. And there were others.

In the Senate, Symington was the quintessential insider, working quietly in committee rooms and corridors. He never chaired a committee, except briefly Armed Services as acting chairman, but as the only senator to serve simultaneously on the Armed Services, Foreign Relations, and Space Committees, he accumulated vast quantities of information and exercised great influence. He chaired a number of important subcommittees, and primarily because of his personal prestige they generated much discussion. The work of the subcommittee on commitments abroad helped to end our entanglement in southeast Asia.

The *Washington Post* summed up his career this way:

> If Hollywood were to make a movie about the life of a United States senator, not only would the events in the life of Stuart Symington provide a great plot, the senator himself would have been the best possible choice

to play the starring role. . . . [He] had the good looks and gracious manners. Fortunately for the country, he also brought to his many government posts an intelligence and dedication that distinguished his career. . . .

He was a tough and generous man, and also not just a little stubborn— a Missourian through and through, for all the years he spent in the capital city.[23]

In Missouri, he increasingly had become a remote figure. When he died he had very few close ties to the state. There was not even a formal recognition of his passing until Sam Hamra, a prominent Springfield attorney and longtime Symington supporter, organized a memorial service, held November 1, 1991, in the Law School Auditorium at the University of Missouri–Columbia.[24] Yet Missourians, proud that one of their own had played such an important national role, also remembered the good he had done everywhere—from securing the Gateway Arch in St. Louis to saving professional baseball in Kansas City to helping bring dams and lakes, parks and waterworks, and other improvements to little towns all across the state.

Missourians have no trouble in giving him a central place in their pantheon of political leaders.

Abbreviations

AFHRC—Air Force Historical Research Center

ASWA—Assistant Secretary of War for Air

CR—Congressional Record

EL—Dwight D. Eisenhower Library

HSTL—Harry S. Truman Library

KCS—Kansas City Star

LBJL—Lyndon Baines Johnson Library

LC—Library of Congress

NARA—National Archives and Records Administration

NYT—New York Times

PPF—President's Personal Files

PSF—President's Secretary's Files

SLGD—St. Louis Globe-Democrat

SLPD—St. Louis Post-Dispatch

SM—Seeley Mudd Manuscripts Library

SP—Symington Papers

SPF—Symington Personal Files

WHMC—Western Historical Manuscript Collection

WP—Washington Post

Notes

Chapter 1. Beginnings

1. Except as otherwise indicated, this account is based generally on two family histories by Charles J. Symington: *Skippin' the Details: Memoirs of Charles J. Symington for His Twenty Grandchildren February 2, 1883–February 2, 1996,* and *Scotch and Soda: A Family History Covering Twenty-Six Generations.* I am grateful to Stuart Symington, Jr., for making them available to me.

2. As is frequently true of family legends, the one about Colonel Stuart saving Fort McHenry is a little overblown. Stuart was in the line of succession at Fort McHenry, commanding approximately six hundred troops of the 38th Infantry. Some thought may have been given to having him relieve the commandant—who was quite ill, but not drunk—although he did not actually do so. Colonel Stuart both accepted and relinquished command on the morning of September 15. It is unknown why he almost immediately gave command of the fort to Major Samuel Lane. Telephone interview, Scott Sheads, historian, Fort McHenry National Monument, by Teresa Koch, July 29, 1996. Melvin G. Holli and Peter d'A. Jones, *Biographical Dictionary of American Mayors, 1820–1980: Big City Mayors* (Westport, Conn.: Greenwood Press, 1981), 344.

3. Frederick L. Harvey Loviad, comp., *History of the Washington National Monument and Washington National Monument Society* (Washington, D.C.: Government Printing Office, 1903), 43.

4. Colonel John Patton, Jr., to George W. Randolph, Secretary of War, May 22, 1862, manuscript in possession of Stuart Symington, Jr.; Lasalle Corbell Pickett, *Pickett and His Men* (Philadelphia: J. B. Lippincott Co., 1913), 189. Great grandson James W. Symington discussed his ancestors' participation in the Civil War on the Ken Burns television series, aired on PBS in 1991.

5. Pickett, *Pickett and His Men,* 398.

6. *Baltimore Sun,* June 11, 1912.

7. See Charles Symington, *Skippin' the Details,* 32–36; see also an extended obituary, with portrait, that appeared in the *Baltimore Sun,* June 11, 1912.

8. Paul Wellman, *Stuart Symington: Portrait of a Man with a Mission,* 61. A social

historian of Baltimore called the marriage, which united the Symington and Harrison families, "a particularly potent blend."

9. Stuart Symington, "Memories," 150–51.

10. For a good description of Roland Park see Karen Lewand, *North Baltimore: From Estate to Development,* Baltimore City Planning Department and the University of Baltimore, April 1969, 11–24.

11. Powers "Pete" Symington had a long and colorful career in the navy. During the Taft administration he was captain of the presidential yacht, and at the time Emily called on him for help he was naval aide to Ambassador Walter Hines Page at the Court of St. James. Stuart Symington, "Diary," copy in possession of James W. Symington.

12. See Robert Coughlan, "Home Front Boss," *Life,* October 2, 1950, cover story.

13. Ralph G. Martin and Ed Plaut, *Front Runner, Dark Horse,* 271.

14. She served as president of the diocesan altar guild and of the Church Service League. In her later years she became interested in church vestments and rituals, lecturing widely on the subject.

15. Symington, "Memories," 60. The black leader was Clarence Mitchell, later head of the National Association for the Advancement of Colored People. He and Symington became good friends.

16. Apparently, Stuart was very possessive of his tennis racquet. Writing to his father from France, he added as a postscript, "Please see that my tennis racket is not used by the Colstons."

17. *The Sun Magazine,* February 21, 1971. Symington recalled the incident this way: "Smith . . . in a 1948 article on national conventions wrote that Stuart Symington, then Secretary of the Air Force, was the first person who ever made him feel important because, he said, "While coming out with a full basket, I ran into him coming down with an empty one; and he shouted, 'Wilson has just been nominated unamminously.' I knew that word was wrong, so I knew it was important."

18. Symington, "Memories," 13.

19. Wellman, *Symington,* 64–65.

20. As will be discussed, Charlotte later started Foxcroft School, one of the most successful of its kind in the country.

21. Symington, "Memories," 8–9; Wellman, *Symington,* 71–72.

22. Symington, "Memories," 16.

23. Wellman, *Symington,* 73.

24. Ibid., 18.

25. Symington, "Memories," 18.

26. Ellery S. Husted, ed., *History of the Class of Nineteen Hundred Twenty Three, Yale College,* 246–47; Martin and Plaut, *Front Runner, Dark Horse,* 270–71, 308.

27. Symington, "Memories," 13–14.

28. Gordon C. Rhea, *The Battle of the Wilderness, May 5–6, 1864,* 447–50, provides a vivid description of General Wadsworth's death.

29. For the relationship between John Hay and Henry Adams, and for a generally unorthodox view of the lives of both men, see Patricia O'Toole, *The Five of Hearts: An Intimate Portrait of Henry Adams and His Friends, 1880–1918* (New York: C. Potter, 1990).

30. James W. Wadsworth to Walter F. Carter, October 5, 1923, Wadsworth papers,

box 34, LC. See also Alden Hatch, *The Wadsworths of the Genesee,* 224. For information on the Wadsworth family, I have relied on this book, and, more heavily, on Martin L., Fausold, *James W. Wadsworth, Jr.: The Gentleman from New York.*

31. Symington, "Memories," 21.

32. Wellman, *Symington,* 78–79.

33. Martin and Plaut, *Front Runner, Dark Horse,* 273; Wellman, *Symington,* 79.

34. Symington, "Memories," 20. Marshall's memory as to his rank was faulty. He was a major in 1924. The account of the wedding is taken from this and from *NYT,* March 2, 1924.

Chapter 2. A Rapid Rise in Business

1. Stanley Fike to John B. Rumsey, *Rochester Times-Union,* June 13, 1960, SPF, box 11; Wellman, *Symington,* 81; Symington, "Memories," 22. Unless otherwise indicated, this chapter is based on "Memories."

2. In the 1930s Symington had his battered nose straightened surgically to relieve sinus troubles. The procedure also improved his appearance. As for his vision, paradoxically, his three brothers all suffered from juvenile macular degeneration of the retina and became legally blind by the time they were twenty-one.

3. "Symington Addresses since 1925," SPF, box 4. For a description of the neighborhood I am indebted to Francis P. O'Neill, reference librarian, Maryland Historical Society, to Teresa Koch, August 8, 1996, in author's files.

4. Of his father's death, Stuart wrote: "My father had been a superb athlete. . . . But he was careless about his health, and years later, after a foot race on a bet in 1925 against a much younger man, he developed a serious heart condition and was dead in a matter of weeks." ("Memories," 23–24.) The *Baltimore Sun* wrote: "The death of Judge W. Stuart Symington, Jr., of the Supreme Bench of this city, brings a sense of personal sorrow to a large circle of friends. Judge Symington's unusual personality won for him a warm place in the hearts of those who came in contact with him, and who admired his many fine qualities of heart and head. . . . Though having served but a short time on the Bench, Judge Symington had shown great industry, clearness of mind, a promptness in decision and a knowledge of the law which made him a real addition to that body."

5. Blake McKelvey, "East Avenue's Turbulent History," 48. The Federal Writers' Project guide to Rochester provides this description: "East Avenue, shaded by over-arching elms, its pretentious homes on spreading lawns almost hidden by foliage, has been called one of the most beautiful residential streets in America," p. 47.

6. There is a 1925 photo of the Parke Lane Apartments, 33 Park Circle, in the Photo Collection, Buffalo and Erie County Historical Society.

7. Charles Symington remembered it this way: "On two occasions Don wanted to fire Stu, but since he was far too valuable a man to lose, we decided instead to make him president of the Colonial Radio Corporation, which was a subsidiary of Symington-Gould." Charles Symington, *Skippin' the Details,* 158–59.

8. For Wadsworth's association with Donovan, see Richard Dunlop, *Donovan: America's Master Spy,* 134, 136, 143, 147, 222.

9. This account is based primarily on Symington's "Memories," 29, and also on Stuart Symington, "Memorandum," September 14, 1959. Years later, Symington sent this memorandum to General Wood with the request, "If there is anything not right to you would you be good enough to let me know?" Wood replied: "Just got your letter of September 14 and can truthfully say that your memorandum was entirely correct and I could not think of any change being made. As a matter of fact, I was delighted to read it."

10. Symington, "Memorandum," March 10, 1948.

11. Loewy and Symington became acquainted in 1936, and, according to Loewy, "got on well." When Symington became secretary of the air force, Loewy designed his office in the Pentagon. Loewy credited Symington with suggesting and making arrangements for a postwar trip to Japan which, he said, "affected the rest of my career. . . . I was exposed for the first time to the Japanese aesthetic by direct experience. And this in many respects has stayed with me in terms of projects I have been involved in." Raymond Loewy, *Industrial Design,* 350.

12. The "Memorandum" of March 10, 1948, cited previously, was written to refute the playboy charges. He wrote, with uncharacteristic defensiveness: "Since 1917 I have been either working or studying winters and summers . . . Since 1933 I have been independent. All money I have has been earned by me. The money inherited from my parents went to my sister and younger brothers, none to me. . . . Any statement that I was at any time in my life living primarily for fun, golf and tennis, is wrong after the age of 13; and any statement that my friends helped me because of playboy tendencies has no basis of truth. . . . I have made many mistakes, and done many things wrong, but I have worked hard, all my life. . . . There has never been even the shadow of any scandal in my private life; and therefore the appellations of playboy, fun lover, etc. hit hard. There is no pleasure in working if you don't enjoy it, and I do; but worse than anything would be loafing."

13. Martin and Plaut, *Front Runner, Dark Horse,* 278, 280; Townsend Hoopes and Douglas Brinkley, *Driven Patriot: The Life and Times of James Forrestal,* 91; Interview with James Symington by Townsend Hoopes, April 16, 1989, quoted in Hoopes and Brinkley, *Driven Patriot,* 91.

14. Symington was sponsored for membership in the River Club by Kermit Roosevelt, second son of Theodore Roosevelt, who was president of the club. The Symingtons and the Roosevelts became close friends, weekending together at Sagamore Hill, the Roosevelt home on Long Island. Kermit's wife, Belle, was a favorite tennis partner. In 1934, they won the mixed doubles club championship. Symington later reminisced: "The finals could never be forgotten. We were playing against George Putnam, husband of Amelia Earhart, and a lady whose name I forget. They had us down one set and five love five forty in the second, but we pulled it out. I still remember Belle's sparkling eyes after the match was over when she murmured, 'That was high adventure,' a special compliment from a Roosevelt." "Memories," 30, 76–77. See especially the interview in Hoopes and Brinkley, *Driven Patriot,* Stuart Symington by Douglas Brinkley, November 17, 1987, cited on 77. Davison material from *Who's Who in America,* vol. 12, 878. Martin and Plaut, *Front Runner, Dark Horse,* 280.

15. David Grafton, *The Sisters: The Lives and Times of the Fabulous Cushing Sisters,* 89–90. Jock Whitney married Betsy Cushing after his divorce from Liz Eastman.

16. See Serge Obolensky, *One Man in His Time; The Memoirs of Serge Obolensky* (New York: McDowell, Obolensky, 1958), 405.

17. Wellman, *Symington,* 90; Symington, "Memories."

18. Stephen Birmingham, *The Right People: A Portrait of the American Social Establishment* (Boston: Little, Brown, 1968), 71. Wellman, *Symington,* 91, has Eve replying to the nightclub question by saying that Place Pigalle was one block east of Broadway. It was at 201 West Fifty-second Street.

19. *New York American,* October 11, 1934. This and other stories about Eve's singing career are from her press scrapbooks, now in the possession of James W. Symington. *New York News,* October 12, 1934; *New York Morning Sun,* October 11, 1934; *New York American,* October 11, 1934.

20. *New Yorker,* October 26, 1935; *New York Journal,* October 22, 1936.

21. *New York Herald-Tribune,* March 11, 1935.

22. *New York Sunday News,* December 22, 1935; *NYT,* November 7, 1937.

23. Coughlan, "Home Front Boss," 107; *The Playbill,* November 8, 1937.

24. *New York Post,* March 20, 1937.

25. *New York Woman,* March 24, 1937.

26. *New York News,* January 31, 1938.

27. *New York Journal-American,* September 19, 1938.

28. Jim remembers that their father frequently was gone on business and when he was home for dinner spent much of his time correcting their manners, etc. *New York News,* October 22, 1938. James Symington recalled that Danton Walker once wrote that his father had "taken a walk" with Katharine Hepburn during one of Eve's shows. He was furious. He went into the office of the *Daily News,* walked up to Danton Walker, hit him in the face and walked away. Late in life, after a phone call, Symington wrote: "Dear Kate: Putting it mildly, it was great hearing your voice the other day. I have watched your incredible career with respect and much pride. . . . Please come and visit an old friend when you have time; better still, come for lunch. You will like my wife. She is much like you, straightaway. Symington to Katherine Hepburn, April 27, 1988, SPF, box 5.

29. *St. Louis Star-Times,* June 15, 1945. Symington's involvement in the parking meter industry became an issue in his confirmation hearing as chairman of the Surplus Property Board, and for a time threatened to derail his appointment.

Chapter 3. Turnaround in St. Louis

1. Unless otherwise indicated, this chapter is based on the following sources: Interview, Stuart Symington, by Larry Keyes, August 1987, in possession of James W. Symington; Symington, "Memories," 35–45; *Emerson Electric Company: A Century of Manufacturing;* Martin and Plaut, *Front Runner, Dark Horse,* 282–93; and Wellman, *Symington,* 97–109.

2. *NYT,* September 6, 1938.

3. Clark Clifford with Richard Holbrooke, *Counsel to the President,* 37–38, describes the meeting and subsequent friendship: "Sometime around 1936 [Clifford's memory is

slightly off here], after a late-afternoon game of squash at the St. Louis Racquet Club, I entered the bar with my opponent for a drink, and was introduced to a new member of the club. I have long forgotten the name of my opponent, but I shall always remember the tall, slender, very handsome man to whom I was introduced. His name was Stuart Symington. He had come from New York to become President of the Emerson Electric Company, at that time the largest employer in Missouri. He was in his mid-thirties, five years older than I. Our chance meeting at the racquet club was the beginning of a fifty-year friendship which eventually would also include close professional collaboration during the unification of the armed services, the creation of the Defense Department and the CIA, the fight against Joseph McCarthy, an unsuccessful presidential campaign, and the Vietnam War. Until his death in 1989 he was my closest friend."

4. Rosemary Feurer, "William Sentner, the UE, and Civic Unionism in St. Louis," 95–117. See also "A Yaleman and A Communist," *Fortune,* November, 1943, 146ff.

5. Stuart Symington, Jr., to the author, January 13, 1993.

6. *How a Union Saved 1500 Jobs, a $2,000,000 Payroll and the Business They Create for St. Louis,* pamphlet published by Local 1102, United Electrical and Machine Workers of America, n.d., William Sentner Papers, John M. Olin Library, Washington University.

7. An important businessman who was favorably impressed was Joseph Pulitzer, publisher of the *SLPD,* who described Symington as "an unusually liberal, honest and patriotic young businessman with a good labor record."

8. *Fortune,* November, 1943, 148.

9. R. E. Petering to Symington, April 22, 1959, SPF, box 10, Profit Sharing, reviews the history of the profit-sharing program at Emerson.

10. Symington, "Memories," 157.

11. "Today's Chit-Chat," *Tulsa Tribune,* November 22, 1938.

12. Eleanor Harris, "Stu Symington—Democratic Glamour Boy," *American Weekly,* June 24, 1960, 36.

13. "Getting the Production Job Done," address by W. Stuart Symington before the spring conference of the Society for the Advancement of Management, Cleveland, April 11–12, 1940, SPF, box 10.

Chapter 4. Five E's for Excellence

1. *Emerson Electric Company,* 106.

2. A booster was a high impact fuse on the nose of the shell.

3. *Emerson Electric Company,* 107; Symington, "Memories," 45.

4. Symington, "Memories." Tucker became bankrupt in 1949. He was indicted for mail fraud but was not convicted. He died in 1956 at the age of fifty-three.

5. Martin and Plaut, *Front Runner, Dark Horse,* 288.

6. Accounts of Symington's "eight days" appear in a number of places. The original probably was in "A Yale Man and a Communist," *Fortune,* November 28, 1943. Symington quoted this article in "Memories," 46–47, and it is followed closely in *Emerson Electric Company,* 107–8, 110.

7. Winston S. Churchill, *Their Finest Hour* (Boston: Houghton Mifflin, 1949), 350–51.

8. Symington to Spreckley, January 21, 1957, SPF, box 12.

9. Symington, "Memories," 48. The situation in Symington's office may not have been typical. Leonard Mosley, for example, wrote: "But the raid did more than just kill and maim the people of London. It all but broke their spirit."

10. Martin and Plaut, *Front Runner, Dark Horse,* 265.

11. Symington, "Memories," 68; *SLGD,* June 8, 1941.

12. James Leutze, ed., *The London Journal of General Raymond E. Lee, 1940–1941,* 272.

13. W. Averell Harriman and Elie Abel, *Special Envoy to Churchill and Stalin, 1941–1946* (New York: Random House, 1975), 57.

14. Wesley G. Craven and James L. Cate, eds., *The Army Air Forces in World War II,* vol. 1, 600–601; Symington, "Memories," 50. AAF leaders tried to downplay the controversy. Colonel Hugh J. Knerr, "We'll Bomb by Daylight," *American Mercury,* October, 1942, 430–35, criticized the British for using their B-17s before they or the crews were ready, arguing that this experience in no way invalidated daylight bombing. He suggested that the basic difference in doctrines, "instead of conflicting," was "beautifully complementary." *Newsweek* (February 23, 1943, 20) published an article by Major General Ira C. Eaker, commanding the Eighth Bomber Command, denying that there was any conflict between British and American doctrines and arguing that "U.S. day raids and RAF night bombings [were] . . . best use of each force."

15. Symington, "Memories," 50.

16. Leutze, *London Journal of General James E. Lee,* 285–86.

17. Symington, "Memories," 52. Except where otherwise indicated my account of the trip home is based on "Memories," 51–53.

18. *NYT,* May 28, 1941.

19. *SLGD,* June 8, 1941.

20. Kelly was killed when his B-17 was shot down after having sunk the battleship *Haruna.* During the ceremonies, much was made of the fact that the turrets to be manufactured at the plant would be attached to the type of plane Kelly was flying.

21. Stuart Symington to William Sentner, June 13, 1941; William Sentner to James J. Matles, June 13, 1941. Sentner papers.

22. *SLPD,* August 4, 1941. Symington recalled that in an effort to deal with the labor shortage, "we decided to take a chance by putting blacks on jobs above that of janitors, etc. Accordingly, over some strong objections from some of our people, we put in an all black semi-skilled department. . . . We were told that it was the first utilization by St. Louis industry of an entire department manned by semi-skilled blacks. Some worried that this would result in unacceptable standards of work. Accordingly, our Personnel Director, Fred Arches, and I talked to black leaders in the community, urging them to give us as able people as possible in our effort to break this color barrier. Some were apprehensive that said department would be below standard, but it turned out to be one of our best." Interview, Stuart Symington, by Larry Keyes.

As a testimony to Emerson's wartime labor relations, when the company received its first "E" for excellence, for example, the employees kept working during the ceremonies that were broadcast throughout the plant, thus saving about five thousand man-hours of labor. *St. Louis Star Times,* November 27, 1942.

23. *Emerson Electric Company,* 114.

24. *Fortune,* November, 1943, 146. Apparently, neither Symington nor Sentner was particularly pleased with the article.

25. *Emerson Electric Company,* 112. When my college roommate, the late Lieutenant Colonel John H. Seward, who piloted a B-24 on thirty missions over Germany, learned that I was writing this book, he said, "Be sure to mention that a lot of us survived the war because of Stu Symington's turrets."

26. *Emerson Electric Company,* 114.

27. Symington, "Memories," 54.

28. Irving Holley, Jr., *Buying Aircraft: Materiel Procurement for the Army Air Forces* (Washington, D.C.: Government Printing Office, 1964), 378. Holley commented: "Under the circumstances, Mr. Symington might have been forgiven had he charged the negotiators at Wright Field with double dealing. It might be interesting to speculate on the reactions of the colonel when Mr. Symington later became Assistant Secretary of War for Air and then Secretary of the Air Force."

29. Symington, "Memories," 54.

30. "Statement of W. S. Symington, President, The Emerson Electric Manufacturing Co., St. Louis, Mo., Before the House Military Affairs Committee, 2:30 p.m., July 28, 1942."

31. Symington, "Memories," 56. Symington identified the "ranking Republican" as "a Congressman Fisher from Pennsylvania." The ranking Republican on the committee was Walter G. Andrews of New York.

32. *CR-House,* July 24, 1942, 6616–17.

33. Symington's testimony before the House—a ringing defense of Emerson and its employees and a scathing denunciation of Congressman May—may be found in Sen 79A–F 30, National Defense Committee, OP–6, War Department Matters, box 208, RG 46, NARA. See also *SLPD,* July 28, 1942; Eleanora W. Schoenebaum, ed., *Political Profiles—Volume I: The Truman Years,* 377.

34. Symington, "Memories," 56–57.

35. *Emerson Electric Company,* 115.

36. Ibid., 116.

37. Symington, "Memories," 58–59.

38. *Emerson Electric Company,* 116.

39. Ibid., 108–19.

Chapter 5. From Business to Government

1. *NYT,* January 14, 1944; *Emerson Electric Company,* 121.

2. *Emerson Electric Company,* 119–22.

3. Symington, "Memories," 67.

4. Ibid.

5. Frederick Lewis Allen, *Since Yesterday: The 1930s in America, September 3, 1929–*

September 3, 1939 (New York: Perennial Library, 1986), 186. Symington's lack of enthusiasm for FDR may have gone back to 1926 and comments which he later attributed to Eleanor Roosevelt during Senator Wadsworth's unsuccessful campaign for reelection. William Sentner, "October 3, 1941—Discussion with WSS," Sentner papers.

6. Martin and Plaut, *Front Runner, Dark Horse,* 293; Symington, "Memories," 79, 80.

7. David McCullough, *Truman,* 346; Symington, "Memories," 80.

8. Symington to the president, April 24, 1945, papers of HST, PPF, HSTL.

9. Truman to Symington, April 30, 1945, papers of HST, PPF, HSTL; *SLGD,* May 1, 1945.

10. Symington, "Memories," 68.

11. Ibid.

12. *SLPD,* June 4, 1945.

13. Symington to Truman, May 22, 1945, PPF, HSTL. The file copy contains this notation: "No correspondence in file re offer of job." SSP, box 13, WHMC.

14. Robert H. Ferrell, ed., *Off the Record: The Private Papers of Harry S. Truman,* 32, 42. Teapot Dome and Forbes were scandals in the Harding administration.

15. For Symington's appointment, see *PM,* June 8, 1945. Other appointments announced on June 7 were: General Omar Bradley, administrator of veterans affairs; John B. Hutson, undersecretary of agriculture; and Paul M. Herzog, chairman of the National Labor Relations Board.

For press reaction to Symington, see, for example, *NYT,* June 8, 1945; *New York World-Telegram,* June 8, 1945; *Washington Daily News,* June 8, 1945; *SLGD,* June 8, 1945; *SLPD,* June 8, 1945. See also George Dixon, "Washington Scene," *Boston American,* June 11, 1945; *Washington Daily News,* June 9, 1945.

16. Drew Pearson, "Washington Merry-Go-Round," *Cleveland News,* June 13, 1945.

17. *St. Louis Star-Times,* June 15, 1945; James Wadsworth, Diary, June 15, 1945, WP, box 116, LC.

18. For Stokes, see, for example, *Washington News,* June 21, 1945. *CR-Senate,* July 3, 1945, 7158; Symington, "Memories," 72.

19. *CR-Senate,* July 12, 1945, 7431; Wadsworth, Diary, July 15, 1945, LC. James W. Wadsworth, who was present, recorded in his diary: "Present were Evelyn and Stuart's sister, and his uncle Symington. Also Secretary Wallace, Secretary Vinson, Secretary Vinson, Secretary Forrestal, Under Secretary Patterson, Assistant Secretary Lovett, Senator O'Mahoney, General Campbell, Chief of Ordnance, Congressman Cochran and several others."

Chapter 6. The World's Largest Merchandiser

1. *Emerson Electric Company,* 121. Symington sold his stock at the going price of $5.68 per share. Years later, Ralph Petering, former treasurer of the company, told him that if he had held the shares, they would be worth $42 million.

Before Eve arrived in Washington, Symington shared quarters with O. Max Gardner, former governor of North Carolina, then serving as undersecretary of the treasury.

Symington knew Gardner before going to Washington—he credited him with being very helpful during the early days at Emerson. In Washington the two men became close friends, and Gardner, an old Washington hand, was most helpful to Symington during his early years in government. President Truman appointed Gardner ambassador to the Court of St. James, but he died of a heart attack en route to London. Symington later wrote: "First I wired our deepest sympathy to his wife Fay then remembered that the Governor had had four excellent seats to the Redskins. Each Sunday he took three of us with him, often including Jimmy Byrnes, former Supreme Court Justice and former Governor of South Carolina, and Jesse Jones, the Texas banker. Believing he would approve, I then cabled the Redskins requesting his four tickets; so for nearly forty years I have had the Governor's fine seats on the 50-yard line, first at the old Griffith stadium, then at RFK." Symington, "Memories," 80–81.

Debra K. Pitts, "Stuart Symington and Harry S. Truman: A Mutual Friendship," provides a useful overview of the relationship between the two men. Clark Clifford, who had the responsibility for setting up the president's poker games, wrote, "He [the president] loved an eight-handed poker game, and played with a core group of regulars, including George Allen, Stuart Symington, and Secretary of Agriculture (later Senator) Clinton Anderson. His favorite poker companion was Fred Vinson, his Secretary of the Treasury, and later Chief Justice of the United States. To this group he added other players on a rotating basis. Through the poker games I first met Averell Harriman, then Secretary of Commerce. Harriman, one of the wealthiest men in the country, guarded his chips as though he were on relief. A rising young protégé of Speaker Sam Rayburn, Congressman (and later Senator) Lyndon Johnson, also joined the game from time to time." Clifford, *Counsel to the President,* 70.

2. *Who's Who in America,* vol. 25, 1026; Bernard M. Baruch and John W. Hancock, *Report on War and Post-War Adjustment Policies, February 15, 1944* (Washington, D.C.: American Council on Public Affairs, 1944), 35. See Jordan A. Schwartz, *The Speculator: Bernard M. Baruch in Washington, 1917–1965,* 457–66, for a good account of the Baruch-Hancock report and reaction to it. See also "History of the War Assets Administration and Predecessor Agencies," RG 270, boxes 82–86, NARA. (This is a long manuscript with 180 exhibits.)

3. George William Steinmeyer, "Disposition of Surplus War Property: An Administrative History, 1944–1949," provides an excellent survey of the establishment and functioning of the Surplus Property Board.

4. Ibid.; Ferrell, ed., *Off the Record,* 42.

5. *St. Louis Star-Times,* June 14, 1945. See also Steinmeyer, "Disposition of Surplus War Property," 108–46.

6. *Time,* July 7, 1945, 5.

7. Symington, "Memories," 60; Steinmeyer, "Disposition of Surplus War Property," 124–25.

8. Symington, "Memories," 70; Interview, Eugene M. Zuckert, by George M. Watson, Jr., April 27, 1982, 1–2; by the author, October 16, 1991, 1–3.

9. Symington, "Memories," 70; Interview, James J. Wadsworth, by John T. Mason, Jr., OH209, EL.

10. Martin and Plaut, *Front Runner, Dark Horse,* 295–96.

11. Symington, "Memories," 71. Symington wrote Attorney General Tom Clark: "I cannot speak too well of him [Joseph Carroll] and hope that his record will show the deep appreciation I have to you and Edgar for lending him to me." Clark sent the letter on to Hoover with this handwritten note: "Edgar: Looks like you are a good 'picker.'" Symington to Clark, June 6, 1948, Tom Clark papers, box 76, HSTL.

12. Martin and Plaut, *Front Runner, Dark Horse,* 297; Interview, Eugene Zuckert, by the author, October 16, 1991.

13. *CR-Senate,* July 12, 1945, 7448; *SLGD,* July 18, 1945; *NYT,* July 13 and 19, 1945.

14. Ibid., September 26, 1945.

15. *Current Biography: Who's News and Why, 1945,* 587.

16. *NYT,* September 6, 1945.

17. Symington to John W. Snyder, September 18, 1945, PSF, box 138, HSTL.

18. Symington to the president, November 29, 1945, OF, box 659, OF 122 G, HSTL.

19. *SLPD,* November 25, 1945.

20. *NYT,* October 20, 1945. Apparently, Wallace was not at all unhappy to be relieved of the responsibility for surplus property. He mentioned in his diary for October 1, 1945, that he "told the President that the relationship between Symington and Schindler [Alfred Schindler, undersecretary of commerce] was not at all good and I strongly advocated, as I had previously, August 17, the transfer of Surplus Property disposal from Commerce to Symington." Then on October 3, Wallace wrote: "Surprisingly enough, Symington agreed with us on transferring Surplus Property disposal to him. Symington is a nice fellow but the more I see of him the happier I am to get out from under his direction. He is a hard-hitting, go-getting type, who doesn't know too much about government." John Morton Blum, ed., *The Price of Vision: The Diary of Henry A. Wallace, 1942–1946,* 487–88.

21. *The Liquidation of War Surpluses, Quarterly Progress Report to the Congress by the Surplus Property Administration,* Y3W19: 20 (1945–7), 8–10.

22. *SLPD,* November 4, 1945.

23. *NYT,* October 12, 1945.

24. F. H. LaGuardia to Symington, September 26, 1945, SPF box 138, HSTL; Symington, "Memories," 73; Interview, Zuckert, by author. Cf., Symington to LaGuardia, October 12, 1945, PSF, box 138, HSTL; Telegram, LaGuardia to Symington, October 17, 1945, Ibid., Symington to Truman, October 25, 1945, Ibid. Symington, sensitive to the public relations difficulties the mayor of New York could engender, sent the president copies of his correspondence with LaGuardia. In acknowledging them, Truman wrote, "Just keep plugging and don't let any of these fellows take the starch out of you. You are going to run into a lot of things worse than this but keep pounding away and I know the job will be done right. The worst you have to deal with are the chiselers and their purported legal representatives. Watch them closely." Memorandum for W. Stuart Symington from the President, October 19, 1945, ibid. Symington, "Memories," 74.

25. Martin and Plaut, *Front Runner, Dark Horse,* 297; *SLPD,* November 4, 1945.

26. *SLPD,* November 25, 1945.

27. *NYT,* October 2, 1945.

28. Martin and Plaut, *Front Runner, Dark Horse,* 298.

29. *NYT,* November 15, 1945.

30. Senate, Hearings before a subcommittee of the Committee on Military Affairs, *Veterans' Priority for Surplus Property,* 79th Cong., 1st sess., December 12 and 14, 1945 (Washington: Government Printing Office, 1946), 27.

31. Steinmeyer, "Disposition of Surplus War Property," 148.

32. Unless otherwise indicated, this account is based on Harold Stein, "The Disposal of the Aluminum Plants," in Harold Stein, ed., *Public Administration and Policy Development,* 313–61. Stein, an economist with long government service, was a special adviser to the director of the Office of War Mobilization, which had supervision of the Surplus Property Board. He had close contacts with Symington and other senior surplus property officials.

33. Clark attended the ceremony at which Symington was sworn in as chairman of the Surplus Property Board. Shortly thereafter, Symington wrote, in longhand, "Dear Tom: Your note [not found] gave me a very warm feeling around the old pump. I was grateful to you for coming to my little ceremony and glad the family had a chance to meet you." Symington to Clark, undated, but received July 19, 1945, Tom C. Clark papers, box 76, HSTL.

34. Actually, unemployment, while severe in the localities where the plants were shut down, did not have much national impact; moreover, earlier fears of a postwar recession were beginning to moderate.

35. Senate, Joint Hearings before the Subcommittee on Surplus Property of the Committee on Military Affairs, Special Committee to Study and Survey Problems of Small Business Enterprises, Industrial Reorganization Subcommittee of the Special Committee on Postwar Economic Policy and Planning, *Aluminum Plant Disposal,* 79th Cong., 1st sess., October 15–19, 1945 (Washington: Government Printing Office, 1945).

36. *NYT,* October 17, 1945; *Public Papers of the Presidents: Harry S. Truman, 1945,* 401–2. See also *NYT,* October 19, 1945.

37. George David Smith, *From Monopoly to Competition: The Transformation of Alcoa, 1888–1986,* 240.

38. *Fortune,* May 1946, 104. See also *NYT,* January 6, 1946; *SLPD,* January 6, 1946.

39. *Fortune,* May 1946, 108. This contains a good account of the events of January 6–10.

40. Smith, *From Monopoly to Competition,* 242.

41. *Nation,* January 26, 1946, 90–91.

42. Symington to Truman, January 11, 1946, OF, box 659, f. 122, HSTL.

43. Interview, Stuart Symington, by James R. Fuchs, May 29, 1981, 19, 21, HSTL.

44. Truman to Symington, January 18, 1946, OF, box 659, f. 122, HSTL.

Chapter 7. Assistant Secretary of War for Air

1. Symington, "Memories," 20–21.

2. The Reminiscences of Kenneth C. Royall, in the Oral History Collection of Columbia University, 107–8.

3. *NYT,* January 19, 1946. At the same time, Truman announced the appointment of Edwin W. Pauley as undersecretary of the navy. While Symington's appointment was easily confirmed, Pauley's raised such a firestorm of opposition among liberals, who decried his connections with the California oil industry, that Truman ultimately was forced to withdraw the nomination. See Robert J. Donovan, *Conflict and Crisis: The Presidency of Harry S. Truman, 1945–1948,* 178–83.

4. According to a note in the Drew Pearson papers, Senators Styles Bridges of New Hampshire and H. Alexander Smith of New Jersey wanted to hold up the nomination while Symington's St. Louis background was investigated, "in line with the policy followed in the Pauley case." The basis for their concern was the belief that Symington was being groomed for appointment as secretary of war. Bridges finally agreed to withdraw his objection with the understanding that he reserved the right to oppose Symington's nomination as secretary of war, "should the circumstances warrant such a position." The Wadsworth quote is from "Diary," February 1, 1946, Wadsworth papers, box 16, LC. Unhappily, Wadsworth in this instance did not follow his usual practice of naming persons who were in attendance at events such as this.

5. Interview, Eugene Zuckert, by the author, October 16, 1991, 2; Richard F. Haynes, "Patterson, Robert Porter," Richard S. Kirkendall, ed., *The Harry S. Truman Encyclopedia,* 270–72; Eleanora Schoenebaum, ed., *Political Profiles: Volume I: The Truman Years,* 431–33. Interview, Stuart Symington, by James R. Fuchs, HSTL. The efforts to unify the armed forces are discussed in chapter 8.

6. Schoenebaum, *Political Profiles,* 480–81; Kenneth S. Royall, "Reminiscences," 108–11; see also chapter 8; Steven L. Rearden, "Memorandum for the Record, Subject: Interview with W. Stuart Symington," May 20, 1981, Historical Office, OSD.

7. Symington to Eisenhower, April 24, 1950, Dwight D. Eisenhower Papers, Pre-Presidential, 1916–1952, Principal File, box 113, Symington, W. Stuart, EL; James W. Symington, conversations with the author. Jacqueline Cochran, the famous aviatrix who was a very good friend of Stuart Symington, recalled an instance when she was giving a party for the Eisenhowers in New York: "Finally it became about 2:00 in the morning and Senator Symington who was then Secretary Symington, Secretary of the Air Force, said: 'Let's go over to a certain night spot and have breakfast' and General Eisenhower wanted to go so badly and Mrs. Eisenhower said, 'As head of the Columbia University I don't think you have any business over there' so the Eisenhowers went home but we took Barbara, John and the rest of us all went over to the club."

8. Symington, "Memories," 76.

9. Ibid., 76–77. See also George M. Watson, Jr., *The Office of the Secretary of the Air Force, 1947–1965,* 35, 45, 46.

10. Watson, *Office of the Secretary of the Air Force,* 36–38.

11. Interview, Eugene Zuckert, by George M. Watson, Jr., April 27, 1982, 3, USAF Oral History Program, K.233.0512–1348, 10.

12. Memos, Symington to Everett L. Butler, March 13, 1946; Butler to Symington, March 29, 1946, RG 107, Ofc Asst Sec War for Air, Decimal File, 1945–46, 210 to 313.7, NARA.

13. Memo, Col. B. L. Boatner to ASWA, July 23, 1946, RG 107, box 182, decimal file, 1945–46, 329 to 334, NARA.

14. Spaatz papers, box 250, August 1–31, 1946, LC.

15. Interview, Zuckert by Watson, April 27, 1982, 7.

16. Watson, *Office of the Secretary of the Air Force,* 40– 41.

17. The 70–Group Program has inspired a substantial body of literature, much of it argumentative. For a balanced, brief account, see Herman S. Wolk, *Planning and Organizing the Postwar Air Force, 1943–1947,* 74–79.

18. Memo, Symington to Patterson, September 16, 1946, SP, box 10, Patterson correspondence, HSTL, as quoted in Watson, *Office of the Secretary of the Air Force,* 43–44, which provides a discussion of AAF manpower problems.

19. See, for example, Spaatz to Lieutenant General Nathan F. Twining, Commanding General, Air Matériel Command, September 5, 1946, Spaatz papers, box 250, September 1–30, 1946, LC; Watson, *Office of the Secretary of the Air Force,* 45–46.

20. Memo, Symington to the Secretary of War, May 28, 1946, SP, box 13, HSTL; Symington to J. H. Whitney, October 30, 1946, SP, box 14, HSTL; Watson, *Office of the Secretary of the Air Force,* 46.

21. Symington, to the Secretary of War, December 30, 1946, SP, box 10, HSTL.

22. Symington to the Secretary of War, January 9, 1947, ibid.

23. Watson, *Office of the Secretary of the Air Force,* 45. See also chapter 8.

24. Symington to Eaker, April 1, 1946, SP, box 5, HSTL.

25. Symington to Eaker, June 15, 1946, Spaatz papers, box 254, ASWA, LC; Symington to Secretary of War, May 24, 1946, RG 107, Office of Asst Secy War for Air, decimal file, 1945–46, box 178, NARA; Symington to Secretary of War, June 11, 1946, Spaatz papers, box 254, ASWA, LC.

26. Symington to the Secretary of War, May 8, 1946, Spaatz papers, box 254, ASWA, LC.

27. Interview, Stephen F. Leo by George M. Watson, 10–11; Watson, *Office of the Secretary of the Air Force,* 56. Symington was highly enthusiastic about the team of O'Donnell and Leo. He wrote Jock Whitney: ". . . O'Donnell is very good on the job. People like him and want to help him and he is enthused. Leo is the best young newspaper man I know—a Republican from Maine who enlisted as a private and rose to Captain in the Air Forces, then was transferred to the Truman Committee." Symington to Whitney, October 30, 1946, loc. cit.

28. See, for example, Drew Pearson papers, Symington, DP G282, LBJL.

29. Symington to Toots Shor, April 20, 1946, SPF, box 3.

30. See George Killion to Symington, February 28, 1946; Symington to Killion, April 19, 1946, SP, box 5, HSTL; Lyndon Johnson to Symington, March 13, April 13, 19, 1946, SP, box 6, HSTL; Robert Dallek, *Lone Star Rising: Lyndon Johnson and His Times, 1908–1960,* 290.

31. Symington to Truman, April 19 and May 16, 1946, SP, box 13, HSTL; Truman to Symington, May 21, 1946, PSF, box 157, HSTL.

32. Symington to Truman, April 12, 1946; Truman to Symington, April 15, 1946, PF, box 12; Symington to Truman, May 2, 1946, SP, box 13, HSTL.

33. Bill Davidson, "Mr. Charm of Washington," *Collier's,* June 15, 1946, 20, 24–25. There is no doubt that Symington's friendship with Quentin Reynolds was at least in part responsible for this article, and especially for its favorable tone. Symington wired Reynolds: "FORGOT TO MENTION HAVE NOT SEEN REVISED DRAFT AND

AM WIRING DAVIDSON. IN ANY CASE HOPE HE GOES THROUGH WITH THE CHANGES HE SAID HE WOULD MAKE AND WOULD MUCH APPRECIATE YOUR SEEING THAT WHATEVER COMES OUT HAS ENOUGH DIGNITY TO IT SO IT DOES NOT AFFECT ANY STANDING I MAY HAVE FROM THE STANDPOINT OF DOING A JOB FOR THESE PEOPLE DOWN HERE YOU AND I BOTH LIKE SO MUCH." Telegram, Symington to Reynolds, April 8, 1946, SP, box 11, file 3, HSTL.

34. Richmond B. Keech, Administrative Assistant to the President, June 17, 1948, PPF 497,1004, HSTL; AAF press release, June 21, 1946, 168.3951, February-June 1946, USAF Collection, USAF Historical Research Center, Maxwell AFB, Alabama; see also War Department Travel Order AGAO-O-E 200.4, June 17, 1946, SP, box 12, HSTL. For an account of Forrestal's trip, see Hoopes and Brinkley, *Driven Patriot,* 295–301. Symington complained that American State Department representatives were more solicitous of Forrestal's group than they were of his, which included the postmaster general, whose position "ranks that of the Secretary of the Navy." This he attributed to the effective work of the naval attachés: "Brass and caste go well around the world, as representation, during the years between wars; and the Navy have considered it primarily their duty to handle America's representation." Unsigned, undated memorandum, SP, box 14, HSTL.

35. *NYT,* June 30, 1946; *Honolulu Star-Bulletin,* June 27, 1946. Baruch was serving as U.S. representative on the United Nations Atomic Energy Commission. For more on the B-36, see below.

36. Symington, "Memories," 107. Unless otherwise indicated, this account of Symington's trip is based on "Memories," 106–14; Symington, Memorandum for the Secretary of War, August 19, 1946, Report of Inspection of Certain Army Air Forces Overseas Installations, SP, box 14, HSTL; and Interview, Stuart Symington, June 8, 1984, by Caroline K. Ehlers, June 8, 1984, 24–41, courtesy Caroline Keith, Bethesda, Maryland. For Senator Tydings's impressions, see Caroline H. Keith, *"For Hell and a Brown Mule": The Biography of Senator Millard E. Tydings,* 344–97. General accounts of the Bikini tests will be found in William A. Shurcliff, *Bombs at Bikini: The Official Report of Operations Crossroads* (New York: W. H. Wise, 1947), and Jonathan M. Weisgall, *Operation Crossroads: The Atomic Tests at Bikini Atoll* (Annapolis, Md.: Naval Institute Press, 1994).

37. For a good account of the acrimonious public-relations battle between the AAF and the navy over "Operation Crossroads" (the code name for the Bikini tests), see Weisgall, *Operation Crossroads,* 182–205.

38. Symington, "Memories," 108. In his report to the secretary of war, Symington wrote: "Perhaps the most important of the information received was the verbal report of the Navy Captain on the Pensacola that the force of the blast down the stacks, bursting the casing of the boilers, would have killed instantly all personnel in the engine rooms of the Pensacola, the Arkansas, and the Nevada." Memo, August 19, 1946, loc. cit.

39. Ibid., 109.

40. Ibid., 109–10, 111. For good descriptions of Marshall's mission to China, see Leonard Mosley, *Marshall, Hero for Our Times,* 382–87; and especially Forrest C. Pogue, *George C. Marshall: Statesman,* 54–143.

41. For a good brief discussion of Clay's isolation from the views of most of the American diplomatic establishment and a summary of his interview with Symington, see Jean Edward Smith, *Lucius D. Clay,* 290–95.

42. "Notes on General Clay's Conference July 25, 1945," Attachment to Memorandum for the Secretary of War, August 19, 1946, SP, box 14, HSTL. See also Smith, *Lucius D. Clay,* 293–94.

43. Interview, Henry A. Wallace, 4910–4912, OHRC. See also John Morton Blum, ed., *The Price of Vision: The Diary of Henry A. Wallace, 1942–1946,* 609–10. For a good brief account of Wallace's Madison Square Garden speech on foreign policy and the events leading up to his dismissal as secretary of commerce, see McCullough, *Truman,* 513–18.

44. Symington, "Memories," 113; Harriman and Abel, *Special Envoy to Churchill and Stalin,* 553.

45. Rosslyn to Major General Clayton Bissell, August 11, 1946, copy in SPF, box 3; Symington, "Memories," 114.

46. Symington to Spaatz, August 5, 1946, SP, box 12, HSTL; Bissell to Symington, August 16, 1946, SPP, box 3.

47. Symington to Spaatz, August 7, 1946, Spaatz papers, box 254, ASWA, LC.

48. Memo, Symington to Spaatz, August 26, 1946, Spaatz papers, loc. cit.

49. *San Antonio Express,* October 10, 1946; *Time,* October 21, 1946, 26.

50. Symington to J. C. Hopkins, February 1, 1956, SPF, box 10; Hopkins to Symington, January 17, 1956, ibid. Major General James C. Selser, Jr., "The Bomber's Role in Diplomacy," *Air Force Magazine* (April 1956): 52, 55–56, is an account of the mission by the man who led the Superfortresses to Germany. Selser attributed considerable diplomatic significance to the mission: "In view of then-existing world conditions, our unprecedented flight of even a small group of B-29s to Europe was a significant event. Although the flight itself could not have been interpreted as a threat to Russia, the implications were obvious to thoughtful observers. Our B-29 was widely recognized as the aircraft capable of delivering the atomic bomb. Furthermore, the appearance of B-29s in Europe was certain to cause speculation about the possibility of stationing the Superfortresses there permanently. . . . It is a matter of record that Mr. Molotov adopted a more amenable attitude during the course of the meetings of the Council of Foreign Ministers, held in New York City in November 1946."

Chapter 8. Unification

1. Memo, Secretary of War to Assistant Secretary of War for Air, April 11, 1946, RG 340, Special Interest File, box 4, NARA.

2. Memo, Symington to the Secretary of War, April 12, 1946, Norstad papers, box 33, Unification Correspondence, Memos for Record, Misc. (3), EL; Memo, Symington to the Secretary of War, April 22, 1946, SP, box 10, Correspondence F-Patterson, R., HSTL.

3. Arnold to Spaatz, August 19, 1945, as quoted in John T. Greenwood, "The Emergence of the Postwar Strategic Air Force, 1945–1953," in Alfred I. Hurley and

Robert C. Ehrhart, eds., *The Proceedings of the 8th Military History Symposium, USAF Academy, 18–20 October 1978,* 215–16.

4. Robert Frank Futrell, *Ideas, Concepts, Doctrine: A History of Basic Thinking in the United States Air Force, 1907–1964,* 169–70.

5. For the views of AAF leaders on reorganization, see, for example, Demetrios Caraley, *The Politics of Military Unification: A Study of Conflict and the Policy Process,* 115–16; Ernest R. May, "Cold War and Defense," in Keith Nielson and Ronald B. Haycock, eds., *The Cold War and Defense* (New York: Praeger, 1990), 29–30. Alice C. Cole, Alfred Goldberg, Samuel A. Tucker, and Rudolph A. Winnacker, eds., *The Department of Defense: Documents on Establishment and Organization, 1944–1978,* provides a highly useful compilation of the various plans and organizational charts relating to the establishment of the Department of Defense. Hoopes and Brinkley, *Driven Patriot,* 321.

6. For a good discussion of Eberstadt's relationship with Forrestal, see Jeffrey M. Dorwart, *Eberstadt and Forrestal: A National Security Partnership, 1909–1949.* The development of the "Eberstadt Report" is covered in 90–107.

7. *Public Papers of the Presidents: Harry S. Truman, 1945,* 546–60.

8. Eberstadt to Forrestal, December 20, 1945, quoted in Dorwart, *Eberstadt and Forrestal,* 126; Caraley, *The Politics of Military Unification,* 129–30.

9. Symington to Forrestal, March 15, 1946, Norstad Papers, box 33, Unification Correspondence, memos for the record, Misc (3), EL.

10. Clark Clifford, *Counsel to the President,* 151.

11. Memo, Symington to the Secretary of War, September 3, 1946, SP, box 10, HSTL.

12. Norstad described his relationship to the AAF at this time as follows: "I was in Air Force matters only to the extent that Hap or Tooey or Vandenberg brought me in—and Symington. We had . . . a sort of informal policy group consisting of Symington, Vandenberg and myself. One of the two of them would invite me up from the War Department to meet with them on some subject. But that was not a formal relationship, that was a people relationship. I think it is safe to say that we were good friends and we could work together well, and there was no pulling of the punches when the three of us got together." Interview, Lauris Norstad by Hugh Ahmann, 1979, 185–86. "Conversation between Mr. Patterson and General Norstad, 14 May '46," Norstad Papers, box 31, EL; Leach to Spaatz, March 21, 1946, Norstad Papers, box 21, EL. See also Spaatz to Leach, March 28, 1946, Spaatz Papers, box 250, LC.

13. For a good summary of Forrestal's testimony, see Caraley, *The Politics of Military Unification,* 131–32.

14. Lauris Norstad, "Meeting—Nite of 7 May 1946," May 8, 1946, Norstad Papers, box 31, EL. This was the first time Norstad had met Clifford except in social gatherings. In a separate memo he wrote: "He displayed a high degree of intelligence, tolerance and an objective approach. In spite of this, I did feel that many of his conclusions were slanted, but realizing his close connection with the Navy on this subject it is appreciated that the Navy side has been stressed throughout and the facts or opinions impressed upon him naturally had been those considered important by Navy people. In spite of this, however, he appeared to be most receptive to new approaches and an independent

thinker." Norstad, "General Reactions to Conference, May 7, 1946—Mr. S's Home," ibid.

15. The letters between the president and the service secretaries are conveniently found in Cole et al., eds., *The Department of Defense*, 22–29.

16. Symington, Memorandum to the Secretary of War, May 17, 1946, SP, box 10, HSTL.

17. Memo, Symington to Major General C. C. Chauncey, September 12, 1946, RG 107, box 179, Office of Assistant Secretary of War for Air, Decimal File 080, Job A48–2, Series 2, NARA.

18. Earlier, he had posed the same question to the president in a letter complaining that the navy had been approved for the purchase of more planes in fiscal 1947 than the AAF. Symington to the President, May 16, 1946, SP, HSTL. Truman responded by saying, "These matters will work out, as they should, if we ever get to the point where we can get a practical result. Things are in better shape than they were except for the statements of Walsh and Vinson yesterday." Truman to Symington, May 21, 1946, PSF, box 157, HSTL.

19. "Remarks by W. Stuart Symington, Assistant Secretary of War for Air, before the Economic Club of Detroit, Book Cadillac Hotel, Detroit, Michigan, 17 June 1946," SPF, box 11.

20. Alvan Macauley to Congressman Louis C. Rabaut, June 20, 1946, Spaatz Papers, box 254, ASWA, LC. Symington, in sending a copy of his speech to the president, wrote, "All but two hands came up for your program." Symington to Truman, June 21, 1946, SP, box 13, HSTL. See also *NYT*, June 18, 1946; Telephone Conversation, General Norstad and Mr. Symington, June 18, 1946, Norstad Papers, box 31, EL.

21. Symington, Memo, Discussion with General MacArthur, July 8, 1946, PSF, box 157, HSTL; Symington, Memo, "Discussion with General Marshall in Nanking," July 10, 1946, SPF, box 157, HSTL.

22. *NYT*, September 12, 1946; *Memphis Commercial Appeal*, November 19, 1946; *Washington Star*, November 28, 1946.

23. Jacqueline Cochran and Maryann Buchnum Brinley, *Jackie Cochran: An Autobiography*, 249.

24. Ibid.

25. Eberstadt had met with former Assistant Secretaries of War John J. McCloy and Robert Lovett to solicit their support for the idea of coordination as opposed to authority, which was based on the British plan with which he (Eberstadt) was much impressed. He thought he obtained their concurrence, and though neither could speak for the War Department, he represented this as a victory for the navy's point of view. Robert Greenhalgh Albion and Robert Howe Connery, *Forrestal and the Navy*, 273–75. Eberstadt's assumption, as reported by Grenhalgh and Connery, went considerably beyond what the facts would warrant. On October 16 McCloy sent Symington, "for your confidential information," a letter which he had sent to Judge Patterson outlining his views. In general, they followed the president's plan, except for an emphasis on "coordination." McCloy also wanted it clearly understood that he did not want "to be quoted as in any way representing the navy, the Air Force, or indeed any group or individual, for I do not in any way whatever." McCloy to Patterson, October 16, 1946; McCloy to Symington,

October 16, 1946, SP, box 8, HSTL. Symington, good friend of both Lovett and McCloy, reminded them that the British had been following a plan which resembled Eberstadt's, but that they had changed it to provide more authority for the air minister, that they had found simple coordination unworkable. Symington to John J. McCloy, November 8, 1946, George M. Elsey Papers, box 82, HSTL.

26. Lauris Norstad, Memorandum for the Record, n.d., Norstad Papers, box 31, Memos for the Record (1), EL; Robert Greenhalgh Albion and Robert Howe Connery, with the collaboration of Jennie Barnes Pope, foreword by William T. R. Fox, Greenhalgh and Connery, *Forrestal and the Navy*, 222–23, describes what must have been this meeting as taking place on November 12. The description is not a Diary entry, but an editorial note, which refers to "Admiral Sherman's notes." It would appear that Norstad's record is more accurate than Millis's editorial notes. Symington was in Texas on November 12.

27. Norstad, Memorandum for the Record, November 14, 1946, Norstad Papers, Ibid.

28. Ibid., November 21, 1946.

29. Walter Millis, ed., *The Forrestal Diaries*, 223–24; Symington to James W. Wadsworth, October 16, 1946, SP, box 2, HSTL.

30. Hoopes and Brinkley, *Driven Patriot*, 342–43.

31. Millis, ed., *The Forrestal Diaries*, 225–26.

32. Memo, Norstad to Symington, December 20, 1946, Norstad Papers, box 33, EL.

33. Millis, ed., *The Forrestal Diaries*, 229–30. Clifford, *Counsel to the President*, 152.

34. Clifford, *Counsel to the President*, 152.

35. Interview, Clark Clifford, by James C. Olson, October 16, 1991; Millis, ed., *The Forrestal Diaries*, 228–30.

36. Cole et al., eds., *The Department of Defense*, 31–33; Millis, ed., *The Forrestal Diaries*, 230–31. See also *NYT*, January 17, 1947, which gave the story a three-line, five-column headline on page one.

37. G.M.E. to C.M.C., Feb[ruary] 5 [1947], George Elsey Papers, box 82, HSTL. Hanson W. Baldwin, the pro-navy military correspondent for the *New York Times*, expressed essentially the same view, writing that ". . . it was—and always has been misleading since the first plan for reorganization was introduced—to describe the agreed-upon reorganization as either 'unification' or 'merger.'" *NYT*, January 18, 1947.

38. Clifford, *Counsel to the President*, 154–55; Forrestal, telephone conversation with Symington, February 12, 1947, quoted in Cecilia Sites Cornell, "James V. Forrestal and the American National Security Policy, 1940–1949," 301.

39. For Wadsworth's role in the Eightieth Congress, see Fausold, *James W. Wadsworth, Jr.: Gentleman from New York*, 359–64.

40. For a general account of Symington's illness and hospitalization, see Wellman, *Stuart Symington*, 129–32. Interview, Eugene M. Zuckert, by George W. Watson, Jr., April 27, 1982, 4; *NYT*, March 15, 1947; Clifford to Symington, February 28, 1947, SP, box 18, HSTL.

41. Dr. R. H. Smithwick to Symington, February 12, 1947, SP, box 11, HSTL.

42. Eisenhower to Symington, March 12, 1947, Pre-Presidential Papers, box 113, EL.

43. Wellman, *Stuart Symington,* 131–32; Eaker to Symington, March 27, 1947, SP, box 5, HSTL.

44. Forrestal to Symington, April 14, 1947, Forrestal Papers, box 76, SM. Having gotten virtually everything he wanted, Forrestal was now prepared to give his unequivocal support to the unification measure.

45. Eisenhower to Mrs. Stuart W. [*sic*] Symington, March 25, 1947, Pre-Presidential Papers, box 113, EL; also in SPF, box 12.

46. Clifford to Symington, March 26, 1947, SP, box 3, HSTL.

47. Symington to Clifford, May 1, 1947, SP, box 3, HSTL; Symington to Spaatz, April 29, 1947, to Truman, April 30, 1947, SP, boxes 12 and 13, HSTL; Truman to Symington, May 7, 1947, PSF, box 322, HSTL.

48. Symington to Douglas, May 2, 1947, SP, box 4, HSTL.

49. Forrestal to Symington, April 24, 1947, Forrestal Papers, box 76, SM; Eisenhower to Symington, May 6, 1947, Pre-Presidential papers, box 113, EL; Symington to Forrestal, April 29, 1947, Forrestal Papers, box 76, SM; Symington to Steve Leo, April 29, 1947, SP, box 7, HSTL; Symington to Kenney, May 30, 1947, SP, box 13, HSTL, quoted in Watson, *Office of Secretary of the Air Force,* 47.

50. Symington to Smithwick, June 24, 1947, SP, box 11, HSTL; Symington to Connelly, June 24, 1947, PPF, box 497, no. 1004, HSTL.

51. Presidential Appointments File, Daily Sheets, PSF, HSTL; Cole et al., eds., *The Department of Defense,* 33; Clifford, *Counsel to the President,* 157; see also Robert E. Ferrell, ed., *Truman in the White House: The Diary of Eben A. Ayers,* 187–88. Ayers indicated that, in addition to those mentioned by Clifford, the president also asked that a pen be given to Senator Chan Gurney of South Dakota, chairman of the Senate Armed Services Committee.

While passing over Cincinnati, the president received word that his mother had died.

52. Clifford to Symington, July 26, 1947, PSF, box 138, HSTL.

53. Symington to Lieutenant General Ennis Whitehead, Commanding Far Eastern Air Forces, September 10, 1947, Whitehead Papers, USAF Collection, USAFHRC.

54. Interview, Stuart Symington, by James R. Fuchs, May 29, 1981, 28, HSTL; Clifford, *Counsel to the President,* 156–57.

Chapter 9. First Secretary of the Air Force

1. Forrestal's observation to Truman is in Millis, ed., *The Forrestal Diaries,* 295. In a memorandum dated October 12, 1951, Symington wrote: "As of yesterday I talked with Mr. X, one of Mr. Forrestal's closest friends. In the discussion the question of [Ferdinand] Eberstadt came up. . . . He said what I already knew, namely, that Eberstadt tried very hard to prevent me, Symington, from becoming Secretary of Air, by working on Forrestal, and that he had asked him to work on Forrestal. He said apparently Eberstadt was bitter against me because I had taken the War Department Administration line in unification, ultimately defeating Eberstadt, the leader of the 'coordination' group in the unification argument as against the 'administration' group." SPF, box 11.

Paul Nitze asserted in later years that General Lauris Norstad had suggested him as the first secretary of the air force, but Truman had turned him down because he was a registered Republican, but then at Norstad's suggestion, he (Nitze) was asked to help organize the office, and that he worked alongside Symington for several weeks. Interviews, Paul Nitze by Lieutenant Colonel John Dirk and Dr. James C. Hasdorf, 1977, 1981, and by James C. Olson, October 16, 1991. I have found nothing in the Truman, Norstad, or Symington papers to support this assertion. *NYT,* August 22, 1947; Memo, Stephen F. Leo to Symington, August 27, 1947, SP, box 7, HSTL. After reporting editorial comment from around the country, Leo added, "I'm sure you will be relieved to know that in the Los Angeles Times and in the Augusta (Maine) Daily Kennebec Journal the story was the lead on page one."

2. SP, box 2, HSTL.

3. Arnold to Symington, August 27, 1947, SP box 2, HSTL.

4. *SLPD,* September 18, 1947. See also *NYT,* September 18, 1947; Clifford, *Counsel to the President,* 159; Symington to "Tim and Jim," September 20, 1947, SPF, box 3.

5. *NYT,* September 19, 1947.

6. Watson, *Office of the Secretary of the Air Force,* 51–58. I have relied heavily on Watson in this chapter.

7. Symington, "Memories," 170; George M. Watson, Jr., "Stuart Symington—the First Secretary of the Air Force, 18 September 1947–24 April 1950," *Aerospace Historian* 34 (September 1987): 185–89; Watson, *Office of Secretary of the Air Force,* 107; Interview, Harold C. Stuart by Charles J. Gross, August 28, 1978, 13, USAF Historical Research Center.

8. Interview, General William F. McKee, by George W. Watson, Jr., March 20, 1984, 24, USAF Center for Air Force History; Interview, Eugene Zuckert, by George M. Watson, Jr., April 27, 1982, 9, USAF Center for Air Force History.

9. Interview, General Lauris Norstad, by Hugh Ahmann, 1979, 119–20; Interview, Zuckert, by Watson, April 27, 1982, 9–10.

10. Interview, Stuart, by Gross, August 28, 1978, 13–14.

11. Interview, Zuckert by Watson, December 9, 1986, 127–29. For a good discussion of Symington as a public administrator, see Rebecca Ann Thomas, "Stuart Symington: Manager and Strategist 1946–1950," 1–24, 96–112.

12. *Time,* January 19, 1948, 24.

13. Shortly after the air force was established, Spaatz wrote in longhand to Symington: "Do you realize that in accepting our new jobs and in the event of war with Russia we will be *hanged as war criminals if we lose?* There had better be some real honest to God thinking about what we need to avoid being on the losing side. The U.S. has already set the pace for the atomic bomb, strategic bombing & hanging war criminals. This is no time to temporize very long with old established prerogatives of the services nor to tolerate interservice rivalry, friction, jealousy. Whoever does not cooperate should be obliterated." Memo, Spaatz to Symington, undated, SP, box 12, HSTL. Symington, "Memories," 76; Interview, Symington, by Caroline K. Ehlers, June 8, 1984, 40. See also David Mets, *Master of Air Power: General Carl A. Spaatz,* 331–32.

14. Clifford, *Counsel to the President,* 167.

15. Robert L. Smith, "The Influence of USAF Chief of Staff Hoyt S. Vandenberg on United States National Security Policy," 230–31.

16. Interview, Zuckert, by Watson, April 27, 1982, 23–24; Watson, *Office of the Secretary of the Air Force,* 51–55.

17. *Time,* January 14, 1948, 24–25.

18. Interview, Symington, by Watson, October 21, 1981, 18.

19. The exchange between Symington and Rogers will be found in RG 340, box 12, Special Interest File, 1948–49, NARA. Memo, Symington to Forrestal, November 13, 1947, SP, box 5, HSTL.

20. Watson, *Office of the Secretary of the Air Force,* 58–59; Interview, Symington, by Watson, October 21, 1981, 21.

21. *NYT,* November 25, 1947; Jack Raymond, *Power at the Pentagon,* 205; Symington to Homer Ferguson, March 24, 1948, Carl Spaatz Papers, box 264, LC.

22. Watson, *Office of the Secretary of the Air Force,* 60, 95, 221; Interview, Zuckert, by Watson, April 27, 1982, 19–22.

23. Minutes of the National Security Council, 3d meeting, December 12, 1947, microfilm, HSTL; Ibid., 5th meeting, January 13, 1948.

24. Memorandum, The President to W. Stuart Symington, January 21, 1948, PSF, box 157, HSTL.

25. Alfred Goldberg, ed., *A History of the United States Air Force, 1907–1957,* 162.

26. Interview, Zuckert, by Watson, April 27, 1982, 31–32.

27. Goldberg, ed., *History of the United States Air Force,* 171–73.

28. In 1948, RAND was separated from Douglas Aircraft and established as a private, not-for-profit corporation. For a good brief history of RAND, see Bruce L. R. Smith, *The RAND Corporaton: Case Study of a Non-Profit Advisory Corporation.* On Spaatz, see Mets, *Master of Airpower,* 326–27.

29. Memo, Symington to Forrestal, October 28, 1947, RG 107, box 187L, file 334, NARA; Memo, Symington to Secretary of Defense, October 31, 1947, RG 107, box 187L, File 334, NARA.

30. Watson, *Office of the Secretary of the Air Force,* 66–67.

31. Symington called John Snyder, who was with the president in Key West, and said, "Look, if the President wants me to leave, I'll be glad to go right now." In a few hours Snyder called back to say Truman had no intention of asking him to resign, "So keep quiet and do your job." Symington commented, with respect to the stories: "Eventually I found who was responsible. . . ; a man who hurt Mr. Truman by always telling him what he thought the President would like to hear. Apparently my contempt for some of his actions and advice had at some time shown through." Symington, "Memories," 126. As was so frequently the case, Symington did not identify the culprit. For the poker games, see Bert Cochran, *Harry Truman and the Crisis Presidency,* 222. The marriage of Stuart Symington, Jr., to Janey Studt on June 21, 1949, was one of the major social events of the summer in St. Louis, and was covered extensively in both the news and "Society" sections of the local papers. *SLGD, SLPD,* June 22, 1949.

32. Symington, "Memories," 167.

33. Truman wrote Baruch, "A great many honors have passed your way, both to you and your family, and it seems when the going is rough it is a one-way street." Bernard M. Baruch, *Baruch: The Public Years;* see also David McCullough, *Truman,* 678.

34. *New York Herald-Tribune,* July 14, 1948.

35. Symington, "Memories," 169–71.

36. For the troubles of the Truman campaign see, for example, Donovan, *Conflict and Crisis,* 388–416; McCullough, *Truman,* 678–79. Interview, Symington, by James R. Fuchs, May 29, 1981, 59, HSTL.

37. Symington, "Memories," 171–72.

38. Ibid., 122–23.

39. See, for example, Donovan, *Conflict and Crisis,* 417–39; McCullough, *Truman,* 653–707; Robert H. Ferrell, *Harry S. Truman: A Life,* 280–81.

40. Symington, "Memories," 125.

41. Dallek, *Lone Star Rising,* 326–27.

42. Interview, Stuart Symington, by Joe B. Frantz, October 6, 1976, 3–4, LBJL; Cochran and Buchnum Brinley, *Jackie Cochran: An Autobiography,* 252–59.

43. Interview, Symington, by Frantz, 4.

Chapter 10. Integrating the Air Force

1. *Federal Register of the United States,* vol. 13, no. 146, 4313. Much has been written on the integration of the air force. See especially Richard M. Dalifiume, *Desegregation of the United States Armed Forces;* Alan L. Gropman, *The Air Force Integrates: 1945–1964; Integration of the Armed Forces, 1940–1965* (Washington, D.C.: Smithsonian Institute Press, 1998); Lee Nichols, *Breakthrough on the Color Front;* Richard J. Stillman II, *Integration of the Negro in the U.S. Armed Forces.*

2. Symington, "Memories," 62.

3. Interview, Eugene Zuckert, by the author, October 16, 1991, 9, author's files.

4. Alan L. Gropman, "The Air Force, 1941–1951, from Segregation to Integration."

5. Nichols, *Break Through on the Color Front,* 74–75.

6. Omar N. Bradley and Clay Blair, *A General's Life: An Autobiography* (New York: Simon and Schuster, 1983), 484–86; Richard F. Haynes, *The Awesome Power: Harry S. Truman as Commander in Chief,* 91; Gropman, *The Air Force Integrates,* 243.

7. Morris J. MacGregor, *Integration of the Armed Forces, 1940–1965,* 338.

8. Nichols, *Break Through on the Color Front,* 76; Symington, "Memories," 156. Pruitt was memorialized in the name of St. Louis's much-heralded public housing project. Unhappily, "Pruitt-Igoe" became synonymous with failure in public housing, and the project was torn down.

9. Gropman, "The Air Force, 1941–1951, from Segregation to Integration," 4–7; MacGregor, *Integration of the Armed Forces,* 288.

10. Nichols, *Break Through on the Color Front,* 76–77.

11. Executive Order 9981, "Establishing the President's Committee on Equality of Treatment and Opportunity in the Armed Services," 13 Federal Register, 4313; Stillman, *Integration of the Negro in the United States Armed Forces,* 44–47.

12. "Meeting of the President and the Four Service Secretaries with the President's Committee on Equality of Treatment and Opportunity in the Armed Services, January 12, 1949," Morris J. MacGregor and Bernard C. Nalty, eds., *Blacks in the United States Armed Forces: Basic Documents,* vol. 9, 3–8.

13. "The President's Committee on Equality. . . , January 13, 1949," ibid., 169–220.

14. Memo, Zuckert to Symington, March 25, 1949, File 168.7061–37, AFHRC, Maxwell AFB.

15. Nichols, *Break Through on the Color Front,* 77.

16. Memo, Symington to Forrestal, February 17, 1949, MacGregor and Nulty, eds., *Blacks in the United States Armed Forces,* vol. 12, 21.

17. Dalifiume, *Desegregation of the United States Armed Forces,* 181–82. Lieutenant Colonel Jack Marr, who wrote the initial paper on desegregation in the air force, recalled that when the air force plan was first presented, Royall "hit the ceiling. He said no, the Army would never go along with anything like this, that it would never go along as long as he was Secretary of the Army. It was brought up more than once, and somebody told me that in one of these meetings, Symington was sufficiently disturbed so that he called Royal [*sic*] stupid." The Reminiscences of Jack Marr, Oral History Collection of Columbia University, 3–4.

18. "The President's Committee on Equality of Treatment and Opportunity in the Armed Services . . . March 28, 1949 . . . ," MacGregor and Nalty, eds., *Blacks in the United States Armed Forces,* vol. 9, 559–601.

19. For a good summary, see Dalifiume, *Desegregation of the United States Armed Forces,* 185–86.

20. USAF Oral History Program, Interview with Lieutenant General Daniel James, Jr., quoted in MacGregor, *Integration of the Armed Forces, 1940–1965,* 401; MATS Hq Ltr No 9, May 1, 1949, quoted in ibid.

21. *WP,* May 9, 1949, quoted in MacGregor, *Integration of the Armed Forces,* 399.

22. Benjamin O. Davis, *Benjamin O. Davis, Jr., American: An Autobiography,* 164. General Davis commanded the 332d Fighter Group during the war, and was in command at Lockbourne for a time. He gave Symington high marks for his role in the integration of the air force, adding, "He was a very great manager and he did a lot for this nation." Telephone interview, General Benjamin O. Davis, by the author, May 14, 1993. In 1974 Lockbourne was renamed Rickenbacker Field and placed under the control of the Ohio Air National Guard. Oscar Alan Osur, *Blacks in the Army Air Forces During World War II* (New York: Arno Press, 1980), 138; MacGregor, *Integration of the Armed Forces,* 403–5.

23. MacGregor, *Integration of the Armed Forces,* 406, 411; "All Answers by Senator Stuart Symington on Air Force Integration," USAF Document 168.7061–23, 46/00/00–50/00/00.

24. Charles Fahy et al. to the President, May 23, 1950, with attachments, MacGregor and Nalty, eds., *Blacks in the United States Armed Forces,* vol. 9, 1358–59, 1369, 1391–1404; MacGregor, *Integration of the Armed Forces,* 408.

25. Symington to MacGregor, May 6, 1970, quoted in MacGregor, *Integration of the Armed Forces,* 339.

26. Nichols, *Break Through on the Color Front,* 76.

Chapter 11. The Berlin Airlift

1. See, for example, Watson, *Office of the Secretary of the Air Force,* 79–82.

2. For an interesting comment on the diplomatic problems arising from the fact that General Clay to a large extent had been given a free hand in Germany, see *SLPD,* August 12, 1948.

3. Steven L. Rearden, *History of the Office of the Secretary of Defense,* vol. 1, *The Formative Years: 1947–1950* (Washington, D.C.: Government Printing Office, 1984), 291.

4. Interview, Stuart Symington, by Hugh N. Ahmann and Herman S. Wolk, May 2 and December 12, 1948, 94–95.

5. Jean Edward Smith, *The Defense of Berlin,* 107.

6. Memorandum for the President, 16th meeting of National Security Council, July 23, 1948, box 220, HSTL; Goldberg, ed., *History of the United States Air Force,* 235. Unless otherwise indicated, my account of the Berlin Airlift is based on Goldberg, 235–41. See also Robert G. Miller, *To Save A City: The Berlin Airlift, 1948–1949.* For the perspective of General Curtis LeMay, commander of United States Air Forces in Europe, see Curtis LeMay, with MacKinlay Kantor, *Mission with LeMay: My Story,* 415–20.

7. Rearden, *The Formative Years,* 294.

8. On the B-29s see, for example, *Los Angeles Times,* from which Symington's press conference quotes are taken, and *WP,* July 17, 1948. As late as the day before the planes were dispatched, the National Security Council was debating the wisdom of the movement. After a fairly extended discussion they somewhat reluctantly agreed that the effort should go forward. Memorandum for the President, Summary of Discussion, 15th Meeting of NSC, July 16, 1948, box 220, HSTL.

The flight of the jet fighters, which covered the 2,193 miles separating Goose Bay, Newfoundland, and Stornoway, Scotland, in four hours and forty minutes, "underlined a prime strategic point—modern United States jet fighters are only a few hours from any sudden trouble in this part of the world." *WP,* July 22, 1948.

9. *Los Angeles Times, WP,* July 23, 1948. See also Letter, Symington to J. C. Hopkins, February 1, 1956, SPF, box 10. The mission lost much of its luster when one of the B-29s crashed in the Arabian Sea off Aden, killing seventeen of the eighteen men aboard. *WP,* July 30, 1948.

10. Avi Shlaim, *The United States and the Berlin Blockade, 1948–1949: A Study in Crisis Decision-Making; NYT,* August 9, 1948.

11. Interview, William H. Draper, by Jerry N. Hess, HSTL. See also Shlaim, *The United States and the Berlin Blockade,* 320. *NYT,* August 9 and 12, 1948; *The Times* (London), August 12, 1948, as quoted in Shlaim. Symington's optimism was not widely shared in the air force. Assistant Secretary C. V. Whitney told the National Security Council on July 16 that the air staff was convinced that the air operation was "doomed to failure." Memorandum for the President, Summary of Discussion, 15th Meeting of NSC, July 16, 1948, box 220, HSTL.

12. Richard Collier, *Bridge across the Sky: The Berlin Blockade and Airlift, 1948–1949,* 79–81.

13. LeMay, *Mission with LeMay*, 416. Tunner's version is considerably different. He thought that neither Clay nor LeMay wanted him, and that he was sent over by General Vandenberg on the recommendation of Lieutenant General Albert C. Wedemeyer, director of plans and operations of the Army General Staff: ". . . Clay was of the opinion that he had all the know-how and all the people necessary to run the Airlift properly. . . . As for LeMay, he had a good thing going, and it was perfectly understandable that he would prefer to remain in control of it." William H. Tunner, *Over the Hump*, 160–62.

14. Interview, Symington, by Ahmann and Wolk, 85; Symington, "Notes on Berlin Airlift," Wiesbaden, Germany, August 11, 1948, SP, box 12, HSTL.

15. Symington, "Memories," 120–23; *NYT*, August 18, 1948.

16. Symington, Memorandum, "Visit with President Inonu, Ankara, Turkey, August 16, 1948, attached to Memorandum, Symington to Forrestal, August 20, 1948, SP, box 5, HSTL; Symington, "Memories," 122.

17. Symington memorandum, "Meetings—Ambassador Harriman—August 17 and 18, 1948," SP, box 5, HSTL.

18. *NYT*, October 21, 1948.

19. Ibid., September 26, 1948.

20. The "Christmas Caravan" marked the beginning of a lifelong friendship between Symington and Hope, a friendship which included their wives as well. Symington and Hope frequently played golf together, and they carried on a fairly active correspondence, largely social. In 1961 Symington introduced, and was instrumental in getting passed, a Congressional joint resolution authorizing the issuance of a gold medal to Hope. President Kennedy presented the medal on September 11, 1963, in a Rose Garden ceremony, with Symington looking on. Hope came to St. Louis to participate in ceremonies honoring Symington for his long years of public service. Symington and Ann Watson, who were married June 14, 1978, were introduced to each other in the home of Bob and Delores Hope, and the Hopes were among the guests at the wedding. SPF, box 5; SP, Subject box 58, WHMC. For Delores Hope's reminiscence of the airlift, see James Brady, "In Step with: Bob and Delores Hope," *Parade*, December 18, 1994, 22. On Barkley's presence, see *NYT*, December 24, 1948. Also in the party were General James H. Doolittle and Elmer Davis. Doolittle to Symington, January 3, 1949, SP, box 4, HSTL. For the show itself, see Collier, *Bridge across the Sky*, 148–49. See also Tunner, *Over the Hump*, 194–95. Apparently, the original plans had called for only two shows, one in downtown Berlin and the other at USAFE headquarters in Wiesbaden. When Tunner heard this, he "exploded." He demanded that the show appear where the airlift troops actually were stationed, or that all references to the airlift be deleted from the publicity. Obviously, the itinerary was changed.

21. Tunner, *Over the Hump*, 196–201. See also Goldberg, ed., *History of the United States Air Force*, 241.

22. Symington, Memorandum for the Chief of Staff, December 30, 1948, SP, box 13, HSTL. The conditions at Burtonwood received wide publicity. See *SLPD*, December 27, 1948.

23. Interview, Major General Leon Johnson, by James C. Hasdoff, 149–51.

24. Symington, Memorandum for the Chief of Staff, December 30, 1948, SP, box 13, HSTL; Colonel Walter I. Miller, Memorandum for the Record, Conference with

Comptroller General Concerning Use of ECA Counterpart Funds at Burtonwood, England, January 12, 1948, SP, box 5, HSTL.

25. Symington, Memoradum for the Chief of Staff, December 30, 1948, SP, box 13, HSTL. Thomas Finletter also was at the luncheon.

26. Ibid. Symington was so impressed with the results of the trip that the next year (Christmas 1949) he persuaded Hope to accompany him on a visit to air force troops stationed in Alaska. In forty-eight hours Hope gave seven shows in sub-zero temperatures, and in such remote places as Kodiak in the Aleutian Islands. *SLGD,* January 1, 1950. Symington spent much of his time visiting with the troops. When he learned that some of their allowances were late, he called Eugene Zuckert on New Year's Eve and told him he wanted them delivered on New Year's Day—"We had people working until midnight on New Year's eve so Symington could give these boys something he felt they deserved." Interview, Eugene Zuckert, by George M. Watson, Jr., January 24, 1948. Symington and Hope apparently shared barracks-type quarters. Frequently in the years to come, Hope addressed Symington as "Dear Cell-Mate."

27. Symington to Lyndon Johnson, February 11, 1949, Lyndon Johnson Papers, box 55, LBJL. Johnson's statement is in *CR- Senate,* February 10, 1949.

28. Rearden, *The Formative Years,* 300.

29. Futrell, *Ideas, Concepts, Doctrine,* 217.

30. *Report of the Secretary of the Air Force to the Secretary of Defense for Fiscal Year 1948,* 7–8. See also air force press release no. 133, January 9, 1949, RG 340, Special Interest File, box 19, NARA. The designation "Four Year Program" replaced the "70-Group Program" as being more descriptive of what the Air Force was trying to do.

Chapter 12. The Fight for Air Power (I)

1. Robert J. Donovan, *Tumultuous Years: The Presidency of Harry S. Truman, 1949–1953* (New York: Norton, 1982), 54–56.

2. W. Barton Leach, "The Bear Has Wings," *Air Force,* February 1947, 17–19, 64, quoted in Futrell, *Ideas, Concepts, Doctrine,* 201; 80th Cong., 1st sess., *Military Establishment Appropriation Bill for 1948, House of Representatives,* 2–4, quoted in ibid.

3. Rearden, *The Formative Years,* 310–11.

4. Wolk, *Planning and Organizing the Postwar Air Force,* 215. Spaatz expressed impatience at the slow pace at which activation of the fifty-five groups proceeded. He told the air staff on July 2, 1947, that he wanted all groups to be fully activated by January 1—"He considers it to be of the highest importance that when we appear before Congress next year for the new budget that the 55 Group Program is in effect." "Minutes of Air Staff Meeting, July 1, 1947," RG 107, box 187K, NARA.

5. Thomas Y. French, "Unification and the American Military Establishment, 1945–1950," 215; William S. Hill, Jr., "The Business Community and National Defense: Corporate Leaders and the Military, 1943–1950," 87–90.

6. Watson, *Office of Secretary of the Air Force,* 30–31.

7. Hill, "The Business Community and National Defense," 210–12. Frank Kofsky, *Harry S. Truman and the War Scare of 1948: A Successful Campaign to Deceive the Nation,*

52–60, treats all this as part of a great conspiracy between industry and the AAF. See memo, Symington to Spaatz, November 19, 1946, loc. cit.

8. Watson, *Office of Secretary of the Air Force,* 44.

9. Memo, Symington to Spaatz, February 12, 1947, SP, box 14, HSTL; Symington to Echols, May 30, 1947, SP, box 14, HSTL.

10. Kofsky, *Truman and the War Scare of 1948,* 47–82, discusses in detail the attitudes and activities of both uniformed and civilian leaders toward the aircraft industry.

11. Ibid., 59.

12. Ibid., 67–70, 76; Futrell, *Ideas, Concepts, Doctrine,* 67–70.

13. Rearden, *The Formative Years,* 80, 314.

14. Memo, Brigadier General B. L. Boatner, September 12, 1947, "Briefing for the President's Air Policy Commission," SP, box 8, HSTL; Memo, Boatner to Spaatz, October 3, 1947, enclosing Memo for Mr. Symington and General Spaatz, "dictated by Mr. John A. McCone in my office this date, after a long distance telephone conversation with Mr. Finletter in New York," Spaatz Papers, box 251, LC.

15. Rearden, *The Formative Years,* 314.

16. Wolk, *Planning and Organizing the Postwar Air Force,* 215; *Aviation Week,* December 15, 1947, quoted in Donald R. Wilson, "The History of President Truman's Air Policy Commission and Its Influence on Air Policy, 1947–1949," 92–93; Wilson, *Kitty Hawk to Sputnik to Polaris,* 92–93.

17. Rearden, *The Formative Years,* 314–15.

18. "The Wildest Blue Yonder Yet," *Fortune,* March 1948, 151.

19. President's Air Policy Commission, *Survival in the Air Age.*

20. Symington to James E. Webb, December 16, 1947, SP, box 14, HSTL.

21. Memo, Symington to Forrestal, December 16, 1947, Symington to Clifford, December 16, 1947, both in Clifford Papers, box 11, HSTL.

22. See, for example, Donovan, *Tumultuous Years,* 132; Letter (not sent), Truman to Stanley Marcus, July 12, 1949, in Ferrell, ed., *Off the Record,* 160–61.

23. Millis, ed., *The Forrestal Diaries,* 387. Kofsky, *Truman and the War Scare of 1948,* 103–22, describes the telegram as the result of a nefarious plot involving Marshall, Forrestal, and Royall. Rearden, *The Formative Years,* 281–84, provides a more balanced view.

24. David Lilienthal, *The Journals of David E. Lilienthal,* vol. 2, 302. For air force estimates of Soviet air strength see, for example, Kofsky, *Truman and the War Scare of 1948,* 113–16, 154–55, 273–74, and Rearden, *The Formative Years,* 284. Kofsky charges that air force intelligence "was mediocre at best and geared primarily to obtaining larger appropriations for that service by exaggerating Soviet air strength" (p. 115).

25. *Public Papers of the Presidents of the United States: Harry S. Truman,* 182–86.

26. Kofsky, *Truman and the War Scare of 1948,* 203.

27. Truman to Symington, March 25, 1948, Symington to Truman, March 29, 1948, both in SP, box 13, HSTL.

28. Truman to Symington, April 1, 1948, PSF, box 295, HSTL.

29. *NYT,* March 9, 1948; *A Program for National Security,* Report of the President's Advisory Commission on Universal Training, 29.

30. House, Hearings before the Committee on Armed Services, *Selective Service,* 80th

Cong., 2d sess., 6138, quoted in French, "Unification and the American Miitary Establishment," 133.

31. Kofsky, *Truman and War Scare of 1948,* 211. For reports on Symington's insubordination see, for example, Hanson W. Baldwin, *NYT,* April 15, 1948. Memo, Symington to Forrestal, April 21, 1948, SP, box 7, HSTL. Symington sent a copy of the memo to Colonel Robert B. Landry, the president's military aide, with this "eyes only" note: ". . . You must realize how sad and bitter I am about this whole situation because of my devotion to the President. Please show it to Matt [Connelley, the president's appointments secretary] and if he thinks advisable, ask him to show it to the President." Symington to Landry, April 21, 1948, ibid. The record does not show whether the president ever saw the letter.

32. *Selective Service,* 6082, 6159–60, 6138, 6216; House, Hearings before the Subcommittee of the Committee on Appropriations, *National Military Establishment Appropriation Bill for 1949,* 80th Cong., 2d sess. (Washington, 1948), vol. 3, 2–4, cited in Warner R. Schilling, Paul Y. Hammond, and Glen H. Snyder, *Strategy, Politics, and Defense Budgets,* 42–43; *NYT,* April 15, 1948.

33. Memo, Symington to Forrestal, March 31, 1948, Spaatz Papers, box 28, LC.

34. Robert Cutler, *No Time for Rest,* 255.

35. Cutler to Symington, April 3, 1948, RG 340, box 4, NARA; Memo, "J.F." to Symington, April 5, 1948, SPF, box 11; Symington to Gurney, April 13, 1948, RG 340, box 4, NARA.

36. Interview, Stuart Symington, by Robert J. Donovan, quoted in Donovan, *Tumultuous Years,* 53.

37. Interview, Stuart Symington, by Douglas Brinkley, November 1 and 17, 1987, quoted in Hoopes and Brinkley, *Driven Patriot,* 375–76.

38. Senate, Stenographic Transcript of Hearings before the Armed Services Committee, UMT, Requirements of the Air Force, April 7, 1948, 61, RG 46, box 6, NARA.

39. *American Magazine,* February 1948, 50. The article was reproduced in *CR-House,* Extension of Remarks of Chester E. Murrow, February 16, 1948, A818.

40. Senate, Stenographic Transcript of Hearings before the Committee on Armed Services, April 7, 1948, 63–64, RG 46, box 6, NARA.

41. *NYT,* April 8, 1948; Memo, Karl Bendetsen [a budgetary assistant who had been brought into Forrestal's office at Robert Cutler's request] to Clark Clifford, April 8, 1948, Clifford Papers, box 11, HSTL.

42. *NYT,* April 8 and 16, 1948.

43. See, for example, Cutler, *No Time For Rest,* 257–58; Arnold Rogow, *James Forrestal: A Study of Personality, Politics, and Policy,* 295–96.

44. *The National Military Establishment,* Conference Held by the Secretary of Defense with the Secretaries of the Army, the Navy, and the Air Force, April 20, 1948, 10 A.M., Room 3E-714, SPF, box 11. The following notation appears on the cover sheet: "File in personal file—Very important—and he is very anxious to keep here, handy and available and safe. vl" [Virginia Laird, Symington's personal secretary.]

45. *New York Herald Tribune,* April 22, 1948.

46. Ibid.; *WP,* April 23, 1948. Vinson, known as the "father" of the modern navy, was a recent convert to the position of the air force. During the struggle over unification,

when he had been serving as chairman of the House Committee on Naval Affairs, he had consistently favored the navy's point of view. By the spring of 1948, however, he had become a strong advocate of air power's important role in national defense. On April 5 Symington wrote him: "I suppose you have received a lot of compliments on your long record of public service, but never in my life have I been more impressed with, or appreciative of, the fairness and gracious kindness of your approach to this problem of America's new Air Force." Spaatz Papers, box 264, LC. *WP,* April 23 and 26, 1948; *CR-Senate,* April 20, 1948, 4695–99; *Washington Evening Star,* April 23, 1948.

47. *CR-Senate,* May 11, 1948, 5586; Eaker to Symington, May 25, 1948, SPF, box 7.

48. "Statement by the President," May 21, 1948, Clifford Papers, box 11, HSTL.

Chapter 13. The Fight for Air Power (II)

1. *Report of the Secretary of the Air Force to the Secretary of Defense for Fiscal Year 1948,* 4–6.

2. Millis, ed., *The Forrestal Diaries,* 390–94; OSD Press Release no. 38–48, March 26, 1948, RG 340, Special Interest File, box 4, NARA; Walter Millis, with Harvey C. Mansfield and Harold Stein, *Arms and the State: Civil-Military Elements in National Policy,* 210–13.

3. Hoopes and Brinkley, *Driven Patriot,* 410–11.

4. Ibid., 411–12; Millis, ed., *The Forrestal Diaries,* 468, 476; Cornell, "James V. Forrestal and the American National Security Policy," 399–400. Hoopes and Brinkley assert that Spaatz's position, a reversal of his earlier views, "was devoid of interservice altruism, but was based on a technological breakthrough. . . . The indications were that by 1950 the United States could have as many as four hundred atomic bombs. Given such prospective abundance, Spaatz concluded that the Navy could share in the strategic bombing mission without encroaching on Air Force primacy."

5. OSD Press Release no. 137–48, August 23, 1948, John H. Ohly Papers, box 69, HSTL.

6. OSD Press Release no. 140–48, August 24, 1948, RG 340, Special Interest Files, box 22, NARA.

7. For an excellent treatment of the budget discussions following the Newport Conference, see Rearden, *The Formative Years,* 335–60.

8. Rearden, *The Formative Years,* 344; Hoopes and Brinkley, *Driven Patriot,* 413; William D. Leahy Papers, Diary, October 4, 1948, Container 8, LC.

9. Symington credited General Curtis LeMay with persuading Forrestal to appreciate the efficacy of strategic bombing. Forrestal called Symington one day and said, "I understand bombers cannot operate without fighter escort." When Symington replied that was a lot of nonsense, Forrestal suggested that he join him for dinner at his home the next night "and bring someone who can demonstrate it isn't true." Symington asked Spaatz whom he should take and was told "LeMay." The next night at dinner, Forrestal raised the question and asked LeMay for his thoughts. Symington remembered that the conversation went like this:

"'Well,' replied LeMay, 'one day in England we got our weather signals switched about a shuttle raid over Germany. The escort fighters didn't come up, so when the bombers, B-17s, broke into the sun around 20,000 feet we had no fighter escort at all.'

Forrestal asked, 'What raid was that?'

LeMay replied either Schweinfurt or Regensberg. 'I can't remember, but it was one of those two.'

Forrestal observed, 'You lost a lot of bombers, didn't you?'

LeMay replied, 'Yes, sir, but we wiped the target off the earth.'

Forrestal asked, 'How do you know that, General?'

LeMay put down the cigar he was chewing on and replied, 'I led the first group, sir.'

Forrestal looked at him a time, then said, 'That's good enough for me.' And we never heard any more about it in any formal way." Interview, Stuart Symington, by James R. Fuchs, May 29, 1981, 49–52.

10. Murray Green, "Stuart Symington and the B-36," 98.

11. Rearden, *The Formative Years,* 435; Greg Herken, *Counsels of War,* 53; Joint Interview, Charles Murphy, Richard Neustadt, David Stowe, James Webb, by Hugh Heclo and Anna Nelson, February 20, 1980, 76–77, HSTL. See also Ferrell, *Harry S. Truman,* 444.

12. Rearden, *The Formative Years,* 425.

13. Lilienthal, *Journals,* entry of June 30, 1948, vol. 2, 377. See also Ferrell, *Harry S. Truman,* 347.

14. Lilienthal, *Journals,* entry of July 21, 1948, vol. 2, 391.

15. Ferrell, *Harry S. Truman,* 347; Millis, ed., *The Forrestal Diaries,* 241. See also Hoopes and Brinkley, *Driven Patriot,* 378–80. David Lilienthal, it will be recalled, was confirmed as chairman of the Atomic Energy Commission only after an acrimonious battle in the Senate and the press, being accused, among other malevolence, of being a Communist. Memo, Major General Hugh Knerr to Symington, March 23, 1949, RG 340, Special Interest File, box 21, NARA; Millis, ed., *The Forrestal Diaries,* 458.

16. McCullough, *Truman,* 650.

17. Memo, JA [Jack Anderson] to DP [Drew Pearson], June 5, 1948, Drew Pearson Papers, F 151, LBJL.

18. *NYT,* July 18, 1948. Symington charged that Hill's version was not corroborated by any other account of the speech. Letter, Symington to Turner Catledge, July 22, 1948, PSF, box 138, HSTL. The *Los Angeles Times*'s extensive account on July 17, 1948, surely bears out this charge.

19. Millis, *The Forrestal Diaries,* 463. Millis notes that this entry of July 18 was not dictated until August 3. I have not been able to find a copy of Forrestal's message in either the Symington or Forrestal papers. When General Eisenhower read Forrestal's diary, shortly after its publication, he made the following handwritten note: "He told me he never demanded resignation of S." Schulz, Memo for the Record, September 27, 1950, DDE papers, Pre-Presidential, box 42, EL.

20. McCone later served as undersecretary of the air force, chairman of the Atomic Energy Commission, and director of the CIA. Rearden, *The Formative Years,* 80n. Steven L. Rearden, Memorandum for the Record, May 28, 1981, subject: Interview

with Stuart Symington, May 27, 1981, Historical Office, Office of Secretary of Defense; Symington to Turner Catledge, July 22, 1948, PSF, box 138, HSTL.

21. Rearden, Memorandum for the Record, May 28, 1981; R. W. Berry to John O'Donnell, July 20, 1948, Pre-Presidential Papers, box 113, EL.

22. Millis, ed., *The Forrestal Diaries,* 465.

23. Symington to Eisenhower, July 23, 1948, Pre-Presidential Papers, box 113, EL.

24. Arthur Krock, *Memoirs: Sixty Years on the Firing Line,* 252; *NYT,* August 27, 1948.

25. Rearden, Memorandum for the Record, May 28, 1981; Interview, Vice Admiral Fitzhugh Lee, by E. B. Kitchen, August 9, 1970, 193–95, U.S. Naval Institute, Annapolis. Admiral Lee was a navy public relations officer. His 1970 interview is not supported by any other evidence I have seen. Moreover, his memory as to details seems to have been faulty. For example, he suggests that Forrestal "called in Mr. Symington" only after John Sullivan had complained about the speech. Also, he identifies the *New York Times* reporter as Hanson Baldwin rather than Gladwin Hill.

26. Hoopes and Brinkley, *Driven Patriot,* 382–83. Walter Lippman, not one of Symington's great admirers, suggested that Forrestal did not insist upon Symington's dismissal "because Mr. Forrestal was not altogether sure that Mr. Symington might not be right." Lippmann, "Today and Tomorrow," *WP,* March 7, 1949.

27. Krock, *Memoirs,* 252.

28. Symington to Forrestal, January 17, 1949, SP, box 5, HSTL. Hoopes and Brinkley, *Driven Patriot,* 440, quote Marx Leva as saying that "it was well known that Symington was a confidant who regularly fed Pearson with Air Force propaganda detrimental to the navy and to Forrestal." They also quote Pearson's widow as saying that her husband and Symington were "very close friends." The Drew Pearson papers in the Johnson Library contain no evidence that Symington "fed Pearson" with anti-navy, anti-Forrestal propaganda. As for the two men being "very close friends," Pearson was highly critical of Symington at the time of his appointment as chairman of the Surplus Property Board, as previously discussed. On April 22, 1949, Pearson wrote in his Diary: "Talked to Stuart Symington. He looks like a phony. He talks like a phony. But I am convinced he is no phony." Tyler Abell, ed., *Drew Pearson Diaries, 1949–1959,* 44. That is hardly the sort of thing one would write about a "very close friend." The pro-navy people, both at the time and in retrospect, have left no innuendo unturned in their effort to discredit Symington and the air force.

29. Ferrell, ed., *Truman in the White House: The Diary of Eben A. Ayers,* 254.

30. "Forrestal's Appointments Calendar, January 3, 1949 to March 28, 1949," in Rogow, *James Forrestal,* 353–64.

31. Interview, Stuart Symington, by James R. Fuchs, May 29, 1981, 44, HSTL. This interview is the only source I have found relating to this matter.

32. Rogow, *James Forrestal,* 364; Memorandum, March 29, 1949, SPF, box 11, Various Personal Memoranda. Hoopes and Brinkley, *Driven Patriot,* 447, relying on interviews with Marx Leva (Interview, Marx Leva, by Jerry N. Hess, December 9, 1969, Oral History Interviews, HSTL) assert that Symington and Forrestal were alone in the car and that "Symington said something that shattered Forrestal's last remaining defenses." This would have to be inferred from Leva's statement. He did not state it. Even so, the interview, twenty years after the event, hardly supersedes Symington's private

memorandum dictated the day of the event, unless, of course, Symington was writing for history, which might have been the case.

33. *NYT,* May 23, 1949.

34. Rearden, Memorandum for the Record, May 28, 1981. This also was the view of John T. Connor, secretary of commerce in the Johnson administration, who was an assistant to Forrestal during the unification struggle and for a time in the Department of Defense. He wrote: "This trying and even humiliating experience of struggling to make work what was in fact an unworkable mechanism, at the same time realizing that he was important contributing factor in bringing his [Forrestal's] life to an abrupt end." John T. Connor, "Impressions of the Secretary," October 23, 1961, Arthur Krock papers, box 57, SM.

35. Hoopes and Brinkley, *Driven Patriot,* 447; Symington to Peter C. Walker, May 27, 1987, SPF, box 5; Interview, Stuart Symington, by Alfred Goldberg, May 27, 1981, 9.

Chapter 14. Showdown with the Navy

1. Much has been written on this unhappy episode. Two of the most comprehensive accounts are Jeffrey G. Barlow, *The Revolt of the Admirals: The Fight for Naval Aviation, 1945–1950,* and Green, "Stuart Symington and the B-36." I have made extensive use of both, particularly of Green.

2. Vandenberg to Forrestal, March 1, 1949, quoted in Green, "Symington and the B-36," 17n.

3. Symington to Wadsworth, April 11, 1949, SPF, box 3.

4. Johnson told Senator Millard Tydings that the decision was made "on the recommendation of not less than a majority of the Joint Chiefs of Staff and with the approval of the President." Johnson to Tydings, April 25, 1949, Records of the U.S. Senate, 81st Congress, Committee on the Armed Services, general correspondence, NARA RG 46, box 127. *NYT,* April 27, 1949; *Washington Evening Star,* April 26, 1949.

5. *U.S. News and World Report,* May 6, 1949.

6. *Washington Evening Star,* April 26, 1949. In his memoirs, Baldwin called Symington one of the "nastiest" politicians in Washington, asserting that his "methods were dirty pool and dirty politics." He made the further absurd claim that Symington had "ganged up on Forrestal" because he wanted to become secretary of defense. Hanson W. Baldwin, *Reminiscences,* vol. 2, 458–68. Baldwin's quote is from *NYT,* April 29, 1949.

7. *CR-House,* May 26, 1949, 6892–94.

8. *SLPD,* June 3, 1949. Colonel Glen W. Martin, Symington's executive officer, recalled that Symington took Van Zandt's charges as "a personal attack on his integrity." "His first action . . . was to go through it, point by point, and then start writing a rebuttal. He would dictate part of it and send it out to get typed while he redrafted the earlier part, and he kept working on that thing literally for hours." Interview, Glen Martin, by Vaughn H. Gallacher and Hugh N. Ahmann, 28–30. Symington to Vinson, June 3, 1949, NARA RG 340, Special Interest File, box 51, NARA.

9. Memo, Barton Leach to General Fairchild, June 2, 1949, RG 340, box 40, Special Interest File, 1949, NARA. See also Watson, *Office of the Secretary of the Air Force,* 91.

10. House, Hearings before the Committee on Armed Services, *Investigation of the B-36 Bomber Program,* 81st Cong., 1st sess., 35; *Los Angeles Times,* August 18, 1944. A detailed chronological account of the B-36's development will be found in an unpublished air force document, "History of B-36 Procurement," attached to memo, General Muir S. Fairchild to Secretary of the Air Force, July 26, 1949, Vandenberg papers, box 42, LC.

11. "History of B-36 Procurement," 67.

12. Ibid., 73; *SLGD,* August 27, 1946, quoted in Green, "Symington and the B-36," 74.

13. Memo, Symington to O'Donnell, November 9, 1946, quoted in Green, "Symington and the B-36," 77.

14. Kenney to Spaatz, December 12, 1946, Memo, Twining to Assistant Chief of Staff A-4, December 27, 1946, Spaatz to Kenney, January 16, 1947, all in RG 340, box 38, Special Interest File, 1949, #11, NARA.

15. Memo, Symington to Barrows, December 29, 1947, SP, box 2, HSTL.

16. Symington, undated, unsigned memorandum, dictated about June 16, 1949, quoted in Green, "Symington and the B–36," 86–87; Memo, Colonel B. C. Kelsey to General [Lieutenant General Howard] Craig, May 13, 1948, RG 340, Special Interest File, 1949, no. 11, NARA; Memo, Norstad to Lieutenant General Howard Craig, April 24, 1948, Ibid.

17. Green, "Symington and the B-36," 89.

18. Symington presented Carter with the Air Force Award, January 13, 1950. Symington to Lyndon Johnson, January 7, 1950, box 55, LBJL.

19. Memorandum, Symington to Forrestal, May 26, 1948, SPF, box 11. Symington took the rather unusual step of communicating with Forrestal through Montgomery because he was becoming increasingly suspicious that his communications on the B–36, as well as other matters, were not reaching the secretary. He later said that, with Forrestal's permission, his communications were increasingly verbal, because when information went to the secretary of defense in writing, "it leaked out to the press, and to aviation magazines, and when it leaked out it was invariably distorted."

20. *NYT,* October 9, 1948. Kenney wrote Symington a long letter reviewing his changed position on the B-36, in which he said, "Since the actual worth of the B–36 became evident about a year ago, I have repeatedly made speeches in public and in private giving the audience the facts. I have yet to find anyone that is willing to listen that isn't convinced." Kenney to Symington, June 18, 1949, RG 340, box 39, Special Interest File, 1949, NARA.

21. Air Force Press Release no. 135–49, January 11, 1949, quoted in Green, "Symington and the B-36," 104.

22. For Symington's relationship with Jackie Cochran, see above.

23. Green, "Symington and the B-36," 130–35.

24. Ibid., 135–40.

25. Watson, *Office of the Secretary of the Air Force,* 92.

26. *Washington Daily News,* July 12, 1949, quoted in Green, "Symington and the B-36," 176.

27. *CR-Appendix,* July 20, 1949, A-4685; *New York Daily Mirror,* July 27, 1949, quoted in ibid., 178.

28. Green, "Symington and the B-36," 181.

29. *Investigation of the B-36 Bomber Program,* 8–9.

30. Ibid., 26.

31. Ibid., 148.

32. Ibid., 172.

33. Ibid., 206, 220, 232.

34. Ibid., 239–40. For Symington's earlier relations with Danton Walker, see above.

35. Ibid., 242–43.

36. Green, "Symington and the B-36," 193. Symington wrote Northrup: "Dear Jack: The Air Force and I personally are grateful to you for your testimony and this is just a line to send you my high regard." Symington to Northrup, September 1, 1949, RG 340, box 39, Special Interest File, 1949, NARA. In a 1980 interview on public television station KETC, John Northrup, then eighty-five years old and very frail, declared that he had perjured himself in his 1949 testimony, that Symington had threatened him with dire consequences if he refused the merger with Convair, and that he (Northrup) believed that the Flying Wing was canceled in retaliation for his refusal. Symington refused to appear on camera in reply, but he was deeply hurt by the whole episode. He said later that he believed his reputation "had been unfairly and perhaps irretrievably damaged" by the broadcast.

In 1984, Francis J. Baker wrote a doctoral dissertation on the subject, exhaustively examining the records and interviewing the few participants who were still alive—notably Generals Curtis LeMay and Lauris Norstad. He concluded that the decision was based entirely on military considerations and that Northrup's belated recollections were wholly unsupportable. General LeMay, not one of Symington's close friends, who as commanding general of SAC had as much to do with the decision as anyone, said flatly, "I don't believe any of it. . . . There may have been hard feelings between Northrup and Symington. I could understand that. Symington wasn't the most likeable guy in the world."

37. *Washington Times-Herald,* August 22, 1949, quoted in Green, "Symington and the B-36," 196.

38. Symington, it will be recalled, had "borrowed" Carroll from the FBI to conduct investigations for him in the Surplus Property Administration. When Symington became secretary of the air force, he persuaded J. Edgar Hoover to transfer Carroll permanently to the air force.

39. *Investigation of the B-36 Bomber Program,* 497–508, 524–28. General Carroll's investigation revealed that Martin had made a substantial effort to try to discredit Symington, including the employment of the Burns Detective Agency to try to dig up any skeletons from Symington's past—an effort in which they were unsuccessful. OSI Report, quoted in Green, "Symington and the B-36," 207–8.

40. *Investigation of the B-36 Bomber Program,* 654–55. See also *New York Herald-Tribune,* August 25, 1949.

41. Memo, Symington to Johnson, August 24, 1949, SP box 6, HSTL. The memorandum was widely printed in the press.

42. Memo, S. E. to Symington, August 24, 1949, SP, box 6, HSTL. Posing an inter-

esting historiographical problem, Symington, in a 1978 interview, said, "Steve Early, Deputy Secretary of Defense, called and said: 'I want you to put out a statement that you have full confidence in the United States Navy.' He wrote the statement, and I signed it." Interview, Stuart Symington, by Hugh N. Ahmann and Herman S. Wolk, 1978, 34. Porter to Symington, SPF, box 11.

43. Green, "Symington and the B-36," 223.

44. Memo, Symington to the Naval Court of Inquiry, September 22, 1949, SP, box 6, HSTL.

45. Memo, Colonel William E. Carpenter to Symington, September 22, 1949, Clifford papers, box 11, HSTL; *NYT,* September 23, 1949.

46. Douglas Cornell, *Washington Star,* September 11, 1949, quoted in Green, "Symington and the B-36," 223–24. See also *NYT,* September 10, 12, October 4, 1949.

47. Franklin D'Olier, president of the Prudential Insurance Company, who had served as chairman of the Strategic Bombing Survey, wrote Louis Johnson a long letter in which he stated: "The document ['The Strategic Bombing Myth'] quotes heavily the Survey out of context; injects parenthetical expressions not in the original work; links together short quotations which establish a train of thought not found in the original documents; alters a Survey chart; omits qualifying phrases; and in general appears to me to paint a picture diametrically opposed to the findings of the Survey." D'Olier to Johnson, August 23, 1949, SP, box 6, HSTL.

48. Address to 4th Annual Joint Civilian Orientation Conference, Washington, D.C., September 19, 1949, cited in Green, "Symington and the B-36," 227.

49. *NYT,* October 4, 1949.

50. Ibid. Secretary Matthews had testified on the opening day, but it was clear that he was not speaking for the admirals. An air force observer reported to Symington that Matthews spoke "with obvious sincerity, but also with an implied admission that he was powerless to control the officers under him." Memo, F. M. Sallagar to Symington, October 6, 1949, quoted in Green, "Symington and the B-36," 239; *Investigation of the B-36 Bomber Program,* 166–70; *New York Herald Tribune,* October 8, 1949; Kenneth W. Condit, *History of the Joint Chiefs of Staff: The Joint Chiefs of Staff and National Policy* (Washington, D.C.: Government Printing Office, 1986), vol. 2, 343.

51. Green, "Symington and the B-36," 240n.

52. Memo, Leach to Symington, October 4, 1949, quoted in ibid., 242.

53. Radford recalled in his memoirs that when he was nominated to be chairman of the Joint Chiefs of Staff in 1953, he was sure that Senator Symington, a member of the Armed Services Committee, would oppose him. Symington, however, asked only one question: "'Admiral, when you were with the Navy, you worked hard for the Navy. What I would like to know is this: In this new job, will you consider it your duty to work as hard for the Army and Air Force as for the Navy?'

"I said: 'Senator Symington, in this new job I will work primarily for the United States and I will do my best not to favor any particular service. I will try to call my shots as impartially as I can.'

"Senator Symington then told the committee Chairman that he had no further questions. I was over that particular hurdle . . .

"For the next four years and since, Senator Symington has been a close friend. While

I was chairman of the JCS he helped me with various problems." Stephen Jurika, Jr., ed., *From Pearl Harbor to Vietnam: The Memoirs of Admiral Arthur W. Radford,* 315.

54. *Investigation of the B-36 Bomber Program,* 443–45.

55. Ibid., 433–34.

56. Ibid., 399–400.

57. Ibid., 404–5.

58. Ibid., 456–57.

59. Ibid., 536. See also *NYT,* October 20, 1949. For a good discussion of Bradley's impact on the hearings, see Donovan, *Tumultuous Years,* 112. Bradley and Blair, *A General's Life,* 506–13, 523–35.

60. Final evaluation of the B-36 was in the hands of the Special Weapons Evaluation Group, an interservice committee created by Forrestal. Symington was worried about their report—there was some fear in the air force that the navy members might mount a last-ditch attack on the plane—but his fears did not materialize. Green, "Symington and the B-36," 291; House, A Report of an Investigation by the Committee on Armed Services, *Unification and Strategy,* 81st Cong., 2d sess., Doc. 600. Shortly after the hearings ended, President Truman announced that he was accepting the recommendation of Secretary Matthews that Admiral Denfield be replaced as chief of naval operations by Admiral Forrest Sherman. Sherman, it will be remembered, had worked closely with General Norstad in hammering out the final unification document in 1947. (See above.) He was a moderate who had not been involved in the "revolt."

61. *WP,* October 15, 1949.

Chapter 15. Reorganization and Resignation

1. Interview, Symington, by Hugh N. Ahmann and Herman S. Wolk, 1978.

2. Leach to Norstad, December 18, 1948, Norstad Papers, box 21, EL; Ferdinand Eberstadt, Diary, May 19, 1948, Eberstadt papers, box 155, SM. Eberstadt wrote: "Later in the day, Symington called me and asked if I thought it was proper to act as Chairman of Hoover's Committee in view of my past relationship to the unification problem and in view of the fact that I had been lined up with the Navy before. I told him that as this was regarded as a reflection on my non-partisanship in the matter that I could not concur; that I did not want the job but had told Hoover that I would do it. I asked Symington if he had talked with Hoover and he said he had put in a call but had cancelled it. I suggested to him that we talk the matter over further on his return to town. He said he was not raising any questions of confidence or integrity, but simply thought that past associations and connections with the problem might slant my views." Ibid., May 22, 1948, Eberstadt papers, box 155, SM. Memo, Symington to Forrestal, May 21, 1948, Eberstadt papers, box 155, SM. This memorandum appears as an attachment to Eberstadt to Herbert Hoover, May 21, 1948. I have not discovered a copy in Symington's papers or air force records.

3. Memo, Royall to the Secretary of Defense, May 21, 1948, Ibid.

4. Symington to Clifford, July 1, 1948, with enclosures, Clifford papers, box 11, HSTL.

5. Memo, J. B. M. [probably Colonel John B. Montgomery] to Symington, October 19, 1948, SP, box 5, HSTL.

6. Memo, Royall to the Secretary of Defense, September 7, 1948, RG 340, box 4, NARA.

7. Symington to Eberstadt, October 25, 1948, RG 340, Special Interest File, box 5, NARA.

8. Eberstadt to Symington, October 28, 1948, RG 330, box 64, file CD 12–1–26, NARA.

9. Symington to Eberstadt, November 1, 1948, RG 340, Special Interest File, box 5, NARA.

10. *NYT,* December 17, 1948.

11. Patterson to Eberstadt, November 9, 1948, attached to Patterson to Eisenhower, November 17, 1948, Pre-Presidential Papers, box 191, EL.

12. Leach to Norstad, December 18, 1948, Norstad papers, box 21, EL.

13. Hanson W. Baldwin, *NYT* military correspondent who usually took a strong pro-navy position and who was a member of the committee, told Eberstadt that he (Baldwin) had "received a severe rebuke" from Symington, who told him that "if the Committee did 'publish the Navy report,' or make recommendations on the subject, he wouldn't want to, but might have to 'knock down' our reports." Dorwart, *Eberstadt and Forrestal,* 165.

14. Senate, Hearings before the Committee on Armed Services, *National Security Amendments of 1949,* 81st Cong., 1st sess., on S. 1269 and S. 1843, April 7, 1949.

15. Memo, Leach to Symington, April 14, 1949, SP, box 7, HSTL. Symington to Eberstadt, July 1, 1958, ibid.

16. For an analysis of the legislation, see United States, Dept. of Defense, Historical Office. Cole et al., eds., *Department of Defense,* 82–111. See also Edwin L. Williams, Jr., *Legislative History of the AAF and USAF, 1941–1951* (Maxwell Air Force Base, Ala.: Research Studies Institute, Air University, 1955), 61–65.

17. Interview, Eugene Zuckert, by George Watson, Jr., 16–17.

18. Ibid., 53–54.

19. Interview, Stuart Symington, by Alfred Goldberg, Roger Trask and Steven Rearden, May 19, 1981, 3, 9–12.

20. For Johnson's approach to his position, see *NYT,* March 30, April 1, 1949.

21. "Washington Calling," *WP,* May 3, 1949.

22. Acheson made no secret of his dislike of Johnson or his disapproval of Johnson's policies. It was widely believed that his influence with Truman was an important factor in the president's decision to dismiss Johnson early in the Korean War.

23. This story was first reported in Joseph W. Alsop and Stewart Alsop, *The Reporter's Trade,* 73–74. It has been frequently repeated, with various embellishments. See, for example, Joseph W. Alsop, with Adam Platt, *I've Seen the Best of It: Memoirs,* 303–4; Edwin M. Yoder, Jr., *Joe Alsop's Cold War: A Study of Journalistic Influence and Intrigue,* 25–26; Robert W. Merry, *Taking on the World: Joseph and Stewart Alsop—Guardians of the American Century,* 183.

24. Martin and Plaut, *Front Runner, Dark Horse,* 307.

25. Interview, Stuart Symington, by Hugh S. Ahmann and Herman S. Wolk, 1978, 96–97.

26. For a good brief account of the process by which the intelligence was gathered and evaluated, see Donovan, *Tumultuous Years,* 98–101. Truman's quote appears in *Public Papers of the Presidents,* 1949, 485.

27. Donovan, *Tumultuous Years,* 102.

28. Draft memo, Symington to Johnson, January 9, 1950, SP, box 6, HSTL.

29. Minutes of Press Conference held by Secretary of Defense Louis Johnson, January 10, 1950–2:30 p.m., Room 3E-869, Pre-Presidential Papers, box 62, EL. See also *NYT,* January 11, 1950.

30. *WP,* January 11, 1950; *SLPD,* January 11, 1950.

31. *Washington Times-Herald,* February 15, 1950; OSD, press release no. 24–508, for release February 22, 1950, SP, box 12, HSTL; *Washington Times-Herald,* February 15, 1950.

32. *SLPD,* January 20, 1950. Symington sent Johnson a handwritten note, commenting on a clipping from the *Ohio State Journal,* February 7, 1950, discussing the differences between the two: "This is silly. I say as of course you do, that the Russians are strong and getting stronger. You say we will beat them if they hit us today. I subscribe 100%. Tomorrow or day after tomorrow, if they continue to throw their wealth into armaments it might be different." Symington to Johnson, February 9, 1950, SP, box 6, HSTL.

33. Robinson to Symington, February 13, 1950, SP, box 10, HSTL. Robinson expressed regret that the *Herald Tribune* had not given the Baylor speech "the kind of play it should have had." Symington was to have lunch at the *Herald Tribune* on January 20 with Robinson, Helen Reid, Whitelaw Reid, Geoffrey Parsons, Walter Millis, Frank Kelley, and Walter Kerr. Robinson hoped that the lunch would provide an opportunity to discuss ways "to get over a comprehensive version of your ideas to the whole American public." There is no record of the lunch-table discussion. In his "thank you" letter, Symington wrote: "It is good to see you inside the four walls of your plant but far better to see you on any of the 18 holes, so don't forget and if you get down this way do let me know." Symington to Whitelaw Reid, February 21, 1950, ibid. For Baruch's relations with Truman's associates, see Margaret L. Coit, *Mr. Baruch* (Washington, D.C.: BeardBooks, 2000), 637–38. Telegram, Baruch to Symington, January 25, 1950, SPF, box 11; Leach to Symington, March 9, 1950, SP, box 6, HSTL.

34. "The Missouri Gang," Symington papers, box 12, HSTL; *SLPD,* March 6, 1950.

35. Interview, Stuart Symington, by James R. Fuchs, 37–38, HSTL.

36. David Lilienthal, chairman of the Atomic Energy Commission since its establishment in 1946, had resigned to go into business.

37. Interview, Symington by Fuchs, 37–38, HSTL.

38. *Washington Evening Star,* March 31, 1950, and numerous other papers; *Washington Evening Star,* April 2, 1950.

39. Associated Press dispatch dated March 31, 1950, in NSRB clipping file, RG 304, box 43, NARA; *CR-Senate,* March 31, 1950, 4522; ibid., April 5, 1950, 4848.

40. Senate, Hearing before the Committee on Armed Services, *Miscellaneous Bills,*

81st Cong., 2d sess., April 6, 1950. Wherry had worked closely with Symington during the establishment of the Strategic Air Command headquarters at Offutt Field, near Omaha, Nebraska. He also was instrumental in passing legislation for more adequate air force housing. For Symington's view of Wherry, see Marvin E. Stromer, *The Making of a Political Leader: Kenneth S. Wherry and the United States Senate* (Lincoln: University of Nebraska Press, 1969), 140–41.

41. Symington, who was playing golf at the Augusta National Golf Club in Georgia, learned of his confirmation by telegram from Colonel Glen Martin, his executive officer. Telegram, Martin to Symington, April 10, 1950, SPF, box 3.

42. Interview, Symington, by Fuchs, 37; Donovan, *Tumultuous Years*, 265. Finletter believed that he was appointed largely because of Symington's recommendation. Watson, *Office of the Secretary of the Air Force*, 105. Symington, Memo, April 5, 1950, SPF, box 11.

43. SP, box 12, HSTL; Associated Press report in the *Washington Evening Star*, April 19, 1950.

44. When Barrows indicated that he was resigning, Symington wrote: "You have done a great job for your country, and for the new, young Air Force. You have showed them that courage and capacity pay off in the procurement function, just as it does in the air." Symington to Barrows, March 9, 1950, SPF, box 11. Mark S. Watson, "Symington Once More Cites Support for 70 Air Groups," *Baltimore Sun*, April 25, 1950; *NYT*, April 25, 1950. Diary, April 24, 1950, Vandenberg papers, box 2, LC; Eaker to Symington, April 10, 1950, SP, box 1, WHMC.

45. McCone to Symington, April 10, 1950, Lovett to Symington, April 24, 1950, both in SP, box 1, WHMC; Vinson and Short to Symington, April 26, 1950, SPF, box 11.

46. Watson, *Office of Secretary of the Air Force*, 100–101.

47. Ibid., 101–2.

Chapter 16. Frustrated Mobilization Boss

1. Public Law 253, 80th Cong., as reproduced in Cole et al., eds., *Department of Defense*, 39–40. For a history of the National Security Resources Board, see Harry B. Yoshpe, *The National Security Resources Board, 1947–1953: A Case Study in Peacetime Mobilization Planning*, Executive Office of the President, April 30, 1953.

2. Executive Order 9905, November 13, 1947; Executive Order 9931, February 19, 1948.

3. See, for example, *Time*, April 20, 1950, 22; *U.S. News and World Report*, April 21, 1950, 32.

4. White House press release, May 9, 1950, RG 304, box 17, NARA.

5. Executive Office of the President, National Security Resources Board, Press Release no. 146, RG 304, box 43, NARA.

6. Achsah Dorshy Smith, "Society," unidentified clipping, April 25, 1950, SP, vol. 1, WHMC.

7. Interview, Stephen Leo, by George M. Watson, Jr., August 18, 1982; Interview,

James J. Wadsworth, by John P. Mason, Jr., April 24, 1957, 54–56, EL. Wadsworth, it will be recalled, had worked for Symington in the Surplus Property Administration.

8. *SLPD,* May 14, 1950.

9. See Marquis Childs, "Symington's Responsibility," *WP,* June 2, 1950, for a good discussion of the problem.

10. Truman wrote Bess: "The St. Louis meeting was a most successful one. . . . The mayor, Stuart Symington, and the French ambassador made excellent speeches, and then I came on. I've never had such profuse statements and congratulations." Robert H. Ferrell, ed., *Dear Bess: The Letters from Harry to Bess Truman, 1910–1959,* 561. It is easy to see why Truman thought that Symington had made a good speech. Referring to Truman and Jefferson as "two of the most famous artillery captains in history," he said: "What extraordinary coincidence . . . that today this other artillery captain, true to the principles of Thomas Jefferson, is guiding the policy to furnish the French nation and all other freedom loving democracies, with tools with which to preserve their dignity and independence; Thomas Jefferson's vision of the west has become a reality, and, in turn, under our fellow Missourian has become a vision for the world." "Remarks at Jefferson Expansion Memorial, St. Louis, June 10, 1950," SPF, box 12.

11. *Washington Evening Star,* May 19, 1950; *Washington Daily News,* May 23, 1950; *WP,* May 24, 1950; Richard G. Hewlett, *Atomic Shield: A History of the United States Atomic Energy Commission,* vol. 2, 487.

12. PSF, box 94, Appointments, HSTL; McCullough, *Truman,* 780; Donovan, *Tumultuous Years,* 208.

13. Matthew Connelley papers, box 1, Notes on Cabinet Meetings, July 21, 1950, HSTL. At the start of the Korean War, Truman brought Harriman back from his post as ambassador at large to the Marshall Plan countries to serve as a special assistant, giving him a wide range of responsibilities in the area of foreign affairs. Donovan, *Tumultuous Years,* 261–62.

14. *WP,* July 11, 1950.

15. Robert Coughlan, "Home Front Boss," *Life,* October 2, 1946, 104–6, 111–12, 115–16, 118.

16. "Mr. Assistant President," *Forbes,* September 1, 1950, 24–26.

17. William Green to Symington, July 14, 1950, PSF, box 146, HSTL; unidentified clipping, July 12, 1950, SP, vol. 1, WHMC.

18. David O. Ives, "Mobilizer Symington," *Wall Street Journal,* August 4, 1950; *U.S. News and World Report,* July 28, 1950, 22.

19. Symington, Memorandum, "Suggested Action by the NSC for Consideration of the President in the Light of the Korean Situation," July 6, 1950, PSF, box 146, HSTL; Symington to Truman, July 7, 1950, ibid.

20. NSC-68 has engendered a daunting body of literature. Among the more useful accounts are: Donovan, *Tumultuous Years,* 158–61; John Lewis Gaddis, *Strategies of Containment: A Critical Appraisal of Postwar American National Security Policy,* 89–106; Herken, *Counsels of War,* 38–43; Paul H. Nitze, "The Development of NSC-68," *International Security* 4 (spring 1980): 170–76; Schilling et al., *Strategy, Politics, and Defense Budgets,* 267–368. Ernest R. May, ed., *American Cold War Strategy: Interpreting*

NSC-68 reproduces the document with commentaries from a wide variety of perspectives.

21. NSC-68, as reproduced in May, ed., *American Cold War Strategy,* 23–81.

22. Nitze wrote in his memoirs: "Despite 'revisionist' historians who have since asserted that the Truman administration overreacted, there was no doubt in my mind at the time that the danger of the war's spreading was serious and that the situation called for more vigorous measures than we had theretofore contemplated. I did not, however, share the view of the 'doom-and-gloom' prophets—Stuart Symington chief among them—that we should prepare ourselves for a full-scale preemptive nuclear attack on the Soviet Union." Paul Nitze, with Ann M. Smith and Steven L. Rearden, *From Hiroshima to Glasnost: At the Center of Decision, a Memoir* (New York: G. Weidenfeld, 1989), 109.

23. House, Hearings before the Committee on Banking and Currency, *Defense Production Act of 1950,* 81st Cong., 2d sess., on H.R. 9176, July 24 and 25, 1950, 19.

24. Executive Order 10161, September 9, 1950, quoted in Harry B. Yoshpe and Stanley L. Falk, *Organization for National Security* (Washington, D.C.: Industrial College of the Armed Forces, 1965), 140.

25. Willard Shelton, "Truman's New Team," *Nation,* September 23, 1950.

26. Cabell Phillips, "Key Man of Our Mobilization," *NYT,* October 1, 1950.

27. Executive Order no. 10172, October 12, 1950, *Federal Register,* October 17, 1950. See also Yoshpe and Falk, *Organization for National Security,* 140. For good discussions of the stockpiling program see Glenn Herald Snyder, "The Stockpiling of Strategic Materials: A Study of Civilian and Military Perspectives in the Formulation of National Security Policy"; Snyder, *Stockpiling Strategic Materials: Politics and National Defense.*

28. Snyder, *Stockpiling Strategic Materials,* 170–71.

29. W. Stuart Symington, "The Importance of Civil Defense Planning," *Bulletin of the Atomic Scientists,* August 1950, 231–33; Symington to Truman, September 8, 1950, RG 304, box 15, NARA.

30. Harry S. Truman to the Congress of the United States, September 18, 1950, RG 304, box 15, NARA.

31. This was the burden of Symington's article in the *Bulletin of the Atomic Scientists.* This also came to be the prevailing view among America's opinion leaders. For a brilliant discussion of the transition in American thinking with respect to the atomic bomb in the years following the end of World War II, see Paul Boyer, *By the Bomb's Early Light: American Thought and Culture at the Dawn of the Atomic Age.*

32. *Washington Evening Star,* October 5, 1950.

33. *U.S. News and World Report,* October 20, 1950, 28–34.

34. *New York Herald-Tribune,* October 26, 1950.

35. Matthew Connelley, Notes on Cabinet Meetings, October 27, 1950, Connelley papers, box 1, HSTL; *Houston Post,* November 3, 1950. See also *WP,* November 3, 1950; *Wall Street Journal,* November 3, 1950.

36. Schwarz, *The Speculator,* 531–32.

37. Donovan, *Tumultuous Years,* 324–27; *Wall Street Journal,* November 3, 1950.

38. Interview, Elmer Staats, by Robert C. Turner, July 13, 1964, JFK Library; Un-

signed memorandum, "Chronology," December 18, 1950, SPF, box 11, Various Personal Memoranda. Although in the third person, this probably was written by Symington himself.

39. Executive Order no. 10193, December 16, 1950, *Federal Register,* December 19, 1950.

40. *NYT, SLGD,* December 19, 1950; Associated Press, *SLGD,* October 6, 1950. One of Drew Pearson's assistants reported that shortly before Robert Lovett was named secretary of defense, Symington was overheard to tell a friend at the Burning Tree Country Club that he (Symington) would be named secretary of defense. Memo, "DP from FP," n.d., Drew Pearson Papers, 172, LBJL.

41. Thomas to Symington, January 13, 1951, RG 304, box 18, NARA.

42. Memorandum, October 15, 1951, SPF, box 11.

43. NSC-100, "A Report to the National Security Council by the Chairman of the National Security Resources Board, on Recommended Policies and Actions in Light of the Grave World Situation," January 11, 1951, RG 273, NSC 100, NARA; also attached to Symington to Truman, January 12, 1951, PSF, box 147, HSTL.

44. Michael J. Lacey, ed., *The Truman Presidency,* 434. Truman created great consternation both at home and abroad when in response to a reporter's question at a press conference, November 30, he indicated that the atomic bomb was "one of our weapons" and that its use would be determined by commanders in the field. This was simply a blunder—one of the worst of his administration. Truman apparently forgot that the Atomic Energy Act of 1946 provided that only the president could authorize use of the atomic bomb, and the record is clear that he would do so only in the direst circumstances. He turned down all suggestions that nuclear weapons be used in the Korean War. See, for example, McCullough, *Truman,* 832–33. For accounts of the unfortunate press conference, see NSC-100, "A Report to the National Security Council by the Chairman of the National Security Resources Board," 821–23; Donovan, *Tumultuous Years,* 307–10.

45. *Report of the Chairman, National Security Resources Board* (Washington: Government Printing Office, 1951).

46. Memo, Robert L. Dennison to John Steelman, May 3, 1951, PSF, box 146, HSTL.

47. At Wilson's first cabinet meeting (December 29, 1950) the two men disagreed on the wisdom of putting a basic industry in New England. Wilson thought an aluminum plant should be put there. Symington said, "You can't put a basic industry in New England because the power costs are way out of line with the costs in other areas." "Notes on Cabinet Meetings, December 29, 1950," Connelley Papers, box 1, HSTL. *Washington Evening Star,* January 22, 1951; *New York Herald Tribune,* January 11, 1951.

48. Interview, Stuart Symington, by James R. Fuchs, 81, HSTL.

Chapter 17. Reforming the RFC

1. U.S. Congress, Senate Committee on Banking and Currency, *Study of Reconstruction Finance Corporation: Favoritism and Influence,* S. Report 76, 82d Cong., 1st sess., 1951. Senate Miscellaneous Reports, vol. 1, cited in Donovan, *Tumultuous Years,* 333.

2. The RFC scandals are covered in Donovan, *Tumultous Years,* 332–39; Ferrell, *Harry S. Truman,* 362–63; and McCullough, *Truman,* 863–70.

3. Fulbright was not one of the president's favorites. Truman never forgave him for suggesting, after the 1946 congressional elections, that he should resign. He referred to him privately as "an over-educated S.O.B." Apparently, he applied the same epithet to Illinois Democratic Senator Paul Douglas, who was a member of the Fulbright committee. Paul H. Douglas, *In the Fullness of Time: The Memoirs of Paul H. Douglas,* 222. James Reston, Special to the *Globe-Democrat* from the *New York Times, SLGD,* April 4, 1951; Truman to Symington, April 17, 1951, PSF, box 148, HSTL; Symington to Truman, April 17, 1951, SPF, box 12.

4. H. I. Phillips, unidentified clipping, SP, scrapbooks, vol. 1, WHMC.

5. Senate, Hearing before the Committee on Banking and Currency, *Nomination of W. Stuart Symington,* 82d Cong., 1st sess., April 26, 1951, 3.

6. The president's reorganization plan had been held up while the Senate considered whether the agency should be abolished.

7. Memo, The President to Administrator Reconstruction Finance Corporation, May 15, 1951, SPF, box 12.

8. Andrew J. Dunar, *The Truman Scandals and the Politics of Morality,* 94; *Washington Times-Herald,* May 22, 1951.

9. *Nomination of Stuart Symington,* 23; Symington to Truman, May 23, 1951, box 975, OF210-B (RFC), HSTL.

10. Interview, Stephen F. Leo, by George M. Watson, Jr., August 18, 1982, 3.

11. Wellman, *Stuart Symington,* 140–41.

12. Ibid., 141. Weaver recalled that when Symington approached him about going to RFC he protested that he didn't know anything about banking. Symington replied, "I don't either . . . but I do know good management when I see it, and from what I have seen and heard from over there, their problem is poor management." Interview, George Weaver, by James C. Olson, October 17, 1991, 5–6.

13. Wellman, *Stuart Symington,* 141–42.

14. Dunar, *The Truman Scandals,* 94; Reconstruction Finance Corporation, *1951 Annual Report and Financial Statements,* 4–5.

15. Charles D. Bright, *The Jet Makers: The Aerospace Industry from 1945 to 1972,* 188–89; Edward V. Rickenbacker, *Rickenbacker,* 395–96.

16. *SLGD,* September 13, 1951.

17. Truman to Symington, September 26, 1951, SPF, box 12. Republican National Chairman Guy Gabrielson had been charged in the press with trying to influence the old RFC board on behalf of his company, Carthage Hydrocol, Inc. Months later, the Senate Permanent Committee on Investigations issued a report that, while not accusing Gabrielson of wrongdoing, did comment on his lack of candor in dealing with the issue. Senate, Interim Report of the Committee on Expenditures in the Executive Departments made by Its Permanent Subcommittee on Investigations, *American Lithofold Corp., William M. Boyle, Jr., and Guy George Gabrielson,* 82d. Cong., 2d sess., Report no. 1142. See also Donovan, *Tumultuous Years,* 339.

18. Dunar, *The Truman Scandals,* 95; *Washington Times-Herald,* May 22, 1951. Symington and Fulbright became close in the Senate, particularly during the Vietnam War.

19. Senate, Sixth Report of the Preparedness Subcommittee of the Committee on Armed Services, *Investigation of the Preparedness Program,* per S. Res. 18, 82d Cong., 1st sess., Doc. 13, March 14, 1951, 51.

20. *El Diario,* La Paz, Bolivia, June 18, 1951, as translated by Guido Pignatelli, Library of Congress, SPF, box 3.

21. Martin and Plaut, *Front Runner, Dark Horse,* 310; Wellman, *Stuart Symington,* 143–44.

22. Memo, Arthur E. de Celles and George L. P. Weaver to Symington, June 28, 1951, SPF, box 3.

23. Transcript, telephone conversation, Symington and Thomas Mann, July 5, 1951, SPF, box 3.

24. Unsigned memorandum, June 15, 1951, transmitted per Dean Rusk to Symington, July 3, 1951, ibid.

25. Symington to Rusk, July 14, 1951, ibid.

26. Senate, Hearing before the Preparedness Subcommittee of the Committee on Armed Services, *Stockpiling of Tin and Rubber,* 82d Cong., 1st sess., July 24, 1951, 28.

27. Ibid., 32.

28. Symington to Truman, July 31, 1951, PSF, box 138, HSTL; Symington to Acheson, July 31, 1951, SPF, box 3; Symington, Personal Memorandum, August 1, 1951, SPF, box 11. In addition to the State Department flap, Truman apparently was irritated by Symington's friendliness toward Senator Fulbright, and especially by a complimentary remark he had made during a speech in Arkansas. In his personal memo Symington wrote: "It is hard to understand how I could have ignored Senator Fulbright, who was sitting on the platform along with Senator McClellan. I therefore complimented him for his counsel and advice on RFC matters. . . . He is in effect my first liaison with the Senate in getting this shattered agency underway; and along with his staff has been of great assistance."

29. Symington to the Ambassador of Bolivia, August 31, 1951, SPF, box 3; *American Metal Market,* September 12, 1951; *NYT,* January 5, 1952.

30. *NYT,* January 5, 1952.

31. Symington to Truman, December 21, 1951, OF, box 746, HSTL.

32. Truman to Symington, January 7, 1952, ibid.

33. See, for example, the *Detroit Free Press,* January 21, 1952; Drew Pearson, *SLPD,* December 18, 1951; *WP,* January 11, 1952; Truman to Anderson, January 12, 1952, PSF, box 148, HSTL. Symington frequently cited his need for a rest in connection with his resignation, but there is no evidence that the operation to which Truman referred, and which was performed in 1946, had anything to do with his condition. Dr. Samuel Grant of St. Louis, who gave Symington a thorough physical examination on February 1, reported, "It was found that you are in excellent condition, and it is particularly notable that in spite of the responsibilities and strenuous activities attendant to your position, your blood pressure has remained normal, the electrocardiogram is normal, and x-ray reveals the heart to be of normal size and contour." Grant to Symington, February 12, 1952, SPF, box 3.

34. Truman to Symington, January 16, 1952, PSF, box 295, HSTL. McDonald, a Michigan Republican, had been serving as chairman of the Securities Exchange Com-

mission. A House committee report had reflected unfavorably on McDonald, and some senators were strenuously opposing his nomination. *SLPD*, January 29, 1952. Truman to Symington, February 15, 1952, box 796, HSTL. The RFC was run by a committee of four (Don Burrows, Solis Horwitz, Leo Nielson, and Edward Welsh). On February 15, Neilson, on Symington's recommendation, became acting administrator. Cross Reference Sheet, 210-B, Symington, Hon. W. Stuart, 12/21/51, PPF 497-PPF 1004, HSTL. Citation, OF, 01049, #3577, HSTL. Apparently Charles E. Wilson, whose appointment as director of the Office of Defense Mobilization had been a major factor in Symington's decision to leave the National Security Resources Board, first suggested to the president that Symington be awarded the Distinguished Service Medal. Wilson to the president, January 18, 1952, Truman to Wilson, January 21, 1952, ibid.; SPF, box 4. The ceremony received extensive press coverage.

35. *SLPD*, January 29, 1952.

Chapter 18. Beating the Odds in Missouri

1. Martin and Plaut, *Front Runner, Dark Horse*, 314.

2. Alonzo L. Hamby, *Man of the People: A Life of Harry S. Truman* (New York: Oxford University Press, 1995), 606–7.

3. Lashly to Symington, January 7, 1952, reproduced in Martin and Plaut, *Front Runner, Dark Horse*, 317. The letter does not appear to be anywhere in the Symington papers.

4. Ibid., n.d., in ibid.

5. Symington, "Memories," 88–89. Clark Clifford, who had been a member of Lashly's law firm before going to Washington, may well have inspired Lashly's original letter. Martin and Plaut, *Front Runner, Dark Horse*, 317–18. In any event, he had warned Symington to treat Lashly with the courtesy he deserved.

6. Meredith, who would later become Symington's campaign manager, recalled that he was in St. Louis on business, "and Johnny Hahn called me. He wanted to know what did I think of Symington running for the Senate. I told him I didn't give a particular damn one way or another. I had a family to think about, and I was getting out of government into law and I had to start making a little money." Martin and Plaut, *Front Runner, Dark Horse*, 320.

7. Symington, "Memories," 89.

8. *SLGD*, January 31 and February 5, 1952.

9. Martin and Plaut, *Front Runner, Dark Horse*, 319.

10. Symington, "Memories," 90. In recounting his conversation with the president, Symington added: "Hardly had I put down the phone, when my friend [Sidney] Salomon called and said, 'This is unbelievable. I was at the airport, put in my dime to make a call, ran into your conversation with the President, and immediately recognized both voices. . . . I heard the discussion and believe you could win, so from a political standpoint, o.k., but from the standpoint of you as my friend, it would be a very rough go in the primary; and if you win that, an even rougher go in the general election. I know

Mr. Truman was not happy when we brought you the message that State Democratic leaders wanted you to run for Governor and you refused. So think it all over carefully.'"

11. *SLPD*, February 10, 1952.

12. *"MEMORANDUM,"* February 12, 1952, "Personal Memorandum, Senatorial," SPF, box 11. The two memoranda of February 12 appear in full in James C. Olson, "Beating the Odds in Missouri: Stuart Symington's First Campaign for the Senate, 1952," 209–13.

13. Memorandum, February 12, 1952, SPF, box 11. This is Symington's second memorandum of February 12 dealing with his conversation with the president.

14. Martin and Plaut, *Front Runner, Dark Horse*, 315.

15. At the time of Symington's conference with him, Truman was in the process of trying to get rid of J. Howard McGrath, a political crony whom he had appointed attorney general and who had soon proven totally unable to handle the job, with some of his problems, at least, being attributed to his fondness for alcohol. Hamby, *Man of the People*, 589–92.

Symington's memorandum was still sealed when I found it while working with the personal files.

16. Symington, "Memories," 91; *SLPD*, February 13, 1952.

17. Symington to Truman, February 29, 1952, PPF, box 497, #1004, HSTL.

18. Truman to Symington, March 4, 1952, ibid.

19. Symington, "Memories," 92.

20. Ibid. See also Martin and Plaut, *Front Runner, Dark Horse*, 322.

21. Martin and Plaut, *Front Runner, Dark Horse*, 322.

22. Paul C. Nagel, *Missouri: A Bicentennial History* (New York: Norton, 1977), 73. This work, particularly chapter 4, "More Than One Missouri," is an excellent discussion of Missouri's complex character.

23. Lawrence H. Larsen and Nancy Hulston, *Pendergast!* (Columbia: University of Missouri Press, 1997) provides a judicious, well-balanced view of Tom Pendergast.

24. Symington, "Memories," 95.

25. Martin and Plaut, *Front Runner, Dark Horse*, 323–29.

26. Aside from brief trips to St. Louis and Kansas City, Weaver had never been in Missouri. The experience was "an education." Jim Meredith and Stanley Fike, for example, had never eaten with a black man. Weaver recalled a time when he and Dowdal Davis, general manager of the *Kansas City Call*, stopped for Symington at the Muehlbach Hotel in Kansas City. Symington wanted to go into the drugstore to get a malted milk and insisted that they go with him: "He asked us if we wanted a malted milk. We said no. He was standing at the end of the counter and he insisted on it. I looked at Donald and Donald looked at me, and I said, O.K., so he ordered another. The guy looked at him, he was known there in the hotel. The chap behind the counter looked at him, but he went ahead and fixed two, and we stood there and drank them. It was sort of shaky, because I could just envision the headlines. I knew what kind of person Symington was. He would not back up at all in a case like that. We got out in the car, and I bluntly told him, look, we are not out here to solve the race issue. We are trying to get you elected." Interview, George Weaver, by James C. Olson, October 17, 1991.

27. For Oliver's efforts in Kansas City, see Martin and Plaut, *Front Runner, Dark Horse,* 344–51.

28. *SLPD,* March 21, 1952; *SLGD,* March 24, 1952; *SLPD,* May 18, 1952; *KCS* as reprinted in the *SLGD,* July 18, 1952.

29. *Monroe County Appeal,* April 17, 1952.

30. "Paris, Mo. Speech," text in SPF, box 11; Symington, "Memories," 94.

31. *Columbia Tribune,* April 15, 1952.

32. Beulah Schacht in *SLGD,* as quoted in Martin and Plaut, *Front Runner, Dark Horse,* 332.

33. Kem once remarked, when asked if he knew Jim Symington, "If it weren't for that young whippersnapper and his fiddle I'd be in the Senate yet." James Symington to author, January 25, 2001.

34. *SLPD,* August 10, 1952.

35. Martin and Plaut, *Front Runner, Dark Horse,* 324.

36. *SLPD,* July 2, 1952.

37. Ibid., August 10, 1952.

38. *SLGD,* July 11, 1952.

39. "The President's News Conference of May 29, 1952," *Public Papers of the Presidents of the United States: Harry S. Truman. 1952–1953,* 389.

40. SLPD, May 29, 1952; Johnson to Symington, May 29, 1952, LBJA Congressional File, box 55, LBJL.

41. Symington to Johnson, June 4, 1952, ibid.; Symington to Truman, May 6, 1952, PSF, box 324, HSTL. For the president's comments, see above. Ibid., July 25, 1952, ibid.

42. Harry Dorsey Watts, the owner of the car, was still alive, and wrote: "At the time, the incident was only a prank, and it is absurd to think that it could be considered anything else thirty-four years later." Watts to Symington, July 1, 1952, SPF, box 5.

43. "Radio Address of Attorney General J. E. Taylor . . . ," William Becker Papers, box 30, WHMC.

44. See note 28.

45. Becker to Symington, August 6, 1952, William Becker Papers, box 30, WHMC.

46. See, for example, *Washington Star,* August 6, 1952; *NYT,* August 7, 1952.

47. "The President's News Conference of August 7, 1952," *Public Papers of the Presidents of the United States: Harry S. Truman, 1952–1953,* 511.

48. Telegram, Truman to Symington, August 6, 1952, PPF 1004, HSTL; Telegram, Symington to Truman, August 7, 1952, PSF, box 324, HSTL.

49. Martin and Plaut, *Front Runner, Dark Horse,* 361. The *SLPD* of August 12, 1958, reprinted favorable editorials from seven major newspapers, including the *New York Times* and the *New York Herald Tribune.*

50. Symington was one of Eisenhower's favorite bridge companions. Chief Justice Fred Vinson was another. They were both Democrats, however; Eisenhower wrote ruefully to a friend that he was afraid that if he continued to play with them and his other Democratic friends, some Republicans might not understand. Stephen E. Ambrose, *Eisenhower: Soldier and President,* 73. Grafton, *The Sisters,* 167; E. J. Kahn, Jr., *Jock: The Life and Times of John Hay Whitney* (Garden City, N.Y.: Doubleday, 1981), 207–12; Eisenhower to Symington, April 9, 1952, Pre-Presidential Papers, box 113, EL.

51. *SLGD,* July 27, 1952. For the McCarthy endorsement see Ambrose, *Eisenhower: Soldier and President,* 2, 85.

52. While in Colorado Springs, Symington wrote Arthur Krock of the *New York Times* to thank him for his comments on the nomination: "I think I have a good chance against Kem. He is not strong with labor or the farmer, or with the foreign policy position of even the Republican newspapers of the state. It would be a pleasure to be back with you all and I hope it works out that way." Symington to Krock, August 15, 1952, Krock papers, box 57, SM. Krock, responding, wrote: "Most earnestly, I wish you success, and not only because Martha [Mrs. Arthur Krock] can't face Washington without Eve." Krock to Symington, August 18, 1952, ibid.

53. Dallek, *Lone Star Rising,* 421. In his biography of Lyndon Johnson, Robert Caro asserts that Johnson's friends in Texas contributed substantial sums in cash to Symington's campaign. Robert A. Caro, *Master of the Senate* (New York: Knopf, 2002), 412–13.

54. Peter Wyden, "What It's Like to Run for Office," *SLPD,* November 11, 1952, is a chatty, anecdotal piece based on an interview with Symington just after the election.

55. Gilpatric to Symington, October 2, 1952, SPF, box 10; *KCS,* October 9, 1952; *SLPD,* October 3, 1952.

56. William Becker wrote from Columbia: "A number of your friends are not satisfied with the turn of events whereby Kem seems to be carrying the fight to you in this campaign. It seems to me it is time for you to come out fighting and strike a few blows in your own behalf. And I think, you are going to have to strike some of them personally." Becker to Symington, September 22, 1952, Becker papers, box 30, WHMC. *SLPD,* October 3 and 22, 1952.

57. Symington, "Memories," 101–2.

58. Irving Dilliard, "Farewell to Mr. Kem," *New Republic,* October 27, 1952, 16–17.

Chapter 19. Not Your Ordinary Freshman

1. The Wadsworths had lived at 2800 Woodland Drive for many years after the Hay house, across from Lafayette Square, became the site of the Hay-Adams Hotel. They had purchased the Georgetown house just before the beginning of World War II. Eve's father died in 1952. Information from Stuart Symington, Jr. Lloyd Grove, "Where Talk Wasn't Cheap," *WP,* August 31, 1998; Bonnie Angelo, *Newsday,* March 17, 1960, 58.

2. Whitney to Symington, January 22, 1953, SPF, box 12.

3. Symington to Wellman, September 7, 1959, SPF, box 11.

4. Hope was in Washington on February 27 to be honored by the Friars Club. Symington was one of the guest speakers, joining such luminaries as George Jessel, Milton Berle, Fred Allen, Alben Barkley, Adolph Zukor, and Bernard Baruch in ceremonies broadcast over NBC. Arthur Marx, *The Secret Life of Bob Hope,* 302–3. Hope to Symington, January 16, 1953, SPF, box 12. Symington and Hope remained close friends throughout Symington's life. During Symington's senatorial years, they frequently visited on the telephone. Interview, Virginia Laird, by James C. Olson.

5. Marshall to Symington, January 25, 1953, SPF, box 12.

6. In a letter congratulating the Fikes on their fiftieth wedding anniversary,

Symington wrote: "To you, Stan, I owe more than to any living person outside of my family." Symington to Mr. and Mrs. Stanley Fike, July 2, 1985, SPF, box 5. See also "The Third Senator," *Mexico Ledger,* December 16, 1976.

7. *SLGD,* January 1, 1953.

8. Information from Stuart Symington, Jr.

9. Memo, Ag to Staff, SP, box 124, WHMC.

10. Memo, Symington to Staff, April 11, 1962, ibid.

11. Interview, Glen Martin, by Vaughn H. Gallacher and Hugh N. Ahmann, US-AFHRC; Memo, Fike to the Staff, March 12, 1964, SP, box 124, WHMC.

12. Interview, Virginia Laird, by James C. Olson; Interview, R. J. Vanderzee, 45–47, Senate oral history interviews, box 9, LC.

13. Fike to Becker, March 11, 1953, William Becker papers, box 29, WHMC.

14. For the range and scope of these efforts, see SP, subject box 95, WHMC.

15. *SLGD,* January 1, 1953.

16. For Johnson's thinking on the matter, see Rowland Evans and Robert Novak, *Lyndon B. Johnson: The Exercise of Power,* 63–64.

17. For an interesting discussion of the process, see John A. Goldsmith, *Colleagues: Richard B. Russell and His Apprentice, Lyndon B. Johnson,* 32–34. Symington was rewarded by appointment to the Armed Services Committee, a post he desired above all.

Chapter 20. Confronting McCarthyism

1. Pogue, *George C. Marshall,* 430–36; Thomas C. Reeves, *The Life and Times of Joe McCarthy: A Biography,* 357–62; Symington to Rosenberg, July 21 and October 26, 1950, RG 304, box 16, NARA.

2. Reeves, *The Life and Times of Joe McCarthy,* 287–346; Keith, *"For Hell and a Brown Mule,"* 425–27. Eve Symington and Eleanor Tydings had been debutantes together in Washington.

3. *NYT,* January 13, 1953; Robert Griffith, *The Politics of Fear: Joseph R. McCarthy and the Senate,* 211.

4. Symington to Mrs. James Wadsworth, February 25, 1953, SPF, box 3.

5. Senate, Hearings before the Permanent Subcommittee on Investigations of Committee on Government Operations, *State Department Information Program—Voice of America,* 83d Cong, 1st sess. (Washington: Government Printing Office, 1953), pt. 4, March 2, 1953, 250–51.

6. "Excerpt from broadcast of Elmer Davis March 2, 1953, American Broadcasting Company," SP, box 348, WHMC.

7. Swope to Symington, March 16, 1953, SP, box 348, WHMC; Alsop to Symington, March 13, 1953, Alsop Papers, box 20, LC. In reply, Symington wrote: "My head and heart are both really in the Armed Services Committee, but I will do my best re that other situation." Symington to Alsop, March 17, 1953, ibid.

8. Symington, Memorandum for file, December 2, 1953, SPF, box 10. Symington's directness was particularly evident in his interrogation of Dr. Bernhard J. Stern, profes-

sor of sociology at Columbia University, who repeatedly took the Fifth Amendment in response to such questions as, "Do you think that a man who refuses to say whether or not he has been a member of an organization which has as its primary motive or one of its primary motives the destruction of our way of government is still a person who can be a good teacher of American youth?" Senate, Hearings before the Permanent Subcommittee on Investigations of the Committee on Government Operations, *State Department Information Program—Information Centers,* 83d Cong., 1st sess., pt. 2, March 27, April 1 and 2, 1953, 106–9.

9. The junket of Cohn and Schine was well covered by the press. For a good, if not altogether impartial, account see Richard H. Rovere, "The Adventures of Cohn and Schine," *The Reporter* 9 (July 21, 1953): 7–16.

10. *State Department Information Program—Information Centers,* 290–305; James A. Wechsler, *The Age of Suspicion* (New York: Random House, 1953), 306–9.

11. Ferald J. Bryan, "Joseph McCarthy, Robert Kennedy, and the Greek Shipping Crisis: A Study of Foreign Policy Rhetoric," *Presidential Studies Quarterly* 24: 93–104; Harold Stassen and Marshall Houts, *Eisenhower: Turning the World Toward Peace,* 247–50.

12. Reeves, *Life and Times of Joe McCarthy,* 486–88; Griffith, *Politics of Fear,* 297–98; Arthur M. Schlesinger, Jr., *Robert Kennedy and His Times,* 102–4; Robert J. Donovan, *Eisenhower: The Inside Story,* 245; Sherman Adams, *Firsthand Report: The Story of the Eisenhower Administration,* 140–41.

13. Press release, June 10, 1953, William H. Becker papers, box 29, WHMC; *SLGD,* June 11, 1953.

14. J. B. Matthews, "Reds and Our Churches," *American Mercury,* July 1953, 3–13.

15. *NYT,* July 3 and 8, 1953.

16. Ibid., July 11, 1953. Potter apparently had been persuaded to go along with his Republican colleagues after McCarthy had accepted Matthews's resignation.

17. Ibid., July 17, 19, and 20, 1953. Jackson and McClellan also labeled McCarthy's charges as false.

18. Most of the letters are in SP, box 347, WHMC.

19. "Memorandum," December 2, 1953, SPF, box 10.

20. Reeves, *The Life and Times of Joe McCarthy,* 533–34; William Prochnau and Richard W. Larson, *A Certain Democrat: Senator Henry M. Jackson,* 140. The Democrats immediately hired as their minority counsel Robert Kennedy, who had resigned as minority counsel shortly after the Democratic walkout, ostensibly to enter private practice but probably because he was tired of playing second fiddle to Roy Cohn, the committee's chief counsel. Kennedy, along with his brother Jack and other members of the family, maintained friendly relations with McCarthy throughout his life. Schlesinger, *Robert Kennedy and His Times,* 104–7.

21. William Bragg Ewald, Jr., *Who Killed Joe McCarthy?* 176.

22. Reeves, *The Life and Times of Joe McCarthy,* 516–17.

23. Ibid., 540–45; John G. Adams, *Without Precedent: The Story of the Death of McCarthyism,* 124–27.

24. Robert Stevens to Karl Mundt, June 17, 1954; *NYT,* June 18, 1954.

25. Symington to McCarthy, February 19, 1954, SPF, box 11; Memo, telephone conversation with Richard O'Melia, February 20, 1954, ibid. When he returned to town,

McCarthy confirmed this by telegram. Telegram, McCarthy to Symington, April 22, 1954, SP, f. 2336, WHMC.

26. Senate, Hearing before the Special Subcommittee on Investigations of the Committee on Government Operations, *Special Senate Investigation on Charges and Counter-charges Involving Secretary of the Army Robert T. Stevens, John G. Adams, H. Struve Hensel, and Senator Joe McCarthy, Roy M. Cohn, and Francis P. Carr,* 83d Cong., 1st sess. (Washington: Government Printing Office, 1954), 2120; hereafter referred to as Army-McCarthy Hearings. The letter as sent, with copies to the Democratic members of the committee, is in SP, f. 2336, WHMC.

27. Ibid., 2120.

28. Ewald, *Who Killed Joe McCarthy?* 200; Army-McCarthy Hearings, 2121–22. The "Bill Rogers" to whom Symington referred was Assistant Attorney General William P. Rogers. It will be recalled that Symington had intervened with Rogers, then serving as counsel to a legislative investigation of the Meyers case, on behalf of the air force.

29. *SLPD,* June 9, 1954.

30. Cablegram, Stevens to Symington, February 21, 1954, SP, f. 2371, WHMC; Cable, SEC OF STATE WASH DC TO DEPTAR WASH DC, 23 FEB 54, ibid.

31. Army-McCarthy Hearings, 2124–25.

32. Adams, *Without Precedent,* 122–23, 142–43; Ewald, *Who Killed Joe McCarthy?* 260.

33. In his memoirs, Cohn implies that Symington actually befriended him. He reported that after his appearance on *Meet the Press,* following his European trip with David Schine, "Senator Symington conveyed a congratulatory message from Bob Hope—they had watched together." Again, he described a January 1954 meeting in Symington's office at which Symington cryptically used the word "crossfire" to warn him that the three Republicans on the committee were conspiring with the Democratic minority to fire him. Roy M. Cohn, *McCarthy,* 92, 114–15, 120. Symington later stated that he had no recollection of these conversations or of any friendly relations with Cohn. Nicholas von Hoffman, *The Life and Times of Roy Cohn: Citizen Cohn,* 239. McCarthy's quote is from Reeves, *The Life and Times of Joe McCarthy,* 592.

34. Keith, *"For Hell and a Brown Mule,"* 440–41.

35. Memo, Robert F. Kennedy to Symington, March 9, 1954, SP, f. 2455, WHMC.

36. Senate, Hearings before the Permanent Subcommittee on Investigations of the Committee on Government Operations, *Army Signal Corps—Subversion and Espionage,* 83d Cong., 2d sess. (Washington: Government Printing Office, 1954), 458–59.

37. Ibid., 462.

38. Thomas Rosteck, *"See It Now" Confronts McCarthyism: Television Documentary and the Politics of Representation* (Tuscaloosa: University of Alabama Press, 1994), 161. Rostock provides a good descriptive analysis of the Moss hearing. Telegram, Mitchell to Symington, March 11, 1954, Telegram, White to Symington, March 12, 1954, both in SP, f. 2456, WHMC; Capp to Symington, March 13, 1954, ibid., f. 2547.

39. *New York Herald Tribune,* March 19, 1954.

40. Von Hoffman, *Citizen Cohn,* 205.

41. *New York Daily News,* August 5, 1954; Stanley Fike, "Statement by Fulton Lewis

on Mutual Wednesday Night," SP, f. 2467, WHMC; Symington to Dilliard, August 10, 1954, ibid., f. 2472; Symington to McCarthy, August 5, 1954, McCarthy to Symington, September 3, 1954, ibid., f. 2474; Charles E. Wilson to The Secretary of the Army, January 18, 1955, DOD press release no. 52–55, January 19, 1955, copies in ibid., f. 2475.

42. Office of Senator Stuart Symington, Press Release, March 20, 1954, SP, f. 2337, WHMC.

43. *SLGD,* March 21, 1954.

44. *U.S. News and World Report,* April 16, 1954, 55–56.

45. Much has been written about the hearings. For a good brief description, see Eric Goldman, *The Crucial Decade and After,* 271–79.

46. Walter Winchell charged on his television program that the Americans for Democratic Action had "gone to work on Sen. Stuart Symington, a member of the McCarthy Comm., because he looms as a dangerous opponent to Adlai Stevenson. ADA favors Adlai for '56. In the party the ADA has started spreading stories that Symington is 'another Tom Dewey.'" "From Walter Winchell's office," April 20, 1954, SPF, box 12. In a letter of thanks, Symington wrote: "You can't win on this McCarthy Committee situation. Those who don't approve of him are criticizing a lack of positiveness on our part; those who do approve him, criticize us for not supporting him in entirety. It's a great world. Eve and I look at you every Sunday night. I must say, when you take those glasses off, you could sell me just about anything." Symington to Winchell, April 20, 1954, ibid.

47. *SLPD,* May 18, 1954; James Allen to Symington, May 24, 1954, SPF, box 10.

48. Abell, ed., *Drew Pearson Diaries,* 309; Richard H. Rovere, *Senator Joe McCarthy,* 220–21.

49. Michael Straight, "The Growth of Stuart Symington," *New Republic,* June 21, 1954, 12–14. See also James W. Symington, *The Stately Game,* 132.

50. Army-McCarthy Hearings, 258.

51. Clark Mollenhoff, *The Pentagon: Politics, Profits, and Plunder,* 170–81.

52. Peter J. Ognibene, *Scoop: The Life and Politics of Henry M. Jackson,* 97.

53. Army-McCarthy Hearings, 1503–5.

54. Ibid., 1507–8.

55. Ibid., 2238–39.

56. Ibid., 2240–41.

57. Ibid., 2281–84.

58. Ibid., 2350–63. Carey wired Mundt, asking to testify. As president of the United Electrical Workers during the time, he was in close touch with the situation at Emerson; he could provide detailed refutation "of McCarthy's lies." He added: " . . . Mr. Symington needs no character reference from our International Union, but I believe I can express the opinions and sentiments of tens of thousands of IUE-CIO members in regard to the Senator from Missouri. . . . When I testify . . . to Symington's high moral and ethical standards, his complete honesty and probity, I speak not only my own opinions but the opinions of thousands of Union employees . . . who know the man and his unquestionable integrity." Telegram, Carey to Mundt, June 9, 1954, copy in SP, f. 2339, WHMC.

59. Army-McCarthy Hearings, 2526–43. See also Clifford, *Counsel to the President,* 289–300.

60. Army-McCarthy Hearings, 2706–7.

61. Ibid., 2970–71.

62. Ibid., 2972–83.

63. Reeves, *The Life and Times of Joe McCarthy,* 636–37.

64. Army-McCarthy Hearings, 2911.

65. Ibid., 2426–30. See also Reeves, *The Life and Times of Joe McCarthy,* 630–32.

66. Reeves, *The Life and Times of Joe McCarthy,* 630.

67. *Toledo Blade,* June 9, 1954.

68. Straight, *Trial by Television,* 219. Later reviews of Symington's position on the censure resolution were not so quite positive. Griffith, *Politics of Fear,* 287. The Democrats had a difficult problem with the censure issue. Some, such as Kennedy, had large Catholic constituencies; the leadership was afraid of making it a party issue for fear of alienating Republican support for the resolution.

69. Abell, ed., *Drew Pearson Diaries,* 328.

70. Clifford, *Counsel to the President,* 300.

71. Ibid. Roy Cohn wrote that McCarthy told him that Symington "visited him in his home during the censure hearing, and said he felt terrible about it. . . . 'Symington told me he hoped I don't get sore at the individuals participating, because there was nothing any of them could do about it.' " Cohn, *McCarthy,* 239. Further—although dubious—evidence of Symington's ambivalence is the statement of Willard Edwards, a friend of McCarthy's, who recalled that one evening during the hearings, "he dropped in at McCarthy's home and was surprised to find Symington there having a drink with the Wisconsin senator." Griffith, *Politics of Fear,* 256. Memorandum for File, January 12, 1955, SPF, box 12.

Chapter 21. Defense—A Voice in the Wilderness

1. Bobby Baker with Larry L. King, *Wheeling and Dealing: Confessions of a Capitol Hill Operator,* 65.

2. Ambrose, *Eisenhower: Soldier and President,* 315.

3. *NYT,* March 12, 1953.

4. Ambrose, *Eisenhower: Soldier and President,* 322.

5. *NYT,* January 17, 1953.

6. Senate, Report of Proceedings, "Hearing Held before Committee on Armed Services, Nomination of Charles E. Wilson to be Secretary of Defense," Executive Session, January 23, 1953, SP, f. 1818, WHMC.

7. Ambrose, *Eisenhower: Soldier and President,* 90.

8. *NYT,* March 31, 1953.

9. Senate Democratic Policy Committee, press release, April 17, 1953, William Becker papers, box 29, WHMC.

10. *NYT,* May 1, 1953.

11. Ibid., May 16, 1953.

12. *Time,* June 29, 1953, 11.

13. *CR–Senate,* June 25, 1953, 7237.

14. Ibid., 7241. Wilson was quoted as saying that Lovett would have submitted a lower figure than he did "if he had not been tired—and very fond of his old friends."

15. Ibid., July 6, 1953, 8014–15.

16. *New Republic,* July 13, 1953, 8–13; Transcript, *American Forum of the Air,* NBC, July 15, 1953, SPF, box 11; *CR-Senate,* July 22, 1953, 9455–9613. See also *NYT,* July 23, 1953.

17. Symington, "Memories," 177.

18. *CR-Senate,* March 30, 1954, 4072. Symington's speech and the colloquy that accompanied it are on 4072–84.

19. For example, in responding to a request for information, Wilson wrote somewhat patronizingly, "I am sure you are aware of the problem from a security standpoint in attempting to provide you with a full and documented report on the subjects in which you have expressed an interest. . . . I share with you a deep concern for this nation's security. I can only add that the program presently under consideration within the Department will reflect our concern for the vital aspects of this over-all problem." Wilson to Symington, April 3, 1953, SPF, box 10.

20. *CR-Senate,* March 30, 1954, 4077.

21. Ibid., 4082. In April 1954, air force intelligence noted the appearance of a new bomber in the skies over Moscow. Although it was later shown that the air force exaggerated the number, Symington used the information as the basis of a charge that the Eisenhower administration was permitting the Soviets to move ahead of the United States in bomber strength. Dino A. Brugioni, *Eyeball to Eyeball: The Inside Story of the Cuban Missile Crisis,* 9–10.

22. Symington to Carl Estes [Longview, Texas, publisher and good friend of Lyndon Johnson], April 5, 1954, Johnson papers, box 55, LBJL; *CR-Senate,* April 9, 1954, 4962.

23. *CR-Senate,* July 21, 1954, 11161–65.

24. Ibid.

25. *U.S. News and World Report,* July 29, 1954, 40, 70–74; *Time,* August 2, 1954, 11–12; *America,* August 7, 1954, 451.

26. *CR-Senate,* August 14, 1954, 14486.

Chapter 22. Into the Mainstream

1. *CR-Senate,* January 28, 1955, 825.

2. Program Transcript, "Meet the Press," April 24, 1955, 8– 9, Lawrence Spivak papers, box 210, LC.

3. Ibid., 11.

4. *CR-Senate,* May 16, 1955, 6403; *KCS,* May 17, 1955.

5. *SLGD,* May 19, 1955, *WP,* May 19, 1955.

6. *NYT,* May 19, 1955. Symington had the article reprinted in the *Congressional Record.* Baldwin was now "the highly respected military analyst" of the *Times.* (*CR-Senate,* May 23, 1955, 6749.)

7. *SLGD,* June 20, 1955.

8. *CR-Senate,* January 28, 1955, 825.

9. Symington to Wilson, August 4, 1955; Robert Tripp Ross to Symington, August 9, 1955; Symington to Wilson, September 13, 1955; Wilson to Symington, October 22, 1955; Symington to Wilson, November 8, 1955; Ross to Symington, December 22, 1955; all in SPF, box 10.

10. Senate Resolution 71, 84th Cong., 1st Sess, *CR–Senate,* March 2, 1955, 2320–2324.

11. Office of Stuart Symington, Press Release, March 8, 1955, Symington papers, f. 3362, WHMC.

12. Chronology, Disarmament Resolution, prepared September 4, 1959, Ibid.

13. Humphrey and Symington generally agreed on issues, and they worked closely together on agricultural problems. Material regarding the work of the Disarmament subcommittee will be found in the Hubert Humphrey papers, Senatorial File, Minnesota Historical Society.

14. Press Release, September 30, 1955, SP, f. 3338, WHMC. See also *SLPD,* September 30, 1955.

15. "The Silent Curtain," Address by Senator Stuart Symington, Centennial Anniversary, *The Mexico Ledger,* October 12, 1955, SP, f. 3305, WHMC.

16. Symington to Johnson, November 28, 1955, Lyndon B. Johnson papers, box 55, LBJL.

17. Memorandum, February 8, 1956, SPF, box 11.

18. Ibid. It is not clear whether Symington made this argument to Johnson or confined it to his private memo.

19. *CR-Senate,* February 10, 1956, 2191–2198.

20. Symington introduced a number of editorials into the *Congressional Record* in connection with his speech. Ibid.

21. *NYT,* February 11, 1956.

22. Symington to Johnson, February 18, 1956, SPF, box 12.

23. Russell to Symington, February 24, 1956, SP, f. 1820, WHMC.

24. *SLPD,* March 6, 1956. Many in the air force, it will be recalled, had been highly critical of the work of the bombing survey.

25. United States Senate, Subcommittee on the Air Force of the Committee on Armed Services, Executive Session, March 5, 1956, RG 46, U.S. Senate Records, 84th Congress, Committee on Armed Services, box 34, NARA.

26. *SLGD,* March 31, 1956.

27. *Washington Star,* April 20, 1956. Fleeson, usually friendly to Symington, suggested that he and Jackson were trying to make up for their poor performance in the Army-McCarthy hearings: "It is, in a way, the second effort for both. They were on the Senate committee holding the McCarthy-Army hearings, and much was hoped for from them. Both young, vigorous liberals, they were unterrified by the Senator from Wisconsin, but they simply did not prove effective in dealing with him."

28. Symington to Johnson, May 25, 1956, SPF, box 12.

29. *Washington Star,* April 20, 1956.

30. "Statement by Senator Stuart Symington, Chairman, Subcommittee on the Air

Force of the Senate Committee on Armed Services, To Be Presented at Opening Hearing, 10:30 A.M., Monday, April 16, 1956," SP, box 6788, f. 1827, WHMC; Hearings before the Subcommittee on the Air Force of the Committee on Armed Services, *Study of Airpower,* Senate, 84th Cong., 2d Sess. (Washington: GPO, 1956), 1–4.

31. Hearings, *Study of Airpower,* 1883.

32. *CR-Senate,* July 12, 1956, 12117.

33. Symington's good friend and steady correspondent, Professor Barton Leach of the Harvard Law School, wrote: "We are building our summer readings for Seminar Students. . . . One word of gratuitous advice. Do see that the Printing Office produces a substantial oversupply. . . These hearings are unique and are producing a great government document which will be in demand for years to come. . . ." (Leach to Symington, 25 July 1956, SP, f. 1819, WHMC.)

Chapter 23. Reluctant Favorite Son

1. Independent Editorial Service, Ltd., *Newsletter,* July 15, 1953, 3; *Evening Star,* Washington, D.C., July 7, 1953.

2. *SLGD,* December 28, 1953.

3. *NYT,* December 2, 1953.

4. *Time,* November 6, 1953, 10.

5. *Santa Barbara* [California] *News-Press,* August 27, 1953.

6. Symington to Clements, September 4, 1953, SPF, box 11.

7. Between February and November 1954, the committee raised $123,779.75. "Senatorial Campaign Committee, 1954—Financial Statement," SPF, box 11.

8. Johnson to Symington, November 19, 1954, box 55, LBJL. Symington and Morse worked well together. Morse strongly supported Symington's efforts to increase air force appropriations. When Morse ran for reelection in 1956, Symington sent him two hundred dollars: "a small contribution from a friend—strictly personal." Symington to Morse, May 29, 1956, SPF, box 12.

9. Symington to Johnson, December 20, 1954, box 55, LBJL.

10. *SLGD,* May 30, 1955.

11. Ibid., July 10, 1955.

12. See Dallek, *Lone Star Rising,* 484–85, 488–97; Caro, *Master of the Senate,* 620. Apparently, there was some evidence that Johnson and Symington were not getting along well. At least, Caro suggests that Rayburn was trying to effect a rapprochement between the two men. Symington to Johnson, July 25, 1955, Symington to Mrs. Lyndon Johnson, July 11, 1955, box 55, LBJL; *CR-Senate,* August 2, 1955, 12916–18.

13. *Christian Science Monitor,* January 18, 1956; Johnson to Symington, September 8, 1955, Symington to Johnson, September 9, 1955, Johnson to Symington, September 14, 1955, and Symington to "Hon. and Mrs. Lyndon Johnson," October 24, 1955, all in box 55, LBJL; *SLPD,* October 24, 1955; *SLGD,* October 24, 1955.

14. *SLGD,* October 11 and November 29, 1955.

15. See, for example, Fike to Meredith, December 29, 1955, James Meredith papers, f. 14, WHMC.

16. *Christian Science Monitor,* January 18, 1956; CMC to Stu, nd, SPF, box 11.

17. Memorandum, January 9, 1956, SPF, box 11.

18. Meredith to James P. Aylward, Jr., January 19, 1956, Meredith papers, f. 16, WHMC; to William H. Becker, January 25, 1956, Becker papers, box 29, WHMC.

19. *SLPD,* January 14, 1956; Oliver to Meredith, January 17, 1956, Meredith papers, f. 16, WHMC.

20. *SLGD,* March 22, 1956; *Washington Star,* March 27, 1956; *New York Herald Tribune,* April 5, 1956; *U.S. News and World Report,* April 6, 1956; Victor Riesel, "Inside Labor," *SLGD,* April 10, 1956.

21. *SLGD,* May 29, 1956; *SLPD,* May 29, 1956.

22. *Washington Star,* May 29, 1956.

23. It was generally believed in Washington that prior to Johnson's coronary, Symington was "a stalking horse for a Johnson candidacy." Ibid.

24. For rather extended discussions of Symington as a dark horse candidate, see Samuel Shaffer and Peter Wyden, "Mr. If of the Democrats," *Newsweek,* June 18, 1956, 45–52; Joe Alex Morris, "Candidate Bubbling With Charm," *Saturday Evening Post,* July 21, 1956, 26–27, 67–68, 70.

25. *SLPD,* August 1 and 2, 1956.

26. The press made much of the fact that in 1952 he had supported Symington's opponent for the Democratic senatorial nomination in Missouri.

27. Wellman, *Stuart Symington,* 188–93.

28. *SLGD,* August 13, 1956.

29. Ibid., August 17, 1956.

30. Ibid.; *SLPD,* August 18, 1956.

31. *SLGD,* August 17, 1956.

32. Meredith to Allen, August 29, 1956, Meredith papers, f. 25, WHMC. The campaign raised $2,179.65 and spent $1,971.89, $800 of which went to cover Symington's hotel bill in Chicago. The $207.76 balance was returned to Symington. True Davis, Jr., to Catherine Roberts, September 4, 1956, Becker papers, f. 26, WHMC.

33. *Newsweek,* June 18, 1956, 50; Symington to William H. Becker, September 7, 1956, Becker papers, box 29, WHMC.

34. Stevenson to Symington, September 1, 1956, SPF, box 12.

35. Symington to Stevenson, September 6, 1956, ibid. Symington wrote Becker: "Stevenson handled himself very well in Chicago—dignity, restraint, sincerity." September 7, 1956, ibid.

36. Mary Rather to Mr. and Mrs. Stuart Symington, October 17, 1956, box 55, LBJL.

37. Interview, Clinton P. Anderson, by John F. Stewart, April 14, 1967, Oral History Program, JFKL; "Televised Discussion of H-Bomb Tests, on October 16, 1956, by Adlai Stevenson and Senators Clinton P. Anderson and Stuart Symington," Publicity Division, Democratic National Committee, senatorial files, Hubert Humphrey papers, Minnesota Historical Society.

38. Symington to Johnson, October 28, 1958, Congressional file, box 55, LBJL.

Chapter 24. The Missile Gap

1. Senate, *Airpower, Report of the Subcommittee on the Air Force of the Committee on Armed Services,* 85th Cong., 1st sess., Doc. 29, February 27, 1957 (Washington: Government Printing Office, 1957), 95–97. A good summary of the hearings and the report will be found in Mollenhoff, *The Pentagon,* 199–209.

2. Mollenhoff, *The Pentagon,* 127–28.

3. National Broadcasting Company, *Meet the Press,* February 3, 1957, SP, f. 3,422, WHMC.

4. Symington to Spivak, February 8, 1957, Lawrence Spivak papers, box 212, LC.

5. Symington to Johnson, February 6, 1957, Johnson papers, box 55, LBJL; *New York Herald Tribune,* January 30, 1957; *SLGD,* February 1, 1957.

6. Symington to Richard Russell, April 30, 1957, SPF, box 12.

7. Symington to Lyndon Johnson, April 30, 1957, ibid., box 55, LBJL.

8. Symington to Stewart Alsop, May 21, 1957, Alsop papers, box 21, LC. Alsop had charged that Symington's Wilkes-Barre speech marked an "end of any serious attempt to make a national issue of what seems to me—and I thought seemed to you—infinitely the most dangerous aspect of the Eisenhower Administration's management of our affairs." The Eisenhower administration, "in the sacred name of economy," had permitted the Soviets to nullify the United States' superiority in "air-atomic power." This "has seemed to me not only unwise, but downright disgraceful and I had thought that you agreed." Stewart Alsop to Symington, ibid. The Alsop brothers had detected a change in Symington's attitude while he was secretary of the air force. Joseph Alsop wrote Lawrence Sommers, an editor at the *Saturday Evening Post,* "last night he [Symington] gave me half an hour of shouting about how 'this country can't do the whole job in the world,' etc., etc." The Alsops, according to their biographer, "considered such talk a new brand of isolationism, and it filled them with anxiety." Merry, *Taking on the World,* 180.

9. *A Modern Concept of Manpower Management and Compensation,* a Report and Recommendation for the Secretary of Defense by the Defense Advisory Committee on Professional and Technical Compensation, 2 vols., May 1957; Henry A. Kissinger, "Force and Diplomacy in the Nuclear Age," *Foreign Affairs* 34 (April 1956): 349–56. Symington had parts of the article inserted in the *CR-Senate,* April 1, 1957, 4837–38.

10. *CR-Senate,* June 13, 1957, 8961–62, July 1, 1957, 10668–73, July 19, 1957, 12121–22; *SLPD,* July 20, 1957. The argument was complex and difficult to follow. The House of Representatives had cut the administration's defense request by $2.5 billion; the administration requested the Senate to restore $1.2 billion. The Senate voted an increase of $970 million, but when the matter went to the conference committee, Secretary Wilson advised that the administration could get along with $142 million less than the Senate had voted.

11. Johnson to Symington, February 4, 1957, LBJA Congressional File, box 50, LBJL; Jackson to Symington, June 11, 1957, SP, f. 1979, WHMC; Symington to James H. Douglas, July 31, 1957, Congressional File, box 55, LBJL; Symington to Johnson, August 15, 1957, ibid.; Johnson to Symington, August 22, 1957, ibid.; Draft letter, not sent, Symington to Johnson, August 28, 1957, SP, f. 1979, WHMC. Tension between

Johnson and Symington surfaced again in connection with the preparation of an interim report from the committee. Symington pushed for a hard-swinging attack on the administration, but Johnson, unwilling to distance himself too far from Eisenhower, insisted on a more moderate tone. *Time,* February 3, 1958, 13–14.

12. Just before leaving Washington for Missouri, Symington held a press conference in which he criticized Secretary of State John Foster Dulles for misleading the public by suggesting that the London conference on disarmament had achieved "significant progress" when nothing had been accomplished. He charged that in the light of this failure and the Soviets' announcement that they had successfully tested an intercontinental ballistic missile, continuing cuts in the defense program "constituted unilateral disarmament." *NYT,* September 13, 1957; see also Ambrose, *Eisenhower: Soldier and President,* 403–4. *SLPD,* September 13, 1957; *Sioux Falls Argus-Leader,* October 11, 1957.

13. Telegram, Symington to Richard Russell, October 5, 1957, SP, f. 1984, WHMC; *SLGD,* October 6, 1957; *NYT,* October 6, 1957.

14. Symington to Eisenhower, October 8, 1957, SP, subject box 28, WHMC.

15. Eisenhower to Symington, October 29, 1957, enclosing a memorandum from the secretary of defense, October 28, 1957, ibid.

16. Statement by Senator Stuart Symington, "The Significance of Sputnik on American Defense Policy," October 14, 1957, SP, f. 3428, WHMC. The text of the statement is in the *SLGD,* October 27, 1957.

17. Stephen E. Ambrose, *Eisenhower,* vol. 2, 430.

18. Arthur Krock, "In the Nation," *NYT,* October 17, 1957.

19. Ibid., November 18 and 24, 1957; "Memorandum to Mr. Krock re Nixon Memorandum," November 12, 1957, attached to Symington to Krock, November 12, 1957, SP, f. 3428, WHMC.

20. Russell had responded to Symington's call for hearings by turning the matter over to the Preparedness Subcommittee, headed by Lyndon Johnson, probably, as his biographer suggests, to further Johnson's presidential ambitions. Gilbert Fite, *Richard B. Russell Jr., Senator from Georgia* (Chapel Hill: University of North Carolina Press, 1991), 362–63.

21. Symington to Johnson, November 21, 1957, SP, f. 1955–57, WHMC.

22. Dallek, *Lone Star Rising,* 529–30. Robert Caro wrote: " . . . after Johnson put Symington on the Armed Services Committee, the experience and 'true expertise' in military matters of the tall, handsome Missourian became apparent . . . and Johnson's aides became aware that he resented it." *Master of the Senate,* 570–71.

23. Frank Zentay, a staff assistant, recalled that Symington was "furious" at being passed over. Interview, Frank Zentay, by James C. Olson, June 14, 2002.

24. Caro, *Master of the Senate.*

25. Senate, Hearings before the Preparedness Investigating Subcommittee of the Committee on Armed Services, *Inquiry Into Satellite and Missile Programs,* 85th Cong., 1st and 2d sess. (Washington: Government Printing Office, 1958), 44–45. This is the public record only. Much of the subcommittee's work was conducted in executive sessions, the records of which are not available.

26. Ibid., 917–20.

27. "Statement by Senate Majority Leader Lyndon B. Johnson," January 23, 1958,

SP, f. 1985, WHMC; *Time,* February 3, 1958, 13–14; Dallek, *Lone Star Rising,* 529–32; Evans and Novak, *Lyndon B. Johnson,* 193–94.

28. Cole et al., eds., *Department of Defense,* 175–86.

29. *CR-Senate,* March 24, 1958, 5076.

30. Symington complained about this on the Senate floor, complaints seconded by Republicans Joseph Clark of Pennsylvania and John Sherman Cooper of Kentucky. Ibid., April 21, 1958, 6755.

31. Cole et al., eds., *Department of Defense,* 187.

32. Senate, Hearings before the Committee on Armed Services, *Department of Defense Reorganization Act of 1958,* 85th Cong., 2d sess. (Washington: Government Printing Office, 1958), 178. After the hearings, Eberstadt wrote Symington a "Dear Stu" letter of appreciation for the manner in which he had been treated, adding: "We have been through many things together and many of those who were with us no longer are. I do not know that we will ever reconcile our differences, but, as you know, I'm not resentful of diverse points of view, setting only one condition—that they be sincere. I believe that yours are, and mine are, too. Thus, in spite of our disagreements, it is comforting and reassuring to me to have your attentive eye guarding Uncle Sam's welfare." Eberstadt to Symington, June 26, 1958, Eberstadt papers, SM. Symington replied: "Dear Ferd: All thanks for your note of June 26th. I myself had determined to write you, and was only prevented from doing so by a trip back to my state. Nobody handles himself before Congressional committees better than you. That is an understatement. As our colloquy continued, Jim's [James Forrestal's] face kept coming up in my mind the deep desire, his great life from a limited start and because I knew how much you meant to him, it was hard to disagree. Twenty-five years from now I hope the three of us can sit on a cloud and continue the discussion." Symington to Eberstadt, July 1, 1958, ibid.

33. Radford and Symington had buried their differences during Radford's tour as JCS chairman. Ibid., 420–21.

34. 85th Cong., Armed Services Committee, July 15, 1958, box 42, RG 46, NARA.

35. *CR-Senate,* July 18, 1958, 14256–62.

36. Cole et al., eds., *Department of Defense,* 187–88.

37. *SLGD,* July 22, 1958.

38. *CR-Senate,* July 30, 1958, 15591–92. For a continuation of Symington's speech on the army, see 15592–600.

39. Ibid., August 18, 1958, 18068–69.

40. Ibid.; *New York Mirror,* August 14, 1958; *WP,* August 14, 1958 (Symington entered both newspaper articles in the *CR,* August 14, 1958, 17510–11); Bruce L. R. Smith, *The RAND Corporation: Case Study of a Non-Profit Advisory Corporation,* 95–97.

41. Symington apparently was the first member of either house to receive a private briefing at CIA headquarters. John Prados, *The Soviet Estimate: U.S. Intelligence Analysis and Russian Strategic Forces,* 83.

42. Symington to Eisenhower, August 29, 1958; "Memorandum," n.d., SPF, box 11. Ambrose, *Eisenhower,* vol. 2, 477, states that Symington's letter was a request for a meeting, and the meeting was held August 30. My reading of the letter and the memorandum, which, unfortunately, was not dated, indicates that Symington handed the letter to the president at the meeting.

43. There is a vast literature on the missile gap. See especially McGeorge Bundy, *Danger and Survival: Choices about the Bomb in the First Fifty Years,* 334–37; Peter J. Roman, *Eisenhower and the Missile Gap,* 35–45, 128–49; Arnold L. Horelick and Myron Rush, *Strategic Power and Soviet Foreign Policy,* 58–70; James C. Dick, "The Strategic Arms Race, 1957–61: Who Opened a Missile Gap?" *Journal of Politics* 34 (November 1972): 1062–1110; Colin S. Gray, "'Gap' Prediction and America's Defense: Arms Race Behavior in the Eisenhower Years," *Orkis* 16 (spring 1972): 257–74; Roy E. Licklider, "The Missile Gap Controversy," *Political Science Quarterly* 85 (December 1970): 600–615.

Chapter 25. Agriculture—The Other Big Issue

1. For a brief history of the two organizations, see Richard S. Kirkendall, *History of Missouri, Volume V, 1919 to 1953,* 58–61; see also Raymond A. Young, *Cultivating Cooperation: A History of the Missouri Farmers Association* (Columbia: University of Missouri Press, 1995).

2. At Symington's insistence, President Kennedy considered Heinkel for appointment as secretary of agriculture. When Heinkel was not appointed, Kennedy is reported to have told Symington, "He is a little too old for this administration." Young, *Cultivating Cooperation,* 166–67. Actually, Heinkel made a poor impression on both the president and Robert Kennedy. Schlesinger, *Robert Kennedy and His Times,* 226.

3. Symington to Meredith, April 16, 1956, Meredith papers, box 10, WHMC.

4. "Senator Stuart Symington, Speech Quotations," n.d., but prepared in connection with the 1960 presidential campaign, Symington papers, f. 3498, WHMC.

5. For a sympathetic account of Benson's years as secretary of agriculture, see Edward L. Schapsmeier and Frederick H. Schapsmeier, *Ezra Taft Benson and the Politics of Agriculture: The Eisenhower Years, 1953–1961.*

6. Press release, office of Stuart Symington, June 11, 1955, SP, box 272, WHMC. Symington discussed the problem in detail on the floor of the Senate. *CR-Senate,* July 29, 1955, 12049–59.

7. Symington wrote Lyndon Johnson from his home in St. Louis: "Sunday Hubert Humphrey comes to town, and after dedicating a Lutheran Hospital we will get our heads together for the hearings he opens Monday at our Capital, Jefferson City re the ASC program in this state. If he does the job I know he will, it will help both Tom Hennings and me." Symington to Johnson, November 11, 1955, Lyndon Johnson papers, box 55, LBJL.

8. Associated Press, December 29, 1955, SP, Scrapbooks, vol. 2, WHMC. The hearings were widely covered in both the urban and rural press of Missouri. A good summary can be found in the *SLPD,* November 21, 1955. See also *SLGD,* November 15, 1955; *Kansas City Times,* November 15, 1955. The rural press is heavily represented in SP, Scrapbooks, vol. 2, WHMC.

9. *Liberty* [Missouri] *Tribune,* December 9, 1955, SP, Scrapbooks, vol. 2, WHMC; *SLPD,* January 4, 1956; Associated Press, January 6 and February 21, 1956.

10. For example, John Sam Williamson, an agricultural leader who farmed on the rich Missouri Valley bottomland near Columbia, wrote: "I am highly pleased and encouraged by your appointment . . . to the Committee on Agriculture. I hope that with your ability and experience we farmers can have more statesmanlike farm legislation. . . . I marvel at your growing popularity and country wide activity." Williamson to Symington, April 1, 1956, SP, f. 175, WHMC. For his move off the Public Works Committee see Symington press release, March 29, 1956, ibid, f. 174.

11. Symington press release, April 18, 1956, ibid., f. 479. Ironically, the fuss over the veto diverted attention from Symington's air power hearings, just getting under way.

12. *SLGD,* June 11, 12, and 13, 1956; June 5, 1957.

13. *CR-Senate,* January 17, 1957, 759–68.

14. Ibid., February 4, 1957, 1451–52.

15. Ibid., February 19, 1957, 2222–23; March 2, 1957, 2918.

16. "Excerpt from Secretary Benson's speech to Republican women, April 2, 1957," SP, f. 296, WHMC.

17. *NYT,* July 21, 1957.

18. *Sioux Falls Argus-Leader,* October 11, 1957. On the evening of his farm speech, Symington spoke to the Sioux Falls Chamber of Commerce on missiles.

19. *CR-Senate,* March 19, 1958, 4715; Symington to Cline Hancock, Cassville, Mo., February 21, 1958, SP, f. 1496, WHMC.

20. *CR-Senate,* 85th Cong., 2d sess., 822.

21. See Schapsmeier and Schapsmeier, *Ezra Taft Benson,* 206–7.

22. *CR-Senate,* July 25, 1958, 15095.

23. Ibid.

24. Ibid., August 28, 1958, 19334–36.

25. *NYT,* December 28, 1957; *SLGD,* December 29, 1957; *SLPD,* December 29, 1957.

26. *SLPD,* June 10, 1958.

27. Ibid., July 27, 1958; *SLGD,* July 27, 1958.

28. *SLGD,* August 10 and September 4, 1958. The *Wall Street Journal,* October 17, 1958, contains a detailed analysis of Republican difficulties in Missouri.

29. *SLGD,* September 3, 1958. Symington wrote Bill Becker: "This has been a rough campaign. The lady is articulate; and it has been impossible for me to answer her." Symington to Becker, November 3, 1958, Becker papers, box 29, WHMC.

30. *SLPD,* October 18, 1958; *SLGD,* September 29, 1958; *KCS,* October 4, 1958; *Sedalia Democrat,* October 19, 1958.

31. *SLGD,* November 6, 1958.

Chapter 26. Half-Hearted Run for the Presidency

1. *SLPD,* March 23, 1958.

2. *WP,* March 25, 1958. Childs was a Washington correspondent of the *St. Louis Post-Dispatch* whose column was syndicated nationally. For another but similar view see Willard Edwards in the *Chicago Sunday Tribune,* April 20, 1958.

3. An Associated Press poll of state Democratic chairmen showed Senator Kennedy leading the race for the nomination, with "Senator Symington of Missouri . . . running a strong second." *SLGD,* November 16, 1958.

4. Ibid., December 16, 1958.

5. Symington to Johnson, August 23, 1958, SPF, box 12.

6. *NYT,* July 19, 1959.

7. Apparently the feeling was mutual, as the following note in Glennan's diary would indicate: "On the Hill again at 4:30 to see Senator Symington. What a demagogue! Acts like a pompous prosecuting attorney. Heaven help the US if he ever makes the Presidency!" T. Keith Glennan, Diary, 1958–1961, January 16, 1959, EL.

8. Address before the National Grange, Long Beach, Calif., November 12, 1959, SP, f. 1649, WHMC.

9. For Symington's views on the missile gap, see, for example, ibid., January 23, 1959, 1101–3; January 27, 1960, 1372–73; *New York Post,* February 22, 1959, containing transcript of *Meet the Press,* February 15, 1959; *Washington Post and Times-Herald,* June 28, 1959. For signs of acceptance for his arguments, see, for example, Thomas R. Phillips, "The Growing Missile Gap," *Reporter,* January 8, 1959, 10–16. See also *CR-Senate,* January 12, 1959, 418; Jack Bell, Associated Press, in *SLGD,* January 13, 1959.

10. *CR-Senate,* January 14, 1959, 639–40; Republican National Committee, *Battle Line,* vol. 3, no. 1, January 16, 1959. This was interpreted as being "an early start on the 1960 campaign." *NYT,* January 17, 1959.

11. *Washington Evening Star,* January 19, 1959; *NYT,* January 18, 1959; *CR-Senate,* January 20, 1959, 910–11; Acheson to Symington, January 21, 1959, and Truman to Symington, January 22, 1959, both in SPF, box 12.

12. For the uncertainty surrounding the missile gap see *CR-Senate,* January 23, 1959, 1101–3, *New York World-Telegram,* January 23, 1959; *NYT,* January 23, 1959; *Christian Science Monitor,* January 24, 1959; *Los Angeles Times,* February 1, 1959. For Lippmann's comments, see *Washington Post and Times-Herald,* February 5, 1959. Symington's viewpoint appears in *CR-Senate,* February 5, 1959, 1840–42.

13. A poll conducted by *Congressional Quarterly* showed Symington the choice of 33 percent of congressional Democrats, with Kennedy the choice of 17 percent. *SLGD,* February 1, 1959. *NYT,* February 22, 1959; *U.S. News and World Report,* February 27, 1959, 46–49.

14. *Washington Daily News,* April 29, 1959; *Wall Street Journal,* March 25, 1959.

15. Clifford, *Counsel to the President,* 312; Douglas Frantz and David McKean, *Friends in High Places: The Rise and Fall of Clark Clifford,* 152–53. Stanley Fike turned down the chance to run for Congress in the heavily Democratic Fourth District when the incumbent, George Christopher, suddenly died. Fike recalled that in response to a direct question "about the middle of January, latter part of January '59," Symington told him that he did plan to run for the presidency in 1960. Fike said, "Well, if you think, then, that I could help you on that, and maybe afterwards when you're elected, I'm going to say no on this congressional nomination." Symington, Fike added, "got up and shook my hand, and there were almost tears in his eyes." Interview, Stanley Fike, by Larry J. Hackman, September 7, 1967, JFKL.

16. William S. White, "Symington: The Last Choice for President," *Harper's*

Magazine, July 1959, 78–81, was a slashing, much-quoted attack on Symington, declaring that of all the contenders, he " . . . [had] shown the weakest qualifications for the job." For Symington's response see Symington to Ernest Kirschten, July 17, 1959, SPF, box 10. Syndicated columnist Holmes Alexander wrote: "My guess is that Symington's rivals will rue the day they stirred him up. . . . Although I have no pipeline to the Senator's office, I make bold to believe that he is far more apt to go after the nomination, and far more likely to win it, before the opposition started shooting at him." "The Symington Equation," *St. Louis Globe-Democrat,* July 29, 1959. This was the first of three articles. See also July 30, 31, 1959.

17. *NYT,* July 14, 1959; Stuart Symington, "Let's Have a West Point for Diplomats," *This Week,* August 2, 1959. Litton went on to become a congressman, and in 1976 won the Democratic senatorial nomination, defeating James Symington in the Democratic primary. His career was tragically cut short in a plane crash on election night. Bonnie Mitchell, *Jerry Litton, 1937–1976: A Biography,* 172–208. James Reston in *SLPD,* August 17, 1959. Eleanor Roosevelt wrote Symington that she thought a foreign service academy was a good idea. A fairly regular correspondence ensued. Eleanor Roosevelt Papers, Franklin D. Roosevelt Library.

18. Clifford: "On Sunday, September 6 1959, Symington and his senior advisers met at my house. We outlined the difficulties of his candidacy, but added that no one appeared to have a lock on the 1960 Democratic nomination. A deadlock between Kennedy, Humphrey, and Johnson was a distinct possibility, and if Symington were part of that game, he could well end up as the nominee." *Counsel to the President,* 313.

19. Interview, Fike, by Hackman, September 13, 1967, 30, JFKL.

20. *NYT,* February 1, 1960. James Reston reported, "The shrewdest political performance of the night was made by Senator Stuart Symington . . . [His speech] went over well and undoubtedly improved his chances." Ibid., January 25, 1960. The speech apparently was written by Charles Brown. Milton Gwirtzman, who wrote most of Symington's political speeches, recalled that Ted Sorenson, Kennedy's principal speechwriter, made a special point of seeking him out after the dinner to congratulate him. Interview, Milton S. Gwirtzman, by Ronald J. Grele, January 19, 1966, JFKL.

21. James Symington quit his job as aide to his uncle, Ambassador John Hay Whitney, in London, to return home to help out.

22. James W. Symington, quoted in Frantz and McKean, *Friends in High Places,* 154. Regarding the Maryland primary, Truman wrote: "You use your own judgment, but Presidential primaries are dynamite and can cause a lot of unnecessary difficulties." Truman to Symington, June 22, 1959, SP, box 178, WHMC.

23. *NYT,* January 3 and 11, 1960.

24. Walter Lippmann, for example, wrote in his syndicated column: "Senator Symington has done the country a great service by rejecting the idea that the candidate of the Democratic party should be chosen in two or three presidential primaries." *Corvallis Gazette-Times,* January 15, 1960, clipping in Hubert Humphrey papers, Senatorial Files, Minnesota Historical Society.

25. *SLPD,* February 11, 1960. The best overall source of information on the campaign is Interviews, Fike, by Larry Hackman, September 7, 13, and November 30, 1967, JFKL. Unless otherwise indicated, I am relying on these interviews.

26. See, for example, *CR-Senate,* February 19, 1960, 2757–87; March 2, 1960, 4167–79.

27. *NYT,* October 29, 1959. Arkansas Governor Orval Faubus told a news conference that Symington's prospects as a Democratic candidate "would have to be reevaluated" as a result of the incident. Ibid., October 30, 1959.

28. *WP,* November 29, 1959.

29. For viewpoints on Symington's shortcomings as a presidential candidate, see Hugh Sidey, "Everybody's No. 2," *Time,* November 9, 1959, 18–22; Benjamin Bradlee, "Symington," *Newsweek,* May 9, 1960, 30–33. On the Kennedy camp's fear of Symington, see Bradlee, *Conversations with Kennedy,* 18.

30. Rudy Abramson, *Spanning the Century: the Life of W. Averell Harriman, 1891–1986,* 576; Douglas Brinkley, *Dean Acheson: The Cold War Years, 1953–71,* 205–6, 346–47.

31. Transcript of press conference, March 24, 1960, SP, box 152, WHMC; *NYT,* March 25, 1960; *Washington Star,* March 25, 1960; *SLGD,* March 25, 1960.

32. Interview, Fike, by Hackman, September 13, 1967, 35. Regarding the Truman-Clifford campaign strategy, Theodore H. White wrote: "Deep, deep, in the approach of Symington's managers was a conviction" almost naive for such seasoned politicians "that ability alone could sell a man for the Presidency." *The Making of the President 1960,* 40. See also Frantz and McKean, *Friends in High Places,* 154.

33. "Statement of former President Harry S. Truman, at a Press Conference, July 2, 1960, Auditorium, Harry S. Truman Library, Independence, Missouri," SP, box 176, WHMC. See also McCullough, *Truman,* 973–74.

34. See, for example, *Meet the Press,* July 10, 1960.

35. *SLPD,* July 8, 1960.

36. For a good brief account of Johnson's preconvention activities, see Dallek, *Lone Star Rising,* 555–74.

37. *SLGD,* July 14, 1960. It was reported that the governor had had too much to drink, but apparently his problem was with the teleprompter rather than the bottle. Richard Amberg to Symington, July 22, 1960, SPF, box 12. Stanley Fike, reflecting on the campaign, said that in retrospect it was a mistake to select Blair, who was a good extemporaneous speaker but not particularly effective at reading a manuscript. He had been chosen on the recommendation of Harry Truman. Interview, Fike, by Hackman, 73–74.

38. There was some feeling in the Missouri delegation, which contained both Kennedy and Johnson supporters, that Symington should release them on the first ballot. Interview, James H. Meredith, by Larry Hackman, July 7, 1967, 7–8.

39. *Wall Street Journal,* June 10, 1960. See also White, *Making of the President,* 126–27. R. J. Vanderzee, administrative assistant to Hubert Humphrey, who joined the Symington effort after Humphrey was defeated in West Virginia, when asked to compare Symington and Humphrey as candidates, said, "Well there really was no comparison as far as their desire to get out there and get among them." Interview, R. J. Vanderzee, Senate oral history interview, 41–43, box 9, LC.

40. *SLPD,* July 8, 1960.

41. *Los Angeles Times,* July 14, 1960.

42. Clifford, *Counsel to the President,* 316–19.

43. Walter Reuther, president of the United Auto Workers, favored Symington, but

the only major figure in the labor movement who actively supported him was James Carey, president of the International Electrical Workers Union. Symington was disappointed in the support he received from labor. Interview, Albert Zack, by Larry Hackman, November 28, 1967, 6, Oral History program, JFKL.

44. Columnist Joseph W. Alsop and *Washington Post* publisher Philip Graham visited Kennedy in Los Angeles to urge him to select Johnson. They were sure that Johnson wanted the vice presidency and he was much too big a man to leave in the Senate, disappointed and resentful. Besides, Alsop added, "Something might happen to you, and you know damn well that Stu Symington is too shallow a puddle for the United States to have to dive into." From Kennedy's smile, Alsop surmised that he had already dismissed Symington. Alsop, *I've Seen The Best of It*, 427–28; Katharine Graham, *Personal History*, 260–67; Merry, *Taking on the World*, 350–51.

45. Chester Bowles told an interviewer in 1965: "I remember a meeting which I attended with Sarge Shriver and Bob Kennedy in Shriver's hotel room. From the discussions at this meeting, I was fully convinced that Stuart Symington would be the VP nominee." Bowles, however, dated the meeting as "the afternoon of day Lyndon Johnson was nominated." Interview, Chester Bowles, by Robert R. R. Brooks, February 2, 1965, 8, Oral History program, JFKL. See also Pierre Salinger, *P.S.: A Memoir*, 80–81.

46. Edwin O. Guthman and Jeffrey Shulman, eds., *Robert Kennedy in His Own Words: The Unpublished Recollections of the Kennedy Years* (New York: Bantam, 1988), 304.

47. There are differing versions of the process by which the decision was made. Among the more credible are: Dallek, *Lone Star Rising*, 574–83; Krock, *Memoirs*, 362–64; Arthur Schlesinger, *A Thousand Days: John F. Kennedy in the White House*, 50–61; Seymour Hersh, *The Dark Side of Camelot*, 121–30, quoting the unpublished memoir of Hyman Raskin, a major Kennedy strategist, implies that Johnson blackmailed Kennedy with threats to go public about his womanizing, etc. As for the public story that Kennedy had to put Johnson on the ticket to assure a win in Texas, Hersh argues that while they won Texas with Johnson, with Symington they probably could have won California, with more electoral votes, which with Johnson they lost.

48. Clifford, *Counsel to the President*, 319.

49. *Official Proceedings of the Democratic National Convention and Committee, 1960*, 232–33.

50. Interview, Fike, by Hackman, 66.

Chapter 27. The Kennedy Years

1. Audio interview, Stuart Symington, by Pat Holt, August 18, 1964, Oral History program, JFKL. There is some evidence that privately Kennedy did not reciprocate Symington's friendship. Laurence Leamer, in *The Kennedy Men*, describes a plane trip with Ben Bradlee of *Newsweek* and Chalmers Roberts of the *Washington Post* during which Kennedy "set off on one of his minor rants, calling Senator Symington "Stubum" and deriding the elegant Missouri politician as little more than a well-dressed fool." Laurence Leamer, *The Kennedy Men, 1901–1963: The Laws of the Father* (New York: William Morrow, 2001), 327–28.

2. As requested, Eve destroyed the letter. Information from James W. Symington.

Interview, Symington, by Holt; Peter Collier and David Horowitz, *The Kennedys: An American Drama* (San Francisco: Encounter Books, 2002), 190–96; Merry, *Taking on the World,* xix. Kennedy had authorized Dr. Janet Travell, his personal physician, to treat the bursitis that occasionally interfered with Symington's golf swing. Memo, Symington to Stanley Fike, April 3, 1963, SP, box 167, WHMC.

3. There were suggestions that Symington went easy on Kennedy because of the influence of Clifford, who was close to the Kennedys and wanted to do nothing to jeopardize his influence with the new administration. Frantz and McKean, *Friends in High Places,* 155–57.

4. Memo, Fike to Symington, August 12, 1960, SP, box 39, WHMC; Symington to Ernest Kirschten, August 23, 1960, SPF, box 10; Address, Kennedy fund-raising dinner, St. Louis, October 2, 1960, SP, box 162, WHMC.

5. Kennedy quotations regarding the missile gap are in SP, f. 3430, WHMC.

6. *New York Herald Tribune,* August 8, 1960.

7. Kennedy press release, "Committee on the Defense Establishment," St. Louis, September 14, 1960, SP, f. 3263, WHMC. See also, Clifford, *Counsel to the President,* 330.

8. Leva seems to have had some difficulty in working with Finletter and Gilpatric, who, he felt, were proposing too elaborate a structure for the Department of Defense, and who had "little receptivity to ideas other than their own." Telegram, Leva to Symington, November 15, 1960, SP, f. 3317, WHMC.

9. Interview, Edward Welsh, by Walter D. Sohier, Addison M. Rothrock, and Eugene M. Emme, May 16, 1964, 1–3, JFKL; *NYT,* November 20, 1960; *SLPD,* November 20, 1960.

10. Report to Senator Kennedy from the Committee on the Defense Establishment, December 5, 1960, *CR-Senate,* February 9, 1961, 1928–30; *NYT,* December 5, 1960.

11. See, for example, *Army Times,* December 17, 1960; *Navy Times,* February 18, 1961; *Wall Street Journal,* December 7, 1960; *NYT,* December 7, 1960.

12. *CR-Senate,* February 9, 1961, 1931–37.

13. Interview, Eugene Zuckert, by George M. Watson, Jr., April 22, 1982, 53.

14. Holmes Alexander, *Boston Herald,* April 5, 1961. See also Harry H. Ransom, "Department of Defense: Unity or Confederation?" in Mark E. Smith III and Claude Johns, Jr., eds., *American Defense Policy,* 371–73.

15. *Army, Navy, Air Force Journal,* October 28, 1961, 6; *SLPD,* January 16, 1962.

16. For a good account of the stir caused by McNamara, see Deborah Shapley, *Promise and Power: The Life and Times of Robert McNamara* (Boston: Little, Brown, 1993), 97–99. Shapley asserts that McNamara offered to resign over the incident, but Kennedy would not consider it.

NYT, February 1, 1961, contains a convenient chronology of the debate on the missile gap.

17. *CR-Senate,* February 9, 1961, 1954.

18. Ibid., 1954–58. The *NYT,* February 10, 1961, reporting Symington's speech, reminded its readers that Kennedy and Johnson both received briefings from Allen Dulles, director of the CIA.

19. Stuart Symington, "Where the Missile Gap Went," *Reporter,* February 15, 1962,

21–23. At the request of Senator Clair Engle of California the article was printed in the *CR-Senate,* February 15, 1961, 2282–83.

20. *CR-Senate,* February 22, 1961, 2559–60. Symington sent a copy of his speech to Pierre Salinger, the president's press secretary, as "my effort . . . to set the record straight." Symington to Salinger, February 22, 1961, SP, subject box 94, WHMC.

21. T. Keith Glennan, first administrator of the space agency, commented frequently in his diary about his difficulties in dealing with Symington, "who was determined to prove that none of us knew very much about what we were doing." Diary, EL.

22. Symington to Lyndon Johnson, December 21, 1960, SPF, box 12, WHMC.

23. Truman Wright, vice president of the Greenbrier, to Symington, July 17, 1963, Fulbright papers; Fulbright to Symington, January 12, 1961, Symington to Fulbright, January 18, 1961, SP, f. 2155, WHMC.

24. *KCS,* January 25, 1961.

25. *CR-Senate,* June 26, 1961, 11294–98; *NYT,* August 9, 1963.

26. *SLGD,* August 13, 1963.

27. For a good history of the stockpile, see Glenn Herald Snyder, *Stockpiling Strategic Materials: Politics and National Defense.* The quotation is from p. 6.

28. Presidential press conference no. 42, January 31, 1962, SP, f. 1846, WHMC; *NYT,* February 1, 1962. Assistant Secretary of State Frederick Dutton wrote: "Congratulations on the President's stockpile announcement. Your perseverance certainly paid off handsomely on this problem. . . . I think a medal should be struck for you from surplus platinum, encrusted with surplus diamonds and edged with surplus duck feathers." Dutton to Symington, February 1, 1962, ibid., f. 1847, WHMC.

29. *NYT,* February 1, 1962.

30. Ibid., February 2, 1962.

31. Ibid., March 24, 1962; transcript, press conference, March 23, 1962, SP, f. 1848, WHMC.

32. Senate, Hearings before the National Stockpile and Naval Petroleum Reserves Subcommittee of the Committee on Armed Services, *Inquiry into the Strategic and Critical Material Stockpiles of the United States,* 87th Cong., 2d sess., 2209–18.

33. Raymond Moley, *Los Angeles Times,* August 27, 1962; *Draft Report of the National Stockpile and Naval Petroleum Reserves Subcommittee. . . on the National Stockpile,* 2209–18.

34. *Miami Herald,* November 20, 1960.

35. For an interesting discussion of Kennedy's thinking, see Interview, Theodore Sorensen, by Carl Kaysen, March 26, 1964, Oral History program, JFKL.

36. Shapley, *Promise and Power,* 106–7.

37. *CR-Senate,* August 3, 1961, 14497.

38. Ibid., July 29, 1961; *NYT,* July 30, 1961.

39. Symington to Russell, May 19, 1961, SP, f. 1759, WHMC.

40. *CR-Senate,* June 12, 1961, 9959.

41. Senate, Hearings, Committee on Foreign Relations. *S. 2180, Disarmament Agency,* 87th Cong., 1st sess. (Washington: Government Printing Office, 1961).

42. *NYT,* September 2, 1961; *CR-Senate,* September 21, 1961, 20629.

43. Symington to Russell, March 27, 1962, Symington to John Stennis, March 27,

1962, both in SP, f. 1994, WHMC; Symington to Foster, April 17, 1962, Foster to Symington, April 30, 1962, both in SP, subject box 29, ibid.

44. Teller to Symington, August 8 and 31, 1962, SP, f. 1963, WHMC. See also letters of August 23 and September 11, 1962; John Foster to Symington, September 14, 1962, ibid., f. 1964.

45. Richard B. Russell, Henry M. Jackson, and Stuart Symington to the President, February 21, 1963, SP, box 84, WHMC. The president replied at length. In his view, the proposal as submitted was "more advantageous, on balance, than our past proposals, because of our greatly increased reliance on our own means of detection." He added: "I share your belief in the necessity as well as the desirability of maintaining unity on national security matters, and appreciate your frank statement of your views. In the interest of this unity, I hope you will withhold final judgment for the time being. I must say the prospects for any agreement are not now bright." Kennedy to Russell, February 28, 1963, ibid.

46. Senate, Hearings before the Preparedness Investigating Subcommittee of the Committee on Armed Services, *Military Aspects and Implications of Nuclear Test Ban Proposals and Related Matters,* 88th Cong., 1st sess. (Washington: Government Printing Office, 1964), 211.

47. The *SLPD* wrote scornfully: ". . . The Senator professes to be a much misunderstood man on this subject, and it is true that some of his statements have been interpreted in directly opposite ways by different interpreters. Perhaps that was due to a certain tendency of his toward built in ambiguity." *SLPD,* August 11, 1963.

48. Memo, "Additional Views," September 6, 1963, SP, f. 3359, WHMC.

49. Senate, Hearings before the Committee on Foreign Relations, *Nuclear Test Ban Treaty,* 88th Cong., 1st sess. (Washington: Government Printing Office, 1963), 145–49; Memo, Manatos to O'Brien, July 24, 1963, office files of Mike Manatos, box 14, LBJL.

50. *CR-Senate,* September 17, 1963, 17148. William C. Foster, director of the arms control and disarmament agency, wrote: "The impressive vote by which the Senate consented to the ratification of this treaty would not have been possible without your support." Foster to Symington, September 27, 1963, SP, f. nuclear test ban treaty, WHMC. *WP,* September 18, 1963. The *SLPD* was grudging in its approval (September 18, 1963), and the *SLGD,* a strong Symington supporter, opposed the treaty (September 13, 1963). The mail showed slightly more in opposition than in favor. Memo, "Diane" to the Senator, August 8, 1963, SP, f. nuclear testing, WHMC.

51. *Nuclear Test Ban Treaty,* 261.

52. Symington had a personal reason for interest in foreign aid. His son Jim was associate director of the Food for Peace program, headed by George McGovern.

53. Interview, Robert Amory, Jr., by Joseph E. O'Connor, February 9, 1966, 41–46, Oral History program, JFKL; *NYT,* January 14, 1963; *CR-Senate,* November 1, 1963, 20880–82.

54. Schlesinger, *A Thousand Days,* 531; *CR-Senate,* July 20, 1962, 14255.

55. *Washington Star,* September 5, 1963; *KCS,* October 4, 1963.

56. Stuart Symington, speeches in the Senate, "The Balance-of-Payments Problem," November 18, 20, 22, December 5, 19, 1963, *Congressional Record, Proceedings and Debates of the 88th Congress, First Session.*

57. *Washington Daily News,* December 20, 1963, quoted in ibid., 11–12; Symington to J. W. McAfee, January 30, 1964, SP, subject box 10, WHMC.

58. *CR-Senate,* September 18, 1961, 19924; *SLPD,* January 16, 1962. Symington included his good friend Undersecretary Roswell Gilpatric in his praise. Later, he vigorously defended Gilpatric against charges of conflict of interest in awarding contracts for the TFX fighter plane. *CR-Senate,* March 21, 1963, 4696–4703. See also Mollenhoff, *The Pentagon,* 298–312. Senate, Hearings, Committee on Foreign Relations, *The Peace Corps,* 87th Cong., 1st sess. (Washington: Government Printing Office, 1961), 95; *CR-Senate,* March 16, 1961, 4110, February 25, 1963, 2927–28; Press release, November 21, 1961, SP, box 162, WHMC.

59. Press release, November 21, 1961, SP, box 162, WHMC. As part of his tribute in the Senate, Symington inserted an article written by Ben Bradlee in *Newsweek.* Acknowledging it, Bradlee wrote: ". . . He [Kennedy] admired you so much, your innate decency, and your grace, too—and so do we." Bradlee to Symington, December 7, 1963, SP, box 84, WHMC.

60. Memo, n.d., attached to Edward Kennedy to Symington, November 28, 1973, SPF, box 5.

Chapter 28. Vietnam—From Hawk to Dove

1. *WP,* April 7, 1969.

2. Much has been written about the Taylor-Rostow mission, important in the chain of events leading to American involvement in Vietnam. Two good short accounts are Douglas Kinnard, *The Certain Trumpet: Maxwell Taylor and the American Experience in Vietnam,* 95–104; and Schlesinger, *A Thousand Days,* 544–50.

3. William Conrad Gibbons, *The U. S. Government and the Vietnam War: Executive and Legislative Roles and Relationships,* 101–2. After Symington returned to Washington, he sent Kennedy a memorandum further elaborating his views. He lamented the decline of American prestige around the world. He warned that the United States was "losing" Vietnam and advocated the prompt establishment of a policy based on "whatever is necessary" to hold the country. See also Richard Reeves, *President Kennedy: Profile of Power,* 256.

4. Robert D. Schulzinger, *A Time for War: The United States and Vietnam, 1941–1975* (New York: Oxford University Press, 1997), 111–12; Gibbons, *U.S. Government and Vietnam War,* vol. 2, 191–92. Symington's commitment to Kennedy's policy can be seen, for example, on September 6, 1963, when he inserted in the *Congressional Record* an editorial from the *St. Louis Globe Democrat* praising "Mr. Kennedy's Sound Vietnam Policy" because he "believed in most if not all of . . . [its] conclusions." *CR-Senate,* September 9, 1963, 16451.

5. Gibbons, *U.S. Government and Vietnam War,* vol. 2, 192; Senate, Committee on Foreign Relations, Executive Session, *Situation in Vietnam,* 88th Cong., 1st sess., October 9, 1963 (Historical Series, 15, 781–822).

6. Johnson to Symington, February 19, 1964, WHCF name file, LBJL. See also Vaughn Davis Bornet, *The Presidency of Lyndon B. Johnson,* 76–77; Symington to the president, February 27, 1964, WHCF subject file, Ex Co 312, LBJL.

7. Transcript, World Affairs Council, St. Louis, Missouri, May 23, 1964, Symington papers, f. 2059, WHMC.

8. *CR-Senate*, August 8, 1964, 18411–12.

9. See, for example, Randall Bennett Woods, *Fulbright: A Biography*, 349–57; Woods, *J. William Fulbright, Vietnam, and the Search for a Cold War Foreign Policy* (New York: Cambridge University Press, 1998), 78–80.

10. For outstate support for Symington's reelection see, for example, *Columbia Daily Tribune*, September 27, 1964; *SLPD*, October 8, 1964. The *Post-Dispatch* wrote that Symington should be reelected, "partly because he can be counted on to back the key elements of the Kennedy-Johnson program, and partly because he has rendered excellent service to Missouri constituents in every part of the state."

Symington, and especially Stanley Fike, had a number of political dealings with Baker but were never involved with his financial activities.

11. Memo, Ken Allen to Symington, December 10, 1964, SPF, box 11.

12. James Deakin, Washington correspondent of the *SLPD*, wrote that Johnson was being constrained by the presence of a large number of "silent senators." *SLPD*, August 8, 1965.

13. Memorandum, July 22, 1965, SP, f. 2104, WHMC. For a statement of Symington's support for Johnson see, for example, *CR-Senate*, October 21, 1965, 27039.

14. Symington to Richard B. Russell and J. William Fulbright, January 24, 1966, enclosing a 122-page report (highly sanitized) of his visit to South Vietnam, January 28–February 6, 1966, SP, box 185, WHMC; *NYT*, January 26, 1966; *CR-Senate*, January 27, 1966, 1304–5, 1460–63.

15. *CR-Senate*, February 1, 1966, 1629–30.

16. See, for example, *Washington Evening Star*, February 4, 1966; *San Diego Union*, February 9, 1966.

17. Bundy to Jones, LBJ archives, name file, LBJL.

18. *SLPD*, February 8, 1966.

19. *U.S. News and World Report*, February 28, 1966, 47–48.

20. Woods, *Fulbright, Vietnam, and Cold War Foreign Policy*, 114–15.

21. Interview of Senator Stuart Symington, Metromedia News, Senate Press Gallery, February 10, 1966, SP, box 116, WHMC.

22. Robert Dallek, *Flawed Giant: Lyndon Johnson and His Times, 1961–1973*, 351–55; Woods, *Fulbright, Vietnam, and Cold War Foreign Policy*, 115–23.

23. Woods, *Fulbright, Vietnam, and Cold War Foreign Policy*, 118.

24. Senate, Hearings before the Armed Services Committee, *Supplemental Foreign Assistance Fiscal Year 1966-Vietnam*, 89th Cong., 2d sess. (Washington: Government Printing Office, 1966), 482–86. Symington also submitted twenty-six questions in writing to Taylor, questions obviously designed to enable Taylor to explain and justify the administration's policies. Ibid., 555–59.

25. Ibid., 22–25.

26. Ibid., 271–79, 315–21. Symington discussed his exchange with Gavin on the Senate floor, calling Gavin's prescriptions "fuzzy." He also reproduced Gavin's letter to

Harper's and the editorial comment. *CR-Senate,* February 10, 1966, 2856–58. See also Schulzinger, *A Time for War,* 223*n31,* 358.

27. Woods, *Fulbright, Vietnam, and the Search for a Cold War Foreign Policy,* 116–17.

28. *Supplemental Foreign Assistance . . . Vietnam,* 419–28.

29. *WP,* February 10, 1966.

30. *Supplemental Foreign Assistance . . . Vietnam,* 429–30.

31. *CR-Senate,* March 4, 1966, 5002–5; *SLGD,* June 25–26, 1966; *CR-Senate,* June 30, 1966, 4802.

32. *NYT,* January 1, 1966; *CR-Senate,* February 28, 1966, 4066–67. Symington placed the names of all the signers in the *Record.* It should be pointed out that by 1967 support on the Missouri campus had given way to protests. Symington to Doris Bolef, July 11, 1966, SP, box 185, WHMC.

33. Symington to Fulbright and Russell, May 4, 1966, SP, box 163, WHMC.

34. Symington to Fulbright and Russell, February 6, 1967, SP, box 185, WHMC. Attached to the letter was a 129-page, extensively sanitized report.

35. *SLGD,* June 29, 1967.

36. Shapley, *Promise and Power,* 431–37.

37. *CR-Senate,* July 27, 1967, 20381; Press release, August 3, 1967, SP, box 163, WHMC; Symington to Johnson, August 21, 1967, ibid., subject box 80.

38. *CR-Senate,* August 29, 1967, 24423–24.

39. His report—heavily censored—was submitted to Senators Russell and Fulbright in December. Stuart Symington, Report of Trip to Far East, Middle East and Europe, September 8–28, 1967, SP, f. 2007, WHMC.

40. Memo, "Position on Vietnam," n.d., sent to Missouri editors, October 24, 1967, and to members of the Senate, October 25, 1967, SP, f. 2080, f. 2106, WHMC.

41. *CR-Senate,* October 3, 1967, 27544–45.

42. *SLPD,* October 22, 1967; *Washington Star,* October 7, 1967. As early as November 1966, Walt Rostow, who had replaced McGeorge Bundy as national security adviser, told the president that Symington had said to him that "you and I have been hawks since 1961. I am thinking of getting off the train soon. . . . We are getting in deeper and deeper with no end in sight. In 1968 Nixon will murder us. He will become the biggest dove of all times. There has never been a man in public life that could turn so fast on a dime." Johnson replied, "I know at least one more fellow who can turn faster on a dime than Nixon. Guess who!" Dallek, *Flawed Giant,* 385–86. *WP,* October 4, 1967; *CR-Senate,* October 5, 1967, 14247–48; *SLPD,* October 3, 1967, *SLGD,* October 4, 1967. The usually supportive *Globe-Democrat,* in an editorial headed "Strange Symington Proposal," concluded: "Most of us will be sympathetic with the Missouri senator, discouraged over the bloody attrition and impasse Washington's political war strategy has caused. But unilaterally quitting in Vietnam, for weeks or a month, would only raise the sacrificial toll of American dead and wounded."

43. *CR-Senate,* October 6, 1967, 28090–91.

44. This figure appears in a long story by Richard Dudman, Washington correspondent of the *SLPD,* "Remarkable Evolution of Symington's Views on the War in Vietnam," *SLPD,* October 22, 1967.

45. Ibid. Symington was much impressed by Ronald Steel's recent book, *Pax Americana*, with its emphasis on the force of nationalism in world affairs. Thus, the Soviet Union's expansionist tendencies derived more from Russian nationalism than from a simple desire to spread communism.

46. Transcript, *Face the Nation*, CBS, October 15, 1967, 19–20, SP, box 173, WHMC.

47. Senate, Hearings before the Committee on Foreign Relations, *Foreign Assistance Act of 1968*, 90th Cong., 2d sess. (Washington: Government Printing Office, 1968), 184–85.

48. Interview, Virginia Laird (Symington's personal secretary), by James C. Olson. For a good brief description of Tet, see Schulzinger, *A Time for War*, 259–63. Clifford, *Counsel to the President*, 498; *Foreign Assistance Act of 1968*, 185–86.

49. Interview, Virginia Laird, by the author; Walter Isaacson and Evan Thomas, *The Wise Men: Six Friends and the World They Made: Acheson, Bohlen, Harriman, Kennan, Lovett, McCloy* (Boston: Faber and Faber, 1986), 685.

50. Senate, Hearing before the Committee on Foreign Relations, *Present Situation in Vietnam*, 90th Cong., 2d sess. (Washington: Government Printing Office, 1968).

51. Symington, "Washington Report," April 10, 1968. For a good brief account of Johnson's efforts, see Dallek, *Flawed Giant*, 536–43; *CR-Senate*, June 4, 1968, 15920–21.

52. Symington to Humphrey, June 13, 1968, SP, subject box 67, WHMC; Symington to Humphrey, August 15, 1968, SP, box 67, WHMC. Humphrey's reply illustrates the problem he had with Vietnam throughout the campaign: "What I said . . . was, 'Three Presidents have thought that it was in the best interests of the United States to be in Vietnam.' I went on to say that only history could give an objective judgment on this, and I continue to say that if I were elected President I would make it my first priority of business to bring this war to an end. I am sure that no one could ever have predicted our degree of involvement. War has a sort of built-in escalation. The only way to check it is by a firm policy that puts on the brakes." Humphrey to Symington, August 20, 1968, ibid.

53. *CR-Senate*, September 27, 1968, 28587.

54. Ibid., October 1, 1968, 28942.

Chapter 29. Laos, Cambodia, and the CIA

1. Linda McFarland, *Cold War Strategist: Stuart Symington and the Search for National Security*, 104; *CR-Senate*, January 17, 1969, 1215; Johnson to Symington, January 18, 1969, WHCF, Name File, LBJL. Although the two old warriors buried the hatchet, they never resumed the easy camaraderie of the early days. After Johnson's death, the Symington family and Lady Bird maintained close and cordial relationships. On a visit to the LBJ ranch in Stonewall, Texas, I noted an autographed photo of Stuart Symington hanging in a prominent position at the entrance to LBJ's study.

2. *NYT,* March 3 and 5, 1971.

3. *CR-Senate*, September 21, 1973, 30822. Symington told the Senate that he had known Kissinger for many years, "long before he became a national and international

figure." He described him as "able, with a brilliant mind." He did not agree with many of his policies, "but everybody knows they were not his policies. In his new post, he may be in a better position to object when he feels that what has been considered is wrong."

4. Although Symington and Fulbright at this time generally were in agreement on matters of foreign policy, having the chairman of the committee as a member of the subcommittee was awkward.

5. John F. Lehman, *The Executive, Congress, and Foreign Policy: Studies of the Nixon Administration* (New York: Praeger, 1976), 108–69, provides an excellent account of the committee's activity.

6. From New York en route to Barbados with Eve for a winter vacation, he wrote Fulbright, "Let me take this opportunity to thank you very much for letting me run these hearings. The facts we are developing will certainly save the taxpayers a lot of unnecessary expenses and in the long run could save the country." Symington to Fulbright, December 1, 1969, Fulbright papers. For an expression of Symington's concern that the United States was overreaching, see, for example, *NYT,* August 31, 1966.

7. *NYT,* February 4, 1969.

8. Senate, Hearings before the Subcommittee on United States Security Agreements and Commitments Abroad, *Broader Aspects of U.S. Commitments,* 91st Cong., 2d sess. (Washington: Government Printing Office, 1971), November 24, 1970, 1.

9. Lehman, *Executive, Congress, and Foreign Policy,* 116.

10. Ibid., 117–18; *NYT,* April 9, 1969.

11. Lehman, *Executive, Congress, and Foreign Policy,* 117–23, 124–25, 127–33. See *CR-Senate,* August 8, 1969, 23080–82 for a colloquy between Fulbright and Symington. Henry Kissinger, *White House Years* (Boston: Little, Brown, 1979), 453–57. Kissinger wrote: "Symington had behaved honorably. . . . [he] would not release classified information without the consent of the Administration."

12. Senate, Hearings, *United States Security Agreements and Commitments Abroad: The Republic of the Philippines* (Washington: Government Printing Office, 1969), 1–599; *NYT,* October 13, 1969. John W. Finney, reporting for the *Times,* wrote, "The dispute is a test case for the Senate subcommittee headed by Senator Stuart Symington." See also Lehman, *Executive, Congress, and Foreign Policy,* 125–27. Lehman recounts the bickering between the Defense and State Departments over which group had the responsibility for dealing with Symington. The White House created a "working group," headed by John Ehrlichman and including Kissinger and General Alexander Haig, to coordinate relations with the subcommittee. Ibid., 130–31. *NYT,* November 19, 1969.

13. Symington later charged on the CBS program *Face the Nation* that the story of the $39 million was "pretty shoddy." He refused to supply details, but hinted that the subcommittee had uncovered evidence of widespread corruption in the administration of President Ferdinand Marcos. Ibid., March 16, 1970. Lehman, *Executive, Congress, and Foreign Policy,* 134.

14. *NYT,* September 20, 1969.

15. Senate, Hearings, *United States Security Agreements and Commitments Abroad: Kingdom of Laos* (Washington: Government Printing Office, 1970); *NYT,* October 21, 1969; Symington to Rogers, February 3, 1970, SP, f. 2216, WHMC; *CR-Senate,* March 26, 1970, 9626–27.

16. Kissinger, *White House Years,* 454–55.

17. *NYT,* February 12, 1970; Office of the White House Press Secretary, "Statement by the President," March 6, 1976, SP, f. 2211, WHMC.

18. NBC, *The Frank McGee Report,* March 8, 1970, ibid.

19. *WP,* April 21, 1970; *SLPD,* April 24, 1970.

20. KMOX radio, St. Louis, May 3, 1973, transcript in SP, f. 2203, WHMC.

21. *NYT,* May 6, 1970.

22. In the extensive maneuvering over the legislation, Symington joined Fulbright in an unsuccessful effort to keep the bill bottled up in the Foreign Relations Committee. Even though that effort failed, Symington offered, and the committee adopted, an amendment requiring the president to give thirty days' notice to Congress before using any authority granted by the bill in Cambodia. Lehman, *Executive, Congress, and Foreign Policy,* 197.

23. *NYT,* October 14, 1971.

24. Schulzinger, *A Time for War,* 297–300, contains a good brief account of the war's effect on the election.

25. Joint Statement by Senator Stuart Symington, Senator Thomas F. Eagleton, and Governor Warren Hearnes, press release, October 7, 1971, SP, f. 1971, WHMC; Symington to Lewis, November 1, 1972, ibid., f. 2221, WHMC; Symington to Fulbright, December 7, 1972; Symington press release, December 8, 1972, SP, f. 2221, WHMC; Symington to Major General John C. Ribaudo, December 8, 1972, SPF, box 4.

26. *Kansas City Times,* December 25, 1972; *SLPD,* December 30, 1972; *Washington Star,* January 8, 1973; *WP,* December 25, 29, 1972. Both ardent sports fans, Stuart and Eve seldom missed a Redskins home game.

27. Symington to J. H. Whitney, March 12, 1973, SPF, box 4.

28. Stanley Fike to William Becker, January 5, 1973, William Becker papers, box 29, WHMC; Clark Clifford to Stephen Ailes et al., January 19, 1973, SP, box 19, ibid; *SLPD,* January 5, 1973.

29. *SLGD,* February 2, 1973; *WP,* February 3, 1973; Symington to John Hampton Stennis (a son), February 8, 1973, SP, f. 1780, WHMC.

30. *NYT,* April 28, 1973; Press Release, "Report on the Air War in Cambodia," April 127, 1973, SP, f. 2226, WHMC.

31. William Shawcross, *Sideshow: Kissinger, Nixon and the Destruction of Cambodia* (New York: Simon and Schuster, 1987), 287–88.

32. Hughes to Symington, July 18, 1973, Goldwater to Symington, July 19, 1973, and Symington to Harold Hughes, July 19, 1973, all in SP, f. 1802, WHMC. Cf., Symington to Goldwater, July 23, 1973, ibid.

33. *WP,* July 24, 1973.

34. Senate, Committee on Armed Services, *Bombing in Cambodia,* 93d Cong., 1st sess.; *WP,* August 10, 1973; American Broadcasting Company, *Issues and Answers,* August 12, 1973, transcript in SP, f. 1782, WHMC; *WP,* August 21, 1973.

35. Senate, Committee on Foreign Relations, *Nomination of Henry Kissinger,* 93d Cong., 1st sess., pt. 1, 31; *NYT,* September 8, 1973.

36. *CR-Senate,* September 21, 1973, 30822; "Statement by Senator Symington," September 10, 1973, SP, subject box 84, WHMC.

37. "Congressional Oversight of the Intelligence Community," unidentified document, November, 1972, 8, SP, f. 1805, WHMC.

38. Symington to Stennis, July 7, 1971, Mansfield papers.

39. *CR-Senate,* November 23, 1971, 42923-32.

40. Unfortunately, there is no record of any personal communication between Symington and Helms at this time. For an account of the relationship between the two men, see Thomas Powers, *The Man Who Kept the Secrets: Richard Helms and the CIA* (New York: Knopf, 1979).

41. Mark Perry wrote that Schlesinger was "continually spurned by Stuart Symington, one of the more powerful members of the Senate Armed Services Committee." *Four Stars,* 260. My research does not support that view. Symington to Stennis, January 15, 1973, SP, f. 1779, WHMC.

42. Symington to John McClellan, May 11, 1973, SP, f. 1781; Clifford P. Case to Symington, May 8, 1973, f. 1805, WHMC.

43. *NYT,* May 9, 1973; Symington to McClellan, May 11, 1973, loc. cit. See also Powers, *The Man Who Kept the Secrets,* 360–61.

44. "Opening Statement, Senator Symington, Acting Chairman, Armed Services Committee, May 11, 1973," SP, f. 1781, WHMC.

45. G. M. Lies wrote in the Capitol Hill newspaper *Roll Call* that in his handling of the case Symington "displayed that true grit brand of class. . . . the CIA issue could have been exploited by a lesser man, but not Stuart Symington. He handled it in true fashion, dexterously answering questions to get at the elusive truth." *Roll Call,* May 17, 1973.

46. Lawrence L. Knutson, Associated Press dispatch, May 14, 1973, SP, f. 1805, WHMC. See also *NYT,* May 15, 1973. Symington was careful to protect the reputation of former director Richard Helms. In reporting on the Walters testimony he said, "I believe that Director Helms and General Walters . . . behaved very well with respect to this." "Statement by Senator Stuart Symington, Acting Chairman, Senate Committee on Armed Services," May 15, 1973, SP, f. 1805, WHMC.

47. *Kansas City Times,* May 19, 1973.

48. Office of the White House Press Secretary, "Accompanying Statement by the President," May 22, 1973, SP, f. 1805, WHMC; *SLPD,* May 24, 1973.

49. Symington to Richardson, May 21, 1973, SP, box 109, WHMC; *SLPD,* May 27, 1973; Office of Senator Stuart Symington, press release, June 3 and September 7, 1973, SP, f. 3758, WHMC.

50. "Statement by Senator Stuart Symington," October 21, 1973, SP, f. 3769, WHMC.

51. Memo, "Chris" to Kathy [Nelson], April 30, 1974, SP, box 132.

Chapter 30. Meanwhile, Back in Missouri

1. Author's conversations with Missourians.

2. Stuart Symington, Jr., has frequently discussed with the author his father's growing

disenchantment with St. Louis. An incident that particularly rankled was the refusal of the St. Louis Country Club to grant him nonresident status, after they had done the same for Jack Danforth, then serving as Missouri's attorney general and living in Jefferson City.

3. *SLPD*, February 15, 1970.

4. These men, distinguished jurists all, referred to themselves as "the Symington court." A photograph of them hangs in the School of Law at the University of Missouri-Columbia.

5. *CR-Senate*, June 20, 1962, 11076; author's conversations with Dr. Sabates; Vera Olson, "A Missouri Woman Who Took on the World," unpublished paper, author's files; Carl Rollyson, *Nothing Ever Happens to the Brave: The Story of Martha Gellhorn* (New York: St. Martin's, 1990), 278. The Symington and Gellhorn families were quite close. Martha's mother, Edna, a prominent St. Louis activist, frequently wrote Symington on political issues. Martha Love Symington, who had been married to Stuart's brother James, had moved to St. Louis after a divorce and was one of Martha Gellhorn's closest friends. Martha also was close to Eve's cousin John Hay Whitney and his wife, Betsey, frequently staying at the embassy in London during Whitney's ambassadorship. Symington and Gellhorn corresponded frequently on behalf of Sandy. Gellhorn's letters are long, rambling, and occasionally quite passionate. See SPF, box 12; Edna Gellhorn papers, Olin Library, Washington University. D. Clayton James, *The Years of MacArthur*, vol. 3 (Boston: Houghton, Mifflin, 1985), 675, 814; *CR-Senate*, December 18, 1973, 24949–53.

6. Good brief accounts of the development of the Jefferson Expansion National Memorial can be found in George B. Hartzog, Jr., *Battling for the National Parks*, 37–57, and James Neal Primm, *Lion of the Valley: St. Louis, Missouri* (Boulder, Colo.: Pruett, 1990), 479–85.

7. Symington, "Memories," 161–62. Former President Truman also urged Green to change his mind on the project. Truman to Green, November 4, 1953, SP, alpha correspondence, WHMC.

8. Symington to Charles Nagel, director of the St. Louis Art Museum, April 15, 1957, SP, alpha correspondence, WHMC.

9. See, for example, Morton May to Symington, May 17, 1956; Bernard F. Dickman to Symington, June 26, 1959, ibid; *SLPD*, November 27, 1960. The entire Missouri delegation supported the project. Representative Tom Curtis, a south St. Louis Republican, was particularly effective with the Eisenhower administration.

10. *SLPD*, August 14, 1964. See also Hartzog, *Battling for the National Parks*, 59–69; *CR-Senate*, January 14, 1963, 236–37.

11. Symington's efforts, combined with those of Senator Long, created quite a stir in the White House. In a note to Larry O'Brien, for example, Mike Manatos commented: "I really believe the Bureau [of the Budget] did not understand the importance of the project to these two senators." Memo, Mike Manatos to Larry O'Brien, February 3, 1964, LBJL. See also Memo, Elmer Staats to [Roy] Jenkins, January 27, 1964; Long and Symington to the president, February 7, 1964; Symington to O'Brien, February 5, 1964; O'Brien to Symington, February 10, 1964; LBJL.

12. SP, Blues hockey folder, subject box 12, WHMC; *CR-Senate*, May 15, 1968, 13308.

13. Symington to William V. Bidwill and Charles Bidwill, July 14, 1964, SP, subject box 15, WHMC. The relationship between the Bidwills and St. Louis remained uneasy. Moreover, Busch Stadium, though a handsome monument, was not well configured for football. The Cardinals moved to Phoenix in 1988.

14. *SLPD,* June 12, 1970; *SLGD,* October 19, 1967. Good articles by Joe McGuff on the efforts to save professional baseball in Kansas City will be found in *KCS,* October 17, 18, 19, and 20, 1967. Fike to Symington, September 20, 1967, SP, subject box 40, WHMC; Ilus W. Davis, Proclamation, February 12, 1970, copy in SP, box 131, WHMC.

15. *Kansas City Times,* April 8 and 9, 1969.

16. *SLGD,* April 29, 1969.

17. Symington to Lawrence F. O'Brien, SPF, box 12.

18. *SLPD,* February 15, 16, 17, and 18, 1970.

19. *SLGD,* February 8, 1970.

20. Ibid., October 20, 1970. Danforth had been urged by Nixon to enter the race, and the Republicans hoped that Missouri might provide one of the seven seats they needed to gain control of the Senate.

21. In February 1971, Symington complained to James S. McDonnell, chairman of the McDonnell-Douglas board, about Douglas's charge against Symington and his staff, adding, "You, of all persons know that it is just not true." *SLPD,* February 9, 1971. He turned the correspondence over to Robert Lasch, editorial page editor of the *Post-Dispatch,* commenting: "Don't guess there is anything to do, but did want you to have facts." Symington to Robert Lasch, February 9, 1971, SP, box 91, WHMC.

22. *SLPD,* August 29, 1970.

23. *KCS,* July 31, 1970; *SLGD,* August 1, 1970; Telegram, Danforth to Symington, August 19, 1970, SPF, James Symington papers.

24. James W. Symington, Speech at Springfield Kiwanis, September 25, 1970, SPF, James Symington papers.

25. On Danforth's lack of campaign issues see, for example, the *National Observer,* September 21, 1970. Associated Press, October 13, 1970; Symington press release, October 2, 1970, William Becker papers, box 29, WHMC.

26. *NYT,* October 6, 1970. Apple filed a long report on the campaign from Hannibal, where Symington was attending a chili feed in the town square: "It was a typical campaign performance by the Senator. . . . (still handsome at 69 years of age, still so slim that he wears suit jackets with no vents. Confident almost to the point of cockiness, the picture of a man for whom success is a habit.) . . . and the audience . . . responded warmly."

27. *SLPD,* September 27, 1970; *SLGD,* October 4, 1970; *KCS,* October 15, 1970; Symington press release, November 1, 1970, SP, f. 504, WHMC.

Chapter 31. The Search for Peace

1. Flora Lewis, "The Education of a Senator," *Atlantic,* December 1971, 53–64.

2. Tom Steinbrenner, "Air Power Is Indivisible," *Armed Forces Journal,* September 1972, 26–28.

3. Ibid., and in many speeches from the 1960s and 1970s.

4. See, for example, J. W. Fulbright to Symington, March 14, 1970, Fulbright to William P. Rogers, March 18, 1970, SP, f. 222, WHMC; *NYT,* March 20, 1970.

5. On Christmas Day in Seoul, Korea, he narrowly escaped death when the automobile in which he was riding was hit by a fire truck. The car was demolished and Symington was knocked unconscious for a time, but otherwise received only minor injuries; after two days in the U.S. military hospital in Seoul he was able to continue his travels.

6. Statement by Senator Stuart Symington regarding thirteen-nation tour, January 19, 1972, SP, box 163, WHMC.

7. *CR-Senate,* April 19, 1968, 10035–36. Much has been written on this subject. I have relied on Christopher Raj, *American Military in Europe: Controversy over NATO Burden Sharing* (New Delhi, India: ABC Publishing House, 1983), 152–81, 187–97, 279–81; Phil Williams, *The Senate and U.S. Troops in Europe,* 143–45; and John S. Duffield, *Power Rules: The Evolution of NATO's Conventional Force Posture,* 186–89.

8. Gregory F. Treverton, *The Dollar Drain and American Forces in Germany: Managing the Political Economics of Alliance,* 107–9.

9. McCloy to Symington, May 20, 1968, and Symington to McCloy, May 20, 1968, both in Fulbright papers.

10. Symington to Fulbright, December 7, 1972, and July 16, 1973, SP, f. 2221.

11. *NYT,* December 2, 1973; *WP,* December 2, 1973; *CR-Senate,* December 7, 1973, 22151–54.

12. *CR-Senate,* February 8, 1972, 2567.

13. Ibid., 2510.

14. See, for example, Symington to Robert Diamond, *Congressional Quarterly,* March 5, 1970, SP, subject box 93, WHMC, written in response to Diamond's request for Symington's position on the Middle East.

15. *CR-Senate,* March 23, 1970, 8737–38; Kissinger, *White House Years,* 558–82; Jacob Javits with Rafael Steinberg, *Javits: The Autobiography of a Public Man* (Boston: Houghton Mifflin, 1981), 467.

16. Seymour M. Hersh, *The Price of Power: Kissinger in the Nixon White House* (New York: Summit Books, 1983), 402–14, quote on p. 405. In *White House Years,* 558–82, Kissinger repeatedly criticizes Rogers' handling of Middle East problems.

17. Symington to Kissinger, September 27, 1974, SP, subject box 84, WHMC, Symington to Mr. and Mrs. Angier Biddle Duke, October 23, 1974, ibid., box 181; Senate, Report to the Committee on Foreign Relations by Senator Stuart Symington, *The United Nations,* 91st Cong., 1st sess. (Washington: Government Printing Office, 1969).

18. Statement by Senator Stuart Symington, "UNGA First Committee, US Statement on Nuclear Issues," October 21, 1974, SP, box 181, WHMC; Yost to Symington, October 24, 1974, ibid.; Kissinger to Symington, December 26, 1974, ibid.

19. Symington developed very cordial relations with Panofsky, director of the Stanford Linear Accelerator Center, referring to him as "Pief" in their rather extensive correspondence. The two men frequently lunched together when Panofsky was in town.

20. Others in the group were John Sherman Cooper, Edward Kennedy, Philip Hart, William Fulbright, Albert Gore, Jacob Javits, Charles Percy, Mike Mansfield, George

McGovern, Frank Church, and Mark Hatfield. Fred M. Kaplan, *The Wizards of Armageddon* (New York: Simon and Schuster, 1983), 349–50. Kathie Nelson of Symington's office worked closely with aides of the other anti-ABM senators as well as with Panofsky. See, for example, Memo, Kathie Nelson to Senator Symington, February 3, 1970, SP, box 1, ABM correspondence, WHMC.

21. See Kaplan, *Wizards of Armageddon,* 350–53, for a good brief discussion of the two models.

22. Vojtech Mastny, ed., *Disarmament and Nuclear Tests, 1964–69* (New York: Facts on File, 1970), 198–200; Richard F. Kaufman, *The War Profiteers* (Indianapolis: Bobbs-Merrill, 1970), 208.

23. "Statement by Senator Stuart Symington," March 20, 1969, before the Committee on Armed Services, SP, f. 2011; *NYT,* March 21, 1969; *CR-Senate,* March 7, 1969, 5602–4; National Broadcasting Company, *Meet the Press,* June 1, 1969; CBS Television, *Face the Nation,* August 3, 1969, reprinted in *CR-Senate,* August 5, 22322–24, at the request of William Proxmire of Wisconsin, who called Symington's remarks "unusually perceptive and thoughtful"; *U.S. News and World Report,* July 14, 1969, 29–31. The *Globe-Democrat's* accusation is in *SLGD,* July 7, 1969; the *Post-Dispatch's* comment is in *SLPD,* July 24, 1969.

24. *NYT,* April 19, 1971.

25. Memo, Kathie Nelson to Senator Symington, September 1, 1971, SP, subject box 1, WHMC; *CR-Senate,* June 30, 1971, 10444; Symington to Stennis, April 23, 1972, SP, subject box 1, WHMC. Some of Symington's colleagues, particularly Senators Cooper and Hart, probably would have gone further, but they were looking to Symington for the lead in the matter. Memo, Nelson, September 1, 1971.

26. Statement by Senator Stuart Symington, "The Case against the F-14," September 23, 1971, SP, box 163, WHMC. Cf. *CR-Senate,* September 23, 1971, 33112–14. He also wrote Charles Schultze of the Brookings Institution, whom he had known when the latter was director of the budget, complaining about a Brookings study that was critical of the F-15. Symington to Schultze, June 19, 1972, SP, subject box 92, WHMC. See also Symington to James S. McDonnell, June 21, 1972, ibid.

27. Draft statement on TRIDENT, prepared by Kathie Nelson, July 20, 1972, SP, f. 4008, WHMC. See also Elmo R. Zumwalt, *On Watch,* 162–63.

28. Statement by Senator Stuart Symington, Senate floor, July 27, 1972, SP, box 178, WHMC; Bentsen to Symington, August 1, 1973, ibid.; *SLGD,* December 11, 1972. Symington was testifying before a special committee on congressional reform. See also Memo, Kathie Nelson to Symington, June 13, 1973, SP, f. 4007, WHMC.

29. Draft of minority report attached to Memo, Nelson to Symington, September 4, 1973, SP, box 178, WHMC.

30. *CR-Senate,* June 28, 1971, 10101–3. Sanford N. McDonnell, president of McDonnell Douglas, wrote: ". . . We appreciate immensely your very effective comments on the Shuttle." McDonnell to Symington, July 9, 1971, SP, subject box 92, WHMC.

31. He wrote Dixie Lee Ray when she left the chairmanship of the Atomic Energy Commission, "For years I have tried to get these people to open up re information that will not help a possible enemy; and yet until you came, it was like butting your head against a stone wall." November 25, 1974, SP, box 8, WHMC.

32. Symington press releases, July 15, 1973, and January 27, 1974, SP, f. 2528, WHMC.

33. Opening Statement by Senator Stuart Symington, "Nuclear Weapons and Foreign Policy," SP, f. nuclear weapons, WHMC.

34. Senate, Committee on Foreign Relations, Subcommittee on U.S. Security Agreements and Commitments Abroad and Subcommittee on Arms Control, International Law and Organization, *Nuclear Weapons and Foreign Policy*, 93rd Cong., 2d sess., March 7, 14, and April 4, 1974, 159–201.

35. Louis René Beres, *Apocalypse: Nuclear Catastrophe in World Politics* (Chicago: University of Chicago Press, 1980), 74. Symington is quoted along with David Lilienthal, in a separate heading at the beginning of chapter 2. See also Symington, *Washington Report*, October 7–11, 1974, SP, subject box 163, WHMC.

36. *Washington Star*, February 24, 1976; *WP*, February 25, 1976. See also *NYT*, February 25, 1976.

37. *CR-Senate*, April 14, 1975, 5720.

38. *SLGD*, July 7, 1976; Kissinger to Symington, July 27, 1976, SP, subject box 84, WHMC. Bill Ashworth, who worked on nuclear matters in Symington's office, wrote that the letter was "the strongest expression of concern in regard to proliferation" he had seen from the State Department. Memo, Ashworth to Symington, July 28, 1976, ibid.

39. Harold Agnew, "Atoms for Lease," *Bulletin of the Atomic Scientists* (May 1976): 22–23. Agnew wrote: "I find it hard to understand why this concept has been to date turned down by our State Department, the Arms Control and Disarmament Agency, and other key officials. Only Senator Stuart Symington has pursued this suggestion." *CR-Senate*, July 28, 1976, 12610.

40. Stuart Symington, "The Washington Nuclear Mess," *International Security* (winter 1977): 71–78.

Chapter 32. The Final Years

1. Statement by Senator Stuart Symington, Chase–Park Plaza Hotel, St. Louis, Missouri, April 22, 1975, William Becker papers, box 29, WHMC.

2. James W. Symington, attending a reception in Washington, told reporters that he knew nothing in advance, he was not even aware that his father had gone to St. Louis. *SLGD*, April 23, 1975.

3. Ibid.; *SLPD*, April 23, 1975.

4. *SLGD*, April 23, 1975; *Kansas City Times*, April 23, 1975. On election night while flying to Kansas City for a victory celebration, Litton and his family were killed in a plane crash. Symington immediately withdrew from further consideration, and the Democratic state central committee named Warren Hearnes as the party's candidate. Jack Danforth easily defeated Hearnes.

5. Memo, Fike to "Senator," April 23, 1975, SPF, box 4.

6. *Washington Star*, February 24, 1976; *WP*, February 25, 1976.

7. *WP*, November 9, 1976. The *Post* gave the story a top front-page position with a two-column picture.

8. Snyder to Symington, January 24, 1976, Symington to Snyder, February 9, 1976,

SPF, box 1; *Kansas City Times,* May 19, 1976. Mrs. Ginn, a personal friend, told the author that she would be eternally grateful for Symington's support: "As he escorted me to the hearing table, he squeezed my arm and said, 'Don't worry, it's all wired.'"

9. *SLGD,* September 30, 1976.

10. Senate, *Tributes to the Honorable Stuart Symington of Missouri in the United States Senate. . . ,* 94th Cong., 2d sess., Doc. 94–276, September 27, 1976 (Washington: Government Printing Office, 1977).

11. Symington to Vice President Nelson Rockefeller, December 17, 1976, SPF, box 4; Danforth to Symington, September 19, 1986, ibid., box 5. The records sent to the University of Missouri became file #3637, Western Historical Manuscripts Collection, and the principal source for this work.

12. Most of the foregoing is from *SLGD,* January 12 and 16, 1977; *SLPD,* December 2, 1976. See also *WP,* November 9, 1976.

13. The correspondence file bulges with letters to and from VIPs from the realms of politics, government, business, and entertainment. SPF, box 5.

14. His notes were put together under the title "Memories," valuable for the earlier years of his life. He also read the manuscript of a book being written by his friend, Thomas Lanphier, writing extensive critiques.

15. *Air Force Magazine,* February 1985, 119. In an exchange of letters after the ceremony, Goldwater wrote: "As I mentioned, you and I have had disagreements, but I've always been a staunch admirer for the guts you showed in getting this country to recognize the Air Force as a separate service." Goldwater to Symington, December 12, 1984, SPF, box 5.

16. Symington to Weinberger, August 4, 1976, Weinberger to Symington, August 7, 1986, ibid.

17. *SLPD,* July 22, 1980.

18. Robert Altman, a rising star in the legal profession, became something of a celebrity by marrying Lynda Carter, the "Wonder Woman" of television fame. The newlyweds were introduced to Washington society at a reception in the F Street Club hosted by James Symington. Frantz and McKean, *Friends in High Places,* 330-31.

19. Symington was close to both men, although he and Gavin had publicly disagreed on the Vietnam War.

20. Frantz and McKean, *Friends in High Places,* 336. Their work contains a good account of the Clifford difficulties.

21. *SLGD,* April 12, 1978.

22. *SLPD,* December 18, 1988, and January 11, 1989; Cathedral Church of Saint Peter and Saint Paul in the City and Diocese of Washington, Memorial Service for Stuart Symington, January 10, 1989, courtesy Stuart Symington, Jr.

23. *WP,* December 15, 1988.

24. Sam Hamra to the author, February 28, 2002, author's files.

Bibliography

Manuscripts

The basic sources used in the preparation of this book are the Stuart Symington papers. The largest collection is in the Western Historical Manuscript Collection, University of Missouri, Columbia: Collection No. C3874, Senatorial Papers; and No. 3637, Symington Scrapbooks, 1945–1976, thirty-seven volumes on microfilm. The Symington Papers, Harry S. Truman Library, Independence, Missouri, cover Symington's service as a government administrator in the Truman administration. A third, most important collection, in the possession of the Symington family, referred to as Symington Personal Files in this work, consists of twelve large manuscript boxes and provides much important information not available elsewhere. "Memories," typed notes dictated by Symington at various times during his retirement, possibly as preparation for an autobiography, is incomplete, but valuable. Official correspondence from Symington's various administrative posts is contained in the files of the National Archives and Records Administration, Washington, D.C., particularly in Record Groups 46, 107, 270, 273, 304, and 340.

In addition to these personal and official papers, the following manuscript collections are cited in the text:

Dwight D. Eisenhower Library, Abilene, Kansas
    Dwight Eisenhower Papers
    T. Keith Glennan Papers
    Lauris Norstad Papers
Franklin D. Roosevelt Library, Hyde Park, New York
    Eleanor Roosevelt Papers
Harry S. Truman Library, Independence, Missouri
    Tom Clark Papers
    Clark Clifford Papers

    Matthew Connelley Papers
    George M. Elsey Papers
    National Security Council, Minutes
    John Ohly Papers
    Harry S. Truman Papers
John M. Olin Library, Washington University, St. Louis
    Edna Gellhorn Papers
    William Sentner Papers
Library of Congress, Washington, D.C.
    Joseph and Stewart Alsop Papers
    William D. Leahy Papers
    Carl Spaatz Papers
    Lawrence Spivak Papers
    Hoyt Vandenberg Papers
    James Wadsworth Papers
Lyndon Baines Johnson Library, Austin, Texas
    Lyndon Baines Johnson Papers
    Drew Pearson Papers
Minnesota Historical Society, St. Paul
    Hubert Humphrey Papers
Seeley Mudd Manuscript Library, Princeton University, Princeton, New Jersey
    Ferdinand Eberstadt Papers
    James Forrestal Papers
    Arthur Krock Papers
Special Collections Division, University of Arkansas Libraries, Fayetteville
    J. William Fulbright Papers
U.S. Air Force, Historical Research Center, Air University, Maxwell Air Force Base, Alabama
    Ennis Whitehead Papers
Western Historical Manuscript Collection, University of Missouri, Columbia
    James H. Meredith Papers
    William Becker Papers

Interviews and Oral Histories

Amory, Robert, Jr., by Joseph E. O'Connor. JFKL.
Anderson, Clinton P., by John F. Stewart. JFKL.
Bowles, Chester, by Robert R. R. Brooks. JFKL.
Clifford, Clark, by James C. Olson.
Davis, General Benjamin O., Jr., by James C. Olson (telephone).
Draper, William H., by Jerry N. Hess. HSTL.
Fike, Stanley, by Larry Hackman. JFKL.
Godfrey, Toby, by James C. Olson.
Graves, Amelia, by James C. Olson.

Lee, Vice Admiral Fitzhugh, by E. B. Kitchen. U.S. Naval Institute, Annapolis.

Leo, Stephen, by George M. Watson, Jr. Albert F. Simpson Historical Research Center, USAF.

Marr, Jack, Reminiscences. Oral History Collection of Columbia University.

Martin, Glen, by Vaughn H. Gallacher and Hugh N. Ahmann. USAF Collection, US-AFHRC.

McKee, William F., by George M. Watson, Jr. USAF Collection, USAFHRC.

Meredith, James, by Larry Hackman. JFKL.

Murphy, Charles, Richard Neustadt, David Stowe, James Webb, joint interview by Hugh Heclo and Anna Nelson. HSTL.

Nelson, Kathryn, by James C. Olson.

Nitze, Paul, by James C. Olson.

———, by Paul Dirk and James Hasdorf. USAF Collection, USAFHRC.

Norstad, Lauris, by Hugh Ahmann. USAF Collection, USAFHRC.

Royall, Kenneth S., Reminiscences. Oral History Collection of Columbia University.

Sorenson, Theodore, by Carl Kaysen. JFKL.

Staats, Elmer, by Robert C. Turner. JFKL.

———, by James C. Olson.

Stuart, Harold C., by Charles J. Gross. USAF Collection, USAFHRC.

Symington, James, by Larry J. Hackman. JFKL.

Symington, Stuart, by Caroline K. Ehlers, for the University of Maryland.

———, by George M. Watson, Jr. USAF Oral History Collection, USAFHRC.

———, by Hugh N. Ahmann and Herman S. Wolk. Albert F. Simpson Historical Resarch Center, Air University.

———, by Joe B. Frantz. LBJL.

———, by James R. Fuchs. HSTL.

———, by Larry Keyes. In possession of James W. Symington.

———, by Metromedia News.

———, by Pat Holt. JFKL.

Vanderzee, R. J. Senate Oral History Interview. LC.

Wadsworth, J., by John P. Mason, Jr. EL.

Wallace, Henry A. Reminiscences, Oral History Research Center, Columbia University.

Weaver, George, by James. C. Olson.

Welsh, Edward, by Walter D. Sohier, Addison M. Rothrock, and Eugene M. Emme. JFKL.

Zentay, John, by James C. Olson (telephone).

Zuckert, Eugene, by George M. Watson, Jr. USAF Oral History Program.

———, by James C. Olson.

Hearings and Reports

Baruch, Bernard M., and John W. Hancock. *Report on War and Post-War Adjustment Policies, February 15, 1944.*

A Modern Concept of Manpower Management and Compensation, a Report and

Recommendation for the Secretary of Defense by the Defense Advisory Committee on Professional and Technical Compensation. 2 vols. May 1957.

President's Air Policy Commission. *Survival in the Air Age.* 1946.

Reconstruction Finance Corporation. *1951 Annual Report and Financial Statements.*

Report of the Chairman, National Security Resources Board. Washington: Government Printing Office, 1951.

Report of the President's Advisory Commission on Universal Training. *A Program for National Security.*

Report of the Secretary of the Air Force to the Secretary of Defense for Fiscal Year 1948. Washington: Government Printing Office, 1949.

U.S. House. *The Liquidation of War Surpluses, Quarterly Progress Report to the Congress by the Surplus Property Administration.* Y3W19: 20 (1945–1947).

U.S. House. Hearings before the Committee on Armed Services, *Investigation of the B-36 Bomber Program.* 81st Cong., 1st sess.

U.S. House. Hearings before the Committee on Banking and Currency, *Defense Production Act of 1950.* 81st Cong., 2d sess.

U.S. House. A Report of an Investigation by the Committee on Armed Services, *Unification and Strategy.* 81st Cong., 2d sess., doc. 600.

U.S. Senate. Hearings before a Subcommittee of the Committee on Military Affairs, *Veterans' Priority for Surplus Property.* 79th Cong., 1st sess.

U.S. Senate. Joint Hearings before the Subcommittee on Surplus Property of the Committee on Military Affairs, Special Committee to Study and Survey Problems of Small Business Enterprises, Industrial Reorganization Subcommittee of the Special Committee on Postwar Economic Policy and Planning, *Aluminum Plant Disposal.* 79th Cong., 1st sess.

U.S. Senate. Hearings before the Committee on Armed Services, *National Security Amendments of 1949.* 81st Cong., 1st sess.

U.S. Senate. Hearings before the Committee on Armed Services, *Miscellaneous Bills.* 81st Cong., 2d sess.

U.S. Senate. Hearings before the Committee on Banking and Currency, *Nomination of W. Stuart Symington.* 82d Cong., 1st sess.

U.S. Senate. Committee on Banking and Currency, *Study of Reconstruction Finance Corporation: Favoritism and Influence. S. Report 76, Eighty-second Congress, First Session, 1951. Senate Miscellaneous Reports, Vol. 1.* Cited in Robert J. Donovan, *Tumultuous Years,* 333.

U.S. Senate. Hearings before the Preparedness Subcommittee of the Committee on Armed Services, *Stockpiling of Tin and Rubber.* 82d Cong., 1st sess.

U.S. Senate. Sixth Report of the Preparedness Subcommittee of the Committee on Armed Services, *Investigation of the Preparedness Program.* 82d Cong., 1st sess., doc. 13.

U.S. Senate. Interim Report of the Committee on Expenditures in the Executive Departments made by Its Permanent Subcommittee on Investigations, *American Lithofold Corp., William M. Boyle, Jr., and Guy George Gabrielson.* 82d Cong., 2d sess., Report No. 1142.

U.S. Senate. Hearings before the Permanent Subcommittee on Investigations of the Committee on Government Operations, *State Department Information Program— Information Centers.* 83d Cong., 1st sess.

U.S. Senate. Hearings before the Permanent Subcommittee on Investigations of Committee on Government Operations, *State Department Information Program—Voice of America.* 83d Cong., 1st sess.

U.S. Senate. Hearings before the Special Subcommittee on Investigations of the Committee on Government Operations, *Special Senate Investigation on Charges and Countercharges Involving Secretary of the Army Robert T. Stevens, John G. Adams, H. Struve Hensel, and Senator Joe McCarthy, Roy M. Cohn, and Francis P. Carr.* 83d Cong., 1st sess.

U.S. Senate. Hearings before the Permanent Subcommittee on Investigations of the Committee on Government Operations, *Army Signal Corps—Subversion and Espionage.* 83d Cong., 2d sess.

U.S. Senate. Report of Proceedings, Hearing Held before Committee on Armed Services, *Nomination of Charles E. Wilson to be Secretary of Defense.* Executive Session, January 23, 1953. SP, f. 1818, WHMC.

U.S. Senate. Subcommittee on the Air Force of the Committee on Armed Services, Executive Session, March 5, 1956, RG 46, U.S. Senate Records, 84th Congress, Committee on Armed Services, box 34, NARA.

U.S. Senate. Hearings before the Subcommittee on the Air Force of the Committee on Armed Services, *Study of Airpower.* 84th Cong., 2d sess.

U.S. Senate. *Airpower, Report of the Subcommittee on the Air Force of the Committee on Armed Services.* 85th Cong., 1st sess., Doc 29.

U.S. Senate. Hearings before the Preparedness Investigating Subcommittee of the Committee on Armed Services, *Inquiry Into Satellite and Missile Programs.* 85th Cong., 1st and 2d sess.

U.S. Senate. Hearings before the Committee on Armed Services, *Department of Defense Reorganization Act of 1958.* 85th Cong., 2d sess.

U.S. Senate. Hearings before the Committee on Foreign Relations, *S. 2180, Disarmament Agency.* 87th Cong., 1st sess.

U.S. Senate. Hearings before the Committee on Foreign Relations, *The Peace Corps.* 87th Cong., 1st sess.

U.S. Senate. Hearings before the National Stockpile and Naval Petroleum Reserves Subcommittee of the Committee on Armed Services, *Inquiry into the Strategic and Critical Material Stockpiles of the United States.* 87th Cong., 2d sess.

U.S. Senate. Hearings before the Committee on Foreign Relations, *Nuclear Test Ban Treaty.* 88th Cong., 1st sess.

U.S. Senate. Hearings before the Preparedness Investigating Subcommittee of the Committee on Armed Services, *Military Aspects and Implications of Nuclear Test Ban Proposals and Related Matters.* 88th Cong., 1st sess.

U.S. Senate. Committee on Foreign Relations, *Situation in Vietnam,* Executive Session of the Senate Foreign Relations Committee. 88th Cong., 1st sess., October 9, 1963, Historical Series 15: 778–79.

U.S. Senate. Committee on Armed Services, *Draft Report of the National Stockpile and Naval Petroleum Reserves Subcommittee . . . on the National Stockpile.* 88th Cong., 2d sess.

U.S. Senate. Hearings before the Senate Armed Services Committee, *Supplemental Foreign Assistance Fiscal Year 1966-Vietnam.* 89th Cong., 2d sess.

U.S. Senate. Hearings before the Committee on Foreign Relations, *Supplemental Foreign Assistance Fiscal Year 1966 Vietnam.* 89th Cong., 2d sess.

U.S. Senate. Hearings before the Committee on Foreign Relations, *Foreign Assistance Act of 1968.* 90th Cong., 2d sess.

U.S. Senate. Hearings before the Committee on Foreign Relations, *Present Situation in Vietnam.* 90th Cong., 2d sess.

U.S. Senate. Report to the Committee on Foreign Relations by Senator Stuart Symington, *The United Nations.* 91st Cong., 1st sess.

U.S. Senate. Hearings before the Subcommittee on United States Security Agreements and Commitments Abroad of the Committee on Foreign Relations, *Broader Aspects of U.S. Commitments.* 91st Cong., 2d sess.

U.S. Senate. Hearings before the Subcommittee on United States Security Agreements and Commitments Abroad of the Committee on Foreign Relations, *United States Security Agreements and Commitments Abroad: Kingdom of Laos.* 91st Cong., 2d sess.

U.S. Senate. Hearings before the Subcommittee on United States Security Agreements and Commitments Abroad of the Committee on Foreign Relations, *United States Security Agreements and Commitments Abroad: The Republic of the Philippines.* 91st Cong., 2d sess.

U.S. Senate. Hearings before the Committee on Armed Services, *Bombing in Cambodia.* 93d Cong., 1st sess.

U.S. Senate. Hearings before the Committee on Foreign Relations, *Nomination of Henry Kissinger.* 93d Cong., 1st sess.

U.S. Senate. Hearings before the Committee on Foreign Relations, Subcommittee on U.S. Security Agreements and Commitments Abroad and Subcommittee on Arms Control, International Law and Organization, *Nuclear Weapons and Foreign Policy.* 93d Cong., 2d sess.

U.S. Senate. *Tributes to the Honorable Stuart Symington of Missouri in the United States Senate . . . , September 27, 1976.* 94th Cong., 2d sess., doc. 94–276.

Newspapers

Most of the newspaper citations are from the Scrapbooks in the Symington Papers, Western Historical Manuscripts Collection, University of Missouri, Columbia. In addition, I made extensive use of the *St. Louis Globe-Democrat* clippings in the St. Louis Mercantile Library, St. Louis. Aside from the *Globe-Democrat,* I made extensive use of the *New York Times* and the *Washington Post* on microfilm, plus the *Kansas City Star* and the *St. Louis Post-Dispatch* in the Newspaper Library of the State Historical Society of Missouri, Columbia.

Books, Articles, Dissertations, and Theses

"A Yale Man and a Communist." *Fortune,* November 1943, 146ff.

Abell, Tyler, ed. *Drew Pearson Diaries, 1949–1959.* New York: Holt, Rinehart and Winston, 1974.

Abramson, Rudy. *Spanning the Century: The Life of W. Averell Harriman, 1891–1986.* New York: Morrow, 1992.

Adams, John G. *Without Precedent: The Story of the Death of McCarthyism.* New York: Norton, 1983.

Adams, Sherman. *Firsthand Report: The Story of the Eisenhower Administration.* New York: Harper and Bros., 1961.

Agnew, Harold. "Atoms for Lease." *Bulletin of the Atomic Scientists* 32 (May 1976): 22–23.

Albion, Robert G., and Robert Howe Connery, with the collaboration of Jennie Barnes Pope. *Forrestal and the Navy.* New York: Columbia University Press, 1962.

Allen, Frederick Lewis. *Only Yesterday: An Informal History of the Nineteen Twenties.* New York: Harper and Row, 1964.

Alsop, Joseph, with Adam Platt. *I've Seen the Best of It: Memoirs.* New York: W. W. Norton, 1992.

Alsop, Joseph, and Stewart Alsop. *The Reporter's Trade.* New York: Reynal and Company, 1958.

Ambrose, Stephen E. *Eisenhower.* 2 vols. Norwalk, Conn.: Easton Press, 1987.

———. *Eisenhower: Soldier and President.* New York: Simon and Schuster, 1990.

Baker, Bobby, with Larry L. King. *Wheeling and Dealing: Confessions of a Capitol Hill Operator.* New York: W. W. Norton, 1978.

Barlow, Jeffrey G. *The Revolt of the Admirals: The Fight for Naval Aviation, 1945–1950.* Washington, D.C.: Naval History Center, Department of the Navy, 1994.

Baruch, Bernard M. *Baruch: The Public Years.* New York: Holt, Rinehart and Winston, 1960.

Blum, John Morton, ed. *The Price of Vision: The Diary of Henry A. Wallace, 1942–1946.* Boston: Houghton Mifflin Co., 1973.

Bornet, Vaughn Davis. *The Presidency of Lyndon B. Johnson.* Lawrence: University Press of Kansas, 1983.

Boyer, Paul. *By the Bomb's Early Light: American Thought and Culture at the Dawn of the Atomic Age.* New York: Pantheon Books, 1985.

Bradlee, Benjamin C. *Conversations with Kennedy.* New York: Norton, 1975.

Brady, James. "In Step With: Bob and Delores Hope." *Parade,* December 18, 1994, 22.

Bright, Charles. *The Jet Makers: The Aerospace Industry from 1945 to 1972.* Lawrence: Regents Press of Kansas, 1978.

Brinkley, Douglas. *Dean Acheson: The Cold War Years, 1953–71.* New Haven, Conn.: Yale University Press, 1992.

Brugioni, Dino A. *Eyeball to Eyeball: The Inside Story of the Cuban Missile Crisis.* New York: Random House, 1991.

Bryan, Ferold J. "Joseph McCarthy, Robert Kennedy, and the Greek Shipping Crisis: A Study of Foreign Policy Rhetoric." *Presidential Studies Quarterly* 24 (1994): 93–104.

Bundy, McGeorge. *Danger and Survival: Choices about the Bomb in the First Fifty Years.* New York: Random House, 1988.

Caraley, Demetrios. *The Politics of Military Unification: A Study of Conflict and the Policy Process.* New York: Columbia University Press, 1966.

Clifford, Clark, with Richard Holbrooke. *Counsel to the President.* New York: Random House, 1991.

Cochran, Bert. *Harry Truman and the Crisis Presidency.* New York: Funk and Wagnalls, 1973.

Cochran, Jacqueline, and Maryann Buchnum Brinley. *Jackie Cochran: An Autobiography.* New York: Bantam Books, 1987.

Cohn, Roy M. *McCarthy.* New York: New American Library, 1968.

Collier, Richard. *Bridge across the Sky: The Berlin Blockade and Airlift, 1948–1949.* New York: McGraw-Hill, 1978.

Cornell, Cecilia Stiles. "James V. Forrestal and the American National Security Policy, 1940–1949." Ph.D. diss., Vanderbilt University, 1987.

Coughlan, Robert. "Home Front Boss." *Life,* October 3, 1950, cover story.

Cutler, Robert. *No Time for Rest.* Boston: Little, Brown, 1965.

Dalfiume, Richard M. *Desegregation of the U.S. Armed Forces.* Columbia: University of Missouri Press, 1965.

Dallek, Robert. *Flawed Giant: Lyndon Johnson and His Times, 1961–1973.* New York: Oxford University Press, 1998.

———. *Lone Star Rising: Lyndon Johnson and His Times, 1908–1960.* New York: Oxford University Press, 1991.

Davidson, Bill. "Mr. Charm of Washington." *Collier's,* June 15, 1946, 20, 24–25.

Davis, Benjamin O., Jr. *Benjamin O. Davis, Jr., American: An Autobiography.* Washington, D.C.: Smithsonian Institution Press, 1991.

Dilliard, Irving. "Farewell to Mr. Kem." *New Republic,* October 27, 1952, 16–17.

Donovan, Robert J. *Conflict and Crisis: The Presidency of Harry S. Truman, 1949–1953.* New York: Norton, 1982.

———. *Eisenhower: The Inside Story.* New York: Harper and Bros., 1956.

Dorwart, Jeffery M. *Eberstadt and Forrestal: A National Security Partnership, 1909–1949.* College Station: Texas A&M University Press, 1991.

Douglas, Paul H. *In the Fullness of Time: The Memoirs of Paul H. Douglas.* New York: Harcourt, Brace, Jovanovich, Inc., 1971.

Duffield, John S. *Power Rules: The Evolution of NATO's Conventional Force Posture.* Stanford, Calif.: Stanford University Press, 1995.

Dunar, Andrew J. *The Truman Scandals and the Politics of Morality.* Columbia: University of Missouri Press, 1984.

Dunlop, Richard. *Donovan: America's Master Spy.* Chicago: Rand McNally and Co., 1982.

Evans, Rowland, and Robert Novak. *Lyndon B. Johnson: The Exercise of Power.* New York: New American Library, 1986.

Ewald, William Bragg, Jr. *Who Killed Joe McCarthy?* New York: Simon and Schuster, 1984.

Fausold, Martin L. *James W. Wadsworth, Jr: The Gentleman from New York.* Syracuse, N.Y.: Syracuse University Press, 1975.

Ferrell, Robert H., ed. *Dear Bess: The Letters from Harry to Bess Truman, 1910–1959.* New York: W. W. Norton, 1983.

———. *Harry S. Truman: A Life.* Columbia: University of Missouri Press, 1994.

———, ed. *Off the Record: The Private Papers of Harry S. Truman*. New York: Harper and Row, 1980.

———, ed. *Truman in the White House: The Diary of Eben A. Ayers*. Columbia: University of Missouri Press, 1991.

Feurer, Rosemary. "William Sentner, the UE, and Civic Unionism in St. Louis." In Steve Rosswurm, ed., *The CIO's Left-Led Unions* (New Brunswick, N.J.: Rutgers University Press, 1992), 95–117.

Frantz, Douglas, and David McKean. *Friends in High Places: The Rise and Fall of Clark Clifford*. Boston: Little, Brown and Company, 1995.

French, Thomas Y. "Unification and the American Military Establishment, 1945–1950." Ph.D. diss., State University of New York at Buffalo, 1972.

Futrell, Robert F. *The United States Air Force in Southeast Asia: The Advisory Years to 1965*. Washington, D.C.: Office of Air Force History, USAF, 1981.

Gaddis, John Lewis. *Strategies of Containment: A Critical Appraisal of Postwar American National Security Policy*. New York: Oxford University Press, 1982.

Gibbons, William Conrad. *The U.S. Government and the Vietnam War: Executive and Legislative Roles and Relationships*. 4 vols. Princeton, N.J.: Princeton University Press, 1995.

Goldberg, Alfred, ed. *A History of the United States Air Force, 1907–1957*. Princeton, N.J.: Van Nostrand Press, 1957.

Goldman, Eric. *The Crucial Decade and After*. New York: Vintage Paperback, 1960.

Goldsmith, John A. *Colleagues: Richard B. Russell and His Apprentice, Lyndon B. Johnson*. Washington: Seven Locks Press, 1993.

Grafton, David. *The Sisters: The Lives and Times of the Fabulous Cushing Sisters*. New York: Villard Books, 1992.

Graham, Katharine. *Personal History*. New York: Alfred A. Knopf, 1997.

Green, Murray. "Stuart Symington and the B-36." Ph.D. diss., American University, 1960; Ann Arbor, Mich.: University Microfilms, 1993.

Greenwood, John T. "The Emergence of the Postwar Strategic Air Force." in Alfred I. Hurley and Robert C. Ehrhart, eds., The Proceedings of the 8th Military History Symposium, USAF Academy, October 18–20, 1958; also *Air Power and Warfare*. Washington, D.C.: Office of Air Force History and the United States Air Force Academy, 1979.

Griffith, Robert. *The Politics of Fear: Joseph R. McCarthy and the Senate*. Lexington: University Press of Kentucky, 1970.

Gropman, Alan L. "The Air Force, 1941–1951, from Segregation to Integration." Paper presented at the 106th annual meeting of the American Historical Association, 1991.

Harris, Eleanor. "Stu Symington—Democratic Glamour Boy." *American Weekly*, June 24, 1960. Clipping in SP, WHMC.

Hatch, Alden. *The Wadsworths of the Genesee*. New York: Coward-McCann, Inc., 1959.

Haynes, Richard F. *The Awesome Power: Harry S. Truman as Commander in Chief*. Baton Rouge: Louisiana State University Press, 1973.

Herken, Gregg. *Counsels of War*. Expanded edition. New York: Oxford University Press, 1987.

Hersh, Seymour. *The Dark Side of Camelot.* Boston: Little Brown, 1997.

Hewlett, Richard G. *Atomic Shield: A History of the United States Atomic Energy Commission. Vol. II, 1947–1952.* University Park: Pennsylvania State University Press, 1990.

Hill, William S., Jr. "The Business Community and National Defense: Corporate Leaders and the Military, 1943–1950." Ph.D. diss., Stanford University, 1980.

Hoffman, Nicholas von. *The Life and Times of Roy Cohn: Citizen Cohn.* New York: Doubleday, 1988.

Hoopes, Townsend, and Douglas Brinkley. *Driven Patriot: The Life and Times of James Forrestal.* New York: Alfred A. Knopf, 1992.

Horelick, Arnold L., and Myron Rush. *Strategic Power and Soviet Foreign Policy.* Chicago: University of Chicago Press, 1965, 1966.

Husted, Ellery S., ed. *History of the Class of Nineteen Hundred Twenty Three.* New Haven, Conn.: Yale College, 1923.

Jurika, Stephen B., Jr., ed. *From Pearl Harbor to Vietnam: The Memoirs of Admiral Arthur W. Radford.* Stanford, Calif.: Hoover Institution Press, 1980.

Keith, Caroline H. *"For Hell and a Brown Mule": The Biography of Senator Millard E. Tydings.* Madison, Wisc.: Lanham, 1991.

Kinnard, Douglas. *The Certain Trumpet: Maxwell Taylor and the American Experience in Vietnam.* Washington: Brassey's, 1991.

Kirkendall, Richard S. *A History of Missouri, Volume V, 1919 to 1953.* Columbia: University of Missouri Press, 1986.

————, ed. *Truman Encyclopedia.* Boston: G. K. Hall and Company, 1989.

Kissinger, Henry A. "Force and Diplomacy in the Nuclear Age." *Foreign Affairs* 34 (April 1956): 349–56.

Knerr, Hugh J. "We'll Bomb by Daylight." *American Mercury,* October 1942, 430–35.

Kofsky, Frank. *Harry S. Truman and the War Scare of 1948: A Successful Campaign to Deceive the Nation.* New York: St. Martin's Press, 1993.

Krock, Arthur. *Memoirs: Sixty Years on the Firing Line.* New York: Funk and Wagnalls, 1968.

Lacey, Michael J., ed. *The Truman Presidency.* Cambridge: Cambridge University Press, 1989.

LeMay, Curtis, with MacKinlay Kantor. *Mission with LeMay: My Story.* Garden City, N.Y.: Doubleday, 1965.

Leutze, James, ed. *The London Journal of General Raymond E. Lee, 1940–1941.* Boston: Little, Brown and Co., 1971.

Lewis, Flora. "The Education of a Senator." *Atlantic,* December 1971, 53–64.

Lilienthal, David E. *The Journals of David E. Lilienthal.* Vol. 2, *The Atomic Energy Years, 1945–1950.* New York: Harper and Row, 1964.

Loewy, Raymond. *Industrial Design.* Woodstock, N.Y.: Overlook Press, 1979.

MacGregor, Morris J. *Integration of the Armed Forces, 1940–1965.* Washington: Center of Military History, 1981.

————, and Bernard C. Nalty, eds. *Blacks in the United States Armed Forces: Basic Documents.* 13 vols. Wilmington, Del.: Scholarly Resources, 1977.

Martin, Ralph G., and Ed Plaut. *Front Runner, Dark Horse.* Garden City, N.Y.: Doubleday, 1960.

Marx, Arthur. *The Secret Life of Bob Hope*. New York: Barricade Books, 1993.

Matthews, J. B. "Reds in Our Churches." *American Mercury,* July 1953, 3–13.

May, Ernest R., ed. *American Cold War Strategy: Interpreting NSC-68*. Boston: Bedford Books of St. Martin's Press, 1993.

McCullough, David. *Truman*. New York: Simon and Schuster, 1992.

McFarland, Linda. *Cold War Strategist: Stuart Symington and the Search for National Security*. Westport, Conn.: Praeger, 2001.

McKelvey, Blake. "East Avenue's Turbulent History." *The Federal Writers' Project Guide to Rochester*.

Merry, Robert W. *Taking on the World: Joseph and Stewart Alsop—Guardians of the American Century*. New York: Viking, 1996.

Mets, David. *Master of Airpower: General Carl A. Spaatz*. Novato, Calif.: Presido Press, 1988.

Miller, Roger G. *To Save a City: The Berlin Airlift, 1948–1949*. Washington, D.C.: Air Force History and Museums Program, 1998.

Millis, Walter, ed., E. S. Duffield, collab. *The Forrestal Diaries*. New York: Viking Press, 1966.

———, with Harvey C. Mansfield and Harold Stein. *Arms and the State: Civil-Military Elements in National Policy*. New York: Twentieth Century Fund, 1958.

Mitchell, Bonnie C. *Jerry Litton, 1937–1976: A Biography*. Chillicothe, Mo.: Jerry Litton Family Memorial Foundation, 1978.

Mollenhoff, Clark R. *The Pentagon: Politics, Profits, and Plunder*. New York: G. P. Putnam's Sons, 1967.

Morris, Joe Alexis. "Candidate Bubbling with Charm." *Saturday Evening Post,* July 21, 1956, 26–27, 67–68, 70.

Mosley, Leonard. *Marshall, Hero for Our Times*. New York: Hearst Books, 1982.

Nichols, Lee. *Break Through on the Color Front*. New York: Random House, 1954.

Nitze, Paul H. "The Development of NSC-68." *International Security* 4 (spring 1980): 170–76.

Olson, Vera. "A Missouri Woman Who Took on the World." Unpublished paper, author's files.

Pitts, Debra K. "Stuart Symington and Harry S. Truman: A Mutual Friendship." *Missouri Historical Review* 90 (July 1996): 453–79.

Pogue, Forrest C. *George C. Marshall*. New York: Viking Press, 1963.

Prados, John. *The Soviet Estimate: U.S. Intelligence Analysis and Russian Strategic Forces*. Princeton, N.J.: Princeton University Press, 1986.

Raj, Christopher. *American Military in Europe: Controversy over NATO Burden Sharing*. New Delhi, India: ABC Publishing House, 1983.

Ransom, Harry H. "Department of Defense: Unity or Confederation?" In Mark E. Smith III and Claude Johns, Jr., eds., *American Defense Policy* (Baltimore: Johns Hopkins Press, 1965), 371–73.

Raymond, Jack. *Power at the Pentagon*. New York: Harper and Row, 1964.

Reeves, Richard. *President Kennedy: Profile of Power*. New York: Simon and Schuster, 1993.

Reeves, Thomas C. *The Life and Times of Joe McCarthy: A Biography*. New York: Stein and Day Publishers, 1982.

Rhea, Gordon C. *The Battle of the Wilderness, May 5–6, 1864.* Baton Rouge: Louisiana State University Press, 1994.

Rickenbacker, Edward V. *Rickenbacker.* Englewood Cliffs, N.J.: Prentice-Hall, 1967.

Rogow, Arnold A. *James Forrestal: A Study of Personality, Politics, and Policy.* New York: Macmillan, 1963.

Roman, Peter J. *Eisenhower and the Missile Gap.* Ithaca, N.Y.: Cornell University Press, 1995.

Rovere, Richard. *Senator Joe McCarthy.* New York: Harcourt Brace, 1959.

———. "The Adventures of Cohn and Schine." *Reporter* 9 (July 21, 1953): 7–16.

Salinger, Pierre. *P.S.: A Memoir.* New York: St. Martin's Press, 1995.

Schapsmeier, Edward L., and Frederick H. Schapsmeier. *Ezra Taft Benson and the Politics of Agriculture: The Eisenhower Years, 1953–1964.* Danville, Ill.: Interstate Printers and Publishers, Inc., 1975.

Schilling, Warner, Paul Y. Hammond, and Glenn A. Snyder. *Strategy, Politics and Defense Budgets.* New York: Columbia University Press, 1962.

Schlesinger, Arthur M., Jr. *Robert Kennedy and His Times.* Boston: Houghton Mifflin, 1978.

———. *A Thousand Days: John F. Kennedy in the White House.* Boston: Houghton, Mifflin, 1965.

Schoenebaum, Eleanora W., ed. *Political Profiles. Volume I: The Truman Years.* New York: Facts on File, Inc., 1978.

Schwartz, Jordan A. *The Speculator: Bernard M. Baruch in Washington, 1917–1965.* Chapel Hill: University of North Carolina Press, 1981.

Selser, James C., Jr. "The Bomber's Role in Diplomacy." *Air Force Magazine,* April 1956, 52, 55–56.

Shaffer, Samuel, and Peter Wyden. "Mr. If of the Democrats." *Newsweek,* June 18, 1956, 45–52.

Shlaim, Avi. *The United States and the Berlin Blockade, 1948–1949: A Study in Crisis Decision-Making.* Berkeley: University of California Press, 1983.

Smith, Bruce L. R. *The RAND Corporation: Case Study of a Non-Profit Advisory Corporation.* Cambridge, Mass.: Harvard University Press, 1966.

Smith, George David. *From Monopoly to Competition: The Transformation of Alcoa, 1888–1986.* New York: Cambridge University Press, 1988.

Smith, Jean Edward. *The Defense of Berlin.* Baltimore: Johns Hopkins Press, 1963.

———. *Lucius D. Clay: An American Life.* New York: Henry Holt and Co., 1990.

Smith, Robert L. "The Influence of USAF Chief of Staff Hoyt S. Vandenberg on United States National Security Policy." Ph.D. diss., American University, 1965.

Snyder, Glenn Herald. *Stockpiling Strategic Materials: Politics and National Defense.* San Francisco: Chandler Publishing Company, 1966.

Stassen, Harold, and Marshall Houts, *Eisenhower: Turning the World Toward Peace.* St. Paul: Merrill/Magnus Publishing Corp., 1990.

Stein, Harold, ed. *Public Administration and Policy Development.* New York: Harcourt Brace and Co., 1952.

Steinbrenner, Tom. "Air Power is Indivisible." *Armed Forces Journal,* September 1972, 26–28.

Steinmeyer, George William. "Disposition of Surplus War Property: An Administrative History, 1944–1949." Ph.D. diss., University of Oklahoma, 1969.

Stillman, Richard J. *Integration of the Negro in the U.S. Armed Forces.* New York: Frederick A. Praeger Publishers, 1968.

Straight, Michael. "The Growth of Stuart Symington." *New Republic,* June 21, 1954, 12–14.

————. *Trial by Television.* Boston: Beacon Press, 1954.

Symington, Charles J. *Skippin' the Details: Memoirs of Charles J. Symington for His Twenty Grandchildren February 2, 1883–February 2, 1996.* Printed and Bound by Clarke and Way, Inc., 1966.

Symington, James W. *The Stately Game.* New York: Macmillan Company, 1971.

Symington, W. Stuart. "The Importance of Civil Defense Planning." *Bulletin of the Atomic Scientists* 6 (August/September 1950): 231–33.

————. "The Washington Nuclear Mess." *International Security* 1 (winter 1977): 71–78.

————. "Where the Missile Gap Went." *Reporter,* February 15, 1962, 371–73.

Thomas, Rebecca Ann. "Stuart Symington: Manager and Strategist 1946–1950." Master's thesis, University of Missouri–Columbia, 1993.

Treverton, Gregory F. *The Dollar Drain and American Forces in Germany: Managing the Political Economics of Alliance.* Athens: Ohio University Press, 1978.

Tunner, William. *Over the Hump.* New York: Duell, Sloan and Pearce, 1964.

Watson, George M., Jr. *The Office of the Secretary of the Air Force, 1947–1965.* Washington, D.C.: Center for Air Force History, 1993.

Watson, George M., Jr. "Stuart Symington—the First Secretary of the Air Force, 18 September 1947–24 April 1950." *Aerospace Historian* 34 (September 1987): 185–89.

Wellman, Paul. *Stuart Symington: Portrait of a Man with a Mission.* Garden City, N.Y.: Doubleday, 1960.

White, Theodore H. *The Making of the President, 1960.* New York: Atheneum, 1961.

White, William S. "Symington: the Last Choice for President." *Harper's Magazine,* July 1959, 78–81.

Williams, Phil. *The Senate and U.S. Troops in Europe.* New York: St. Martin's, 1985.

Wilson, Donald R. "The History of President Truman's Air Policy Commission and Its Influence on Air Policy, 1947–1949." Ph.D. diss., University of Denver, 1978.

Wolk, Herman S. *Planning and Organizing the Postwar Air Force.* Washington: Office of Air Force History, 1984.

Woods, Randall Bennett. *Fulbright: A Biography.* New York: Cambridge University Press, 1995.

Yoder, Edwin M., Jr. *Joe Alsop's Cold War: A Study of Journalistic Influence and Intrigue.* Chapel Hill: University of North Carolina Press, 1995.

Index